THE CAMBRIDGE HANDBOOK OF ENVIRONMENTAL JUSTICE AND SUSTAINABLE DEVELOPMENT

Despite the global endorsement of the Sustainable Development Goals, environmental justice struggles are growing all over the world. These struggles are not isolated injustices, but symptoms of interlocking forms of oppression that privilege a few while inflicting misery on the many and threatening ecological collapse. This handbook offers critical perspectives on the multidimensional, intersectional nature of environmental injustice and the cross-cutting forms of oppression that unite and divide these struggles, including gender, race, poverty, and indigeneity. The work sheds new light on the often-neglected social dimension of sustainability and its relationship to human rights and environmental justice. Using a variety of legal frameworks and case studies from around the world, this volume illustrates the importance of overcoming the fragmentation of these legal frameworks and social movements in order to develop holistic solutions that promote justice and protect the planet's ecosystems at a time of intensifying economic and ecological crisis.

SUMUDU A. ATAPATTU is Director of Research Centers and International Programs at University of Wisconsin Law School, and Executive Director of the Human Rights Program. She is affiliated faculty with Raoul Wallenberg Institute for Human Rights, Sweden, and lead counsel for human rights at Centre for International Sustainable Development Law, Canada.

CARMEN G. GONZALEZ is the Morris I. Leibman Professor of Law at Loyola University Chicago School of Law, and Professor Emerita at Seattle University School of Law. She has published widely on international environmental law, human rights and the environment, and environmental justice. Professor Gonzalez has chaired the Environmental Law Section of the Association of American Law Schools, and served as member and deputy chair of the Governing Board of the IUCN Academy of Environmental Law. She is currently a member of the Board of Trustees of Earthjustice, the largest public interest environmental law firm in the United States.

SARA L. SECK is an associate professor with the Schulich School of Law and Marine & Environmental Law Institute, Dalhousie University. In 2015, she received the IUCN Academy of Environmental Law's Emerging Scholarship Award. She is a regional director with the Global Network for the study of Human Rights and the Environment.

D1611516

The Cambridge Handbook of Environmental Justice and Sustainable Development

Edited by

SUMUDU A. ATAPATTU

University of Wisconsin Law School

CARMEN G. GONZALEZ

Loyola University Chicago School of Law
and Seattle University School of Law

SARA L. SECK

Dalhousie University (Nova Scotia) Schulich School of Law

CAMBRIDGE
UNIVERSITY PRESS

CAMBRIDGE
UNIVERSITY PRESS

University Printing House, Cambridge CB2 8BS, United Kingdom

One Liberty Plaza, 20th Floor, New York, NY 10006, USA

477 Williamstown Road, Port Melbourne, VIC 3207, Australia

314-321, 3rd Floor, Plot 3, Splendor Forum, Jasola District Centre, New Delhi - 110025, India

103 Penang Road, #05-06/07, Visioncrest Commercial, Singapore 238467

Cambridge University Press is part of the University of Cambridge.

It furthers the University's mission by disseminating knowledge in the pursuit of education, learning and research at the highest international levels of excellence.

www.cambridge.org
Information on this title: www.cambridge.org/9781009281935
DOI: 10.1017/9781108555791

First published 2021
First paperback edition 2022

A catalogue record for this publication is available from the British Library

ISBN 978-1-108-47000-1 Hardback
ISBN 978-1-009-28193-5 Paperback

Contents

PART III CONCLUSION

Contributors

Sumudu A. Atapattu is the Director of Research Centers and International Programs at University of Wisconsin Law School, and Executive Director of the Human Rights Program. She is lead counsel for Human Rights at the Centre for International Sustainable Development Law, Canada, affiliated faculty at the Raoul Wallenberg Institute for Human Rights, Sweden and formerly, Senior Lecturer, Faculty of Law, University of Colombo, Sri Lanka.

Rebecca M. Bratspies teaches at the CUNY School of Law and directs the CUNY Center for Urban Environmental Reform. Her research explores the role of individuals and communities in the regulatory state, human rights, environmental democracy, and food justice. Her environmental justice comic books (*Mayah's Lot*, *Bina's Plant*) have been used widely in classrooms and by state environmental agencies. She serves on the US Environmental Protection Agency's Children's Environmental Health Protection Advisory Committee, is a member-scholar with the Center for Progressive Reform and the Environmental Law Collective. She blogs with the Nature of Cities. She is past chair of the AALS Section on Environmental Law.

Robert W. Collin is an author, environmental justice activist, and retired professor, with master's degrees in law, social work, and urban planning. He is a former member of the National Environmental Justice Advisory Committee at the US Environmental Protection Agency. Robert was appointed to the Oregon Environmental Justice Task Force, serving continuously since its formation in 2009, and is currently vice chair.

Barbara Cosens is a University Distinguished Professor Emerita with the University of Idaho College of Law, where she has taught for the sixteen years. Her LLM is from Lewis and Clark Law School, JD from the University of California, Hastings, MS in geology from the University of Washington, and BS in geology from the University of California, Davis. Her teaching and research expertise is in water law, the law–science interface and water dispute resolution. She is co-PI on the UI Water Resources IGERT focused on adaptation to climate change. She cochaired the Adaptive Water Governance project made possible through support from the NSF funded National Socio-Environmental Synthesis Center, SESYNC, and spent spring 2015 at the Goyder Institute in Australia comparing water law reform in western USA and Australia during drought. In her outreach and engagement, she provides education and expertise on the Columbia River Treaty as part of the Universities Consortium on Columbia River Governance.

Erin Daly is Professor of Law at Delaware Law School and Executive Director of Dignity Rights International; she also serves as the Director of the Global Network for Human Rights and the Environment. With James May, she has written extensively on human rights and the environment and on environmental constitutionalism. She is the author of *Dignity Rights: Courts, Constitutions, and the Worth of the Human Person* (2012) and numerous other publications on the emerging law of dignity rights. She and Professor May are working on the first global casebook on dignity rights.

Jackie Dugard is an associate professor at the School of Law, University of the Witwatersrand (Wits), where she focuses on power and exclusion. Jackie was a cofounder and the first Executive Director (2010–2012) of the Socio-Economic Rights Institute of South Africa, where she is a board member. Jackie was the founder and first Director of the Gender Equity Office at Wits (2014–2016). She is on the Advisory Board of the Southern Centre for Inequality Studies at Wits, and she is a global fellow at the Centre on Law and Social Transformation (Bergen University), and an associated senior researcher at the Chr. Michelsen Institute in Norway. In May 2019, Jackie became a member of the South African Ministerial Task Team to advise on matters related to sexual harassment and gender-based violence at South African universities.

Patrícia Galvão Ferreira is an assistant professor in transnational law at the University of Windsor Faculty of Law, in Canada. She teaches environmental law and international environmental law, and is the Director of the Transnational Environmental and Policy Clinic. Dr. Galvão Ferreira holds an LLB from the Federal University of Bahia in Brazil and an LLM from the University of Notre Dame in the USA. She holds an SJD from the Faculty of Law, University of Toronto, which she earned concurrently with an interdisciplinary PhD in dynamics of global change from the Munk School of Global Affairs, University of Toronto. Dr. Galvão Ferreira's research interests include transnational environmental law, transnational climate change law, environmental justice, human rights law, and law and development.

Joshua C. Gellers is an associate professor in the Department of Political Science and Public Administration at the University of North Florida, research fellow of the Earth System Governance Project, and Fulbright Scholar to Sri Lanka. He is the author of *The Global Emergence of Constitutional Environmental Rights* (2017).

Carmen G. Gonzalez is the Morris I. Leibman Professor of Law at Loyola University Chicago School of Law. She is Professor Emerita at Seattle University School of Law. She has published widely in the areas of international environmental law, human rights and the environment, environmental justice, and food security. Professor Gonzalez holds a BA from Yale University and a JD from Harvard Law School.

Lakshman Guruswamy is the Nicholas Doman Professor of International Law at the University of Colorado at Boulder. His work explores how and why energy justice calls for the fashioning of practical solutions for the energy poor inhabiting the least developed parts of the developing world.

Angela P. Harris is Professor Emerita at the University of California, Davis School of Law. Her work is centered on critical legal theory, including critical race theory, feminist legal theory, and law and political economy. Her current work considers the impact of climate catastrophe on theories of social justice.

Stellina Jolly is a senior assistant professor at the Faculty of Legal Studies South Asian University, a Fulbright Scholar at the University of San Francisco, and a recipient of the

International Visitors Leadership Program. Dr. Jolly's research focuses on international environmental law and conflict of laws.

Alice Kaswan is Professor and Associate Dean for Faculty Scholarship at the University of San Francisco School of Law. An expert on climate justice, federalism, and US climate policy, she received her BS in Conservation and Resource Studies from UC Berkeley and her JD from Harvard Law School.

Sabaa A. Khan is an attorney member of the Barreau du Québec (Canada) and senior researcher at the Center for Climate Change, Energy and Environmental Law (University of Eastern Finland). She specializes in public international law as it relates to trade, environment, and labor.

Louis J. Kotzé is Research Professor of Environmental Law at North-West University, South Africa, and Senior Visiting Professorial Fellow in Earth System Law at the University of Lincoln, United Kingdom. His research focuses on law and the Anthropocene, environmental constitutionalism, and earth system law.

Konstantia Koutouki is a full professor at the Université de Montréal, Senior Fellow at the McGill University Centre for Inernational Sustainable Development Law, and Executive Director of Nomomente Institute. She has extensive expertise in international law as it relates to the social, economic, and cultural development of local and Indigenous communities, as well as the preservation of natural spaces and ancient knowledge. In particular she is interested in traditional medicine, living soils, cultural expressions, and human/ecosystems well-being.

Elizabeth Ann Kronk Warner is the Dean of the S.J. Quinney College of Law at the University of Utah, where she is also a professor of law. She is an enrolled citizen of the Sault Ste. Marie Tribe of Chippewa Indians.

Katherine Lofts is a Research Associate with McGill University's Disability-Inclusive Climate Action Research Program and with the Canada Research Chair in Human Rights, Health, and the Environment. She holds master's degrees in both law and English literature, and has worked at the intersections of environmental governance, human rights, and climate change for more than a decade.

Deborah McGregor joined York University's Osgoode Hall law faculty in 2015 as a cross-appointee with the Faculty of Environmental Studies. Professor McGregor's research has focused on Indigenous knowledge systems and their various applications in diverse contexts including water and environmental governance, environmental justice, health, and climate justice.

Mario Mancilla is a law professor at the Universidad de San Carlos, at the Universidad Mariano Gálvez, and at the Escuela de Estudios Judiciales de Guatemala. He teaches environmental law, international environmental law, constitutional law, sociology of law, and philosophy of law. He has been a visiting professor in several universities in Central America and the Dominican Republic. Professor Mancilla holds an M.Sc. in constitutional law from the Universidad de San Carlos de Guatemala, a PhD in law from the Universidad Mariano Gálvez de Guatemala, and is doctoral candidate in political science and sociology at the Universidad Pontificia de Salamanca in Spain. He is also an attorney and public notary for the Universidad de San Carlos de Guatemala.

James R. May is Distinguished Professor of Law and Cofounder and Codirector of the Dignity Rights Project and the Environmental Rights Institute at Widener University Delaware Law

School, the Cofounder and Codirector of Dignity Rights International, and past inaugural chief sustainability officer at Widener University, where he founded the Widener Sustainability Initiative. He is an inductee of Phi Kappa Phi National Honor Society, and the American College of Environmental Lawyers, and has served as consultant to the United Nations Environment Programme and the International Senior Lawyers Project, among others.

Tamar Meshel is an assistant professor at the University of Alberta Faculty of Law. Dr. Meshel's research focuses on international water law, international arbitration, and various areas of public international law. She also teaches and researches in tort law, corporate law, and securities law.

Robin Morris Collin is the Norma J. Paulus Professor of law at Willamette University College of Law. She is the first US law professor to teach sustainability courses in a US law school. Her publications include "Restoration and Redemption," in *Moral Ground: Ethical Action for a Planet in Peril* (2011).

Usha Natarajan is Edward W Said Fellow at Columbia University, Global South Visiting Scholar at the University of British Columbia, and Senior Fellow at Melbourne Law School. Natarajan was tenured at the American University in Cairo as Associate Professor of International Law and Associate Director of the Center for Migration and Refugee Studies. Previously, she worked with UNDP, UNESCO and the World Bank.

Quoc Nguyen is an attorney-adviser at the US Environmental Protection Agency Office of General Counsel. She provides legal counsel and litigates on environmental information law issues.

Damilola S. Olawuyi, SAN, is an associate professor of petroleum, energy and environmental law at Hamad Bin Khalifa University (HBKU) College of Law, Doha, Qatar. He is also Chancellor's Fellow and Director of the Institute for Oil, Gas, Energy, Environment and Sustainable Development (OGEES Institute), Afe Babalola University, Ado Ekiti, Nigeria. He is an Independent Expert of the Working Group on Extractive Industries, Environment, and Human Rights Violations in Africa formed by the African Commission on Human and Peoples' Rights.

Mona Paré is Associate Professor at University of Ottawa's Faculty of Law, Civil Law Section. She holds a PhD in law from Queen Mary College, University of London. She is cofounder of the Interdisciplinary Research Laboratory on the Rights of the Child at uOttawa.

Antoni Pigrau is Professor of Public International Law, Universitat Rovira i Virgili (Tarragona, Spain), Director of the Tarragona Centre for Environmental Law Studies, and Director of the *Catalan Journal of Environmental Law*. Antoni is a member of the European Environmental Law Forum Advisory Board, and member of the Advisory Board of the Network on Business, Conflict and Human Rights.

Shyami Puvimanasinghe is Human Rights Officer, Right to Development Section, Office of the United Nations High Commissioner for Human Rights, Geneva, Switzerland, and a senior research fellow, Centre for International Sustainable Development Law. Formerly senior lecturer, Faculty of Law, University of Colombo, Sri Lanka.

Jacinta Ruru (Raukawa, Ngāti Ranginui) is Professor of Law at the University of Otago, Codirector of Ngā Pae o te Māramatanga New Zealand's Centre of Māori Research Excellence, fellow of the Royal Society Te Apārangi, and recipient of New Zealand Prime Minister's Supreme Award for Excellence in Tertiary Teaching.

Boaventura de Sousa Santos is a full professor at the University of Coimbra, School of Economics, Department of Sociology, in Portugal, and a Distinguished Scholar of the Institute for Legal Studies at the University of Wisconsin Law School. He has published prolifically on issues related to law and globalization, legal pluralism, multiculturalism, and human rights, and has taught at law schools and graduate programs in Brazil, England, Mexico, Argentina, Colombia, Angola, Mozambique, and Spain, in addition to his current Coimbra, Portugal and Madison posts.

Dayna Nadine Scott is an associate professor at Osgoode Hall Law School and the Faculty of Environmental and Urban Change at York University. She is also the York Research Chair in Environmental Law & Justice in the Green Economy. Professor Scott's research focuses on contestation over extraction, the distribution of pollution burdens, and climate justice.

Sara L. Seck is an associate professor with the Schulich School of Law and Marine & Environmental Law Institute, Dalhousie University, Canada. Her research considers environmental and climate justice with attention to gender, Indigenous law, and insights from relational theorists; business, human rights, and transnational law; and critical approaches to public and private international law and sustainable development.

Andrea C. Simonelli is an assistant professor of human security at Virginia Commonwealth University and Founder of Adaptation Strategies International. Her research investigates climate-induced migration as well as the relationship between island resilience, adaptation, and governance in the Maldives and greater Pacific, which includes extensive fieldwork.

Penelope Simons is an associate professor at the Faculty of Law (Common Law Section) at the University of Ottawa. Her research focuses on business and human rights and in particular on: the human rights implications of domestic and transnational extractive sector activity; state responsibility for corporate complicity in human rights violations; the regulation of transnational corporations; gender and resource extraction; as well as the intersections between transnational corporate activity, human rights, and international economic law.

Adrian A. Smith is an associate professor at Osgoode Hall Law School in Toronto, Canada. He is currently serving as Academic Director of the Intensive Program in Poverty Law. His research addresses labor, law, and political economy in colonial and settler colonial contexts.

Linda Tsang is a legislative attorney at the Congressional Research Service of the Library of Congress. She works on legal issues related to environmental, energy, climate change, administrative, and constitutional law.

Tseming Yang is Professor of Law and Director of the Center for Global Law and Policy at the Santa Clara University School of Law. In 2010–2012, he served as deputy general counsel of the US Environmental Protection Agency. His research focuses on environmental justice as well as comparative and international environmental law.

Acknowledgments

This project would not have been possible without the collaboration and support of many people and institutions. We would like to thank all our contributors, who produced their chapters amidst many demands on their time. They were very gracious about the editorial comments and suggestions and worked with us to ensure that the central themes of the book – environmental justice and sustainable development – were highlighted in their chapters. We would like to thank them for their contribution to our volume as well as their continued dedication to scholarship and advocacy.

We owe a particular debt of gratitude to Sarah MacLeod, a recent JD graduate from the Schulich School of Law, Dalhousie University, who worked tirelessly to ensure that all the chapters were formatted properly and were ready for submission. Without her, we would have been lost and this book would not have seen the light of day. Her dedication and meticulous attention to detail as well as her editorial skills, were invaluable. Sara Seck is very grateful to the Schulich School of Law, Dalhousie University for research funding in support of Sarah MacLeod's contributions.

We are most grateful to Professor Boaventura de Sousa Santos for writing the Foreword. We would also like to acknowledge the support of Cambridge University Press, especially Matt Gallaway, who very graciously accommodated our many requests for extensions.

Sumudu Atapattu would like to thank University of Wisconsin Law School for research support and the students of the *Wisconsin International Law Journal* who hosted a symposium in 2018 based on the book project in which many of the contributors participated. She gratefully acknowledges the support of the Laurie Carlson Progressive Ideas Forum for supporting a workshop following the symposium to discuss the edited volume.

Carmen G. Gonzalez would like to thank Seattle University School of Law and Loyola University Chicago School of Law for the research support that made it possible to present the ideas in this volume at several scholarly conferences and workshops.

Finally, we would like to thank our families for their continued love, patience, and ongoing support and encouragement.

Foreword (on Living in an Interregnum)

This book deals with two main topics, one with an already long and controversial history (sustainable development) and another with a shorter but equally controversial history (environmental justice). It could therefore be one more book about conceptual history (the narratives, discourses, and practices unfolding from such mainstream concepts) and a rereading of the controversies that make up such history. The importance of this book lies in the fact that it is not such a book. It is rather a book which, however fully accounting for the contemporary histories of these topics and the controversies surrounding them, is dialectically (and tragically) aware that it is coming at the end of an epoch dominated by these topics, an epoch consisting of both the issues these topics credibly highlighted and the issues they cunningly obscured or made invisible. In this way, the discussion on sustainable development slides into the discussion on the highly problematic development of sustainability, as much as the discussion on environmental justice slides into the discussion on the highly dubious justice in/of conceiving of the environment as a separate entity, added to many other conditions that make life on earth possible in a dignifying way for both humans and nonhumans.

The deep flaws of the mainstream renditions of the controversial trajectory of these topics come out very clearly in this book. I identify three of them. First, as long as infinite economic growth remains as a dogma we will be cruising the *Titanic* and be part of its fateful destiny. If escaping is still possible, an intellectual and political move imposes itself: from alternative development to alternatives to development. Second, this move is extremely difficult because it demands confronting the three main modes of modern domination: capitalism (exploitation of labor power), colonialism (racism, slave labor, accumulation by dispossession), and patriarchy (sexism and all forms of gender discrimination). Third, global social justice is not possible without global cognitive justice. If I am allowed to quote myself, "the quest for the recognition and celebration of the epistemological diversity of the world underlying the epistemologies of the south requires that these new (actually, often ancestral and newly reinvented) repertoires of human dignity and social liberation be conceived of as being relevant far beyond the social groups that caused them to emerge from their struggles against oppression" (*The End of the Cognitive Empire* (Durham, NC: Duke University Press, 2018), p. 11).

This book sometimes suggests, sometimes cries loudly that we live in an interregnum, a period similar to the one analyzed by Antonio Gramsci in the early 1930s and characterized by the fact that the old is not yet completely dead while the new is not yet fully born. The antinomies of the old go on causing much damage and suffering in the world to both humans and nonhumans, while the new is forcing its entry into history more and more convincingly. The morbidity of our time lies in this historical and existential ambiguity. This book is by far the best I have read in years about the antinomies of our historical and existential condition. It is therefore a must-read for those who want to understand why so much rhetorical investment in the topics of sustainable development and environmental justice have accomplished so little. And equally for those for whom a new beginning is necessary, a new gestalt, with new concerns, radically different objectives, discourses, practices, and, above all, different ways of knowing and living.

Boaventura de Sousa Santos

1

Intersections of Environmental Justice and Sustainable Development

Framing the Issues

Sumudu A. Atapattu, Carmen G. Gonzalez, and Sara L. Seck

1.1 INTRODUCTION

Humanity stands at a critical juncture. It has entered a new geologic era called the "Anthropocene,"[1] in which unbridled economic activity threatens irreversible ecological harm. In the name of "development," human beings have caused massive ecosystem destruction and species extinction, disrupted the planet's climate, and generated vast amounts of toxic waste – exceeding the assimilative and regenerative capacity of nature.

Global statistics are sobering. The world has entered a sixth wave of mass extinction where, according to some estimates, 27,000 species vanish every year[2] and about one million species currently face extinction.[3] Climate change is accelerating more rapidly than scientists predicted, leading the World Meteorological Organization to warn that lack of aggressive mitigation measures will likely result in a catastrophic temperature increase of 3–5 degrees Celsius (5.4–9.0 degrees Fahrenheit) above preindustrial levels by 2100.[4] In 2016, the world generated 242 million tons of plastic waste.[5] If present trends continue, there will be more plastic in the oceans than fish by 2050.[6] Between 1945 and the present, the worldwide generation of hazardous

---

[1] See P. J. Crutzen, "Geology of Mankind – The Anthropocene" (2002) 415 *Nature* 23; C. Gonzalez, "Global Justice in the Anthropocene," in L. Kotzé (ed.), *Environment Law and Governance for the Anthropocene* (Oxford: Hart, 2017); C. Jefferies, S. L. Seck, and T. Stephens, "International Law, Innovation, and Environmental Change in the Anthropocene," in N. Craik, C. Jefferies, S. L. Seck, and T. Stephens (eds.), *Global Environmental Change and Innovation in International Law* (Cambridge, UK: Cambridge University Press, 2018), pp. 1–18.

[2] See E. O. Wilson, "The Diversity of Life 280 (1992)," referred to in D. Hunter, J. Salzman, and D. Zaelke, *International Environmental Law and Policy* 5th ed. (Sunderland, UK: Foundation Press, 2015), p. 8.

[3] E. S. Brondizio, J. Settele, S. Díaz, and H. T. Ngo (eds.), "Global Assessment Report on Biodiversity and Ecosystem Services of the Intergovernmental Science-Policy Platform on Biodiversity and Ecosystem Services" (IPBES secretariat, Bonn, Germany: IPBES, 2019), p. 12.

[4] "Global Temperatures on Track for 3–5 Degree Rise by 2100: U.N.," Nov. 29, 2018, www.reuters.com/article/us-climate-change-un/global-temperatures-on-track-for-3-5-degree-rise-by-2100-u-n-idUSKCN1NY186. See also, World Bank, "Series: Turn Down the Heat," www.worldbank.org/en/topic/climatechange/publication/turn-down-the-heat.

[5] The World Bank, "Global Waste to Grow by 70 Percent by 2050 Unless Urgent Action Is Taken: World Bank Report," Sept. 20, 2018, www.worldbank.org/en/news/press-release/2018/09/20/global-waste-to-grow-by-70-per cent-by-2050-unless-urgent-action-is-taken-world-bank-report.

[6] R. Harrington, "By 2050, the Oceans Could Have More Plastic than Fish," Jan. 26, 2017, www.businessinsider .com/plastic-in-ocean-outweighs-fish-evidence-report-2017-1.

waste increased from 5 million to 400 million tons *per year*.[7] Much of this waste is generated in affluent countries (the Global North) and is exported to poor and middle-income countries (the Global South) for disposal[8] – a practice that has been denounced as "toxic colonialism." From heavy metals in soils to the chemical contamination of air and water, the extraction of wealth from nature and the disposal of wastes has rendered some places on earth so toxic that they are not suitable for human habitation.[9] Every year, air pollution kills more than seven million people, while lack of access to fresh water and sanitation has been linked to the death of five million people per year.[10]

It is important to recognize that not every person or every state contributed equally to environmental destruction. Nor do all segments of society lead unsustainable lifestyles. Sadly, those who contributed the least to environmental degradation are disproportionately exposed to the resulting harm. In affluent and impoverished countries alike, it is the poor and vulnerable who pay the price for the consumption-driven lifestyles of national and global elites. This imbalance between those who benefit from economic activity and those who bear its adverse social and environmental impacts is one of the hallmarks of environmental injustice.

This volume seeks to examine the complex and multidimensional forms of oppression that produce environmental injustice at the national and international level and the legal frameworks and strategies that have been deployed to combat these injustices. The goal is to develop a more robust conception of environmental justice by engaging with the literature on sustainable development and human rights – particularly the often-neglected social pillar of sustainable development. As many of the case studies in this volume illustrate, environmental justice struggles overlap with struggles for other forms of justice. Despite these overlaps and intersections, the literature on environmental justice often treats them as single, isolated challenges without taking the larger context and underlying historical causes into consideration. As a result, the "solutions" that are adopted or proposed do not address the structural issues that give rise to intersecting forms of injustice, many of them dating back to the colonial era.[11] And the separation of environmental law from other bodies of law makes it impossible to address the root causes of many of these injustices in economic, trade, and investment law.[12]

This chapter proceeds as follows. Section 1.2 describes the evolution of the concept of sustainable development from the 1987 report of the World Commission on Environment and Development (WCED) to the Sustainable Development Goals (SDGs). It discusses contemporary degrowth and green growth movements, before introducing the relatively novel concept of just sustainabilities, a synthesis of environmental justice and sustainable development. Section 1.3 defines environmental justice and discusses its relationship to human rights and the social pillar of sustainable development, reflecting on which dimensions of environmental justice are well reflected in this book and which proved more difficult to address. Section 1.4 then provides an outline of the volume, and assesses limitations, challenges, and areas for further research.

---

[7] The World Counts, "Hazardous Waste Statistics," www.theworldcounts.com/counters/waste_pollution_facts/hazardous_waste_statistics.

[8] The disposal of hazardous waste can cost as much as US$2,000 per ton in developed country versus just US$40 per ton in Africa (Hunter et al., note 2, p. 11).

[9] For example, La Oroya in Peru, the site of a lead smelter, is regarded as one of the world's most polluted places. B. Walsh, "The World's Most Polluted Places: La Oroya, Peru," http://content.time.com/time/specials/2007/article/0,28804,1661031_1661028_1661020,00.html.

[10] See Hunter et al., note 2, p. 15.

[11] See Chapters 3 and 18 in this volume.

[12] See ibid., Chapters 5 and 29.

1.2 SUSTAINABLE DEVELOPMENT FROM BRUNDTLAND
TO THE SDGS

Prior to the advent of sustainable development, the right to development was promoted by the Global South as a manifestation of their right to self-determination.[13] The right to development and sustainable development operated in parallel until the adoption of the SDGs in 2015.[14] Sustainable development has emerged as the overarching framework for environmental govern-ance[15] and a potential alternative to the dominant economic development paradigm.[16] It has come a long way since it was first popularized by the 1987 report of the WCED, also known as the Brundtland Commission.[17]

Defined as "development that meets the needs of the present without compromising the ability of future generations to meet their needs,"[18] sustainable development initially required the balancing of two pillars – economic development and environmental protection.[19] The binary nature of sustainable development was modified at the 1995 World Summit for Social Development, which added a third pillar: social development.[20] As explained in the Summit's Declaration:

> [E]conomic development, social development and environmental protection are interdepend-ent and mutually reinforcing components of sustainable development, which is the framework for our efforts to achieve a higher quality of life for all people. Equitable social development that recognizes empowering of the poor to utilize environmental resources sustainably is a necessary foundation for sustainable development. We also recognize that broad-based and sustained economic growth in the context of sustainable development is necessary to sustain social development and social justice.[21]

Influenced by the Copenhagen Declaration, the 2002 Johannesburg Declaration on Sustainable Development[22] affirmed "collective responsibility to advance and strengthen the interdependent and mutually reinforcing pillars of sustainable development – economic devel-opment, social development and environmental protection – at the local, national, regional and global levels."[23]

---

[13] See K. Mickelson, "The Stockholm Conference and the Creation of the South–North Divide in International Environmental Law," in S. Alam, S. Atapattu, C. G. Gonzalez, and J. Razzaque (eds.), *International Environmental Law and the Global South* (Cambridge, UK: Cambridge University Press, 2015), p. 109.

[14] R. Gordon, "Unsustainable Development," in Alam et al., note 13, p. 50. See UN General Assembly, *Transforming Our World: The 2030 Agenda for Sustainable Development*, Oct. 21, 2015, UN Doc. A/RES/70/1.

[15] See Hunter et al., note 2, p. 114.

[16] See UN World Commission on Environment and Development, *Our Common Future, Report of the World Commission on Environment and Development* (Oxford: Oxford University Press, 1987).

[17] Ibid.

[18] Ibid., p. 43.

[19] Ibid.

[20] UN, *Report of the World Summit for Social Development, Copenhagen*, Mar. 6–12, 1995, UN Doc. A/CONF.166/9 [Copenhagen Declaration].

[21] Ibid.

[22] UN World Summit on Sustainable Development, *Johannesburg Declaration on Sustainable Development*, Sept. 4, 2002, UN Doc. A/CONF.199/20.

[23] Ibid., para. 5. While the Copenhagen Declaration added the social pillar to sustainable development, Agenda 21 adopted at the 1992 United Nations Conference on Environment and Development (UNCED) recognized the importance of social development. It recognized the need to combat poverty, address consumption patterns, and protect health, as well as promoting sustainable human settlements as coming within the social

Thus, sustainable development now comprises three pillars and requires the balancing of all three. But what does social development mean? This third pillar remains under-theorized,[24] but seems to encompass basic human needs such as access to food, water, healthcare, shelter, and education.[25] The social pillar intersects with human rights because many of these basic needs are expressed in rights language.[26]

The commitments made by states in the Copenhagen Declaration elucidate the meaning of the social pillar. These commitments include: creating an economic, political, social, cultural, and legal environment that will enable people to achieve social development; eradicating poverty; promoting the goal of full employment to enable men and women to attain sustainable livelihoods; promoting social integration by fostering societies that are stable, safe, and just, based on the promotion and protection of all human rights and nondiscrimination; promoting full respect for human dignity to achieve equality and equity between men and women; and promoting and attaining the goals of universal and equitable access to quality education and the highest attainable standard of physical and mental health.

Sustainable development is said to embrace the "triple bottom line approach to human wellbeing."[27] It aims for a combination of economic development, environmental sustainability, and social inclusion. Social inclusion includes principles such as nondiscrimination, gender equality, and participation. While states have the "sovereign right to exploit their own resources pursuant to their own environmental and developmental policies,"[28] this right is neither absolute nor limitless and "cannot lawfully be exercised without regard for the detrimental impact on human rights or the environment."[29]

If sustainable development resembles a three-legged stool, giving equal weight to each leg (environmental protection, economic development, and social development) is necessary to ensure that the stool (sustainable development) is stable. However, this depiction of sustainable development has been criticized for placing humanity *outside* the environment and failing to encourage us to recognize our place within the biosphere:[30]

> [I]t perpetuates an even older myth that the environment is something apart from humanity, humanity's economy, and its social well-being. We do not discuss whether sustainable development itself is an oxymoronic concept. We do assume that sustainable development represents a real change in the way humans choose to live so that the viability and subsistence of all living species and their places are ensured.[31]

---

and economic dimensions of sustainable development. UN Sustainable Development, "United Nations Conference on Environment and Development: Agenda 21, June 3–14, 1992.

[24] C. G. Gonzalez, "Environmental Justice, Human Rights and the Global South" (2015) 13 *Santa Clara Journal of International Law* 151.

[25] See Copenhagen Declaration, note 20.

[26] See J. Knox, "Human Rights, Environmental Protection and Sustainable Development Goals" (2015) 24 *Washington International Law Journal* 517 at 518 who argues that while (draft) SDGs set out many worthwhile goals, "the targets often do not contain language that is concrete and focused enough to effectively promote human rights or environmental protection."

[27] See J. Sachs, "From Millennium Development Goals to Sustainable Development Goals" (2012) 379 *Viewpoint* 2206–2211 at 2206.

[28] UN General Assembly, *Rio Declaration on Environment and Development*, Aug. 12, 1992, UN Doc. A/CONF.151/26 (Vol. I), Principle 2.

[29] See P. Birnie, A. Boyle, and C. Redgwell, *International Law and the Environment* 3rd ed. (Oxford: Oxford University Press,2009), p. 115.

[30] See N. Dawe and K. Ryan, "The Faulty Three-Legged-Stool Model of Sustainable Development" (2003) 17 *Conservation Biology* 1458.

[31] Ibid.

In other words, "the environment is not and cannot be a leg of the sustainable development stool. It is the *floor* upon which the stool, or any sustainable development model, must stand."[32] Because humanity and the economy cannot survive without the ecosystem services provided by nature,[33] environmental protection must be the foundation of all development activities. Critics question whether we will ever understand our place on the planet and choose to live within the limits set by the biosphere. Perhaps we can do it, but not by relying on the three-legged stool model "because it continues to place us outside those limits. And while we may be able to think outside the limits, we cannot live outside the limits."[34]

In short, one of the most significant critiques of sustainable development is that it fosters the illusion of unlimited economic growth on a finite planet.[35] Critics point out that the concept of sustainable development has been deployed by global elites to continue to subordinate nature to the imperatives of economic growth, while ignoring ecological limits and planetary boundaries.[36] An economic model based on perpetual economic growth and unbridled extraction of wealth from nature is ill-suited for the achievement of sustainable development. Relying on the same system that created the problem to fix the problem is shortsighted, to say the least. The case studies in this volume illustrate how states continue to give primacy to economic development over environmental protection and social development – to the detriment of species, ecosystems, and vulnerable human beings.

In many respects, sustainable development came of age with the adoption of the 2030 Agenda for Sustainable Development, with its seventeen SDGs and 169 targets.[37] The SDGs build on the Millennium Development Goals (MDGs) and seek to complete what the MDGs failed to achieve. However, the SDGs go much further. Never before have world leaders pledged common action across such a broad and universal policy agenda based on economic, social, and environmental targets within a human rights framework. The SDGs seek to realize human rights for all and to achieve gender equality and the empowerment of all women and girls. They are integrated and indivisible and balance the three dimensions of sustainable development: economic, social, and environmental. Agenda 2030 further recognized that each country faces specific challenges in its pursuit of sustainable development and that vulnerable people must be protected, including children, youth, persons with disabilities, people living with HIV/AIDS, older persons, Indigenous peoples, refugees, and internally displaced persons, and migrants.

Unlike the MDGs, the 2030 agenda and the SDGs are explicitly based on human rights:

We envisage a world of universal respect for human rights and human dignity, the rule of law, justice, equality and non-discrimination; of respect for race, ethnicity and cultural diversity; and of equal opportunity permitting the full realization of human potential and contributing to shared prosperity. A world which invests in its children and in which every child grows up free from violence and exploitation. A world in which every woman and girl enjoys full gender equality and all legal, social and economic barriers to their empowerment have been removed. A just, equitable, tolerant, open and socially inclusive world in which the needs of the most vulnerable are met.[38]

---

[32] Ibid. p. 1459.

[33] See Hunter et al., note 2.

[34] See Dawe and Ryan, note 30.

[35] See Gordon, note 14, pp. 50, 63–64; W. Haydn, *Demystifying Sustainability: Towards Real Solutions* (London: Earthscan, 2015), p. 36.

[36] M. Redclift and G. Woodgate, "Sustainable Development and Nature: The Social and the Material" 21 *Sustainable Development* 92–100 at 92.

[37] This section draws from S. Atapattu, "From 'Our Common Future' to Sustainable Development Goals: Evolution of Sustainable Development under International Law" (2019) 36 *Wisconsin International Law Journal* 215.

[38] UN General Assembly, note 14.

It remains to be seen how much progress the international community will make toward achieving the SDGs by 2030. Although reducing poverty and improving the living standards of people has been on the global agenda since the creation of the UN, over one billion people continue to live in poverty.[39] The problem is not the failure to generate wealth, but the uneven distribution of this wealth, including its concentration in fewer and fewer hands.[40] In addition, the SDGs continue to envisage economic growth as the primary engine of poverty reduction. Goal 8, for example, seeks to increase gross domestic product (GDP) growth in the least developed countries along with higher levels of economic productivity in all countries.[41] By failing to acknowledge the need to reduce economic growth in affluent countries in order to improve living standards in poor countries without exceeding ecological limits, the SDGs "fail to reconcile the contradiction between growth and sustainability at the core of sustainable development."[42]

Because the current capitalist economic model, with its emphasis on unlimited growth, is the main cause of the current environmental crisis, scholars, activists, and grassroots environmental justice movements have begun advocating for "degrowth."[43] The idea of degrowth is emerging as a response to the triple crisis – environmental, social, and economic – we are facing. Degrowth is slowing down economic growth based on the narrow economic measure of GDP growth,[44] which, as the feminist movement pointed out, does not value what is not in the market, such as unpaid domestic work and voluntary work.[45] It questions the way of life linked to growth and asks what makes people really prosperous?[46] The production of goods and services and improving standards of living is the focus of the current economic model. However, "the ecological crisis tells us that this story of social progress through economic growth is highly questionable."[47] Sustainable degrowth is defined as: "[a]n equitable down-scaling of production and consumption that increases human well-being and enhances ecological conditions at the local and global level."[48] Proponents of sustainable degrowth do not propose degrowth across the board; they recognize that certain social and small-scale economic activities and impoverished

---

[39] See FINCA, "World Poverty Facts," https://finca.org/campaign/world-poverty/?gclid=CjwKCAiA5 8fvBRAzEiwAQW-hzeffdCSfYqP7dqmdBtUEqVTn_ajwIyTEK5cbbMVsmPmmwo-Hx5kiuBoCa7wQAvD_ BwE. However, according to the World Bank, "in 2015, 10 percent of the world's population lived on less than \$1.90 a day, down from nearly 36 percent in 1990. Progress has been uneven, and the number of people in extreme poverty remains unacceptably high. Given growth forecasts, the world is not on track to end extreme poverty by 2030" ("Poverty at a Glance," www.worldbank.org/en/topic/poverty).

[40] According to Oxfam, twenty-six billionaires currently control as much wealth as the poorest half of the world's population. Oxfam, "Public Good or Private Wealth?" Jan. 2019, p. 12.

[41] See Target 8.1, https://sustainabledevelopment.un.org/sdg8#targets.

[42] S. Adelman, "The Sustainable Development Goals, Anthropocentrism and Neoliberalism," in D. French and L. Kotzé (eds.), *Global Goals: Law, Theory & Implementation* (Cheltenham, UK: Edward Elgar, 2018), p. 34.

[43] F. Demaria, G. Kallis, and K. Bakker, "Geographies of Degrowth: Nowtopias, Resurgences and the Decolonization of Imaginaries and Places" (2019) 2 ENE: *Nature and Space* 431; B. Akbulut, F. Demaria, J. F. Gerber, and J. Martinez-Alier, "Who Promotes Sustainability? Five Theses on the Relationships between the Degrowth and Environmental Justice Movements" (2019) 165 *Ecological Economics* 106418.

[44] J. Martinez-Alier, "Environmental Justice and Economic Degrowth: An Alliance between Two Movements, Capitalism, Nature, Socialism" (2012) 23 *Capitalism Nature Socialism* 51.

[45] F. Schneider, G. Kallis, and J. Martinez-Alier, "Crisis or Opportunity? Economic Degrowth for Social Equity and Ecological Sustainability" (2010) 18 *Journal of Cleaner Production* 511.

[46] See C. Bauhardt, "Solutions to the Crisis? The Green New Deal. Degrowth, and the Solidarity Economy: Alternatives to the Capitalist Growth Economy from an Ecofeminist Economics Perspective" (2014) 102 *Ecological Economics* 60.

[47] Ibid.

[48] See Schneider et al., note 45, p. 512

groups or regions may still need to grow. However, growth that externalizes its costs elsewhere is not sustainable.[49]

While there is an urgent need to reduce the overall consumption of resources, it is no secret that most of this consumption takes place in the Global North, while much of the world's population remains mired in poverty. As the Degrowth Declaration of 2008 recognized: "By using more than their legitimate share of global environmental resources, the wealthiest nations are effectively reducing the environmental space available to poorer nations, and imposing adverse environmental impacts on them."[50] The Declaration also recognized that global economic growth has not succeeded in reducing poverty, that "unequal exchange in trade and financial markets" has increased inequality between countries,[51] and that we need to bring economic activity in line with the capacity of our ecosystems and to redistribute wealth and income globally.[52] The Declaration defines degrowth as "a voluntary transition towards a just, participatory and ecologically sustainable society."[53] Degrowth must occur in wealthy parts of the world through a transformation of the global economic system. The objectives of degrowth are "to meet basic human needs and ensure a high quality of life, while reducing the ecological impact of the global economy to a sustainable level, equitably distributed between nations."[54]

Thus, the objectives of sustainable development and degrowth are similar. Degrowth, with its emphasis on reducing consumption in affluent countries, advocates for an alternative economic model that respects planetary boundaries.[55] Sustainable development has a similar objective at least in theory, even though it has failed to explicitly call for degrowth.

A second approach to the interlocking economic and ecological crises is the concept of the "green economy" or "green growth," often used interchangeably. This approach ranges from a narrow emphasis on eco-industry and environmentally friendly production to a redefinition of a country's entire economy.[56] Between these two extremes are policies that promote low-carbon economies with dematerialization, decoupling of resource use and environmental impacts from economic growth, valuing ecosystem services, or simply increasing energy efficiency.[57] United Nations Environment Programme (UNEP) has been a great proponent of the green economy as "an engine for growth," generating jobs and eradicating poverty. It defines green economy as "one that results in improved human well-being and social equity, while significantly reducing environmental risks and ecological scarcities."[58] According to UNEP:

> In its simplest expression, a green economy can be thought of as one which is low carbon, resource efficient and socially inclusive. In a green economy, growth in income and employment should be driven by public and private investments that reduce carbon emissions and pollution, enhance

---

[49] Ibid.

[50] Research and Degrowth, "Degrowth Declaration of the Paris 2008 Conference" (2010) 18 *Journal of Cleaner Production* 523, s. 7. The Declaration was adopted at the Economic Degrowth for Ecological Sustainability and Social Equity Conference in Paris in April 2008.

[51] Ibid., s. 3.

[52] Ibid.

[53] Ibid.

[54] Ibid.

[55] See J. C. J. M. van den Bergh and G. Kallis, "Growth, A-Growth or Degrowth to Stay within Planetary Boundaries?" (2012) 46 *Journal of Economic Issues* 909–920; J. Martinez-Alier, "Environmental Justice and Economic Degrowth: An Alliance between Two Movements" (2012) 23 *Capitalism Nature Socialism* 51.

[56] O. Bina, "The Green Economy and Sustainable Development: An Uneasy Balance?" (2013) 31 *Environment and Planning C: Government and Policy* 1023 at 1024.

[57] Ibid.

[58] UN Environment Programme (UNEP), "Towards a Green Economy: Pathways to Sustainable Development and Poverty Eradication. A Synthesis for Policy Makers," 2011, p. 2; Bina, note 56.

energy and resource efficiency, and prevent the loss of biodiversity and ecosystem services. These investments need to be catalysed and supported by targeted public expenditure, policy reforms and regulation changes. The development path should maintain, enhance and, where necessary, rebuild natural capital as a critical economic asset and as a source of public benefits, especially for poor people whose livelihoods and security depend on nature.[59]

The UNEP report points out that the green economy does not replace sustainable development but creates an enabling framework for its realization. "Decades of creating new wealth through a 'brown economy' model have not substantially addressed social marginalization and resource depletion."[60] In order to transition to a green economy, specific enabling conditions will be required but these conditions are currently heavily weighted toward the prevailing brown economy, which depends excessively on fossil fuel energy. The report seeks to debunk certain myths surrounding the green economy, the most widespread being that there is a trade-off between environmental sustainability and economic progress. UNEP insists that the "greening" of economies neither inhibits wealth creation nor employment opportunities.[61]

However, the notion of a green economy appears to pour old wine into new bottles, essentially preserving the status quo with a few minor tweaks. Indeed, since the green economy was floated as "an alternative" to the existing economic development model (brown economy as the UNEP report calls it) at Rio+20 conference in 2012, nothing much seems to have changed. In fact, as the UNEP's own "Emissions Gap" report shows, greenhouse gas emissions have increased to a historic high level,[62] and global dependence on fossil fuels has not declined.

The SDGs do not endorse the green economy or green growth. On the contrary, while SDG 12 refers to the need to ensure sustainable consumption and production patterns, SDG 8 continues to use GDP as a measure of economic success.[63] Rather than degrowth, SDG 8 promotes the need to *increase* the rate of economic growth:

> Inclusive and sustainable economic growth can drive progress and generate the means to implement the Sustainable Development Goals. Globally, labour productivity has increased and unemployment is back to pre-financial crisis levels. However, the global economy is growing at a slower rate. More progress is needed to increase employment opportunities, particularly for young people, reduce informal employment and the gender pay gap and promote safe and secure working environments to create decent work for all.[64]

In sum, while sustainable development might accommodate both degrowth and the green economy, degrowth is more likely to achieve sustainable development by slowing down the global economy and reducing consumption in affluent countries in order to give poor countries the ecological space to improve living standards. Regrettably, the SDGs preserve the status quo by calling for an increase in economic growth and merely labeling it "sustainable economic growth." Unless we recognize that the current environmental crisis is due to an economic system premised on the unbridled extraction of wealth from nature and the exploitation and dispossession of human beings, we will only be tinkering at the margins without seeing any positive results. Real change requires recognizing that the environment is the floor on which both society and the economy rest.

---

[59] UNEP, note 58, p. 2.
[60] Ibid.
[61] Ibid.
[62] UN Environment Programme, "Emissions Gap Report 2019, Executive Summary," 2019.
[63] Target 8.1, note 41.
[64] "Progress of Goal 8 for 2019," https://sustainabledevelopment.un.org/sdg8.

This volume seeks to fill a significant gap in the scholarly literature by examining the relationship between environmental justice and sustainable development, particularly its social pillar. One of the few frameworks that does attempt to address this relationship is the "just sustainabilities" framework proposed by Agyeman *et al.* The authors define "just sustainabilities" as "the need to ensure a better quality of life for all, now, and into the future, in a just and equitable manner, while living within the limits of supporting ecosystems."[65] This framing encompasses fairness, equity including inter and intragenerational equity, precaution, environmental sustainability, and social justice. The authors acknowledge that:

> In recent years it has become increasingly apparent that the issue of environmental quality is inextricably linked to that of human equality. Wherever in the world environmental despoliation and degradation is happening, it is almost always linked to questions of social justice, equity, rights and people's quality of life in its widest sense.[66]

The authors make three interrelated arguments in support of their framework. First, they point out that countries with more equal distributions of income, better rights, and higher literacy rates tend to have higher environmental quality than those who do not.[67] Second, they note that environmental problems tend to affect the poor disproportionately, even though the poor are not the major polluters. While the rich are better able to insulate themselves from the negative impacts of pollution and other environmental degradation, poor people lack the resources to do so.[68] Finally, they emphasize that sustainability "cannot be simply an 'environmental' concern, important though 'environmental' sustainability is. A truly sustainable society is one where wider questions of social needs and welfare, and economic opportunity, are integrally connected to environmental concerns."[69]

The "just sustainabilities" framework is a useful reminder that sustainability and environmental justice are inextricably intertwined. Sustainability cannot be achieved without considering social justice, economic opportunity, and environmental protection. But just what is environmental justice?

1.3 ENVIRONMENTAL JUSTICE

Environmental justice has become the rallying cry of subordinated communities throughout the world who are disproportionately burdened by environmental degradation. While social justice struggles with an environmental dimension can be found throughout history, the discourse of environmental justice emerged in the United States in the 1980s, as poor people and racial and ethnic minorities mobilized to combat the siting of polluting facilities and hazardous waste disposal sites in their communities.[70] In recent decades, vulnerable communities in both affluent and poor countries and even vulnerable states, such as the small island states, have embraced the discourse of environmental justice.[71]

---

[65] See J. Agyeman, R. D. Bullard, and B. Evans, (eds.), *Just Sustainabilities: Development in an Unequal World* (Boston, MA: MIT Press, 2003), p. 7 who believe that "one explanation for the success of the environmental justice movement can be seen in the mutual benefits of a coalition between environmental and social concerns."

[66] Ibid., p. 1.

[67] Ibid.

[68] Ibid.

[69] Ibid., p. 2.

[70] C. G. Gonzalez, "Environmental Racism, American Exceptionalism, and Cold War Human Rights" (2017) 26 *Transnational Law and Contemporary Problems* 281 at 282–283.

[71] L. Temper, D. del Bene, and J. Martinez-Alier, "Mapping the Frontiers and Front Lines of Global Environmental Justice: The EJAtlas" (2015) 22 *Journal of Political Ecology* 255–278.

The language of environmental justice is morally compelling and has given a voice to marginalized communities. However, much of the literature on environmental justice has failed to develop a rigorous analysis of the complex ways that poverty, race, gender, indigeneity, age, and disability, among other identity characteristics, many of which are subject to protection under international human rights law, intersect to produce environmental injustice in specific contexts. In other words, the social pillar of sustainable development and its relationship to environmental justice is under-theorized.

Environmental justice scholars and activists have attempted to address this shortcoming by articulating a four-part definition of environmental justice consisting of distributive justice, procedural justice, corrective justice, and social justice.[72] Distributive justice requires the fair allocation of the benefits and burdens of economic activity among and within nations.[73] Procedural justice calls for transparent, informed, and inclusive environmental decision-making processes.[74] Corrective justice requires governments to enforce environmental laws, compensate those whose rights are violated, and terminate the harm-producing conduct.[75] Social justice emphasizes that environmental struggles are inextricably intertwined with struggles for social and economic justice.[76] In other words, environmental injustice cannot be separated from economic exploitation, race and gender subordination, the marginalization of children, the elderly, immigrants, and persons with disabilities, the ongoing dispossession of Indigenous peoples, and the colonial and postcolonial domination of the Global South. As the case studies in this volume illustrate, environmental conflicts frequently involve multiple dimensions of environmental justice, and do not fit neatly into one of the four categories. Yet, it cannot be said that the case studies in this volume grapple with the full intersectional dimensions of environmental justice; rather, different dimensions are explored in different chapters, with some dimensions untouched, perhaps most notably disability.

The chapters in this volume expand upon the four-fold definition of environmental justice. For example, several of the chapters address the failure of Western law and policy to recognize and respect the lived experiences and world views of subaltern communities, particularly Indigenous peoples[77] – a phenomenon known as epistemic injustice. Coined by philosopher Miranda Fricker,[78] the concept of epistemic injustice has been used by prominent legal scholars, such as Rebecca Tsosie, to explain the harms caused by "the uncritical application of Western values, categories, and standards to the very different social experience" of Indigenous peoples.[79] The chapters in this volume shed light on the concept of epistemic

[72] See R. R. Kuehn, "A Taxonomy of Environmental Justice" (2000) 30 *Environmental Law Reporter* 10681; C. G. Gonzalez, "Environmental Justice and International Law," in S. Alam, J. H. Bhuiyan, T. M. R. Chowdury, and E. J. Techera (eds.), *Routledge Handbook of International Environmental Law* (Abingdon, UK: Routledge, 2013), p. 77 (applying this definition to environmental conflicts between affluent and poor countries).

[73] See D. French, "Sustainable Development and the Instinctive Imperative of Justice in the Global Order," in D. French (ed.), *Global Justice and Sustainable Development* (Leiden: Martinus Nijhoff, 2010), p. 8.

[74] See Kuehn, note 72, p. 10688.

[75] Ibid., pp. 10693–10698; M. Burkett, "Climate Reparations"(2009) 10 *Melbourne Journal of International Law* 513 at 522–523.

[76] See C. G. Gonzalez, "An Environmental Justice Critique of Comparative Advantage: Indigenous Peoples, Trade Policy, and the Mexican Neoliberal Economic Reforms" (2011) 32 *University of Pennsylvania Journal of International Law* 728; R. Guha, *Environmentalism: A Global History* (New York: Longman, 2000), p. 105.

[77] See for example Chapters 4, 14, and 23 in this volume.

[78] M. Fricker, *Epistemic Injustice: Power and the Ethics of Knowing* (Oxford: Oxford University Press, 2007).

[79] R. Tsosie, "Indigenous Peoples and Epistemic Injustice: Science, Ethics and Human Rights" (2012) 87 *Washington Law Review* 1133 at 1201; B. de Sousa Santos, *Epistemologies of the South: Justice against Epistemicide* (Boulder, CO: Paradigm, 2014).

injustice by explaining the differences between Indigenous and Western knowledge, the ways in which Indigenous communities have been harmed by the subordination of their world views, and the importance of Indigenous epistemologies and cosmologies not only to Indigenous self-determination, but also to the achievement by all communities of environmental justice and sustainable development. In Latin America and Canada, for example, Indigenous cosmovisions have served as the foundation for alternatives to Eurocentric notions of development. Known as *buen vivir* or living well,[80] these alternative approaches deny the human–nature binary, reject the Western obsession with economic growth, and adopt a communitarian and participatory vision of environmental justice.[81]

The chapters in this volume also expand our understanding of environmental racism.[82] Developed by the environmental justice movement in the United States, the term environmental racism refers to the disproportionate concentration of environmental hazards in racial and ethnic minority communities.[83] Who is racialized and how they are racialized is socially constructed, rather than phenotypically predetermined, and varies substantially from country to country and over time in relation to changing economic and political circumstances.[84] In the United States, for example, African Americans, Latinos, and Indigenous communities have long been racialized and subjected to inequitable environmental burdens.[85] Conversely, Jews and the Irish, who are currently usually classified as White, have a long history in Europe and the United States of being regarded as non-White.[86]

Racialization is a global phenomenon embedded in the life cycle of fossil fuel–based capitalism. The extraction of wealth from nature was implemented through the dispossession and conquest of Indigenous peoples, through slavery, through the "slow violence" inflicted by the fossil fuel industry on marginalized communities, through the bloody resource wars instigated by the Global North in the Middle East, and through the colonial and postcolonial domination by White Euro-American elites of large segments of the world's population.[87] These practices targeted populations constructed as non-White and were justified through a variety of legal doctrines, including *terra nullius*, the doctrine of discovery, the mandate system after World War I, and the trusteeship system after World War II. These doctrines depicted racialized peoples as so primitive and in need of "modernization and development" that their livelihoods and world views were not worthy of protection.[88] Ironically, those most susceptible to climate

---

[80] See Chapters 4, 11, and 12 in this volume.

[81] A. Acosta, "El Buen (con) Vivir, una utopía por (re)construir: Alcances de la Constitución de Montecristi" Otra Economía: Revista Latinoamericana de economía social y solidaria" (2010) 4 *Otra Economía* 8–31; A. Acosta and E. Gudynas, "La renovación de la crítica al Desarrollo y el buen vivir como alternativa" (2011) 16 *Utopía y Praxis Latinoamericana* 71–83; E. Gudynas, "Buen Vivir: Today's Tomorrow" 54 *Development* 441.

[82] See Chapters 5 and 8 in this volume.

[83] Gonzalez, note 70, pp. 282–283. Environmental racism was invoked by the petitioners in the *Mossville* case filed before the Inter-American Commission of Human Rights and the complaint filed before the UN Committee against Racial Discrimination. This is the first time that environmental justice groups used environmental racism in a human rights complaint against the USA. See Report No 43/10, Petition 242-05, Admissibility, *Mossville Environmental Action Now* v. *USA*, Mar. 17, 2010. See also www.enrichproject.org/about/background.

[84] A. Reed. Jr., "Marx, Race, and Neoliberalism" (2013) 22 *New Labor Forum* 49 at 50.

[85] See Chapter 8 in this volume.

[86] See generally N. Ignatiev, *How the Irish Became White* (New York: Routledge, 1995); K. Brodkin, *How Jews Became White Folks and What that Says about Race in America* (New Brunswick, NJ: Rutgers University Press, 1998).

[87] See Chapter 5 in this volume.

[88] See A. Anghie, *Imperialism, Sovereignty and the Making of International Law* (Cambridge, UK: Cambridge University Press, 2014).

change-related displacement (and to detention, criminalization, and deportation if they attempt to migrate to the Global North) are also overwhelmingly persons classified as non-White.[89] A race-conscious analysis of the capitalist world economy highlights the intersection of environmental justice struggles with other social movements, including movements for Indigenous rights, economic justice, immigrant rights, peace, reparations for slavery and colonialism, and for the restructuring of international economic laws and institutions that facilitate the plunder of nature and the impoverishment of the Global South.[90]

Other intersecting forms of oppression are also crucial to consider,[91] and yet are often not fully explored by environmental justice scholars. For example, several contributions to this volume consider the gender dimensions of environmental justice in detail,[92] while others merely touch upon it in passing,[93] or not at all. Gender, like race, is socially constructed, and gender roles are therefore historically contingent. As noted in the Gender Guidance of the United Nations Working Group on Business and Human Rights:

> The term "gender" refers to socially constructed roles of and power relations among men, women and gender non-binary persons, all of whom may be affected differently by business activities. However, considering that women have historically been discriminated against owing to patriarchal norms and power structures, the guidance in the report focuses only on women, although the gender framework proposed herein could be used in relation to any group of rights holders.[94]

Similarly, yet more expansively, the understanding of gender embraced by Canada's National Inquiry into Missing and Murdered Indigenous Women and Girls is an inclusive one that goes well beyond the biological binary of women and men, encompassing all identities and diverse sexualities, including, *inter alia*, gay, lesbian, bisexual, transgender, queer, and Two-Spirit, among other ways in which people self-identify.[95] While several chapters in the book address injustices involving violations of the human rights of women and girls, our contributors generally do not explicitly explore gender-based environmental injustices in this more fulsome manner.

Vulnerable communities do frequently frame their demands for environmental justice in the language of human rights, even though most human rights treaties do not contain explicit

---

[89] See Chapter 5 in this volume.

[90] Ibid.

[91] On intersectionality, see K. Crenshaw, "Demarginalizing the Intersections of Race and Sex: A Black Feminist Critique of Antidiscrimination Doctrine, Feminist Theory, and Antiracist Politics" (1989) *University of Chicago Legal Forum* 139–167.

[92] See Chapters 14, 21, and 24 in this volume.

[93] See ibid., Chapters 25 and 27.

[94] UN General Assembly, *Gender Dimensions of the Guiding Principles on Business and Human Rights*, May 23, 2019, UN Doc. A/HRC/41/43, para. 9 regarding scope and limitations. The report contains gender guidance for states and business enterprises in relation to all three pillars of the UN Guiding Principles on Business and Human Rights. The paragraph continues: "The guidance should be read together with other relevant standards, such as the standards of conduct for business, published by the Office of the United Nations High Commissioner for Human Rights, aimed at tackling discrimination against lesbian, gay, bisexual, transgender and intersex persons, and the Children's Rights and Business Principles."

[95] See National Inquiry into Missing and Murdered Indigenous Women and Girls, "Reclaiming Power and Place: The Final Report of the National Inquiry into Missing and Murdered Indigenous Women and Girls: Volume 1a," 2019, p. 58 [MMIWG Final Report] where the National Inquiry interpreted its mandate widely "to include 2SLGBTQQIA people (people who are Two-Spirit, lesbian, gay, bisexual, transgender, queer, questioning, intersex, and asexual). This is particularly important for people who don't fit the gender binary of 'male' or 'female,' since their gender isn't reflected in a simple statement of 'Indigenous women and girls' . . . and as an explicit reminder that gender-diverse people's needs must equally be taken into account."

environmental provisions. National and international tribunals have concluded that environmental degradation violates existing human rights, including the rights to life, health, food, and water; the procedural rights to information, participation, and access to justice; the collective rights of Indigenous peoples to their ancestral lands and resources; and the right to a healthy environment, which is recognized in a large number of national constitutions as well as legislative provisions.[96]

State obligations to protect, respect, and fulfil environmental human rights are often thought to be essential to achieving environmental and climate justice. For example, the 2018 Framework Principles on Human Rights and the Environment,[97] developed by the former Special Rapporteur on Human Rights and the Environment, note in Principles 1 and 2 that "States should ensure a safe, clean, healthy and sustainable environment in order to respect, protect, and fulfil human rights" while at the same time "States should respect, protect and fulfil human rights in order to ensure a safe, clean, healthy and sustainable environment." The concept of a sustainable environment must also include a sustainable earth system, although it is rare for international legal instruments to state this with clarity.

Nondiscrimination is a cross-cutting theme in the 2018 Framework Principles, with Principle 3 calling upon states to "prohibit discrimination and ensure equal and effective protection against discrimination in relation to the enjoyment of a safe, clean, healthy, and sustainable environment." Meanwhile, Principle 14 elaborates upon the need for states to take "additional measures to protect the rights of those who are most vulnerable to, or at particular risk from, environmental harm, taking into account their needs, risks, and capabilities." The commentary points out that vulnerability may arise due to the unusual susceptibility of some to environmental harm, or due to a denial of human rights, or both.[98] Those who are at increased risk from environmental harm "often include women, children, persons living in poverty, members of indigenous peoples and traditional communities, older persons, persons with disabilities, ethnic, racial or other minorities and displaced persons."[99]

While women are among those identified as often vulnerable due to both susceptibility to environmental harm and denial of human rights, a full analysis of women's rights violations will require attention to social and cultural dimensions. For example, not all women have the same relationship with land and water as the many Indigenous women who self-identify as water keepers or land protectors.[100] As a result, a women's empowerment and equality response that

---

[96] See D. R. Boyd, *The Environmental Rights Revolution: A Global Study of Constitutions, Human Rights, and the Environment* (Vancouver: UBC Press, 2012); L. Kotzé, *Global Environmental Constitutionalism in the Anthropocene* (Oxford: Oxford University Press, 2016); J. R. May and E. Daly, *Global Environmental Constitutionalism* (Cambridge, UK: Cambridge University Press, 2016); S. Atapattu and A. Schapper, *Human Rights and the Environment: Key Issues* (Abingdon, UK: Routledge, 2019), ch. 7; J. C. Gellers, *The Global Emergence of Constitutional Environmental Rights* (Abingdon, UK: Routledge, 2017).

[97] UN General Assembly, *Report of the Special Rapporteur on the issue of human rights obligations relating to the enjoyment of a safe, clean, healthy and sustainable environment*, Jan. 24, 2018, UN Doc. A/HRC/37/59. Arguably this framework applies also to business responsibilities to respect and support environmental human rights. See S. L. Seck, "Transnational Labour Law and the Environment: Beyond the Bounded Autonomous Worker" (2018) 33 *Canadian Journal of Law and Society* 137–157; S. L. Seck, "Indigenous Rights, Environmental Rights, or Stakeholder Engagement? Comparing IFC and OECD Approaches to the Implementation of the Business Responsibility to Respect Human Rights" (2016) 12 *McGill Journal of Sustainable Development Law* 48–91.

[98] UNGA, note 97, para. 40.

[99] Ibid., para. 41.

[100] S. Morales, "Digging for Rights: How Can International Human Rights Law Better Protect Indigenous Women from Extractive Industries?" (2019) 31 *Canadian Journal of Women and the Law* 58; S. L. Seck, "Relational Law: Re-imagining Tools for Environmental and Climate Justice" (2019) 31 *Canadian Journal of*

advocates increasing female representation in upper management of mining companies, for example, may not fully respond to the gender blindness of the mining industry if none of those women are Indigenous.[101] Similarly, if the call for women's equality and empowerment, in keeping with SDG 5, is linked exclusively to ensuring access to education in science and technology disciplines, without embedding equal respect for local and Indigenous knowledge often held by Indigenous women, then the vital importance of two-eyed seeing for environmental and climate justice will be missed.[102] The importance of education on environmental matters is noted in Framework Principle 6, as without the capacity to understand environmental risks, the public is not able to fully exercise their rights to express their views and participate effectively in environmental decision-making. Yet, whose knowledge is valued in decision-making matters as well.

The Framework Principles highlight other vulnerable groups who should be considered as part of an intersectional analysis, including children (the girl child), older people (grandmothers), those with disabilities, those living in poverty, and those who experience discrimination on the basis of race, ethnic, or other minority status, as well as those subject to environmental or climate-induced displacement. Principle 15 separately addresses the importance of compliance with obligations "to indigenous communities and members of traditional communities'" in many ways, including through respect and protection of their rights to traditional lands, territories and resources, consulting them to obtain their free, prior, and informed consent, and respecting and protecting traditional knowledge and practices in conservation and sustainable use. This principle and commentary are silent on gender, although the United Nations Declaration on the Rights of Indigenous Peoples (UNDRIP) is not,[103] yet it is important to consider the gender dimensions of its implementation more deeply. Many Indigenous feminist scholars have noted the vital importance of not placing Indigenous women in the position of being seen to undermine their own community's self-determination and self-governance by seeking protection from the state (or a company) against their community.[104] A nuanced response is therefore required, and one that does not position the state (or company) as the savior of women against the uncivilized "other" that underlies international law's colonial history.[105] In some cases patriarchal norms have infiltrated local community governance as a result of colonial histories. Challenges to these social norms must come from within and are best supported – but not necessarily mandated – from outside. Similarly, women who take on the responsibility of serving as environmental human rights defenders may face challenges both from within and outside

---

Women and the Law 151–177 (citing writings by Deborah McGregor, Janice Makokis, and Isabel Altamirano-Jiménez). See generally S. L. Seck and P. Simons, "Resource Extraction and the Human Rights of Women and Girls: Introduction to Special Issue" (2019) 31 *Canadian Journal of Women and the Law*, special issue edited by S. L. Seck and P. Simons, pp. i–vii.

[101] See K. MacMaster and S. L. Seck, "Mining for Equality: Soft Targets and Hard Floors for Boards of Directors," in O. Fitzgerald (ed.), *The Corporation in International, Transnational, and Domestic Law and Governance – Canadian Perspectives on Globalized Rule of Law* (Centre for International Governance Innovation, forthcoming).

[102] On the importance of two-eyed seeing, see MMIWG Final Report, note 95, pp. 132–133. According to L'nu Mi'kmaq scholar Tuma Young, the concept of two-eyed seeing is very important: "An issue has to be looked at from two different perspectives: the Western perspective and the Indigenous perspective, so that this provides the whole picture for whoever is trying to understand the particular issue" (ibid., p. 132).

[103] UN, Declaration on the Rights of Indigenous Peoples, Sept. 13, 2007, UN Doc. A/RES/61/295, Arts. 21 and 22.

[104] I. Altamirano-Jiménez, "The State Is Not a Saviour: Indigenous Law, Gender and the Neoliberal State in Oaxaca," in J. Green (ed.), *Making Space for Indigenous Feminism*, 2nd ed. (Halifax: Fernwood, 2017) pp. 215, 228–229.

[105] See Seck, note 100, pp. 165–166, citing the work of I. Altamirano-Jiménez.

their communities, at times opposing development projects which are supported by others within their community, and subject to harassment if not violence for challenging gender norms.[106] These women must be supported, but this can only be achieved if intersectional dimensions are integrated into the response.

Beyond poverty, gender, and race, there are other environmental justice vulnerabilities to consider. A frequently missing one, including from this book, is disability. According to the World Health Organization (WHO), "vulnerability is the degree to which a population, individual or organization is unable to anticipate, cope with, resist and recover from the impacts of disasters."[107] Disability should play a key role in the application of intersectionality, and an intersectional environmental justice framework should help us see disability justice and racial justice "as not separate but rather interconnected and at times the very same project."[108] For example, in addition to poor people of color who were disproportionately affected by Hurricane Katrina, people with disabilities were also disproportionately affected, yet this did not receive much attention.[109]

As the world experiences more and more adverse consequences of climate change, especially disasters and extreme weather events, we need to pay particular attention to those who will be trapped due to disability or age.[110] The elderly are more prone to extreme weather events than younger age groups as they are less mobile and may not have support networks. For example, in the deadly heatwave in Europe in 2003, during which a record number of 30,000 people perished (15,000 in France alone), the elderly and chronically ill were the most susceptible to the heat.[111] Indeed, as the Deputy Director of Regional Programs of the Global Greengrants Fund has stated: "We are not truly an environmental justice organization unless we have the full understanding of fifteen percent of the world's population. People with disabilities need to be a full part of finding solutions to unequal access to natural resources and right to a healthy environment."[112]

As Kimberlé Crenshaw points out in her pioneering work on intersectionality:

> If [we] began with addressing the needs and problems of those who are most disadvantaged and with restructuring and remaking the world where necessary, then others who are singularly disadvantaged would also benefit. In addition, it seems that placing those who are currently marginalized in the center is the most effective way to resist efforts to compartmentalize and undermine potential collective action.[113]

Closely aligned with the intersectionality theory is compound injustice. Proposed by Henry Shue, "compound injustice" occurs when an initial injustice paves the way for a second. An example is when colonial exploitation weakens the colonized nation to such an extent that the

---

[106] K. Deonandan and C. Bell, "Discipline and Punish: Gendered Dimensions of Violence in Extractive Development" (2019) 31 *Canadian Journal of Women and the Law* 24.

[107] B. Wisner, J. Adams, and WHO, "Environmental Health in Emergencies and Disasters: A Practical Guide" (WHO, 2002).

[108] See C. Jampel, "Intersections of Disability Justice, Racial Justice and Environmental Justice, Environmental Sociology" (2018) 4 *Environmental Sociology* 122–135.

[109] Ibid.

[110] UNGA, note 97.

[111] The editors of *Encyclopaedia Britannica*, "European Heat Wave of 2003," www.britannica.com/event/ European-heat-wave-of-2003.

[112] "Why the Environmental Justice Movement Must Include Persons with Disabilities," Mar. 18, 2019, www .greengrants.org/2019/03/18/disability-and-environment.

[113] See Crenshaw, note 91, p. 167.

colonizer can impose unequal treaties upon it even after it gains independence.[114] The current economic subordination of the Global South[115] is a good example of compound injustice.

Finally, environmental justice movements have recognized the limitations of human-centric conceptions of justice, and have embraced intergenerational justice (the rights of future generations)[116] and the rights of nature to address some of these deficiencies.[117] For example, the principles of environmental justice developed by the delegates to the 1991 First National People of Color Environmental Leadership Summit held in Washington, DC, recognized both intergenerational justice and the rights of nature.[118] Principle 1 "affirms the sacredness of Mother Earth, ecological unity and the interdependence of all species, and the right to be free from ecological destruction."[119] Principle 3 "mandates the right to ethical, balanced and responsible uses of land and renewable resources in the interest of a sustainable planet for humans and other living things."[120] Principle 17 "requires that we, as individuals, make personal and consumer choices to consume as little of Mother Earth's resources and to produce as little waste as possible; and make the conscious decision to challenge and reprioritize our lifestyles to ensure the health of the natural world for present and future generations."[121] In order to operationalize these principles, some scholars have proposed specific criteria for equitably allocating the planet's resources between humans and other living creatures.[122]

In sum, while the environmental justice movement seeks to achieve justice for human beings, increasing attention is being paid to justice for other species.[123] Even the human rights framework, which until recently, was about protecting rights of *human beings*, is increasingly according rights to other species and to nature itself as seen in the 2017 Advisory Opinion of the Inter-American Court of Human Rights.[124]

1.4 OUTLINE OF THE BOOK, CHALLENGES, OPTIONS, AND AREAS FOR FURTHER RESEARCH

This volume is divided into three parts. Part I examines the relationship among environmental justice, sustainable development, and human rights, through several theoretical frameworks. We begin with Erin Daly and James R. May's exploration of human dignity and sustainability, in which they propose that the economic, social, and environmental pillars of sustainability are best

---

[114] See H. Shue, *Climate Justice: Vulnerability and Protection* (Oxford: Oxford University Press, 2014), p. 4.

[115] A. Anghie, "The Evolution of International Law: Colonial and Postcolonial Realities" (2006) 27 *Third World Quarterly* 739 at 747.

[116] See generally E. Brown Weiss, *In Fairness to Future Generations: International Law, Common Patrimony, and Intergenerational Equity* (New York: Transnational, 1989).

[117] See generally R. Nash, *The Rights of Nature* (Wisconsin: University of Wisconsin Press, 1989).

[118] See First People of Color Environmental Leadership Summit, "Principles of Environmental Justice," Oct. 24–27, 1991, www.ejnet.org/ej/principles.html.

[119] Ibid., Principle 1.

[120] Ibid., Principle 3.

[121] Ibid., Principle 17.

[122] See J. Riechmann, "Tres principios básicos de la justicia ambiental" (2003) 21 *Revista Internacional de Filosofía Política* 103 at 107–108, 112–115.

[123] See J. Ebbesson, "Introduction: Dimensions of Justice in Environmental Law," in J. Ebbesson and P. Okowa (eds.), *Environmental Law and Justice in Context* (Cambridge, UK: Cambridge University Press, 2009), p. 7.

[124] See Inter-American Court of Human Rights, "Environment and Human Rights, Advisory Opinion OC-23/17 of November 15, 2017," requested by the Republic of Colombia; M. Banda, "Inter-American Court of Human Rights' Advisory Opinion on the Environment and Human Rights" (2018) 22 *American Journal of International Law Insights*; S. Atapattu, "An Idea Whose Time Has Come: On an Emerging Right to a Healthy Environment," Oct. 29, 2019, https://verfassungsblog.de/an-idea-whose-time-has-come.

understood as indivisible aspects of a right to human dignity, rather than being seen as in competition. Usha Natarajan's chapter highlights the usefulness of an environmental justice framework for the Global South, as it facilitates resistance to the universalization that is dominant in international lawmaking, and calls attention to the experiences of subaltern communities so as to build solidarity and foster global change. Deborah McGregor then introduces an Indigenous environmental justice framework drawing upon Anishinabek knowledge systems that have existed for millennia, and questions whether sustainability could ever be achieved based only on human knowledge that ignores reciprocal relations with the natural world, ancestors, and future generations.

Next, Carmen G. Gonzalez introduces a racial capitalism framework for the Anthropocene, crafted to clarify how racial subordination, environmental degradation, and the capitalist world economy are interrelated, with the climate crisis serving to illuminate the links between forms of oppression that are otherwise seen as disconnected. The relationship between human rights and socioecological justice, informed by vulnerability theory, is explored in the chapter written by Louis J. Kotzé, who proposes that vulnerability's embodied yet post-identity approach could inform a move away from Western neoliberal human rights toward a more contingent understanding of the entire living order's vulnerability. Socioecological resilience and its relationship to the social pillar of sustainable development is the subject of Barbara Cosens's framework chapter, in which she clarifies that as a theory of system properties, resilience theory cannot be a substitute for normative goals evident in concepts such as sustainable development, yet resilience theory can confirm that just societies are better equipped to adapt to change. Finally, we conclude Part I with a coauthored contribution by Robin Morris Collin and Robert W. Collin, who provide a history of the US environmental justice movement and call for intergenerational and transformative development by linking place-based reparations with ecosystems and communities.

Part II, the heart of the book, consists of a series of case studies on selected environmental justice struggles in the Global North and the Global South. The case studies examine the intersecting forms of oppression that produce environmental injustice in specific contexts, and the legal strategies that can and have been developed to combat these inequities. Given the wide range of intersecting issues and the sheer number of environmental justice struggles around the world, this book can only scratch the surface of this topic. In order to provide some structure, the case studies are divided into five, at times, overlapping and interrelated sections: Strategies, Challenges, and Vulnerable Groups; Toxic Substances and Hazardous Wastes; Resource Extraction; Energy; and Climate Change.

Our first case study in the Strategies, Challenges, and Vulnerable Groups section is Shyami Puvimanasinghe's exploration of public interest litigation in South Asia and the role of selected environmental justice cases in realizing sustainable development, including through the adoption of the right to development. We then turn our attention to children's rights in a contribution by Mona Paré who considers the environmental justice implications of approaching the rights of children in sustainable development through an intergenerational equity lens as compared to a child rights lens. Moving to Latin America, Patrícia Galvão Ferreira and Mario Mancilla offer a case study of water as life from the perspective of the Indigenous communities in Totonicapán, Guatemala, and argue that the new Escazú Agreement on procedural environmental rights missed an opportunity to fully integrate the type of Indigenous cosmovision evident in Totonicapán's water governance system. Jacinta Ruru provides further insights into Indigenous environmental justice in her chapter on legislative changes in Aotearoa, New Zealand, that recognize the legal personality of land, a river, and a mountain, in keeping with

Māori Indigenous laws. Next, strategies to achieve water justice in Israel and the West Bank are explored by Tamar Meshel, who concludes that water justice for the Bedouin and Palestinians will not be forthcoming while the right to water is narrowly interpreted and divorced from historic contexts and socioeconomic conditions, as well as obligations of antidiscrimination. Damilola S. Olawuyi then considers how preexisting vulnerabilities of gender and indigeneity in postcolonial Africa combine to magnify risks in the context of climate change mitigation and adaptation in two Nigerian case studies. Finally, Lakshman Guruswamy, Joshua C. Gellers, and Sumudu Atapattu turn to the failure to date of varied environmental justice strategies in Sri Lanka to successfully challenge the construction of the Colombo International Financial City, part of China's Belt and Road Initiative.

Our second set of case studies turns to environmental injustice in relation to toxic substances and hazardous wastes. First, Sabaa Ahmad Khan explores international trade in hazardous chemicals and waste, concluding in part that a lack of transparency in global commodity chains inhibits our capacity to protect human and ecosystem health, but that embedding responsibility and accountability into a life cycle approach, including the business responsibility to respect human rights, could be transformative. Next, Quoc Nguyen, Linda Tsang, and Tseming Yang tell the story of the Wengyuan County Cancer Villages in China's Guangdong Province, revealing how the economic and social marginalization of some communities makes them less resilient to adverse environmental and health consequences, while also less able to seek legal recourse. Finally, Antoni Pigrau turns our attention to the Marshall Islands and its colonial history of nuclear testing as illustrative of how colonialism and a failure to remedy historic environmental injustice combine to prevent future realization of sustainable development.

The third set of case studies examines environmental justice challenges in the resource extraction context. Stellina Jolly first introduces the Vedanta case study in which the Indian Supreme Court embraced a new interpretation of tribal rights as an essential component of effective participation in sustainable development. Jackie Dugard examines the historic injustice of the Tudor Shaft case in South Africa and highlights the ineffectiveness of the South African government's single-axis approach to dealing with intersectional social and ecological disadvantage. Finally, Sara L. Seck and Penelope Simons examine Canada's role as both home and host state in the context of sustainable mining and environmental justice, drawing attention to the failure of Canada's domestic and transnational legal and policy responses to fully embrace respect for the human rights of women and girls.

Next, we consider four case studies involving energy. Rebecca M. Bratspies explores the environmental justice dimensions of the successful campaign to close the Poletti Power Plant in New York City, leading to improved environmental quality for an overburdened environmental justice community, yet failing to be truly transformative due to its failure to openly confront related legacies of racism. This is contrasted with Elizabeth Kronk Warner's recounting of the Dakota Access Pipeline story and the unsuccessful efforts of Tribes and water protectors to halt its construction, due to the failure of decision makers to take seriously the unique issues that Indigenous peoples face, including applicable domestic and international law, tribal sovereignty, and connection to land and waters. Next, Lakshman Guruswamy considers the challenges confronting the energy poor and the disproportionate impact of energy poverty on women, in violation of international justice and sustainable development. Finally, Adrian A. Smith and Dayna Nadine Scott examine the transformative potential of participation by Indigenous communities in large-scale renewable energy generation, when community led, drawing upon the experiences of the Batchewana First Nation in Ontario, Canada.

Our final set of three case studies explores the challenge of climate change. The first, by Alice Kaswan, considers climate justice implications in the Californian context of climate mitigation policies, with attention to participatory and distributive justice and the importance of climate transition initiatives recognizing underlying historic and socioeconomic contexts. The second case study, a chapter coauthored by Katherine Lofts and Konstantia Koutouki, turns to the Canadian Arctic and considers how integration of eco-health concerns in environmental impact assessment processes could help to better incorporate Inuit world views and knowledge, and so provide for greater adaptability to a rapidly changing environment. Finally, Sumudu Atapattu and Andrea C. Simonelli conclude with a study of small island states, focusing on the challenges facing the poor and marginalized in the Maldives due to both climate change and changing political agendas that prioritize mass tourism and mega-development over climate justice.

Part III of the book addresses cross-cutting issues and topics based on the case studies in Part II. It offers reflections on the case studies that tease out their practical and theoretical ramifications for strategic litigation and political mobilization. Angela P. Harris' contribution reflects on how a law and political economy approach to these environmental justice case studies reveals the common roots of these struggles in an economic order that treats nature as an infinite resource for human domination and exploitation and creates seemingly intractable human hierarchies. The final chapter by the editors considers the lessons offered by the case studies (including topics for further research) in order to overcome the fragmentation of legal frameworks and social movements and develop holistic solutions that are both just and sustainable.

PART I

Frameworks

The Indivisibility of Human Dignity and Sustainability

*Erin Daly and James R. May**

2.1 INTRODUCTION

Human dignity means that all people have equal worth and deserve to live in dignity. This chapter posits that human dignity and a healthy environment are indivisible rights essential to the three dimensions of sustainability – environmental, social, and economic. A healthy environment is a necessary component of living in dignity: all have an equal claim to healthy air, water, and surroundings. Dignity is elemental to social sustainability, that is, building strong and resilient communities under the rule of law. Dignity is also essential to economic sustainability.[1] That is, the ability to earn, support, and gain economic autonomy. Thus, dignity is the thread that binds the three dimensions of sustainability and evinces their indivisibility: if any one pillar is sacrificed or compromised, the ability to live with dignity is threatened. These relationships are becoming increasingly clear and enforceable as constitutions and constitutional courts around the world are protecting environmental and dignity rights for present and future generations, all of which advance sustainability.

It can be impractical (if not impossible) to realize dignity rights in conditions of unsustainable environmental, social, and economic conditions: ask people who live near toxic dumps and experience higher than normal rates of cancer, or in deforested areas whose shelters get washed away in the rains, or anyone who has lost a home, a limb, or a loved one in record-setting freezes, droughts, fires, and storms. Simply, unsustainable practices diminish individual and collective quality of life and, with it, human dignity. This chapter demonstrates that the three pillars of

---

* Portions of what appears in this chapter draw from: E. Daly, *Dignity Rights: Courts, Constitutions, and the Worth of the Human Person* (Philadelphia: University of Pennsylvania Press, 2d ed. 2020); E. Daly and J. May, "Environmental Dignity Rights," in S. Maljean-Dubois (ed.), *The Effectiveness of Environmental Law* (Cambridge, UK: Intersentia, 2017); E. Daly and J. May, "Bridging Constitutional Dignity and Environmental Rights Jurisprudence" (2016) 7 *Journal of Human Rights and the Environment* 218–242.

[1] We mean "economic sustainability" as one that reconciles the right to development and to earn a living with environmental and social sustainability, including intergenerational equity. See generally, R. N. Stavins, A. F. Wagner, and G. Wagner, "Interpreting Sustainability in Economic Terms: Dynamic Efficiency Plus Intergenerational Equity" (2003) 79 *Economics Letters* 339 (proposing a definition of "economic sustainability" that combines "dynamic efficiency and intergenerational equity"); J. Moreilli, "Environmental Sustainability: A Definition for Environmental Professionals" (2011) 1 *Journal of Environmental Sustainability* 1 ("sustainability requires that current economic activity not disproportionately burden future generations . . . Economic sustainability should involve analysis to minimize the social costs of meeting standards for protecting environmental assets but not for determining what those standards should be" (internal references omitted).

sustainability are best interpreted not as in competition with one another but as three aspects of the same indivisible interest in human dignity.

The right to human dignity embodies the fundamental notion that all individuals in present and future generations are entitled to equal respect from others, to live life well, with choices, and free from arbitrary action by those in positions of power. Dignity is not simply an aspiration or a wish; it is an actionable right that is being recognized by courts in thousands of cases around the world. Indeed, courts have applied the right and the value of human dignity in a wide variety of factual and legal settings that span the catalogues of both civil and political rights and socioeconomic and cultural rights, that now include environmental rights.

This chapter has four sections. Section 2.2 provides an introduction to the right to human dignity under law, a concept nearly as old as humanity and as fresh as the most recent cases. Section 2.3 then pivots to environmental rights, including domestic, regional, and emerging international means for recognition as a way of advancing environmental and social sustainability. Section 2.4 demonstrates the indivisibility of sustainability and the right to dignity as reflected in the UN Sustainable Development Goals (SDGs). Section 2.5 samples judicial decisions from around the globe that bridge these concepts. We conclude that it is instructive to recognize that advancing human dignity is sustainability's core function.

2.2 THE RIGHT TO HUMAN DIGNITY

With deep roots in philosophic and religious traditions, dignity is also a legal right that is enforceable in courts around the world.[2] The first and most important recognition of human dignity in an international legal instrument is in the 1948 Universal Declaration of Human Rights, whose preamble begins with an emphatic acknowledgment of every person's dignity and a commitment to its centrality to human rights: "Whereas recognition of the inherent dignity and of the equal and inalienable rights of all members of the human family is the foundation of freedom, justice and peace in the world."[3] From there, the recognition of human dignity dispersed into the next generation of international law in the common language of both international covenants, which begin by recognizing that the rights enumerated therein "derive from the inherent dignity of the human person."[4]

---

[2] See for example E. Daly, *Dignity Rights: Courts, Constitutions, and the Worth of the Human Person* (Philadelphia: University of Pennsylvania Press, 2013; J. May and E. Daly, "Why Dignity Rights Matter" (2019) 2 *European Human Rights Law Review* 15; E. Daly and J. May, "A Dignity Rights Primer" (2018) 3 *Juriste internationale* 21; E. Daly and J. May, *Dignity Law: Global Recognition, Cases and Perspectives* (New York: W. S. Hein, 2020); J. May and E. Daly, Advanced Introduction to Human Dignity And Law (London: Edward Elgar, 2020).

[3] UN General Assembly, Universal Declaration of Human Rights, Dec. 10, 1948, UN Doc. A/Res/217 (III), Preamble.

[4] UN, International Covenant on Civil and Political Rights, Dec. 16, 1966, 999 UNTS 171, Preamble [ICCPR] and International Covenant on Economic, Social and Cultural Rights, Dec. 16, 1966, 993 UNTS 3, Preamble [ICESCR]. "Dignity" appears twice in the preambles in both covenants, and one additional time in each. In the ICCPR, it appears in connection with liberty: "All persons deprived of their liberty shall be treated with humanity and with respect for the inherent dignity of the human person" (Art. 10 (1)). In the ICESCR, it appears in connection with education: "The States Parties to the present Covenant recognize the right of everyone to education. They agree that education shall be directed to the full development of the human personality and the sense of its dignity, and shall strengthen the respect for human rights and fundamental freedoms. They further agree that education shall enable all persons to participate effectively in a free society, promote understanding, tolerance and friendship among all nations and all racial, ethnic or religious groups, and further the activities of the United Nations for the maintenance of peace" (Art. 13).

Dignity is thus both an inherent quality of being human and a legal entitlement. It signifies, in the simple but profound words of Hannah Arendt, "the right to have rights"[5] – recognized as both a right in and of itself and the progenitor and justification for all other rights, whether social or political, individual or collective, or environmental. These various ways of thinking about dignity rights are reflected in current global constitutionalism: more than 160 of the world's constitutions have incorporated dignity in some fashion, and hardly a new constitution is adopted without reference to the right to dignity. Many of these constitutions address dignity in multiple ways – as a foundational value, as a general personality right, and/or as a right associated with some specific interest (work, detention, etc.) or with a particularly vulnerable segment of the population (disabled, elderly, children, etc.). Some constitutions, either by text or by judicial implication, make it clear that the obligation to respect the dignity of every human being is imposed on all the organs of the state.[6] Thus, dignity, the common ancestor of all modern human rights law, is also its future – informing and implicating most other human rights at the international and national levels.[7]

Because of these provisions and the global movement to appreciate the fundamental role that recognition of dignity plays in the application of human rights, litigants around the world are framing claims in terms of human dignity and courts are responding. In the last two decades alone, dignity rights have been invoked, interpreted, and applied by courts in thousands of cases and in a wide variety of factual settings.[8] Notable examples include: Argentina, where dignity is the foundation for freedom of speech and right of association;[9] South Africa, where civic dignity protects voting rights and other rights associated with the political process;[10] Israel, where it is a "mother right" whose "daughters" include the right of family unity as well as the right of prisoners to be treated humanely, among many other rights;[11] Colombia, where dignity is a measure of the state's obligation to provide healthcare;[12] Germany, where the level of pension benefits must allow a person to live in dignity;[13] and India, where dignity guarantees the right to

---

[5] H. Arendt, *The Origins of Totalitarianism* (Cleveland, OH: World Publishing, 1958), p. 296.

[6] See for example Basic Law of Germany, Art. 1: "Human dignity shall be inviolable. To respect and protect it shall be the duty of all state authority." See also "This means that the principle of human dignity must be understood: (i) as a founding principle of the legal system; (ii) as a constitutional principle, and (iii) as an autonomous fundamental right. Additionally, the Court has established that the 1991 Charter is essentially humanistic, insofar as the entire normative system has been constructed to protect dignity and personal autonomy, not in the abstract, but from a material and concrete dimension: that is why the respect for human dignity should inspire all actions of the State." *Center for Social Justice Studies et al.* v. *Presidency of the Republic et al.*, Judgment T-622/16, Constitutional Court of Colombia (Nov. 10, 2016).

[7] I. Currien and J. De Waal, *Bill of Rights Handbook* (Cape Town, SA: Juta, 2005). See also M. H. Cheadle, D. H. Davis, and N. R. L. Haysom, *South African Constitutional Law: The Bill of Rights* (Durban, SA: LexisNexis, 2014), s. 5.1; see also s. 5.2.2: "The right to dignity, a core value from which other rights derive, is frequently invoked together with the specific enumerated right relied upon to challenge conduct or laws. Dignity, thus, stands as a forensic reinforcement to the other specified rights. Not infrequently, constitutional litigation brought primarily on the grounds of another fundamental right has been decided on the question of the right to dignity. In other instances, the court has referred to or enquired into the impact on the right to dignity of the conduct or law complained of."

[8] See generally Daly, note 2.

[9] *Asociación Lucha por la Identidad Travesti-Transexual* v. *Inspección General de Justicia*, Argentina Supreme Court of Justice (Nov. 21, 2006).

[10] *August and Another* v. *Electoral Commission and Others* (CCT8/99) [1999] ZACC 3; 1999 (3) SA 1; 1999 (4) BCLR 363 (Apr. 1, 1999).

[11] *Golan* v. *Prison Services* (1996) IsrSC 50 (4) 136; *Gal-On* v. *Attorney General*, HCJ 466/07 (2012).

[12] Sentencia T-292/09 (Constitutional Court of Colombia).

[13] BVerfG, Judgment of the First Senate of Feb. 9, 2010, 1 BvL 1/09, paras. 1–220, www.bverfg.de/e/ ls20100209_1bvl000109en.html.

travel.[14] These broad statements about the role of human dignity in all state action also reveal the indivisibility of human rights – a characteristic that is all the more poignant in the context of sustainable environmental health and environmental justice.

Indeed, as detailed below, courts are increasingly recognizing the relationship between unsustainable environmental, social, and economic conditions and the ability to live with dignity.[15] What we see is that depending on the nature of the claim and the orientation of the judges and advocates, courts may or may not invoke the SDGs, but even where the reference is not explicit, the effort is to move toward the fulfillment of the SDGs and more generally of the social aspects of sustainability.[16]

2.3 ENVIRONMENTAL RIGHTS

Although environmental rights and human rights have been defined and protected at the international level for decades, only recently have the orbits of the two bodies of law begun to intersect so that environmental rights are being seen *as* human rights.[17] The Stockholm Declaration in 1972 declared that "[b]oth aspects of man's environment, the natural and the man-made, are essential to his well-being and to the enjoyment of basic human rights, even the right to life itself."[18] But it took twenty years for the international community to follow up: in 1992 in Rio, participants in the Earth Summit proclaimed that "[h]uman beings . . . are entitled to a healthy and productive life in harmony with nature."[19] At the same time, more attention was being paid to the mechanisms by which international economic, social, and cultural human rights could be enforced, culminating in the Limburg and Maastricht principles relating to how governments should respect, protect, and fulfill such rights, as well as in the San Salvador Protocol in the Americas.[20] Increasingly, the worlds of environmental and human rights have

---

[14] *Maneka Ghandi v. Union of India* (1978) 2 SCR 621.

[15] *Nigeria: Gbemre v. Shell Petroleum Development Company Nigeria Limited and Others* (2005) AHRLR 151 (NgHC 2005); *Merriman and Others v. Fingal County Council and Others; Friends of the Irish Environment Clg v. Fingal County Council and Others* [2017] IEHC 695 at 292, citing Constitution of Ireland (Bunreacht Na Héireann), Art. 40.3.1; *Ashgar Leghari v. Federation of Pakistan* (Lahore High Court, Pakistan, 2018).

[16] In this chapter, we focus primarily on the relationship between sustainability and the substantive aspects of human dignity, although there are also important procedural aspects of human dignity that are pertinent to sustainability and environmental claims generally. For instance, the right to human dignity entails access to justice, as well as rights to information and participation in environmental decision-making. These issues, however, are beyond the scope of this chapter. See for example *Center for Social Justice Studies et al. v. Presidency of the Republic et al.*, note 6.

[17] E. Daly and J. May, *Implementing Environmental Constitutionalism* (Cambridge, UK: Cambridge University Press, 2018); E. Daly and J. May, "Learning from Constitutional Environmental Rights," in J. H. Knox and R. Pejan, (eds.), *The Human Right to a Healthy Environment* (Cambridge, UK: Cambridge University Press, 2018).

[18] UN, Stockholm Declaration of the United Nations Conference on the Human Environment, June 16, 1972, UN Doc. A/CONF.48/14/Rev. 1, p. 3. Principle 1 further confirms that "Man has the fundamental right to freedom, equality and adequate conditions of life, in an environment of a quality that permits a life of dignity and well-being."

[19] UN, Rio Declaration on Environment and Development, June 3–14, 1992, UN Doc. A/CONF.151/26. See also Agenda 21 (relating to sustainable development) at www.un.org/esa/dsd/agenda21/res_agenda21_00.shtml [Rio Declaration].

[20] UN Commission on Human Rights, *Note verbal dated 5 December 1986 from the Permanent Mission of the Netherlands to the United Nations Office at Geneva addressed to the Centre for Human Rights* [Limburg Principles], Jan. 8 1987, UN Doc. E/CN.4/1987/17; UNCESCR, *Maastricht Guidelines on Violations of Economic, Social and Cultural Rights*, Jan. 22–26, 1997, UN Doc. E/C.12/2000/13; Organization of American States [OAS], Additional Protocol to the American Convention on Human Rights in the Area of Economic, Social and Cultural Rights [Protocol of San Salvador], Nov. 16, 1999, A-52.

intersected, with the result that more and more attention is being paid to the impact on human rights of environmental degradation and climate change, and on the positive impact that sustainability might have for human development. At the same time, at the domestic level, more than half the nations of the world have rewritten their constitutions, or adopted new ones since the late 1980s, usually including extensive bills of rights. According to the UN Environment Programme, about 150 countries currently have environmental provisions in their constitutions, expressed in a variety of ways.[21] As of 2018, approximately eighty-eight of these countries have adopted an express constitutional right to a healthy environment.[22] About a dozen more countries recognize a fundamental right to a healthy environment implicitly.[23]

Moreover, about 130 nations are subject to regional agreements that recognize a right to a healthy environment,[24] such as the Additional Protocol to the American Convention on Human Rights in the Area of Economic, Social and Cultural Rights ("Everyone shall have the right to live in a healthy environment");[25] the African Charter on Human and Peoples' Rights ("all peoples shall have the right to a general satisfactory environment favorable to their development");[26] and the Association of South East Asian Nations (ASEAN) Human Rights Declaration ("Every person has . . . the right to a safe, clean and sustainable environment").[27] Among these, the African Charter on Human and Peoples' Rights "is the only human rights treaty, albeit a regional one, to include a justiciable right to a healthy environment."[28] The 2004 Arab Charter on Human Rights includes a right to a healthy environment as part of the right to an adequate standard of living that ensures well-being and a decent life.[29]

There is an ongoing debate as to whether and how environmental rights should be recognized and implemented at the international level.[30] One school of thought advocates recognizing a right to a healthy environment at the international level.[31] As a normative matter, formal recognition of such a right would confirm the indivisibility of human and environmental rights and, in particular, the ways in which the harms caused by environmental degradation constitute violations of well-recognized human rights, such as the right to life, to health, and to dignity. This is reflected in human experience throughout the world, in all natural and social settings. For example, the illegal dumping

---

[21] UN Environment, "Environmental Rule of Law: First Global Report," UN Environment Programme, Nairobi, Jan. 24, 2019, p. 159. See also J. May and E. Daly, *Global Environmental Constitutionalism* (Cambridge, UK: Cambridge University Press, 2015) (putting the number at seventy-six as of 2013); J. May and E. Daly, "Vindicating Fundamental Environmental Rights: Judicial Acceptance of Constitutionally Entrenched Environmental Rights" (2009) 11 *Oregon Review of International Law* 365 (sixty-five as of 2009); J. May, "Constituting Fundamental Environmental Rights Worldwide" (2006) 23 *Pace Environmental Law Review* 113 (sixty as of 2005).

[22] UN Environment, note 21, p. 2; see also, Envirorights Map, http://envirorightsmap.org.

[23] UN Environment, note 21, p. 2.

[24] Ibid., p. 161.

[25] OAS, Protocol of San Salvador, note 20, Art. 11.

[26] Organization of African Unity [OAU], African Charter on Human and Peoples' Rights [Banjul Charter], June 27, 1981, CAB/LEG/67/3 rev.5, 21 ILM 58 (1982), Art. 24.

[27] Association of Southeast Asian Nations [ASEAN], ASEAN Human Rights Declaration, Nov. 18, 2012, Art. 28 (f).

[28] S. Atapattu and A. Schapper, *Human Rights and the Environment* (Abingdon, UK: Routledge, 2019), p. 122.

[29] League of Arab States, Arab Charter on Human Rights, May 22, 2004 (entered into force Mar. 15, 2008), reprinted in (2005) 12 *International Human Rights Report* 893, para. 38.

[30] E. Daly, "Environmental Human Rights: Paradigm of Indivisibility" (2011) *Widener Law School Legal Studies Research Paper No. 11-05*.

[31] See generally J. Knox and R. Pejan, *The Human Right to a Healthy Environment* (Cambridge, UK: Cambridge University Press, 2018); M. Prieur, M. A. Mekouar, and E. Daly, "An International Covenant on the Right of Human Beings to the Environment," in J. May and E. Daly (eds.), *Human Rights and the Environment: Legality, Indivisibility, Dignity and Geography* (Cheltenham, UK: Edward Elgar, 2019).

of toxic waste endangers the surrounding ecosystems, as it contaminates drinking water, arable soils, and habitable land, and otherwise threatens people's right to life, health, work, property, culture, dignity, and so on. Likewise, mining, deforestation, and environmental degradation brought about by climate change threaten both environmental and human interests and needs. As the former Special Rapporteur on Human Rights and the Environment has observed: "Human rights are grounded in respect for fundamental human attributes such as dignity, equality and liberty. The realization of these attributes depends on an environment that allows them to flourish . . . Human rights and environmental protection are inherently interdependent."[32]

As a legal matter, an internationally recognized human right to a healthy environment would impose supranational obligations on states to observe or protect rights that otherwise may not be reflected in domestic law or in regional instruments.[33] Given the resistance that many states have to protecting their own natural environments, the argument goes, only a supranational legal norm can effectively control national urges to sacrifice their environments in the name of short-term financial or political gain. Inexorably – if belatedly – international law is beginning to recognize the interdependence and indivisibility of human dignity and environmental rights.[34]

The indivisibility of human dignity and environmental sustainability can also be seen in the context of climate- and environment-related migration. The 2018 Global Compact for Safe, Orderly and Regular Migration recognizes that migration must be "safe, orderly and regular" to ensure the dignity and the protection of human rights of all migrants, whether the source of the migration is economic, environmental, or otherwise, noting that there is "unity of purpose" in working "together to create conditions that allow communities and individuals to live in safety and dignity in their own countries."[35]

In actuality, the link between human dignity and environmental rights has pedigree in the concept of sustainability. Since the concept of sustainability was first promoted as a single-sentence principle of international law at the Stockholm Conference in 1972, it is now a common if not ubiquitous feature in legal expressions at the international, national, and subnational levels.

Sustainability has long served as a principle of international environmental law, including as an interpretive principle in international accords[36] and with international tribunals resolving

---

[32] Human Rights Council, *Report of the Independent Expert on the Issue of Human Rights Obligations Relating to the Enjoyment of a Safe, Clean, Healthy and Sustainable Environment*, Dec. 24, 2012, UN Doc. A/HR/22/43. See also, D. J. Whelan, *Indivisible Human Rights: A History* (Philadelphia: University of Pennsylvania Press, 2010); Daly, note 30 ("The constitutional right to a healthy environment is perhaps the paradigmatic example of the indivisibility claim. Environmental rights are inseparable from many other rights, including (depending on the factual nature of the claim) the right to life, to health, to dignity, to subsistence, to employment, to property and so on").

[33] See generally P. Allott, "The Emerging Universal Legal System," in J. Nijman and A. Nollkemper (eds.), *New Perspectives on the Divide between National and International Law* (Oxford: Oxford University Press 2007), pp. 63–83.

[34] E. Daly and J. May, "Environmental Dignity Rights," in J. May and E. Daly, *Encyclopedia of Human Rights and the Environment: Legality, Indivisibility, Dignity, and Geography* (Cheltenham, UK: Edward Elgar, 2019); E. Daly and J. May, "Exploring Environmental Justice through the Lens of Human Dignity" (2019) 25 *Widener Law Review* 167; J. May and T. Dayo, "Environmental Dignity Rights in Nigeria" (2019) 25 *Widener Law Review* 183; E. Daly and J. May, "Environmental Dignity Rights" in S. Maljean-Dubois (ed.), *The Effectiveness of Environmental Law* (Cambridge, UK: Intersentia, 2017); E. Daly and J. May, "Bridging Constitutional Dignity and Environmental Rights Jurisprudence" (2016) 7 *Journal of Human Rights and the Environment* 218–242"; D. Lupin Townsend, "The Place of Human Dignity in Environmental Adjudication" (2016) 3 *Oslo Law Review* 27–50.

[35] Global Compact for Migration, "Global Compact For Safe, Orderly and Regular Migration," July 11, 2018.

[36] See for example R. K. L. Panjabi, *The Earth Summit at Rio: Politics, Economics, and the Environment* (Lebanon, NH: Northeastern University Press, 1997), p. 17 (describing how the Earth Summit in Rio led to a new global consciousness of sustainability in treaty making).

environmental disputes.[37] Sustainability advances environmental, social, and economic equity in a variety of contexts, including dignity,[38] human rights,[39] climate change, access to and availability of fresh water,[40] shale gas development,[41] corporate practices, and higher education.

Sustainability has also infiltrated constitutionalism around the globe. Presently, more than three-dozen countries incorporate sustainability in their constitutions by advancing "sustainable development," the interests of "future generations," or some combination of these themes.[42] These constitutional provisions help bridge the gap left by international and domestic laws, even given the array of sustainability provisions already in existence. Moreover, they advance the prospect of enforcing claims of sustainability.

Despite or perhaps because of sustainability's diaspora, the concept has a growing cadre of critics who hold the view that it is neither workable nor relevant, has done little if anything to improve environmental outcomes, and is no match for the Anthropocene.[43] The relative merits and second thoughts about sustainable development as a concept are beyond this chapter. What is within scope is the idea that sustainability can be better understood and utilized by viewing it through the lens of the role of human dignity under law. To be sure, sustainability's virtue is in promoting the equal worth of everyone, everywhere, and for all time.

2.4 SUSTAINABILITY AND THE INDIVISIBILITY OF DIGNITY AND ENVIRONMENTAL RIGHTS

Whether at the international or national constitutional level, the protection of the human right to a healthy environment demonstrates the indivisibility of rights. Indivisibility describes the *integral* nature of a set of human rights.[44] The image might be that of a diamond: no single facet can be separated from a diamond, and the diamond does not exist without its many facets. It is only if the relationship among the rights is that close that we can say that human rights are indivisible. As such, indivisibility does not describe the entire system of rights: not all rights are indivisible, though they might be interrelated or interdependent. But the right to dignity and the right to environmental protection are indivisible: one cannot exist without the other.

---

[37] See R. Higgins, "Natural Resources in the Case Law of the International Court," in Alan Boyle and David Freestone (eds.), *International Law and Sustainable Development* (Oxford: Oxford University Press, 1999), pp. 87, 111 (using the International Court of Justice to highlight environmental sustainability in international courts and other arenas).

[38] Daly and May (2016), note 34.

[39] See J. Knox, *Report of the Independent Expert on the Issue of Human Rights Obligations Relating to the Enjoyment of a Safe, Clean, Healthy and Sustainable Environment*, Feb. 3, 2015, UN Doc. A/HRC/28/61, pp. 11–12.

[40] J. R. May, "Of Development, daVinci and Domestic Legislation: The Prospects for Sustainable Development in Asia and Its Untapped Potential in the United States" (1998) 3*Widener Law Symposium Journal* 197.

[41] J. C. Dernbach and J. R. May, *Shale Gas and the Future of Energy: Law and Policy for Sustainability* (Cheltenham, UK: Edward Elgar, 2016) (suggesting laws and policies needed to ensure that shale gas development fosters transition to sustainability).

[42] May and Daly (2015), note 21; Appendix E and associated text (denoting role of sustainability in the development of international and national law, and analyzing constitutional provisions that embed sustainability from around the world); J. R. May, "Constituting Fundamental Environmental Rights Worldwide" (2006) 23 *Pace Environmental Law Review* 113, Appendix B (listing countries that have constitutionally entrenched environmental policies as governing principles, some including sustainability).

[43] See for example M. H. Benson and R. K. Craig, *The End of Sustainability Resilience and the Future of Environmental Governance in the Anthropocene* (Lawrence: University of Kansas Press, 2017) ("The time has come for us to collectively reexamine – and ultimately move past – the concept of sustainability in environmental and natural resources law and management").

[44] See generally Whelan, note 32.

To say that some rights are indivisible is to pose significant challenges to the interpretation and vindication of that right. The right to vote, to free expression, and other rights that are sometimes referred to as "negative rights" are comparatively simple to vindicate, usually by ordering the removal of barriers to the exercise of the right. And socioeconomic rights are becoming increasingly amenable to judicial interpretation and vindication thanks to the development of the law of progressive realization.[45] Thus, when a court or international tribunal finds that the right to housing has been violated, it may order the government to take reasonable legislative measures to develop a plan that would progressively realize that right in accordance with the nation's available resources.[46] Likewise, when the right to water is viewed as a *human* right, then the court will vindicate the right by determining whether the claimant's access to clean water is adequate to ensure the person's dignity or other human right.[47]

As applied to environmental rights, indivisibility means that claims of environmental wrongs – deforestation, water pollution, mining, oil spills, climate change – in and of themselves, have consequences for other human rights, such as the right to life, to live with dignity, to health, to privacy and family life, as well as for civil and political rights like the right to political participation and the right to free expression, and for collective and solidarity rights like those of indigenous communities or of future generations, with implications for environmental and climate justice.[48] When there is a violation of an environmental right, the effect is experienced as a deprivation of human dignity. For this reason, environmental rights provide a paradigmatic example of the thesis of indivisibility.

Current constructions of sustainability well support this observation. The United Nations' 2015 SDGs are the culmination of four decades of multidisciplinary thinking about what sustainable development means, and grasping that, how to put it into place.[49] The sustainability framework features seventeen "Goals" to achieve by 2030, including protecting biodiversity, ensuring clean water, air, land and food, ending poverty, hunger and discrimination, and providing access to justice and opportunity for the future.[50]

While the seventeen SDGs are indivisible insofar as it is not possible either to realize human rights in a degraded environment or to protect the environment in the absence of human rights, the SDGs are often treated as if they are independent of one another. For example, the High-Level Political Forum focuses on two connected SDGs at a time, such as (in 2019) achieving SDGs 13 (climate action) and 17 (peace, justice, and strong communities).[51] But what can be lost in conversations about the SDGs and its component parts is the elegant idea that dignity is the thread that stitches the SDGs together, reflected in the SDGs' core provisions:[52]

> We are determined to end poverty and hunger, in all their forms and dimensions, and to ensure that all human beings can fulfil their potential in dignity and equality and in a healthy environment.[53]

---

[45] ICESCR, note 4, Art. 2(1). See also for example *Mazibuko and Others* v. *City of Johannesburg and Others* (CCT 39/09) [2009] ZACC 28; 2010 (3) BCLR 239 (CC); 2010 (4) SA 1 (CC) (Oct. 8, 2009).

[46] See *Government of the Republic of South Africa and Others* v. *Grootboom and Others* 2001 (1) SA 46 (CC), CCT 11/2000.

[47] See for example *Mazibuko and Others* v. *City of Johannesburg and Others*, note 45.

[48] Daly and May (2019), note 34.

[49] See UN Sustainable Development Goals, adopted by all UN member states in 2015, https://sustainabledevelopment.un.org/?menu=1300.

[50] Ibid.

[51] UN Sustainable Development Goals Knowledge Platform, "High-Level Political Forum 2019 under the Auspices of ECOSOC," https://sustainabledevelopment.un.org/hlpf/2019.

[52] Ibid.

[53] UN General Assembly, *Transforming Our World: The 2030 Agenda for Sustainable Development*, Oct. 21, 2015, UN Doc. /RES/70/1, Preamble.

As we embark on this great collective journey, we pledge that no one will be left behind.[54] Recognizing that the dignity of the human person is fundamental, we wish to see the Goals and targets met for all nations and peoples and for all segments of society. And we will endeavour to reach the furthest behind first.[55]

We envisage a world of universal respect for human rights and human dignity, the rule of law, justice, equality and non-discrimination; of respect for race, ethnicity and cultural diversity; and of equal opportunity permitting the full realization of human potential and contributing to shared prosperity.[56]

We are meeting at a time of immense challenges to sustainable development. Billions of our citizens continue to live in poverty and are denied a life of dignity. There are rising inequalities within and among countries. There are enormous disparities of opportunity, wealth and power. Gender inequality remains a key challenge. Unemployment, particularly youth unemployment, is a major concern. Global health threats, more frequent and intense natural disasters, spiralling conflict, violent extremism, terrorism and related humanitarian crises and forced displacement of people threaten to reverse much of the development progress made in recent decades. Natural resource depletion and adverse impacts of environmental degradation, including desertification, drought, land degradation, freshwater scarcity and loss of biodiversity, add to and exacerbate the list of challenges which humanity faces. Climate change is one of the greatest challenges of our time and its adverse impacts undermine the ability of all countries to achieve sustainable development. Increases in global temperature, sea level rise, ocean acidification and other climate change impacts are seriously affecting coastal areas and low-lying coastal countries, including many least developed countries and small island developing States. The survival of many societies, and of the biological support systems of the planet, is at risk.[57]

The recognition in 2002 by the UN Committee on Economic, Social and Cultural Rights (CESCR) of the right to water is another example of the indivisibility of dignity and environmental rights.[58] In its General Comment 15, the CESCR recognized that while the right to water is protected by specific international instruments, it is indispensable to many rights protected by human rights instruments.[59] Throughout the text of the General Comment, the CESCR noted the relationship between water and other recognized rights. The Comment begins: "Water is a limited natural resource and a public good fundamental for life and health. The human right to water is indispensable for leading a life in human dignity. It is a prerequisite for the realization of other human rights."[60] But this does not merely describe a familial relationship (a pristine environment has a relationship with human dignity) nor even an interdependence (human life depends on forests, or forests depend on life); rather, it manifests an inextricable link between the two concepts that makes one virtually meaningless without the other. The nature of the environmental right is bound up in the nature of the social and economic rights. The Comment shows how the right to water also necessarily requires recognition of other rights, such as political rights,[61] rights against

---

[54] Ibid.

[55] Ibid., Introduction (para. 4).

[56] Ibid., para. 8.

[57] Ibid., Introduction (para. 14).

[58] UN Committee on Economic, Social and Cultural Rights [CESCR], *General Comment No. 15: The Right to Water*, Jan. 20, 2003, UN Doc. E/C.12/2002/11, para. 2.

[59] See for example *Report of the United Nations Conference on Environment and Development, Rio de Janeiro, 3–14 June 1992* (New York: United Nations, 1993).

[60] CESCR, note 58, para. 1.

[61] Ibid., para. 48: "The formulation and implementation of national water strategies and plans of action should respect, inter alia, the principles of non-discrimination and people's participation. The right of individuals and

discrimination,[62] and even due process rights,[63] all of which help to reinforce the enjoyment of the right to water. Rights to water, food, health, and a healthy environment are all inter-dependent, as are the rights to secure and protect them. And all are aspects of the right to live with dignity as it has been recognized by courts. These are the conditions for survival of present and future generations.[64]

Thus, water as described in the General Comment instantiates the indivisibility thesis at several different levels. First, it confirms the connection among different rights: health, life, employment, food, safety, discrimination, due process, and so on. Second, at another level, it bridges the divide between the two types (or generations) of rights by implicating both civil and political rights, as well as economic, social, and cultural rights, without distinguishing in any way between the two or privileging one over the other. Water is as important to equal protection and political participation as it is to housing, food, and health.[65] This is evident, too, in the General Comment's discussion on implementation of water rights, where the CESCR noted that "While the Covenant provides for progressive realization and acknowledges the constraints due to the limits of available resources, it also imposes on States parties various obligations which are of immediate effect,"[66] invoking the general principle of implementation associated with the ICCPR. Third, it unifies the disparate geopolitical interests of the world, as it transcends temporal interests. Water rights have national, as well as international, implications as water sources often cross-national boundaries, and resource and management plans to ensure adequate access to clean water may have to take into account the interests of a wide range of stakeholders: local and global interests, industrial and rural uses, personal and commercial uses, and so on. Moreover, as the CESCR and many courts have recognized, water rights must be assured not only for the current burgeoning population, but for future generations as well.

What is true of water is also true of other rights relating to the environment: the right to clean air is also essential not only to the effective enjoyment of other rights but to *any* enjoyment of

---

groups to participate in decision-making processes that may affect their exercise of the right to water must be an integral part of any policy, programme or strategy concerning water. Individuals and groups should be given full and equal access to information concerning water, water services and the environment, held by public authorities or third parties"; UN Committee on Economic, Social and Cultural Rights, *General Comment No. 14: The Right to the Highest Attainable Standard of Health*, Aug. 11, 2000, UN Doc. E/C.12/2000/4, para. 37(f), requiring governments "To adopt and implement a national water strategy and plan of action addressing the whole population; the strategy and plan of action should be devised, and periodically reviewed, on the basis of a participatory and transparent process."

[62] CESCR, note 58, para. 13: "The obligation of States parties to guarantee that the right to water is enjoyed without discrimination (art. 2, para. 2), and equally between men and women (art. 3), pervades all of the Covenant obligations. The Covenant thus proscribes any discrimination on the grounds of race, colour, sex, age, language, religion, political or other opinion, national or social origin, property, birth, physical or mental disability, health status (including HIV/AIDS), sexual orientation and civil, political, social or other status, which has the intention or effect of nullifying or impairing the equal enjoyment or exercise of the right to water."

[63] Ibid., para. 10: "The right to water contains both freedoms and entitlements. The freedoms include the right to maintain access to existing water supplies necessary for the right to water, and the right to be free from interference, such as the right to be free from arbitrary disconnections or contamination of water supplies."

[64] Ibid., para. 3.

[65] See also Rio Declaration, note 19: "Environmental issues are best handled with the participation of all concerned citizens, at the relevant level. At the national level, each individual shall have appropriate access to information concerning the environment that is held by public authorities, including information on hazardous materials and activities in their communities, and the opportunity to participate in decision-making processes. States shall facilitate and encourage public awareness and participation by making information widely available. Effective access to judicial and administrative proceedings, including redress and remedy, shall be provided."

[66] CESCR, note 58, para. 17.

other rights. If the air is so polluted as to cause ill health, then the right to a clean environment and the right to health are simultaneously and jointly violated and to the same extent. Likewise, when a government authorizes companies to clear-cut forests or to mine mountains, the right to sustenance of those who depend on the forests for food, or the right to development for those who depend on the mountainside for farming or maintaining their communities may, to that extent, be compromised. Climate change in general presents new challenges to the human rights regime as it increases human vulnerability to poverty and disease, which in turn creates opportunities for political oppression and myriad forms of human rights abuses. Climate change may well turn entire populations into refugees, raising human rights issues to a new level. Increasingly, courts are entertaining claims that liberty includes the right to a climate capable of sustaining human life.[67]

The effects of climate change provide vivid examples of how environmental conditions affect human dignity. Climate change "directly and indirectly implicates" important human rights and responsibilities because it "connects the many dangerous climate impacts to the human rights commitments states have already undertaken."[68] The right to life is increasingly threatened as floods, landslides, and fires become more common and more severe; the right to health is impacted when droughts make access to food less secure or when pollution makes potable water less available, which in turn threatens the right to employment and education; rights relating to property (including agricultural, inheritance, and development rights) are threatened when rising sea levels erode land; cultural rights may be threatened by reckless logging, overfishing, or mining, as may be labor and employment rights – to give just a few examples.

And, yet, the law can sometimes be slow to catch on, particularly when the impacts are most acutely and chronically felt by the poor and the disenfranchised. Thus, it is a welcome advance that courts around the world are beginning to occupy the space where environmental rights and the right to live with dignity meet.

2.5 JUDICIAL RECOGNITION OF THE INDIVISIBILITY OF HUMAN DIGNITY AND THE ENVIRONMENT

As constitutional courts around the globe are turning their attention to environmental human rights, they are becoming increasingly aware of the impact that environmental degradation has on human dignity. Dignity can be a useful concept in environmental litigation for several reasons:

> First, it provides a vocabulary for foregrounding the damage *to people* of environmental and climate harms. Second, it draws attention to how environmental harms affect all of the essential aspects of a person's life: where food security, access to clean water, and breathable air are threatened, a person's ability to design her own life plan is weakened and her ability to live in material comfort is impossible . . . Thus, it draws attention to *how* people live in their environments and seeks to ameliorate the impacts that adverse environmental conditions have on people's ability to live *as people of worth*.[69]

Third, and relatedly, inherent in the concept of human dignity is that the right must be enjoyed by every person on an equal basis, a principle that has particular salience in the context

---

[67] *Juliana v. United States*, 6:15-cv-1517 (D.Or., 2016).

[68] M. Burkett, "A Justice Paradox: On Climate Change, Small Island Developing States, and the Quest for Effective Legal Remedy" (2013) 35 *Harvard Law Review* 633, 646–647.

[69] Daly and May (2019), note 34, p. 187.

of environmental injustice which visits the burdens of environmental destruction disproportionately on communities of color and poor communities. Advancing the SDGs requires taking seriously the challenge of ensuring that environmental benefits and burdens are experienced by all without privilege or discrimination.[70]

One of the earliest cases to see the connection between environmental conditions and the ability to live with dignity is from Nigeria. In *Gbemre v. Shell Petroleum Development Company Nigeria Limited and Others*, the lower court held that gas flaring violated the petitioners' constitutional "right to respect for their lives and dignity of their persons and to enjoy the best attainable state of physical and mental health as well as [the] right to a general satisfactory environment favourable to their development" and that the gas flaring activities formed "a violation of their said fundamental rights to life and dignity of human person and to a healthy life in a healthy environment."[71] Although a declaratory judgment without remedy or continuing judicial oversight, the case signals a growing appreciation of the connection between dignity and environmental conditions.

More recently, the High Court of Lahore in Pakistan recognized the connection between life, dignity, and environmental and climate justice in 2015, and again when it revisited the same case in 2018:

> Fundamental rights, like the right to life (article 9) which includes the right to a healthy and clean environment and right to human dignity (article 14) read with constitutional principles of democracy, equality, social, economic and political justice include within their ambit and commitment, the international environmental principles of sustainable development, precautionary principle, environmental impact assessment, inter and intra-generational equity and public trust doctrine.[72]

Other courts have followed a similar path recognizing the indivisibility of human dignity and the environment. Kenya's Environmental and Land Court in Nairobi acknowledged that environmental rights must be read in light of the constitutional commitment to human dignity:[73]

> The Preamble to the Constitution . . . proclaims that the people of Kenya, when making the Constitution were committed to nurturing and protecting the well-being of the individual, the family, communities and the nation. Likewise, the national values and principles that bind this Court . . . include human dignity, equity, social justice, human rights, non-discrimination, protection of the marginalized and sustainable development.[74]

The Nepalese Supreme Court has articulated a similar commitment to environmental dignity:

> Article 12(1) of the Interim Constitution has also incorporated the right to live with dignity under the right to life. It shall be erroneous and incomplete to have a narrow thinking that the right to

---

[70] Ibid.

[71] *Gbemre v. Shell Petroleum Dev Corp & the Nigerian National Petroleum Corporation* [2005] 6 AHRLR 152 (Nigeria). See J. May and T. Dayo, "Dignity and Environmental Justice in Nigeria: The Case of Gbemre v. Shell" (2019) 25 *Widener Law Review* 183–197.

[72] *Ashgar Leghari*, Lahore High Court, 2018.

[73] Kenya Const., Art. 10(2)(b) and (d).

[74] *Friends of Lake Turkana Trust v. Attorney General & Two Others* [2014] KLR, in the Environment and Land Court at Nairobi ELC Suit No. 825 of 2012 (finding insufficient evidence of actual violations of the right to dignity, life, livelihood, and cultural and environmental heritage by the Gibe III hydroelectric project at the planning and implementation stages, but finding that the risks involved in "the harnessing of such electricity in Ethiopia is likely to affect its right to life and [] livelihood and its cultural and environmental heritage . . . [and this] imposes a positive duty upon the Respondents and Interested Party to provide the Petitioner with the all relevant information in relation to importation and/or purchase and transmission of electric power from Ethiopia").

life is only a matter of sustaining life. Rather it should be understood that all rights necessary for living a dignified life as a human being are included in it. Not only that, it cannot be imagined to live with dignity in a polluted environment rather it may create an adverse situation even exposing human life to dangers.[75]

Beyond mere statements acknowledging the interdependence of human dignity and environmental and climate rights, courts could acknowledge the right to dignity in at least two phases of constitutional litigation: defining the cause of action and fashioning remedies.

2.5.1 *Establishing a Violation*

One of the most pressing challenges for environmental constitutionalism is definitional. Most substantive environmental rights provisions are vague, which can deter judicial officers from applying them: judges are often unwilling to make judgments about what is a "quality environment" or a "healthy environment,"[76] a "sound" environment,[77] or a "healthy and ecologically balanced human environment."[78] Applying these terms to a given situation can also be daunting: How can a court decide whether a timber license violates a healthy environment, or whether pollution levels in a river or bay or in the air reaches a point where the air or water is no longer clean?

In the face of such interpretive challenges in environmental adjudication, dignity can alleviate the nebulous nature of environmental rights by providing a benchmark against which a violation or a remedy should be judged: in implementing, enforcing, and vindicating constitutional environmental rights, dignity rights can help a court determine when the right to a quality (or healthy or balanced) environment is violated. While all human activity impairs the environment, a constitutional violation would occur when the impairment impacts the dignity of those affected – a standard of evaluation that is loose, but still more familiar to the judiciary. A timber license might be constitutional, but not if the clear-cutting removed trees that people relied on for shelter and protection against storm damage, or food or natural water were imperiled. Dams could be constructed to provide electricity, but a violation of the constitutional right to dignity might be found where the construction of the dam displaced communities without meaningful compensation and without opportunities for participation in discussions about timing and impact. Government policies that destroyed the aesthetic or recreational value of natural environments would also come under scrutiny for the impact they would have on the dignity interest in social and cultural self-development, for example.

A dignity-based definition of harm would apply similarly to procedural environmental rights: absolute transparency and infinite participation is impracticable, but information and opportunities to participate in environmental decision-making would need to be sufficient to enable those affected to exercise their civic dignity.[79] Plaintiffs would still have to show harm, but the harm in question would be to their dignity interests – whether individual or collective, and whether sounding in civil and political rights or social, economic, and cultural rights. In many cases, it might be easier for plaintiffs to allege harm to their dignitary interests because they would not

---

[75] *Pro Public* v. *Godavari Marble Industries Pvt. Ltd. and Others* (Supreme Court of Nepal, 2015).

[76] See for example Nicaragua Const., Title IV, Ch. 3, Art. 60; Colombia Const., Title II, Ch. 3, Art. 79.

[77] Montenegro Const., Art. 23.

[78] See for example Portugal Const., Part I, Section 3, Ch. 2, Art. 66(1); Dominican Republic Const., Art. 67(1); Costa Rica Const., Title V, Art. 50.

[79] *August and Another* v. *Electoral Commission*, Case CCT 8/99 [1999] ZACC 3; 1999 (3) SA 1; 1999 (4) BCLR 363 (Apr. 1, 1999).

need to show the causal effects of adverse health impacts or scientific evidence about water shortages, for instance, but could rely instead on subjective and objective testimony that draws attention to the impact of environmental degradation on the ability of individuals, families, and communities to live in dignity. Such a dignity-based approach would enable courts to be more sensitive and holistic in pursuing a rights-protective role in both substantive and procedural terms.

2.5.2 *Fashioning Remedies*

Environmental cases are among constitutional law's most complicated to remedy because the injuries can be multifaceted, layered, and interdependent; defendants can be recalcitrant and are often among the country's most politically powerful and economically resourceful; and the damage to both humans and their environment can be literally irremediable. In addition, it can be daunting to quantify the damage not only to present but also to future generations. Most courts are keenly aware of the limitations of their own power – of the fact, namely, that courts have no particular resource other than their own legitimacy to ensure respect for or compliance with judicial orders.[80]

But just as recourse to the right to dignity can help identify violations, it can also help define remedies. And, again, dignity-based remedies can be both substantive and procedural. When the Supreme Court of India ordered the closure of tanneries that had been polluting the River Ganga, it required that the new operation protect the jobs and rights of the displaced workers, including requiring that they be paid during the period of closure and that they be given a substantial "shifting bonus" to help them settle at the new location.[81] Similarly, when landfills were being closed in Colombia, the Court took special care to assure the dignity of those individuals whose only means of support had been collecting recyclables from the landfill. The Court's extensive remedial order required each affected municipality to, within a few months, adopt necessary measures to "protect the recyclers' rights to health, education, dignified living, and food, ensuring in each particular case that the means were connected to specific social programs."[82] And, without risking charges of judicial activism, courts could even go further: they could ensure that governmental decisions that impact the environment would be made only on the basis of human dignity, in its various manifestations. And when courts issue orders in cases involving procedural environmental rights, they can advance the civic dignity of individuals who would seek to participate meaningfully in the environmental protection of their communities. Indeed, one could even ask how a remedy could reasonably be designed except by reference to human dignity. After all, the protection of human dignity is arguably how we know how much clean water is needed or what constitutes appropriate environmental safeguards for the extraction of natural resources, or how to advance climate justice.

And, yet, while the right to dignity is universal, its application in the context of litigation would be left to courts to decide and define based on the facts of the case and according to the existing dignity jurisprudence that is judicially relevant.

To say that the human and environmental interests are interlocked leaves open the question of whether the interests are mutually reinforcing or antagonistic. We might call a mutually reinforcing relationship "positive" in that understanding the claim in both its dimensions makes the claim stronger. Ordering the closure of tanneries on the Ganges River unless they stop

---

[80] Ibid., p. 149.
[81] *M.C. Mehta (Calcutta Tanneries' Matter)* v. *Union of India and Others*, Writ Petition (C) No. 3727 of 1985 (1996).
[82] Sentencia T-291/09 (Colombia Constitutional Court, 2009), para. 9.2.5.

discharging pollutants illustrates the indivisibility of environmental and human rights: respecting the environment invariably promotes the human right to life.[83] Indeed, the effort to incorporate environmental rights into the catalogue of human rights assumes that what is good for one is good for the other and that relying on both will strengthen the arguments of claimants who seek to vindicate environmental rights. Making explicit their indivisibility with rights to life, health, dignity, and so on, the conventional wisdom goes, will encourage courts to recognize the claimants as legitimate plaintiffs, to see their injuries as cognizable, and to see the violation as remediable. Positive indivisibility does not present any significant juridical problems because both the harms and the remedies are interlinked.

But not all environmental rights relate positively with other dignity-reinforcing rights. For instance, in the tanneries case, the Supreme Court of India recognized that "Closure of tanneries may bring unemployment and loss of revenue, but life, health and ecology have greater importance to the people."[84] Thus, environmental rights must be considered in light of employment, life, and health, and in that sense they are indivisible with these latter human rights. But while they positively reinforce claims to life and health, they detrimentally impact claims to employment, also a human and constitutionally protected right closely associated with the right to live with dignity. Or, in the case of *Maria Elena Burgos* v. *Municipality of Campoalegre (Huila)*, the Constitutional Court of Colombia upheld a lower court's order to destroy pig stalls that caused respiratory distress and fevers in neighbors.[85] While the environmental claim supported the right to life and health, it impaired the pig stall owners' right to employment and to the free enjoyment of their property. The environmental claimant should understand that the environmental claim, and its remedy if it is successful, will necessarily *affect* some human rights, but the effect will be positive in the case of some human rights and negative in the case of others. Indeed, in many cases the environmental claim will detrimentally affect the right to property and economic development. The indivisibility is no less relevant where the claim is made first from the standpoint of the human right rather than the environmental right. For instance, when the South African Constitutional Court ruled that the residents of Johannesburg are entitled to access to a certain amount of water per day, the claim was made in terms of the *human* right to water and it was thus partially vindicated. But this victory for human rights may be a defeat for environmental rights: to secure a certain amount of water may very well require irrigation toward the population center that will have adverse environmental consequences on the surrounding watershed area. Thus, environmental rights and human rights are interlocked, but, in this case, they correlate negatively. The issues get more complicated when we think of dignity in all its substantive dimensions. Human dignity, as it has been recognized in the courts, affects all civil as well as social and economic and cultural rights: when we think about dignity, we should be thinking not only about the environment, but also about health, livelihood, food and water security, and all other aspects of a life that implicate the ability to live with dignity. Moreover, dignity is judicially understood not only as the right of autonomous individuals, but as rights to live in community with family and others.[86] Thus, the impacts

---

[83] See M.C. Mehta v. Union of India (1987) 4 SCC 463, discussed in May and Daly (2009), note 21, p. 400.

[84] Ibid.

[85] *María Elena Burgos* v. *Municipality of Campoalegre (Huila)*, Constitutional Court, Feb. 27, 1997.

[86] In one Colombian case about the right to water, the Court said that "the water that people use is indispensable to guarantee physical life and human dignity, understood as the ability to enjoy the material conditions of life that permit the development of an active role in society." Colombia Constitutional Court, Sentencia T-81/02. "El agua que usan las personas es indispensable para garantizar la vida física y la dignidad humana, entendida esta como la posibilidad de gozar de condiciones materiales de existencia que le permitan desarrollar un papel activo en la sociedad." See also Colombia Constitutional Court, Sentencia C-793/09 (discussing dignity as "convivencia ciudadana" (i.e. living together as citizens)).

of environmental decision-making on the whole social fabric should also be taken into consideration. These all matter, indivisibly.

2.6 CONCLUSION

Human dignity is essential to sustainability's environmental, social, and economic pillars; attention to the equal worth of all those involved in environmental outcomes evidences a respect for the human dignity of each person in present and future generations, something the SDGs capture in their core provisions. Courts have increasingly recognized the links between environmental protection and the enjoyment of human rights, in large part by reference to human dignity and to the rights that human dignity entails. As a conceptual matter, attention to human dignity foregrounds the impacts on human beings of environmental decisions, including decisions that contribute to climate change, and requires courts to address ways in which those decisions diminish the ability of people to manage their own lives, often in ways that disproportionately affect those who are already the most vulnerable and marginalized. Thus, in the context of judicial implementation, attention to dignity can also help shape the contours of environmental human rights by providing a measure of when a violation of an environmental right has occurred. Dignity can also serve as a benchmark for remedies, ensuring that environmental harms are remedied in ways that protect the dignity interests of all those who are affected.

3

Environmental Justice in the Global South

Usha Natarajan

3.1 INTRODUCTION

The concept of environmental justice has its origins in the United States in the 1980s when it was used to describe the unequal impact of industrial pollution on racial minorities. From these beginnings, over the last four decades the idea has blossomed, expanding both geographically and historically to encompass variegated environmental struggles worldwide, including those from centuries past. Why does this concept have such resonance and wherein lies its usefulness? This chapter examines these questions from the point of view of the Global South. I begin with some background on what is meant by the Global South and by environmental justice. I then use the customary four-pillar formulation of environmental justice – distributive justice, procedural justice, corrective justice, and social justice – to explain the different theoretical and practical ways in which this concept is helpful for understanding environmental struggles across the Global South.

3.2 BACKGROUND

We are witnessing environmental change unseen in millions of years: the sixth mass extinction of species, the changing climate, the dying oceans, and dwindling forests, the spreading deserts, the increasing toxicity of our water, air and soil, and the complex interrelatedness between these phenomena. In attempting to formulate adequate responses, communities, activists, technical experts, academics, as well as law and policymakers, are increasingly turning to the notion of environmental justice for guidance. Before examining reasons for such a turn, it is worth stating that I am among those making this move, and this Chapter is self-reflexive participation in constructing what environmental justice means for the Global South. I am an international law scholar and practitioner in the Global South and part of the Third World Approaches to International Law (TWAIL) movement.[1] My assessment of environmental justice is colored by my location, profession, and politics. I judge the utility of environmental justice against the

---

[1] TWAIL is a network of international law scholars and practitioners committed to the interests of the peoples of the Global South. For its political commitments, see B. S. Chimni, "Third World Approaches to International Law: A Manifesto" (2006) 8 *International Community Law Review* 3. For a description, see J. T. Gathii, "TWAIL: A Brief History of Its Origins, Its Decentralized Network and Tentative Bibliography" (2011) 3 *Trade, Law and Development* 26.

backdrop of how effective international law has heretofore been for addressing the environmental concerns of the Global South.

My comfort in using the term "Global South" stems from my participation in the TWAIL
movement, which is a network of international law scholars and practitioners committed to
solidarity along these lines.[2] The term "Global South" can be used interchangeably with "less-
developed," "developing," "underdeveloped," or indeed "Third World," to refer to states and
peoples marginalized in international society – lagging behind in terms of prosperity and power.[3]
States of the Global South have sometimes formed political coalitions, such as the Group of 77
(G-77) and the Non-Aligned Movement,[4] and peoples of the South have also been loosely
linked at various times by social movements of protest by the poor against the rich.[5] While the
term Global South has more contemporary purchase, its Cold War antecedent was the term
"Third World." Nyerère described the Third World as the majority of the world's population,
possessing the largest part of certain important raw materials, and yet having no control and
hardly any influence over the manner in which nations of the world arrange their economic
affairs.[6]

By the late twentieth century, when many Third World states such as South Korea, Taiwan,
Hong Kong, and Singapore successfully developed export-oriented processes of industrialization,
analysts declared that the Third World no longer existed.[7] Rapid economic growth in Brazil,
China, India, Indonesia, Russia, South Africa, and other emerging economies, raises similar
issues today for the term Global South. When using broad and crosscutting terms such as Third
World or Global South, there is a risk of impreciseness and elision of the growing diversity
amongst developing states and the fracturing and reshaping of alliances between them. Thus,
scholars have critiqued the risk of camouflaging the differences between and within nations.[8]
Hardt and Negri famously declared that globalization had made the Third World obsolete as
there is a First World in every Third World, and a Third in the First, and the Second almost
nowhere at all.[9]

These challenges are not new. Postcolonial scholars have always negotiated them. In the
1980s, Anand observed of the Third World that:[10]

> They cover a whole range of economic, political and cultural diversities, even antagonisms. The
> family of underdeveloped countries include both producers and consumers of energy, importers
> and exporters of raw materials, nations which can feed their populations as well as those which

---

[2]   The subsequent five paragraphs are abridged from U. Natarajan, "TWAIL and the Environment," in A.
      Philippopoulos-Mihalopoulos & V. Brooks (eds.), *Research Methods in Environmental Law: A Handbook*
      (Cheltenham, UK: Edward Elgar, 2017).
[3]   K. Mickelson, "Rhetoric and Rage: Third World Voices in International Legal Discourse" (1998) 16 *Wisconsin
      International Law Journal* 353 at 356.
[4]   The G-77 was formed on June 15, 1964 through the Joint Declaration of the 77 Countries issued at the United
      Nations Conference on Trade and Development (UNCTAD). The Non-Aligned Movement was founded in
      Belgrade in 1961 to advocate a middle course for states of the developing world between the Western and
      Eastern blocs during the Cold War. See further www.g77.org/ and http://csstc.org.
[5]   Mickelson, note 3, p. 357.
[6]   J. Nyerère, "South–South Opinion," in A. Gauhar (ed.), *The Third World Strategy: Economic and Political
      Cohesion in the South* (Westport, CT: Praeger, 1984), pp. 9–10.
[7]   N. Harris, *The End of the Third World* (Harmondsworth, UK: Penguin, 1987); M. T. Berger, "End of the Third
      World" (1994) 15 *Third World Quarterly* 257; M. Berger, "After the Third World? History, Destiny and the Fate
      of Third Worldism" (2004) 25 *Third World Quarterly* 9.
[8]   See references in note 7.
[9]   M. Hardt and A. Negri, *Empire* (Cambridge, MA: Harvard University Press, 2000), pp. 263–264.
[10] R. P. Anand, *International Law and the Developing Countries: Confrontation or Cooperation?* (Dordrecht:
      Martinus Nijhoff, 1987), p. 120 (emphasis added).

almost always face the spectre of famine. They differ among themselves so greatly in economic promise that they are sometimes divided into 'third,' 'fourth' and 'fifth' worlds . . . In fact, for many purposes it is more misleading than illuminating to lump together countries of Asia, Africa and Latin America. And yet, for a variety of purposes *these countries perceive themselves as a group*, a perception made more impressive because it overcomes an underlying, undeniable diversity.

Many decades after Anand helped pioneer Third World scholarship in international law, his observations on the self-identified and self-constituted nature of the Third World remain insightful. Terms such as Third World or Global South retain their political and scholarly purchase today because of their enduring relevance for peoples across geographical, social, and cultural divides. People everywhere continue to be drawn together by shared concerns for the poorest and most vulnerable peoples in their societies, by common struggles against transnational and systemic patterns of domination and subordination, and by finding a usefulness in working together.

The utility of terms such as Global South lie in the way they are employed by postcolonial scholars, to breakdown dichotomies rather than to reinforce them. In this chapter, the term Global South is used to help reveal that there are no rigid boundaries between the South and North, colonized and colonizer, or between Third World and First. The identities of victim and victor were rarely pure in colonial times, and the postcolonial world has seen a continuation of mutual cultural transference and hybridity of identities.[11] Rather than asserting an inflexible boundary between North and South, my intent is to break down this boundary and contest any claims to the stability of meaning and identity.[12] Postcolonial scholars understand colonialism as a project of cultural control. Colonized societies were classified and labeled. New distinctions and oppositions came into being between colonizers and colonized, Europe and Asia, Europe and Africa, modern and primitive, West and East, and North and South.[13] One of the purposes of a chapter such as this is to complicate contemporary understandings of the South and North, rejecting simplistic characterizations of non-Western and Western states and peoples. After all, as Baxi accurately observed, long before Hardt and Negri identified globalization as scrambling the composition of the Three Worlds, scrambling had already occurred through centuries of colonialism, settlement colonies, enforced diasporas of laboring classes, slavery, slave-like labor, and forced relocations.[14]

One of the strengths of a term such as Global South is its flexible porous meaning, which enables reference to transnational underclasses, movements, and solidarities that are in a process of continual flux geographically. While the term Global South may be problematic in some ways, the alternatives are too, and the concept is used in this chapter because of its usefulness for counter-hegemonic knowledge production. It provides what Darby calls a "conceptual tripwire against colonizing tendencies of much dominant discourse."[15]

---

[11] L. Gandhi, *Postcolonial Theory: A Critical Introduction* (New York: Columbia University Press, 1998), pp. 126, 131, 137.

[12] A. Riles, "Aspiration and Control: International Legal Rhetoric and the Essentialisation of Culture" (1993) 106 *Harvard Law Review* 723; D. Otto, "Subalternity and International Law: The Problems of Global Community and the Incommensurability of Difference" (1996) 5 *Social and Legal Studies* 337.

[13] N. Dirks, *Castes of Mind: Colonialism and the Making of Modern India* (Princeton, NJ: Princeton University Press, 2001), p. 9.

[14] Hardt and Negri, note 9; U. Baxi, "What May the 'Third World' Expect from International Law?" (2006) 27 *Third World Quarterly* 713 at 717.

[15] P. Darby, "Pursuing the Political: A Postcolonial Rethinking of Relations International" (2004) 33 *Millennium: Journal of International Studies* 1 at 2–3.

The term environmental justice has a more precise origin. It was a movement that gained prominence in the United States in the 1980s for its organized opposition to situating hazardous waste facilities and polluting industries in poor, minority communities.[16] Environmental justice was a response to environmental racism – the disproportionate impact of environmental hazards on people of color – and beyond race environmental justice also encompasses issues of class, gender, and other intersectional markers of identity.[17] As the US government started to engage with some of the movement's demands, activists became wary of cooption of their message, and clarified that they do not accept a mere redistribution of environmental harms but rather demand their abolition.[18] Advocates identified four aspects of environmental injustice experienced by historically marginalized communities. First, distributive injustice arising from disproportionate exposure to environmental hazards and limited access to environmental services. Second, procedural injustice caused by exclusion from environmental decision-making. Third, corrective injustice due to inadequate enforcement of environmental legislation and inadequate redress for harm done. Fourth, social injustice because environmental degradation is inextricably intertwined with deeper structural ills such as poverty and racism.[19]

Given its origins in the heartlands of the long-industrialized United States with its particularities of race and class, at first glance it may seem surprising that the concept of environmental justice has been so readily taken up across the Global South. However, the connections become evident when considering the US development pathway and its indivisibility from the exploitation of labor and resources worldwide. US particularities of race and class were produced by centuries of settler colonialism, genocide of Indigenous populations, slavery and forced labor, apartheid, access to labor and resources across the globe, and environmental degradation. Indeed, when the People of Color Environmental Leadership Summit formulated their *Principles of Environmental Justice* in 1991, they explicitly acknowledged this historical and geographical link, stating that they are[20]

> gathered together . . . to build a national and *international movement of all peoples of color* to fight the destruction and taking of our lands and communities . . . to respect and celebrate each of our cultures, languages and beliefs about the natural world and our roles in healing ourselves . . . and, *to secure our political, economic and cultural liberation that has been denied for over 500 years of colonization and oppression*, resulting in the poisoning of our communities and land and the genocide of our peoples.

That is to say, environmental justice did not begin only in the United States. It stems from centuries of environmental degradation as a result of colonization and the oppression of communities of color worldwide – communities that carried the burden of Western industrialization through loss of land, livelihood, and even life so that elites could profit. For this reason, environmental justice is an idea well attuned to the needs of Global South, as both environmental justice and the Global South are ideas based on an awareness of patterns of exploitation that are longstanding and transnational.

Environmental struggles have been the ubiquitous and inescapable companion of mass industrialization everywhere. Such efforts did not label themselves environmental justice until

---

[16] L. W. Cole and S. R. Foster, *From the Ground Up: Environmental Racism and the Rise of the Environmental Justice Movement* (New York: New York University Press, 2001), pp. 19–33.

[17] Ibid. See also R. W. Collin, "Review of the Legal Literature on Environmental Racism, Environmental Equity, and Environmental Justice" (1994) 9 *Journal of Environmental Law and Litigation* 121.

[18] EJnet.org: Web Resources for Environmental Justice Activists, www.ejnet.org/ej.

[19] R. R. Kuehn, "A Taxonomy of Environmental Justice" (2000) 30 *Environmental Law Reporter* 10681 at 10688.

[20] People of Color Environmental Leadership Summit, *Principles of Environmental Justice*, Oct. 24–27, 1991, Washington, DC, www.ejnet.org/ej/principles.html (emphasis added) [hereafter, *Principles*].

recent decades, when communities in the North and later the South adopted this terminology in a variety of grassroots movements; frequently in the context of equitable access to basic resources such as clean water, food, energy and land, as well as in opposition to extractive industries and dams.[21] As in the USA, environmental justice is used in the South to describe an evaluative framework as well as a social movement when environmental impact on communities is disparate. This duality reflects the praxis of environmental justice and its commitment to evaluation and action. Extending to the Global South a framework developed in the Global North can be tactical as it provides an established paradigm within which research can be conducted. Using accepted concepts, methods, and networks allows Southern voices to participate more easily in knowledge production and advocate for change. However, foreign frameworks may miss, obfuscate, and prevent the articulation of context-specific issues and stifle creativity. The abovementioned *Environmental Justice Principles* address this risk, declaring that global solidarity is built on the celebration of diverse understandings of nature and different roads to self-healing.[22] This approach values and is respectful of difference, inviting movements worldwide to participate in shaping the evolution of the concept of environmental justice.[23] Rather than subsuming contradictions and diversities and focusing only on commonalities, environmental justice is defined as multiplicity rather than unity, ensuring its usefulness for subalterns worldwide that may be facing challenges in unique contexts, that may have no or limited parallels in other places and times, and that may be in flux.

From this embrace of cultural difference stems the hopefulness of the concept of environmental justice, particularly for international lawyers in the Global South. International law is not a progressive discipline.[24] It is deeply conservative, useful to power, and struggles with tackling contemporary environmental challenges.[25] In this context, environmental justice provides a language of resistance for the disempowered masses to articulate their needs on their own terms within a framework not yet coopted by international lawmakers and their institutions. Through its origins in grassroots activism, environmental justice provides a paradigm that grounds law in social praxis as rooted in particular contexts. The extension of the concept to the transnational and global sphere is occurring in fields such as political ecology, globalization studies, and the study of transnational social movements.[26] Edited collections such as this ensure that

---

[21] See for example D. Schlosberg, *Defining Environmental Justice: Theories, Movements, and Nature* (New York: Oxford University Press, 2007); J. Ebbeson and P. Okowa (eds.), *Environmental Law and Justice in Context* (Cambridge, UK: Cambridge University Press, 2009); G. Walker, *Environmental Justice: Concepts, Evidence and Politics* (Basingstoke, UK: Routledge, 2012).

[22] *Principles*, note 20.

[23] See for example R. D. Bullard (ed.), *The Quest for Environmental Justice: Human Rights and the Politics of Pollution* (San Francisco: Sierra Club, 2005); D. V. Carruthers (ed.), *Environmental Justice in Latin America: Problems, Promise, and Practice* (London: MIT Press, 2008); J. A. Carmin and J. Agyeman (eds.), *Environmental Inequalities beyond Borders: Local Perspectives on Global Injustices* (Cambridge, MA: MIT Press, 2011); R. Ako, *Environmental Justice in Developing Countries: Perspectives from Africa and Asia-Pacific* (Abingdon, UK: Routledge, 2013); H. Shue, *Climate Justice: Vulnerability and Protection* (Oxford: Oxford University Press, 2014).

[24] See for example J. Linarelli, M. E. Salomon, and M. Sornarajah, *The Misery of International Law* (Oxford: Oxford University Press, 2018); A. Orford, "Scientific Reason and the Discipline of International Law" (2014) 25 *European Journal of International Law* 369; H. Charlesworth, "International Law: A Discipline of Crisis" (2002) 65 *Modern Law Review* 377.

[25] For a fuller elaboration of this argument, see U. Natarajan and K. Khoday, "Locating Nature: Making and Unmaking International Law" (2014) 27 *Leiden Journal of International Law* 573.

[26] G. Walker and H. Bulkeley, "Geographies of Environmental Justice" (2006) 37 *Geoforum* 655; R. Nixon, *Slow Violence and the Environmentalism of the Poor* (Cambridge: Harvard University Press, 2011); J. Sze and J. K. London, "Environmental Justice at the Crossroads" (2008) 2 *Sociology Compass* 1331.

international law also benefits from this traction. The challenge is to do so while ensuring the concept is not coopted and subsumed within the dominant disciplinary discourse, robbing it of radical and transformative potential. With this in mind, the subsequent sections articulate what environmental justice means in the context of the Global South, considering each of the four aspects of environmental injustice as experienced by marginalized communities: distributive injustice, procedural injustice, corrective injustice, and social injustice. While this chapter identifies transnational structures of environmental injustice, it must be kept in mind that the Global South is most of the world and thus encompasses a staggering diversity of experiences. The nuances of each local situation, with its particular dynamics of gender, sexuality, class, caste, religion, and other intersectional markers of identity, are beyond the scope of this chapter. Instead, this chapter identifies thematic commonalities across the South, providing a conceptual framework for subsequent chapters that undertake context-based analyses through specific case studies.

3.3 DISTRIBUTIVE JUSTICE

Environmental justice within the USA analyzes domestic social dynamics that produce racial inequalities in exposure to pollution and access to resources. Similarly, when applied at the global scale, the framework of environmental justice is useful for identifying transnational patterns of environmental winners and losers. Environmental justice traces the global distributive outcomes of environmental goods and bads, and whether/how this distribution correlates with race, culture, class, gender, and other possible markers of inequality internationally. It is worth noting that the divide between the Global South and Global North when it comes to environmental issues is well known and longstanding.[27] Indeed, this division precedes the US environmental justice movement, and has shaped international efforts to tackle environmental problems since the early days of international environmental law in the 1970s. Thus, for communities in the Global South that lack access to ecological services and are on the frontlines of environmental harm, the usefulness of environmental justice is not so much its ability to point out a North–South divide when it comes to the distribution of environmental benefits and harms as this is old news. Rather, environmental justice helps situate and explain their plight within a more useful framework for change. It provides a much-needed alternative given the extant failure of international laws and institutions to address environmental harm. It also shows the intersectionality between various markers of identity and discrimination and, by tracing how this operates transnationally, enables more effective solidarity-building and mobilization for change.

Distributive justice is a particularly helpful aspect of environmental justice for international lawyers because our discipline is at an impasse when it comes to addressing environmental challenges. The specialized and fast-growing field of international environmental law has identified the leading environmental challenges of our time – climate change, species extinction, desertification, deforestation, hazardous wastes, and so on.[28] Yet each of these problems have significantly worsened since international environmental laws have attempted to address them. This woeful record is because the rich and powerful are unwilling to embrace economic

---

[27] See generally S. Alam, S. Atapattu, C. Gonzalez, and J. Razzaque (eds.), *International Environmental Law and the Global South* (Cambridge, UK: Cambridge University Press, 2015).

[28] See the International Environmental Agreement Database Project for a catalog of laws: https://iea.uoregon .edu.

development models less harmful to nature. However, failure has not prevented the legal specialization from growing. The opposite has occurred, with increasing interest and investment in international environmental law, and a marked increase in jobs, textbooks, research centers, grants, degrees, and a proliferation of technical expertise. This paradox is troubling for those concerned with addressing environmental problems because of the risk that the field may be contributing to these problems rather than solving them. In light of this concern, distributive justice provides a timely and necessary reminder to focus on the reasons why we have not been able to tackle global challenges, as a productive way of moving forward.

Gonzalez, a scholar at the vanguard of introducing the discourse of environmental justice to international law, provides this succinct explanation of why environmental justice is grounded in distributional justice: the richest 20 percent of the world consumes 80 percent of its natural resources and generates over 90 percent of its hazardous waste.[29] For most of the world, the poorer 80 percent, their grossly unequal access to natural resources is compounded by also bearing the brunt of the pollution generated by the rich. To briefly illustrate the scale of the inequality, I draw on an example from climate change. The United Kingdom, with a population of 60 million, emits more greenhouse gases than Egypt, Nigeria, Pakistan, and Vietnam, that have a total population of 472 million. The US state of Texas with a population of 23 million has a deeper carbon footprint than the whole of sub-Saharan Africa with total a population of 720 million. And the 19 million people in New York state emit more than the 766 million people living in the 50 least developed countries.[30] Inequality at such a scale is not happenstance. It is systemic. Globalized capitalism ensures that the profligate wealthy sectors of society not only stay rich but get richer.[31] As environmental burdens are borne by others, there is no immediate incentive for the rich to change their behavior. The poor contribute very little to environmental problems but are on the frontlines of environmental harm because of their vulnerable geographic locations, lack of resources and regulatory capacity to protect themselves, ongoing extraction of their natural resources and labor to fuel an unequal global economy, and a systemic transfer of pollution from the North to the South.

A system so unequal in its economic and ecological impact has its origins in European colonialism. Imperial control of land and labor in the colonies was justified not through an ethics of brute force but through the purported superiority of the White race, used to rationalize genocide, slavery, forced labor, apartheid, discrimination, and other types of cruelty in the colonies.[32] Imperial centers industrialized through extracting labor and resources from their colonies, building much of their wealth on the suffering of lands and peoples elsewhere.[33] In the

---

[29] C. G. Gonzalez, "Environmental Justice, Human Rights and the Global South" (2015) 13 *Santa Clara Journal of International Law* 151 at 154; C. G. Gonzalez, "Environmental Justice and International Environmental Law," in S. Alam et al. (eds.), *Routledge Handbook of International Environmental Law* (Abingdon, UK: Routledge, 2013), p. 77.

[30] K. Watkins, "Human Development Report 2007/2008 Fighting Climate Change: Human Solidarity in a Divided World," United Nations Development Programme, 2007).

[31] See for example Oxfam, "An Economy for the 99%," Jan. 2017: in the USA, the bottom 50 percent has not seen its income grow in the last thirty years, whereas the richest 1 percent has seen its income grow by 300 percent. In Vietnam, the richest person earns more in a day than the poorest earns in ten years.

[32] See for example A. Anghie, *Imperialism, Sovereignty and the Making of International Law* (Cambridge, UK: Cambridge University Press, 2007); S. N. Grovogui, *Sovereigns, Quasi-Sovereigns and Africans: Race and Self-Determination in International Law* (Minneapolis: University of Minnesota, 1996).

[33] See for example K. Sanyal, *Rethinking Capitalist Development: Primitive Accumulation, Governmentality and Post-Colonial Capitalism* (New Delhi: Routledge, 2007); A. Stanziani, *Labor on the Fringes of Empire: Voice, Exit and the Law* (London: Palgrave Macmillan, 2018); P. Hudson, *Industrial Revolution* (London: Edward Arnold, 1992); G. K. Bhambra, "Undoing the Epistemic Disavowal of the Haitian Revolution: A Contribution

postcolonial era, the wealthy and powerful conditioned the independence of their former colonies on a commitment to industrial development. This ensured that, in exchange for self-determination, Europe would retain access to the labor and natural resources of the Global South so as to help promote industrialization, but this time with ostensible consent. Peoples in the South gained self-determination through committing to a development model they did not shape – a model inescapably wedded to economic inequality and ecological destruction. As in colonial times, in the postcolonial era Southern elites are incentivized to collaborate with their Northern counterparts through mutual enrichment, to the detriment of transnational laboring classes.[34]

The environmental justice framework highlights commonalities and historic connections between disempowered communities within rich and poor states. It allows for a reconfigured understanding of where the Global South really is: a transnational and evolving place where solidarity can be built between lower class and caste communities in poor and rich states, Indigenous communities, and poor peoples of color. In comparison with its origins in the USA, when extended to the Global South environmental justice is no longer only about disproportionately impacted minority communities. While minority communities in the Global North such as Indigenous peoples are disproportionately burdened by environmental degradation (most notably climate change and extractive industries), a focus on distributive injustice globally also reveals the alignment of elite interests across the so-called North–South divide, and the enrichment of the powerful few at the economic and environmental cost of the many. Here too the legacies of colonialism are extant, such as in South Africa where the majority Black population bears the burden of deprivation rather than the White minority.[35] Additionally, postcolonial states often kept in place or replicated colonial practices, disenfranchising parts of their population to control and exploit their natural resources and labor. For example, in India this is evident in corporate land grabs that disproportionately impact lower-caste and Tribal peoples,[36] and in China the oppression of religions and ethnic minorities in the mineral rich Western regions of Tibet and Xinjiang;[37] in both cases to the benefit and enrichment of metropole elites.

A distributive justice focus is crucial for the Global South because of the tendency to shift environmental problems and "solutions" across national borders. For example, the climate change regime promotes market mechanisms such as the Clean Development Mechanism

to Global Social Thought" (2016) 37 *Journal of Intercultural Studies* 1; M. Badia-Miró, V. Pinilla, and H. Willebald (eds.), *Natural Resources and Economic Growth: Learning from History* (New York: Routledge, 2015); W. J. Ashworth, "The British Industrial Revolution and the Ideological Revolution: Science, Neoliberalism and History" (2014) 52 *History of Science* 178.

[34] For a fuller elaboration of this argument, see U. Natarajan, "TWAIL and the Environment: The State of Nature, the Nature of the State, and the Arab Uprisings" (2012) 14 *Oregon Review of International Law* 177.

[35] D. A. McDonald (ed.), *Environmental Justice in South Africa* (Cape Town: University of Cape Town Press, 2002); H. Stacy, "Environmental Justice and Transformative Law in South Africa and Some Cross-Jurisdictional Notes about Australia, the United States and Canada" (1999) *Acta Juridica* 36.

[36] K. Bahuguna, M. Ramnath, K. Sambhav Shrivastava, R. Mahapatra, M. Suchitra, and A. Chakravartty, "Indigenous People in India and the Web of Indifference," Aug. 10, 2016) www.downtoearth.org.in/cover age/governance/indigenous-people-in-india-and-the-web-of-indifference-55223; G. C. Rath (ed.), *Tribal Development in India: The Contemporary Debate* (New Delhi: Sage, 2006); D. Kapoor, "Adivasis (Original Dwellers) 'in the way' of State-Corporate Development: Development Dispossession and Learning in Social Action for Land and Forests in India" (2009) 44 *McGill Journal of Education* 55.

[37] A. Bhattacharya, "China and Its Peripheries: Strategic Significance of Tibet," Institute of Peace and Conflict Studies Issue Brief #220, May 2013; special issue on Xinjiang (2010) 14 *Himalayan and Central Asian Studies*; K. Mukherjee, "Comparing China's Contested Borderland Regions: Xinjiang and Tibet" (2015) 6 *Millennial Asia* 61.

(CDM), Reducing Emissions from Deforestation and Forest Degradation (REDD), and carbon-trading schemes.[38] These allow the rich to pay the poor to take environmentally responsible actions on their behalf so that the rich can maintain their high-consumerist, carbon-intensive lifestyles. Similarly, Western countries responded to the environmental consequences of industrialization by relocating their polluting facilities and exporting their hazardous wastes to developing countries.[39] The newly industrialized countries (NICs) such as South Korea and Taiwan likewise relocated their polluting industries to mainland China and Southeast Asia.[40] Within states, it is important to bear in mind that the distributive inequities that triggered the environmental justice movement persist four decades later. In both rich and poor countries, environmentally noxious land uses continue to be disproportionately located within poor and marginalized communities.[41] These regressive schemes are the natural product of a global economic system that rewards and thrives on exploitative practices.

Environmental justice movements call for more than moving problems around, demanding fairness and genuine sustainability, not a shallow, short-term veneer. This approach was evident in many of the environmental justice movements that began in Southeast Asia in the 1970s, preceding the region's industrialization into Asian Tiger economies. Movements in Indonesia, Philippines, and Thailand were often related to energy issues, in opposition to nuclear power and hydroelectric mega dam projects; as well as against deforestation and marine pollution.[42] Local communities fought not only the developmentalism of the state, but the conditionalities of the World Bank and the structural adjustment policies of the International Monetary Fund. Environmental movements included small farmers and fisherfolk, Tribal, and Indigenous communities, but also broader mobilization by the poor and working-class masses. They opposed industries that relocated to their communities because the harmful socioeconomic and environmental impacts of these industries were no longer welcome in richer areas. They also opposed the export-oriented growth model pursued by the state and encouraged by international financial institutions, as this type of development exploited local natural resources and cheap labor to benefit local elites and pay international debts. The collaboration of central governments with local monopoly capital and transnational capital was opposed by an alliance between the workers, the urban poor, and environmentalists.[43] It would be a mistake to conclude that the subsequent rise of the Asian Tiger economies evidences the failure of such mass movements. On the contrary, environmental movements in the 1970s, 1980s, and 1990s not

[38] All three are endorsed under the UN Framework Convention on Climate Change (UNFCCC), with CDM and carbon trading falling under the flexible and joint-implementation mechanisms of the Kyoto Protocol to the UNFCCC, and REDD+ developed by UNFCCC state parties.

[39] K. Kanemoto, D. Moran, M. Lenzen, and A. Geschke, "International Trade Undermines National Emission Reduction Targets: New Evidence from Air Pollution" (2014) 24 *Global Environmental Change* 52; A. K. Jorgenson, C. Dick, and M. C. Mahutga, "Foreign Investment Dependence and the Environment: An Ecostructural Approach" (2007) 54 *Social Problems* 371–394.

[40] See generally W. Bello and S. Rosenfeld, *Dragons in Distress: Asia's Miracle Economies in Crisis* (San Francisco: Food First, 1990); Y. F. Lee and A. Y. So (eds.), *Asia's Environmental Movements: Comparative Perspectives* (New York: Armonk, 1999); R. P. Weller and H. H. M. Hsiao, "Culture, Gender and Community in Taiwan's Environmental Movement," in A. Kalland and G. Persoon (eds.), *Environmental Movements in Asia* (Richmond, UK: Curzon Press, 1998), p. 83.

[41] L. M. Collins, "Security of the Person, Peace of Mind: A Precautionary Approach to Environmental Uncertainty" (2013) 4 *Journal of Human Rights and the Environment* 79; D. N. Scott and A. A. Smith, "Sacrifice Zones in the Green Energy Economy: The 'New' Climate Refugees" (2017) 62 *McGill Law Journal* 861; I. Waldron, *There's Something in the Water: Environmental Racism in Indigenous and Black Communities* (Black Point: Fernwood, 2018).

[42] Lee and So, note 40; Kalland and Persoon, note 40.

[43] A. Kalland and G. Persoon (eds.), *Environmental Movements in Asia* (Richmond: Curzon Press, 1998).

only scuttled many transnational megaprojects, they also contributed to radical political transformation away from dictatorships within many Southeast Asian countries and a deepening of democracy across the region.[44]

China is an extreme example of the redistribution of environmental ills to the Global South, its lax environmental and labor laws attracting industries from across the Global North as well as from the NICs. As a result, the last two decades have seen consistent and massive environmental protests across the nation. The concentration of industries within special economic zones has meant high levels of persistent organic pollutants (POPs) and heavy metals within certain communities. Special zones are often located in coastal areas and waterways, not only destroying ecosystems in these regions, but also exposing large populations clustered in these vulnerable geographic areas to climate change hazards such as super typhoons and sea level rise. China's unrestrained export-oriented industrialization has united low-wage internal migrant laborers, farmers losing their land, and environmentalists, who together protest a fusion of environmental, land-loss, income, and political injustices.[45] The most extreme case of distributive inequality in China is the taking of water and mineral resources from Xinjiang and Tibet to fuel the Chinese economy, which occurs under harsh military oppression, apartheid, settler colonialism by the Han Chinese majority, and cultural genocide, fueling the longstanding resentment of these ethnic communities that demand self-determination.[46]

In India, environmental justice movements are often connected with public health issues, exemplified in the Bhopal disaster in 1984 for which some victims still await compensation.[47] Demands for transnational corporate accountability have also surfaced in the fight against Coca-Cola and Pepsi Cola for overuse and contamination of groundwater;[48] against intensive aquaculture industries in coastal states;[49] and in the determined struggle by Indian farmers against the use of genetically modified crops or GMOs.[50] The anti-dam movement in India is one of the more internationally well-known aspects of local environmental justice struggles. Independent India undertook industrialization with missionary zeal, building dams and new irrigation systems that destroyed traditional water management systems sustained for millennia. In its drive to modernize, services were increasingly centralized, inevitably benefiting urban industrial elites at the expense of farmers and the rural and urban poor. The infrastructure for mass

---

[44] M. Ford (ed.), *Social Activism in Southeast Asia* (London: Routledge, 2013).

[45] P. Stalley and D. Yang, "An Emerging Environmental Movement in China?" (2006) 186 *China Quarterly* 333; L. Xie, *Environmental Activism in China* (Abingdon, UK: Routledge, 2009); Q. Huan, "Development of the Red–Green Environmental Movement in China: A Preliminary Analysis" (2014) 25 *Capitalism Nature Socialism* 45; L. Xiea and P. Hob, "Urban Environmentalism and Activists' Networks in China: The Cases of Xiangfan and Shanghai" (2008) 6 *Conservation and Society* 141; L. Zhu, "Social Media and Public Diplomacy: Foreign to China's Environmental Movements" (2013) 4 *Exchange: The Journal of Public Diplomacy Art* 7.

[46] See note 36.

[47] Amnesty International, "Injustice Incorporated: Corporate Abuses and the Human Right to Remedy," Mar 7, 2014, p. 33; E. Grossman, "Thirty Years Later, Victims of Bhopal Gas Disaster Are Still Waiting for Justice," Dec. 3, 2014, www.earthisland.org/journal/index.php/articles/entry/thirty_year_later_victims_of_bhopal_gas_disaster_are_still_waiting_for_just.

[48] P. Parmar, *Indigeneity and Legal Pluralism in India: Claims, Histories, Meanings* (New York: Cambridge University Press, 2015).

[49] Mukul, "Aquaculture Boom: Who Pays?" (1994) 29 *Economic and Political Weekly* 3075; M. Flaherty and K. C. Samal, *Coastal Aquaculture in India: Poverty, Environment and Rural Livelihood* (New Delhi: Concept, 2009).

[50] G. Thomas and J. De Tavernier, "Farmer-Suicide in India: Debating the Role of Biotechnology" (2017) 8 *Life Sciences, Society and Policy* 8n T. Yamaguchi, "Controversy over Genetically Modified Crops in India: Discursive Strategies and Social Identities of Farmers" (2007) 9 *Discourse Studies* 87.

industrialization also displaced millions, disproportionately affecting Tribal and lower-caste Indians.[51] Social movements against dam building and the associated displacement have not only stopped mega dam projects, including those financed by the World Bank and powerful international investors; they have helped deepen Indian democracy and accountability, as was the case in Southeast Asia.[52] Tribal movements opposing corporate access to mineral resources are gradually gathering steam not only across India but transnationally, as companies exploit the mineral-rich band across Afghanistan, Pakistan, India, Nepal, and Western China.[53] The impact of climate change is being felt across South Asia, but particularly in Himalayan areas with the retreat of glaciers and increased stream runoff, and coastal areas with rising sea levels submerging islands and displacing coastal villages.[54] Again, as urban elites insulate themselves from climate impacts, those on the frontlines have organized to demand relocation and redress.[55]

Environmental justice movements across the Global South oppose the global alliance between economic and political elites that obfuscates local needs. US negotiators at environmental summits insist that emerging economies such as Brazil, China, and India play their part in tackling global environmental problems. Brazilian, Chinese, and Indian political elites shoot back with old Third-Worldist arguments that they are entitled to industrialize and pollute as much as Western states.[56] Divisions of this kind characterize international environmental lawmaking for the last five decades and disguise transnational unity among elites that profit from the economic and ecological suffering of the masses. The concept of sustainable development, as gradually refined over the last three decades, intends to guide communities toward balanced social, economic, and environmental sustainability. Sadly, the outcome thus far has been a paying of lip service to the concept of sustainable development, while pursuing economic growth based on the exploitation of the poor and of nature.[57]

A focus on distributive justice is useful to the Global South because it emphasizes an ethics of fairness and equity between and within states. Distributive justice redirects development policymakers from their enduring obsession with transforming the developing world, asking them to focus instead on transforming those transnational structures that produce and maintain patterns of inequality and environmental degradation across poor, disempowered, and marginalized

[51] S. Khagram, *Dams and Development: Transnational Struggles for Water and Power* (Ithaca, NY: Cornell University Press, 2004); P. Basu, "Scale, Place and Social Movements: Strategies of Resistance along India's Narmada River" (2010) 13 *Revista NERA* 96; A. Roy, *The Cost of Living* (London: Flamingo, 1999).

[52] See references in note 51.

[53] S. Widmalm, *Political Tolerance in the Global South: Images of India, Pakistan and Uganda* (Abingdon: Routledge, 2016); M. Mandal, *The Rise of Revolution: Internal Displacement in Contemporary Nepal* (Abingdon, UK: Routledge, 2018); K. Mukherjee, "Comparing China and India's Disputed Borderland Regions: Xinjiang, Tibet, Kashmir, and the Indian Northeast" (2015) 32 *East Asia* 173.

[54] K. Khoday, "Climate Change and the Right to Development. Himalayan Glacial Melting and the Future of Development on the Tibetan Plateau," Human Development Occasional Papers, HDOCPA-2007-28, UN Development Programme, 2007; S. S. Mahdi (ed.), *Climate Change and Agriculture in India: Impact and Adaptation* (Cham: Springer, 2019); K. Jörgensen, A. Mishra, and G. K. Sarangi, "Multi-level Climate Governance in India: The Role of the States in Climate Action Planning and Renewable Energies" (2015) 12 *Journal of Integrative Environmental Sciences* 267; N. K. Dubash, *Handbook of Climate Change and India: Development, Politics and Governance* (Abingdon, UK: Earthscan, 2012); S. Narain, P. Ghosh, N. C. Saxena, J. Parikh, and P. Soni, "Climate Change Perspectives from India," UN Development Programme India, Nov. 2009.

[55] See references in note 54; A. Srinivas, "Why Farmer Protests May Be the New Normal," July 19, 2018, www .livemint.com/Politics/cjW8GmkZpCq8TzSpeDkyoH/Why-farmer-protests-may-be-the-new-normal.html.

[56] For a discussion of these dynamics, see generally M. Prost and A. T. Camprubi, "Against Fairness? International Environmental Law, Disciplinary Bias, and Pareto Justice" (2012) 25 *Leiden Journal of International Law* 379.

[57] See further R. Gordon, "Unsustainable Development," in Alam et al., note 27, p. 50.

communities everywhere. With concepts such as the Anthropocene gaining currency (the Anthropocene denotes the current geological age as a period where human activity is the dominant influence on the environment), distributive justice is even more crucial as a reminder that only a small sector of humanity – the rich – are responsible for environmental damage on a planetary scale. Distributive justice prevents an ahistorical approach to contemporary problems, insisting that ecological debts are paid. It helps contest the trend in international environmental law toward an increasingly technical specialization that obfuscates its own failures. Distributive justice requires a convergence between the ecological footprints of the rich and poor. It places responsibility on those who caused environmental harm and demands they change their behavior. It ensures that those who overconsume and over-pollute are in the limelight and asked to reduce their environmental harm; with their progress scrutinized, classified, and calculated. It reverses international lawyers' longstanding disciplinary attention to transforming the developing world. Rather than focusing on how to change the poor, distributional justice instead demands that the rich – both states and individuals – reduce their consumption and waste, so that in a planet with finite resources everyone has equal access to environmental benefits and experiences an equal distribution of environmental harms.

3.4 PROCEDURAL JUSTICE

Environmental justice foregrounds the procedures that underlie distributive outcomes to show why certain communities tend to come out on the losing side of environmental decision-making. When considering decision-making on the global level, the Global South has not had an equal say in making international laws and institutions. The Western origins of international law, and the continuing socioeconomic, political, and cultural dominance of the West conditions the participation of non-Western peoples in international lawmaking in various ways.[58] At its most fundamental level, participation in international lawmaking requires sovereign statehood, the conditions of which were set by Western states. To gain their independence, communities of the Global South underwent significant transformation to meet Western demands for social organization into the Westphalian model. Those entities unwilling or unable to make these capitulations still lack sovereignty today, as evidenced by the plight of most Indigenous and Tribal peoples.[59] A lawmaking process that is predominantly state-centric poses representation challenges for subnational and transnational forms of social organization. Such forms encompass not only Tribal and Indigenous communities but also many social groupings in the Global South whose borders do not correspond to those set by Western powers as a condition of decolonization.[60]

The sources of international law – treaties, custom, general principles, judicial decisions, and scholarly treatises – were selected by Western states.[61] In the postcolonial era, non-Western states can also participate in creating these sources of international law. However, they joined an existing framework they did not shape, which has created two types of procedural problems.

---

[58] M. Prost, "Hierarchy and the Sources of International Law: A Critique" (2017) 39 *Houston Journal of International Law* 285; J. T. Gathii, "Imperialism, Colonialism, and International Law" (2006–2007) 54 *Buffalo Law Review* 1013; J. T. Gathii, "Assessing Claims of a New Doctrine of Pre-emptive War under the Doctrine of Sources" (2005) 43 *Osgoode Hall Law Journal* 67.
[59] Anghie, note 32.
[60] See generally V. Nesiah, "Placing International Law: White Spaces on a Map" (2003) 16 *Leiden Journal of International Law* 1; Grovogui, note 32.
[61] Statute of the International Court of Justice, Art. 38.

First, where they participate in international lawmaking, they struggle to implement laws that are in the interests of the Global South. Second, deeper and more troubling, they struggle to express their needs within the confines of a lawmaking process based on a Western conception of environmentalism.

On the first issue, international law is a regime based on sovereign equality, yet the world it purports to govern is increasingly unequal. One of the reasons for this paradox is the difficulties of international lawmaking by the Global South. From international economic law to human rights,[62] from law of the sea to the laws of war,[63] from international laws on migration to labor,[64] and in the operations of international institutions,[65] the unequal influence of rich and powerful entities remains a systemic structural presence, whether states, corporations, NGOs, or individuals. For the purposes of this chapter, I focus on international laws addressing the global environment. International environmental law was a result of the middle classes of the USA and Western Europe feeling the effects of industrial pollution on daily life. Western environmentalism gathered momentum in the 1960s and eventually led to international environmental lawmaking summits, most famously in Stockholm in 1972 and the Rio Earth Summit in 1992.[66] From the early days of this specialization, Third World states played a strong role, shaping formative concepts such as sustainable development and the principle of common but differentiated responsibilities for the global environment. These laws require rich states that caused environmental problems to take the lead in finding solutions. They also require rich states to take the lead in providing technical and financial support for environmental solutions because of their capacity to do so. However, rich states have not observed these laws. Indeed, the USA has concertedly pushed international environmental law frameworks away from commitment to these foundational principles.[67] This is most evident in the climate change regime, in the move away from the defunct Kyoto Protocol's firm commitments for rich states toward the present voluntary regime under the Paris Agreement. That is to say, despite the close involvement of the Global South in international environmental lawmaking, the Global North has been able to selectively ignore laws with impunity.[68] Additionally, as international environmental law proliferates into an increasingly complex and specialized web of negotiations occurring almost every month, many poor states cannot afford to send large (or sometimes any) delegations or obtain the necessary expertise to represent their interests, fomenting systemic disadvantage over time.

---

[62] J. T. Gathii and I. Odumosu, "International Economic Law in the Third World" (2009) 11 *International Community Law Review* 349; M. Fakhri, *Sugar and the Making of International Law* (Cambridge, UK: Cambridge University Press, 2014); O. Okafor, "Praxis and the International (Human Rights) Law Scholar: Towards the Intensification of TWAILian Dramaturgy" (2016) 33 *Windsor Yearbook of Access to Justice* 1.

[63] S. Ranganathan, *Strategically Created Treaty Conflicts and the Politics of International Law* (Cambridge, UK: Cambridge University Press, 2014); U. Natarajan, "A Third World Approach to Debating the Legality of the Iraq War" (2007) 9 *International Community Law Review* 405.

[64] B. S. Chimni, "The Geopolitics of Refugee Studies: A View from the South" (1998) 11 *Journal of Refugee Studies* 350; O. Okafor, "Re-Configuring Non-Refoulement? The *Suresh* Decision, 'Security Relativism,' and the International Human Rights Imperative" (2003) 15 *International Journal of Refugee Law* 30; A. A. Smith, "Migration, Development and Security within Racialised Global Capitalism: Refusing the Balance Game" (2016) 37 *Third World Quarterly* 2119.

[65] B. Rajagopal, *International Law from Below* (Cambridge, UK: Cambridge University Press, 2003); Anghie, note 32.

[66] K. Mickelson, "The Stockholm Conference and the Creation of the North–South Divide in International Law and Policy," in Alam et al., note 27, p. 109.

[67] For similar trends in human rights law, see A. Brysk and G. Shafir (eds.), *National Insecurity and Human Rights* (Berkley: University of California Press, 2007); and in international trade law, see Gonzalez, note 29.

[68] This argument is further elaborated in Natarajan and Khoday, note 25.

The second issue is that the procedures and institutions of international environmental law do not welcome different understandings of environmentalism. Rooted in Western environmentalism, international environmental law remains wedded to a modern, anthropocentric, and obsessively controlling understanding of nature. The "environment" as an object over which we can acquire knowledge and govern reflects a specific type of knowledge production that stems from the European Enlightenment.[69] The ability to accumulate scientific knowledge and control over as many aspects of life as possible is a defining trait of Enlightenment thinking and indeed of Western modernity.[70] In this sense, when international environmental law identifies the "environment" – that is to say, everything – as an object of governance, international law has made the ultimate modern move.[71] By limitlessly extending international law's scope of operations, international environmental law may make things worse not better, by creating new unbounded arenas for the expansion of governmentality, institutionalism, expertise, and structural violence.

A troubling example of such expansion is the tendency to utilize economic incentives for environmental solutions. Environmental lawyers increasingly turn to the "green economy" and "green growth" to solve environmental crises, in hopes that capitalism can simultaneously solve the problems it creates. This contradiction is epitomized in ostensibly virtuous environmentalist calls for more efficient use of natural resources, instead of directly tackling the problem of overconsumption. Such approaches ultimately exacerbate environmental crises through enabling even greater consumption by making more resources available for unlimited (albeit more efficient) usage. Indeed, many so-called green solutions, from biofuels to electric vehicles, from carbon offsets to carbon trading are creative ways to fuel economic growth but do not stand up to scrutiny when it comes to environmental protection. These approaches provide new markets for globalized capitalists to expand and diversify, enabling their further enrichment and allowing environmentalism itself to be captured by the rich in their untrammeled pursuit of wealth.

To understand the environment as something we control, rather than that which controls and gives life to us, is inaccurate. This approach to environmental problems excludes and erodes less hubristic world views that could help us find more harmonious ways of living in nature. For instance, many Tribal and Indigenous cultures understand themselves as part of nature, with no clear demarcation between themselves and their environment.[72] For cultures that more fully appreciate the interconnection between all things, the anthropocentrism of distinct specializations such as international environmental law and human rights has no meaning. Where does the autonomous person begin and end when they consistently depend on the world around them for air, water, and sustenance? A world of sovereign states peopled by autonomous individuals is a comforting disciplinary conceit, allowing us the illusion of order and comprehension.[73] But environmental crises confront us with the limits of Western knowledge production and the need for a new paradigm that understands nature and our place in it. For cultures in the Global South to bring their own experiences and knowledge to international law requires

---

[69] G. Rist, *The History of Development: From Western Origins to Global Faith*, trans. P. Camiller (London: Zed Books, 2014).

[70] V. Argyrou, *The Logic of Environmentalism: Anthropology, Ecology and Postcoloniality* (New York: Berghahn, 2005).

[71] Ibid.

[72] G. J. Coulthard, *Red Skins, White Masks: Rejecting the Colonial Politics of Recognition* (Minneapolis: University of Minnesota Press, 2014); J. Borrows, *Drawing Out Law: A Spirit's Guide* (Toronto: University of Toronto Press, 2010).

[73] On the search for order, see further P. Fitzpatrick, *Modernism and the Grounds of Law* (Cambridge, UK: Cambridge University Press, 2001); Riles, note 12; Otto, note 12; Argyrou, note 70.

procedures and institutions that allow for evolution into radically different modes of social organization and knowledge production. Rather than a specialized technocracy that only those with elite training can access, environmental justice demands an openness to completely different world views and the fundamental transformation this entails. In addition to being fair and just, such an evolution will foster the type of innovative thinking that the discipline desperately needs.[74]

With a view to disrupting conventional lawmaking processes, civil society organizations increasingly target treaty-based meetings, such as the annual "Climate COPs" – the Conference of the Parties to the United Nations Framework Convention on Climate Change. Denied equal access and participation in these meetings, civil societies instead set up parallel fora alongside the COPs, such as the Mother Earth Summits in Cochabamba after COP 15 in Copenhagen,[75] and alongside COP 20 in Lima.[76] Similar points are made effectively and dramatically by endeavors such as the Rights of Nature Tribunals, which purport to determine and enforce an alternative set of laws that protect nature.[77] More conventionally, notable scholarly endeavors from the Global South to engage more fully in lawmaking include the Separate Opinion of Justice Weeramantry in the *Gabčíkovo–Nagymaros Project* case, that infuse into the jurisprudence of the International Court of Justice diverse cultural understandings of sustainable development.[78]

3.5 CORRECTIVE JUSTICE

Redress for environmental suffering endured transnationally or internationally – whether past, present, or future harm – has proven elusive. Environmental problems are often transboundary in nature and can have global implications. The absence of a consistent global approach that provides remedies encourages irresponsible and unaccountable behavior. Those least to blame suffer most, and those responsible seemingly infinitely defer their day of reckoning. To disrupt this pattern, environmental justice demands corrective justice. Perhaps the most extreme case is that of small island developing states, where climate change has destroyed ecosystems, livelihoods, and in some cases entirely engulfed islands under rising seas.[79] Island inhabitants did not cause climate change and have no way to prevent it. They cannot survive without assistance. Yet, the rich states that caused climate change, and that have the ability to help with finance, land, and technology, have not done so at any significant level. International climate instruments

---

[74] This argument is further elaborated in K. Khoday and U. Natarajan, "Fairness and International Environmental Law from Below: Social Movements and Legal Transformation in India" (2012) 25 *Leiden Journal of International Law* 415.

[75] World People's Conference on Climate Change and the Rights of Mother Earth: Building the People's World Movement for Mother Earth, press release, "Bolivia Calls for Urgent High-Level Talks on Cutting Climate Pollution," June 17, 2011, https://pwccc.wordpress.com.

[76] Peoples' Summit on Climate Change COP20, "For Climate Justice and a World Fit to Be Lived in Lima, December 8 to 11, 2014," Sept. 27, 2014, http://rio20.net/en/iniciativas/peoples%E2%80%99-summit-on-climate-change-cop20.

[77] Rights of Nature Tribunals often occur alongside major international summits: http://therightsofnature.org/rights-of-nature-tribunal.

[78] Separate Opinion of Vice-President Weeramantry, *Gabčíkovo–Nagymaros Project (Hungary v. Slovakia)* [1997] ICJ Rep 7.

[79] S. Albert, A. Grinham, J. Blythell, A. Olds, A. Schwartz, K. Abernathy, K. Aranani, M. Sirikolo, C. Watoto, N. Duke, J. McKenzie, C. Roelfsema, L. Liggins, E. Brokovich, O. Pantos, J. Oeta, B. Gibbes, "Building Social and Ecological Resilience to Climate Change in Roviana, Solomon Islands," final report to Department of Climate Change and Energy Efficiency, Australian Government, University of Queensland School of Civil Engineering, WWF, World Fish Center, Dec. 23, 2010–Mar. 30, 2012.

contemplate addressing loss and damage yet without acknowledgment of liability or promise of compensation,[80] and meaningful corrective justice at anything resembling the levels owed or needed has yet to occur.

Corrective justice in situations such as the one described above for small island states cannot be merely monetary. The loss of entire states cannot be corrected with just financial support. Rather, they require the restoration of self-determination, independence, and dignity. Beyond the stark predicament of small island developing states, displacement from environmental change is widespread. While these gradual movements are not always noticed, they are massive and protracted. The median projection is that approximately 200 million people are being displaced by climate change.[81] This number does not include those displaced by other forms of environmental degradation such as non-climate-related cases of desertification, deforestation, pollution, and development-induced displacement. While monetary remedy compensates to a limited extent, in the long term this phenomenon reconfigures our planet's habitable zones. In the past, people (and other animals) have adapted to climate change by moving. The difficulty today is that rich states do not allow people to move freely even at times of great peril. Currently, most rich states are strengthening border controls.[82] Corrective justice for environmentally and developmentally induced displacement caused by rich states could include a requirement that displaced populations be welcomed into the territories of responsible states.[83] This would not only ensure that states take responsibility for their transboundary actions but it provides displaced persons the opportunity to establish anew a dignified and sustainable life.

Previous sections explain the ecological debt the Global North owes the Global South for centuries of plundering its resources and labor, dumping waste, and destroying its natural and cultural heritage. Northern development models premised on infinite economic growth and accumulation of wealth through control and exploitation of nature were universalized through international laws and institutions, destroying more sustainable ways of life.[84] Reparations were never provided to the Global South for colonialism, genocide, slavery, apartheid, and other destructive practices. Instead, upon decolonization, the South was blamed for its own under-development and asked to "catch up" to richer states, although the violent and exploitative means by which the Global North had developed were forbidden to the South.[85] Environmental justice calls for a change from the unaccountable and irresponsible patterns of the past in international relations through providing remedies for environmental harms.

---

[80] UNFCCC COP 18 in Doha established a Loss and Damage plan that was consolidated during UNFCCC COP 19 into the Warsaw International Mechanism for Loss and Damage. UN Framework Convention on Climate Change, Paris Agreement, Dec. 12, 2015, UN Doc. FCCC/CP/2015/L.9/Rev.1, Art. 8, paras. 48–52.

[81] P. Alston, *Climate Change and Poverty: Report of the Special Rapporteur on Extreme Poverty and Human Rights*, June 25, 2019, UN Doc. A/HRC/41/39, p. 5; O. Brown, "Climate Change and Forced Migration: Observations, Projections and Implications," Human Development Report 2007/2008, Office Occasional Paper, UN Development Programme, 2008.

[82] M. Vargas, "Globalisation du contrôle des frontières et résistance des peuples" (2018) 139 *France Amerique Latine* 27; D. S. Massey, J. Durand, and K. A. Pren, "Why Border Enforcement Backfired" (2016) 121 *American Journal of Sociology* 155; I. Angelescu and F. Trauner, "10,000 Border Guards for Frontex: Why the EY Risks Conflated Expectations," European Policy Center, European Migration and Diversity Programme, Sept. 21, 2018; Government Europa, "EU to Triple Border Security, Management, and Migration Funding," June 12, 2018, www.governmenteuropa.eu/eu-border-security-management-migration/88377.

[83] Indeed, the UN Framework Convention on Climate Change in Article 4 calls upon developed countries to help developing countries adapt to climate change.

[84] Natarajan, note 34.

[85] Rist, note 69; Anghie, note 32.

It is a general principle of international law – a legal principle shared by all legal systems of the world – that reparation be made for harm done.[86] The operability of this principle for transboundary environmental harm was famously confirmed in the *Trail Smelter* case.[87] It is also codified and expanded in the International Law Commission's Draft Articles of State Responsibility and Principles on the Allocation of Loss in the Case of Transboundary Harm Arising Out of Hazardous Activities.[88] Thus, demands for corrective justice in the Global South are not an unheard-of innovation, but stem from basic understandings of the rule of law and its applicability to everyone equally. This is most especially necessary in cases where the weak need protection from the careless and irresponsible actions of the strong. Movements focusing on corrective justice are surging, including endeavors at the International Court of Justice,[89] the Inter-American Court of Human Rights,[90] and the European Court of Human Rights,[91] as well as various domestic jurisdictions.[92] Domestically, environmental tribunals have proliferated in India and China and across the Global South to address the fast-growing numbers of disputes.[93] While actual redress often remains elusive, demands for corrective justice are easier to articulate within existing legal systems because they use conventional legal arguments, compared with more complex distributive and procedural demands that entail disciplinary upheaval.[94]

---

[86] *Chorzow Factory Case (Germany v. Poland)* (1928) PCIJ Series A No. 17.

[87] *Trail Smelter Arbitration (United States v. Canada)* (1941) 3 RIAA 1905.

[88] International Law Commission, *Draft Articles on Responsibility of States for Internationally Wrongful Acts*, Supplement No. 10 (A/56/10), Ch IV E (Nov. 2001); *Prevention of Transboundary Harm from Hazardous Activities*, Supplement No. 10 (A/56/10), Ch IV E (Nov. 2001). For the relationship between the two, see S. L. Seck, "Transnational Business and Environmental Harm: A TWAIL Analysis of Home State Obligations" (2011) 3 *Trade, Law & Development* 164.

[89] International Union for the Conservation of Nature (IUCN), *Request for an Advisory Opinion of the International Court of Justice on the Principles of Sustainable Development in View of the Needs of Future Generations*, WCC-2016-Res-079-EN (Sept. 10, 2016); *MOX Plant Arbitration (Ireland v. UK)* (2003) 23 RIAA 59; *Southern Bluefin Tuna Arbitration (Australia v. Japan)* (2000) 23 RIAA 3; *Gabčíkovo–Nagymaros Project (Hungary v. Slovakia)* [1997] ICJ Rep 3; *Pulp Mills on the River Uruguay (Argentina v. Uruguay)* [2010] ICJ Rep 14; *Whaling in the Antarctic (Australia v. Japan)* [2014] ICJ Rep 226; see generally T. Stephens, *International Courts and Environmental Protection* (Cambridge, UK: Cambridge University Press, 2009).

[90] Environment and Human Rights, Inter-American Court of Human Rights Advisory Opinion OC-23/18 (Ser. A) No. 23 (Nov. 15, 2017); S. Thériault, "Environmental Justice and the Inter-American Court of Human Rights," in A. Grear and L. Kotzé (eds.), *Research Handbook on Human Rights and the Environment* (Cheltenham, UK: Edward Elgar, 2015), p. 309.

[91] O. Pedersen, "The European Court of Human Rights and International Environmental Law," in J. H. Knox and R. Pejan (eds.), *The Human Right to a Healthy Environment* (Cambridge, UK: Cambridge University Press, 2018).

[92] *Massachusetts v. EPA* (2007) 549 US 497; *American Electric Power v. Connecticut* (2011) 564 US 410; *Kivalina v. Exxon Mobil* (2012) 696 F3d 849; *Juliana v. United States* (2016) WL 183903; *Friends of the Earth v. Canada* [2008] FC 1183; *Leghari v. Pakistan* (2015) WP No 25501; *Gbemre v. Shell Nigeria* [2005] African Human Rights Law Reports 151; *Greenpeace New Zealand v. Northland Regional Council* [2006] NZHC CIV 2006-404-004617; *Genesis Power v. Franklin District Council* [2005] NZRMA 541; *Urgenda v. Netherlands* [2015] ECLI:NL:RBDHA:2015:7196. See further United Nations Environment Programme, *The Status of Climate Change Litigation: A Global Review* (2017). A compendium of climate litigation is maintained by Climate Justice at Climate Law Database: www.climatelaw.org.

[93] G. N. Gill, "Environmental Justice in India: The National Green Tribunal and Expert Members" (2015) *Transnational Environmental Law* 1; R. E. Stern, "The Political Logic of China's New Environmental Courts" (2014) 72 *China Journal* 53.

[94] While allowing for an articulation of corrective justice demands, most laws remain unhelpful for providing actual redress because, among other things, they have not evolved to encompass new challenges such as climate change. For instance, state responsibility principles do not encompass collective liability, adequately account for climate change causality, or adequately incorporate the polluter pays principle.

3.6 SOCIAL JUSTICE

The experience of colonialism has meant that in the postcolonial era environmental justice in the Global South remains inextricable from transnational exploitation of labor along the lines of race, gender, class, and caste, among other things. Environmental justice is understood as part of the longstanding social struggles against practices that impoverish the South to empower the North. A high proportion of ecological harm in the Global South is the result of export-oriented production rather than domestic consumption and is related to the unrelenting transnational corporate quest for natural resources and labor in the South.[95] As in the USA, communities at the frontlines of environmental harm in the Global South are often those most impoverished, marginalized, politically disenfranchised, and treated as expendable in the endless quest for economic growth.[96] People in such situations have no choice but to accept risks of pollution, toxicity, and other environmental harms. Serious environmental hazards may be known but may not seem immediate. Communities beset by a multitude of harrowing problems may perceive economic needs as a more immediate priority and easier to organize around. Complex latent environmental risks may seem like "luxury" concerns or else too difficult to address, provoking denial or hopelessness. To overcome such systemic barriers to action, environmental justice provides an understanding of economic and ecological concerns as interlinked and best addressed together.

Environmental justice emphasizes the inextricability of our ecological and economic choices, an emphasis particularly crucial given the growth of the so-called green economy. Domestic and international laws and policies overly rely on economic incentives to solve environmental problems, lauding the potential that environmental challenges provide for economic growth, whether through trading systems that allow rich states to pay poor states to offset their emissions; through more energy-efficient homes, transport, construction, and green consumerism; or more cynically through disaster economies of climate insurance and reconstruction. While each of these endeavors provides short-term benefit, in the long term they are harmful to the global environment; and together they point to our inability or unwillingness to think outside the confines of consumer capitalism. Offsetting schemes exacerbate inequality because only the rich can benefit from them. Energy efficiency is unhelpful when consumption grows at a rate that uses all available energy and still demands more. Disaster economies are symptomatic of an economic system so self-destructive that it profits from its own decay. Scott and Smith point to how the power dynamics of the green economy may reproduce or proliferate the "sacrifice zones" of the fossil fuel economy.[97] Environmental justice reminds us that an economic system that causes global inequality and environmental destruction cannot be relied upon to solve either of these problems and, most importantly, systemic change requires addressing both these concerns together.

Environmental consciousness across the South has a long, rich, and varied history and for some Southern communities, including many Tribal and Indigenous communities, there is no distinction between social, economic, and environmental concerns.[98] For instance, when Tribal

---

[95] W. E. Rees and L. Westra, "When Consumption Does Violence," in J. Agyeman, R. D. Bullard, and B. Evans (eds.), *Just Sustainabilities* (Cambridge, MA: MIT Press, 2003), p. 99.

[96] J. Klugman, "Human Development Report 2011: Sustainability and Equity: A Better Future for All," United Nations Development Programme, 2011.

[97] Scott and Smith, note 41.

[98] See note 72.

and Indigenous communities resist mining and oil companies,[99] and transnational agrarian and peasant movements oppose trade policies,[100] their concerns are holistic, effortlessly connecting cultural, livelihood, and environmental matters. World views that do not separate ecology and economy are unamenable to capitalism and, while they face an existential threat, such alternatives provide hope for imagining postcapitalist life.

3.7 CONCLUSION

Environmental justice is helpful to communities in the Global South because it focuses on issues that international law, particularly international environmental law, has failed to address. Through a commitment to distributive justice, environmental justice emphasizes the need for equity and fairness in access to natural resources and exposure to environmental harm. It pushes against the tendency to geographically relocate environmental problems, prioritizing instead fairness and sustainability globally. An emphasis on procedural fairness and equal participation in the law and policymaking process helps infuse ideas from the South into international laws and institutions, allowing for much-needed solutions to global environmental problems from outside Western environmentalism. Corrective justice fosters a rule-of-law culture in international relations, where those who cause harm take responsibility for providing the remedy. Lastly, social justice is a reminder that environmental harm in subaltern communities is inextricable from the socioeconomic processes that construct their subalternity, and requires holistic solutions.

Environmental justice is a social movement as well as a scholarly field and this bipartite nature presents some challenges. Disciplines such as international law, which are conservative in nature and useful to the powerful, can hollow out revolutionary ideas to become insipid and depoliticized shells. The relatively fast conceptual uptake of environmental justice globally has occurred among scholarly elites as well as civil society organizations, but this does not necessarily reflect synchronicity and collaboration between the two groups. To fulfill the emancipatory potential of environmental justice, scholarly elites need to reflect the experiences of subaltern communities, rather than appropriate them as cultural capital in international lawmaking and research forums. The commitment of environmental justice to social praxis requires attentiveness to the distributive, procedural, corrective, and social consequences of our habitual operations as international lawyers and scholars, and a commitment to everyday changes toward a radical restructuring of knowledge production and fearless embrace of difference. Through resisting the disciplinary tendency toward universalization and welcoming a variety of cultural inflections, environmental justice can remain a language of resistance that enables us to build solidarity and effect change globally.

---

[99] A. Chandrashekhar, "The Anatomy of a Fake Surrender: A Movement Against Bauxite Mining in Odisha's Niyamgiri Hills and the State's Efforts to Circumvent It," Aug. 4, 2017, https://caravanmagazine.in/vantage/odisha-bauxite-mining-fake-surrender-niyamgiri; A. George, "Claiming Niyamgiri: The Dongria Kondh's Struggle against Vedanta," Dec. 18, 2014, www.ritimo.org/Claiming-Niyamgiri-the-Dongria-Kondh-s-Struggle-against-Vedanta.

[100] See La Via Campesina (international peasants' movement), https://viacampesina.org/en.

4

Indigenous Environmental Justice and Sustainability

Deborah McGregor

4.1 INTRODUCTION

This chapter offers an alternative vision for sustainable futures involving self-determined Indigenous environmental justice (EJ). It builds upon a distinct understanding of Indigenous EJ which asserts that the components necessary for Indigenous EJ are Indigenous knowledge systems, legal orders, and conceptions of justice that have existed for thousands of years.[1] This contribution will also offer preliminary thoughts on the need to decolonize internationally adopted conceptions of sustainable development expressed more recently through the post-2015 United Nations sustainable development agenda. Indigenous environmental injustice is very much an outcome of "unsustainable" and detrimental "development," as well as gross violations of human and Indigenous rights as pointed to by Indigenous peoples globally for decades. Indigenous peoples have formulated alternative forms of sustainable development based in part on anti-colonial critiques of "sustainable development," and have asserted their own self-determined sustainable future since the Earth Summit in 1992.

I will address the points above by analyzing key international Indigenous environmental declarations of the past two decades that offer anti-colonial critiques and insights, thus creating the space for alternative sustainable futures from an Indigenous perspective. I will then offer a distinct conception of sustainability and environmental justice through the Anishinabek ideal of *mino-mnaamodzawin* (living well) through the use of stories.[2] Importantly, I am not suggesting that I have the ability to pose the definitive Indigenous EJ framework; each nation *already* has its own intellectual and legal traditions to draw upon. In this contribution, I focus on the Anishinabek tradition. Realizing well-being with the Earth is a plural endeavor, as evident in the concept of *buen vivir* which calls for living well within a community, but an expanded view of community that includes, nature, animals, plants – the Earth itself (or what I would refer to as all of Creation). *Buen vivir* has found expression in Indigenous international sustainable development declarations, such as the outcome document from Rio+20 International Conference of Indigenous Peoples on Self-Determination and Sustainable Development.[3]

---

[1] D. McGregor, "Honouring Our Relations: An Anishinabe Perspective on Environmental Justice," in J. Agyeman, R. Haluza-Delay, P. Cole, and P. O'Riley (eds.), *Speaking for Ourselves: Constructions of Environmental Justice in Canada* (Vancouver, BC: UBC Press, 2009), pp. 27–41.

[2] See V. Napoleon and H. Friedland, "An Inside Job: Engaging with Indigenous Legal Traditions through Stories" (2016) 61 *McGill Law Journal* 727; H. Stark, "Stories as Law: A Method to Live by," in C. Anderson and J. O'Brien (eds.), *Sources and Methods in Indigenous Studies* (New York: Routledge, 2017), pp. 249–256.

[3] At Earth Summit 2 in Rio De Janeiro, twenty years after the first summit in 1992, Indigenous Peoples gathered to formulate their own declaration as part of Rio + 20 International Conference of Indigenous Peoples on Self-

4.2 DECOLONIZING SUSTAINABLE DEVELOPMENT

Two decades after the Earth Summit in Rio de Janeiro, the outcome document "The Future We Want"[4] was released following the UN Conference on Sustainable Development at Rio 2012, also known as Rio+20. Indigenous peoples were immediately critical of the view of sustainable development offered in the document. As an example, the portrayal of the earth as "natural capital" which would drive the "green economy" was viewed as problematic and contributing to the further institutionalization of colonialism.[5] Access to key discussions and inclusion in decision-making at Rio+20 were also major concerns for Indigenous peoples at the conference, who had experienced ongoing procedural injustices at these international forums.

In spite of this, Indigenous peoples at Rio+20 were able to meet and produce some key outcome documents of their own. Chief among these, the Kari-Oca 2 Declaration: Indigenous Peoples Global Conference on Rio+20 and Mother Earth, points to a self-determined and desirable future from an Indigenous point of view.

> In the absence of a true implementation of sustainable development, the world is now in a multiple ecological, economic, and climatic crisis; including biodiversity loss, desertification, de-glaciation, food, water, energy shortage, a worsening global economic recession, social instability, and crisis of values. In this sense, we recognize that much remains to be done by international agreements to respond adequately to the rights and needs of Indigenous Peoples. The actual contributions and potentials of our peoples must be recognized by a true sustainable development for our communities that allows each one of us to *Live Well.*[6]

In short, as long as significant Indigenous environmental injustices go unresolved under current sustainable development initiatives, self-determination for Indigenous peoples remains seriously compromised.[7] The more recent post-2015 United Nations sustainable development agenda "Transforming Our World: The 2030 Agenda for Sustainable Development" offers some improvement, yet while Indigenous peoples called for a more human rights-based approach this time around, many Indigenous people remain dissatisfied and have offered further recommendations for improving the Sustainable Development Goals.[8]

Determination and Sustainable Development. The Declaration specifically engages the term *buen vivir* as offering an ancient yet alternative vision of how to achieve sustainability, stating: "Indigenous peoples call upon the world to return to dialogue and harmony with Mother Earth, and to adopt a new paradigm of civilization based on Buen Vivir – Living Well. In the spirit of humanity and our collective survival, dignity and well-being, we respectfully offer our cultural world views as an important foundation to collectively renew our relationships with each other and Mother Earth and to ensure Buen Vivir/ living well proceeds with integrity" (Rio+20 International Conference of Indigenous Peoples on Self-Determination and Sustainable Development June 19, 2012, Rio De Janeiro) Kari-Oca Declaration 2, 2012. Indigenous Peoples Global Conference on Rio +20 and Mother earth, Kari-Oca, Brazil, https://rightsandresources.org/wp-content/exported-pdf/rio20finalpoliticaldeclaration.pdf.

4 UN, "The Future We Want: Outcomes Document of the United Nations Conference on Sustainable Development," RIO+20 United Nations Conference on Sustainable Development, June 20–22, 2012.

5 M. A. Frank, "The Future We Don't Want: Indigenous Peoples at RIO+20," *Cultural Survival Quarterly Magazine*, Sept. 2012, www.culturalsurvival.org/publications/cultural-survival-quarterly/future-we-dont-want-indigenous-peoples-rio20.

6 Kari-Oca 2 Declaration, Indigenous Peoples Global Conference on Rio+20 and Mother Earth, Kari-Oka Village at Sacred Kari-Oka Púku, Rio de Janeiro, Brazil, June 17, 2012, p. 4 (italics added).

7 D. McGregor, "Living Well with the Earth: Indigenous Rights and Environment," in C. Lennox and D. Short (eds.), *Handbook of Indigenous Peoples' Rights* (New York: Routledge, 2016), pp. 167–180.

8 "Indigenous Peoples Major Group: Policy Brief on Sustainable Development Goals and Post-2015 Development Agenda: A Working Draft," 2015.

The achievement of Indigenous environmental justice continues to be an elusive and challenging target in international sustainable development forums. Resolving this situation necessarily involves conversations around human rights and Indigenous rights in particular. This has been expressed over the last decade through the United Nations Declaration on the Rights of Indigenous Peoples (UNDRIP),[9] UN Resolution 64/292, Human Right to Water and Sanitation;[10] and other instruments developed internationally to protect Indigenous and other vulnerable and marginalized peoples. As critically important as these instruments are for guiding humanity toward a just and sustainable future, they are not based on Indigenous intellectual or legal traditions (although in some cases, such as UNDRIP, they are informed by them). What these important instruments point to is the responsibility of the international Indigenous and human rights community to support the stated and desired aspirations of Indigenous peoples by compelling global governance structures (United Nations, World Bank, etc.), nation-states and others to comply with such instruments. The reality for most (if not all) Indigenous peoples is that they remain subject to foreign law (as opposed to their own legal orders) and thus realizing the "future they want" requires international actors to fully implement UNDRIP and other Indigenous declarations in support of Indigenous aspirations, rather than simply inserting and subsuming Indigenous peoples in dominant frameworks.

As other scholars have pointed out, extending conventional notions of environmental justice and sustainable futures to a narrative that considers or is inclusive of nonhuman entities through a "rights of nature" discourse demonstrates innovation based perhaps in part on Indigenous world views, such as the Universal Declaration on the Rights of Mother Earth.[11] However, EJ seen from an Indigenous point of view is more than this: it involves a unique set of considerations which draws Indigenous sovereignty, law, justice, and governance into the conversation.[12] It requires an examination of not only power relations among peoples, but also of the colonial legacy that continues to play out in laws, litigation, and policies that systematically, institutionally, and structurally enable ongoing assaults on Indigenous lands and lives.[13] Furthermore, Indigenous communities have never been homogeneous and this remains so; different communities are impacted differently by environmental injustices.[14] Some groups are typically more vulnerable to the impacts of environmental injustice, and broader legal, institutional colonial and capitalist structures often further exacerbate this fact. Gender, for example, can be a defining characteristic for how a person or group may experience environ-

---

[9]   UN General Assembly, United Nations Declaration on the Rights of Indigenous Peoples, Dec. 13, 2007, UN Doc. A/RES/61/295.

[10] UN General Assembly, *The Human Right to Water and Sanitation*, 29 May 2014, UN Doc. A/RES/64/292.

[11] See R. Bratspies, "Do We Need a Human Right to a Healthy Environment?" (2015) 13 *Santa Clara Journal of International Law* 31 at 68; C. G. Gonzalez, "Human Rights, Environmental Justice, and the Global South" (2015) 13 *Santa Clara Journal of International Law* 151 at 168.

[12] L. Westra, *Environmental Justice & the Rights of Indigenous Peoples: International & Domestic Legal Perspectives* (Padstow, UK: Earthscan, 2008); K. Whyte, "Indigenous Climate Change Studies: Indigenizing Futures, Decolonizing the Anthropocene" (2017) 55 *English Language Notes* 153.

[13] Whyte, note 12.

[14] B. Jacobs, "Environmental Racism on Indigenous Lands and Territories," Canadian Political Science Association, May 20, 2010; K. Whyte, "Our Ancestors' Dystopia Now: Indigenous Conservation and the Anthropocene," in U. K. Heise, J. Christensen, and M. Niemann (eds.), *Routledge Companion to the Environmental Humanities* (Abingdon, UK: Routledge, 2017).

mental injustice.[15] Furthermore, gender also informs distinct approaches to addressing environmental injustice.[16]

It is not enough to put forward alternative (often ancient) models of Indigenous EJ frameworks and expect them to flourish, as these must operate in a capitalist and colonial context. The more commonly accepted environmental justice conceptions must also be decolonized to generate the space for how we might "know" about these other conceptions of justice.[17] From an Indigenous point of view, environmental injustices are symptomatic of ongoing processes of colonialism and dispossession, coupled with a literal transformation of the natural environment, that have been at work for over 500 years.[18] Even though these destructive forces have shape-shifted and taken different forms over time, they have continued throughout to support the development and maintenance of an unsustainable global world order, politically, legally, economically, and environmentally. Western and colonial laws have thus failed and continue to fail Indigenous peoples.[19] Indigenous peoples cannot be expected to rely solely on Western legal orders to achieve justice.

International actors and nation-states do, however, still have a critical role to play in support of Indigenous self-determined, sustainable futures, as they must challenge and decolonize their own laws and legal systems. Such measures are called for in UNDRIP, which presents opportunities to address certain aspects of Indigenous environmental justice, in particular by offering redress for the dispossession of Indigenous peoples of their lands, territories, and resources (something that continues to this day, as evidenced by ongoing resource extraction and development on Indigenous lands and waters without Indigenous consent or adequate consultation). UNDRIP seeks to address such injustices through a number of provisions, free, prior, and informed consent being an important principle for contributing to procedural justice. As UNDRIP states:

> Indigenous peoples shall not be forcibly removed from their lands or territories. No relocation shall take place without the free, prior and informed consent of the indigenous peoples concerned and after agreement on just and fair compensation and, where possible, with the option of return.[20]

It is increasingly clear that current global and national environmental protection regimes are failing, with increasing species extinction, water pollution, contamination of the natural environment, scarcity, climate change, and other forms of environmental degradation all vying for our immediate attention.[21] Ongoing and increasing conflict for control over lands and resources

---

[15] Assembly of First Nations Environmental Stewardship Unit, "Environmental Health and First Nations Women: Research Paper," March 2009; K. Vinyeta, K. P. Whyte, and K. Lynn, "Climate Change through an Intersectional Lens: Gendered Vulnerability and Resilience in Indigenous Communities in the United States," United States Department of Agriculture, US Forest Service, Pacific Northwest Research Station, General Technical Report PNW-GTR-923, Dec. 2015; L. Williams, "Climate Change, Colonialism, and Women's Well-being in Canada: What Is to Be Done?" (2018) 109 *Canadian Journal of Public Health* 268.

[16] For example, to address water justice, the Ontario Native Women's Association (ONWA) Indigenous Women's Water Commission developed a specific tool kit for Indigenous women, drawing on specific women's responsibilities and knowledge: Ontario Indigenous Women's Water Commission, "Water Commission Toolkit," Nov. 2014.

[17] D. McGregor, "Mino-Mnaamodzawin: Achieving Indigenous Environmental Justice in Canada" (2018) 9 *Environment and Society* 7.

[18] H. Davis and Z. Todd, "On the Importance of a Date, or Decolonizing the Anthropocene" (2017) 16 *Archives of Civil and Mechanical Engineering* 761; Whyte, note 12.

[19] J. Borrows, *Freedom and Indigenous Constitutionalism* (Toronto: University of Toronto Press, 2016).

[20] Art. 10.

[21] M. Barlow, "Building the Case for the Universal Declaration of The Rights of Mother Earth," in Council of Canadians, Fundacion Pachamama, and Global Exchange (eds.), *Does Nature Have Rights? Transforming*

throughout the world further demonstrates that existing environmental governance, policy, legal, and regulatory frameworks are floundering at every scale. Such points have been highlighted in Indigenous and non-Indigenous international, national, and regional environmental declarations over the past three decades.[22] For example, the Mandaluyong Declaration of the Global Conference on Indigenous Women[23] stated that from the perspective of Indigenous women:

> The worsening conflicts over ownership and access to our land and resources brought about by past and present discriminatory legal, political and economic systems, some conservation regimes and some climate change responses, as well as the unregulated behavior of corporations, are taking a serious toll on us. We have to continue nurturing our families and communities under such difficult situations.[24]

These systems in fact aggressively undermine Indigenous peoples, in particular Indigenous women, in systemic, ongoing, and violent ways. The Mandaluyong Declaration adds that "The Bagua Massacre in Peru in June 2009 where the military fired upon Indigenous peoples protesting against discriminatory laws which favored mining corporations over them represents what is happening to many Indigenous peoples in Africa, Latin America and Asia."[25] It is simply not rational for Indigenous peoples to rely on these global, national, and regional economic and political frameworks for environmental justice and a sustainable future. Various Indigenous international environmental declarations over the decades have articulated similar sentiments and challenges and have offered calls to action to reorient the dominant world order's unsustainable paradigms.[26]

4.3 INDIGENOUS ENVIRONMENTAL JUSTICE

The environmental justice contributions included in this volume, several of which address Indigenous rights and Indigenous law, are important and will remain so for years to come, particularly in diagnosing injustice and advocating for its elimination. Through my own contribution I hope to generate a nuanced understanding of *Indigenous* EJ by building on my earlier work which establishes that environmental justice is relevant beyond the human dimension. In so doing, I will draw upon knowledge and laws that originate from the lands and waters themselves.[27]

In earlier theoretical explorations, I examined how Indigenous EJ is not a new concept and has existed for millennia.[28] I pointed out that simply decolonizing or indigenizing the concept of EJ will not

---

Grassroots Organizing to Protect People and the Planet (Ottawa: Council of Canadians, Fundacion Pachamama, and Global Exchange, 2010), pp. 6–11.

[22] McGregor, note 7; Whyte, note 13.

[23] TEBREBBA, Indigenous Peoples' International Centre for Policy Research and Education, *Mandaluyong Declaration of the Global Conference on Indigenous Women, Climate Change and REDD Plus*, Legend Villas, Mandaluyong, Metro Maila, Philippines, Nov. 18–19, 2010.

[24] Ibid., p. 2.

[25] Ibid., p. 3.

[26] McGregor, note 7.

[27] Indigenous legal orders convey that it is not ethical to take credit for knowledge that already exists in "Nature" or on the "Land." J. Dumont, *Indigenous Intelligence* (Sudbury: University of Sudbury, 2006). For humans to claim ownership over knowledge of the "more-than-human," see M. Nelson, "The Hyrdomythology of the Anishinaabeg: Will Mishipizhu Survive Climate Change, or Is He Creating It?," in J. Doerfler, J. Sinclair, and H. Stark (eds.), *Centering Anishinaabeg Studies: Understanding the World through Stories* (East Lansing, MI: Michigan State University, 2013), pp. 213–233.

[28] McGregor, note 1.

fully illuminate a profound understanding and practice of EJ.[29] The foundation of Indigenous thought lies in the theories, philosophies, principles, and values of Indigenous peoples, in all their diversity, around the world. Processes of "decolonizing" or "indigenizing" are indeed necessary undertakings, and UNDRIP and other human rights instruments present opportunities for the reform of dominant legal orders to address injustice. However, these instruments are intended to decolonize global actors and nation-states, and their epistemological origins differ from those of Indigenous peoples. Indigenous legal orders flow from Indigenous peoples' own long-standing relationships to and understandings of the natural/spiritual world. Further insights into this fundamental dichotomy are required to articulate, from an Indigenous perspective, the laws, norms, protocols, and traditions essential for achieving Indigenous EJ.

Although diverse, one of the major commonalities of Indigenous perspectives in relation to justice, and a key way in which Indigenous perspectives differ markedly from their non-Indigenous counterparts, involves the conception of humanity's relationships with "other orders of beings,"[30] or what Melissa Nelson calls the "more-than human world."[31] Indigenous intellectual and legal systems draw on a set of Indigenous metaphysical, ontological, and epistemological assumptions about the place of humanity in the world which describe how people should relate to all of Creation.[32] As illustrated by the stories at the conclusion of this chapter, the instructions, protocols, laws, and ethics that are conveyed in Anishinabek *inaakonigewin* (law),[33] for example, guide humanity in proper conduct, and these instructions often come directly from the natural world (water, plants, wind, animals, etc.). The Anishinabek[34] take clan names (*dodem*) from among the first animals that are said to have died for the people, and as such are considered "relatives."[35] As well, many Anishinabek characterize the Earth as a living entity with feelings, thoughts, and agency.[36]

Anishinabek legal scholar John Borrows affirms that, "Anishinabek law provides guidance about how to theorize, practice, and order our associations with the Earth, and does so in a way

---

[29] McGregor, note 17.

[30] C. King, *Balancing Two Worlds: Jean-Baptiste Assiginack and the Odawa Nation, 1768–1866* (Saskatoon: Articulate Eye, 2013), p. 11.

[31] Nelson, note 27. For the Anishinabek, our sources of knowledge are thousands of years old, or even millions or more when you consider who some of our relatives are. Over time, we have developed our own epistemologies for understanding and relating to these relatives and teachers. Academic scholarship increasingly refers to these teachers/relatives as the "other-than-human," the "more-than-human," or the "non-human." S. C. Larsen and J. T. Johnson, *Being Together in Place: Indigenous Coexistence in a More Than Human World* (Minnesota: University of Minnesota Press, 2017). Because such terminology continues to place humanity at the "center," Indigenous scholars such as Robin Kimmerer and Kyle Whyte choose other terms (e.g. "teachers" and "relatives") to refer to other beings/entities (R. Wall Kimmerer, *Braiding Sweetgrass: Indigenous Wisdom, Scientific Knowledge and the Teachings of Plants* (Minneapolis: Milkweed Editions, 2013); Whyte, note 12.

[32] J. Borrows, *Canada's Indigenous Constitution* (Toronto: University of Toronto Press, 2010).

[33] A. Craft, "Giving and Receiving Life from *Anishinaabe nibi inaakonigewin* (Our Water Law) Research," in J. Thorpe, S. Rutherford, and A. Sandberg (eds.), *Methodological Challenges in Nature-Culture and Environmental History Research* (New York: Routledge, 2017), pp. 105–119.

[34] The Anishinabek, historically and in the present day, have lived and continue to live around the middle of North America, particularly in the Great Lakes region and the prairies northwest of the Lakes (Borrows, note 32). Prior to this, however, Anishinabek ancestors migrated from their original homeland on the eastern shores of North America and thus currently live along the shores of St. Lawrence to the Great Lakes and further west. E. Benton-Banai, *The Mishomis Book: The Voice of the Ojibway* (Hayward, WI: Indian Country Communications, 1988).

[35] D. Johnston, *Respecting and Protecting the Sacred*, prepared for the Ipperwash Inquiry, Ministry of the Attorney General, 2006.

[36] Ibid.

that produces answers that are very different from those found in other sources."[37] In this sense, by grounding conceptions of Indigenous justice (and injustice) in Anishinabek law, possibilities open up for innovation in Indigenous conceptions of justice and sustainability.

4.4 SOURCES OF KNOWLEDGE

Ontologically, an important aspect of Indigenous knowledge systems, and Anishinabek knowledge systems in particular, is that we acknowledge the lands and the waters themselves as relatives and teachers, and that they are a significant source of knowledge.[38] We learn from them about how to be in the world, and they also form a critical source of law.[39]

Utilizing Indigenous knowledge systems as a framework for analysis, EJ applies to all "relatives" in Creation, not just people. Indigenous EJ encompasses the duties and responsibilities of people to all beings, and conversely their responsibilities to people. EJ is regarded as a question of balance and harmony, of reciprocity and respect, among all beings in Creation; not just between humans, but among all "relatives."

Indigenous laws flow from different sources (from the land, the Creator, the spiritual realm) and are embedded in Place, although laws can be negotiated across nations and large geographic spaces, as seen in nation-to-nation treaties. They convey particular types of relationships with and responsibilities to each other as peoples, the natural world or environment, the ancestors, the spirit world, and future generations.[40]

Inherent in Anishinabek law are reciprocal responsibilities and obligations that are to be met to ensure harmonious relations. With rights come responsibilities. Responsibilities lie at the heart of Anishinabek legal structure, according to Aimee Craft.[41] Anishinabek legal obligations and responsibilities consider relationships among all our relations, including the spirit world, the ancestors, those yet to come, and other powerful beings that inhabit the peopled cosmos. These legal considerations are supported by Indigenous knowledge systems (IKS), which emphasize not just the practice of acquiring knowledge and perhaps utilizing it, but also acquiring the knowledge needed to ensure harmonious and just relationships. The Anishinabek developed laws, protocols, and practices over time to ensure that relationships with other orders of beings remained in balance, and that life would continue. In this sense, as knowledge can come directly from Creation, or the "natural world," all beings/entities/peoples have responsibilities to carry out to ensure the continuance of Creation to support life.

The idea of Place/Land/Peopled Landscape[42] is paramount in this theoretical framework.[43] IKS and laws are read from the land.[44] The primary sources of Anishinabek laws are experiences from

---

[37] Borrows, note 32, p. 269.

[38] Kimmerer, note 31.

[39] Borrows, note 32; A. Craft, *Anishinaabe Nibi Inaakonigewin Report: Reflecting the Water Laws Research Gathering*, University of Manitoba Human Rights Research (CHRR) and the Public Interest Law Centre, Spring 2014.

[40] Borrows, note 32; Johnston, note 35.

[41] Craft, note 39.

[42] In this sense, knowledge can come directly from the Land (and by this I mean all of Creation). As expressed by Indigenous scholar Sandra Styres and collaborator Dawn Zinga, "For us, this refers to land as a living entity providing the central underpinnings for all life, the understanding of interconnected relationships, and is underscored by her capitalization as a proper name" (D. Zinga and S. Styres, "Pedagogy of the Land: Tensions, Challenges, and Contradictions" (2011) 4 *First Nations Perspectives* 59 at 62). All beings/entities/peoples have responsibilities to carry out in order to ensure the continuance of Creation.

[43] Ibid.; Larsen and Johnson, note 31.

[44] Borrows, note 31; Kimmerer, note 31.

living in and observing the natural world/Creation.[45] Natural law comes from a natural, spiritual place.[46] Law, then, is all around us, if we know how to read it. In other words, properly understanding and enacting natural law requires vast knowledge of the natural world/environment, the "more-than-human" world, and how it functions in ensuring the continuance of all of Creation.

Anishinabek EJ would include obligations and responsibilities to all of Creation, including all beings, the ancestors and those yet to come, and the spirit world; it is not limited to the living or the "natural" world as seen through Western eyes.[47] Anishinabek justice would be supported by Anishinabek conceptions of legal and knowledge systems which require that people must cooperate with all beings in Creation. Fundamentally, Indigenous conceptions of EJ, based on Indigenous knowledge, convey a profound understanding of humanity's place in the world, extending beyond the aspirations and needs of humanity to other beings/persons/relatives/teachers (plants, animals, moon, stars, etc.). Such world views and ontologies, in which everything is alive and must be related to as such,[48] require distinct understandings and practices to influence conceptions of laws, knowledge, and justice. It is, therefore, not enough to simply incorporate Indigenous perspectives into existing EJ theoretical and methodological frameworks (as valuable as these are). Explicit effort must be made to decolonize EJ theoretical frameworks and underlying assumptions about human–nature relationships. Furthermore, the narrative must go beyond "indigenizing" EJ to envisioning distinct formulations of Indigenous EJ based on the diversity of Indigenous world view, theory, ontology, epistemology, and intellectual and legal traditions.

Indigenous legal traditions reflect a set of reciprocal relationships and a coexistence with the natural world.[49] Balanced relationships are sought between humans and other entities in the natural world (animals, plants, birds, forests, waters, etc.) as well as with the ancestors[50] and future generations.[51] The outcome of these relationships is *mino-mnaamodzawin*, the ideal that ensures a sustainable future for all life.

4.5 MINO-MNAAMODZAWIN

The Anishinaabe concept of *mino-mnaamodzawin* (the "good life," or "living well") offers protocols for ensuring that balanced relationships among all beings of Creation are maintained. Concepts such as this could provide significant guidance as we work toward achieving a more sustainable society. *Mino-mnaamodzawin* (some communities use "minobimaatasiiwin"), broadly speaking, is considered to be the overriding goal of the Anishinabek, both individually and collectively. Dr. Cecile King describes *mino-mnaamodzawin* as the "art of living well [which] forms the ideal that Anishinabek strive for."[52] Living well requires maintaining good and balanced relations with each other as humans, as well as with "other than human persons."[53] Anishinaabe leader and activist Winona LaDuke, who began applying the concept to

[45] King, note 30.
[46] Craft, note 39.
[47] McGregor, note 1.
[48] Dumont, note 27.
[49] Larsen and Johnson, note 31.
[50] Johnston, note 35.
[51] D. McGregor, "Indigenous Women, Water Justice and Zaagidowin (Love)" (2015) 30 *Canadian Woman Studies/les cahiers de la femme* 71.
[52] King, note 30.
[53] T. Smith, *The Island of the Anishnaabeg: Thunderers and Water Monsters in the Traditional Ojibwe Life-World* (Moscow: University of Idaho Press, 1995).

environmental justice issues, pointed out that the ideal is supported by Indigenous knowledge systems, legal orders, and especially natural law.[54]

Mino-mnaamodzawin, then, does not apply to humanity alone. Seeking redress, restoration, or reconciliation purely for humans and their environmental abuses, violations, and destruction will not result in balanced relationships. All beings have the potential to realize *mino-mnaamodzawin*.[55] The purpose of reconciliation in this context is to sustain life for all "relations"; it is not strictly a human endeavor. Many stories point to humans' tendency to be the most destructive and thus in need of more guidance than other entities or beings.[56] However, the obligations to attain *mino-mnaamodzawin* are *mutual* and other beings or entities also have their obligations and duties to perform. *Mino-mnaamodzawin* recognizes that other beings or entities in Creation also have their own laws (natural laws) that they must follow to ensure balance. A commitment to *mino-mnaamodzawin* has the potential to reconfigure and reclaim appropriate relationships with other orders of beings to achieve justice.

The relationships that Anishinabek are responsible for include those with all entities and beings in the world, some of which have far more power than humans.[57] *Mino-mnaamodzawin* points to the responsibility to seek well-being with other orders of beings or persons through processes of relational accountability. Relational accountability extends beyond nurturing relations among humans and includes "limitless 'nonhuman' entities that are usually described in western contexts as elements, animals, trees, landscapes, and so on."[58]

As noted above, I am not in any way suggesting that I have the ability to pose the definitive Indigenous EJ framework as each nation *already* has its own intellectual and legal traditions to draw upon. In this contribution I focus on the Anishinabek tradition, a tradition that shares common features with the concept of *buen vivir* as expressed in Indigenous international sustainable development declarations, such as the outcome document from the Rio+20 International Conference of Indigenous Peoples on Self-Determination and Sustainable Development.[59]

I will share stories that illustrate the intersection between knowledge and legal orders. Utilizing stories as a source of knowledge to convey Indigenous legal orders is a defining characteristic of emerging Indigenous legal, governance, and political scholarship.[60] In any story there are multiple layers and meanings to be derived, depending on how prepared the listener (or, in this case, the reader) is to process and make sense of the story. The next section provides insight into the epistemology and ontology of Indigenous knowledge systems.

---

[54] W. LaDuke, "Traditional Ecological Knowledge and Environmental Futures" (1994) 5 *Colorado Journal of International Environmental Law and Policy* 126.

[55] Indigenous peoples' continued assertion of the rights of Mother Earth to live can no longer be seen as simply philosophical, unrealistic reflections. On the contrary, they are becoming a reality in certain state legal systems. Emerging conceptual frameworks such as Earth Jurisprudence, Earth Justice, and Wild Law are gaining currency and increasingly becoming the topic of much debate. For example, Earth Jurisprudence is a legal philosophy that emphasizes the interconnections and interdependence of humanity and the natural world. A. L. Schillmoller and A. Pelizzon, "Mapping the Terrain of Earth Jurisprudence: Landscape, Thresholds and Horizons" (2013) 3 *Environmental and Earth Law Journal* 1. Earth Jurisprudence challenges the human-focused nature of current legal systems and promotes laws that protect nature in its own right (nature not as property). McGregor, note 7.

[56] Craft, note 33.

[57] Smith, note 53.

[58] S. Suchet-Pearson, S. Wright, K. Lloyd, L. Burarrwanga, and P. Hodge, "Footprints across the Beach: Beyond Researcher-Centered Methodologies," in J. Johnson and S. Larson (eds.), *A Deeper Sense of Place: Stories and Journey of Indigenous-Academic* Collaboration (Corvallis: Oregon State University Press, 2013), p. 33.

[59] See note 3.

[60] Borrows, notes 19 and 32; Napoleon and Friedland, note 2; Stark, note 2.

The stories below illustrate how knowledge and legal orders are derived directly from the natural and spiritual world, two sources of Anishinabek law. It is up to humans to act on the knowledge shared through these realms by enacting the duties and responsibilities that come with the knowledge. The other orders of being share knowledge with people, and as seen below, humans deliberate on the best course of action (another source of Anishinabek law). It is recognized that, although it has been shared with them, the knowledge is not owned by the people.[61] Knowledge in this context is not necessarily of a human origin.

4.6 STORY 1: A WOMAN'S VOICE[62]

Ishigamizige Giizis (the boiling sap moon) is in the springtime, when the snow and ice begin to melt, and water begins to flow. The days are warm with the sunshine, but the nights are still cold. During one such time, the Anishinabek were suffering and in a state of crisis. It had been a long and difficult winter and there was little food available. The winter stores had been used up and the people were desperate. The children were crying from hunger.

There was little hope, the hunters came up empty, and could not travel far, as all were weak from hunger. Many people died. One day, a woman began to get herself and her three children ready to leave the camp. The night before they left, she went out a ways from the camp and put down tobacco. Under the full moon, she prayed for strength and direction, for she knew that her children would die of starvation if she did not do something. Some of the other women, Mothers and Grandmothers, followed her and began to pray with her. While they were praying, a voice began to sing. When the prayer was finished, the voice, that seemed to come from a huge tree, spoke and said "*Waaban nanaawwneg omaagibzhak*," "Tomorrow at mid day come here."[63]

Some women were afraid and left, while others stayed to discuss what had occurred. These latter women decided to do what the spirit voice had instructed them to do, hopeful that the voice/spirit would help guide them in this time of great need. The next day was sunny and warm and the remaining people gathered at the huge tree. A prayer was offered by an Elder asking for direction and assistance. As the Elder prayed, water flowed from the sunny side of the tree, much to the surprise of those gathered. Not sure what to do, it was the children, curious and fearless, who tasted the water first and told the others the water tasted good. The water was sap from the maple tree: *zhiiaagamide* – sweet water.

The people used birch bark vessels, *makaks*, to catch the sap, Elders were nourished, and children were so happy and grateful for the gift. And so it was the people were saved from starvation. The sap is often referred to as the sweet medicine water and the tree is referred to as the tree of life. The trees offer food and nourishment in the spring when there is little food available. The *Aniaatig* (maple tree) is honored for its gift to the people and the knowledge for how to obtain the sap.[64]

The story of how sweet sap, maple syrup, and maple sugar came to the people, at a time of year when the need was great, conveys many teachings. It is partly a warning not to romanticize the past, and that life for the Anishinabek for thousands of years was intellectually and physically challenging as well as beautiful. It also recognizes that people, in this case the Anishinabek, had

---

[61] In this world view, the natural world can be said to have intellectual property rights. Laws and protocols already exist in the Anishinabek governance system to address such concerns.

[62] This story is a summary of the version told by Edward Benton-Banai in E. Benton-Banai, *The Anishinaabe Almanac: Living through the Seasons* (M'Chigeen, ON: Kenjgewin Teg Educational Institute, 2008).

[63] Ibid.

[64] Ibid., p. 17.

to seek new knowledge in order to flourish. When necessary, knowledge would come to the Anishinabek or be sought in different ways.[65]

The source of the knowledge in this story is of particular interest here. The teachings come from the tree itself; the *Aniaatig* has agency and decides to share its life force with the people and conveys this message as knowledge of how to survive and enjoy a great gift during that difficult time of year. The *Aniaatig* comes to the aid of the people, particularly because of the women who were seeking guidance and instruction through prayer and contemplation. The knowledge comes from the natural and spiritual world, yet it is up to the humans to decide what do with the knowledge that has been shared with them. Innovation is therefore still required (e.g. utilizing the birch bark vessels, boiling the sap to produce maple syrup and sugar).

In the sharing of the knowledge, a relationship is developed between the people and the trees. A set of mutual obligations and responsibilities is established. The Anishinabek honor the *Aniaatig* by creating ceremonies, songs, and prayers to remember its gifts. In another version of this story, also told by Anishinabe Elder Benton-Banai, it is the bear (*mukwa*) that shares knowledge of how to obtain sap from the trees with the people to again save them from sure starvation. The bear teaches the Anishinabek how to find nourishment at the time of year (spring) when food is scarce.

In both these stories it is the tree (plant being) or the bear (animal being) that shares its knowledge. The knowledge shared is a gift to support the continuance of life. A gift obligates the receiver to "know" how to honor the gift appropriately. For example, in our family, at the *ziizaakodokeng* (where we make maple syrup), we tap the trees and make syrup every year during the time of the *Ishigamizige Giizis*. An important obligation to the *Aniaatig* on our part (as humans) is to receive the gift of the *ziizabaakodaabo* (sap) and to *know* how to *miizhiyaang* (receive) that gift that saved my ancestors from certain starvation. In my family, based on our knowledge and understanding of the gift of *ziizabaakodaabo*, the legal obligation to the *Aniaatig* is to refrain from "taking" from the trees. The legal obligation is to the tree, not only its spirit, but its very being. In other words, we have an obligation to sustain the biology and ecology of the *Aniaatig*. We must also sustain the ecological system that supports the trees/forest. In order to fully honor the gift of *Ziizabaakodaabo*, we also have to obtain and act on Anishinabek *Gikensowin*/knowledge (which encompasses ecological/environmental knowledge).

This means, for example, that we do not "take" sap by setting up a "pipeline" system, where lines are hooked up to the trees and sap sent to a central location for boiling. We, as Anishinabek, have the capacity to do so, but we do not. There is a profound intergenerational understanding that each tree must be approached every day (as in when tapping and collecting the sap) and its well-being observed. Is each tree still prepared to "give" sap, or does it need a rest? Such relationships are lost when more automated systems are used, and when the well-being of each tree is unknown. It becomes tempting when using a pipeline system to take more than is actually needed to nourish the family and others in need (greed may arise). The legal principal of *knowing how* to receive a *gift* from the *Aniaatig*, rather than to *take or extract a resource* is fundamental to understanding law that supports justice, well-being, or *mino-mnaa-modzawin* for the *Aniaatig*. *Ziizabaakodaabo* is not a resource; it is life, it is nourishment. Similarly, the *Aniaatig* is not a resource, but the tree of life. Ensuring well-being for the

---

[65] D. McGregor and S. Plain, "Anishnabe Research Theory and Practice: Place Based Research," in A. Corbiere, M. A. Corbiere, D. McGregor, and C. Migwans (eds.), *Anishnaabewin niiwin: Four Rising Winds* (M'Chigeeng, ON: Ojibew Cultural Foundation, 2013).

Aniaatig, the knowledge and legal principles gained from the tree/bear therefore support sustainability.[66]

4.7 STORY 2: THE PIPE AND THE EAGLE[67]

The following story illustrates that sometimes it is not humans who are the arbiters of justice. We lack the capacity on occasion, despite our great intelligence, to ensure justice for all beings in Creation. Sometimes it is the compassion, knowledge, actions, and interventions of other beings (plants/animals, etc.) that must be deployed to ensure the continuance of life.

The Anishinabek received many gifts (knowledge, laws, drums, pipes, ceremonies, *semma* (tobacco)) from the Creator/Creation to provide them with the spiritual strength to support the continuance of life. There were also various helpers and teachers sent to assist the people in learning how to live well and coexist with the rest of Creation. Over time, however, the Anishinabek came to forget the teachings of love, respect, honor, generosity, humility, truth, and bravery. Instead, they began to disregard the natural laws and to behave disrespectfully toward other orders of beings. The people became vain and arrogant, and used the gifts from the Creator/Creation, that were supposed to remind us of our duties, obligations, and responsibilities to Creation, against other life for their own gain and personal power, and to feed their own ego and greed.

The Creator/Creation became upset about the abuse and corruption of these vitally important gifts that were intended to engender peace, humility, and generosity, and to support life-giving ways. A spirit was therefore sent to destroy the Earth after the Sun rose four times. On the fourth day, just before the Sun rises, the Creator/Creation is about to set forth destruction.

Just before dawn on the fourth day, the *Mi-gi-zi'* (eagle) flew out of the crack between darkness and light – that edge between night and day. He flew straight into the sky. He flew so high that he flew completely out of sight. He flew to talk with the Creator. The Sun was about come over the rim of the Earth. The eagle screamed four times to get the Creator's attention. The Creator saw the eagle and held back the Sun. At the time of this *be-da'-bun* ("false dawn"), the eagle talked to the Creator.[68]

The Eagle petitioned the Creator/Creation in an effort to save the people. *Mi-gi-zi'* acknowledged that while indeed there was corruption and evil in the world and people had forgotten their instructions, the unborn could still learn and therefore there was still hope. The Eagle reported that although things looked grim there were still a few who were humble and trying to live in harmony with the Earth. The Eagle appealed to the Creator/Creation and asked that, if he could find any people who still followed the original instructions, who cared for and lived well with the Earth, who knew how to use the gifts respectfully and to support life, would life then be spared on Earth?

> Let me fly over the Earth each day at dawn and look over the people. As long as I can report to you each day that there is still one person who sounds the Waterdrum or uses Tobacco and the Pipe in the proper way, I beg you to spare the Earth for the sake the unborn. It is in these unborn that there is still hope for the Earth's people to correct their ways.[69]

---

[66] This story also challenges the view that Indigenous peoples were simply too primitive to cause widespread environmental destruction. We could have, but we did not. We could commercialize the Ziizaakodokeng, but we do not. Doing so would cross the line and become "taking" rather than "receiving." The laws of nature are intended to support life.

[67] Adapted from Benton-Banai, note 34.

[68] Ibid., p. 80.

[69] Ibid., pp. 80–82.

The Creator/Creation thus holds back the destruction and entrusts the Eagle with the responsibility to fly over the Earth each day to find at least one good person who continues to live according to *mino-mnaamodzawin* and report back to the Creator/Creation his observations. Every day, the Eagle flies over the Earth to find at least one family or person who still practices the traditions. The unborn, the Eagle says, can learn from the few who still follow the instructions to live in harmony with the Earth, and life is spared. As Benton-Benai observes "We owe our lives and the lives of our children to the Eagle."[70]

There are many important teachings and messages associated with this story. For example, we must remember that it is Eagle who petitions on our behalf; we are not able to save ourselves as humanity. Despite our intelligence, we are destructive; yet we have been spared despite doing everything to cause our own demise. We are saved again by our relatives, who have compassion and pity for us. Second, through our arrogance, we have orchestrated our own destruction. Yet we continue to ignore our responsibilities to life and the unborn. Third, the Eagle only needs to find one person still using the gifts as instructed to support life. If there is one family, or even one person, there is still hope, and life will continue for another day.

The knowledge and interventions in the story of the Pipe and the Eagle are not human-derived or enacted. Indigenous, or in this particular case, Anishinabek, legal orders can account for this phenomenon through natural law – the laws that are derived from our knowledge of Creation and life. The knowledge and laws that have a profound influence on our lives as humans are enacted through spiritual and natural laws and our obligations to the future – the unborn.[71]

4.8 CONCLUSION

We have relied, and I suggest continue to rely, on knowledge being shared by our relatives, including the lands and the waters, in order to survive. But we must relearn how to receive these gifts and knowledge and not to abuse them for our own gain or vanity. As the stories point to above, we have faced our demise before and counted on our relatives to intercede on our behalf. As people, we have duties and obligations to deliberate on the knowledge and laws from other sources and learn how to honor and enact them to ensure harmonious relations in Creation. These laws may be codified in various ways and passed down from generation to generation. The stories also convey that despite the gifts of will and intelligence given to us, we can be highly destructive, to which the current planetary ecological crisis attests. We, in other words, have choices to make.

I suggest that the knowledge we need to survive as humanity may not derive strictly from the "human realm"; we need to revitalize and relearn the traditions that will ensure all knowledge is respected, including that from our various nonhuman relatives. We have not been able to solve the greatest challenges of our time on our own, despite great advances in science and technology. Human-centered and generated knowledge has not proven to be enough.

If Indigenous knowledge and legal traditions with respect to such concepts as *mino-mnaa-modzawin* remain invisible or unacknowledged, then how can environmental justice be

---

[70] Ibid., p. 82.
[71] I also understand this story as a climate justice story. Our unsustainable development/destruction mode of living threatens current and future generations. It is the "love" born by the Eagle that spares us despite our arrogance as humanity. Love for humanity, all beings, and all life is rarely offered as a motivation for environmental justice or sustainability.

achieved? Can sustainability be attained based on human knowledge only? The stories related here and the knowledge they convey may offer appropriate approaches to achieving the justice and sustainability that is so desperately needed. Thus far, it is the people who have failed; the *Aniaatig* and the Eagle continue to do their work. Without fail, they continue to fulfil their obligations.

5

Racial Capitalism and the Anthropocene

Carmen G. Gonzalez[*]

5.1 INTRODUCTION

This chapter introduces the framework of racial capitalism as a means of exploring the under-theorized relationship among environmental degradation, racial subordination, and the capitalist world economy. Using climate change as an example, the chapter illuminates the links between seemingly disparate forms of oppression in order to foster collaboration among scholars, policymakers, and social justice movements seeking systemic change.

Climate change is one of the cruelest manifestations of injustice confronting humanity. Caused primarily by the greenhouse gas emissions of the world's most affluent populations, its consequences are being borne disproportionately by the planet's most vulnerable states and peoples, including the small island developing states (SIDS), Indigenous peoples, and the poor.[1] Philip Alston, the United Nations (UN) Special Rapporteur on Extreme Poverty and Human Rights, has used the term "climate apartheid" to describe the divide between the affluent (who possess the resources to protect themselves from climate-related heat waves, food shortages, and conflict) and the rest of humankind (who will be left to suffer).[2]

The climate crisis is unfolding at a time of growing economic inequality and rising racial tensions. Since 1980, income inequality has soared in all regions of the world, squeezing the global middle class and enriching the top 1 percent of earners.[3] According to Oxfam, twenty-six billionaires currently control as much wealth as the 3.8 billion people who constitute the poorest half of the world's population.[4] As the gap between the rich and the poor increases, authoritarian leaders and right-wing social movements are increasingly directing public anger at racial and ethnic minorities, not only in the United States and across much of Europe, but also in India,

[*] This chapter is adapted from an article titled "Racial Capitalism, Climate Justice, and Climate Displacement" to be published in the Oñati Socio-Legal Series.

[1] See generally S. N. Islam and J. Winkel, "Climate Change and Social Inequality," United Nations Department of Economic and Social Affairs, DESA Working Paper No. 152, UN Doc. ST/ESA/2017/DWP/152, Oc. 2017; R. Gordon, "Climate Change and the Poorest Nations: Further Reflections on Global Inequality" (2007) 78 *University of Colorado Law Review* 1559.

[2] UN Human Rights Council, Climate Change and Poverty, *Report of the Special Rapporteur on Extreme Poverty and Human Rights*, June 25, 2019, UN Doc. A/HRC/41/39, p. 14, para. 50.

[3] F. Alvaredo, L. Chancel, T. Piketty, E. Saez, and G. Zucman, "World Inequality Report 2018," World Inequality Lab, p. 11.

[4] Oxfam, "Public Good or Private Wealth?" Jan. 2019, p. 12.

Brazil, and China.[5] The scapegoating of minority populations for the ills of capitalism has resulted in mass incarceration, rising state violence against darker-skinned and poorer populations, ongoing dispossession of Indigenous peoples, and detention and deportation of immigrants.[6]

While recognizing the valuable contributions of critical race theory to our understanding of racial subordination, this chapter adopts a structural approach to race and racism grounded in political economy. The remainder of this chapter is divided into three sections. Section 5.2 defines key terms and concepts, including racism, racial capitalism, the coloniality of power, and the abyssal line. Section 5.3 applies these concepts to climate change and the Anthropocene. It explains the violence that carbon capitalism inflicts on marginalized communities in both affluent and poor countries throughout the life cycle of fossil fuels – from cradle (extraction) to grave (climate change). Section 5.4 examines the complicity of law in racial capitalism as well as its emancipatory potential.

5.2 FOUR CRITICAL CONCEPTS: RACISM, CAPITALISM, COLONIALITY, AND THE ABYSSAL LINE

The term racism is used in this chapter to refer to the dehumanization and objectification of human beings based for the most part on physical characteristics (such as skin color), but also on ethnicity, indigeneity, culture, language, religion, geographic location, and geographic origin.[7] Racialization is the process through which specific bodies are classified as superior or inferior on the basis of the distinct set of markers adopted in a particular region or nation at a particular time.[8] Which groups are racialized and the narrative that accompanies that racialization varies substantially across place and time in relation to changing economic and political conditions.[9] For example, some groups that are currently recognized as White (such as Jews and the Irish) have a long history of being classified as non-White.[10]

Racial hierarchies serve distinct economic objectives and maintain population-specific modes of control. In the US, for example, the founding logic of anti-Black racism was labor exploitation.[11] When slavery was abolished, other mechanisms of exploitation and control became dominant, including share-cropping, debt peonage, convict-leasing, lynching, and segregation.[12] By contrast, the logic of anti-Native racism was the elimination of the Native in order to appropriate Indigenous lands.[13] Consequently, settler-colonial states like the USA, Australia,

---

[5]   H. Winant, "Preface: New Racial Studies and Global Raciality," in P. Bacchetta, S. Maira, and H. Winant (eds.), *Global Raciality: Empire, Postcoloniality, and Decoloniality* (New York: Routledge, 2019), pp. viii–ix; see generally M. Bergmann, C. Kenney, and T. Sutton, "The Rise of Far-Right Populism Threatens Global Democracy and Security," Nov. 2, 2018, www.americanprogress.org/issues/security/news/2018/11/02/460498/rise-far-right-populism-threatens-global-democracy-security.

[6]   P. Bacchetta, S. Maira, and H. Winant (eds.), *Global Raciality: Empire, Postcoloniality, and Decoloniality* (New York: Routledge, 2019), p. 2.

[7]   R. Grosfoguel, "What Is Racism?" (2016) 22 *Journal of World-Systems Research* 9 at 10; R. Grosfoguel, L. Oso, and A. Christou, "'Racism', Intersectionality and Migration Studies: Framing Some Theoretical Reflections" (2014) 22 *Identities: Global Studies in Culture and Power* 1 at 2–3.

[8]   Grosfoguel et al., note 7, pp. 2–3.

[9]   A. Reed. Jr., "Marx, Race, and Neoliberalism" (2013) 22 *New Labor Forum* 49 at 50.

[10] See generally N. Ignatiev, *How the Irish Became White* (New York: Routledge, 1995); K. Brodkin, *How Jews Became White Folks and What that Says about Race in America* (New Brunswick, NJ: Rutgers University Press, 1998).

[11] P. Wolfe, *Traces of History: Elementary Structures of Race* (New York: Verso, 2016), pp. 2–5.

[12] Ibid., pp. 75–93; S. Sassen, *Expulsions: Brutality and Complexity in the Global Economy* (Cambridge, MA: Harvard University Press, 2014), p. 68; see generally D. A. Blackmon, *Slavery by Another Name: The Re-enslavement of Black Americans from the Civil War to World War II* (New York: Knopf/Doubleday, 2009).

[13] Wolfe, note 11, p. 33

and Canada sought to dissolve Native societies and extirpate Native land claims through genocide and various forms of ethnocide, including "the breaking-down of Native title into alienable individual freeholds, Native citizenship, child abduction, religious conversion, resocialization in total institutions such as missions or boarding schools, and a whole range of biocultural assimilations."[14]

Drawing upon the work of political theorist Cedric Robinson[15] and sociologist Aníbal Quijano,[16] this chapter recognizes that racism and capitalism are inextricably intertwined. The extraction of wealth from nature was operationalized through slavery, the conquest and dispossession of Indigenous peoples, and the colonial and postcolonial domination by White Euro-American elites of large segments of the world's population.[17] Robinson uses the term racial capitalism to denote this symbiotic relationship between racism and capitalism.[18] He argues that capitalism emerged from a feudal order thoroughly infused with racial hierarchies, and then evolved into a world system that transforms regional and cultural differences into racial forms of domination.[19]

Quijano introduces the term "coloniality of power" to refer to the Eurocentric racial and cultural hierarchies and institutional forms of domination (such as the nation-state) imposed through colonialism that constitute the contemporary capitalist world system – including the North–South divide.[20] These hierarchies persist long after the departure of the colonial administration, and continue to structure economic and social relations.[21] Scholars in a variety of disciplines have extended Quijano's definition of the coloniality of power to encompass interlocking systems of oppression, including those that privilege core (North) over periphery (South), humans over nonhuman nature, men over women, Christians over non-Christians, Europeans over non-Europeans, heterosexuals over homosexuals, and Western knowledge over non-Western knowledge.[22] What distinguishes this decolonial perspective from Robinson's approach is that it emphasizes race and racism as a cross-cutting principle of the capitalist world system while also recognizing other intersecting forms of subordination.[23] For example, racial hierarchies shape the national and international division of labor, consigning those constructed as non-White to the most precarious, dirty, dangerous, and least desirable forms of employment.[24] Similarly, gender hierarchies relegate women to the unpaid domestic labor that reproduces the workforce, including cooking, cleaning, and raising children.[25] However, racialized poor women face additional forms of subordination,

---

[14] Ibid.

[15] See generally C. Robinson, *Black Marxism: The Making of the Black Radical Tradition* (Chapel Hill: University of North Carolina Press, 2000).

[16] See generally A. Quijano, "Coloniality of Power, Eurocentrism, and Latin America" (2000) 1 *Nepantla: Views from the South* 533; A. Quijano, "Coloniality and Modernity/Rationality" (2007) 21 *Cultural Studies* 168; A. Quijano, *Cuestiones y horizontes: de la dependencia histórico-estructural a la colonialidad/descolonialidad del poder* (Buenos Aires: CLACSO, 2014).

[17] G. Battacharyya, *Rethinking Racial Capitalism* (New York: Rowman & Littlefield, 2018), pp. 71–79.

[18] Robinson, note 15, p. 2.

[19] Ibid., pp. 26–27, 66–68.

[20] Quijano (2000), note 16, pp. 536–540; Quijano (2007) note 16, pp. 168–171.

[21] Quijano (2014), note 16, pp. 757–775.

[22] R. Grosfoguel, "World-Systems Analysis in the Context of Transmodernity, Border Thinking, and Global Coloniality" (2006) 29 *Review (Fernand Braudel Center)* 167 at 171; L. E. Figueroa Helland and T. Lindgren, "What Goes around Comes around: From the Coloniality of Power to the Crisis of Civilization" (2016) 22 *Journal of World-Systems Research* 430 at 439.

[23] Grosfoguel, note 22, p. 172; Quijano (2000), note 16, pp. 533–580; Quijano (2007), note 16, pp. 168–178.

[24] Battacharyya, note 17, pp. 107–108; D. Faber, "Global Capitalism, Reactionary Neoliberalism, and the Deepening of Environmental Injustices" (2018) 29 *Capitalism, Nature, Socialism* 8 at 14; N. Fraser, "Expropriation and Exploitation in Racialized Capitalism: A Reply to Michael Dawson" (2016) 3 *Critical History Studies* 163 at 175.

[25] Battacharyya, note 17, p. 40.

including trafficking, coerced sex work, and the hyper-exploitative domestic and care work that enables more privileged women to enter elite labor markets.[26] In other words, racial and gender hierarchies intersect, conferring greater status on some White women than many non-White men and generally placing non-White women in a subordinate position in relation to both groups.[27]

Eurocentric racial and cultural hierarchies correspond, at least in part, to Boaventura de Sousa Santos's notion of the "abyssal line" demarcating those deemed fully human from those deemed less than human.[28] Conflicts involving those above the abyssal line are managed through discourses of liberty, equality, and autonomy.[29] Those below the abyssal line are treated as nonhumans/subhumans and occupy zones of violence and dispossession.[30]

The racialized abyssal line is mapped onto space in the form of stigmatized geographic locations – including ghettos, reservations, export-processing zones, extractive zones, and the Third World – where the land and the people have been rendered expendable, disposable, and, in the words of Fanon, "wretched."[31] Indeed, the current stage of racial capitalism is marked by growing expendability as people are expelled from gainful employment by contracting global labor markets,[32] expelled from society through mass incarceration,[33] and displaced from their homes in record numbers not only by poverty and conflict but also by extreme weather events triggered by climate change (such as hurricanes, drought, and floods) as well as the degradation of air, land, and water.[34] Racialization renders abyssal exclusions "socially and legally acceptable,"[35] and "allows both capital and the state to pursue policies and practices that are catastrophic to the planet and its many life forms because much of the cost is borne by 'surplus' people and places."[36] Thus, "[t]o be rendered surplus is not to be paid less, it is to be left dying or for dead."[37]

This chapter focuses on the dehumanization of those below the abyssal line while recognizing that abyssal and non-abyssal exclusions exist on a continuum and that some groups cross between these two forms of exclusion in their daily lives. Santos provides examples that illustrate the distinction between abyssal and non-abyssal exclusion.

> First example: In a predominantly white society, a young Black man in secondary school . . . may well consider himself excluded, whether because he is often avoided by his schoolmates or because the syllabus deals with materials that are insulting to the culture or history of peoples of African descent. Nonetheless, such exclusions are not abyssal; he is part of the same student community and, at least in theory, has access to mechanisms that will enable him to argue

---

[26] Ibid., p. 47; Bacchetta et al., note 6, pp. 2–3.

[27] Grosfoguel, note 22, p. 172; K. Crenshaw, "Demarginalizing the Intersections of Race and Sex: A Black Feminist Critique of Antidiscrimination Doctrine, Feminist Theory, and Antiracist Politics" (1989) *University of Chicago Legal Forum* 139–167.

[28] B. S. Santos, *Epistemologies of the South: Justice against Epistemicide* (New York: Paradigm, 2014), pp. 118–135.

[29] Grosfoguel, note 7, p. 13.

[30] Ibid.

[31] L. Gahman and E. Hjalmarson, "Border Imperialism, Racial Capitalism, and Geographies of Deracination" (2019) 18 *ACME: An International Journal for Critical Geographies* 107 at 115; L. Pulido, "Flint, Environmental Racism, and Racial Capitalism" (2016) 27 *Capitalism, Nature, Socialism* 1 at 8, citing F. Fanon, *The Wretched of the Earth* (New York, Grove, 1963).

[32] Battacharrya, note 17, pp. 63, 122–123.

[33] Sassen, note 12, pp. 63–75.

[34] Ibid., pp. 149–210.

[35] J. Sundberg, "Placing Race in Environmental Justice Research in Latin America" (2008) 21 *Society and Natural Resources* 569 at 570.

[36] Pulido, note 31, p. 8.

[37] Battacharrya, note 17, p. 20.

against discrimination. On the other hand, when the same young man on his way back home is stopped by the police, evidently due to ethnic profiling and is violently beaten, at such a moment, the young man crosses the abyssal line . . . Second example: In an overwhelmingly Christian society bearing strong Islamophobic prejudices, a migrant worker holding a work permit . . . may feel discriminated against because the worker next to him earns a higher salary, even though they both perform the same tasks. As in the previous case, and for similar reasons, such discrimination prefigures a non-abyssal exclusion. However, when he is assaulted on the street just because he is Muslim and therefore immediately deemed to be a friend of terrorists, at that moment the worker crosses the abyssal line.[38]

The abyssal line operates on a global scale between centers and peripheries – racializing and impoverishing the Global South and rendering much of it population surplus and disposable.[39] In the Global North, Indigenous peoples, racial and ethnic minorities, and immigrants from the Global South are disproportionately classified as subhuman/nonhuman.[40] In the Global South, westernized elites frequently engage in internal colonialism – exploiting, dispossessing, and abusing racialized social groups.[41] The abyssal line is perhaps most evident in the zones of extreme violence and dehumanization – such as Guantánamo, Darfur, Iraq, Palestine, and Yemen. It is also evident in the prisons, migrant detention camps, and over-policed ghettos of the Global North as well as in the communities in both the North and the South whose homes have been rendered uninhabitable as a consequence of environmental degradation. The distinction between abyssal and non-abyssal exclusions is not grounded in the intensity of the pain and deprivation experienced by individual or collective bodies, but "refers to the indifference with which suffering is inflicted, indifference meaning both cold-bloodedness and impunity."[42] The following section examines climate change and the Anthropocene through a race-conscious decolonial lens.

5.3 CLIMATE CHANGE AND THE ANTHROPOCENE

Climate change is perhaps the most familiar example of anthropogenic interference with earth system processes in an era that has become known as the Anthropocene. The Anthropocene is a term introduced by scientists Paul Crutzen and Eugene Stoermer to refer to a new geological epoch of unprecedented human breach of planetary boundaries essential to the flourishing of human and nonhuman life.[43] The authors attribute the emergence of the Anthropocene to the destructive technologies developed by humanity and seek "to guide [hu]mankind towards, global, sustainable, environmental management"[44]

At heart of the Anthropocene is the anthropos, the human whose economic activity is exceeding ecosystem limits. Portraying the Anthropocene as a crisis to which all humans have contributed obscures the fact that only a small minority of humankind caused the problem –

---

[38] B. S. Santos, *The End of the Cognitive Empire: The Coming of Age of Epistemologies of the South* (Durham, NC: Duke University Press, 2018), pp. 22–23.

[39] Battacharrya, note 17, pp. 79, 122; see also N. Fraser and R. Jaeggi, *Capitalism: A Conversation in Critical Theory* (Cambridge, UK: Polity, 2018), pp. 42–43.

[40] Santos, note 38, p. 95.

[41] Ibid., p. 3; C. G. Gonzalez, "Environmental Justice, Human Rights, and the Global South" (2015) 13 *Santa Clara Journal of International Law* 151 at 160.

[42] Santos, note 38, p. 95.

[43] P. J. Crutzen and E. F. Stoermer "The 'Anthropocene'" (2000) *Global Change Newsletter* 41 at 17–18.

[44] Ibid., p. 18.

primarily persons who are White, affluent, and located predominantly in the Global North.[45] Scholars in a variety of disciplines have criticized this undifferentiated view of humanity, and have emphasized the underlying social and economic drivers of anthropogenic earth system disruption, including colonial conquest, imperial dispossession, and the imposition of a global capitalist order that systematically abuses nature and exploits large segments of the world's population.[46] Some scholars proposed the notion of the Capitalocene to better address the role of capitalism as the underlying cause of contemporary social and ecological crises.[47] Others have emphasized the role of racism and colonial violence as the means through which humans and nature are objectified and exploited.[48]

An analysis of climate change through a race-conscious decolonial lens reveals the ways that race is inscribed in the history of capitalism and in the sacrifice zones of both the fossil fuel economy and the emerging green energy economy. The domination of nature and the dispossession and exploitation of racialized human beings are deeply interconnected.

First, the colonization of the Americas and the transatlantic slave trade established the material and ideological foundations of capitalism – a system based on extraction, accumulation through dispossession, and White supremacy.[49]

> The Anthropocene is the epoch under which 'humanity' – but more accurately, petrochemical companies and those invested in and profiting from petrocapitalism and colonialism – have had such a large impact on the planet that radionuclides, coal, plutonium, plastic, concrete, *genocide* and other markers are now visible in the geologic strata.[50]

Indeed, the genocide of the Indigenous populations of the Americas in the 1500s was so massive (nearly fifty million deaths) that farming collapsed and forests rebounded.[51] The removal by forests of enormous amounts of carbon from the atmosphere caused a significant dip in atmospheric carbon dioxide levels in the 1600s, measurable in Antarctic ice cores.[52] Due to the magnitude of this early human modification of the environment, some scholars have proposed 1610 as the beginning of the Anthropocene.[53]

This early marker of the Anthropocene coincided with the importation of enslaved Africans to extract gold, silver, and copper in the Americas and to produce the sugar and cotton that fueled the Industrial Revolution.[54] "Plantation agriculture and cotton in particular were key to the emergence of the industrial power of England first and quickly much of the rest of Europe."[55]

---

[45] L. Pulido, "Racism and the Anthropocene," in G. Mitman, M. Amiero, and R. Emmett (eds.), *Future Remains: A Cabinet of Curiosities* (Chicago: University of Chicago Press, 2018), pp. 116–117.

[46] See generally J. Baskin, "Global Justice and the Anthropocene: Reproducing a Development Story," in F. Biermann and E. Lövbrand (eds.), *Anthropocene Encounters: New Directions in Green Political Thinking* (Cambridge, UK: Cambridge University Press, 2019), pp 150–168; D. Haraway, *Staying with the Trouble: Making Kin in the Chthulucene* (Durham, NC: Duke University Press, 2016); J. W. Moore (ed.), *Anthropocene or Capitolocene? Nature, History, and the Crisis of Capitalism* (Oakland, CA: PM Press, 2016).

[47] See generally Moore, note 46.

[48] See generally K. Yusoff, *A Billion Black Anthropocenes or None* (Minneapolis: University of Minnesota Press, 2018).

[49] Fraser and Jaeggi, note 39, pp. 40–47, 91–96; Yusof, note 48, pp. 23–64; H. Davis and Z. Todd, "On the Importance of a Date, or Decolonizing the Anthropocene" (2017) 16 *ACME: An International Journal of Critical Geographies* 761–780.

[50] Davis and Todd, note 49, p. 765 (emphasis added).

[51] S. Lewis and M. Maslin, "Defining the Anthropocene" (2015) 519 *Nature* 171 at 176.

[52] Ibid., p. 175.

[53] S. Lewis and M. Maslin, *The Human Planet* (London: Penguin, 2018), pp. 318–321.

[54] Yusof, note 48, pp. 14–16.

[55] S. Dalby, "Environmental Geopolitics in the Twenty-First Century" (2014) 39 *Alternatives: Global, Local, Political* 3 at 6.

The slave plantation colonies of the Americas supplied not only food and industrial inputs but also markets for British manufactured goods.[56] Between 1600 and 1800, slaves in the Americas comprised less than 1 percent of the world's population, but produced the commodities that dominated world trade.[57] Slavery, genocide, and colonialism were thus central rather than peripheral to the Industrial Revolution, the birth of carbon capitalism, and the beginning of the Anthropocene.[58] These systems of domination relied on lethal force as well as the ideology of White supremacy.[59]

Second, the "slow violence" inflicted by the fossil fuel industry on racialized and poor communities throughout the world remains a central feature of contemporary capitalism.[60] The extraction, processing, transportation, refining, and combustion of fossil fuels has placed disproportionate environmental burdens on racialized communities in both the Global North and the Global South. From the Niger Delta to the Canadian tar sands to the countless communities living in the shadow of polluting petrochemical facilities and power plants, the life cycle impacts of fossil fuels include eviction from ancestral lands; desecration of sacred sites; poisoning of air, land, and water; fires, explosions, and industrial accidents; loss of subsistence fishing and hunting rights; and exposure to significant health hazards.[61] Thus, local and transnational environmental justice struggles against coal mining, petroleum drilling, fracking, oil and gas pipelines, and polluting refineries and power plants are an integral part of the struggle for climate justice.

Third, fossil fuels are concentrated in particular countries and regions, such as the Middle East, that have been targeted over and over for invasion, occupation, and exploitation. The North's bloody resource wars, its collusion with despotic petrostates, and the resulting death, destruction, and displacement of racialized Muslim and Arab populations are among the most violent ongoing manifestations of climate injustice.[62] When persons displaced by these conflicts seek refuge in the Global North, they are branded as potential terrorists and subjected to restrictive border controls, including the notorious "Muslim ban" on travel to the USA from certain predominantly Muslim countries.[63]

Fourth, those most susceptible to climate-related disasters and slow-onset events are over-whelmingly persons classified as non-White.[64] They reside in geographic locations (such as low-lying coastal zones, small island states, and agriculture-dependent nations) disproportionately

---

[56] Lewis and Maslin, note 53, pp. 193–194; R. Blackburn, *The Making of the New World Slavery* (London: Verso, 1997), p. 375; E. Williams, *Capitalism and Slavery* (Chapel Hill: University of North Carolina Press, 1994), pp. 51–85.

[57] S. Beckert, *Empire of Cotton: A Global History* (New York: Vintage, 2015), p. 21.

[58] Lewis and Maslin, note 53, pp. 318–320; Yusof, note 48, pp. 40–41; Davis and Todd, note 49, 770–772.

[59] Pulido, note 45, p. 125.

[60] R. Nixon, *Slow Violence and the Environmentalism of the Poor* (Cambridge, MA: Harvard University Press, 2013), pp. 68–102.

[61] N. Klein, *This Changes Everything: Capitalism vs the Climate* (New York: Simon & Schuster, 2014), pp. 302–334.

[62] See generally N. Klein, "Let Them Drown: The Violence of Othering in a Warming World" (2016) 11 *London Review of Books* 1; M. T. Klare, *Blood and Oil: The Dangers and Consequences of America's Growing Dependence on Imported Petroleum* (New York: Henry Holt, 2004).

[63] A. Liptak and M. D. Shear, "Trump's Travel Ban Is Upheld by Supreme Court," June 26, 2018, www.nytimes .com/2018/06/26/us/politics/supreme-court-trump-travel-ban.html; A. Telford, "A Threat to Climate-Secure European Futures? Exploring Racial Logics and Climate-Induced Migration in US and EU Climate Security Discourses" (2018) 96 *Geoforum* 268 at 268–277.

[64] Pulido, note 45, pp. 117–118; N. Barhoum, E. Elsheikh, R. Galloway-Popotas, and S. Menendian (eds.), "Moving Targets: An Analysis of Global Forced Migration," Haas Institute for a Fair and Inclusive Society, University of California, Berkeley, Research Report, Sept. 2017, pp. 28–31.

exposed to hurricanes, floods, drought, desertification, and rising sea levels.[65] In addition, they have been *rendered* socially and economically vulnerable to climate change by the North's economic and military interventions.[66] The North's "under-development" of the Global South during the colonial and postcolonial era, so eloquently described by Walter Rodney[67] and Eduardo Galeano[68] has been exacerbated by decades of neoliberal economic reforms imposed initially by the World Bank and the International Monetary Fund (IMF) and subsequently through regional and multilateral trade agreements and bilateral investment treaties.[69] These reforms increased poverty; reduced access to healthcare, education, and other social services; undermined the development of climate-resilient urban and rural infrastructure; created mass displacement; and deprived states and communities of the resources necessary for climate adaptation and disaster response and recovery.[70]

Fifth, racialized communities in the Global South are being displaced not only by climate change, military interventions, and neoliberal economic policies, but also by the measures deployed to mitigate greenhouse gas emissions. For example, wind farms are being developed in Oaxaca, Mexico on Indigenous lands to provide energy to Walmart, Coca-Cola, Heineken, and Cemex (a Mexican cement manufacturer) without public debate; adequate compensation; free, prior, and informed consent; equitable sharing of benefits with local communities; and mechanisms to provide compensation for damage and loss of land.[71] In Canada, a controversial proposal to build an enormous hydroelectric dam on the Peace River threatens to displace

---

[65] R. Anand, *International Environmental Justice: A North–South Dimension* (Burlington, VT: Ashgate, 2004), pp. 35–39.

[66] Barhoum et al., note 64, pp. 28–31.

[67] W. Rodney, *How Europe Underdeveloped Africa* (London: Bogle-L'Ouverture Press, 1972).

[68] E. Galeano, *Open Veins of Latin America: Five Centuries of the Pillage of a Continent* (New York: Monthly Review Press, 1997).

[69] Gonzalez, note 41, pp. 167–172; see generally J. Linarelli, M. E. Salomon, and M. Sornarajah, *The Misery of International Law: Confrontations with Injustice in the Global Economy* (Oxford: Oxford University Press, 2018).

[70] Linarelli et al., note 69, pp. 11–17; Barhoum et al., note 64, pp. 29–30; M. Thomson, A. Kentikelenis, and T. Stubbs, "Structural Adjustment Programmes Adversely Affect Vulnerable Populations: A Systematic-Narrative Review of Their Effect on Child and Maternal Health" (2017) 13 *Public Health Reviews* 1–18; M. Lahsen, R. Sanchez-Rodriguez, P. Romero Lankao, P. Dube, R. Leemans, O. Gaffney, M. Mirza, P. Pinho, B. Osman-Elasha, and M. Stafford Smith, "Impacts, Adaptation and Vulnerability to Global Environmental Change: Challenges and Pathways for an Action-Oriented Research Agenda for Middle-Income and Low-Income Countries" (2010) 2 *Current Opinion in Environmental Sustainability* 364–374.

[71] See generally S. H. Baker, "Project Finance and Sustainable Development in the Global South," in S. Alam, S. Atapattu, C. G. Gonzalez, and J. Razzaque (eds.), *International Environmental Law and the Global South* (New York: Cambridge University Press, 2015), pp. 338–355; E. Zárate-Toledo, R. Patiño, and J. Fraga, "Justice, Social Exclusion and Indigenous Opposition: A Case Study of Wind Energy Development on the Isthmus of Tehuantepec, Mexico" (2019) 54 *Energy Research & Social Science* 1–11. The International Labor Organization Convention 169 Concerning Indigenous and Tribal Peoples in Independent Countries (ILO Convention No. 169) recognizes the rights of Indigenous peoples to consultation with respect to legislative or administrative measures that may affect them directly and to participation and benefit-sharing concerning the use, management, and conservation of natural resources on Indigenous lands (ILO, Convention concerning Indigenous and Tribal Peoples in Independent Countries (ILO No. 169), June 27, 1989, 28 ILM 1382, arts. 6 and 15). The United Nations Declaration on the Rights of Indigenous Peoples (UNDRIP) emphasizes the duty of states to obtain the free, prior, and informed consent of Indigenous peoples prior to approving or undertaking projects affecting Indigenous peoples, lands, territories, or resources (UN General Assembly, United Nations Declaration on the Rights of Indigenous Peoples, September 13, 2007, UN Doc. A/RES/61/295, arts. 19, 23, 28, 30, and 32). Mexico is a party to ILO Convention No. 169 and endorsed UNDRIP. C. G. Gonzalez, "An Environmental Justice Critique of Comparative Advantage: Indigenous Peoples, Trade Policy, and the Mexican Neoliberal Economic Reforms" (2011) 32 *University of Pennsylvania Journal of International Law* 723 at 781, nn. 276 and 277.

Indigenous peoples and replicate the sacrifice zones of carbon capitalism – but this time in the name of "green energy."[72] In Brazil and throughout the Global South, forest conservation schemes developed through the climate regime's Reducing Emissions from Deforestation and Forest Degradation (REDD+) program are interfering with the rights of local and Indigenous communities to harvest plants, timber, or fish in their ancestral territories.[73] Lastly, the legislation in the United States[74] and the European Union[75] requiring the blending of biofuels into transportation fuels has diverted land from food to fuel production, increased food prices, and incentivized large-scale land transactions in the Global South that destroy forests and displace rural dwellers in order to make way for large plantations to cultivate biofuel feedstocks (such as oil palm).[76] These mandates remain in place even though the life-cycle greenhouse gas emissions of many biofuels exceed those of the fossil fuels they replace.[77]

Finally, racialized persons displaced by poverty, conflict, and environmental degradation face death, detention, and deportation when they attempt to migrate to the Global North.[78] The Trump administration has portrayed the Central American families seeking refuge in the United States as "an unstoppable invasion of social parasites and criminals,"[79] and has threatened to close the US–Mexican border.[80] The US government has criminally prosecuted migrants, separated migrant children from their families, and confined thousands of migrant children in kennel-like, ice-cold cells.[81] European states are adopting increasingly aggressive measures to deter the entry of African and Middle Eastern migrants, who are depicted as violent, patriarchal, and likely to commit act of terrorism.[82] These policies have resulted in the death of thousands of

[72] D. N. Scott and A. A. Smith, "The Abstract Subject of the Climate Migrant Displaced by the Rising Tides of the Green Energy Economy" (2017) 8 *Journal of Human Rights and the Environment* 30–50.

[73] E. A. Kronk Warner, "South of South: Examining the International Climate Regime from an Indigenous Perspective," in S. Alam, S. Atapattu, C. G. Gonzalez, and J. Razzaque (eds.), *International Environmental Law and the Global South* (New York: Cambridge University Press, 2015), pp. 451–468; Klein, note 62, pp. 221–223.

[74] See Energy Independence and Security Act of 2007, Public Law 110–140, 42 USC, s. 7545(o) (2009) (requiring the blending of 36 billion gallons of biofuels into US transportation fuels by 2022).

[75] Directive 2009/28/EC of the European Parliament and of the Council of 23 April 2009 on the promotion of the use of energy from renewable sources and amending and subsequently repealing Directives 2001/77/EC and 2003/30/EC (2009) *Official Journal of the European Union* L 140/16 (requiring each EU member state to derive at least ten percent of its transportation fuels from biofuels by 2020).

[76] C. G. Gonzalez, "The Environmental Justice Implications of Biofuels" (2016) 20 *UCLA Journal of International Law and Foreign Affairs* 229, 251–262.

[77] Ibid., pp. 238–240.

[78] C. G. Gonzalez, "Climate Justice and Climate Displacement: Evaluating the Emerging Legal and Policy Responses" (2019) 36 *Wisconsin International Law Journal* 366 at 367–369, 381.

[79] M. Chen, "Trump's Caravan Problem Isn't Which People Are Coming, But What Kind of Country America Will Choose to Be," Dec. 2018, www.nbcnews.com/think/opinion/trump-s-caravan-problem-isn-t-which-people-are-coming-ncna945816.

[80] S. Collinson, "Trump Seems Inclined to Close Border Despite Potential Chaos," Apr. 2, 2019, www.cnn.com/2019/04/02/politics/donald-trump-immigration-border-closure-crisis/index.html.

[81] M. Chalabi, "How Many Migrant Children Are Detained in US Custody?" Dec. 22, 2018, www.theguardian.com/news/datablog/2018/dec/22/migrant-children-us-custody; N. Cummings-Bruce, "Taking Migrant Children from Parents Is Illegal, U.N. Tells U.S.," June 5, 2018, www.nytimes.com/2018/06/05/world/americas/us-un-migrant-children-families.html; E. Delgado, "Trump Administration Still Separating Families at Border, Advocates Say" Feb. 12, 2019, www.theguardian.com/us-news/2019/feb/12/trump-el-paso-family-separations-migrants-immigration; S. J. Nawyn, "Refugees in the United States and the Politics of Crisis," in C. Menjívar, M. Ruiz, and I. Ness (eds.), *The Oxford Handbook of Migration Crises* (New York: Oxford University Press, 2019), pp. 163–180.

[82] See generally Telford, "Threat to Climate-Secure European Futures?" note 63; E. Gutierrez Rodríguez, "The Coloniality of Migration and the 'Refugee Crisis': On the Asylum–Migration Nexus, the Transatlantic White European Settler Colonialism-Migration and Racial Capitalism" (2018) 34 Refuge 16 at 19; P. Boghani, "The

migrants at sea as smugglers select more dangerous routes and less seaworthy vessels to avoid detection.[83] Finally, Australia continues to indefinitely detain migrants and refugees in offshore processing centers located in Nauru and on Manus Island in Papua New Guinea under conditions that Amnesty International has denounced as "a human rights catastrophe."[84]

In Europe, the United States, and other settler-colonial nations, the population is generally divided "between those whose movement is a manifestation of liberty, and should therefore be maximized, and those whose freedom is a problem, and should therefore be tightly regulated."[85] While corporations freely roam the world, racialized bodies are policed, detained, incarcerated, and deported. Ironically, even though the mobility of the affluent (including air travel) contributes disproportionately to climate change,[86] it is the mobility of the non-White poor that states restrict.[87] Climate change is anticipated to displace between twenty-five million and one billion people by 2050.[88] The North's exclusionary immigration policies do not bode well for climate-displaced racialized communities.

An analysis of climate change grounded in the coloniality of power reveals a key thread that unites these abuses – the abyssal line dividing those deemed human from those deemed nonhuman/subhuman. While everyone is vulnerable to climate change, those who occupy the sacrifice zones of racial capitalism are particularly susceptible to harm due to their classification as subhuman and disposable. Racialization justifies and naturalizes violence and dispossession – in war zones, in resource extraction zones, in the green energy economy, and in the refugee camps and migrant detention centers of the Global North. As Naomi Klein observes:

> A culture that places so little value on black and brown lives that it is willing to let human beings disappear beneath the waves, or set themselves on fire in detention centres, will also be willing to let the countries where black and brown people live disappear beneath the waves, or desiccate in the arid heat. When that happens, theories of human hierarchy – that we must take care of our own first – will be marshalled to rationalize these monstrous decisions.[89]

Even though they have uprooted "the darker races"[90] throughout the world through the ecological and economic crises of colonialism, militarism, and predatory capitalism, Northern governments use a variety of border controls to exclude "those whose very recourse to migration results from the ravages of capital and military occupations."[91] For those below the abyssal line,

'Human Cost' of the EU's Response to the Refugee Crisis," Jan. 23, 2018, www.pbs.org/wgbh/frontline/article/the-human-cost-of-the-eus-response-to-the-refugee-crisis.

[83] M. Birnbaum, "Could the Flow of Migrants to Europe Be Stopped?" Oct. 3, 2017, www.washingtonpost.com/world/europe/could-the-flow-of-migrants-to-europe-be-stopped/2017/10/02/e76ac66e-a2ce-11e7-b573-8ec86cd fe1ed_story.html?noredirect=on&utm_term=.8b9b2aff2822.

[84] H. Davidson, "Offshore Detention: Australia's Recent Immigration History a 'Human Rights Catastrophe,'" Nov. 13, 2016, www.theguardian.com/australia-news/2016/nov/13/offshore-detention-nauru-immigration-history-human-rights.

[85] H. Kotef, *Movement and the Ordering of Freedom: On Liberal Governance of Mobility* (Durham, NC: Duke University Press, 2015), p. 100.

[86] J. Gabbatiss, "Tourism Is Responsible for Nearly One Tenth of the World's Carbon Emissions," May 7, 2018, www.independent.co.uk/environment/tourism-climate-change-carbon-emissions-global-warming-flying-cars-transport-a8338946.html; M. Le Page, "It Turns Out Planes Are Even Worse for the Climate than We Thought," *New Scientist*, June 27, 2019.

[87] M. Sheller, *Mobility Justice: The Politics of Movement in an Age of Extremes* (London: Verso, 2018), p. 135.

[88] B. Kamal, "Climate Migrants Might Reach One Billion by 2050," Aug. 21, 2017, https://reliefweb.int/report/world/climate-migrants-might-reach-one-billion-2050.

[89] Klein, note 62, p. 9.

[90] W. E. B. Du Bois, "To the Nations of the World," Jan. 29, 2017, www.blackpast.org/african-american-history/1900-w-e-b-du-bois-nations-world.

[91] H. Walia, *Undoing Border Imperialism* (Chico, CA: AK Press, 2013), p. 5.

racism is not simply prejudice or discrimination, but "state-sanctioned or extralegal production and exploitation of group-differentiated vulnerability to premature death."[92] The following section examines international law in creating and maintaining the abyssal exclusions of racial capitalism and its utility as a tool of resistance.

5.4 THE WAY FORWARD

International law has been deeply complicit in the project of racial capitalism. As Antony Anghie explains, international law originates in the colonial encounter and has justified successive Northern interventions in the Global South through a variety of doctrines – including *terra nullius*, the doctrine of discovery, the mandate system, trusteeship, modernization, development, humanitarian intervention, and preemptive self-defense.[93] International law has depicted Southern peoples as so primitive, savage, uncivilized, backward, and underdeveloped that their lives, livelihoods, and cultures are unworthy of protection.[94]

From the colonial era to the present, international law has also created the rules and institutions of the capitalist world system through which Northern states and transnational corporations maintain an iron grip on the states and people of the South,[95] including trade law,[96] foreign investment law,[97] and finance law.[98] As discussed in the introductory chapter to this volume, the concept of sustainable development, which aims to integrate economic development, environmental protection, and social development, has been hijacked by elites to promote economic growth at the expense of the poor and of the planet's fragile ecosystems.[99] The social pillar of sustainable development has failed to deliver minimum socioeconomic rights to those below the abyssal line because it does not challenge the structural inequities of the international economic order that perpetuate poverty, inequality, and social exclusion.[100] Even human rights law, which has been used by grassroots activists in environmental justice struggles, mitigates specific abuses but leaves intact the larger system.[101]

Scholars have long recognized that international law is constrained as a tool of resistance due to its epistemological complicity with structural violence against humans and nonhuman nature.[102] Influenced by Enlightenment philosophers, international law universalized the idea that humans are obligated to dominate nature, and created racial hierarchies that justify the

---

[92] R. Gilmore, *Golden Gulag: Prisons, Surplus, Crisis, and Opposition in Globalizing California* (Berkeley: University of California Press, 2007), p. 28.

[93] See generally A. Anghie, *Imperialism, Sovereignty and the Making of International Law* (Cambridge, UK: Cambridge University Press, 2004).

[94] Ibid.; Gonzalez, note 41, pp. 161–175.

[95] See generally Linarelli et al., note 69, pp. 159–163.

[96] Linarelli et al., note 69, pp. 110–144.

[97] Ibid., pp. 145–174.

[98] Ibid., pp. 175–225.

[99] R. Gordon, "Unsustainable Development," in S. Alam, S. Atapattu, C. G. Gonzalez, and J. Razzaque (eds.), *International Environmental Law and the Global South* (Cambridge, UK: Cambridge University Press, 2015), pp. 60–73; S. Adelman, "The Sustainable Development Goals, Anthropocentrism and Neoliberalism," in D. French and L. J. Kotzé (eds.), *Sustainable Development Goals: Law, Theory and Implementation* (Cheltenham, UK: Edward Elgar, 2018), pp. 21–27.

[100] Linarelli et al., note 69, pp. 250–255.

[101] See S. Marks, "Four Human Rights Myths," in D. Kinley, W. Sadurski, and K. Walton (eds.), *Human Rights: Old Problems, New Possibilities* (Cheltenham, UK: Edward Elgar, 2013), pp. 217–235; Gonzalez, note 41, pp. 188–190.

[102] T. Lindgren, "Ecocide, Genocide and the Disregard of Alternative Life-Systems" (2018) 22 *The International Journal of Human Rights* 525–549; Gonzalez, note 41, pp. 185–186.

objectification, dehumanization, dispossession, and exploitation of societies whose world views and practices differ from Euro-American norms.[103] In addition, the Western legal model's individualistic focus is ill-equipped to recognize and remedy systemic injustice, such as slavery, genocide, colonial exploitation, and decades of austerity imposed under the auspices of the IMF and the World Bank.[104]

Despite these limitations, international law has also been used in counterhegemonic ways by social movements in the Global South.[105] Plaintiffs in environmental cases have harnessed the power of national and international human rights law to achieve important victories.[106] The case studies in this volume provide context-specific examples of the variety of legal and extralegal tools used by subordinated communities to resist abyssal exclusion. This chapter concludes with four insights that can guide critical legal scholars who seek to approach environmental injustice through the lens of racial capitalism in the service of emancipatory struggles.

First, it is important to provide concrete, context-specific analyses of the ways that law produces abyssal exclusion in order to articulate the best ways that social movements can intervene. Scholars often err by depicting systems of extreme violence and dehumanization as so totalizing and overwhelming that resistance is futile. For example, Guantánamo, a paradigmatic case of abyssal exclusion, has been portrayed as a legal black hole, a zone of lawlessness and unfettered sovereign discretion.[107] On closer inspection, the cruelty inflicted on the detainees is governed by an elaborate set of legal classifications, substantive and procedural regulations, and legal institutions.[108] By analyzing the ways in which domestic and international law facilitates injustice, it is possible to identify the cracks in the armor and the strategies that can be deployed to resist systems of oppression and dehumanization.

Second, while environmental justice case studies often focus on racialized and poor communities, a racial capitalism analysis suggests that we should also identify the beneficiaries of this injustice and the mechanisms that sustain their wealth and privilege.[109] Confining our analysis to the poor and marginalized obscures the role of domestic and international law in maintaining racialized systems of exclusion. A socially just and environmentally sustainable world order cannot be achieved unless we dismantle and reconfigure the systems that allow the rich and powerful to continue to accumulate capital at the expense of nature and of the planet's most vulnerable communities. "Under globalised conditions, the principal problem of the poor is not their poverty, but rather the wealth of others, and the mechanics through which their dispossession is made possible."[110]

Third, racial capitalism objectifies, exploits, and degrades not only human beings but also nonhuman nature – breaching planetary boundaries and threatening ecological collapse. A race-conscious decolonial critique of the global economic order must interrogate and reimagine foundational legal concepts that portray humans as separate from nature and justify human domination and abuse of nature. These legal concepts include Western regimes of land tenure,

[103] Gonzalez, note 41, pp. 168–169.

[104] Ibid., pp. 188–190.

[105] See generally B. Rajagopal, *International Law from Below: Development, Social Movements and Third World Resistance* (Cambridge, UK: Cambridge University Press, 2003).

[106] Gonzalez, note 41, pp. 191.

[107] F. Johns, "Guantanamo Bay and the Annihilation of the Exception (2005) 16(4) *European Journal of International Law* 613 at 614, 619–621.

[108] Ibid., p. 618.

[109] See S. Marks, "Human Rights and the Bottom Billion" (2009) 1 *European Human Rights Law Review* 37 at 48–49.

[110] M. E. Salomon, "Why Should It Matter that Others Have More? – Poverty, Inequality and the Potential of International Human Rights Law" (2011) 37 *Review of International Studies* 2137 at 2146.

state sovereignty over "natural resources," and human rights premised on the bounded, autonomous individual.[111] Ironically, one source of alternatives to the dominant legal order is critical engagement with the philosophies, legal traditions, and technologies of racialized peoples, including Indigenous peoples and precolonial societies in Asia, Africa, the Americas, Australia, and the Pacific that thrived in harmony with the environment.[112]

Finally, in an insightful and provocative article titled "Human Rights and Root Causes,"[113] Susan Marks analyzes the perils of treating human rights abuses as random misfortunes that can be remedied if only the perpetrators adopted better practices, laws, and policies. Marks calls for an examination of the systemic causes of injustice and proposes that scholars and activists spend less time pursuing state-oriented reforms that demobilize oppositional activity and more time channeling grievances into organized and coherent action.

A race-conscious decolonial narrative of climate change that examines the cradle-to-grave impacts of carbon capitalism has the potential to unite diverse and powerful social movements that reject militarism, extractivism, economic inequality, and racism. As Naomi Klein observes, social justice struggles are often compartmentalized. "The anti-austerity people rarely talk about climate change, the climate change people rarely talk about war or occupations. We rarely make the connection between the guns that take Black lives on the streets of US cities and in police custody and the much larger forces that annihilate so many Black lives on arid land and in precarious boats around the world."[114] Racial capitalism, including the notion of the racialized abyssal line, can serve as the glue that holds these diverse social movements together and provides a framework for transnational mobilization.

5.5 CONCLUSION

Racialized communities have borne the brunt of carbon capitalism from its origins in genocide and slavery to the contemporary climate crisis and are increasingly being displaced by the emerging green energy economy. Their location below the abyssal line subjects these communities to the "slow violence" of the extractive and polluting fossil fuel industry; resource wars; predatory economic policies; climate-induced disasters; and criminalization, detention, and state-sanctioned death when they attempt to cross the militarized borders of the Global North. Racialization undermines solidarity by portraying large segments of humanity as inferior, unworthy, expendable, and a threat to national security. As one observer astutely notes:

> A divided population is more easily controlled. It turns its venom on itself. The march of corporate totalitarianism . . . skilfully manufactures scapegoats – immigrants, Muslims, black people and others of color, dissidents, the poor – so the rising fury of a betrayed population will vent against a demonized target.[115]

A race-conscious decolonial analysis of environmental injustice based on the recognition of a common vulnerability to the depredations of carbon capitalism can bring together diverse social

---

[111] See for example S. Seck, "Relational Law and the Reimagining of Tools for Environmental and Climate Justice" (2019) 31 *Canadian Journal of Women and the Law* 151 at 156 (critiquing approaches to human rights law that construct the individual as "an autonomous political subject that is separate from its environment").

[112] See C. G. Gonzalez, "Bridging the North–South Divide: International Environmental Law in the Anthropocene," (2015) 32 *Pace Environmental Law Review* 407 at 423–425 (citing Judge Christopher Weeramantry's separate opinion in the *Gabčíkovo–Nagymaros* case).

[113] S. Marks, "Human Rights and Root Causes" (2011) 74 *Modern Law Review* 57.

[114] Klein, note 62, p. 10.

[115] C. Hedges, "Burning Down the Future," June 24, 2019, www.truthdig.com/articles/burning-down-the-future.

movements by articulating the links among extractivism, poverty, economic inequality, displacement, mass incarceration, police brutality, immigrant detention/deportation, militarism, racism, Indigenous dispossession, and a global economic order that systematically subordinates the Global South, undermines the livelihoods of many in the Global North, and sparks ecological crises of epic proportions. As Martin Luther King, Jr. noted decades ago, "[i]njustice anywhere is injustice everywhere . . . In a real sense all life is inter-related."[116] Only through collective struggle can genuinely emancipatory solutions be achieved.

[116] M. L. King Jr., "Letter from Birmingham Jail," in M. L. King Jr., *Why We Can't Wait* (New York: Signet, 1963), pp. 77–100.

6

Human Rights and Socioecological Justice through a Vulnerability Lens

*Louis J. Kotzé**

6.1 INTRODUCTION

I suggest here, as I have done elsewhere, that our legal institutions have been complicit in causing the Anthropocene, while they are unable to address the multiple inter and intraspecies injustices that arise as a result of the decay of earth system integrity.[1] Human rights cannot convincingly stand insulated from the criticism leveled at law more generally.[2] Indeed, uncritical reliance upon the human rights paradigm as a central strategy to achieve the objectives of the social pillar of sustainable development, or, in more contemporary terms, of *socioecological justice*,[3] has failed to meaningfully address in any comprehensive way, the plights of billions of oppressed human and nonhuman beings, despite many human rights "victories."[4]

The Anthropocene predicament makes clear the vulnerability of the living order, and for this reason, I suggest that a reimagination of human rights could be accomplished by utilizing vulnerability theory, which is an emerging epistemic framework (if not – as yet – a powerful normative construction).[5] Vulnerability theory offers an embodied post-identity approach, which could provide an alternative lens through which to critically revisit human rights.[6] As a heuristic, it has the potential to inform an ontological change of stance away from a human-centered, neoliberal, and impregnably Western understanding of human rights, toward an altogether more porous and contingent understanding of the vulnerability of the entire living order as a starting

---

* Research for this chapter was supported by the author's European Commission Marie Skłodowska–Curie project titled: "Global Ecological Custodianship: Innovative International Environmental Law for the Anthropocene" (GLEC-LAW) under grant agreement No. 751782 and it was completed in August 2019. This chapter is based on L. Kotzé "The Anthropocene, Earth System Vulnerability and Socio-ecological Injustice in an Age of Human Rights" (2019) 10 *Journal of Human Rights and the Environment* 62–85.

[1] L. Kotzé, "Rethinking Global Environmental Law and Governance in the Anthropocene" (2014) 32 *Journal of Energy and Natural Resources Law* 121–156.

[2] L. Kotzé, "Human Rights and the Environment in the Anthropocene" (2014) 1 *Anthropocene Review* 252–275.

[3] J. Agyeman, R. Bullard, and B. Evans, "Exploring the Nexus: Bringing Together Sustainability, Environmental Justice and Equity" (2002) 6 *Space and Polity* 77–90.

[4] R. Bratspies, "Claimed Not Granted: Finding a Human Right to a Healthy Environment" (2016–2017) 26 *Law and Transnational Problems* 263.

[5] Despite its occurrence in international climate laws as well as its recurrent appearance in the case law of the European Court of Human Rights, it cannot be said that the concept has any binding normative properties (yet). See, F. Ippolito and S. Iglesias Sánchez (eds.), *Protecting Vulnerable Groups: The European Human Rights Framework* (Oxford: Hart, 2015).

[6] M. Fineman, "The Vulnerable Subject: Anchoring Equality in the Human Condition" (2008) 20 *Yale Journal of Law and Feminism* 1–23.

point from which to critique the epistemological closures and regulatory failures of the current human rights paradigm. Vulnerability theory thereby offers a fresh imagination of alternative potential ways to (re)engage more critically with, and to use, human rights to confront the Anthropocene's socioecological crisis.

This chapter commences by offering a vision of the myriad injustices and associated patterns of vulnerability that marginalized human and nonhuman entities experience as a result of the current socioecological crisis. It argues that any adequate future conception of "socioecological justice" will need to embrace "earth system vulnerability" if it is to be conceptually fit for the Anthropocene epoch. Based on this initial contextual framing, the chapter then offers a critique of human rights as prominent juridical constructs that pursue, but ultimately fail to sufficiently achieve, socioecological justice for humans and nonhuman beings. The discussion will show that human rights as currently constituted cannot fully respond to the Anthropocene, and that human rights have been complicit in contributing to the markers of the Anthropocene, its socioecological injustices and earth system vulnerability. The final part of this chapter explores the potential power of using vulnerability theory as a heuristic to reinterrogate and critique the dominant human rights paradigm and suggests possible ways in which human rights could be reimagined (but not necessarily replaced) alongside vulnerability theory.

6.2 SOCIOECOLOGICAL INJUSTICE AND VULNERABILITY IN THE ANTHROPOCENE

Humans as geological agents have become, at least since the Industrial Revolution, a destructive, powerful, and dominant part of the earth system, and the identification of the Anthropocene epoch makes it likewise clear that humans are responsible for the massive historical and continuing degradation of earth system integrity.[7] As a result, the Anthropocene reveals the full extent of human responsibility for upsetting earth system equilibrium and for impacting its integrity, while it also reveals human responsibility for preventing further harm to the earth system, restoring earth system integrity, designing measures for adapting to and coping with earth system changes, and ensuring that those most vulnerable to such changes are adequately protected.

The Anthropocene's powerful Promethean human, assumed to operate such telluric force on the earth, is, however, also a *vulnerable* subject. It is vulnerable not least because it impacts earth system integrity to such an extent that the quality and longevity of all life on earth are being jeopardized, its own included. If vulnerability could be understood in overtly simplified terms as the "precarity found on the ground when hazards arrive,"[8] a precarity which also bears on the susceptibility of something or someone to damage,[9] then humans have created a range of profound, potentially irreversible disasters such as climate change. These disasters dislodge earth system harmony and cause precarity and damage to which humans and nonhuman entities are increasingly susceptible. Even anthropos cannot escape such vulnerability.

Injustice is key to the Anthropocene and to an understanding of vulnerability in the Anthropocene. Deeply intertwined and mutually reinforcing practices of legally sanctioned

---

[7] J. Zalasiewicz, C. M. Waters, C. P. Summerhayes, et al., "The Working Group on the Anthropocene: Summary of Evidence and Interim Recommendations" (2017) 19 *Anthropocene* 55–60.

[8] J. Ribot, "Cause and Response: Vulnerability and Climate in the Anthropocene" (2014) 41 *Journal of Peasant Studies* 667–705 at 667.

[9] H. Eakin and A. Lynd Luers, "Assessing the Vulnerability of Social–Environmental Systems" (2006) *Annual Review of Environmental Resources* 365–394 at 366.

extractivism, colonialism, imperialism, industrialization, and slavery (all exemplars of modern progress), have been identified as key drivers of the Anthropocene, and as generators of multiple injustices and vulnerabilities.[10] But while the imagery of the Anthropocene tends to be universalistic, it is not the unqualified and generalized "human" that is responsible for the signatures of the Anthropocene and its associated patterns of injustices. Anthropos is thus most accurately to be understood as being a specific type of human: the ontologically disembodied, consumptive, politically dominant, property-owning, "Northern," "White," "male" human subject privileged by neoliberal socioeconomic structures of entitlement (such as through its laws regulating economic, political, and social participation and through empowering "fictions" such as transnational corporations it itself creates to stand in its service).[11]

This historically privileged subject is a persistent construct, marginalizing a host of "others," including for example, nonhuman living beings (popularly understood as "nature"), women, children, the poor, the elderly, the sick, non-Whites, and LGTBQ+ people.[12] A range of critical scholarship, and the historical record, reveals that the "we" at the heart of the Anthropocene's universalized "humans as a geological force of nature" is, in reality, a very small and particularly privileged subset of the past and present global human population.[13] The Anthropocene's anthropos cannot therefore be universalized in an unqualified way and should instead be understood as a privileged subject enjoying a disproportionate share of socioeconomic and environmental benefits. It remains the case that privileged humans are the least vulnerable to earth system disruptions such as climate change, while, for billions of "others" who are oppressed, marginalized, and not beneficiaries of the corporatized neoliberal fossil fuel economy, this is not the case.[14] Universal vulnerability in the Anthropocene must therefore be calibrated by critical attention to profound patterns of *differentially distributed vulnerability*, where everyone is vulnerable but some are – and will be – more resilient than others.

The Anthropocene's crisis of hierarchy also enables us to see that its differentially distributed patterns of vulnerability do not exclusively apply to humans, despite a general tendency to rely on anthropocentrism in some vulnerability theorization.[15] Instead, because it relates to the entire earth system, including its human–social and ecological elements, earth system vulnerability also responds to the vulnerability of nonhuman entities – and to the interdependent nature of human–nonhuman systems. Harris has suggested that "[H]umans are dependent not only on one another but [also] on a series of trans-human systems, and this interdependence is a source of resilience – and vulnerability."[16]

Responding to the all-embracing nature of vulnerability in the Anthropocene briefly elaborated above, I offer the term "earth system vulnerability."[17] While terms such as environmental justice focus on the social aspects of vulnerable humans, earth system vulnerability is a concept

---

[10] A. Harris, "Vulnerability and Power in the Age of the Anthropocene" (2014) *Washington and Lee Journal of Energy, Climate, and the Environment* 98–161 at 103.

[11] A. Grear, "Deconstructing Anthropos: A Critical Legal Reflection on 'Anthropocentric' Law and Anthropocene 'Humanity'" (2015) 26 *Law and Critique* 225–249.

[12] A. Grear, "Foregrounding Vulnerability: Materiality's Porous Affectability as a Methodological Platform," in A. Philippopoulos-Mihalopoulos and V. Brooks (eds.), *Research Methods in Environmental Law* (Cheltenham, UK: Edward Elgar, 2017), pp. 1–28.

[13] L. Rickards, "Metaphor and the Anthropocene: Presenting Humans as a Geological Force" (2015) 53 *Geographical Research* 280–287 at 286.

[14] A. Malm and A. Hornborg, "The Geology of Mankind? A Critique of the Anthropocene Narrative" (2014) 1 *Anthropocene Review* 62–69.

[15] As is the case, for example, in Fineman's work discussed later in this chapter.

[16] Harris, note 10, p. 126.

[17] The "socioecological" referent has been invoked elsewhere in the legal domain but in different contexts. See, for example, J. Ebbesson, "Social–Ecological Security and International Law in the Anthropocene," in

that potentially more fully embraces the human–social and ecological elements of the earth system, explicitly emphasizing the stakes of the Anthropocene and the fact that human vulnerability is ontologically intertwined with nonhuman vulnerability.[18] As we shall see immediately below, a concept of earth system vulnerability in the Anthropocene opens up the prospect of rethinking the practical and conceptual suitability of human rights to address the numerous complex socioecological injustices and associated vulnerabilities in the Anthropocene. Such a critical position brings into view the implications of the anthropocentric focus of human rights, including concerns about their regulatory failures and their potential to shut out alternative and more inclusive modes of socioecological justice responsive to the Anthropocene's crisis of human hierarchy, and its crisis of differentially distributed vulnerability among humans, among nonhuman entities, and between humans and nonhumans.

6.3 SOCIOECOLOGICAL JUSTICE THROUGH HUMAN RIGHTS?

Human rights have been a cornerstone of the world order at least since the adoption of the Universal Declaration of Human Rights in 1948 and the subsequent International Covenants on Civil and Political Rights and on Economic, Social and Cultural Rights of 1966. Several regional human rights instruments have been developed alongside the foregoing "International Bill of Rights," with some even claiming that collectively the global human rights regime could form the core of a nascent international constitutional legal order.[19] As a consequence of this global regime, human rights have been entrenched in the legal systems of countries all over the world. As an epistemological framework and as potentially powerful juridical protective measures, human rights have played a role in revealing the many dimensions of human suffering. They have been important in achieving some justice for some people, and in realizing individual human potential for some, while also serving as useful epistemic tools for "measuring deficiencies in the experience of particular groups in relation to these objectives."[20]

This remains true for environment-related aspects of human suffering, where human rights have been invoked, at least since the 1970s, as a common framework within which to situate the ever-deepening crisis of environmental and social injustices that threaten certain communities. "Environmental human rights" have emerged as a link between environmental protection and the human rights agenda, and ultimately, as a language within which to frame environment-related social justice claims. It is after all now generally accepted that environmental degradation impacts many of the core interests protected by human rights such as human life, human equality, and human dignity.[21] As a result, the right to a healthy environment, despite its not (yet) forming part of binding public international law,[22] has been included in various regional human

---

J. Ebbesson, M. Jacobsson, M. A. Klamberg, D. Langlet, and P. Wrange, *International Law and Changing Perceptions of Security: Liber Amicorum Said Mahmoudi* (Leiden: Brill Nijhoff, 2014), pp. 71–92.

[18] A. Grear, "The Vulnerable Living Order: Human Rights and the Environment in a Critical and Philosophical Perspective" (2011) 2 *Journal of Human Rights and the Environment* 23–44 at 42.

[19] E. de Wet, "The International Constitutional Order" (2006) 55 *International and Comparative Law Quarterly* 51–76.

[20] H. Mannan, M. MacLachlan, J. McVeigh, and EquitAble Consortium, "Core Concepts of Human Rights and Inclusion of Vulnerable Groups in the United Nations Convention on the Rights of Persons with Disabilities" (2012) 6 *Alter* 159–177 at 160.

[21] UN General Assembly, *Report of the Special Rapporteur on the Issue of Human Rights Obligations Relating to the Enjoyment of a Safe, Clean, Healthy and Sustainable Environment*, Jan. 24, 2018, UN Doc. A/HRC/37/59.

[22] The former Rapporteur on Human Rights and the Environment, John Knox, recommended in his final report that the Human Rights Council must "consider supporting the recognition of the right in a global instrument" (ibid., para. 14).

rights instruments as well as in the majority of domestic constitutions the world over, often with the explicit objective of enhancing environmental justice.[23]

Despite their common concerns, the relationship between human rights and environmental protection is an uneasy one. Regardless of its widespread endorsement and incorporation into legal systems the world over, the effectiveness of the human rights approach to achieve socio-ecological justice remains a concern. Although blame can obviously not exclusively be pinned on human rights for such failures, practically, despite their lofty ideals and higher-order consti-tutional normative superiority, human rights have been unable to improve the lived realities of many communities the world over, or to advance formal and substantive equality and to confront head-on discrimination against marginalized people who are particularly vulnerable. Billions of people all around the world continue to live in dirty slums often situated close to polluting industries, without sufficient access to schools, medical care, water, sanitation, and energy. Many continue to be deprived of possibilities to earn an adequate living in safe and healthy working conditions, while they have no meaningful ability to respond to hazards and the resultant social precarity. These marginalized people are most often uneducated, female, young, poor, old, unemployed, and non-White. They are impacted by a complex mix of surrounding environmental, social, and economic conditions that add to an already toxic situation of disempowerment, stereotyping, stigmatizing, exclusion, and ultimately multiple forms of injust-ices.[24] The invocation of rights language has not led to justice for many such marginalized communities and individuals in any meaningful way, despite the power of human rights to "articulate and advance the aspirations and resistance strategies of diverse grassroots social justice movements."[25] One reason for this state of affairs might be the notion of individual autonomy underlying human rights, which is not always appropriate for addressing the collective nature of socioecological justice: "[H]uman rights law, with its emphasis on individual rights, may be ill-suited to the task of advancing the collective rights of Indigenous peoples, racial and ethnic minorities, and other subordinated communities disparately burdened by environmental degradation."[26]

In addition to failing to adequately address the particularized and individualized local manifestation of injustices, human rights have also been unable to address the global dimensions of socioecological injustice, or the North–South divide. This divide is an expression of the deeply pervasive environmental and other inequalities and injustices that prevail between rich, developed states in the global "North" and poor developing states in the global "South." The divide is vividly explicated in terms of systemic global income disparities: since 2015, the world's richest 1 percent has owned more wealth than everyone else on the planet, clearly showing the unequal distribution of resources across the globe.[27] Much of this wealth has historically been, and continues to be, generated on the back of slavery, colonialism, carbon-intensive practices, and the widespread exploitation of people living in poor but resource-rich countries, mainly hailing from the global South.[28] A large question mark looms over the ability of human rights to adequately counter such destructive practices and to address the resultant global socioecological

---

[23] D. Boyd, *The Environmental Rights Revolution: A Global Study of Constitutions, Human Rights and the Environment* (Vancouver: UBC Press, 2011).

[24] D. Hulme, *Global Poverty: How Global Governance is Failing the Poor* (Abingdon, UK: Routledge, 2010).

[25] C. Gonzalez, "Environmental Justice, Human Rights, and the Global South" (2015) 13 *Santa Clara Journal of International Law* 151–195 at 152.

[26] Ibid., p. 183.

[27] D. Hardoon, "Oxfam Briefing Paper: An Economy for the 99%," OXFAM Policy and Practice, Jan. 2017.

[28] Malm and Hornborg, note 14.

injustices that continue to be driven by the forces of exploitation that originally gave rise to the Anthropocene.

Relatedly, there are also concerns, now more evident than ever before amidst a deepening North–South divide, that human rights have been captured by powerful Northern states and corporations to advance their own political and economic agendas, with some indicating that human rights have been co-opted by the neoliberal, corporate agenda that encourages developmentalism, consumerism, and extractivism.[29] This agenda is driven by what is perceived (notably by TWAIL scholars) to be historically embedded, but continuing, hegemonic and oppressive, imperial, colonial power structures of Northern descent, that are deeply vested in the broader international law paradigm of which human rights are a critical part.[30] While the many legacies of colonialism remain evident despite the formal end of colonial rule, there is a worrying rise in neocolonialism the world over. Land-grabbing (also characterized as the "foreignization of space")[31] by governments, and perhaps more notoriously by corporate actors, is an example of neocolonialism in the quest for, among others, the expansion of agro-investment and so called "food and energy security" through the production of palm oil and biofuels.[32] Although these practices are often cunningly veiled as "development aid," "energy security," and "low-carbon development,"[33] they can be more accurately described as "modern euphemism[s] for imperialism."[34] The corporate neocolonial exploitation and oppression of the Global South's nondominant humans, its nonhuman world, and its 'surplus,' 'degraded,' 'idle,' 'waste,' 'abandoned,' 'underutilized'"[35] lands, is instead real, more pervasive and far grimmer than what we are often led to believe:

> the vectors of oppression linking intra- and inter-species hierarchies are particularly pronounced in industrial corporate capitalism, which has become a globally hegemonic system in which such patterns are increasingly extreme: neoliberal capitalist globalisation is a highly uneven process still exhibiting pathological patterns of domination.[36]

Clearly, under such conditions, human rights are unlikely to offer socioecological justice, while such an accusation reveals how socio-juridico structures such as human rights and their discourses have been disingenuously used to appropriate, in a highly effective way, social, economic, and environmental benefits for a small "Northern" elite.

As alluded to above, human rights has also failed to address corporate human rights violations – a highly significant failure given that the neoliberal corporation, perhaps even more than the state, has been and continues to be a key driver of Anthropocene signatures and earth system decay.[37] This failure of the human rights framework to hold (especially transnational)

[29] Gonzalez, note 25, pp. 153, 170.
[30] Ibid., p. 158.
[31] A. Zoomers, "Globalisation and the Foreignisation of Space: Seven Processes Driving the Current Global Land Grab" (2010) 37 *The Journal of Peasant Studies* 429–447.
[32] A. Scheidel and A. Sorman, "Energy Transitions and the Global Land Rush: Ultimate Drivers and Persistent Consequences" (2012) 22 *Global Environmental Change* 588–595.
[33] C. Oguamanam, "Sustainable Development in the Era of Bioenergy and Agricultural Land Grab," in S. Allam, S. Atapattu, C. Gonzalez, and J. Razzaque (eds.), *International Environmental Law and the Global South* (Cambridge, UK: Cambridge University Press, 2015), p. 239.
[34] A. Hornborg, "Colonialism in the Anthropocene: The Political Ecology of the Money-Energy-Technology Complex" (2019) 10 *Journal of Human Rights and the Environment* 7–21 at 12.
[35] Oguamanam, note 33, p. 240.
[36] Grear, note 11, p. 233.
[37] S. Wheeler, "The Corporation and the Anthropocene," in L. Kotzé (ed.), *Environmental Law and Governance for the Anthropocene* (Oxford: Hart, 2017), pp. 289–307.

corporations to account for the massive socioecological injustices they cause the world over,[38] is even more problematic because the corporation is essentially a legal person "forged precisely in the service of the promotion and protection of [neoliberal] capitalistic interests."[39] The corporation, unlike animals or trees, is one of the very few nonhuman entities that the law affords the benefits of legal subjectivity to, and in some instances, even the benefits of human rights.[40] This paradox is deeply troubling: human rights are protecting and reinforcing the interests of corporate entities that contribute to the socioecological injustices that human rights are meant to address in the first place.[41] To date, corporations still do not incur any meaningful, direct, and binding human rights obligations despite high-level initiatives to this effect, such as the 2011 UN Guiding Principles on Business and Human Rights.[42] While there is a valid view that the Guiding Principles does create a form of responsibility on the part of corporations to at least respect human rights (a responsibility that is derived from societal expectations),[43] it is the case, as Simons argues, that corporate impunity for human rights violations is firmly entrenched in the international legal system and in the structure of international law itself.[44] Such a deeply troubling reality further emphasizes the extent to which human rights have been captured by the "Northern" neoliberal agenda. Corporate entitlement is sanctioned in many cases by governments (and even encouraged – as government support of Shell's devastating activities in Nigeria's oil fields suggests),[45] to the detriment of vulnerable human and nonhuman beings. Law generally and human rights specifically have thus missed the opportunity to create a global order in which human rights obligations to "respect, protect, and to remedy"[46] are imposed on corporations.

Human rights remain, additionally, overwhelmingly anthropocentric. Despite the encouraging but slow emergence of rights of nature, both practically in some legal systems (such as in India, Bolivia, Ecuador, Colombia, New Zealand, and some states in the USA) and as a discursive theme,[47] human rights retain the entitled, hierarchically superior human as their main referent and beneficiary while failing to address injustices thereby occasioned. As a general rule, nonhumans do not count as the beneficiaries of human rights and only benefit indirectly from human rights law if their interests align with human interests.[48] While the justice that

---

[38] P. Simons, "Selectivity in Law-making: Regulating Extraterritorial Environmental Harm and Human Rights Violations by Transnational Extractive Corporations," in A. Grear and L. Kotzé (eds.), *Research Handbook on Human Rights and the Environment* (Cheltenham, UK: Edward Elgar, 2015), pp. 473–507.

[39] A. Grear, "Vulnerability, Advanced Global Capitalism and Co-symptomatic Injustice: Locating the Vulnerable Subject," in M. Fineman and A. Grear (eds.), *Vulnerability: Reflections on a New Ethical Foundation for Law and Politics* (Farnham, UK: Ashgate, 2013), p. 45.

[40] A. Grear, *Redirecting Human Rights: Facing the Challenge of Corporate Legal Humanity* (London: Palgrave Macmillan, 2010), p. 7.

[41] See, for a discussion of human rights as simultaneously rights-denying constructs, U. Baxi, *The Future of Human Rights*, 3rd ed. (Oxford: Oxford University Press, 2008).

[42] See UN Human Rights Council, *Report of the Special Representative of the Secretary-General on the issue of human rights and transnational corporations and other business enterprises, John Ruggie*, Mar. 21, 2011, UN Doc. A/HRC/17/31, Annex, "Guiding Principles on Business and Human Rights: Implementing the United Nations 'Protect, Respect, Remedy' Framework."

[43] S. Seck, "Business, Human Rights, and Canadian Mining Lawyers" (2015) 56 *Canadian Business Law Journal* 208–237.

[44] Simons, note 38, p. 477.

[45] H. O. Yusuf, "Oil on Troubled Waters: Multinational Corporations and Realising Human Rights in the Developing World, with Specific Reference to Nigeria" (2008) 8 *African Human Rights Law Journal* 79–107.

[46] UNHRC, note 42.

[47] P. Villavicencio Calzadilla and L. Kotzé, "Living in Harmony with Nature? A Critical Appraisal of the Rights of Mother Earth in Bolivia" (2018) 7 *Transnational Environmental Law* 397–424.

[48] M. Deckha, "Initiating a Non-anthropocentric Jurisprudence: The Rule of Law and Animal Vulnerability under a Property Paradigm" (2013) 50 *Alberta Law Review* 783–814 at 784.

human rights seek to achieve is generally speaking not overtly focused on the nonhuman subject, some Indigenous approaches to justice do more fully embrace a non-anthropocentric approach, such as the rights of nature paradigm and the Principles of Environmental Justice declared by delegates to the First National People of Color Environmental Leadership Summit held in 1991, in Washington, DC.[49] Principle 1 of this document, for example, affirms "the sacredness of Mother Earth, ecological unity and the interdependence of all species, and the right to be free from ecological destruction." While it is mostly Indigenous Peoples that drive the rights of nature paradigm and endeavors to include nonhumans under the protective umbrella of human rights and justice, their voices are often muted. This much is clear from the exclusion of Indigenous Peoples' participation, and the noninclusion of Indigenous worldviews, in the drafting process and draft text of the recent Global Pact for the Environment of 2017 – a document touted as possibly becoming the environmental pillar of the International Bill of Rights, but which embraces a Western and anthropocentric world-view, including in the formulation of its right to a healthy environment.[50] More worryingly, Indigenous voices are sometimes even deliberately silenced in political and legal reform processes, as exemplified by the victimization and sidelining of Indigenous Peoples during the tumultuous and exclusionary process that led to the adoption of the Ecuadoran Constitution's rights of nature clause.[51]

Human rights have also been unable to fully accommodate the justice interests of future human generations, and, as a result of their anthropocentrism, create little space for the consideration of the interests of future human and nonhuman generations. It is important though to concede that some moves toward the juridical recognition of the rights and interests of future human generations are occurring. One example is *Oposa* v. *Factoran*, where the Philippines Supreme Court determined in 1993 that consequent on that country's right to a healthy environment, there is an intergenerational responsibility to protect the environment for future generations.[52] Another example is *Juliana* v. *United States*, where youth plaintiffs are suing the US government on behalf of future generations for its destructive climate change actions that threaten a range of the present and future generations' rights.[53]

6.4 HUMAN RIGHTS AND THE VULNERABLE LIVING ORDER

Vulnerability as a heuristic potentially fosters a deeper appreciation of the destabilization processes we are witnessing in the Anthropocene and its changing socioecological conditions.[54]

---

[49] "Principles of Environmental Justice," First People of Color Environmental Leadership Summit, Washington, DC, USA, Oct. 24–27, 1991.

[50] L. Kotzé and D. French, "A Critique of the Global Pact for the Environment: A Stillborn Initiative or the Foundation for *Lex Anthropocenae*?" (2018) 18 *International Environmental Agreements: Politics, Law and Economics* 811–838.

[51] L. Kotzé and P. Villavicencio Calzadilla, "Somewhere between Rhetoric and Reality: Environmental Constitutionalism and the Rights of Nature in Ecuador" (2017) 6 *Transnational Environmental Law* 401–433.

[52] D. Gatmaytan, "The Illusion of Intergenerational Equity: *Oposa v Factoran* as Pyrrhic Victory" (2003) 15 *Georgetown International Environmental Law Review* 457–485. The rights of future generations are also recognized in some constitutions such as those of Bolivia, Ecuador, Germany, South Africa, and Kenya. See Gonzalez, note 25, p. 186.

[53] M. Powers, "*Juliana v United States*: The Next Frontier in US Climate Mitigation?" (2018) 27 *Review of European, Comparative and International Environmental Law* 199–203.

[54] J. Birkmann, "Measuring Vulnerability to Promote Disaster-resilient Societies and to Enhance Adaptation: Discussion of Conceptual Frameworks," in J. Birkmann (ed.), *Measuring Vulnerability to Natural Hazards: Towards Disaster Resilient Societies*, 2nd ed. (Japan: United Nations University Press, 2013), p. 17.

I adopt Fineman's vulnerability theory to make out a case in support of developing a more complex vulnerable human/nonhuman subject.[55] Envisioning a vulnerable, complex human/ nonhuman subject for human rights, I suggest, could enable a reimagination of the form, function, and purpose of human rights in the Anthropocene, especially the extent to which human rights might play a role as part of the juridical measures needed to address earth system vulnerability and socioecological injustices.

Not to be confused with vulnerability science, vulnerability theory as a heuristic (the focus of this inquiry) is a critical evaluative or explanatory approach "seeking directly to address the inadequacy and distortion produced by the dominant assumptions of the existing liberal legal and political order"[56] in which human rights play a key role. In the social sciences domain, vulnerability theory is applied in various disciplinary areas ranging, among others, from (1) studies exploring the social welfare obligations of government;[57] (2) to the socioecological aspects of climate change;[58] (3) to ways to situate theories of political obligation within care for the natural world;[59] (4) to vulnerability as a heuristic tool to interrogate the concepts and findings of liberal legal and political subjectivity and their associated structural arrangements; and (5) to alternative ways to understand and, ultimately to address, injustice, inequality, and disadvantage.[60]

It is especially the latter two areas that are most useful for the present reflection on human rights, with much of the work done in this regard stemming from Fineman's vulnerability thesis (for which vulnerability arises from our ontologically factual embodiment which carries with it the ever-present possibility of harm, injury, and misfortune, the possibility of dependency and the possibility to be harmed by forces outside our bodies).[61] The life cycle of vulnerable embodied human entities is "characterized by its finite possibilities (and is thus inescapably tragic)"[62] – and humans have an organic propensity to disease, death, and disability. Fineman's vision of vulnerability, she suggests, provides the theoretical foundation for "transforming social values to enable us to reshape public institutional forms and behaviors."[63] Her theory can, therefore, be applied to any regulatory institution concerned with questions of justice, and its relevance for human rights in the pursuit of socioecological justice is promising. I, therefore, briefly draw together relevant strands of the vulnerability thesis with some of the critical themes noted above in relation to human rights to indicate its potential for their reimagination.

6.4.1 *Rethinking the Invulnerable Human Subject*

Fineman explicitly exposes the limitations of the US equality framework, which she finds is mostly formal in nature and draws upon strong visions of autonomy and individual liberty reinforced by liberal human rights. Her theory, which she says aims to be an "independent

---

[55] Fineman, note 6.
[56] Grear, note 39, p. 42.
[57] N. Kohn, "Vulnerability Theory and the Role of Government" (2014) 26 *Yale Journal of Law and Feminism* 1–27.
[58] H. Füssel, "Vulnerability: A Generally Applicable Conceptual Framework for Climate Change Research" (2007) 17 *Global Environmental Change* 155–167.
[59] Harris, note 10, pp. 98–161.
[60] M. Fineman and A. Grear (eds.), *Vulnerability: Reflections on a New Ethical Foundation for Law and Politics* (Farnham, UK: Ashgate, 2013).
[61] Fineman, note 6, p. 9.
[62] B. Turner, *Vulnerability and Human Rights* (Pennsylvania: Pennsylvania State University Press, 2006), p. 29.
[63] M. Cloud, "More than Utopia," in Fineman and Grear, note 60, p. 77.

universal approach to justice,"[64] arguably directly confronts anthropos by challenging the liberal, self-interested, quasi-disembodied, hyperrational (and therefore relatively *invulnerable*) human subject. Developments of Fineman's vulnerable subject (offered by her in the place of the autonomous subject) move it explicitly beyond a Cartesian ontology of disembodiment where invulnerable, invincible humans who are emboldened by their hubris, are able to master nature, control natural disasters, and (ironically) the fate of humanity itself.[65] As we have seen in the previous section, such hubris, autonomy, and control are legitimized by liberal, individualist human rights built on assumptions that place everyone at odds with one another as "antagonists in a bitter fight over limited state resources"[66] – a fight often fought by using human rights. The relative invulnerability of the liberal human subject is problematic, not least because "it produces systemic injustice through its mediation of a formal liberal equality that systematically excises the messy social conflict that it both enacts and simultaneously operates to occlude."[67]

Instead of this separative vision, the vulnerable subject is understood to be enmeshed in a web of relationships expressing interdependence and is responsive to the fact that everyone has variously different degrees of absence of capacity to act. Unlike liberal autonomy, the vulnerability thesis is alive to the constant haunting possibility for everyone "to become dependent based upon our persistent susceptibility to misfortune and catastrophe."[68] It also sits strongly with accounts of vulnerability that expose human rights' liberal individualist ontology.[69]

It is increasingly evident in the light of the Anthropocene's imagery of earth system decay that the human – even understood as masterful – is not invulnerable. To the extent that human rights endorse a conception of vulnerability conditioned by liberal autonomy and its underlying ontological suppositions, they are ill-suited for the present socioecological predicament. What is required is an alternative vision of human rights' quintessential subject. The current liberal human rights bearer needs to be replaced, rather than merely complicated by, an altogether more complex *vulnerable* human/nonhuman subject. Vulnerability theory offers a "powerful secular model for reconstructing a society that extols individual acquisitiveness and control of social goods into one that thrives because its forms and norms rest on notions of interdependency."[70] To this extent, it holds out hopeful foundations for a reimagined vision of human rights that focuses more explicitly – and adequately – on protecting the entire vulnerable living order – rights that richly celebrate and facilitate new modes of sharing, mutual respect, and reciprocal obligations of care that work to promote the collective interests of an interdependent community of human–nonhuman life.

6.4.2 *Universal and Intergenerational Socioecological Justice*

Vulnerability, in Fineman's view, is universal and shared (not only some, but all human beings are vulnerable): "as a state of constant possibility of harm, vulnerability cannot be hidden."[71] Although universal, vulnerability is not a generalized condition. It is non-monolithic, and

---

[64] M. Fineman, "Equality, Autonomy, and the Vulnerable Subject in Law and Politics," ibid., p. 13.
[65] A. Assiter, "Kierkegaard and Vulnerability," ibid., p. 30.
[66] A. Timmer, "A Quiet Revolution: Vulnerability in the European Court of Human Rights," ibid., p. 170.
[67] Grear, note 12, p. 9.
[68] Fineman, note 6, p. 11.
[69] K. Nadakavukaren Schefer, "The Ultimate Social (or Is It Economic?) Vulnerability: Poverty in European Law," in Ippolito and Sánchez, note 5, pp. 407–408.
[70] Cloud, n 63, pp. 77, 87.
[71] Fineman, note 6, p. 11.

responds to differences in embodiment as well as in status, and to institutional differences in resilience:

> Because we are positioned differently within a web of economic and institutional relationships, our vulnerabilities range in magnitude and potential at the individual level. Undeniably universal, *human vulnerability is also particular*: it is experienced uniquely by each of us and this experience is greatly influenced by the quality and quantity of resources we possess or can command.[72]

This universal but differentiated view of vulnerability aligns well with the Anthropocene's differentially distributed vulnerability, and has the flexibility to be able to respond to the fact that earth system vulnerability is multidimensional and differential, scale dependent, and dynamic.[73] Such an account would emphatically eschew the false equivalence of the liberal plane of relations:

> Far from negotiating contractual relations across an 'even' plane of individualised formal juridical equivalence, the vulnerable subject is ineluctably embedded within the messy, contextual, concrete, fleshy imperatives, potentialities and limitations of a fully embodied, particular and collective life – a life lived fully open to the draughts, predations and complexities, moreover, of a distinctly uneven globalised world.[74]

By invoking the idea of universal vulnerability, Fineman explicitly encourages "comprehensive approaches to addressing inequality and vulnerability, not simply piecemeal population-by-population interventions that fail to create fundamental change."[75] While their localized focus will remain important, going forward, human rights will have to be rethought in such a way as to address the earth system's global socioecological crisis in a comprehensive manner. Vulnerability theory points suggestively toward the need for human rights to be responsive not only to particularized vulnerabilities, but also to earth system vulnerabilities in a larger sense, that at once can address the causally interdependent structural causes of socioecological injustice globally – and enable human rights to form a realistic strand in a more empirically responsible account of the vulnerabilities in play in any given situation. A focus on providing access to water and sanitation to poor people living in a slum will remain critical, but equally critical is a vulnerability-responsive meta-view of the deeper structural causes of injustice – including, for example, the role of privatized multinational corporate water services providers and the global systems and assumptions facilitating their structural power. Analysis, in other words, becomes more inclusive and attentive – refusing to shut out complexities, connections and interdependencies that might otherwise go unaccounted for.

Furthermore, the idea that vulnerability is constant, non-episodic and thus *continuing* provides an opportunity to transcend the temporally misaligned limitations of human rights. The radical continuities between present and future generations become framed by a thread of connection, *central*, rather than merely incidental, to the analysis. Vulnerability theory potentially opens the space, more than does the current human rights paradigm, for a clear focus upon the fact that generations not yet born are also vulnerable, that their vulnerability is exacerbated by our present actions, and that the state must act to address future vulnerability. If human rights are part of the state's regulatory tools to achieve this, as they presumably would be, they might

---

[72] Ibid., p. 10 (own emphasis).
[73] Birkmann, note 55, p. 13.
[74] Grear, note 39, p. 53.
[75] Kohn, note 57, p. 10.

thus better be configured to accommodate the temporal demands that arise from within the broader context of past, present, and future socioecological justice. As mentioned above, some legal systems are already articulating ways in which human rights could protect future generations. This is an encouraging trend, and it is possible that a focus on the continuity of vulnerability might extend the intergenerational reach of human rights and their protective reach to future human–nonhuman generations.

6.4.3 *Post-Identity Human Rights?*

Fineman's vulnerability theory is, she suggests, a post-identity approach that rejects identity categories that are deeply entrenched in "racialized" social justice paradigms. In this sense, her approach is distinct from the identity-based approaches found in the genesis of the environmental justice movement, which can be traced back to the 1980s in the United States. The US environmental justice movement rose on the back of the civil rights movement as a movement determined to fight environmental injustice claims framed in terms of racial discrimination in pursuit of formal equality (i.e. equality resulting from the sameness of treatment and in this specific context, inequality arising from discrimination).[76] The identity categories of such social justice movements, however, are potentially problematic from the point of view of Fineman's vulnerability thesis. Fineman is suspicious of the deployment of identity categories, arguing that identity-based approaches run the risk of stigmatizing categories of people as being "lesser, imperfect, and deviant [placing] them somehow outside of the protection of the social contract as it is applied to others."[77] She argues that ignoring the universality and "sharedness" of vulnerability, an identity-based approach to equality and justice also suggests that only the victims in these stigmatized categories are vulnerable, which of course is not the case.[78] Fineman prefers to deploy vulnerability as a shared universal characteristic of being. On this view, vulnerability could replace group identities based on age, class, race, income, and gender when it comes to social welfare and justice programs.[79]

The implications for the present reflection is that if "vulnerability is a particular dynamic concept that encompasses, but also transcends, the notions of minority groups,"[80] as a post-identity approach, then the future-facing, vulnerability-centered focus of efforts to achieve socioecological justice will be placed less on concerns for a stigmatized group of some "minority victims," and more on ways to achieve deeper structural reform that dismantles the barriers resulting from systems of social stratification while maximizing opportunities for everyone.[81] And, because everyone is vulnerable, it is possible to disconnect the victims of injustice from their usual negative connotations. This removal of negative connotations also applies to vulnerability itself, in so far as vulnerability is "in many ways generative: it forges bonds between human beings and leads us to create institutions,"[82] as Timmer says, that enable us to address our

---

[76] S. Ryder "A Bridge to Challenge Environmental Inequality: Intersectionality, Environmental Justice, and Disaster Vulnerability" (2017) 34 *Social Thought and Research* 85–115.

[77] Fineman, note 64, p. 16.

[78] Ibid.

[79] Kohn, note 57, p. 4.

[80] F. Ippolito and S. Iglesias Sánchez "Introduction," in Ippolito and Sánchez, note 5, p. 1.

[81] M. Fordham, W. E. Lovekamp, D. S. K. Thomas, and B. D. Phillips, "Understanding Social Vulnerability," in D. Thomas, B. Phillips, W. Lovekamp and A. Fothergill (eds.), *Social Vulnerability to Disasters*, 2nd ed. (Florida: CRC Press, 2013), p. 16.

[82] Timmer, note 66, p. 149.

shared vulnerability. Vulnerability is thus a "common and positive quality of life around which social institutions should be shaped."[83]

This shaping reimagines the *sociality* underlying social institutions – and human rights. Through the vulnerability lens, human beings are repositioned "in relation to each other as human beings"[84] because the universality of vulnerability embraces all human beings, countering the individualism of human rights and moving ethical attention toward a more collective, universal vulnerability as a condition of the living order – indeed, of the entire earth system. Clearly, "this framing avoids a pull towards sameness logic or problematic comparisons among groups to demonstrate disadvantage that traditional equality discourse generates"[85] – enabling a richer conceptualization of human rights for the socioecological justice context. This chimes, albeit less anthropocentrically, with Fineman's claim that vulnerability theory has "the potential to move us beyond the stifling confines of current discrimination-based models toward a more substantive [and comprehensive] vision of equality."[86]

A vulnerability-centered vision of equality also potentially enables a far more nuanced consideration of relationships between vulnerability, equality, and the nonhuman. The identity-focused approach of human rights, and a liberal emphasis on formal equality, "has proven an inadequate tool to resist or upset persistent forms of subordination and domination."[87] Indeed, the quest for formal equality has all but ignored existing institutional arrangements that privilege some and disadvantage others, but an injustice-sensitive appreciation of the entire living order's universal vulnerability in the Anthropocene presents the possibility of a post-identity human rights paradigm in the pursuit of a more expansive vision of substantive equality for all earth system subjects, as Dekha's work demonstrates.[88]

6.4.4 *From Privileging to All-Embracing Human Rights*

Because vulnerability theory suggests that it is not multiple identities that intersect to produce compounded inequalities, "but rather systems of power and privilege that interact to produce webs of advantages and disadvantages",[89] the focus shifts to critique of these systems of power and privilege. Human rights, as I have argued, can be read as being such a system, or minimally as facilitative of structural relations of power and privilege. Fineman's theory focuses on how social institutions can be redesigned to create a more just society where entrenched advantages for a privileged few are eliminated and comfort, security and opportunity are created for everyone.[90] Her theory is concerned with "privilege and favor conferred on limited segments of the population by the state and broader society through their institutions"[91] – a focus compatible with critiques of human rights. Critique of social institutions through the vulnerability lens therefore sits well with critiques of "privileging" performed by human rights. With its focus on the aspects of the adequacy of social institutions, Fineman's vulnerability theory is also

---

[83] M. Deckha, "Vulnerability, Equality, and Animals" (2015) 27 *Canadian Journal of Women and the Law* 47–70 at 58.

[84] D. Estrada-Tanck, *Human Security and Human Rights under International Law: The Protections Offered to Persons Confronting Structural Vulnerability* (Oxford: Hart, 2016), p. 49.

[85] Deckha, note 83 p. 60.

[86] Fineman, note 6, p. 1.

[87] Ibid., p. 3.

[88] Deckha, note 41.

[89] Fineman, note 6, p. 16.

[90] Cloud, note 63, p. 85.

[91] Fineman, note 6, p. 1.

a framework within which to devise the creation of juridical, governance, economic, and social systems that increase earth system resilience, including of humans and nonhumans, across populations.[92] Resilience – and the distributive justice of the foundations of resilience – also quite naturally invites reflection on questions of resilience relative to the vulnerability of the earth system, suggesting that in the Anthropocene, human rights analysis should focus more inclusively on patterns of vulnerability and resilience and on the structural unevenness attending them.

6.4.5 *Nonhuman Vulnerability*

Finally, it should be noted that Fineman's theory does not explicitly relate to the nonhuman subject and seemingly does not embrace nonhuman vulnerability in any obvious way. Her vulnerable subject is unmistakably human. Vulnerability, on Fineman's account, therefore, fails at first glance to destabilize human centrality and to "explicitly disturb the fundamental subject–object relations underlying law [and human rights]."[93] Yet, as Grear argues, Fineman's theory in some way reformulates subject–object relations, "if only by dint of destabilizing the character of the political and legal subject – at least, by re-embodying it and situating it within a social matrix characterized by the presence of vulnerable institutions and structures. To that extent, Fineman's implicit ontology is promisingly materialist."[94] On that reading it is clear that vulnerability theory can be applied to the nonhuman world. Deckha, for example, argues that the opening that vulnerability extends to nonhumans is its focus on the material needs of embodied and corporeal existence: "[A]nimals can matter in vulnerability theorizations because they are beings leading precarious lives."[95] Through the vulnerability lens and its focus on material embodiment it is thus possible to value the nonhuman world and its diverse entities, not for their proximity to humans, but because the nonhuman world is itself materially vulnerable – a universal vulnerability that is intimately shared with the human world.

Deckha consequently rejects post-humanist critiques and equality discourses as approaches that insist on the worth of nonhuman beings, and instead chooses vulnerability as a critical framework: "[V]ulnerability discourse, which focuses on the dependence that embodiment engenders, thus has a better chance of respecting difference and avoiding the problematic sameness logic and other anthropocentric premises that block juridical attention from seeing full interests and experiences of injustice that animals can have."[96] Vulnerability theory offers a more inclusive and potentially more powerful narrative within which to reinterrogate the incompatibility of human rights and social justice movements with the socioecological justice concerns of the nonhuman living world, allowing as it does a deeper critique of the "liberal humanist tradition . . . whose application to animals, however animal friendly, is an instantiation of human sovereign power over animal lives."[97] In short, if it is recognized that the nonhuman world is vulnerable, as it surely is, then it would be easier for human rights and social justice movements to be reconfigured so that they also impose obligations on humans in relation to the nonhuman world as well as rights for nonhumans. Through the vulnerability lens, the rights of

---

[92] Kohn, note 57, p. 13.
[93] Grear, note 11, p. 11.
[94] Ibid.
[95] Deckha, note 83, p. 60.
[96] Ibid., p. 50.
[97] Ibid., p. 69.

nature paradigm and its gradual development in some countries does not seem all that radical or improbable.

6.5 CONCLUSION

The reflections offered here suggest that vulnerability is a potential alternative framework for the critical interrogation of the achievements and continued suitability of human rights in the Anthropocene. Vulnerability theory is increasingly gaining traction as a post-identity approach providing a point of entry for discussions about justice and equality that can "make visible the embodied result of unsupported frailty."[98] Invoking vulnerability does not automatically mean that the many shortcomings associated with the human rights framework (some of which are deeply troubling) would be meaningfully addressed in a concrete way any time soon. Nor does it mean that human rights will soon be conceptually reformed in a wholesale and meaningful way. But as a heuristic device, the vulnerability framework does open up many stifling closures preventing the epistemic traveler from moving forward in her journey toward a richer under-standing of the "complexity, affectability and vulnerability of the living order and of the multiple beings co-constituted by and within it."[99] Exposing the deficiencies and failures of human rights and opening to the potential significance of vulnerability allows for the richer understanding now being demanded by the Anthropocene situation and by the increasing visibility of human and nonhuman socioecological injustices and earth system vulnerability.

[98] Ibid., p. 62.
[99] Grear, note 39, p. 41.

7

Social–Ecological Resilience and Its Relation to the Social Pillar of Sustainable Development

Barbara Cosens

7.1 INTRODUCTION

Sustainable development is a value-based goal for reconciling interconnected social, environmental, and economic systems in a manner that preserves options for future generations.[1] Similar to sustainable development, resilience captures the integrated nature of society and the environment on which it relies. However, beyond the similarity in the systems they apply to, the terms are of a different nature. Resilience (as defined in the line of literature beginning with the work of ecologist Dr. C. S. (Buzz) Holling[2] and relied on in this chapter)[3] is an emergent property of complex social–ecological systems as the result of their internal and cross-scale interactions and feedbacks, and their responses to disturbance. Human views of social systems are essentially normative with goals such as equity, fairness, justice, and sustainability. As a result, the tendency in scholarly writing related to resilience and social systems is to use "resilience" as a normative term, which in turn leads to the concern that resilience scholarship fails to adequately address social and more specifically, environmental justice.[4] This chapter avoids that trap by remaining true to the ecological roots of resilience theory as a nonnormative system property, leaving concepts such as sustainable development and justice as human constructed goals. Thus, resilience is defined here as the measure of the ability of a system to retain structure and function in the face of disturbance because of a combination of resistance to change and adaptation.[5]

---

[1] World Commission on Environment and Development, *Our Common Future* (London: Oxford University Press, 1987).

[2] C. S. Holling, "Resilience and Stability of Ecological Systems" (1973) 4 *Annual Review of Ecology and Systematics* 1.

[3] For an excellent review of the use of the term "resilience" across multiple disciplines, see A. E. Quinlan, M. Berbés-Blázquez, L. J. Haider, and G. D. Peterson, "Measuring and Assessing Resilience: Broadening Understanding through Multiple Disciplinary Perspectives" (2016) 53 *Journal of Applied Ecology* 3 at 677–687. This chapter does not enter the debate over whether there is a correct definition of resilience. Rather, it uses the C. S. Holling, "Engineering Resilience versus Ecological Resilience," in P. Schulze (ed.), *Engineering within Ecological Constraints* (Washington, DC: National Academy Press, 1996), pp. 31–44 definition and line of literature that is most useful in this context.

[4] M. Cote and A. J. Nightingale, "Resilience Thinking Meets Social Theory: Situating Social Change in Socio-Ecological Systems (SES) Research" (2012) 36 *Progress in Human Geography* 4 at 475–489.

[5] Holling, note 3; L. Gunderson, "Ecological Resilience – In Theory and Application" (2000) 31 *Annual Review of Ecology and Systematics* 425; C. Folke, "Resilience: The Emergence of a Perspective for Social–Ecological Systems Analyses" (2006) 16 *Global Environmental Change* 253; C. Curtin and J. Parker, "Foundations of Resilience Thinking" (2014) 28 *Conservation Biology* 912.

This chapter begins with the understanding of resilience theory as a means of describing certain properties of complex systems relying on the work of systems ecologists.[6] It then explores how this differs from sustainable development and yet complements it by providing deeper understanding of the behavior of social–ecological systems seeking that goal. While resilience theory is well developed in the study of ecosystems, and the understanding of its application to social–ecological systems is increasing,[7] it is poorly developed in its connection to social justice and empirical work has not been done to relate it more specifically to environmental justice.

In seeking to understand the social pillar of sustainable development, the question to explore within resilience theory is: What is the relationship between resilience and environmental justice defined as: (1) distributive injustice: disproportionate exposure to environmental harm as well as fewer opportunities to reap the benefits of natural resource development; (2) procedural injustice: lack of access to environmental decision-making; (3) corrective injustice: disproportionate burden from failure to enforce environmental legislation or to remedy environmental harm: and (4) social injustice: linkage between the disproportionate effects of the other three areas of environmental injustice and broader issues of inequity?[8]

This chapter will seek to explore whether theory or empirical evidence lends support to the idea that a society that addresses environmental injustice is more capable of navigating the surprising and uncertain response of social–ecological systems to change (i.e. more capable of managing resilience). New empirical studies are needed to fully answer these questions. It is possible, however, to use theory and existing case studies to identify those aspects of social–ecological system capacity to manage change that are enhanced through attention to environmental justice. Specifically, the capacity to adapt is one aspect of system resilience that may increase with improvement in environmental justice. This is explored in three areas of social justice that appear to strongly correlate to adaptive capacity: social stability; community capacity to respond quickly, innovate, and evolve through learning; and the governance capacity to resolve conflict and agree on tradeoffs peacefully and equitably.

7.2 RESILIENCE: A PROPERTY OF COMPLEX SYSTEMS

The concept of resilience made its appearance in the study of ecological systems in the work of C. S. Holling, who recognized that ecosystems have emergent properties that include the capacity to adapt through self-organization to maintain structure and function in response to disturbance.[9] Narrowly defined, "[r]esilience is the capacity of a system to absorb disturbance and reorganize while undergoing change so as to still retain essentially the same function, structure, identity, and feedbacks."[10] In contrast to engineering resilience, which focuses on resistance to change and is measured by the return time to a static equilibrium, ecological resilience is a function of both resistance and adaptive capacity in recognition of the fact that

---

[6] See references in note 5.

[7] D. Davidson, "The Applicability of the Concept of Resilience to Social Systems: Some Sources of Optimism and Nagging Doubts" (2010) 23 *Society and Natural Resources* 1135; L. Olsson, A. Jerneck, H. Thoren, J. Persson, and D. O'Byrne, "Why Resilience Is Unappealing to Social Science: Theoretical and Empirical Investigations of the Scientific Use of Resilience" (2015) 1 *Science Advances* 4; S. Lockie, "Beyond Resilience and Systems Theory: Reclaiming Justice in Sustainability Discourse" (2016) 2 *Environmental Sociology* 2 at 115.

[8] R. R. Kuehn, "A Taxonomy of Environmental Justice" (2000) 30 *Environmental Law Reporter* 10681.

[9] Holling, note 2.

[10] B. Walker, C. S. Holling, S. R. Carpenter, and A. Kinzig. "Resilience, Adaptability and Transformability in Social–Ecological Systems" (2004) 9 *Ecology and Society* 5.

ecosystems may evolve while maintaining structure, function, and feedbacks.[11] The importance of adaptive capacity to the understanding of resilience was developed through empirical work on ecosystems[12] and cannot be overstated. The engineering definition of resilience focuses solely on resistance, or return time to a former state.[13] In contrast, complex systems (including complex engineered systems such as artificial intelligence) adapt and transform.[14] Their capacity to adapt is a major component in determining their ability to retain structure and function.[15] In application to social systems and governance, adaptive capacity becomes the core aspect of managing resilience.[16]

Resilience theory focuses on the processes controlling interaction of system components as opposed to the components themselves, which might be better understood through application of disciplines such as biology, soil science, forestry, sociology, and political science. It captures a set of interrelated concepts in addition to "resilience" that describe the abrupt and nonlinear behaviors observed in ecosystems.[17] It focuses on both the capacity of the system to return to its prior state following a disturbance; its capacity to adapt, or transform;[18] and the degree to which that capacity is influenced by or sensitive to changes at smaller and larger scales, a concept referred to as "panarchy."[19] In addition, resilience theory helps make sense of nonlinear behavior of complex systems in response to disturbance. It recognizes that systems may reorganize into alternative regimes or states in response to a disturbance that exceeds system "resilience," and the stability of this new regime makes it more difficult for the system to return to its prior state.[20]

Resilience theory uses the adaptive cycle as a heuristic to describe the path dependency of systems.[21] Systems on a trajectory of exploitation and accumulation of resources may produce their own scarcity and lose adaptive capacity if they continue on this path. Thus, a society dependent on a water supply that varies between abundance and drought may become vulnerable if it maximizes development during a period of wet years. The adaptive cycle is also useful in understanding the potential pathways when a system crosses a threshold. The system may reorganize, innovate, and begin a new cycle in a different system state, or through the provision of external resources, it may return to its earlier state.[22] Thus, an agricultural system may end after many years of drought and its farmers suffer or move to urban areas, or through innovation and knowledge and financial resources from higher levels of government, may reorganize under new livelihoods or a new approach to farming.

Resilience theory focuses on the interaction of system components. Thus, the extension of resilience theory to social–ecological systems is intended to capture the interdependence of

---

[11] Holling, note 3; Quinlan et al., note 3.
[12] Gunderson, note 5; Walker et al., note 10.
[13] Holling, note 3; Quinlan et al., note 3.
[14] Gunderson, note 5; Walker et al., note 10.
[15] Gunderson, note 5.
[16] Ibid.
[17] L. H. Gunderson and L. Pritchard (eds.), *Resilience and the Behavior of Large-Scale Systems* (Washington, DC: Island Press, 2002).
[18] Walker et al., note 10.
[19] L. H. Gunderson and C. S. Holling (eds.), *Panarchy: Understanding Transformations in Human and Natural Systems* (Washington, DC: Island Press, 2001). The application of panarchy to social–ecological systems illustrates that the capacity of a system to adapt increases if external resources are available.
[20] Holling, note 2; Gunderson et al., note 19; Walker et al., note 10; B. Walker and D. Salt, *Resilience Thinking: Sustaining Ecosystems and People in a Changing World* (Washington, DC: Island Press, 2006).
[21] Gunderson et al., note 19.
[22] Ibid. One of the best explanations of the adaptive cycle for those more familiar with social than ecological systems is found in Davidson, note 7.

human and natural systems.[23] This application is less well developed.[24] Ostrom and others have documented that social systems also self-organize and adapt.[25] The work of the Stockholm Resilience Centre, Australia Resilience Centre, and the Resilience Alliance have vastly increased our understanding of the application of resilience theory to social–ecological systems through numerous case studies.[26] Davidson relates the observation of wealth accumulation and increasing institutional complexity followed by collapse or reorganization to the adaptive cycle and argues that the application of resilience to social systems has promise.[27]

Similar to ecosystems, social systems adapt and resist in the face of disturbance, and if the disturbance is sufficient, may pass into a new regime. When this occurs as the result of a disturbance, it is referred to as regime shift in resilience theory.[28] Thus, the changes in upland forests brought about by drought and an increasing wildfire regime in the Middle Rio Grande of New Mexico USA as a result of climate change is altering the mix of species and is thought to represent a regime shift in those ecosystems.[29] Yet there are also times when society is intentional about changing to a new system state, by, for example, reengineering a river system for navigation, hydropower, and flood control.[30] To separate the two concepts, deliberate change is referred to as transformation (as opposed to "regime shift"). The act of intentional transformation requires the exercise of agency and power and thus application of theories in addition to resilience.[31]

Similar to ecosystems, social systems can also be thought of as nested within larger scales from the individual to the global, as contemplated by panarchy. Nevertheless, the power structures within and controlling this nesting are also not well captured by resilience. Agency may not only change the feedbacks in social systems in ways that are not analogous to the response of ecosystems, but may be the driving force behind the response of social systems to change.[32] For example, agency as well as power may drive the response of a social system to a disaster such as Hurricane Katrina.[33] Whereas an ecosystem might adapt to a new floodplain configuration, the city of New Orleans may choose to rebuild rather than adapt to that new configuration.

Thus, the application of resilience theory to social systems has been criticized in part due to its failure to capture unique human and social attributes such as agency, power, knowledge, and conflict.[34] Criticism also results from the confusion between a normative and objective

---

[23] Walker et al., note 10; Folke, note 5.

[24] Davidson, note 7.

[25] E. Ostrom, *Governing the Commons: The Evolution of Institutions for Collective Action* (Cambridge: Cambridge University Press, 1990).

[26] Stockholm Resilience Centre, www.stockholmresilience.org/; Australian Resilience Centre, www.ausresilience .com.au/; Resilience Alliance, Resilience Assessment Projects, www.resalliance.org/assessment-projects. For a summary of six North America water basin assessments, see L. Gunderson, B. A. Cosens, B. C. Chaffin, et al., "Regime Shifts and Panarchies in Regional Scale Social–Ecological Water Systems" (2017) 22 *Ecology and Society* 31.

[27] Davidson, note 7.

[28] Gunderson et al., note 19.

[29] M. H. Benson, D. Llewellyn, R. Morrison, and M. Stone, "Water Governance Challenges in New Mexico's Middle Rio Grande Valley: A Resilience Assessment" (2014) 51 *Idaho Law Review* 195.

[30] B. Cosens and A. Fremier, "Assessing System Resilience and Ecosystem Services in Large River Basins: A Case Study of the Columbia River Basin" (2014) 51 *Idaho Law Review* 91.

[31] B. C. Chaffin, A. S. Garmestani, L. H. Gunderson, et al., "Transformative Environmental Governance" (2016) 41 *Annual Review of Environment and Resources* 399.

[32] Davidson, note 7.

[33] Hurricane Katrina was a Category 3 hurricane that made landfall on the Gulf Coast of the United States on August 29, 2005, near the city of New Orleans. The failure of storm surge infrastructure resulted in flooding of nearly 80 percent of the city. Hurricane Katrina, www.history.com/topics/hurricane-katrina.

[34] Olsson et al., note 7; Lockie, note 7.

definition of resilience.[35] For example, while psychology uses "resilience" to capture the ability of a human to recover from a trauma, tragedy, or stress,[36] the fact that recovery is often the goal when human life is concerned results in conflation of the system response to the goal. The same is true in the disaster relief literature – despite support for transformation following an event like Hurricane Katrina to a system less reliant on engineered solutions and therefore less vulnerable, often the political will cannot overcome the human desire to return lives and livelihoods to their pre-disaster state.[37] High resilience speeds that desired recovery, and once again, the term is conflated with the goal.

This chapter will not resolve, or even engage in that debate. Instead, it will rely on the definition of resilience out of systems ecology that focuses on the properties and processes of complex systems. This allows the question to be explored: Does a deeper understanding of system behavior, even with the qualifications on application to social systems, improve our understanding of how to achieve sustainable development, a normative goal?

7.3 SUSTAINABLE DEVELOPMENT AND RESILIENCE THEORY IN CONTRAST

Sustainable development is defined in this volume as "development that meets the needs of the present without compromising the ability of future generations to meet their needs."[38] While its early manifestation focused on the relation between economic development and environmental protection, the third leg of social justice was added to the stool in 1995.[39] The three-legged stool paradigm, however, does not accurately depict the relationship between environmental protection and social and economic development. Increased understanding of the absolute dependency of society on a functioning environment has led to a modern framework placing the environmental pillar as the floor on which development and environmental justice must stand or fall.[40] Sustainable development is therefore a product of social organization articulated as a goal for deliberate transformation of society and laden with values guiding society's view of what should be. Both the act of reaching consensus on the goal and the efforts to achieve it require the exercise of agency and power, attributes unique to the human species and, as noted above, arguably not adequately captured by the system properties described by resilience theory.

Resilience, in contrast, is the measure of the ability of a system to retain structure and function in the face of disturbance because of a combination of resistance to change and adaptation. Rather than a synonym for sustainability, resilience theory describes the properties that must be managed to achieve the goal of sustainability. Resilience theory captures the complex feedbacks and self-organization of systems that may allow them to resist or adapt or, conversely, undergo nonlinear change in the face of disturbance. Resilience is not always desirable. Thus, a field of invasive species, a military dictatorship, or an impoverished community may be highly "resilient" in the face of efforts to invoke change, yet this property has no relation to the value we place on the system state.

---

[35] Ibid.

[36] Olsson et al., note 7.

[37] Davidson, note 7.

[38] WCED, note 1.

[39] United Nations, Report of the World Summit for Social Development, Copenhagen (Mar. 6–12, 1995) available at www.un.org/development/desa/dspd/world-summit-for-social-development-1995.html; Lockie, note 7.

[40] D. Hunter, J. Salzman, and D. Zaelke, *International Environmental Law and Policy* (5th ed.) (St. Paul, MN: West Academic Publishing, 2015), p. 114.

For social systems society seeks to retain in their current state, attention to adaptive capacity is critical.[41] For social systems society seeks to transform to a new state, often erosion of resistance is necessary for transformation and building adaptive capacity must follow to maintain the new system state.[42] Thus, the military dictatorship mentioned as highly resilient will need to be undermined and viable alternatives placed in reach before transformation may occur. The field of invasive species may require human intervention to remove the highly resilient invasive species and reintroduce native species. Finally, and of greater relevance to the theme of this book, a community trapped in a cycle of poverty may need outside intervention to reverse the social injustices that have placed them in this cycle and to introduce viable opportunities that can reverse the cycle. In the context of the goal of sustainable development, a social–ecological system that is achieving the goal of sustainable development and is highly resilient (i.e. has substantial adaptive capacity and seeks to continue to achieve the goal of sustainable development), is likely to continue achieving that goal in the face of disturbance. In contrast, a system that is not achieving the goal of sustainable development and yet is highly resilient will require substantial intervention to erode resilience and transform to a new, more sustainable state.

The implication of an equilibrium state in the term "sustainability" drives some to seek its replacement with "resilience."[43] This is particularly relevant where the law has adopted an equilibrium view of nature.[44] Thus a requirement of a "sustained yield" based on past timber records for a forest undergoing regime shift in the face of climate change is outdated.[45] A static social–ecological system in the face of climate change is also an obsolete concept.[46] In this context the term "resilience" that recognizes system evolution and thus the need for social–ecological systems to adapt is a valid replacement term for "sustained" or "sustainable."

However, in most contexts "sustainable development" or "sustainable livelihoods" as an overarching societal goal is not so narrowly construed and does not contemplate a static system.[47] It is not a specific state or regime that is to be sustained, but a level, distribution, and process of development that achieves economic security and environmental justice without compromising the options of future generations.[48] Evolution and transformation are therefore not anathema to the concept of sustainable development, and it is possible to retain both a cleaner line between goal and system attributes by keeping sustainable development and resilience theory as distinct concepts. Keeping this distinction allows focus on resilience theory to explain system properties helping guide understanding of the aspects of a social–ecological system that must change to transform toward sustainable development.[49] If sustainable development is to be achieved in this time of accelerating change in which those societies that have developed the earth's natural

[41] Gunderson, note 4.

[42] Chaffin et al., note 31.

[43] See for example M. H. Benson and R. K. Craig, *The End of Sustainability: Resilience and the Future of Environmental Governance in the Anthropocene* (Lawrence, KS: University of Kansas Press, 2017

[44] Ibid.

[45] Ibid.

[46] Davidson, note 7.

[47] J. C. Dernbach and F. Cheever, "Sustainable Development and Its Discontents" (2015) 4 *Transnational Environmental Law* 247.

[48] WCED, note 1.

[49] It should be noted that resilience has also been criticized for a preference for a static system (Lockie, note 7), but this confuses the engineering definition of resilience (focused on system resistance to change) with the definition used in ecology and with reference to social–ecological systems in which adaptive capacity and change to alternative states is of equal importance (Holling, note 3).

resources now dominate the earth,[50] and certain planetary boundaries may be approaching,[51] a platform for discussing the response of complex coupled human and natural systems is essential.[52]

Thus, it is potentially more important to ask whether resilience theory is useful in its application to social systems rather than whether it is a precise fit for explaining all aspects of their behavior while at the same time paying rigorous attention to its failings. Contrary to the claim that resilience scholars seek a unified theory,[53] this approach recognizes that resilience is only one pathway for making sense of complexity. If resilience theory helps the understanding of the behavior of interdependent social and ecological systems absent the exercise of agency and power, then it can inform the exercise of agency and power to achieve societal goals, such as sustainable development. Panarchy may help the understanding of how the exercise of agency in cross-scale interactions may play a role in transformations in social–ecological system configurations.[54] Although regime shift is predicted by resilience theory, deliberate transformation requires agency and is thus a unique behavioral aspect of the social system not captured by resilience theory. Yet, an understanding of the system resilience, including the potential for assistance through cross-scale interactions, is critical to achieving transformation. In short, resilience theory helps unpack how systems respond to change and thus can aid in understanding how to achieve sustainable development. However, the question remains whether resilience, or, more to the point, factors necessary to manage resilience, have any bearing on environmental justice.

7.4 RESILIENCE AND ENVIRONMENTAL JUSTICE

Using the system property definition of resilience theory, the broad question to consider is whether an understanding of system resilience can facilitate achievement of environmental justice. Lebel et al. (2006) explored the question: "How do certain attributes of governance function in society to enhance the capacity to manage resilience?"[55] They specifically looked for empirical evidence that participation, polycentricity (or multilayered governance) and accountability in governance improves that capacity. The authors focused on existing studies that did not necessarily address this question but found some evidence to support increased capacity to manage resilience with each of the attributes. This chapter will focus on a narrow aspect of that question: What is the relationship between resilience and environmental justice? Is there any theory or empirical evidence supporting the proposition that a just and equitable society has greater capacity to adapt and transform in the face of change – that is to manage resilience?

In asking these questions it is important to be cognizant of the criticisms of resilience theory in application to social systems discussed above and be cautious about extending the metaphor too far. Thus, the following discussion will focus on two system properties that have meaning in both

---

[50] W. Steffen, P. J. Crutzen, and J. R. McNeill, "The Anthropocene: Are Humans Now Overwhelming the Great Forces of Nature?" (2007) 36 *Ambio* 614; W. Steffen, Å. Persson, L. Deutsch, et al., "The Anthropocene: From Global Change to Planetary Stewardship" (2011) 40 *Ambio* 739.

[51] W. Steffen, K. Richardson, J. Rockström, et al., "Planetary Boundaries: Guiding Human Development on a Changing Planet" (2015) 347 *Science* 736.

[52] Davidson, note 7.

[53] Olsson et al., note 7.

[54] B. C. Chaffin and L. H. Gunderson, "Emergence, Institutionalization and Renewal: Rhythms of Adaptive Governance in Complex Social–Ecological Systems" (2016) 165 *Journal of Environmental Management* 81; Chaffin et al., note 31.

[55] L. Lebel, J. M. Anderies, B. Campbell, C. Folke, S. Hatfield-Dodds, T. P. Hughes, and J. Wilson, "Governance and the Capacity to Manage Resilience in Regional Social–Ecological Systems" (2006) 11 *Ecology and Society* 19.

resilience and social justice literature: stability and adaptive capacity. It will then discuss an area of literature with its roots in resilience theory, but its more recent development in legal scholarship which must consider the social attributes of agency, power, and conflict – that is adaptive governance.

7.4.1 *Stability and Environmental Justice*

A stable society with sustainable livelihoods is essential to the goals of sustainable development. Injustice and disparity in wealth are destabilizing, and poverty erodes the productivity and hope of those trapped within it. Yet resilience theory tells us that governance and management in the face of change requires flexibility. In a time of accelerating change,[56] attempts to maintain static systems may also be destabilizing. Thus, the key to managing change imposed on complex systems is to balance stability and flexibility.[57] This premise could have been arrived at without reference to resilience theory. The key, therefore, is to ask: Does the understanding of complex systems provided by resilience theory inform how to achieve this balance, and, if so, does the approach have anything to do with environmental justice?

The answer to the first question is, in part, yes: certainly, political theory, social science, and legal scholarship have a lot to say about whether, how, why, and should political systems evolve as societal norms and needs change. Resilience theory addresses whether and how, leaving why and should to normative frameworks. Specifically, panarchy aids in unpacking the cross-scale interactions of governance systems necessary to provide flexibility within a stable framework.[58] Thus, higher scales may provide stability and support for local innovation. Similarly, diversity in innovation at small scales risks less in system stability than large-scale efforts to transform. Successful innovation may then scale up. The adaptive cycle helps to understand the system trajectory by focusing attention on the degree to which external assistance and facilitation of small-scale innovation may be needed by a system approaching a threshold.[59]

The second question – does understanding system resilience have anything to do with environmental justice? – is more difficult to answer. Hans Rosling documented the fact that the clear divide between the Global South and the Global North no longer exists, particularly as countries like India and China develop.[60] Yet he also documented that this applies at the scale of the nation-state – that is when viewing indicators of wellbeing as country averages. If broken down domestically, nation-states in both the North and South show disparities in distributive justice (and likely in the other areas of environmental justice not reflected in the statistics relied on).[61] Thus it is clear that marginalization and poverty within sectors of society persist even though their governments are relatively stable.[62] Leaving aside the question of whether part of this continuing discrepancy is tied to the possibility that the current rapid development in many

---

[56] Steffen et al. (2007), note 50; Steffen et al. (2011), note 50.

[57] R. K. Craig, A. S. Garmestani, C. R. Allen, et al., "Balancing Stability and Flexibility in Adaptive Governance: An Analysis of Tools Available in U.S. Environmental Law" (2017) 22 *Ecology and Society* 3.

[58] Chaffin and Gunderson, note 54.

[59] See generally, L. Gunderson, C. S. Holling, and S. Light (eds.), *Barriers and Bridges to the Renewal of Ecosystems and Institutions* (New York: Columbia University Press, 1995).

[60] H. Rosling, *Factfulness: Ten Reasons We're Wrong about the World – And Why Things Are Better than You Think* (New York: Flatiron Books, 2018).

[61] Ibid.

[62] Even in the wealthiest nations, environmental justice remains an aspirational goal for certain sectors of society such as Indigenous communities (J. Robison, B. Cosens, S. Jackson, K. Leonard, and D. McCool, "Indigenous Water Justice" (2018) 22 *Lewis and Clark Law Review* 873).

nation-states does not meet the goal of sustainable development, and also leaving aside the normative overlay on resilience made by those asking "resilience for whom?,"[63] is it possible to make the argument that the destabilizing effects of accelerating change render it no longer possible (if it ever was) to achieve sustainable development without attention to environmental justice? Possible answers to this question may be found by looking at the disparate impacts of change already occurring as a result of climate change.

Climate change is occurring overall at an intermediate rate of change,[64] but, once again, averages are misleading. The increase in atmospheric energy leading to climate change is already leading to greater extremes in the magnitude of both storms and drought.[65] When you add this to other factors of the twenty-first-century acceleration – consumption, population growth, globalization, and the digital revolution – the changes society must adapt to in order to achieve sustainable development are rapid.[66] This has given rise to the popular term "the great acceleration."[67] Vulnerability studies and the disaster relief literature are useful in considering the impact on marginalized sectors of society to the overall response to disturbance that unfolds rapidly.[68] This is an issue of adaptive capacity.

7.4.2 *Adaptive Capacity and Environmental Justice*

A static view of sustainable development will fail in the face of accelerating change. Resilience theory posits that complex social–ecological systems encountering change will evolve, adapt, and undergo nonlinear reorganization. A society undergoing rapid change will be slow to adapt from the top down whether through the incremental change of democratic societies or the response of totalitarian governments that operate at larger scales.[69] The feedbacks within an integrated social–ecological system are initially felt where change is occurring – that is at the local or bioregional scale. Thus, for the same reasons economic markets are faster to adapt than top-down planning, response to rapid change requires the capacity to act locally.

Social, or more specifically, governance adaptive capacity consists of two important components: the tools necessary to adapt and to navigate social–ecological regime shifts[70] (e.g. knowledge, authority to experiment including through adaptive management,[71] and financial

[63] Cote et al., note 4; Olsson et al., note 7.

[64] B. E. Jiménez Cisneros, T. Oki, N. W. Arnell, et al., "Freshwater Resources," in C. B. Field, V. R. Barros, D. J. Dokken, et al. (eds.), *Climate Change 2014: Impacts, Adaptation, and Vulnerability. Part A: Global and Sectoral Aspects. Contribution of Working Group II to the Fifth Assessment Report of the Intergovernmental Panel on Climate Change* (Cambridge: Cambridge University Press, 2014), p. 229.

[65] C. B. Field, V. R. Barros, D. J. Dokken, et al. (eds.), *Climate Change 2014: Impacts, Adaptation, and Vulnerability. Part A: Global and Sectoral Aspects. Contribution of Working Group II to the Fifth Assessment Report of the Intergovernmental Panel on Climate Change* (Cambridge: Cambridge University Press, 2014).

[66] Steffen et al. (2007 and 2011), note 50.

[67] See references in note 66; T. L. Friedman, *Thank You for Being Late: An Optimist's Guide to Thriving in the Age of Accelerations* (New York: Farrar, Straus and Giroux, 2016).

[68] See for example T. W. Collins and B. Bolin, "Characterizing Vulnerability to Water Scarcity: The Case of a Groundwater-Dependent, Rapidly Urbanizing Region" (2007) 7(4) *Environmental Hazards* 399–418; P. M. Kelly and W. N. Adger, "Theory and Practice in Assessing Vulnerability to Climate Change and Facilitating Adaptation" (2000) 47(4) *Climatic change* 325–352.

[69] See for example F. Ostroff, "Change Management in Government," May 2006, https://hbr.org/2006/05/change-management-in-government.

[70] Gunderson, note 4.

[71] R. K. Craig and J. B. Ruhl, "Designing Administrative Law for Adaptive Management" (2014) 67 *Vanderbilt Law Review* 1.

resources to invest in adaptation and transformation); and the rights and resources for effective citizen participation in decision-making.[72] Resilience theory predicts that change resulting from both environmental and social disturbance may play out in unexpected ways. This requires the tools, rights, and resources to provide an enhanced local capacity to adapt. Rapid response can occur through the cumulative effect of community and local action. For example, local farmers and irrigation cooperatives experience the immediate feedback from climate change and are best able to experiment with new crops and changes in timing of planting and irrigation.

Empirical evidence of the need to increase the capacity of marginalized communities has been documented through the work of rural agricultural extension researchers. Flora et al. developed the Community Capitals framework from empirical observations of the attributes of entrepreneurial communities.[73] The researchers observed "that the communities that were successful in supporting healthy sustainable community and economic development . . . paid attention to seven types of capital: natural, cultural, human, social, political, financial and built."[74] Emery and Flora found that, rather than the traditional development approach to investment in financial and built capital, communities that were able to sustain positive change invested initially in social capital (i.e. "the connections among people and organizations or the social 'glue' to make things, positive or negative, happen").[75] They found that the increase in leadership and interaction then led to increases in the other capitals, but was built on a base of social capital within the community (Emery and Flora refer to this as "spiraling up").[76] While external resources were ultimately accessed, this occurred as an exercise of political capital and thus was more likely to lead to additional resources than the one-time provision of development aid. These findings are consistent with the notion that managing resilience requires capacity building from the bottom up, but a gap remains in whether the social capital in these studies is equitably distributed and inclusive. Other studies have begun looking at this issue.

Building on the work of Flora et al., a case study in a watershed with legacy and ongoing impacts from heavy metal mining which has fallen disproportionately on rural low-income groups, researchers found that disparities in capacity had adverse impacts on access to and understanding of health information.[77] Importantly, even where efforts at communication were made, lack of capacity to take action prevented low-income communities from reducing exposure to toxic metals, reducing the capacity of their region in general.[78]

---

[72] G. T. Raadgever, E. Mostert, N. Kranz, E. Interwies, and J. G. Timmerman, "Assessing Management Regimes in Transboundary River Basins: Do They Support Adaptive Management?" (2008) 13 *Ecology and Society* 14; D. Huitema, E. Mostert, W. Egas, S. Moellenkamp, C. Pahl-Wostl, and R. Yalcin, "Adaptive Water Governance: Assessing the Institutional Prescriptions of Adaptive (Co-)Management from a Governance Perspective and Defining a Research Agenda" (2009) 14 *Ecology and Society* 26.

[73] C. B. Flora, M. Emery, S. Fey, and C. Bregendahl, "Community Capitals: A Tool for Evaluating Strategic Interventions and Projects," North Central Regional Center for Rural Development, Iowa State University, Ames, Iowa, 2005.

[74] C. Flora, J. Flora, and S. Fey, *Rural Communities: Legacy and Change* (2nd ed.) (Colorado: Westview Press, 2004); Flora et al., note 73.

[75] M. Emery and C. Flora, "Spiraling-Up: Mapping Community Transformation with Community Capitals Framework" (2006) 37 *Journal of the Community Development Society* 19 at 21.

[76] Ibid.

[77] C. Wardropper, C. Cooper, J. Langman, C. Vella, and D. Sarathchandra "Assessing Health Beliefs and Health Protective Behaviors in Mining-Impacted Communities" (June 2019) 6th Annual Mountain West (MW) Clinical & Translational Research Infrastructure Network (CTR-IN) Programmatic Meeting, Las Vegas, NV USA; see also, S. E. Austina, J. D. Forda, L. Berrang-Forda, R. Biesbroek, and N. A. Rossa "Enabling Local Public Health Adaptation to Climate Change" (2019) 220 *Social Science & Medicine* 236–244.

[78] Austina et al., note 77.

Lebel et al.[79] demonstrate that accountable authorities who pursue equitable distribution of benefits enhance adaptive capacity by empowering socially vulnerable groups. They found that in the Malinau District, formed in East Kalimantan, Indonesia to decentralize forestry and mining concessions and reverse the flow of benefits away from local communities, "the absence of direct elections, deliberative public meetings, and an independent press," significantly reduced the accountability of the local district and had destabilizing effects.[80] Recent efforts to build local capacity have begun to reduce these effects.[81]

Lebel et al.[82] also found support for the proposition that protecting rights and pursing justice for ethnic minorities are key actions in building the capacity to manage resilience. The recognition of hunting rights to caribou for the Chisasibi First Nation of Cree, Quebec, Canada resulted in development of the Chisasibi Cree Trappers Association that now manages the caribou hunt pursuant to the James Bay Agreement with the federal government of Canada. The result is that the decline of caribou has reversed.[83] Similarly, Indigenous capacity building following the recognition of fishing rights has played a major role in the increased numbers of Columbia River salmon[84] and has been a significant factor in the US commitment to place a greater emphasis on ecosystem functions in renegotiation of the Columbia River Treaty.[85]

Lebel et al. found remarkably little reporting on gender issues in the case studies reviewed. The INGENAES Project (Integrating Gender and Nutrition within Agricultural Extension Services) undertaken with multiple partners with the University of Illinois Urbana-Champaign and under the auspices of USAID's Feed the Future initiative[86] was aimed at reducing gender inequity as a means of achieving development goals. Preliminary results from an INGENEAS project in Liberia suggest that women play a large role in smallholder farm management and their empowerment is essential to achieving sustainable livelihoods.[87]

Not only does empowerment reduce dependency, but it also brings the detection and understanding of local environmental change to the fore. Only through local capacity building of all communities, including those marginalized, will the response to disturbance be both swift enough and sufficiently tailored to meet the complex ways in which resilience theory posits that change will unfold. Managing uncertain and nonlinear change requires local innovation supported and guided by higher levels of governance that assist in building adaptive capacity.

7.4.3 *Adaptive Governance*

While the intergenerational aspect of sustainable development contemplates a check on the type of development that occurs by seeking development that does not reduce the options of future

---

[79] Lebel et al., note 55.

[80] Ibid.

[81] Ibid.

[82] Ibid.

[83] Ibid.

[84] Cosens and Fremier, note 30.

[85] "U.S. Entity Regional Recommendation for the Future of the Columbia River Treaty after 2024," Dec. 13, 2013; B. Cosens, "The Columbia River Treaty: An Opportunity for Modernization of Basin Governance" (2016) 27 *Colorado Natural Resources, Energy & Environmental Law Review* 1.

[86] U.S. Government, Global Hunger and Food Security Initiative: Feed the Future, "INGENEAS: Integrating Gender and Nutrition within Agricultural Extension Services," www.agrilinks.org/activities/ingenaes-integrat ing-gender-and-nutrition-within-agricultural-extension-services.

[87] R. Witinok-Huber and C. Nyaplue-Daywhea "Enhancement of Rural–Urban Linkages and Gender Equity through Agricultural Extension and Advisory Services to Liberian Smallholder Farmers," in L. Vasseur (ed.), *Ecosystem Governance and Urban & Rural Linkages* (Gland, Switzerland: IUCN Publication, 2020 in press).

generations, it does not provide guidance on how to make the necessary tradeoffs to achieve this goal. While balancing the economic and environmental prongs of sustainable development can provide broad general guidelines, it is the social pillar that explores the question of: Development for whom? Top-down processes, whether democratic or totalitarian, seem to be driven at times by science – that is quantifiable metrics and optimization for specified goals – and at times by influence – that is what sectors have the power to access and affect decision-making. Either way the resulting tradeoffs are unlikely to consider the needs of marginalized communities. In contrast, bottom-up processes catalyzed by both self-organization and governmental facilitation can serve to identify those tradeoffs that each sector of the society affected can live with. The solutions are often more nuanced and innovative than those imposed through top-down decision-making. As described in the following paragraphs, the bottom-up collaborative processes are observed to help build adaptive capacity, a key aspect of resilience, and they may help society navigate environmental change.

The emerging literature on adaptive governance as a form of governance that may be suited to the complex and nonlinear ways in which change will unfold – that is suited to managing resilience – is relevant in this context. In particular, the work that recognizes the differing roles of governmental and nongovernmental actors in adaptive governance[88] serves to inform this aspect of the relation between resilience and environmental justice. As a preliminary matter, some clarification on terminology is necessary.

Environmental governance is the means through which collective goals related to society's interaction with natural systems are chosen and implemented.[89] Adaptive governance is a form of environmental governance characterized by the emergence of collective action at the biophysical scale of a problem or disturbance, the capability to facilitate response to change and surprise, and the capacity to learn and evolve.[90] Dietz et al.[91] built on the work of coauthor Elinor Ostrom,[92] when they introduced the term adaptive governance. Their work documented community-scale self-organization to manage common pool resources. Adaptive governance is

[88] B. Cosens and L. Gunderson (eds.), *Practical Panarchy for Adaptive Water Governance: Linking Law to Social–Ecological Resilience* (New York: Springer, 2018); B. C. Chaffin, L. Gunderson, and B. Cosens, "Special Feature Practicing Panarchy: Assessing Legal Flexibility, Ecological Resilience, and Adaptive Governance in Regional Water Systems Experiencing Rapid Environmental Change" (2018) 23 *Ecology and Society* 4, www.ecologyandsociety.org/issues/view.php?sf=122.

[89] P. Rogers and A. W. Hall, "TEC Background Papers No. 7: Effective Water Governance," Global Water Partnership, Sweden, Feb. 2003; M. A. Delmas and O. R. Young (eds.), *Governance for the Environment: New Perspectives* (Cambridge: Cambridge University Press, 2009); UN System Task Team, "U.N. System Task Team on the Post-2015 UN Development Agenda: Governance and Development" (Mar. 2012), www.un.org/millenniumgoals/pdf/Think%20Pieces/7_governance.pdf.

[90] T. Dietz, E. Ostrom, and P. C. Stern, "The Struggle to Govern the Commons" (2003) 302 *Science* 1907; C. Folke, T. Hahn, P. Olsson, and J. Norberg, "Adaptive Governance of Social–Ecological Systems" (2005) 30 *Annual Review of Environment and Resources* 441; C. Pahl-Wostl, J. Sendzimir, P. Jeffrey, J. Aerts, G. Berkamp, and K. Cross, "Managing Change toward Adaptive Water Management through Social Learning" (2007) 12 *Ecology and Society* 30; B. C. Chaffin, H. Gosnell, and B. A. Cosens, "A Decade of Adaptive Governance Scholarship: Synthesis and Future Directions" (2014) 19 *Ecology and Society* 56; B. Cosens, L. Gunderson, and B. Chaffin, "The Adaptive Water Governance Project: Assessing Law, Resilience and Governance in Regional Socio-Ecological Water Systems Facing a Changing Climate" (2014) 51 *Idaho Law Review* 1; O. O. Green, A. S. Garmestani, C. R. Allen, et al., "Barriers and Bridges to the Integration of Social–Ecological Resilience and Law" (2015) 13 *Frontiers in Ecology and the Environment* 332; L. Schultz, C. Folke, H. Österblom, and P. Olsson, "Adaptive Governance, Ecosystem Management, and Natural Capital" (2015) 112 *Proceedings of the National Academy of Sciences* 7369.

[91] Dietz et al., note 90.

[92] Ostrom, note 25.

an alternative path[93] to Hardin's identification of property rights and government regulation for governance of the commons.[94] It is the form of governance considered essential to managing resilience.[95]

Initial literature on adaptive governance focused on its collaborative, bottom-up approach to environmental governance with primary focus on its ability to prevent overexploitation of resources.[96] However, the rise of legal and institutional research using resilience theory as a bridging concept has introduced the importance of "good governance" to provide legitimacy to any mode of governance that requires a high level of flexibility.[97]

Lebel et al.[98] proposed that adaptive governance would require certain attributes of good governance including participation and a just distribution of benefits, both components of environmental justice. They reason that participation builds trust and leads to the understanding necessary to mobilize as change occurs. They assert that a just distribution of benefits by accountable authorities increases the capacity of vulnerable communities, enhancing the ability to respond to change in society as a whole.

In addition to considering arguments as to why social justice may enhance the capacity of society to implement adaptive governance and thus navigate change, it is important to consider the literature that relies on normative values to argue it is the right thing to do. The broader governance literature uses the term "new governance" to capture the move to distributed governance that involves collaboration across governmental and nongovernmental sectors.[99] The increased complexity resulting from collaboration across governmental scales, across sectors, and between governmental and nongovernmental organizations has given rise to concerns about the "erosion of democratic process, entrenchment of local power elites, problems with accountability and legitimacy, and insufficient attention to public good outcomes."[100] Although this literature expressly turns to normative values to argue for processes that ensure legitimacy to avoid this erosion, it is also possible to reason that the erosion of these checks on corruption might be destabilizing, and thus reduce the adaptive capacity of society.

In a project co-led by the author focused on the role of law in facilitating adaptive governance to manage resilience in six North American water basins, the research team found that the absence of good governance principles as collaborative processes emerge could jeopardize their ultimate success.[101] In that study, good governance was defined to include participatory capacity (including access to information), legitimacy, accountability, transparency, a right to seek

---

93 Dietz et al., note 90.

94 G. Hardin, "The Tragedy of the Commons" (1968) 162 *Science* 3859.

95 Folke et al., note 90; Huitema et al., note 72; Chaffin et al., note 90.

96 Dietz et al., note 90.

97 Lebel et al., note 55; M. J. Lockwood, J. Davidson, A. Curtis, E. Stratford, and R. Griffith, "Governance Principles for Natural Resource Management" (2010) 23 *Society & Natural Resources* 986; B. Cosens, "Legitimacy, Adaptation, and Resilience in Ecosystem Management" (2013) 18 *Ecology and Society* 3.

98 Lebel et al., note 55.

99 M. Lee, "Conceptualizing the New Governance: A New Institution of Social Coordination," Institutional Analysis and Development Mini-Conference, Workshop in Political Theory and Policy Analysis, Indiana University, Bloomington, Indiana, USA, May 3–5, 2003; B. C. Karkkainen, "'New Governance' in Legal Thought and in the World: Some Splitting as Antidote to Overzealous Lumping" (2004) 89 *Minnesota Law Review* 471; Lockwood et al., note 97.

100 Lebel et al., note 55.

101 Cosens and Gunderson, note 88. The Adaptive Water Governance project resulting in this book was funded by the US National Socio-Environmental Synthesis Center (SESYNC) under funding from the US National Science Foundation, NSF DBI-1052875.

review, equity, and justice,[102] each of which is reflected in the procedural justice aspect of environmental justice.

7.5 DISCUSSION AND CONCLUSION

Achieving the goals of sustainable development at a time of accelerating change in ecosystems and the social systems that rely on them requires new approaches to understanding how complex systems respond to change and governance systems that act accordingly. As a theory of system properties, resilience theory is not a substitute for normative goals like sustainable development. Instead, it provides an understanding of complex systems that can help society achieve that goal. Resilience theory captures the behavior of complex systems, providing insights on the type of behavior social–ecological systems may experience with the intersections of climate change, increasing rates of consumption, population growth, globalization, and the digital revolution.

In exploring the relationship between resilience and sustainable development, this chapter specifically considered if resilience theory can inform whether just societies are more capable of navigating change. The short answer is yes. In particular, the critical balance between stability and flexibility in governance necessary to navigate change may be upset if attention is not paid to equity and justice. The rapid local response and innovation necessary to adapt as change accelerates requires adaptive capacity in all local communities and particularly those at the interface with agriculture and nature. The growing literature on adaptive governance, a form of new governance that arose out of the literature on resilience theory, provides both guidance on how to navigate change and support for the argument that participatory capacity (including access to information), legitimacy, accountability, transparency, the right to seek review, equity, and justice are key to its implementation. In short, the linkage between resilience and environmental justice informs the actions necessary to achieve the goal of sustainable development.

---

[102] B. Cosens, R. K. Craig, S. Hirsch, et al., "The Role of Law in Adaptive Governance" (2017) 22 *Ecology and Society* 30, table 1.

8

Environmental Justice and Sustainability

The United States Experience

Robin Morris Collin and Robert W. Collin

8.1 INTRODUCTION

Sustainable development recognizes that the environment is the foundation for all human well-being.[1] In the United States, environmental justice, environmental racism, and environmental equity are all terms that have been used to describe the social movement uniting low-income, African-American, Native American, Asian Pacific Islander, and Latino communities (environmental justice communities) in challenging the distribution of environmental burdens and benefits. Through the efforts of the environmental justice movement, the USA has been forced to address its history of racism and conquest – a history so toxic that it has left indelible marks on both the environment and people. That history is not over yet.

The present-day inequitable distribution of social and environmental burdens is the direct result of the preceding industrial, colonial age. Current social inequities in income, health, housing, transportation, and access to clean water and healthy food have their origins in deliberate political, economic, and social decision-making that treated both nature and environmental justice communities as sacrifice zones. Climate change, toxic wastes, and other environmental problems are caused by industrial policies prioritizing profits over ecosystems and over the well-being of people of color. These approaches to vulnerable communities and to nature have destabilized our environment and our communities. To restore the environment, the environmental movement must engage people of color, environmental justice communities, including women and Indigenous peoples, the nations of the Global South, and the poor; these are the peoples upon whom industrial production externalized its worst concentrations of pollution, toxins, and waste. Development cannot become sustainable without a commitment to restore and repair both the environment and vulnerable communities.

The chapter proceeds in three sections. Section 8.2 provides a chronological snapshot of some of the key events and foundational research that launched the US environmental justice movement. Section 8.3 discusses the root causes of these injustices and their legacy in landscapes and human bodies. Section 8.4 examines the relationship between environmental justice and the social pillar of sustainable development and argues that these can be achieved through the repair and restoration of the communities and ecosystems targeted for sacrifice and extinction.

---

[1] N. K. Dawe and K. L. Ryan, "The Faulty Three-Legged-Stool Model of Sustainable Development" (2003) 17 *Conservation Biology* 1458–1460.

8.2 THE STRUGGLE FOR ENVIRONMENTAL JUSTICE IN THE USA: COMMUNITY: RESISTANCE, FAILED JUDICIAL REMEDIES, FOUNDATIONAL RESEARCH

The US environmental justice movement arose from the resistance of communities disproportionately burdened by pollution and subjected to genocide, colonization, racial segregation, and discrimination as a matter of public policy and private practice. For most of its history, racial segregation and race-based discrimination was US law and became the national default custom in housing, education, employment, public accommodations, and criminal justice following a history of slavery and colonialist expansion.[2]

Racism shaped the places where people live, work, play, and worship, and all racial and cultural groups experience the resulting physical and psychological consequences. Racism transformed landscapes, polluted air and water, and affected all living forms. Cities became the loci of inequality; a place where the impacts of institutional racism in housing, education, employment, transportation, and environmental policy were more apparent.[3] However, non-urban environmental justice communities also suffered environmental injustice. Indigenous populations who bore the brunt of colonialism and genocide continue to suffer deadly environmental injustices and military-style assaults as they defend their land and water.[4]

In the USA, perhaps more so than anywhere else in the world, it is traditional to seek redress of wrongs through litigation. Regrettably, environmental justice communities have rarely found vindication in the courts for several reasons, including lack of adequate legal protections for disproportionately burdened communities under US antidiscrimination law and limited access to legal representation.[5] By contrast, mainstream environmental organizations (such as the Sierra Club and the Natural Resources Defense Council) have been able to make use of environmental statutes that permit citizen enforcement, such as the Clean Water Act and the Clean Air Act.[6] Furthermore, access to judicial forums is prohibitively expensive for poor communities, and the adversarial model of litigation focusing on two stakeholders, the plaintiff and the defendant, may be disadvantageous. Environmental justice disputes typically involve stakeholders from the community, government, and business. They are not necessarily locked into an adversarial posture, and these disputes may be amenable to collaborative solutions.[7] Finally, there is very little post-decision monitoring of environmental justice disputes as lawsuits

---

[2]   R. W. Collin and R. M. Collin, "Sustainability and Environmental Justice: Is the Future Clean and Black?" (2001) 31 *Environmental Law Reporter* 10968–10985 (brief history of US slavery and Jim Crow in a US environmental context).

[3]   R. W. Collin and R. A. Morris, "Racial Inequality in American Cities: An Interdisciplinary Critique" (1989) 11 *National Black Law Journal* 176–197 at 181 (discrimination in housing and its relationship to other urban problems); R. W. Collin and R. M. Collin, "Urban Environmentalism and Race," in J. M. Thomas and M. Ritzdorf (eds.), *Urban Planning and the African American Community: In the Shadows* (Thousand Oaks, CA: Sage, 1997), pp. 220–238 (racism in urban planning).

[4]   S. Work, "The Supply Side of Nuclear Energy," in R. M. Collin and R. W. Collin (eds.), *Energy Choice: How to Power the Future* (Oxford: Praeger Press, 2014) pp. 58, 62–78 (uranium mining and the Spokane Tribe's experience).

[5]   *Seif* v. *Chester Residents Concerned for Quality Living*, 524 US 974 (1998) (no right to private enforcement of Title VI of the Civil Rights Act of 1968) [*Seif*]; M. Burkett, "Climate Reparations" (2009) 10 *Melbourne Journal of International Law* 509; C. Gonzalez, "Environmental Racism, American Exceptionalism and Cold War Human Rights" (2017) 26 *Transnational Law & Contemporary Problems* 281, pp. 301–305.

[6]   Clean Air Act, 42 USC §§7401 and following, is the comprehensive federal statute that regulates air emissions from stationary and mobile sources. Clean Water Act, 33 USC §§1251 and following, is the federal statute that regulates discharges of pollutants into the waters of the United States.

[7]   E. Gauna, "The Environmental Justice Misfit: Public Participation and the Paradigm Paradox" (1998) 17 *Stanford Environmental Law Journal* 3.

tend to conclude with a new legal rule or with the award of damages. The failure to find an adequate remedy in the courts has forced environmental justice communities to mobilize protests of unequal environmental treatment.[8]

Studies by government, nonprofit organizations, and academics have validated claims about underlying racism and its consequences, providing the basis for organized resistance to environmental burdens, such as polluting facilities and abandoned hazardous waste sites. In addition to these studies, a variety of publications, including church bulletins, articles, books, and conference proceedings have given the movement greater visibility and power. By chronologically examining the role of protest, lawsuits, mobilization of community resistance, and important studies, this chapter traces the emergence of the environmental justice movement in the USA.

8.2.1 *No Home in Environmental Protection: Origins of the US Environmental Justice Movement*

The USA began formulating national environmental policy on a separate track and later in time than the civil rights movement of the 1960s.[9] The US Environmental Protection Agency (EPA) was established in 1970 and became the lead governmental agency on the environment. The EPA was unprepared to engage cities or address racial discrimination even though both were embedded in the fabric of the "environment."[10] Similarly, the civil rights movement did not address issues of urban environmentalism, even though these issues had occasionally been raised in the early formative years of the EPA.[11] The rise of community-right-to-know laws and the Toxics Release Inventory dramatically increased community awareness of the unequal distribution of environmental harms and their public health risks.[12] But these new environmental laws and policies did not protect environmental justice communities even as the risks became known.

Many of the early environmental justice protests that began the movement were over waste siting, transfer, treatment, and storage.[13] These issues persist in many environmental justice communities in the USA and globally. Extreme weather events will increase with climate change, spreading hazards that were once confined to environmental justice communities to the general population with disastrous consequences for all. As hurricanes, floods, droughts, and landslides increase both in intensity and frequency, exposure to wastes released by these disasters

[8] Ibid.

[9] B. Bryant and E. Hockman, "A Brief Comparison of the Civil Rights Movement and the Environmental Justice Movement," in D. N. Pellow and R. J. Brulle (eds.), *Power, Justice and the Environment* (Cambridge, MA: MIT Press, 2005), pp. 23–36.

[10] R. W. Collin, *The Environmental Protection Agency: Cleaning up America's Act* (Westport, CT: Greenwood Press, 2006).

[11] Bryant and Hockman, note 9, pp. 23–36.

[12] R. W. Collin and R. M. Collin, "Role of Communities in Environmental Decisions: Communities Speaking for Themselves" (1998) 13 *Journal of Environmental Law and Litigation* 37; Collin and Collin, note 2, p. 10971 (community right to know mechanisms in environmental law).

[13] In 1983, a congressionally authorized US General Accounting Office study, "Siting of Hazardous Waste Landfills and Their Correlations with Racial and Economic Status of Surrounding Communities," revealed that three out of four off-site, commercial hazardous wastes landfills in the southeastern USA were located within predominantly African-American communities, even though African Americans made up only one-fifth of the population (US General Accounting Office, "Siting of Hazardous Waste Landfills and Their Correlations with Racial and Economic Status of Surrounding Communities," GAO/RCED-83–168, June 1, 1983, p. 1). See also R. W. Collin, "Review of the Legal Literature on Environmental Racism, Environmental Equity and Environmental Justice" (1994) 9 *Journal of Environmental Law and Litigation* 121 at 128–130.

spreads hazards to people and the environment.[14] For example, flooding in areas with nuclear repositories or hog and chicken farms will compound the public health consequences of storms and hurricanes.

Environmental justice claims have rarely succeeded in the courts. An early environmental justice lawsuit was *Bean* v. *Southwestern Waste Management Corp.*[15] In that case, a solid waste facility was permitted close to an African-American high school and community. While holding that the community had established that siting was "illogical" and that the risk of irreparable harm had been proven, the court refused a remedy because it did not find that the defendant had acted with the requisite discriminatory intent. In most cases, plaintiffs must prove racial animus or discriminatory purpose in order to prevail in a race discrimination action, although the environmental statutes were previously thought to allow a remedy based upon disparate impact or disparate effects.[16] In *Bean*, and other cases, environmental justice communities confronted judicial unwillingness to find that standard of intent applied to their claims of environmental violations.[17] Trying to prove a corporation or municipality acted with animus or discriminatory purpose was made virtually impossible by judicial interpretation of the specific discriminatory intent requirement.

In the absence of judicial remedies, protests have played a major role in environmental justice struggles. A well-known example was the 1982 protest in Warren County, North Carolina, over a PCB (polychlorinated biphenyl) landfill in a majority African-American town. The waste dumped in this landfill was soil laced with PCBs from 200 miles of state highways. The state of North Carolina decided to deposit it in an area where the greatest concentration of African Americans lived, despite the fact that it was geologically unsafe due to sandy soils and a high water table. Several hundred protestors gathered including national civil rights activists, bringing national attention to this issue for the first time. Several hundred protestors were arrested. Protesters called for a study of environmental racism in the South, which the US General Accounting Office conducted one year later.[18] Decades later, after unrelenting struggle between the community and state and federal agencies, the landfill site was cleaned up in 2003.[19] This environmental justice struggle was an early demonstration of the power of racism in hazardous-waste-siting decisions, the long-term, continuous nature of the assault on communities, and the determination of environmental justice communities not to give up the fight.[20]

Indigenous people have always played a unique role in the environmental justice movement. Genocide of Indigenous peoples and relocation far from their ancestral lands was part of US territorial expansion. Tribes resisted this expansion, and continue to fiercely protect their sovereignty, their lands, and their culture.[21]

---

[14] M. Pelling, *The Vulnerability of Cities: Natural Disasters and Social Resilience* (London: Earthscan, 2003), p. 133 (health impacts of flooding).

[15] *Bean* v. *Southwestern Waste Management Corp*, 482 F. Supp. 673 (SD Tex. 1979), *aff'd without opinion*, 782 F. 2d 1038 (5th Cir. 1986) [*Bean*].

[16] Title VI of the Civil Rights Act as implemented in EPA regulations was thought to be a major exception to this rule; however, the US Supreme Court closed the door to private rights of action using this statute in *Seif*, note 5.

[17] See for example Collin, note 13, pp. 134–138.

[18] R. D. Bullard, "25th Anniversary of the Warren County PCB Landfill Protests," May 29, 2007, https://dissidentvoice.org/2007/05/25th-anniversary-of-the-warren-county-pcb-landfill-protests/.

[19] Ibid.

[20] K. Geiser and G. Waneck, "PCBs and Warren County," in R. D. Bullard (ed.), *Unequal Protection: Environmental Justice and Environmental Justice Communities* (San Francisco: Sierra Club Books, 1994), pp. 43–52.

[21] "The Alcatraz Proclamation," 1969, pp. 164–168; Southwest Organizing Project, "Letter to Big Ten Environmental Groups," Mar. 16, 1990, www.ejnet.org/ej/swop.pdf; T. Benally, "So a Lot of the Navajo

Indigenous communities have also felt pressure to accept hazardous wastes.[22] For example, in 1983, Yucca Mountain, Nevada was named as a potential site for a long-term nuclear waste repository. Yucca Mountain contains important traditional and cultural sites for many Indigenous peoples.[23] There were also concerns about radioactive contamination of drinking water given the area's dry, desert environment. In 1996, Yucca Mountain was found geologically unfit for hazardous waste storage and the project proponent was required to develop engineered barriers to keep the wastes separate from the water sources. However, concerns arose about whether the engineered barriers would be sufficient to prevent seepage and drinking-water contamination if an earthquake occurs in this seismically unstable area.[24] Many lawsuits have been filed in this longstanding environmental justice controversy.[25] In August 2013, a federal appeals court authorized the resumption of the licensing process for a nuclear waste storage facility on Yucca Mountain.[26] Even though the US government removed funding to the Yucca Mountain project, the possibility remains that it will be refunded in the future.[27] Currently, the USA has about 80,000 tons of nuclear waste sitting in about seventy above-ground sites around the country. Each year adds a further 2,000 tons. The pressure on environmental justice communities in the USA and globally to accept nuclear waste has increased and so has the community resistance.[28]

Native American lands have also been the site of illegal dumping from outside sources – a practice known as midnight dumping. The relationship of Indigenous people to their environment, their understanding and local knowledge, and their human rights are all violated when US environmental laws fail to address this dumping.[29]

Ladies Became Widows," in C. W. Wells (ed.), *Environmental Justice in Postwar America: A Documentary Reader* (Seattle: University of Washington Press, 2018), pp. 95–96.

[22] Work, note 4; J. T. Roberts and M. M. Toffolon-Weiss, "The Nation's First Major Environmental Justice Judgment: The LES Uranium Enrichment Facility," in *Chronicles from the Environmental Justice Frontline* (Cambridge: Cambridge University Press, 2001), pp. 63–100.

[23] I. Zabarte, "Tribal Concerns about the Yucca Mountain Repository: An Ethnographic Investigation of the Moapa Band of Paiutes and the Las Vegas Paiute Colony," prepared for the Clark County Department of Comprehensive Planning Nuclear Waste Division, Urban Environmental Research, LLC, Oct. 20, 2002, pp. 3–33 (Southern Paiute, Western Shoshone, and Owens Valley Paiute and Shoshone peoples assert historical, religious, and cultural interests in Yucca Mountain).

[24] G. Mone, "Scientists Voice Concerns about Yucca Mountain Repository," Apr. 26, 2002, www.scientificamerican.com/article/scientists-voice-concerns/; Nevada Attorney General Aaron Ford, "The Fight against Yucca Mountain," http://ag.nv.gov/Hot_Topics/Issue/Yucca/ (scientists joined by the Attorney General of Nevada have raised continuing concerns about the design strategy for protecting water from nuclear waste).

[25] "The Major Yucca Mountain Lawsuits," www.yuccamountain.org/court/case.htm.

[26] In a decision by now US Supreme Court Justice Brett Kavanaugh, US Court of Appeals for the District of Columbia Circuit voted 2–1 to force NRC "promptly" to continue the licensing process (*In Re: Aiken County, et al., Petitioners State of Nevada, Intervenor*, No. 11–1271 (Court of Appeals for the District of Columbia Circuit, Aug. 13, 2013)).

[27] In March 2019, Energy Secretary Rick Perry set aside $116 million to restart licensing hearings on a permanent nuclear waste repository at Yucca Mountain (D. Broze, "Yucca Mountain in Focus: Trump Is Trying to Revive the Yucca Mountain Nuclear Waste Site: Nuclear Waste Repository Opposed by Native Activists, Environmentalists," July 16, 2019, https://intercontinentalcry.org/trump-is-trying-to-revive-the-yucca-mountain-nuclear-waste-site/); S. Zhang, "The White House Revives a Controversial Plan for Nuclear Waste," Mar. 21, 2017, www.theatlantic.com/science/archive/2017/03/yucca-mountain-trump/519972/.

[28] O. Milman, "We're Not a Dump," Apr. 15, 2019, www.theguardian.com/us-news/2019/apr/15/were-not-a-dump-poor-alabama-towns-struggle-under-the-stench-of-toxic-landfills.

[29] R. A. Williams, Jr., "Large Binocular Telescopes, Red Squirrel Piñatas, and Apache Sacred Mountains: Decolonizing Environmental Law in a Multicultural World" (1994) 96 *West Virginia Law Review* 1133 at 1134 (discussing the siting of an astronomical observatory on a pristine mountain and environmental spirituality).

8.2.2 *Research Validation of Environmental Racism Claims*

Numerous studies have documented environmental racism and provided data to support community mobilization. In 1983, a congressionally authorized US General Accounting Office study revealed that three out of four off-site, commercial hazardous wastes landfills in the southeastern USA were located within predominantly African-American communities, even though African Americans made up only one-fifth of the entire population.[30] Subsequent studies revealed that industry specifically targeted communities that were least able to resist unwanted land uses. These environmental justice communities lacked the financial, scientific, and technical resources, the political connections, the information, and the opportunity to partici-pate in the governmental decision-making process regarding the siting of polluting facilities in their neighborhoods.[31] Industry specifically avoided more educated, affluent, and activist com-munities likely to contest these noxious land uses.[32]

In 1987, the United Church of Christ Commission for Racial Justice issued the first national study to correlate waste facilities and demographic characteristics.[33] Titled *Toxic Wastes and Race*, the study found that race was the most significant factor in determining where waste facilities were located to a 99.9 percent certainty. Among other findings, the study revealed that three of five African Americans and Hispanic Americans lived in communities with one or more uncontrolled hazardous waste sites as did half of Asian Pacific Islander Americans and Native Americans. A follow-up study in 1994 concluded that this trend had worsened.[34]

In 1990, a Greenpeace report on incinerator siting practices, *Playing with Fire*,[35] concluded that communities with existing incinerators had minority populations 89 percent higher than the national average, and communities with proposed incinerators had minority populations 60 percent higher than the national average. In 1992, a study by the *National Law Journal*, "Unequal Protection," uncovered significant disparities in the way the US EPA enforced its laws in environmental justice communities.[36] White communities saw faster action, better results, and the imposition of stiffer penalties on the perpetrators than African Americans, Latinos, and other minority communities.

In 2007, Robert D. Bullard et al., authored *Toxic Wastes and Race at Twenty: 1987–2007*.[37] The report concluded that people of color make up the majority of those living within 2 miles of a hazardous waste facility and about 66 percent of the people near clustered industrial and waste facilities. After reviewing many studies and new data, the authors concluded that the burdens of hazardous waste facilities continued to fall disproportionately on environmental justice

---

[30] USGAO, note 13; Collin, note 13.

[31] "Political Difficulties Facing Waste-to-Energy Conversion Plan Siting, 1984," in Wells, note 21, pp. 137–141; Cerrell Associates, Inc. and J. S. Powell, "Targeting 'Cerrell' Communities: Political Difficulties Facing Waste-to-Energy Conversion Plant Siting,"1984.

[32] See also R. W. Collin, "Environmental Challenges of Emerging Energy Choices," in R. M. Collin and R. W. Collin (eds.), *Energy Choices: How to Power the Future* (Oxford: Praeger, 2014), pp. 186–187.

[33] Commission for Racial Justice, United Church of Christ, "Toxic Wastes and Race in the United States: A National Report on the Racial and Socio-Economic Characteristics of Communities with Hazardous Waste Sites," 1987; Wells, note 21; R. D. Bullard, P. Mohai, R. Saha, and B. Wright, "Toxic Wastes and Race at Twenty 1987–2007," report prepared for the United Church of Christ Justice & Witness Ministries, Mar. 2007.

[34] Bullard et al., note 33.

[35] P. Costner and J. Thornton, *Playing with Fire: Hazardous Waste Incineration* (2nd ed.) (Washington, DC: Greenpeace USA, 1990).

[36] M. Lavelle and M. Coyle, "Unequal Protection: The Racial Divide in Environmental Law – A Special Investigation" (1992) 15(3) *National Law Journal* S1–S12.

[37] Bullard et al., note 33.

communities. This report fueled another generation of academic research and community mobilization.[38] Finally, in February 2018, a report issued by EPA confirmed that "a focus on poverty to the exclusion of race may be insufficient to meet the needs of all burdened populations."[39] The report concluded that people of color are more likely to live near polluters and to breathe polluted air, and that on all national, state, and county scales non-Whites tend to be burdened disproportionately as compared to Whites.[40]

8.2.3 *Challenging Environmental Racism*

As studies continued to document environmental racism, environmental justice communities were engaged in struggles all across the USA. In 1987, in Virginia, Residents Involved in Saving the Environment (RISE) protested the siting of a large regional landfill in a predominantly African-American community, and ultimately and unsuccessfully pursued a judicial remedy.[41] In 1988, two landmark events in New York and Louisiana took place; in New York City, the West Harlem Environmental Action group, actively opposed the city's North River Sewage Treatment Plant, and the Great Louisiana Toxics March went from Baton Rouge to New Orleans.[42] Environmental justice communities were becoming organized and mobilized around environmental injustices, strengthening the movement and facilitating its national presence.

Despite the overwhelming evidence of racially disproportionate exposure to environmental hazards, the mainstream environmental movement in the USA remained predominantly White, middle to upper-middle class, and did not embrace or support the growing environmental justice movement. In 1990, several environmental justice organizations sent scathing letters to the "Group of Ten" national environmental organizations, criticizing their monocultural perspective on environmentalism, their lack of racial and ethnic diversity in their membership, staffs and boards of directors, and their blindness to the plight of people of color struggling against environmental racism.[43]

In 1991, the First National People of Color Environmental Leadership Summit in Washington, DC brought together hundreds of environmental justice activists from around the USA and other countries to forge the "Principles of Environmental Justice."[44] One of the goals of the conference was to advocate for local and regional environmental activism in the form of regional and ethnic networks. After this foundational conference, many networks formed, including the Asian Pacific Environmental Network (1994), and the Southern Organizing Committee for Economic and Environmental Justice (1992).[45]

---

[38] Ibid.

[39] I. Mikati, A. F. Benson T. J. Lubn, J. D. Sacks, and J. Richmond-Bryant, "Disparities in Distribution of Particulate Matter Emission Sources by Race and Poverty Status" (2018) 108 *American Journal of Public Health* 480–485 at 485.

[40] Mikati et al., note 39.

[41] *RISE Inc v. Kay*, 768 F. Supp. 1141 (ED Va. 1991); R. W. Collin, "Environmental Equity: A Law and Planning Approach to Environmental Racism" (1992) 11 *Virginia Environmental Law Review* 493 at 527–546 (one of the first law review articles on environmental justice, the *RISE* case context). See also C. M. Kaiman, "Environmental Justice and Community-Based Reparations" (2016) 39(4) *Seattle University Law Review* 1327, at 1355.

[42] Bullard et al., note 33, p. 18.

[43] Southwest Organizing Project, "Letter to Big Ten Environmental Groups," in Wells note 21, pp. 164–168.

[44] Delegates to the First National People of Color Environmental Leadership Summit, "Principles of Environmental Justice," 1991, www.ejnet.org/ej/principles.html.

[45] R. D. Bullard, *Dumping in Dixie: Race, Class, and Environmental Quality* (2nd ed.) (Boulder, CO: Westview Press, 1994), p. 31.

In addition, in 1991, El Pueblo para Aire y Agua Limpio won a landmark case against Chemical Waste Management over a Kettleman City, California, incinerator that was proposed to be sited in a predominantly Latino community without providing Spanish translations of the key public documents.[46] The translation of documents and meetings is an important part of the procedural due process required to engage environmental justice communities. The court held that the environmental impact statement was inadequate in terms of the analysis of the impacts on air quality and crops and its analysis of alternatives to the proposed action (including alternative sites). While a significant victory for environmental justice communities, winning a procedural due process case does not ensure a just environmental result. Nevertheless, the plaintiff won a new process with translations into Spanish, but the ultimate decision remained unchanged. This case helped increase access by environmental justice communities to public participation processes.[47]

In the early 1990s Flint, Michigan, was facing a continuous barrage of polluting industrial facilities like many other environmental justice communities. Genesee Power Station Limited Partnership, incinerated wood waste to generate electricity for sale to the Power Company in Genesee County, Michigan. This facility released air pollution containing lead and other unknown chemicals into a community primarily comprising African-American and low-income people. This community was already home to three hazardous waste disposal facilities, two facilities that emit toxic air pollution, and three facilities that deal with multiple forms of toxic waste. In 1998, Michigan's Court of Appeal rejected a challenge to the permitting of the incinerator, concluding that the Michigan Department of Environmental Quality did not act with the requisite racially discriminatory intent when it issued a permit to Genesee Power.[48] Even though the community had gained access to major environmental decision-making processes, the road to substantive environmental justice was closed in court. On January 19, 2017, after multiple decades, the EPA concluded its investigation into the Genesee Power Station and found that race had been a factor in permitting the building of the incinerator.[49] While a step forward, this decision came far too late, as many people involved in the Genesee Power Station case had died and the issue of exposure to lead in Flint had arisen again. In the 1990s, it was lead in the air. Later, it had become lead in the water.[50]

The permitting process for polluting facilities became a battleground for the environmental justice movement during this period.[51] In 1996, Shintech, the largest producer of PVC (polyvinyl chloride) in the USA, announced it was seeking a permit to construct an $800 million polyvinyl chloride plant in Convent, Louisiana. The site where Shintech wanted to build the chemical manufacturing and on-site incinerator was a few hundred yards from the nearby African-American community of Romeville. Convent's population is 82 percent African American and 40 percent of the residents live at or below the poverty line. The area in Romeville nearest to the

---

[46] *El Pueblo para Aire y Agua Limpio v. County of Kings*, No. 366045 (Cal. Super. Ct. Dec. 30, 1991).
[47] L. W. Cole, "The Struggle of Kettleman City for Environmental Justice: Lessons for the Movement" (1995) 5 *Maryland Journal of Contemporary Legal Issues* 67 at 68–80 (discussing Kettleman City case).
[48] L. Kelly, "Environmental Justice Case Study: An Incinerator in Flint, Michigan," Dec. 8, 2000, http://umich .edu/~snre492/Jones/flint.htm.
[49] S. Yeo, "Environmental Racism in Flint Is Much Older than the Water Crisis," June 18, 2018, https://psmag .com/environment/flints-other-lead-crisis.
[50] NRDC, "Flint Water Crisis," www.nrdc.org/flint.
[51] R. W. Collin and R. M. Collin, "The Role of Communities in Environmental Decisions: Speaking for Themselves" (1998) 13 *Journal of Environmental Law and Litigation* 37 at 45–48 (environmental decision-making dynamics).

proposed site was 95 percent African American. The facility would be located less than 2 miles from an elementary school whose student population was 98 percent African American.[52]

Convent is in an area of Louisiana known as "Cancer Alley" because of its high levels of industrial pollution and high rates of cancer.[53] The Shintech plant would have been permitted to emit an additional 611,700 pounds of toxic air contaminants each year. Nearby communities already had been forced to sell their houses and relocate because of groundwater contamination and industrial pollution from the plants.[54] In 1998, the Shintech permit was defeated, not by litigation, but instead through the combined efforts of local, state, and national environmental justice groups and organizations. For example, local opponents to the Shintech plant organized coalition groups, such as the St. James Citizens for Jobs and the Environment, to educate the community, lawmakers, and the nation about the impact and implication of allowing the Shintech plant. In addition, the coalition groups were able to receive endorsement from national players, such as the EPA, through filing complaints and petitions alongside a local law clinic and environmental groups.[55]

Environmental injustice is not confined to the US mainland. The small island of Vieques lies off the coast of Puerto Rico, a US territory. Until 2003, the US Navy used the island as a bombing range.[56] It became a toxic waste site littered with exploded and unexploded ordnance.[57] On April 19, 1999 Navy bombs hit nearby civilians, killing David Sanes-Rodríguez, and Vieques became the site of continued community protests.[58] By 2000, several groups of protestors were established on the island and more than 200 of these protestors were forcibly removed by the military.[59] In February 2000, more than 150,000 people participated in the Peace for Vieques March in San Juan, the capitol of Puerto Rico.[60] Although the bombing stopped the environmental burdens did not. In 2005, Vieques was added to the US Superfund list, which allocates funds for cleanup of the nation's most polluted sites.[61] There are still dangerous amounts of hazardous and nonhazardous wastes in Vieques making it unsuitable for human habitation or economic development.[62]

---

[52] Roberts and Toffolon-Weiss, note 22, pp. 101–136.

[53] O. Laughland and J. Lartey, "Cancer Town: Rev William Barber Challenges Presidential Hopefuls to Visit," July 28, 2019, www.theguardian.com/us-news/2019/jul/27/cancer-town-rev-william-barber-democrats-president. These cancer clusters have been confirmed by epidemiologists (S. P. Tsai, K. M. Cardarelli, J. K. Wendt, and A. E. Fraser, "Mortality Patterns among Residents in Louisiana's Industrial Corridor, USA, 1970–99" (2004) 61 *Occupational and Environmental Medicine* 295–304).

[54] Timmons and Toffolon-Weiss, note 52.

[55] But Shintech did site its factory in a nearby community close to Convent further contributing to the industrial pollution of Cancer Alley (R. I. Hines, "African Americans' Struggle for Environmental Justice and the Case of the Shintech Plant: Lessons Learned from a War Waged" (2001) 31 *Journal of Black Studies* 777–789 (history and environmental justice analysis of the Shintech case)).

[56] R. O'Rourke, "Vieques, Puerto Rico Naval Training Range: Background and Issues for Congress," 2001, www.history.navy.mil/research/library/online-reading-room/title-list-alphabetically/v/vieques-puerto-rico-naval-training-range.html.

[57] US Environmental Protection Agency, National Center for Environmental Research, "Addressing Environmental Concerns in Vieques, Puerto Rico through Community Participatory Research," www.epa.gov/research-grants/addressing-environmental-concerns-vieques-puerto-rico-through-community#Background.

[58] O'Rourke, note 56.

[59] Ibid.

[60] J. Marino, "Puerto Ricans March against US Pact," Feb. 22, 2000, www.washingtonpost.com/wp-srv/WPcap/2000-02/22/069r-022200-idx.html?noredirect=on.

[61] K. T. McCaffrey, "The Struggle for Environmental Justice in Vieques, Puerto Rico," in D. V. Carruthers (ed.), *Environmental Justice in Latin America: Problems, Promise, and Practice* (Cambridge, MA: MIT Press, 2008).

[62] US EPA, note 57.

US military presence on the Vieques island has left Puerto Rico with a major toxic cleanup and public health concerns. The cancer rate in Vieques is about 27 percent higher than the main island.[63] Hair samples studies from residents show toxic levels of arsenic, mercury, and lead, among many other heavy metals (66%, 38%, and 55% above reference level, respectively).[64]. The USA has removed more than 16.5 million pounds of munitions so far, and the cleanup is expected to take until 2025 and cost about $350 million.[65] However, this timeline and cost estimate was developed before the impacts of several major hurricanes. These severe weather events may have spread ecologically destructive wastes across a broader geographic area.[66] A recent amendment, presented by Rep. Alexandria Ocasio-Cortez, D-NY, has approved $10 million to be used for closed detonation chambers to continue the cleanup effort in Vieques.[67]

In 2002, the Second People of Color Environmental Leadership Summit convened in Washington, DC where "Principles of Working Together" was developed.[68] One of the goals of this conference was to advocate for national environmental activism in the form of a national environment justice movement.[69] This summit produced one of the earliest commissioned resource papers proposing environmental reparations to environmental justice communities.[70]

Climate change is an increasingly important environmental justice issue. When Hurricane Katrina hit the US Gulf Coast on August 29, 2005 it was one of the deadliest hurricanes ever to make landfall on the US mainland.[71] Its devastation revealed how the history of racial discrimination in the provision of municipal services cost lives at previously unthinkable levels in the USA. The same situation exists in many US cities. US audiences watched while people pleaded for help on roof tops and in the New Orleans Superdome. An estimated 1,833 people died, and a significant part of New Orleans was destroyed.[72]

The aftermath of Hurricane Katrina also drew attention to some of the broader social and environmental impacts of racially discriminatory environmental decision-making. As flooding

[63] N. R. Figueroa, E. Suarez, T. DE La Torre, M. Torres, and J. Perez, "Incidencia Y Mortalidad De Cancer En Vieques 1990–2004," Centro Comprensivo de Cancer, Nov. 25, 2009.

[64] US Department of Health and Human Services, Agency for Toxic Substances and Disease Registry, Division of Community Health Investigation, "An Evaluation of Environmental, Biological, and Health Data from the Island of Vieques, Puerto Rico," Mar. 19, 2013, p. 88.

[65] B. Fox, "US Rattles Puerto Rico with Bomb Site Cleanup Plan," Nov. 11, 2012, www.cnbc.com/id/100139768.

[66] U. Irfan, "Puerto Rico Is Slipping into an Environmental Crisis," Oct. 26, 2017, www.vox.com/energy-and-environment/2017/10/26/16523868/toxic-waste-hurricane-maria-epa-superfund-puerto-rico (hurricane damage included seeping Superfund sites, and leaking landfills).

[67] N. Acevedo, "AOC Proposal Calls for Environmentally Safer Military Cleanup Efforts in Vieques, Puerto Rico," July 12, 2019, www.nbcnews.com/news/latino/aoc-proposal-calls-environmentally-safer-military-cleanup-efforts-vieques-puerto-n1029351.

[68] People of Color Environmental Justice, "Principles of Working Together," Oct. 27, 1991.

[69] The National Environmental Justice Advisory Council (NEJAC) is a federal advisory committee to EPA. It was established to advise EPA about issues related to environmental justice. The Council involves stakeholders from all interests involved in the environmental justice dialogue (US Environmental Protection Agency, National Environmental Justice Advisory Council, www.epa.gov/environmentaljustice/national-environmental-justice-advisory-council).

[70] R. W. Collin and R. M. Collin, "Environmental Reparations for Sustainability and Justice," Second National People of Colour Environmental Leadership Summit, Resource Paper Series, Oct. 23, 2002; R. W. Collin and R. M. Collin, "Environmental Reparations," in R. D. Bullard (ed.), *The Quest for Environmental Justice: Human Rights and the Politics of Pollution* (San Francisco: Sierra Club Books, 2005), pp. 209–221.

[71] "Hurricane Katrina," www.sciencedaily.com/terms/hurricane_katrina.htm.

[72] L. Murray, "Hurricane Katrina," www.britannica.com/event/Hurricane-Katrina (overall death toll is debated because numbers may not include all states affected, and deaths causally related may not have happened immediately. Ultimately, the storm caused more than $160 billion in damage, and the population of New Orleans fell by 29 percent between the fall of 2005 and 2011).

from Hurricane Katrina inundated the industrial corridor known as "Cancer Alley," toxic and hazardous wastes and materials were released, spreading far beyond the places where they had been sighted in environmental justice communities. Hurricane Katrina also introduced the term "environmental refugees" to the USA, meaning people displaced by, inter alia, a severe weather event who cannot go back home and who have no other place to go. In Louisiana, these were primarily people of color and low-income people.[73]

Climate change is also having a significant impact on Native American subsistence-based communities. As land-connected sea ice in the Arctic forms later in the fall and melts earlier in the spring, coastal erosion is accelerating, and hunting and fishing on increasingly thin ice is becoming more and more dangerous.[74] One severely impacted community is the Native Village of Kivalina. Kivalina, a very small island, lies between the Chukchi Sea and Kivalina Lagoon in northeastern Alaska. It is 10 feet above sea level its highest point. Concerned about severe coastal erosion, island residents first voted to move in 1992, locating a new place to call home in 1998. However, there was no way to relocate without substantial financial assistance. In 2007, the village was forced to temporarily evacuate. By 2010, villagers could not hunt on the thin ice, yet without assistance the community remains forced to stay on the island.[75] This community's tragedy illustrates a central characteristic of all environmental justice struggles: this community is suffering the burden of climate change while others have benefited enormously from the greenhouse gas emissions that contributed to the problem.[76] In February 2006, lawyers for the community sued the nation's top twenty-four greenhouse gas emitters and fossil fuel corporations, seeking damages and resources to move the village.[77] The case ended in 2013 when the US Supreme Court refused to review dismissals by the lower courts.[78]

Meanwhile environmental justice struggles continued to receive national and international media attention. In Flint, Michigan, in 2016, government officials knowingly exposed African-American and low-income residents to lead-contaminated drinking water.[79] Agency officials would eventually be charged with crimes including involuntary manslaughter.[80] The Dakota Access Pipeline controversy, described in detail in Elizabeth Kronk Warner's contribution to this volume, drew thousands of protesters, many of whom were subjected to pepper spray, rubber bullets, sound cannons, water hoses, and attack dogs.[81] Despite the protests and the

---

[73] Burkett, note 5, p. 539 (migration of communities due to severe weather events). It is important to note that climate refugees are not limited to those who are displaced due to severe weather events. Slow onset events like sea level rise can also give rise to climate refugees.

[74] Arctic Alien, "Thin Ice," Feb. 27, 2019, https://arcticalien.net/thin-ice/; C. Restino, "Opinion: Alaskans Are Proceeding on Thin Ice through a Changing Climate," Apr. 19, 2019, www.thearcticsounder.com/article/1916alaskans_are_proceeding_on_thin_ice_through_a.

[75] C. Shearer, *Kivalina: A Climate Change Story* (Chicago: Haymarket Books, 2011) (background of events).

[76] Burkett, note 5; Collin and Collin (2005), note 70, p. 217 (the case for environmental sustainability and justice reparations).

[77] *Native Village of Kivalina* v. *ExxonMobil Corp.*, 696 F.3d 849 (9th Cir. 2012), *cert. denied*, 569 US 1000 (2013).

[78] Ibid.

[79] On March 23, 2016, the *New York Times* reported that the water crisis in Flint, Michigan was a case of environmental injustice (J. Bosman, "Flint Water Crisis Inquiry Finds State Ignored Warning Signs") www.nytimes.com/2016/03/24/us/flint-water-crisis.html.

[80] S. Atkinson and M. Davey, "5 Charged with Involuntary Manslaughter in Flint Water Crisis," June 14, 2017, www.nytimes.com/2017/06/14/us/flint-water-crisis-manslaughter.html.

[81] See Chapter 23 in this volume; D. Smith, "Native Americans Protesting Pipeline Attacked by Goon Squad Using Dogs and Pepper Spray," Sept. 4, 2016, https://jonathanturley.org/2016/09/04/native-americans-protesting-pipeline-attacked-with-dogs-and-pepper-spray/; "Dakota Access Pipeline Co. Attacks Native Americans with Dogs & Pepper Spray," Sept. 6, 2016, www.democracynow.org/2016/9/6/full_exclusive_report_dakota_access_pipeline.

litigation,[82] the crude oil pipeline was ultimately constructed.[83] Finally, the US government's inadequate response when Hurricane Maria hit Puerto Rico in September 2017 left thousands of people without electricity, healthcare, and access to safe drinking water, resulting in a death toll of approximately 2,975 people.[84]

8.3 FOLLOWING THE FOOTPRINTS OF SLAVERY AND CONQUEST: THE ROOT CAUSES OF ENVIRONMENTAL INJUSTICE

The environmental justice struggles described in the preceding section follow the footprints of racist social policies from North American slavery,[85] colonial expansion,[86] seizure of Mexican territory,[87] colonization of Puerto Rico,[88] the Virgin Islands,[89] and Guam,[90] to segregation and "Jim Crow Laws."[91] In the USA, these policies and their continuing effects are identifiable on a geographical map of isolated, exploited, economically starved, and vulnerable communities. For example, Indigenous communities were herded into reservation lands and separated from the landscapes and resources essential for subsistence, cultural, and spiritual practices.[92] Former slaves migrated to urban areas in search of opportunities for economic improvement and greater freedom, only to find a new world of laws and policies relegating them to segregated urban enclaves and denying them economic opportunities on the basis of race.[93] Mexican territories

---

[82] *Standing Rock Sioux Tribe* v. *Army Corps of Engineers*, Case, No. 1:16-cv-01534, (United States District Court for the District of Columbia, 07/27/16). A full list of court documents and proceedings may be viewed online at "Key Legal Documents," https://earthjustice.org/features/faq-standing-rock-litigation.

[83] B. A. McCown, "What Ever Happened to the Dakota Access Pipeline?" June 24, 2018, www.forbes.com/sites/brighammccown/2018/06/04/what-ever-happened-to-the-dakota-access-pipeline/#19d6f6454055. (DAPL has been quietly transferring crude oil from the Bakken fields in North Dakota at a rate of over 500,000 barrels per day.)

[84] Milken Institute of Public Health, George Washington University, "Ascertainment of the Estimated Excess Mortality from Hurricane María In Puerto Rico," in collaboration with University of Puerto Rico Graduate School of Public Health, Aug. 28, 2018 (the official death toll from Hurricane Maria was raised to 2,975 following the release of this report. The revised figure, which encompasses all Maria-related fatalities during the six months following the September 2017 storm, is more than 46 times higher than the previous official estimate of 64 and more than twice as high as the government's later, unofficial estimate of 1,400).

[85] See for example C. Merchant, "Shades of Darkness: Race and Environmental History" (2003) 8 *Environmental History* 380–394.

[86] See for example T. Mahmud, "Colonialism and Modern Constructions of Race: A Preliminary Inquiry" (1999) 53 *University of Miami Law Review* 1219.

[87] See for example J. F. Perea, "A Brief History of Race and the US–Mexican Border: Tracing the Trajectories of Conquest" (2003) 51 *UCLA Law Review* 283.

[88] See for example J. M. Atiles-Osoria, "Environmental Colonialism, Criminalization and Resistance: Puerto Rican Mobilizations for Environmental Justice in the 21st Century" (2014) 6 *Revista Crítica de Ciencias Sociais* 3–21.

[89] See for example M. F. Krigger and L. Roopnarine, "Race Relations in the US Virgin Islands: St. Thomas – A Centennial Perspective" (2017) 42 *Ethnic and Racial Studies* 2387.

[90] See for example J. Go, "'Racism' and Colonialism: Meanings of Difference and Ruling Practices in America's Pacific Empire" (2004) 27 *Qualitative Sociology* 35.

[91] "Jim Crow laws were a collection of state and local statutes that legalized racial segregation. Named after an insulting song lyric regarding African Americans, the laws – which existed for about 100 years, from the post-Civil War era until 1968 – were meant to return Southern states to an antebellum class structure by marginalizing black Americans. Black communities and individuals that attempted to defy Jim Crow laws often met with violence and death" (History.com Editors, "Jim Crow Laws," Mar. 13, 2019, www.history.com/topics/early-20th-century-us/jim-crow-laws).

[92] See for example M. L. Walls and L. B. Whitbeck, "The Intergenerational Effects of Relocation Policies on Indigenous Families" (2012) 33 *Journal of Family Issues* 1272–1293.

[93] R. Rothstein, *The Color of Law: A Forgotten History of How Our Government Segregated America* (New York: Liveright, 2017).

were seized, and laborers forced into agricultural itinerant livelihoods reminiscent of slavery, while policies and laws proclaimed the inevitable domination of North American land and its peoples by the White, Anglo-Saxon settlers.[94] Governmental policies that expressly embraced racism became accepted social norms – and not the other way around.[95]

Both nature and people (particularly Indigenous and enslaved people) were converted by industrialism and capitalism into profit-making commodities in the development of the New World. Colonialism, and its companion ideology of racial supremacy, provided moral cover for the predations on nature and people. As noted in *Moral Ground*, a work devoted to examining the philosophical basis for activism on behalf of nature:

> The systems we inherited were the products of empires political, military, and economic; empires with an agenda of conquest. In them, greed acquired the royal clothing of formal religion and the power of a gun. Armed and winged, greed marched mercilessly over the Earth and her people. Religion clad this army with vindication, not redemption. Winged like angels and armed like demons, greed became the organizing principle of our lives. Nature and poor people were trampled underfoot like the grass when elephants fight. We made systems that carved up people and land into commodities. We inherited systems from another age that poisoned the air, destroyed the cycles of temperature controls of the Earth, and sickened our children and elders. From transportation to agriculture, from housing to employment, we created systems that venerated greed without qualifications or limits. You will learn that greed and the systems modeled by greed never will restore what we have lost.[96]

In *The Color of Law*, Richard Rothstein documents how American cities using the power of municipalities over housing intentionally segregated American cities beginning in the 1920s shaping the conduct of banks, insurance and real estate agencies.[97] Public zoning and public service decisions placed the path of waste and pollution deliberately into these communities, already isolated by law and policy. Industrial and business decisions followed the footprints of these governmental policies, extracting resources without benefiting the communities dependent on those resources, and situating streams of pollution and waste where environmental justice communities lived, worked, played, and practiced spirituality. Business decisions about benefits and burdens of development discounted the value of lives in environmental justice communities, depositing the wastes and toxins of development into these enclaves, the bodies of the people who live there, and the children who grow there.

This pattern of business and governmental decision-making burdening environmental justice communities continues to the present.[98] The most pernicious legacy of this history remains in our land, air, water, and in the bodies of people most closely connected to the earth, including the inheritable genetic consequences of trauma to the land and cultures of environmental justice communities.

The field of epigenomics explores the ways in which social conditions may affect the way in which the cells of a human body use genes. While genes do not contain a specific racial identity, the way society has imposed conditions upon the lives and livelihoods of people can create a

---

[94] Perea, note 87.

[95] Rothstein, note 93.

[96] R. M. Collin, "Restoration and Redemption," in K. D. Moore and M. P. Nelson (eds.), *Moral Ground: Ethical Action for a Planet in Peril* (San Antonio, TX: Trinity University Press, 2010), pp. 84–85.

[97] Rothstein, note 93.

[98] Mikati et al., note 39. Researchers in the EPA's National Center for Environmental Assessment released a 2018 study finding "[A] focus on poverty to the exclusion of race may be insufficient to meet the needs of all burdened populations."

chemical basis for modifying DNA. In this sense, the epigenome is a multitude of chemical compounds that tell the genome what to do. These epigenomic compounds attach to DNA and modify them, by changing the way cells use DNA to assemble proteins that carry out functions in the body.[99] What is now clear from epigenetic study is that these compounds respond to social conditions and can be passed from one generation to future generations.[100] And what is also now clear is that the social conditions of slavery, conquest, and exploitation have left indelible markers on the bodies of people of color that are affecting contemporary and future generations.[101] These markers make populations of color sicker from diseases ranging from asthma, low birthweight babies, maternal mortality, diabetes, heart disease, and other lung conditions.[102]

Race is an iconic social construct that is deeply embedded in US history and in contemporary law, politics, and institutions. While race has no immutable genetic foundation, according to the Human Genome Project, US law and policies made fundamental distinctions based upon immutable labels often derived from disputed genealogies.[103] Understanding the power and the consequences of this social construct must continue, in order to understand the ways in which it expresses in contemporary life. These policies, their geographical consequences, and their physical consequences ensure that future generations will experience the harms from the original American legacy of conquest and exploitation.

8.4 ENVIRONMENTAL JUSTICE, SUSTAINABLE DEVELOPMENT, AND REPARATIONS

This section examines the role of the social pillar of sustainable development in forging solutions to environmental injustice in the USA. The traditional definition of sustainable development is development that meets the needs of present generations without compromising the ability of future generations to meet theirs.[104] This definition recognizes intergenerational equity as an essential constituent of sustainable development.[105] The goal of sustainability is to integrate and align human communities, and their economic activities within the natural systems that support them. As explained in the Copenhagen Declaration on Social Development:

> [E]conomic development, social development and environmental protection are interdependent and mutually reinforcing components of sustainable development, which is the framework for our efforts to achieve a higher quality of life for all people. Equitable social development that recognizes empowering of the poor to utilize environmental resources sustainably is a necessary foundation for sustainable development. We also recognize that broad-based and sustained

---

[99] National Institute of Health, US National Library of Medicine, Genetics Home Reference, "What Is Epigenetics?" https://ghr.nlm.nih.gov/primer/howgeneswork/epigenome; National Human Genome Research Institute, "Epigenomics Fact Sheet," www.genome.gov/about-genomics/fact-sheets/Epigenomics-Fact-Sheet#main-content.

[100] National Human Genome Research Institute, "Epigenomics," www.genome.gov/27532724/epigenomics-fact-sheet/National.

[101] I. Karpin, "Vulnerability and the Intergenerational Transmission of Psychological Harm" (2018) 67 *Emory Law Journal* 1115; S. Sullivan, "Inheriting Racist Disparities in Health Epigenetics and the Transgenerational Effects of White Racism" (2013) 1 *Critical Philosophy of Race* 190–218.

[102] S. H. Woolf, J. M. Buchanich, K. J. Bobby, E. B. Zimmerman, and S. M. Blackburn, "Changes in Midlife Death Rates across Racial and Ethnic Groups in the United States: Systematic Analysis of Vital Statistics" (2018) 362 *British Medical Journal* 3096.

[103] National Human Genome Research Institute, "Race," www.genome.gov/genetics-glossary/Race?id=171.

[104] UN General Assembly, *Report of the World Commission on Environment and Development: Our Common Future*, Aug. 4, 1987, UN Doc. A/42/427.

[105] Ibid.

economic growth in the context of sustainable development is necessary to sustain social development and social justice.[106]

The social pillar of sustainable development encompasses equity, social cohesion, economic growth, combating poverty, good governance, health, anti-corruption, and other goals.[107] In 2015, the United Nations member states adopted seventeen Sustainable Development Goals (SDGs) to implement its 2030 Agenda for Sustainable Development.[108] These goals address a variety of social concerns, including poverty, sanitation, climate action, peace and justice.

The SDGs promote environmental justice because they strive to remedy the primary social consequences of exploitive governmental and business policies and practices that condemn people of color to poverty, poor health, food and water insecurity, and lead to the collapse of ecosystems and livelihoods, and public health hazards. However, the SDGs neglect to evaluate the impacts on future generations of unfettered economic growth.[109] In order to avoid conflicts over access to water, energy, and food triggered by environmental depletion and pollution, it is necessary to emphasize the rights of future generations to healthy ecosystems.[110]

Sustainable development in environmental justice communities cannot be akin to disaster relief. Disaster relief addresses the immediate needs of contemporary generations without engaging the needs of future generations. Incorporating the intergenerational dimension of sustainable development requires greater attention to protecting and restoring natural ecosystems.

Sustainable development cannot be achieved without recognizing the primacy of a healthy environment as the foundation for economic and social development.[111] Both *Our Common Future* and *Toxic Wastes and Race* were published in 1987.[112] *Our Common Future* marked important linkage of development theory with healthy ecosystems. The *Toxic Wastes and Race* study documented environmental damage done to communities on account of racism. The fundamental connection between environmental justice communities and healthy ecosystems capable of satisfying basic human needs was severed by governmental policies and practices that recklessly exploited nature for profit.[113]

Neither disaster relief nor social welfare programs will provide the intergenerational restoration of nature that is required now. Sustainable development requires the restoration of nature in places and within communities that have been targeted for sacrifice and extinction. Take the example of access to clean water.[114] Water is essential for life. As populations increase and

---

[106] UN World Summit for Social Development, Copenhagen Declaration on Social Development, Mar. 14, 1995, UN Doc. A/CONF.166/9, para. 6.

[107] K. Murphy, "The Social Pillar of Sustainable Development: A Literature Review and Framework for Policy Analysis" (2012) 8 *Sustainability: Science, Practice, and Policy* 15–29 at 18 (a comprehensive review of European Union and United Nations sustainable development social policy).

[108] UN, "Sustainable Development Knowledge Platform," www.un.org/sustainabledevelopment/?ajaxCalendar=1&mo=7&yr=2016.

[109] Murphy, note 107, p. 22.

[110] Ibid., p. 25.

[111] Ibid., p. 20.

[112] UNGA, note 104; Bullard et al., note 33.

[113] Intergovernmental Panel on Climate Change predicts unavoidable climate disasters by 2040 (IPCC, "Summary for Policymakers," in V. Masson-Delmotte, P. Zhai, H. O. Pörtner, et al. (eds.), *Global Warming of 1.5 °C. An IPCC Special Report on the impacts of global warming of 1.5 °C above pre-industrial levels and related global greenhouse gas emission pathways, in the context of strengthening the global response to the threat of climate change, sustainable development, and efforts to eradicate poverty* (Geneva, Switzerland: World Meteorological Organization, 2018)).

[114] V. Shiva, *Water Wars: Privatization, Pollution, and Profit* (Cambridge, MA: South End Press, 2002), pp. 39–54 (climate change and impacts on water availability).

climate change and pollution limit access to clean water, water scarcity will degrade the quality of life of present and future generations, leading to conflicts and displacement. Reparations to water sources and communities dependent on them must be made to ensure both intragenerational and intergenerational equity.

Providing reparations for environmental harm is essential to the achievement of environmental justice. The US EPA Office of Environmental Justice promulgated its definition of environmental justice in 1998 as "fair treatment of people of all races, cultures, incomes, and education levels with respect to the development and enforcement of environmental laws, regulations, and policies. Fair treatment implies that no population should be forced to shoulder a disproportionate share of exposure to the negative effects of pollution due to lack of political or economic strength."[115] Robert Kuehn offered a four-part definition of environmental justice that consists of distributive, procedural, corrective, and social justice.[116]

The environmental justice movement has demanded the restoration of communities and repair of nature as a form of corrective justice.[117] Corrective justice entails the rectification of harm and the elimination of suffering. This requires that the wrongdoer pay the true and full costs of the wrongdoing to all victims and ensure that the harms caused by its activities will no longer be externalized onto the rest of society.

Restoration of nature in particular places and within certain communities is the equitable, intergenerational response needed to provide sustainable solutions for vulnerable communities. Environmental reparations for environmental justice communities provide a key link between environmental justice and sustainable development. Environmental reparations should be made explicitly to communities injured by governmental and industrial policies and practices described in the preceding sections so as to provide justice to present and future generations.[118]

The USA already has a land use mechanism that could be adapted to reparations in environmental justice communities to restore ecosystems and mitigate harms caused by industrial activities and by climate change.[119] Historic Preservation Districts use land use laws and processes to preserve historic areas registered on the US National Register of Historic Places. A local board oversees building changes within the districts. Similarly, environmental preservation boards comprised of community members and others could review land use practices within their district for their impacts on the environment. Baselines could be established, the environment could be monitored, mitigation plans could be implemented, and adaptation and restoration plans could be developed.[120] Consistent with procedural justice, such plans should be adopted with the participation of the affected environmental justice communities.

---

[115] US Environmental Protection Agency, "What Is Environmental Justice," www.epa.gov/environmentaljustice.
[116] R. R. Kuehn, "A Taxonomy of Environmental Justice" 30 *Environmental Law Reporter* 10681 (2000).
[117] Burkett, note 5, pp. 522–524 (reparations defined).
[118] Collin and Collin, "Environmental Reparations," note 70.
[119] R. M. Collin and R. W. Collin, "Waste and Race: An Introduction to Sustainability and Equity," in K. Benesch and K. Schmidt (eds.), *Space in America: Theory, History, Culture* (New York: Rodopi Press, 2005) p. 139, pp. 149–151 (environmental reparations); R. W. Collin and R. M. Collin, "Sustainable Development: Environmental Justice and Sustainability," in M. Redclift and D. Springett (eds.), *Routledge International Handbook of Sustainable Development* (London: Routledge, 2015), pp. 219–220 (environmental preservation districts).
[120] Kaiman, note 41, pp. 1368–1371 (community-based environmental reparations in practice, at 1372–1373); Commission to Study and Develop Reparation Proposals for African Americans Act, HR 40, 115th Cong. (1st Sess., 2017).

8.5 CONCLUSION

Race remains a major determining factor in business and government environmental decisions. As EPA recognized in its 2018 report on air pollution, an analysis of environmental injustice that focuses exclusively on poverty and disregards race will not be adequate to address the needs of environmentally burdened communities.[121] The effects of environmental injustice transcend human generations through the impacts on the human genome[122] and produce fundamental changes to the planet.[123]

Social justice efforts cannot remedy landscape and epigenetic harms without an explicit connection to nature. Linking reparations to ecosystems and communities provides the inter-generational and transformative development needed to achieve environmental justice. Such a reparative connection must be place-based and operate through the environmental justice communities that live and continue to struggle in specific landscapes and locations.

---

[121] Mikati et al., note 39; Collin and Collin, note 2, p. 10983 (why race matters to past, present, and future sustainability).

[122] Karpin, note 101; Sullivan, note 101.

[123] Woolf et al., note 102 (mortality in midlife in the USA has increased across racial–ethnic populations for a variety of conditions, especially in recent years, offsetting years of progress in lowering mortality rates. This reversal carries added consequences for racial groups with high baseline mortality rates, such as for non-Hispanic Blacks and non-Hispanic American Indians and Alaskan Natives. That death rates are increasing throughout the US population for dozens of conditions signals a systemic cause and warrants prompt action by policymakers to tackle the factors responsible for declining health in the USA).

PART II

Case Studies

Strategies, Challenges, and Vulnerable Groups

9

The Role of Public Interest Litigation in Realizing Environmental Justice in South Asia

Selected Cases as Guidance in Implementing Agenda 2030

Shyami Puvimanasinghe

9.1 INTRODUCTION

Alongside the evolution of the idea and principles of sustainable development in international law and policy from the 1980s to date,[1] judiciaries in some regions also engaged in defining sustainable development and designing tools to achieve it. In the process, they have clarified the linkages between economic, social, and environmental justice, and development. In South Asia, a vibrant body of jurisprudence evolved during this time, catalyzed by public interest litigation (PIL). PIL has become a viable medium to address the grievances of poor and marginalized communities.

This chapter will discuss selected jurisprudence of the apex courts in South Asia (in particular India, Pakistan, Nepal, Bangladesh, and with a particular focus on Sri Lanka).[2] It will illustrate how public interest lawsuits moved by civil society action combined with innovation by the legal profession, and a certain degree of judicial activism, have served to integrate human rights, environmental protection, and development issues on the ground. It will also discuss the right to development (RTD), and related jurisprudence in South Asia, arising mostly in response to discrimination and marginalization of vulnerable communities. The chapter will close with some conclusions on how jurisprudence on the RTD and on sustainable development has served to reconcile conflicting interests in the quest for justice – social, environmental, and developmental. The cases offer guidance in implementing the 2030 Agenda and the Sustainable Development Goals (SDGs).[3]

In the United States, where the discourse of environmental justice originated, it has been defined[4] as "the principle that all people and communities are entitled to equal protection of

The views expressed herein are those of the author and do not necessarily reflect the views of the United Nations.

[1] See S. Atapattu, "From 'Our Common Future' to Sustainable Development Goals: The Evolution of Sustainable Development under International Law" (2019) *Wisconsin International Law Journal.*

[2] For South Asia as a region, see South Asian Association for Regional Cooperation (SAARC), "Charter of the South Asian Association for Regional Cooperation," http://saarc-sec.org/saarc-charter/5/; SAARC, "Dhaka Declaration," Thirteenth SAARC Summit, Nov. 13, 2005, http://saarc-sec.org/uploads/digital_library_docu ment/13_-_Dhaka_-_13th_Summit_12–13_Nov_2005.pdf.

[3] UN General Assembly, *Transforming Our World: The 2030 Agenda for Sustainable Development,* Oct. 21, 2015, UN Doc. A/RES/70/1.

[4] R. D. Bullard, *Dumping in Dixie: Race, Class, and Environmental Quality* (Boulder, CO: Westview Press, 2000), cited in C. Gunaratne, "Using Constitutional Provisions to Advance Environmental Justice – Some Reflections on Sri Lanka" (2015)11 *Law, Environment and Development Journal* 1, 3.

environmental and public health laws and regulations." In the context of the developing world, this idea needs to transcend its conventional contours of poverty and race, pollution, and discrimination:

> While the validity of its original focus on pollution and discrimination is not disputed, in the context of the wider concerns of the development process in countries of the global South, the principle needs to be broadened beyond its limited boundaries . . . into one which defines development models founded on environmental and economic sustainability, social equity and human rights . . . The principle of environmental justice must therefore address the fundamental paradigms of development with particular emphasis on ensuring that the benefits as well as the brunt of the development process are shared equally for the greater good.[5]

Robert Kuehn's definition of environmental justice, comprising distributive justice, procedural justice, corrective justice, and social justice is of particular relevance here.[6] Respectively, these mean fair allocation of the benefits and burdens of natural resource exploitation among and within nations; open, informed, and inclusive decision-making processes; obligations to provide compensation for historic inequities and refrain from repeating the conduct that caused the harm; and the inextricable interlinkages of struggles for environmental, social, and economic justice.[7]

As has been noted, this broader perspective:

> enables the principle of environmental justice . . . to be also used as a tool for transformative change in developing countries . . . [It] should also encompass rights to sustainable development, to equal access to natural resources, and to freedom from poverty, hunger and deprivation. Importantly, it must also reinforce the capacity and autonomy of citizens to determine the sustainable use and protection of natural resources and the equitable sharing of such resources. Thus, procedural rights that empower peoples and communities also come within the ambit of the principle.[8]

The innately human and social elements of environmental justice and sustainable development give rise to intrinsic links with human rights, most notably the human RTD. Enshrined in the 1986 United Nations Declaration on the Right to Development,[9] "the right to development" is an essential, intertwined, yet inconspicuous part of the history of sustainable development, which includes economic and social justice. Its link to environmental justice and sustainable development was highlighted in the Rio Declaration on Environment and Development and the Vienna Declaration and Programme of Action, both of which declared that "the right to development must be fulfilled so as to equitably meet developmental and environmental needs of present and future generations."[10] The human RTD will be discussed in the following section.

9.2 THE RTD AND THE SOCIAL PILLAR OF SUSTAINABLE DEVELOPMENT

The right to development stands enunciated as an "inalienable human right" of all human beings and peoples everywhere. The UNDRD [United Nations Declaration on the Right to Development] enunciates

---

[5] Gunaratne, note 4.
[6] R. R. Kuehn, "A Taxonomy of Environmental Justice" (2000) 30 *Environmental Law Reporter* 10681.
[7] Ibid.
[8] Gunaratne, note 4.
[9] UN General Assembly, *Declaration on the Right to Development*, Dec. 4, 2015, UN Doc. A/RES/41/128.
[10] UN, *The Rio Declaration on Environment and Development*, June 3–14, 1992, UN Doc. A/CONF.151/26/ Annex.1, Principle 3; UN, Vienna Declaration and Programme of Action, June 25, 1993, UN Doc. A/CONF.157/24, Part I.

a human rights-based conception of human and social development; development being a process that ought to lead to the full realization of "all human rights and fundamental freedoms." This enunciation marks an epistemic break from the ideology of developmentalism, one that perfects the vision of top-down "development" process in which also the major costs of development stand assigned to the developees.[11]

The RTD evolved from a quest for global justice by developing countries. In 1966, Doudou Thiam, Foreign Minister of Senegal, referred to the "right to development" of the "Third World" at the UN General Assembly. He highlighted that the achievement of political and legal sovereignty by newly decolonized states did not resolve the growing economic imbalance between the developing and developed worlds.[12] Attempts to overcome global economic and power imbalances, including through a New International Economic Order,[13] saw progressive and incremental developments in the United Nations over two decades. In 1986, the General Assembly proclaimed that the RTD is "an inalienable human right by virtue of which every human person and all peoples are entitled to participate in, contribute to, and enjoy economic, social, cultural and political development, in which all human rights and fundamental freedoms can be fully realized."[14]

The UN Declaration on the Right to Development (DRTD) adopts a human and people-centered approach to development. It defines development as "a comprehensive economic, social, cultural and political process, which aims at the constant improvement of the well-being of the entire population and of all individuals on the basis of their active, free and meaningful participation in development and in the fair distribution of benefits resulting therefrom."[15] Justice and equity, fair distribution, and meaningful participation are core elements of the DRTD, and thus have the innate potential to advance social, developmental, and environmental justice. The RTD applies at both the national and international levels; mandating the integration of all human rights – civil, political, economic, social, and cultural – in the process of development.[16] It is an entitlement of both individuals and groups (including nations) and it calls for a balance between the interests of the collective and the individual for the enjoyment of the right.[17]

The RTD has since been repeatedly reaffirmed as a human right in international law and policy including in the 1992 Rio Declaration on Environment and Development;[18] the 1993 Vienna Declaration and Programme of Action;[19] and the contemporary development policy framework – notably, the 2030 Agenda and SDGs,[20] the Addis Ababa Action

---

[11] U. Baxi, *Human Rights in a Posthuman World: Critical Essays* (New Delhi: Oxford University Press, 2007), p. 132.

[12] UN General Assembly, *Official Records, 1414th Plenary Meeting, Twenty-first Session*, Sept. 23, 1966, UN Doc. A/PV.1414.

[13] See D. J. Whelan, "'Under the Aegis of Man": The Right to Development and the Origins of the New International Economic Order' (2015) 6 *Humanity: An International Journal of Human Rights, Humanitarianism, and Development* 93–108 at 93; G. A. Sanchez Moretti and S. Puvimanasinghe, "The Right to Development" (2018) *Max Planck Encyclopedia for Comparative Constitutional Law*.

[14] UNGA, note 9, Art. 1.

[15] Ibid., Preamble.

[16] See OHCHR, "Frequently Asked Questions on the Right to Development: Fact Sheet No. 37," 2016.

[17] Report of the Secretary-General, "Chapter 1: The Emergence of the Right to Development. Report of the Secretary-General," in OHCHR *Realizing the Right to Development: Essays in Commemoration of 25 Years of the United Nations Declaration on the Right to Development* (New York: United Nations, 2013), p. 11.

[18] UN, note 10.

[19] Ibid.

[20] UNGA, note 3.

Agenda,[21] the Paris Climate Agreement,[22] and the Sendai Framework for Disaster Risk Reduction of 2015.[23]

The 2030 Agenda with its seventeen universally applicable goals and 169 corresponding targets, as well as indicators, is grounded in international human rights standards,[24] and is "informed by" the DRTD.[25] This Declaration can potentially play a vital role in guiding the implementation of the Agenda, and in particular its social pillar, for several reasons. Among them, its call for an enabling environment for development and removal of obstacles to realizing the RTD and an "order," in which all human rights and fundamental freedoms can be advanced. The RTD addresses systemic and structural obstacles to development, including local and global inequalities and asymmetries, which comprise root causes of challenges to sustainable development. The DRTD highlights the obligation of states under the UN Charter to promote universal respect for and observance of human rights and fundamental freedoms for all without distinction of any kind, such as race, color, sex, language, religion, political or other opinion, national or social origin, property, birth, or other status.[26] It mandates elimination of massive and flagrant violations of human rights of peoples and individuals affected by situations, such as those resulting from colonialism, neocolonialism, apartheid, all forms of racism and racial discrimination, foreign domination and occupation, aggression and threats against national sovereignty, national unity and territorial integrity, and threats of war. These would also be obstacles to development, because development as defined by the Declaration, must advance human rights,[27] equality, and nondiscrimination. The DRTD requires equality of opportunity for both nations and individuals who make up nations.[28]

The RTD and all human rights, which shape the social pillar of sustainable development, must be integral in implementing the 2030 Agenda. They provide pathways to social justice and inter and intragenerational equity. Likewise, the SDGs provide an opportunity to galvanize global, regional, and local actions and resources to implement universal goals and targets that could contribute substantially to the promotion and implementation of the RTD[29] and all human rights. The intrinsic links between the RTD and the social pillar of sustainability and economic, social, and environmental justice, will be illustrated further in the following section.

9.3 PIL AND THE RTD

In this section, selected cases illustrate how courts have dealt with the intersection of the social pillar of sustainable development and economic, social, and environmental justice. The DRTD in its Article 8 mandates that appropriate economic and social reforms must be carried out with a view to eradicating social injustice. This provision, and the DRTD in its entirety, have powerful potential. In India, the RTD has been invoked to support the rights of women, children, persons

---

[21] UN General Assembly, *Addis Ababa Action Agenda of the Third Intentional Conference on Financing for Development*, July 27, 2015, UN Doc. A/Res/69/313.

[22] UNFCCC, Paris Agreement, Dec. 13, 2015, UN Doc. FCCC/CP/2015/10/Add.1.

[23] UN International Strategy for Disaster Reduction (UNISDR), "Sendai Framework for Disaster Risk Reduction 2015–2030," Mar. 18, 2015.

[24] UNGA, note 3, para. 10.

[25] Ibid.

[26] UNGA, note 9, Preamble.

[27] Ibid., Art. 5.

[28] Ibid., Preamble.

[29] F. Cheru, "Developing Countries and the Right to Development: A Retrospective and Prospective African View" (2016) 37 *Third World Quarterly* 1268 at 1279.

with disabilities, Dalits,[30] Adivasis,[31] and minorities including religious minorities, in the face of discrimination in education, labor, succession, land acquisition, and property, among other issues.[32] It has supported victims of discrimination, exclusion, and injustice. Indian courts of law have applied the RTD in relation to Constitutional Article 21 on the right to life, and the rights to property, shelter, and food, as well as to Articles 14, 15, and 16 on the rights to equality, equal status, and equal opportunity of minorities.[33] In *Madhu Kishwar* v. *State of Bihar*,[34] the defendant had excluded Adivasi women from inheriting property. The court called for an amendment of the discriminatory law to ensure that women have an active role in the development process, as required by DRTD Article 8.

In India, the RTD has been mentioned in twenty-nine Supreme Court judgments and seventy-seven High Court judgments between 1990 and 2015.[35] In 1992, Judges Kasliwal and Ramaswamy in *Peerless General Finance and Investment Company* v. *Reserve Bank of India*, speaking in the context of the right to life, stated that, "the right to development is one of the most important facets of basic human rights."[36] In *Murlidhar Dayandeo Kesekar* v. *Vishwanath Pandu Barde*,[37] Justice Ramaswamy cited various sources to illustrate the idea of justice with emphasis on the rights of the "less privileged," especially Dalits and Adivasis. He cited inter alia the Universal Declaration of Human Rights (Articles 1, 3, 17, 22, and 25); the DRTD, including its definition of development in the Preamble and Articles 1, 2, 3, 4, 8, and 10; and Articles 14, 15, 16, and 21 of the Indian Constitution (on the right to equality, nondiscrimination, and the right to life).

Justice Ramaswamy in *Mrs. Valsamma Paul* v. *Cochin University*,[38] opined that the RTD has become part of the Indian Constitution and is, thus, enforceable. He stated that section 2(d) of the Indian Protection of Human Rights Act (1993) defines human rights as "the rights relating to life, liberty, equality, and dignity of the individual guaranteed by the Constitution or embodied in the International Covenants and enforceable by courts in India" and thereby, "the principles embodied in the Covenant on the Elimination of the Discrimination against Women and the concomitant right to development became an integral part of the Constitution of India and the Human Rights Act and became enforceable."[39]

On the other hand, there have been cases which interpreted the RTD in favor of pure economic development. For example, in *Nand Kishore Gupta* v. *State of U.P.* concerning the building of the Yamuna Expressway between Greater Noida (close to Delhi) and Agra, the Supreme Court stated that "The scales of justice must tilt towards the right to development of the millions who will be benefited from the road and the development of the area, as against the human rights of 35 petitioners therein."[40] Economic justice trumped social and environmental justice.

---

[30] Means "oppressed." Also known as "untouchables." People of the lowest caste in India (https://en.oxforddictionaries.com/definition/dalit).

[31] Means "first inhabitants." Aboriginal tribal peoples in India before the second millennium BC and their descendants (https://en.oxforddictionaries.com/definition/Adivasi).

[32] "MANU/SC/0468/1996," cited in A. Wolf, "Juridification of the Right to Development in India" (2016) 49 *VRÜ Verfassung und Recht in Übersee* 175–192.

[33] Ibid., p. 191; Constitution of the Republic of India, Jan. 26, 1950 (as amended May 28, 2015).

[34] Ibid., p. 190.

[35] Ibid., p. 184.

[36] Ibid., p. 188.

[37] Ibid.

[38] Ibid., p. 189.

[39] Ibid.

[40] Ibid., p. 191.

The above cases illustrate how the RTD links the social pillar of sustainable development with economic, social, and environmental justice. It has been invoked to balance the scales of justice in favor of poor, excluded, and disempowered individuals and communities. It has also helped to guide decisions addressing dilemmas of development, environment, and human rights. Race and gender, class, poverty, and indigeneity, and other markers of identity intersect to produce economic, social, and environmental injustice. Most cases discussed in this chapter reflect issues which typically arise in postcolonial societies in the developing world, where the pursuit and possibilities of progress intertwine with histories and heritages of poverty and inequality, environmental degradation, and human rights challenges. Pathways to justice – economic, social, environmental, climate, intergenerational, as well as structural – must be pursued in parallel.

9.4 PIL AND ENVIRONMENTAL JUSTICE

Environmental justice is best implemented within a constitutional framework of human rights. Constitutional rights provide the substantive and procedural foundation to conceptualize and interpret this idea, to offer practical responses to immediate issues and to articulate paradigms of environmental protection and development processes. Environmental rights reflect the universality and indivisibility of human rights,[41] and can provide courts with the basis to substantiate the principle of environmental justice and realize its objectives.[42]

Sustainable development jurisprudence in South Asia[43] was born out of PIL which evolved in the aftermath of the Bhopal disaster of 1984. One of the worst industrial accidents in human history, 40 tons of the lethal gas methyl isocyanate leaked from a pesticide plant belonging to an Indian subsidiary of Union Carbide (a transnational cooperation based in the USA) in an area of widespread poverty. Although the ensuing case *In re Union Carbide Corp. Gas Plant Disaster*,[44] wherein the Indian government filed suit on behalf of the victims against the parent company in the USA for liability and compensation for thousands of deaths and personal injuries was settled out of court,[45] this case catalyzed PIL in the region. Earlier, PIL had begun to emerge as a tool in cases of social injustice, like bonded and child labor, and failures of public accountability. Poverty and vulnerability of the victims were common features of PIL suits. The realization of the total incapacity of the host state legal system to deal with the Bhopal disaster – including lack of legislation, enforcement capacity, and legal resources, led to the emergence of environmental laws and litigation in the ensuing years.[46]

In the Indian case of *Subhash Kumar v. Bihar and Others*,[47] the petitioner filed a PIL pleading infringement of the right to life arising from the pollution of the Bokaro River by the sludge discharged from the Tata Iron and Steel Company, alleged to have made the water unfit for drinking or irrigation. The court construed the right to life to include the right to enjoyment

---

[41] See D. R. Boyd, "The Constitutional Right to a Healthy Environment" (2012) 54 *Environment, Science and Policy for Sustainable Development* 3–15.

[42] See Gunaratne, note 4, p. 4.

[43] This section draws from S. Puvimanasinghe, "Towards a Jurisprudence of Sustainable Development in South Asia: Litigation in the Public Interest" (2009) 10 *Sustainable Development Law and Policy* 41–49; S. Atapattu and S. Puvimanasinghe, "Guidance from the Ground up: Lessons from South Asia for Realizing the Sustainable Development Goals," in W. Zhang (ed.), *The Right to Development and Sustainable Development* (Leiden: Brill, 2019), pp. 141–167.

[44] *In re Union Carbide Corp. Gas Plant Disaster*, 634 F. Supp. 842, 844 (SDNY 1986) (aff'd as modified); *In re Union Carbide Corp. Gas Plant Disaster*, 809 F.2d 195, 197 (2d Cir. 1987).

[45] *Union Carbide Corp. v. Union of India*, AIR 1990 SC 273.

[46] Puvimanasinghe, note 43, p. 41.

[47] *Subhash Kumar v. Bihar and Others*, AIR 1991 SC 420 (1991).

of pollution-free water and air. It stated that if anything endangers or impairs the quality of life, an affected person, or a genuinely interested person, can bring a public interest suit, which involves legal proceedings for vindication or enforcement of fundamental rights of a group or community unable to enforce its rights on account of incapacity, poverty, or ignorance of the law. PIL has taken diverse forms, including representative standing, where a concerned person or organization comes forward to espouse the cause of the underprivileged, and citizen standing, which enables any person to bring a suit as a matter of public interest, as a concerned member of the citizenry.[48] Given the dynamics that divide the social fabric in this region, it is in the interest of justice and equity that poor, illiterate, legally illiterate, minority, low-caste, and other vulnerable and marginalized persons and groups gain access to justice through expansive interpretations of standing doctrines.[49] The test for *locus standi* in these cases has, within limits, been liberalized from the need to be an aggrieved person, to simply being a person with a genuine and sufficient concern. Further, class actions allow one suit in the case of multiple plaintiffs and/or defendants.[50]

In *Municipal Council Ratlam v. Vardichand and Others*,[51] the Supreme Court extended the frontiers of public nuisance through innovative interpretation in light of India's constitutional embodiment of social justice and human rights. The facts arose from a "Third World Humanscape," where overpopulation, large-scale pollution, ill-planned urbanization, abject poverty, and dire need of basic amenities combined with official inaction and apathy to create a miserable predicament for slum and shanty dwellers.[52] The lower court had ordered the municipality to provide toilets, drainage facilities, and access to fresh water. Upholding the order, the Supreme Court said that the judiciary must be informed by the broader principle of access to justice, required by the conditions of developing countries and obligated by the Indian Constitution. Justice Krishna Iyer stated that the nature of the judicial process is not merely adjudicatory and that affirmative action to make the remedy effective is the essence of the right, which otherwise becomes sterile. In the face of extreme poverty and injustice, the court stressed the need for economic, social, and environmental justice.

In *Shehla Zia and Others v. WAPDA*,[53] Pakistan residents living close to a grid station had alleged that the electromagnetic field created by high-voltage transmission lines would pose a serious health hazard to local communities who would face a grave and unfair risk. The court held that the right to life included a right to a healthy environment, and an adequate standard of living. Noting that energy is essential for life, commerce, and industry, it found that a balance in the form of a policy of sustainable development was required. In *Bokhari v. Federation of Pakistan*[54] the court stated that PIL, as it had evolved in India and Pakistan, was useful because of the lived realities of poverty, illiteracy, and institutional fragility. In Pakistan, it had been used to address various issues ranging from environmental pollution to prevention of child exploitation.

In *Ashgar Leghari v. Federation of Pakistan*, a farmer filed a public interest suit alleging that the Pakistani government's inaction and delay in implementing the National Climate Change Policy and in addressing vulnerabilities associated with climate change violated fundamental

[48] Puvimanasinghe, note 43, p. 41.
[49] Ibid.
[50] Ibid.
[51] *Municipal Council Ratlam v. Vardichand and Others*, AIR 1980 SC 1622 (1980).
[52] Ibid., p. 5.
[53] *P.L.D.*, 1994 SC 693.
[54] *Dr. Amjad H. Bokhari v. Federation of Pakistan (Karachi Oil Spill Case)* (Constitutional Petition 45/2003).

constitutional rights to life and dignity. In September 2015, the Green Bench of the Lahore High Court in a lucid reference to environmental justice, declared:

> Climate Change is a defining challenge of our time and has led to dramatic alterations in our planet's climate system. For Pakistan, these climatic variations have primarily resulted in heavy floods and droughts, raising serious concerns regarding water and food security. On a legal and constitutional plane this is clarion call for the protection of fundamental rights of the citizens of Pakistan, in particular, the vulnerable and weak segments of the society who are unable to approach this Court.[55]

The court granted several time-bound remedial measures for implementation. In January 2018, the court noted that only 66 per cent of the priority actions from the Framework for Implementation of Climate Change Policy had been implemented.[56]

Bangladesh Environmental Lawyers Association v. *Secretary, Ministry of Environment and Forests*,[57] concerned the neglect, misuse, and lack of coordination by governmental authorities in relation to Sonadia Island off the coast of Bangladesh, a precious forest area and rich ecosystem. Authorities were said to be preparing for industrial activities which would destroy the environment and the natural habitat for fauna and flora and weaken natural disaster prevention benefits. Apart from injustice to present generations, including through lack of disaster risk reduction, this raises issues of environmental injustice to future generations and to nature itself. In *Bangladesh Environmental Lawyers Association* v. *Ministry of Shipping et al.*,[58] the Supreme Court ordered the closing of ship-breaking yards that were operating without environmental clearance. In these cases, social and environmental justice were sought for nature and present and future generations.[59]

In Nepal, over a twenty-year period, advocate Prakash Mani Sharma and the NGO Pro Public had pursued PIL to close a marble mine in the Godavari hills outside Kathmandu which is considered a "living museum" of cultural and biological significance but has been negatively impacted by mining operations.[60] In 2001, the Department of Mines and Geology had allowed the mining company to continue operations until 2021. In *Pro Public* v. *Godavari Marble Industries*,[61] Pro Public challenged the decision, asking the Supreme Court to cancel the permit. The court determined that the mining operations are inconsistent with constitutional rights to a healthy environment and to live with dignity, and national environmental protection laws. The court applied the principles of sustainable development, including: intergenerational equity and the precautionary principle; it also recognized the values of nature, ecosystems, and equilibrium; natural, religious, and cultural heritage; and the biological diversity of the life-giving Godavari hills. The court stated that although significant profit may accrue from development activities, nothing causing negative impact or destruction of nature can be allowed to continue. The Supreme Court quashed the Department's decision and directed the government to designate the area closed to mining and make recommendations to restore the area to its natural state.

---

[55] *Ashgar Leghari* v. *Federation of Pakistan*, WP No. 25501/2015.

[56] Ibid.

[57] *Bangladesh Environmental Lawyers Association* v. *Secretary, Ministry of Environment and Forests, and Others* (Writ Petition _/2009) (protection of the Pian, Dawki, and Dhala rivers for Jaflong and Bholaganj stone quarries) (original petition).

[58] *BELA* v. *Ministry of Shipping et al.*, WP 3916/2006 (*MT Alfaship Case*, orders dated May 2006).

[59] See also M. S. Karim, O. B. Vincents, and M. M. Rahim, "Legal Activism for Ensuring Environmental Justice" (2012) 7 *Asian Journal of Comparative Law*.

[60] *Pro Public* v. *Godavari Marble Industries*, 068–WO–0082 (Apr. 15, 2016).

[61] Ibid.

Sri Lanka also has a large body of jurisprudence that has interpreted and innovated constitutional rights and can guide further expansion into environmental justice. Despite limited fundamental rights provisions, its courts have creatively used them to develop case law which has defined social justice and human rights in the context of development and the environment. This has been facilitated by PIL and driven largely by nongovernmental organizations (NGOs).[62] In *Deshan Harinda (a minor) et al.* v. *Ceylon Electricity Board et al.*[63] a group of minor children filed a fundamental rights application alleging that the noise from a thermal power plant generator exceeded national noise standards and would cause hearing loss and other injuries. Children are highly vulnerable in this context, given the potential for long-term damage. This case illustrates the gravity of dangers posed to potential victims and communities who may have no redress. Standing was granted on the basis of a violation of their right to life although the Sri Lankan Constitution does not include this right. The case was settled with an *ex gratia* payment. In *Gunarathne* v. *Homagama Pradeshiya Sabha et al.*,[64] the court stated that: "Publicity, transparency and fairness are essential if the goal of sustainable development is to be achieved," referred to the salient elements of good governance intrinsic to sustainable development, and applied principles of natural justice. It found that the Central Environmental Authority and local authorities must notify the neighborhood and hear objections, as well as inform the industrialists and hear their views in deciding whether to issue an environmental protection license. It thus imported this requirement into the licensing process though the law was silent on the matter. It also required that agencies give reasons for their decisions and inform the parties of such reasons, thereby introducing elements of natural justice.

Tikiri Banda Bulankulama v. *Secretary, Ministry of Industrial Development*[65] concerned a joint venture agreement between the Sri Lankan government and the local subsidiary of a transnational corporation for the mining of phosphate in the North Central Province. The terms of the mineral investment agreement were highly beneficial to the company with little concern for human rights, environmental protection, and sustainable development, nor for Indigenous culture, history, religion, and value systems. It was the subject of a public interest suit by the local villagers (including rice and dairy farmers, owners of coconut land, and the incumbent of a Buddhist temple) at the Supreme Court. The power differentials between the parties in cases like this one are considerable – transnational corporations and their subsidiaries command substantial wealth and power vis-a-vis developing countries. Yet more vulnerable, local communities in these countries have little or no voice in the state-investor setting, calling for appropriate measures to redress the many imbalances.

The proposed project would have displaced over 2,600 families, consisting of around 12,000 persons. The Supreme Court found that at previous rates of extraction, there would perhaps be enough deposits for 1,000 years, but that the proposed agreement would lead to complete exhaustion of phosphate in around thirty years. Stating that fairness to all, including the people of Sri Lanka, was the basic yardstick in doing justice, the court held that there was an imminent infringement of the following constitutionally entrenched fundamental rights of the petitioners and all local residents: equality and equal protection of the law under Article 12(1); freedom to engage in any lawful occupation, trade, business, or enterprise under Article 14(1)(g); and

---

[62] Gunaratne, note 4, p. 4.

[63] *Kotte Kids Case* (1998) 5 *South Asian Environmental Law Reports* 116.

[64] *Gunaratne v. Homagama Pradeshiya Sabha and Others*, SLR – 11, vol. 2 of 1998 [1998] LKSC 35; (1998) 2 Sri LR 11 (Apr. 3, 1998).

[65] *Bulankulama and Others v. Secretary, Ministry of Industrial Development and Others*, 3 Sri LR 243 (June 2, 2000).

freedom of movement and of choosing a residence within Sri Lanka under Article 14(1)(h). The court cited sustainable development, intergenerational equity, and human development, and analyzed the agreement with reference to principles of international environmental law, including Principles 14 and 21 of the Stockholm Declaration[66] and Principles 1, 2, and 4 of the Rio Declaration.[67] The court stopped the project from proceeding unless and until legal requirements were followed, including the preparation of an environmental impact assessment (EIA). It found that the proposed project would harm health, safety, livelihoods, and cultural heritage. Cultural heritage, the court noted, was not renewable, nor were the historical and archaeological value and the ancient irrigation tanks that would be destroyed if the project proceeded as planned. Highlighting the social and environmental pillars, the decision emphasized that pure economic growth cannot measure human welfare, which goes beyond "rupees and cents."[68]

The notion of justice – environmental, inter, and intragenerational – is seminal to this case, which illustrates how environmental justice in Third World realities includes justice to nature and to future generations. In these societies, many interests must be balanced to achieve economic progress, deliver basic needs and human rights, especially economic and social rights in a climate-constrained world, and conserve the environment, which is the resource base for development – this requires a very delicate balance. The court drew on the international law of sustainable development, ancient wisdom, and the local history of conservation, sustainability, and human rights. The company's exemption from submitting its project to an EIA was held to be an imminent violation of the equal protection clause. Although the constitution provided only for civil and political rights to be justiciable, the court expanded it to include socio-economic rights. While natural resources were deemed to be held in guardianship and public trust by the government for the benefit of the people, the court emphasized the shared responsibility of all to protect them.[69]

Mundy v. Central Environmental Authority and Others[70] concerned appeals relating to the building of Sri Lanka's first modern highway, the Southern Expressway. Protracted litigation involved allegations of potential damage to human rights, including large-scale displacement and injury to the environment including sensitive ecosystems. The Court of Appeal had held that when balancing competing interests, the conclusion must favor the larger interests of the community, which would benefit immensely from the infrastructure project. Upon appeal by people who were losing their lands without compensation, the Supreme Court ordered compensation under the audi alteram principle of natural justice and Constitutional Article 12(1) on

---

[66] UN, Declaration of the United Nations Conference on the Human Environment, UN Doc. A/CONF.48/14/Rev.1, June 5–16, 1972, Principle 14 makes rational planning an essential tool in reconciling development and the environment; under Principle 21 states have the sovereign right to exploit their own resources pursuant to their own environmental policies, and the responsibility to ensure that activities within their jurisdiction or control do not cause damage to the environment of other states or of areas beyond the limits of national jurisdiction.

[67] UN, note 10, Principle 1 places human beings at the center of concerns for sustainable development; under Principle 2, states have the sovereign right to exploit their own resources pursuant to their own environmental and developmental policies, and the responsibility to ensure that activities within their jurisdiction or control do not cause damage to the environment of other states or of areas beyond the limits of national jurisdiction; Principle 4 makes environmental protection an integral part of the development process.

[68] *Bulankulama v. Min. of Industrial Development (Eppawala Case)*, SC Application No. 884/99 (FR). Despite an effort by a subsequent government to revive the project, so far, the project has not materialized. No EIA was ever prepared, per interview with Hemantha Withanage, Executive Director, Centre for Environmental Justice, Colombo.

[69] Ibid.

[70] *Mundy v. Central Environmental Authority and Others* (SC Appeal 58/2003) (decided Jan. 20, 2004).

equality and equal protection. In a remarkable pronouncement for social, environmental, and developmental justice, the court stated:

> If it is permissible in the exercise of a judicial discretion to require a humble villager to forego his right to a fair procedure before he is compelled to sacrifice a modest plot of land and a little hut because they are of "extremely negligible" value in relation to a multi-billion rupee national project, it is nevertheless not equitable to disregard totally the infringement of his rights: the smaller the value of his property, the greater his right to compensation.[71]

Environmental Foundation Ltd. v. *Urban Development Authority et al.*,[72] concerned the proposed leasing of the Galle Face Green, a popular seaside promenade in Colombo, by the Urban Development Authority to a private company to build a "mega leisure complex."[73] In a fundamental rights application, the Supreme Court upheld the argument of the petitioner NGO to preserve the island's national heritage for use of the public, not just for those who can afford the mega leisure facilities. It thereby favored social and environmental justice, protecting the public interest, because this concerned a public place which was open free of charge to all classes of society without distinction. It also found that there was an infringement of the right to information by reading the Constitutional Article 14(1), on the freedom of speech and expression, to encompass a right to information (which at that time, was not provided for in the Constitution). The court further held that the petitioner's rights to equality under Article 12 (1) had been infringed. Several later cases involved adverse impacts on nature and on local communities and their livelihoods which in turn, are a matter of survival (e.g. for local fishermen).[74]

In several Sri Lankan cases, the court highlighted the link between the RTD and good governance. *Dissanayaka* v. *Gamini Jayawickrema Perera* (*Thuruwila* case)[75] addressed the validity of the decision to transfer water from a tank to urban areas for urban use. The court found a lack of transparency in the decision-making process, and violations of Articles 12(1) (on equality) and 14(1)(g) (on the right to a livelihood) of the Constitution. It highlighted the need for participatory decision-making and the equitable sharing of resources, which are also key elements of the RTD. In *Watte Gedara Wijebanda* v. *Conservator General of Forests*,[76] the court observed that "government accountability is the corner stone of good governance." In *Mendis* v. *Kumaratunga*[77] it was found that a wetland acquired for a public purpose had been sold to a private entrepreneur to build a golf resort, in violation of Article 12(1). The court found an abuse of executive power and held that the public interest is of paramount importance. In upholding the public trust, the court meted out justice to the local community, rather than favoring a few who stood to benefit from the golf resort.

The Sri Lankan Supreme Court has interpreted fundamental rights provisions to redefine the idea of environmental justice. Likewise, litigation on environment and development has contributed to fundamental rights jurisprudence. Environmental justice has been premised on equality and nondiscrimination. Its evolution has been closely linked to the interpretation of Article 12, including nondiscrimination, equal protection of the law, and the principle of

---

[71] Ibid, p. 13.
[72] *Environmental Foundation Ltd.* v. *Urban Development Authority et al.*, 47/2004 (Nov. 28, 2005).
[73] Ibid.
[74] Also see *Kottabadu Durage Sriyani Silva* v. *Chanaka Iddamalgoda* (Sri Lanka, Aug. 8, 2003).
[75] *Dissanayaka* v. *Gamini Jayawickrema Perera* (*Thuruwila Case*) SC (FR) No. 329/2002.
[76] *Watte Gedara Wijebanda* v. *Conservator General of Forests* (2009) 1 SLR 337.
[77] *Mendis* v. *Kumaratunga* SC (FR) No. 352/2007.

arbitrary action. The Supreme Court has extended the application of environmental justice beyond the aggrieved parties before the court whose rights to environmental and social justice have been violated, to those of a community, public, or nation. It has been used to review the development model and processes.[78]

PIL has been useful in balancing development, environment, and human rights in the region and in providing relief to the poor and marginalized in society. As stated by Justice Matthew in *Kesavananda Bharthai* v. *State of Kerala*,[79] the scope of human rights is not static, and its contents must be guided by the experience and context of each generation. Conventional notions of justice have seen some extension in keeping with regional realities. Meaningful public participation, along the lines of the RTD's core principle of free, active, and meaningful participation – including giving voice to groups who are often not actively engaged in decision-making such as women,[80] youth,[81] children,[82] persons with disabilities,[83] minorities,[84] and Indigenous peoples[85] – is key to sustainable development. Participation and voice can empower the disempowered. Judicial measures in the region have inter alia liberalized *locus standi* to include any person genuinely concerned for the environment,[86] placed a public trust obligation on states over natural resources,[87] imposed absolute liability for accidents arising from ultra-hazardous activities,[88] applied international environmental law principles including the polluter-pays and precautionary principles,[89] and promoted good governance and sustainable development[90] reconciling and integrating its three pillars.

Following the Bhopal disaster and ensuing struggles for justice, including accountability and remedy to address adverse effects of economic activities, most states in South Asia invoked legislative, constitutional, and judicial mechanisms as strategies to reconcile human rights, environmental protection, and economic development.[91] The realities of poverty, underdevelopment, and environmental degradation coupled with the intersectionality of discrimination, including gender and race, make PIL a useful tool in addressing the root causes of injustice.

More recently, commentators have observed some retrogressive trends in judicial activism in the region.[92] They rightly point out that, ideally, solutions must rather lie in law and policy reform. It may be wiser, therefore, to avoid looking at judicial activism as a tool to promote

---

[78] Gunaratne, note 4, pp. 17–18.
[79] *Kesavananda Bharthai* v. *State of Kerala* AIR 1973 SC 1461.
[80] See F. Banda, "Women, Human Rights and Development," in OHCHR, note 17, pp. 149–158.
[81] OHCHR, "Information Note: The Right to Development, Children and Youth," Declaration on the Right to Development, www.ohchr.org/Documents/Issues/RtD/InfoNote_ChildrenYouth.pdf.
[82] Ibid.
[83] OHCHR, "Information Note: The Right to Development and Persons with Disabilities," Declaration on the Right to Development, www.ohchr.org/Documents/Issues/RtD/PersonsWithDisabilities.pdf.
[84] Wolf, note 32.
[85] OHCHR, "Information Note: The Right to Development and Indigenous Peoples," Declaration on the Right to Development, www.ohchr.org/Documents/Issues/RtD/RTD_IndigenousPeoples.pdf.
[86] See, for example, *M.C. Mehta* v. *Kamal Nath and Others* (1997) 1 SCC 388.
[87] Ibid.
[88] In the *Shriram Gasleak Case*, the ideas of cost internalization, polluter pays, and absolute liability long preceded the Rio Declaration. Another case in point is *Indian Council for Enviro-Legal Action* v. *Union of India and Others*, AIR. 1996 SC 1446.
[89] *Vellore Citizens' Welfare* v. *Union of India* (1996) 5 SCC 647.
[90] *Gunaratne* v. *Homagama Pradeshiya Sabha and Others*, note 64.
[91] C. G. Weeramantry, "Private International Law and Public International Law" (1998) 34 *Rivista di Diritto Internazionale Private e Processuale* 313 at 324.
[92] N. Kamaardeen, "The Honeymoon Is Over: An Assessment of Judicial Activism in Environmental Cases in Sri Lanka" (2015) 6 *Jindal Global Law Review* 73–91.

environmental rights and see it for what it probably really is: a reflection of a legal system that is tardy and lacks effective solutions. This would compel lawmakers to treat law reform as a serious subject that must be undertaken regularly, and not only when a crisis looms ahead. The evolution of the subject of environmental law, as well as the changes that are taking place in the global environment, mandate great changes in the near future. Lawmakers and policymakers would do well to comprehend this and prepare to take adequate measures to face these new challenges. The honeymoon of judicial activism is over: it is now time to face reality.[93]

At the same time, the cases spanning the region over recent decades still provide practical lessons for implementing the SDGs, especially their social and environmental pillars. They point to some good practices and success stories. In the absence of appropriate laws and policies, and/or their effective implementation, judicial intervention has served to scrutinize governmental and private sector activities and abate administrative apathy.[94] It addresses a lacuna in the law and policy domain, and when there is law and policy in place, can still continue to support their implementation and interpretation. Environmental laws are now in place in most of South Asia, including on EIAs, pollution control, and emissions standards.[95] However, these lay down procedures and technocratic solutions, rather than representing the bigger picture or the plight of marginalized communities. Environmental justice is part of these bigger challenges, and PIL can help to address them. The business and human rights movement may also potentially provide future solutions. The Guiding Principles on Business and Human Rights[96] invoke the state's duty to protect against human rights abuses by third parties, including business; the corporate responsibility to respect human rights, requiring business to act with due diligence; and the need for greater access to effective remedies. They support policy coherence between economic activities and human rights and have regional counterparts in South Asia.[97]

9.5 REFLECTIONS

Globally, progress on economic development has been uneven particularly for Africa, least developed countries, landlocked developing countries, and small island developing states,[98] and for developing countries more generally, including those in South Asia. Within countries, vulnerable and marginalized individuals and groups face discrimination and exclusion, often involving intersectionality of discrimination on multiple grounds. The DRTD and sustainable development provide an alternative paradigm in development thinking that places human rights including equality and nondiscrimination, at the center of national and international develop-ment,[99] strengthening the social pillar. The infusion of human rights values in the development process helps prevent or minimize negative externalities like environmental harm and

---

[93] Ibid, p. 91.

[94] For example, the *Ratlam* case in India (see Section 9.4).

[95] For example, the National Environmental Act No. 47 of 1980 as amended by Act No. 56 of 1988 in Sri Lanka (Puvimanasinghe, note 43, p. 49).

[96] OHCHR, *Report of the Special Representative of the Secretary General on the issue of human rights and transnational corporations and other business enterprises, John Ruggie: Guiding Principles on Business and Human Rights: Implementing the United Nations "Protect, Respect and Remedy" Framework*, Mar. 21, 2011, UN Doc. A/HRC/17/31.

[97] See for South Asia and ASEAN region, OHCHR, "2019 UN South Asia Forum on Business and Human Rights," Mar. 14–15, 2019, www.ohchr.org/EN/Issues/Business/Pages/SouthAsiaRegionalForum.aspx.

[98] UNGA, note 3, para. 16.

[99] B. Ibhawoh, "The Right to Development: The Politics and Polemics of Power and Resistance" (2011) 33 *Human Rights Quarterly* 76 at 103.

distributional inequalities, and promote economic, social, and environmental justice. The RTD, with human rights at its core, is essential for both social justice, a core component of environmental justice, and sustainable development, especially its social pillar. PIL in South Asia has been a powerful tool that has given a voice to the voiceless and empowered the disempowered.

Development plans are created and implemented at the national level often without the participation of the people, especially the poor and marginalized. Constitutional entrenchment of the RTD, buttressed by legislative and policy reform to support its implementation, including in national development plans, and its invocation in litigation, will help to advance an enabling environment for sustainable development from the bottom up. The critical links between the RTD and the SDGs, including SDG 10 on inequalities within and among nations, call for the operationalization of the RTD in implementing the SDGs.

In South Asia, PIL has helped to inject a more informed, participatory, and transparent approach to development, and governmental and private sector actions involving public resources. PIL enables people's empowerment through participation in development. It supports accountability in development and governance, toward inclusive, equitable, and sustainable development. The South Asian jurisprudence provides lessons learned for implementing Principle 10 of the Rio Declaration, as well as SDG 16. Principle 10 states:

> Environmental issues are best handled with the participation of all concerned citizens, at the relevant level. At the national level, each individual shall have appropriate access to information concerning the environment that is held by public authorities, including information on hazardous materials and activities in their communities, and the opportunity to participate in decision-making processes. States shall facilitate and encourage public awareness and participation by making information widely available. Effective access to judicial and administrative proceedings, including redress and remedy, shall be provided.[100]

SDG 16 aims to promote peaceful and inclusive societies, provide access to justice for all, and build effective, accountable, and inclusive institutions at all levels. It includes targets to promote the rule of law and ensure equal access to justice for all: develop effective, accountable, and transparent institutions at all levels; ensure responsive, inclusive, participatory, and representative decision-making; ensure public access to information and protect fundamental freedoms, in accordance with national legislation and international agreements; and promote and enforce nondiscriminatory laws and policies for sustainable development. Realizing sustainable development is key to achieving the SDGs. All human rights, including the RTD, are essential to achieving sustainable development. The cases discussed herein point to pathways to progress, by addressing poverty, environmental degradation, adverse impacts on poor, local, marginalized, discriminated, excluded and vulnerable communities, and other injustices.

Environmental justice in its broader connotations as articulated above, opens doors to transformative change – equal access, equitable sharing and sustainable use of natural resources, people's meaningful participation, and empowerment through PIL, as well as the fair

---

[100] UN, note 10. These principles find expression in legally binding instruments in the 1998 Arhus Convention (UN, Convention on Access to Information, Public Participation in Decision-Making and Access to Justice in Environmental Matters, June 25, 1998, 2161 UNTS 447) and the 2018 Escazú Regional Agreement on Access to Information, Public Participation, and Justice in Environmental Matters in Latin America and the Caribbean (UN, Regional Agreement on Access to Information, Public Participation and Justice in Environmental Matters in Latin America and the Caribbean, Mar. 4, 2018, C.N.195.2018.TREATIES-XXVII.18).

distribution of development benefits and burdens, can support justice – social, economic, and environmental. Value judgments in environment versus development dilemmas would ideally be made preemptively in rational planning. These could include environmental and human rights (or social) impact assessments and the effective implementation of the human rights responsibilities of business in realizing sustainable development, including the SDGs. Where holistic and preventive planning processes are still lacking, the above cases provide guidance to achieving sustainable development and social, environmental, and developmental justice, especially in the Third World.

Children's Rights or Intergenerational Equity?

Exploring Children's Place in Environmental Justice

Mona Paré*

10.1 INTRODUCTION

The notion of environmental justice, which emerged in the United States in the 1970s and 1980s to draw attention to the disproportionate environmental burden carried by poor and minority communities, has joined the sustainable development parlance as part of the social pillar of sustainability.[1] Economic development cannot happen at the expense of the environment and of the well-being of humans. Thus, development needs to be concerned with social development and with environmental protection. While the protection of the environment is a well-understood concept, despite the lack of consensus on the extent and means of protection, social development is less clear. Some components of social development can be found in the UN Sustainable Development Goals (SDGs), and include access to food, clean water and sanitation, education, and health, poverty-reduction, and attention to inequalities of income.[2] Social development is thus connected to internationally recognized human rights, and this link has been expressly recognized since the 1995 Copenhagen Declaration on Social Development.[3] In addition, the concept of environmental justice adds an important equality component to human development. It is interested not just with income inequality but with disparities in relation to environmental contamination. There is ample research to show that poor and minority families and communities are more at risk to suffer from environmental degradation, including air and water pollution, since they are more likely to live close to high-polluting industries and waste facilities.[4] Concern for environmental justice gives a chance to pay attention to different groups of people and how they are affected by decisions that impact the environment. It also goes hand in hand with respect for the human rights principles of equality and nondiscrimination.

---

* I would like to acknowledge the University of Ottawa Centre for Academic Leadership for its writing days, and Julie Ada Tchoukou for her research assistance.

[1] On the merging of environmental justice and sustainable development, see O. Pedersen, "Environmental Principles and Environmental Justice" (2010) 12 *Environmental Law Review* 26.

[2] UN General Assembly, *Transforming Our World: The 2030 Agenda for Sustainable Development*, Oct. 21, 2015, UN Doc. A/RES/70/1.

[3] UN Documents, Copenhagen Declaration on Social Development, Mar. 14, 1995, UN Doc. A/CONF.166/9

[4] See for example G. Di Chiro "Nature as Community: The Convergence of Environment and Social Justice," in W. Cronon (ed.), *Uncommon Ground: Rethinking the Human Place in Nature* (New York: Norton, 1996), p. 298. L. Cole and S. Foster, *From the Ground up: Environmental Racism and the Rise of the Environmental Justice Movement* (New York: New York University Press, 2001); R. Bullard, *Dumping in Dixie: Race, Class, and Environmental Quality* (Boulder, CO: Westview, 2000).

Children could be the main beneficiaries of environmental justice initiatives.[5] Many reports highlight the special vulnerability of children to pollution and toxins, and point to the fact that on a global level, children bear the burden of environmental degradation.[6] This observation is based on the fact that developing countries are disproportionately affected by environmental degradation, and children in developing countries make up a much larger portion of the population than in industrialized countries. Yet, some authors have rightly noted that children are absent as a stakeholder group from discussions on sustainable development, and they are not considered as actors in the context of environmental justice, which is concerned with empowering the marginalized.[7] Instead of focusing on children, the notion of intergenerational equity has been increasingly dealt with as part of environmental justice. Intergenerational justice directs attention to long-term development, considering equally the interests and rights of present and future generations. It is not equitable for future generations to have to pay the price for the mindless economic development and environmental degradation caused by today's generations. Children are understood to be one of the future generations whose interests we must protect. While children have not been the focus of intergenerational justice, the latter allows consideration of children's interests with regards to sustainable development.

This chapter examines children's place in environmental justice and sustainable development-related literature. Given the well-documented and widely accepted notion of children's vulnerability and victimhood in relation to environmental degradation, it analyzes the ways in which children are considered and included in research and initiatives that foster environmental justice. The chapter first gives an overview of the importance of including children in research and discussions related to the environment. Then, it examines children in relation to intergenerational equity. How are children placed in relation to current generations and generations not yet born? The chapter looks at theories that have been advanced to include children's interests as part of the interests of future generations, and even to justify our obligations toward children in light of the interests of generations still unborn. The final section lays out the main argument of the chapter. In light of the strong links between environmental justice, social development, and human rights, the section compares the advantages of a child rights–based approach (CRBA), a type of human rights–based approach (HRBA) that focuses on children, in relation to an intergenerational equity approach. It argues that while both can exist simultaneously, a child rights approach facilitates the determination of legal obligations, and in the end contributes to intergenerational equity and environmental justice.

10.2 CHILDREN AND ENVIRONMENTAL DEGRADATION

It is widely recognized that children are vulnerable to environmental degradation, to exposure to toxins, air, and water pollution. Yet, children are underrepresented in research, whether in law, social sciences, or public health. This section sheds light on the importance of focusing more research on children, including for demographic, medical, legal, and social reasons.

---

[5] Children refer to children and adolescents, as they are defined as minors in law, meaning generally persons under 18 years of age. This is the approach taken by the Convention on the Rights of the Child (CRC), Art. 1.

[6] See for example Committee on the Rights of the Child, "Report of the 2016 Day of General Discussion: Children's Rights and the Environment," May 2017; UNICEF, "Climate Change and Children: A Human Security Challenge," Innocenti Research Centre, Florence, Italy, Nov. 2008.

[7] See S. Cutter, "The Forgotten Casualties: Women, Children and Environmental Change" (1995) 5 *Global Environmental Change* 181; S. Stephens, "Reflections on Environmental Justice: Children as Victims and Actors" (1996) 23 *Social Justice* 62; E. Gibbons, "Climate Change, Children's Rights, and the Pursuit of Intergenerational Climate Justice" (2014) 16 *Health and Human Rights Journal* 19.

It demonstrates that environmental justice cannot reach its objectives of fair distribution of environmental benefits and burdens, if it does not consider children as one of the groups that has been overlooked and unfairly treated in the development and implementation of laws, regulations, and policies related to the environment.

First, one must pay heed to the sheer number of children in the world. In our aging societies, we may forget that children represent close to half of the population in many societies, and especially those communities that suffer most from environmental degradation.[8] Literature points to the fact that developing countries bear a disproportionate burden of environmental degradation, and it is in these countries that children represent the largest segments of the population.[9] In fact, while children represent about a third of the world's population, they amount to half of the world's poor, which shows how they are disproportionately affected by poverty.[10] As Stephens point out, the responsibility of developing countries for environmental degradation does not match the degradation that affects them – be it in relation to the effects of climate change or toxic or hazardous waste dumping; cognizant of children's lack of responsibility for this situation, the children of those countries suffer most injustice in the world in relation to the environmental degradation they endure.[11] Children who represent the "South within the North" face a similar situation. Inuit children, particularly, are disproportionately affected by the accumulation of toxic substances that do not originate from their environment.[12]

Second, children's experience is different from that of adults with regard to environmental degradation, climate change, exposure to toxins, and pollution, including effects on the quality of air and water, the presence of pesticides, herbicides and chemical fertilizers, toxic waste, and heavily polluting industries. The World Health Organization (WHO) reports great numbers of premature deaths that are related to pollution.[13] Causes of death include especially respiratory infections and diarrheal diseases. A UNICEF report describes how air pollution affects the brains of young children.[14] The younger the children, the more vulnerable they are to polluting substances. Because of their development, their organs and immune system are not mature, and this makes them more vulnerable. Because of their size, children breathe more air, and drink more water in relation to their weight than adults do.[15] In addition, the foods and liquids that children ingest contribute directly to their healthy development: height and weight, and cognitive abilities. Children's exposure to toxins thus has more long-term health effects than is the case with adults, and these effects are sometimes irreversible.[16]

---

[8] S. Bartlett, "Children in the Context of Climate Change: A Large and Vulnerable Population," in J. Guzman et al. (eds.), *Population Dynamics and Climate Change* (New York: UNFPA, 2009), p. 133.

[9] Bartlett, note 8; Stephens, note 7; Cutter, note 7.

[10] UNICEF and the World Bank Group, "Ending Extreme Poverty: A Focus on Children," Oct. 2016

[11] Stephens, note 7.

[12] S. Thompson, "Sustainability and Vulnerability: Aboriginal Arctic Food Security in a Toxic World", in F. Berkes et al. (eds.), *Breaking Ice: Renewable Resource and Ocean Management in the Canadian North* (Calgary, AB: University of Calgary Press, 2005), pp. 47, 57; A. Sheppard and R. Hetherington, "A Decade of Research in Inuit Children, Youth, and Maternal Health in Canada: Areas of Concentrations and Scarcities" (2012) 71 *International Journal of Circumpolar Health* 18383.

[13] WHO, "Inheriting a Sustainable World? Atlas on Children's Health and the Environment," Geneva, 2017; A. Prüss-Ustün, J. Wolf, C. Corvalan, R. Bos, and M. Neira, "Preventing Disease through Healthy Environments: A Global Assessment of the Burden of Disease from Environmental Risks," Geneva, 2016.

[14] UNICEF, "Danger in the Air: How Pollution Can Affect Brain Development in Young Children," Division of Data, Research and Policy, Dec. 2017.

[15] WHO, note 13, p. 66.

[16] P. Landrigan, V. Rauh, and M. Galvez, "Environmental Justice and the Health of Children" (2010) 77 *Mount Sinai Journal of Medicine* 178; Cutter, note 8; UN Human Rights Council, *Report of the Special Rapporteur on the issue of human rights obligations relating to the enjoyment of a safe, clean, healthy and sustainable*

Children are not only more vulnerable because of biological reasons, but also because of their behavior, including hand-to mouth behavior, playing outside, and using dangerous items found as toys.[17] Children in poor countries and disadvantaged neighborhoods are more at risk, because of the lack of safe play spaces, open air landfill sites, lack of sanitation, or conflict-zone-related dangers. In addition, children may not pay attention to warning signs, or may not be able to read. Older children and adolescents are also more at risk than adults, because they may pay less attention to security instructions, and taking risks is part of their development.[18] Examples of concrete risks include badly managed and discarded electronic waste that can have effects on children's cognitive development, or contamination of water and lack of sanitation that can cause diarrhea, which may be fatal to infants and young children. In industrialized countries, there is an increase in allergies and asthma in children, which is linked to pollution and environmental degradation.[19] Increased cases of childhood cancer and developmental disabilities can also be connected to environmental degradation. While direct causes cannot always be determined, it is clear that environmental dangers increase the risk of developing pathologies.

In addition to environmental degradation caused by pollution or hazardous substances, children are especially vulnerable to the effects of climate change, including natural disasters, storms, erosion, drought, floods, mudslides, and heatwaves. These situations can affect children's life, development, and health, because of increased risk of accidents, malnutrition, waterborne diseases, etc. For example, both drought and flooding affect the quantity and quality of safe water, and food production. In addition, global warming widens the zone of malaria, which affects children disproportionately and can have long-lasting consequences on their cognitive development and their susceptibility to other diseases.[20]

Third, children are dependent, both socially and legally. Children are characterized by their status as legal minors with lesser legal capacity, as well as belonging to a family (ideally). These characteristics mean that children may be invisible and unheard. Just as women have traditionally been restricted to the home, children tend to be confined within the private sphere, which is given less visibility in policymaking. Children's spheres of life are restricted mostly within the family and educational institutions. Their interests may be subsumed with those of the family as a whole, or the head of the family. As children lack legal capacity, they are not consulted, they cannot vote, and their access to justice is dependent upon the good will of adults.[21] It is thus specifically important to conduct research on and with children to make sure that their viewpoints, rights, and interests are taken into consideration. For example, a children's consultation project on the local environment in a disadvantaged London neighborhood in the 1990s showed how adult assumptions fail to take into consideration children's reality. While children were eager to get more greenery, they rejected the local council's suggestion for a grass-covered

environment, John Knox, Mar. 29, 2018, UN Doc. A/HRC/37/58; UN Human Rights Council, *Report of the Special Rapporteur on the implications for human rights of the environmentally sound management and disposal of hazardous substances and wastes*, Aug. 2, 2016, UN Doc. A/HRC/33/41.

[17] Landrigan et al., note 16; Stephens, note 7; J. Grigg, "Environmental Toxins; Their Impact on Children's Health" (2003) 89 *Disease in Childhood* 244.

[18] On adolescent development, see for example UNICEF, "The State of the World's Children 2011: Adolescence: An Age of Opportunity," New York, Feb. 2011.

[19] I. Buka, S. Koranteng, and A. Osornio-Vargas, "The Effects of Air Pollution on the Health of Children" (2006) 11 *Paediatrics and Child Health* 513; Landrigan et al., note 16; Stephens, note 7.

[20] Bartlett, note 8; S. Sanz-Caballero, "Children's Rights in a Changing Climate: A Perspective from the United Nations Convention on the Rights of the Child" (2013) 13 Ethics in Science and Environmental Politics 1; E. Back and C. Cameron, *Our Climate, Our Children, Our Responsibility* (London: UNICEF UK, 2008).

[21] M. Paré, "Children's Rights Are Human Rights and Why Canadian Implementation Lags Behind" (2017) 4 *Canadian Journal of Children's Rights* 25, p. 33.

playground, because grass could hide broken glass, dog excrement, and discarded needles.[22] Gibbons notes that "Children have a unique capacity to perceive risks that are particular to their age and circumstances, and propose child-friendly ways overcome [*sic*] them."[23]

Children are thus specifically vulnerable to environmental degradation and environmental hazards, including those caused by climate change. They are more exposed to risks and their exposure to pollution, toxins, and effects of climate change have more long-term harmful effects on them. Yet, they receive less attention, because of their social and legal status.

10.3 CHILDREN AND INTERGENERATIONAL EQUITY

Children have not been given much attention in the field of environmental law, at least until recently, and they are not included in initiatives that shed light on and combat environmental discrimination. It is interesting to note that international environmental law documents are more likely to refer to future generations than to children, drawing attention to the long-term effects of environmental degradation that will span generations.[24] Agreements and declarations emphasize the moral obligation of the current international community to consider those who will come after us and who will have to live with the consequences of our decisions and actions. We should not strive to improve our level of development in a way that depletes or destroys natural resources, as this would be unfair to the generations that succeed us. Authors have been suggesting since the 1980s that we should leave the earth in no worse condition to the future generations than it is during our lifetime.[25] The moral call for intergenerational equity has been taken up at the international level. Thus, for example, the *Report of the World Commission on Environment and Development* declares that sustainable development ensures "that it meets the needs of the present without compromising the ability of future generations to meet their own needs."[26] Similarly, Principle 3 of the Rio Declaration on Environment and Development states that "[t]he right to development must be fulfilled so as to equitably meet developmental and environmental needs of present and future generations."[27]

Are children part of present or future generations? Children must be part of present generations because they exist today. While intergenerational equity places a moral obligation on present generations, owed to future generations, it could also be understood as seeking equity between different present generations, thus giving attention to the situation of children and young people, as well as the aging.[28] Are all present generations on an equal footing when it

---

[22] G. Lansdown, "Promoting Children's Participation in Democratic Decision-Making," UN Children's Fund, Innocenti Research Centre, Florence, Italy, Feb. 2001, p. 5, referring to the Stepney and Wapping Community Child Health Project, research and development programme 1993–1995; G. Lansdown, "Implementing Children's Rights and Health" (2000) 83 *Archives of Disease in Childhood* 286, p. 287.

[23] Gibbons, note 7, p. 25.

[24] CRC, note 7, pp. 11, 13.

[25] E. Brown Weiss, *In Fairness to Future Generations: International Law, Common Patrimony, and Intergenerational Equity* (New York: Transnational, 1989).

[26] UN General Assembly, *Annex: Report of the World Commission on Environment and Development: Our Common Future*, Aug. 4, 1987, UN Doc A/42/427, para. 27.

[27] UN General Assembly, *Report of the United Nations Conference on Environment and Development*, Annex I, Aug. 12, 1992, UN. Doc. A/CONF.151/26 (Vol. I).

[28] Some authors distinguish between *intra*generational and *inter*generational when differentiating between existing and unborn generations (see B. Weston, "Climate Change and Intergenerational Justice: Foundational Reflections" (2008) 9 *Vermont Journal of Environmental Law* 375). However, the use of intragenerational justice seems wrong when comparing children and adults, as the two groups cannot be part of the same generation.

comes to the benefits and risks stemming from environment-related decisions? How does environmental justice apply to generations, beyond attention to ethnic minorities or poor communities? Of course, children from ethnic minorities, and especially Indigenous children, as well as children living in poverty, are generally more disadvantaged than other children. However, even within each of these communities, one should pay attention to the different generations. As noted earlier, children are disadvantaged in many regards, making it difficult for them to be empowered to address environmental injustices.

Children are present generations, but they can also be considered as future generations, since they are not part of the current decision-making generation and will have to live with the consequences of decisions made by today's adults. While the focus of intergenerational equity is on generations yet to come, it is at least implied that children are future generations. Weston specifically includes children among future generations, because "children are little better positioned than unborn persons to determine their future."[29] Moreover, children are born every minute, and those who were literally future humans a few minutes ago, arrive on our planet at this very moment. By examining the situation of children, it is easy to see that generations are interlinked. Being exposed to harm suffered by mothers in the womb may compromise children's development before they are even born. Children, whose healthy development is compromised, and who suffer from chronic disease or disabilities, will perpetuate the cycle, as their health may impact on the health of their own children. Authors discussing children in the context of intergenerational justice tend to see children as a link between current and future generations, as well as a specific category of future generations. Brown Weiss calls children "the first representatives of the future generations," who "embody their interests."[30]

Other authors question children's place in our world in the context of intergenerational justice by discussing the right or the opportunity to have children.[31] While these authors are more focused on world demographics, the plight of abandoned children, the risk of disability, gender preference, and related ethical issues, the question may also be asked in relation to environmental degradation: Should we have children knowing that they will be living in conditions that are worse than the ones we live in? Should we avoid having children in a context where overpopulation will certainly make the environmental situation worse? Are we being fair to future generations if we keep making the population grow at an unsustainable rate? Such ethical issues extend beyond the question "to have or not to have children," and the numbers of children that should be created, to include questions about the conditions in which children should come into this world.

One of the ways to look at children's place in intergenerational equity is to consider children as one of the present generations that has responsibilities toward future generations. Can children be duty-bearers? Bohman argues that one reason that children have rights is precisely because of their duties to the future generations.[32] This is in line with Howarth's chain of obligation theory.[33] These theories help to explain the need to include children within intergenerational justice, so that we may address long-term environmental conservation needs. From this perspective, children

---

[29] Weston, note 28, p. 388.

[30] E. Brown Weiss, "In Fairness to Our Children: International Law and Intergenerational Equity" (1994) 2 *Childhood* 22.

[31] L. Doyal and S. McLean, "Choosing Children: Intergenerational Justice?" (2005) 10 *Reproductive BioMedicine Online* 119; E. Bartholet, "Intergenerational Justice for Children: Restructuring Adoption, Reproduction and Child Welfare Policy" (2014) 8 *Law & Ethics of Human Rights* 103.

[32] J. Bohman, "Children and the Rights of Citizens: Nondomination and Intergenerational Justice" (2011) 633 *Annals of the American Academy of Political and Social Science* 128.

[33] R. Howarth, "Intergenerational Justice and the Chain of Obligation" (1992) 1 *Environmental Values* 133.

become agents of intergenerational justice, more than its beneficiaries. According to Howarth, if we don't make the right environmental decisions that allow us to properly provide for children, then we are preventing them from fulfilling their obligation in the future to ensure the welfare of their own children.[34] In this way, attention to children allows us to look forward, and it also helps to bypass the awkward question of having obligations toward people who do not exist yet. However, from a human rights perspective this approach is problematic. As we will see in the next section, focusing on children's rights is another – more tangible – way to address future needs and common interests without getting bogged down in complicated demonstrations of the existence at the present time of the beneficiaries of our obligations.[35]

10.4 A CRBA TO ENVIRONMENTAL JUSTICE

10.4.1 *Advantages of a CRBA*

As seen in the previous section, children are a present generation as well as a future generation. It is important not to consider childhood only as a mere temporary state or a link between generations. Children are not only developing beings, whose ultimate objective is to grow up. Children are human beings today, and they are subjects of rights, whether they will have children or not, and regardless of how they will care for their children. One advantage of focusing on children's rights as opposed to future generations is being able to guide and justify our actions based on the needs and rights of existing rights-holders. One of the main aspects of an HRBA, is to identify rights-holders and duty-bearers.[36] In the context of our common concern for the environment, children are one of the rights-holding groups, and adults – more commonly identified as institutions – are duty-bearers. While it is a traditional approach to recognize the state as a duty-bearer in international human rights law, and indeed, states are parties to human rights treaties, international human rights law also recognizes the responsibility of civil society. The Universal Declaration of Human Rights, upon which the UN human rights treaties are based, states in its Preamble that "every individual and every organ of society" shall promote respect for human rights, and secure, by progressive measures, their effective observance.[37] Article 29 proclaims that "Everyone has duties to the community." The CRC gives parents an active role in helping children exercise their rights (Art. 5).[38] Article 27 clarifies that parents and those responsible for the child have the primary responsibility to secure the necessary conditions for the child's development. It is understood that the state needs to step in when parents are not capable of providing the necessary conditions for their child's development, by helping to create those conditions. Children are thus legally recognized rights-holders with the CRC providing the most comprehensive and widely recognized expression of their rights.[39] A CRBA makes the protection

---

[34] Ibid.

[35] Authors are bending backwards to justify obligations toward future generations. See for example G. Bos and M. Düwell (eds.), *Human Rights and Sustainability: Moral responsibilities for the Future* (London: Routledge, 2016); Weston, note 28.

[36] I refer here indiscriminately to HRBA and CRBA, which is an HRBA focused on children and the principles of the CRC. On the definition of HRBA and CRBA, see T. Collins and M. Paré, "A Child Rights-Based Approach to Anti-Violence Efforts in Schools" (2016) 24 *International Journal of Children's Rights* 762. For an application of the HRBA to environmental health, see M. Ryan, "The Politics of Risk: A Human Rights Paradigm for Children's Environmental Health Research" (2006) 114 *Environmental Health Perspectives* 1613.

[37] UN General Assembly, Universal Declaration of Human Rights, Paris, 1948, Res. 217 A (III).

[38] United Nations, *Treaty Series*, Vol. 1577, p. 3.

[39] The CRC is among the most ratified treaties with 196 states parties.

of this present and future generation much more tangible than the reliance on moral duties toward people who do not yet exist.

Another advantage of the CRBA is that it allows empowerment of rights-holders. As noted earlier, children lack agency because of their social and legal status. While previous child rights protection instruments focused only on the protective side of children's rights, the CRC recognizes that children have autonomy and citizenship rights, including the right to freedom of expression (Art. 13), freedom of association (Art. 15), and the right to be heard on matters that concern them (Art. 12). This means that children should have a say in relation to decision-making that impacts the environment. Given that children are disproportionately affected by environmental degradation, this is clearly a matter affecting the child, as understood in the CRC. The Committee on the Rights of the Child – monitoring body of the CRC – has clarified that the right of children to express their views applies not only to individual decisions concerning a specific child, but also to decisions affecting certain children as a group, or all children.[40] This means that since children do not vote, they should be given other opportunities to express their views, for example through consultations in public decision-making processes. As noted earlier, children, as experts of their own lives and immediate surroundings, can add relevant perspectives to discussions on the environment and its preservation.[41]

The fact that human rights address inequalities is also an empowering aspect of the HRBA. The CRC requires respect for children's rights without discrimination based on prohibited grounds of discrimination that may affect the child directly or the child's parents, legal guardians, or family members. This is an important addition to other nondiscrimination clauses. Children can be negatively affected by the discrimination suffered by their parents and other family members, for example because of their political activities or expressed opinions. This may include children of environmental activists, or children of parents who are resisting activities of mining companies in their community. Complying with the nondiscrimination clause requires not only abstaining from negatively discriminating measures, and protecting children from discrimination by private entities, but also giving special attention to children in disadvantaged situations and taking positive measures to ensure that they can effectively exercise their rights.[42] By drawing attention to discrimination, inequalities, and the situation of vulnerable and marginalized groups, human rights law, including child rights, confronts the issue of power. It identifies those who are powerless and addresses the causes of their vulnerabilities. It also encourages tackling different forms of discrimination, including indirect and systemic discrimination. In this vein it joins some of the objectives of environmental justice, which also identify groups that are at a specific disadvantage with regards the environmental effects of decisions made at different levels of government. Thus, a CRBA requires not only giving special attention to children, but also identifying children who are more at risk, examining patterns of discrimination and taking measures to ensure that these children can enjoy their human rights and thereby become empowered. Children who are most disadvantaged may not only be those who are identified in the context of environmental justice, such as children belonging to racial

---

[40] UN, *Committee on the Rights of the Child, General Comment No. 12: The Right of the Child to Be Heard*, July 20, 2009, UN Doc. CRC/C/GC/12.

[41] Lansdowne (2003), note 22; C. Wilson Outley, "The Challenge of Environmental Justice for Children: The Impact of Cumulative Disadvantageous Risks" (2006) 23 *George Wright Forum* 49; Human Rights Council 2018, note 16, para. 48; S. Meucci and M. Schwab, "Children and the Environment: Young People's Participation in Social Change" (1997) 24 *Social Justice* 1.

[42] UN, *Committee on the Rights of the Child, Treaty-specific guidelines regarding the form and content of periodic reports to be submitted by States parties under article 44, paragraph 1 (b), of the Convention on the Rights of the Child*, Mar. 3, 2015 UN Doc. CRC/C/58/Rev.3, para. 24.

minorities and children living in poverty. One also needs to examine the environmental effects of our decision-making on children with disabilities, on children living in street situations, or on Indigenous children, and ask whether girls are more at risk than boys.

Finally, an HRBA is interesting, as it encourages linkages between different rights. The recognition of the indivisibility and interdependence of human rights is one of the key components of an HRBA and it is particularly well illustrated by children's rights. Indeed, the CRC includes all types of rights without a hierarchy and without preset priorities. For example, it is clear that the possibility for children to express their views about a matter that concerns them is related to the right to freedom of expression (Art. 13), to the right to access information specifically produced for them (Art. 17), to the right to education (Art. 28), to the right to protection from violence (Art. 19), and the right to an adequate standard of living (Art. 19). A CRBA entails identifying and implementing relevant human rights. This leads us to discuss several children's rights that are directly related to environmental justice, and to highlight linkages between human rights instruments and environmental law documents.

10.4.2 *Children's Rights and Respect for the Environment*

First, the right to participation seems obvious as it is directly related to empowerment and a CRBA. Article 12 of the CRC has been identified by the Committee on the Rights of the Child as one of the four general principles of the convention.[43] This article is the basis for child participation generally, as it entails that children be given opportunities to express their views on matters that concern them, and that their views be taken into consideration, the weight of their opinion increasing with age and maturity. This provision is complemented by the right to freedom of expression (Art. 13) which includes the freedom to seek, receive, and impart information. Several international documents call explicitly for general consultation on environmental matters. Principle 10 of the Rio Declaration[44] on environment and development calls for the participation of all concerned citizens, and for access to information for each individual, concerning the environment and the opportunity to participate in decision-making processes. Principle 21 adds that the "creativity, ideals and courage of the youth of the world should be mobilized." Agenda 21, the action plan adopted at the 1992 UN Conference on Environment and Development, includes details on the participation of children in sustainable development. Chapter 25 states that it is "imperative that youth . . . participate actively in all relevant levels of decision-making processes, because it affects their lives today and has implications for their futures . . . they bring unique perspectives that need to be taken into account."[45] Accordingly, governments are asked to establish procedures allowing for consultation and possible participation of youth in decision-making processes with regard to the environment. The 1998 Aarhus Convention on Access to Information, Public Participation in Decision-Making and Access to Justice in Environmental Matters, includes the principle of participation in a legally binding document.[46] States commit to inform the public about all relevant projects that have an effect on the environment, and the authorities must make arrangements to allow the public to

---

[43] UN Convention on the Rights of the Child, *Committee on the Rights of the Child, General Guidelines regarding the form and content of initial report to be submitted by States parties under article 44, paragraph 1(a) of the Convention*, Oct. 30, 1991, UN Doc CRC/C/5, p. 4.

[44] UN, Rio Declaration on Environment and Development, June 14, 1992, UN Doc. A/CONF.151/26 (Vol. 1)

[45] UNGA, note 27.

[46] UNECE, Convention on Access to Information, Public Participation in Decision-Making and Access to Justice in Environmental Matters, June 25, 1998, UNTS Vol. 2161, p. 447.

participate in decision-making processes. More generally, the outcome document of the UN Special Session on children in 2002 provides for children's participation in decision-making processes at different levels. In the Plan of Action, states commit to respect children's right to express their views freely, and to nurture children's creativity "so that they can actively take part in shaping their environment, their societies and the world they will inherit."[47] States will thus "strive to develop and implement programmes to promote meaningful participation by children . . . in decision-making processes."[48] References to public participation in relation to the environment, to children's participation generally, or in connection with the environment more particularly abound in international law.

The right to education is relevant and linked to the right to express one's opinion and to receive information. First, access to education, as provided in CRC Article 28, enables children to read and understand information, and to improve their capabilities to express themselves. Second, according to Article 29, education has important objectives, including preparing children for a responsible life in society in the spirit of understanding, peace, equality of sexes, and friendship among all peoples, and developing children's respect for the natural environment. In its first General Comment, the Committee on the Rights of the Child specified that "education must link issues of environment and sustainable development with socio-economic, sociocultural and demographic issues," and added that "respect for the natural environment should be learnt by children at home, in school and within the community, encompass both national and international problems, and actively involve children in local, regional or global environmental projects."[49] Education is thus dependent upon participation. Some environmental law instruments also address the importance of education. Principle 19 of Stockholm Declaration of the United Nations Conference on the Human Environment, adopted in 1972, proclaims that education in environmental matters is "essential for an enlightened opinion and responsible conduct."[50] More recently, the Paris Agreement requires states to take measures "to enhance climate change education, training, public awareness, public participation and public access to information."[51] Here again, participation, education, and access to information are linked.

Finally, there is the right to an adequate or healthy environment. This right is not expressly recognized in UN human rights treaties.[52] However, it is considered as the most developed among the so-called solidarity or third-generation rights.[53] While it is not a stand-alone right in human rights treaties, it can be composed of different rights, including the right to life, the right to health, as well as procedural rights, such as the right to information, consultation, and access to justice and reparation.[54] The CRC is noteworthy in relation to other universally applicable human rights treaties, as it mentions the environment explicitly. Article 24 on the right to health asks states to take measures, inter alia, to combat disease and malnutrition "taking into consideration the

---

[47] UN General Assembly, *A World Fit for Children*, Oct. 11, 2002, Res. S-27/2, para. 32.

[48] Ibid.

[49] UN Human Rights Council, *Committee on the Rights of the Child, General Comment No.1: The Aims of Education*, Apr. 17, 2001, UN Doc. CRC/GC/2001/1, para. 13.

[50] UN, *Report of the United Nations Conference on the Human Environment*, June 5–16, 1972, UN Doc. A/CONF.48/14/Rev.1.

[51] UNFCCC, Paris Agreement, Jan. 29, 2016, FCCC/CP/2015/10/Add.1.

[52] It is included in the African Charter on Human and Peoples' Rights as a collective right (Art. 24: "All peoples shall have the right to a general satisfactory environment favourable to their development"); and in the "Protocol of San Salvador" in the Inter-American system, as an individual right to live in a healthy environment, with the obligation for states to "promote the protection, preservation, and improvement of the environment" (Art. 11).

[53] M. Paré, *Droit international des droits de la personne: systèmes et enjeux* (Montréal: LexisNexis, 2016), p. 247.

[54] Ibid. The procedural rights are all topics covered by the Aarhus Convention.

dangers and risks of environmental pollution," and to ensure that parents and children have "access to education and are supported in the use of basic knowledge of child health and nutrition . . . hygiene and environmental sanitation." However, reports and resolutions adopted by various UN bodies recognize the right to live in a healthy environment more explicitly.[55] Most of these stress the links between the environment and existing human rights, especially the rights to life, health, and to an adequate standard of living.[56] In the last few years, some have focused specifically on children's rights and the environment.[57] These UN bodies, including the General Assembly, the Human Rights Council, human rights treaty bodies and special procedures refer to environmental law instruments, and recognize the threat of climate change, toxic waste, pollution, and other forms of environmental degradation on human rights.[58]

Children themselves, when empowered to access courts and supported by adults, have claimed their environmental rights, including the right to a healthy environment and a balanced ecology, the rights to life, liberty and property, health, food, and water.[59] These cases demonstrate the importance of helping children exercise their procedural rights, as children have fought deforestation and pollution, and have shown the interlinkages between the various rights that make up environmental rights within their respective domestic legal contexts. Finally, these cases show how a CRBA supports intergenerational equity, as children have successfully claimed their environmental rights not only in their own names, but also for the sake of future generations.

The social pillar of sustainable development, including environmental justice, is thus intimately linked to the respect of human rights. A CRBA is a type of HRBA that focuses on children. As human rights are better embedded in law than intergenerational equity, a CRBA offers advantages as an approach that is based on the most universally accepted human rights treaty, and addresses the same concerns of environmental preservation, public education, and consultation, combating discrimination, and empowering the marginalized.

10.5 CONCLUSION

There is no doubt that threats to the environment are threats to children, and it has been made equally clear that environmental degradation affects the enjoyment of human rights. Environmental law instruments do not give much attention to children, yet researchers have

[55] UN Human Rights Council, *Report of the Special Rapporteur on the issue of human rights obligations relating to the enjoyment of a safe, clean, healthy and sustainable environment: framework principles, John Knox,* Jan. 24, 2018, A/HRC/37/59; see notably UN General Assembly, Dec. 14, 1990, A/RES/45/94.

[56] UNHRC, *Report of the Independent Expert on the Issue of Human Rights Obligations Relating to the Enjoyment of a Safe, Clean, Healthy and Sustainable Environment, Individual Report on the United Nations Convention on the Elimination of All Forms of Discrimination against Women,* Dec. 2013. See for example UN General Assembly, *Report of the Working Group on the Universal Periodic Review,* Dec. 27, 2017, A/HRC/37/8.

[57] UN Convention on the Rights of the Child, *Committee on the Rights of the Child, General Comment No. 15: The Right of the Child to the Enjoyment of the Highest Attainable Standard of Health,* Apr. 17, 2013, UN Doc. CRC/C/GC/15; UN Convention on the Rights of the Child, *Committee on the Rights of the Child, General Comment No. 16 on State Obligations Regarding the Impact of the Business Sector on Children's Rights,* Apr. 17, 2013, UN Doc. CRC/C/GC/16; CRC, note 6; Human Rights Council (2016), note 16; Human Rights Council (2018), note 16.

[58] See for example the Human Rights Council's renewed calls for states to ratify treaties on climate change: UN General Assembly, *Resolution adopted by the Human Rights Council on 1 July 2016: 32/33. Human rights and climate change,* July 18, 2016, A/HRC/RES/32/33.

[59] See for example *Minors Oposa v. Secretary of the Department of Environmental and Natural Resources,* 33 ILM 173 (Supreme Court of the Philippines, 1994); Sala de Casación Civil no. 11001-22-03-000-2018-00319-01 (Supreme Court of Colombia, 2018); *Juliana v. United States,* District Court of Oregon, Civ. No. 6:15-cv-01517-AA.

pointed to the importance of including children in environmental research. Children should be a separate stakeholder group, because they are affected differently than adults, and also because children's interest may not be represented by other groups that have a voice in the public sphere. Some have argued that children should be considered because they are one of the future generations who are affected by intergenerational equity. In a similar logic, children are to be regarded as guardians of the interests of the generations unborn, and we have obligations toward them, because they will in turn have obligations toward their children, grandchildren, and great grandchildren. Children are thus a chain link that connects us – current generations – to the generations yet to come. However, children are not only important because they are developing to become full-fledged adults and citizens. They are human beings with equal worth to those who belong to the current decision-making generations. At the basis of human rights lies the principle that all human beings are born equal in dignity and rights. This includes those who were born decades ago and those who are being born this minute. Based on this principle, children's human rights should be given equal importance to the human rights of adults. Choosing a CRBA does not contradict or rule out intergenerational equity. Intergenerational equity and attention to the interests of people yet to be born, including in the distant future, are important moral considerations that can be translated into laws and policies with political will.

Yet, such an approach should not prevent a CRBA, which has many advantages. First, it makes it easier to identify rights-holders and duty-bearers, as both currently exist. If we adhere to the principles of international human rights law, theorizing to justify children's rights is not necessary,[60] while such theorizing is required to grant rights to categories of people who do not yet exist. Second, the rights related to a healthy environment have now been well developed internationally by various human rights bodies, whose interpretation of existing treaties should be prioritized. These rights require a holistic approach, concerned not only with the quality of air, food, and water, for example, but also education, attention to social status, power relations, and vulnerabilities, and the right to be heard and included in decision-making processes. Third, respecting children's rights in the context of environmental protection is a way to ensure that children will do the same, and so on. As children's education is geared toward respect for their environment, as their environment is protected so that they can enjoy good-quality water, sanitation, safe food, and shelter, as they receive appropriate information on environmental issues, and are consulted in decision-making processes that may affect the environment, they will surely become environmentally conscious parents and decision makers. As exemplified by the class action suits led by children,[61] respecting children as human beings today, contributes to intergenerational equity and environmental justice.

[60] Paré, note 21.
[61] See cases cited in note 59.

Indigenous Environmental Rights and Sustainable Development

Lessons from Totonicapán in Guatemala

Patrícia Galvão Ferreira and Mario Mancilla

11.1 INTRODUCTION

International environmental law (IEL) has been slow to incorporate the social dimension of sustainable development. In this chapter, we seek to unpack the process of integration of international human rights norms and IEL.[1] We focus on the integration of Indigenous rights and IEL, by looking at the recent Escazú Agreement on environmental rights.[2] We argue that, while Escazú represents an important step toward integrating human rights and IEL, not all human rights have been equally integrated. Indigenous rights were largely left outside the Escazú Agreement.[3] We use a case study from Guatemala to illustrate what this left unprotected, and to shed light on the persisting dominance of Western/Eurocolonial epistemologies in shaping IEL.

The chapter is structured as follows. In Section 11.2, we describe the various reasons why Latin America is the perfect context to unpack the nuances relating to the integration of human rights and environmental law and the social dimension of sustainable development. First, environmentalism in the region has historically developed alongside social justice activism. Second, Latin American countries went through a wave of adoption of new constitutions in the 1980s, 1990s, and 2000s, which allowed many of them to incorporate substantive environmental rights

---

[1] On the linkages between human rights and the environment, see S. Kravchenko and J. E. Bonive, *Human Rights and the Environment: Cases, Law, and Policy* (Durham, NC: Carolina Academic Press, 2008); S. Atapattu and A. Schapper, *Human Rights and the Environment: Key Issues* (Abingdon, UK: Routledge, 2019); S. J. Turner, D. L. Shelton, J. Razzaque, O. McIntyre, and J. R. May (eds.), *Environmental Rights: The Development of Standards* (Cambridge: Cambridge University Press, 2019). See also UN General Assembly, *Report of the Independent Expert on the issue of human rights obligations relating to the enjoyment of a safe, clean, healthy and sustainable environment, John H. Knox: Mapping Report*, Dec. 30, 2013, UN Doc. A/HRC/25/53.

[2] Regional Agreement on Access to Information, Public Participation and Justice in Environmental Matters in Latin America and the Caribbean, Escazú, Costa Rica, Mar. 4, 2018, LC/CNP10.9/5 [Escazú Agreement].

[3] While international human rights norms are designed to protect the human rights of all individual human beings, international law concerning the rights of Indigenous peoples seeks to address a set of problems that are particular to Indigenous peoples, including protection of their cultural integrity and self-determination, and strong connection with land and natural resources. S. J. Anaya, *International Human Rights and Indigenous Peoples* (Austin: Wolters Kluwer Law & Business, 2009); S.J. Anaya, *Indigenous Peoples in International Law* (2nd ed.) (New York: Oxford University Press, 2004); F. MacDonald and B. Wood, "Potential through Paradox: Indigenous Rights as Human Rights" (2016) 20 *Citizenship Studies* 710–727; P.K. Kulchyski, *Aboriginal Rights Are Not Human Rights: In Defence of Indigenous Struggles* (Semaphore Series) (Winnipeg: ARP Books, 2013).

(such as the right to a healthy environment and rights of nature) at the highest level of domestic legal systems. Third, Latin American countries also incorporated Indigenous rights in their constitutions. Despite these advances in constitutional law, implementation of both environmental rights and Indigenous rights have proved elusive in the region, leading social groups to look for international law mechanisms to complement efforts to make norms effective on the ground.

In Section 11.3, we analyze the Escazú Agreement, which has been rightly lauded as an important step forward in the integration of human rights and environmental law in Latin America.[4] Escazú's procedural environmental rights (right to access to environmental information, participation in environmental decision-making and access to environmental justice), and reaffirmation of a region-wide substantive right to a healthy environment, are expected to offer new legal and political tools to social groups in Latin America seeking to push governments to give effect to constitutionally recognized substantive environmental rights. We argue, however, that Escazú missed the opportunity to fully integrate Indigenous rights into the substantive and procedural provisions of this Agreement. In Section 11.4, we use a case study of alternative Indigenous water governance systems in Totonicapán, Guatemala to illustrate the type of cosmovision that justifies Indigenous environmental rights being integrated into international environmental rights agreements.

The chapter argues that in order to contribute to a more comprehensive theoretical understanding of the many nuances of the social dimension of sustainable development, IEL scholars should engage more systematically with emerging national and international research on Indigenous alternative perspectives on environmental governance. The approach highlighted here is distinct from existing discussions related to environmental justice and Indigenous peoples, which highlights the disproportionate environmental impacts Indigenous peoples suffer as a racialized social group, because of their close cultural and existential interaction with the environment. The aim is to move from treating Indigenous peoples as victims of environmental racism, to appreciating their active role in shaping alternative forms of natural resources management and environmental stewardship that better integrate the social dimension of sustainable development.

We recognize that this is just a first exploration of the theme, which deserves more scrutiny and further empirical research. We intend this exploratory work to be an invitation to other environmental law scholars to engage in more systematic conversations with the scholarship on Indigenous rights and Indigenous legal traditions, when carrying out research on the social dimension of sustainable development, particularly the cutting-edge work Indigenous law scholars in the Americas are undertaking.[5]

---

[4] B. O. Giupponi, "Fostering Environmental Democracy in Latin America and the Caribbean: An Analysis of the Regional Agreement on Environmental Access Rights" (2019) 28 Review of European, Comparative & International Environmental Law 136–151; E. Barritt, "Global Values, Transnational Expression: From Aarhus to Escazú," in V. Heyveart and L. A. Duvic-Paoli (eds.), Research Handbook on Transnational Environmental Law (Cheltenham, UK: Edward Elgar, 2020), p. 198.

[5] See for example R. Joseph, M. Rakena, M. Te Kuini Jones, R. Sterling, and C. Rakena, "The Treaty, Tikanga Māori, Ecosystem-Based Management, Mainstream Law and Power Sharing for Environmental Integrity in Aotearoa New Zealand – Possible Ways Forward," Māori and Indigenous Governance Center, Te Piringa-Faculty of Law at the University of Waikato for Ngā Moana Whakauka – Sustainable Seas National Science Challenge, Nov. 30, 2018; J. Borrows, "Seven Gifts: Revitalizing Living Laws through Indigenous Legal Practice" (2016–2017) 2 *Lakehead Law Journal* 2–14; D. McGregor, "Lessons for Collaboration Involving Traditional Knowledge and Environmental Governance in Ontario, Canada" (2014) 10 *AlterNATIVE: An International Journal of Indigenous Peoples* 340–353; A. Walkem, "Indigenous Peoples Water Rights: Challenges and Opportunities in an Era of Increased North American Integration," Canada and the New

11.2 ENVIRONMENTAL RIGHTS AND INDIGENOUS RIGHTS
IN LATIN AMERICA: THE UNFINISHED PROCESS

Latin America is a perfect illustration of the importance of paying close attention to the social dimension of sustainable development because their economies are largely reliant on natural commodities including minerals, oil and gas, and agricultural products. These economic sectors produce a heavy environmental footprint which affects a region that has rich biodiversity and ecosystems.[6] Diversity is also a hallmark of the Latin American population. There are around forty-two million Indigenous peoples of various ethnicities living in the region,[7] alongside descendants of Europeans, Africans, and Asians that came as settlers, immigrants, or slaves during colonial times or more recently. On the other hand, income inequality in the region remains high despite important gains in economic growth and improvements in social indicators (like life expectancy and literacy rates) in the last decades.[8] The region also ranks high with regard to various other inequality indicators, including measures of political influence and voice, and health and education outcomes.[9]

A substantial part of Latin America's economic elites relies on the exploitation of natural resources for their wealth and political might, while many rural and Indigenous communities still depend on environmental services and environmental goods to survive. Historically, international financial institutions and donor countries, particularly the USA, have promoted legal reforms or have intervened to facilitate international trade of natural commodities from the region, to the benefit of national and international economic elites, even if it meant supporting or overlooking military interventions or authoritarian regimes. Too often these military governments and authoritarian regimes in Latin America have stripped Indigenous peoples of access to their ancestral lands and their associated environmental benefits, threatening their existence and well-being,[10] or promoted environmental degradation in rural communities, resulting in their impoverishment. In Latin America, inequitable access to land, natural resources, and environmental benefits has been, throughout history, linked to social injustice.[11]

The combination of plentiful land and resources-based economic potential with forced social exclusion helps to explain the extraordinary number of environmental conflicts in the region, with Indigenous peoples being particularly affected due to their intrinsic and close relationship to the land and the natural environment. These environmental conflicts often turn violent in a

American Empire, Centre for Global Studies, University of Victoria, BC, Nov. 2004; R. Kuokkanen, *Restructuring Relations: Indigenous Self-Determination, Governance, and Gender* (Oxford: Oxford University Press, 2019). For a series of publications on Indigenous water governance in Canada, see the Decolonizing Water project, online: http://decolonizingwater.ca/category/articles-and-reports/.

[6] OECD, *Biodiversity Conservation and Sustainable Use in Latin America: Evidence from Environmental Performance Reviews* OECD Environmental Performance Reviews (Paris: OECD Publishing, 2018), https://doi.org/10.1787/9789264309630-en.

[7] The World Bank, "Indigenous Latin America in the Twenty-First Century," Mar. 12, 2018, www.worldbank.org/en/region/lac/brief/indigenous-latin-america-in-the-twenty-first-century-brief-report-page.

[8] A. Bárcena, M. Cimoli, R. García-Buchaca, L. Abramo, and R. Pérez, Economic Commission for Latin America and the Caribbean (ECLAC), *Social Panorama of Latin America*, 2019, LC/PUB.2019/3-P.

[9] D. De Ferranti, F. H. G. Ferreira, G. E. Perry, and M. Walton, "Inequality in Latin America: Breaking with History?" World Bank Latin America and Caribbean Studies, 2004.

[10] Continuing a process of violence and dispossession against Indigenous peoples that began during colonial times (P. Bille Larsen, "The 'New Jungle Law': Development, Indigenous Rights and ILO Convention 169 in Latin America" (2016) 7 *International Development Policy/Revue internationale de politique de développement*).

[11] D. V. Carruters (ed.), *Environmental Justice in Latin America: Problems, Promise and Practice* (Cambridge, MA: MIT Press, 2008).

context of institutional mechanisms that are inadequate to mediate disputes and to ensure accountability for rights violations. The origins of weak and captured institutions in Latin America can be traced to a legacy of extractive colonization,[12] followed by periods of civil wars and authoritarian regimes. Latin America has consistently ranked as the leading region in documented killings of environmental defenders compiled by Global Witness since 2012. The region is responsible for more than half of environmental defenders killed globally in 2018, many of them members of Indigenous nations.[13]

Guatemala alone saw a jump from three environmental defenders killed in 2017 to sixteen killings in 2018, making it the most dangerous country for environmental defenders, in per capita terms.[14] Violence against environmental defenders in Guatemala, including Indigenous leaders, is part of a broader scenario of extremely high violence rates that many authors[15] link to the brutal civil war (1960–1996) that had its roots in the CIA-orchestrated overthrow of democratically elected president Jacobo Arbenz in 1954.[16] Indigenous peoples have been particularly affected by violence in Guatemala. In 1999, a Truth Commission released a ten-volume report, *Guatemala, Memoria del Silencio* ("Guatemala, Memory of Silence"), documenting the killing of 200,000 civilians during the civil conflict, mostly by the government. These killings included massacres and *scorched earth* anti-insurgency operations that decimated whole villages.[17] The report concluded that the Guatemalan military had conducted genocide against four ethnic groups of Mayan Indigenous peoples because their villages had been primarily targeted by the military for *scorched earth* operations and other massacres (83 percent of their victims were from these four Indigenous groups).[18]

Yet Latin America is also characterized by the resilience, the strength, and the innovation of its inhabitants. A critical mass of social movements, nongovernmental organizations (NGOs), academics, progressive courts, and politicians have continuously fought for social, economic, and environmental justice in the face of this challenging geopolitical and institutional context. Latin Americans have systematically resorted to international law as one of many tools to help in domestic efforts to create national legal regimes to promote social justice, economic inclusion, and environmental protection.[19] Following decades of systematic human rights violations and environmental degradation in the name of economic development under postcolonial authoritarian regimes, many countries in Latin America transitioned to democracy in the 1980s and

---

[12] D. Acemoglu and J.A. Robinson, *Why Nations Fail: The Origins of Power, Prosperity, and Poverty* (Redfern, NSW: Currency Press, 2012).

[13] Global Witness, "Enemies of the State? How Governments and Business Silence Land and Environmental Defenders," July 2019, www.globalwitness.org/en/campaigns/environmental-activists/enemies-state/.

[14] Ibid.

[15] D. J. Yashar, "High Violence in Post-Civil War in Guatemala," in D. J. Yashar, *Homicidal Ecologies: Illicit Economies and Complicit States in Latin America* (Cambridge, MA: Cambridge University Press, 2018), p. 149; B. Manz, "The Continuum of Violence in Post-war Guatemala" (2008) 52 *Social Analysis* 151–164.

[16] R. Brett, "Peace without Social Reconciliation? Understanding the Trial of Generals Ríos Montt and Rodriguez Sánchez in the Wake of Guatemala's Genocide" (2016) 18 *Journal of Genocide Research* 285–303; M. E. Vela Castañeda, *Los pelotones de la muerte: la construcción de los perpetradores del genocidio guatemalteco* (Mexico, DF: El Colegio de México, Centro de Estudios Sociológicos, 2014); D. Rothenberg, "Special Double Issue: Guatemala, the Question of Genocide" (2016) 18(2/3) *Journal of Genocide Research*.

[17] Comisión para el Esclarecimiento Histórico, *Memory of Silence: The Guatemalan Truth Commission Report* (New York: Palgrave Macmillan, 2012).

[18] B. Kiernan, "Wall of Silence: The Field of Genocide Studies and the Guatemalan Genocide," in N. Brandal and D. Einar Thorsen (eds.), *Den dannede opprører: Bernt Hagtvet* (Oslo: Dreyers Forlag, 2016), pp. 169–198; P. Garcia, *El Genocidio de Guatemala a la luz de la Sociología Militar* (Madrid: Sepha, 2008).

[19] V. Abramovich, "From Massive Violations to Structural Patterns: New Approaches and Classic Tensions in the Inter-American Human Rights System" (2009) 6 *Sur: International Journal on Human Rights*.

1990s. These transitions represented a critical juncture that enabled the adoption of new progressive constitutions in the region.[20]

The new democratic constitutions in Latin America enshrined basic guarantees to protect and promote human rights, including civil and political rights like freedom of association and expression, and prohibition against torture, as well as socioeconomic rights, such as right to health and education. In tandem with the adoption in the late 1970s and 1980s of the first IEL declarations recognizing the importance of protecting the environment and promoting sustainable development, a process of "greening" of Latin American constitutions also took place.[21] Many constitutions incorporated explicit environmental rights for the first time – including the right to a healthy environment,[22] and some even recognized rights of nature (meaning rights of nonhuman elements of the natural world like rivers, lakes, and forests).[23] Environmental rights are here understood as proclamations or obligations of states to respect, protect, and promote the rights of individuals, groups, and nonhuman elements of nature to live under environmental conditions that are conducive to a healthy and productive existence.[24]

The new constitutional wave in Latin America has also advanced on another front, with the formal recognition of ethnic and cultural diversity as important values to be protected at the higher legal level. Organized Indigenous movements and their allies in many countries in Latin America had been participating in processes for the inclusion of constitutional guarantees to protect their specific rights at the national level,[25] in parallel to global efforts to create an international framework for Indigenous rights.[26] The constitutional incorporation of Indigenous rights in Latin America has happened progressively over the decades. Raquel Yrigoyen Fajardo argues that the process can be divided into three phases.[27] The first phase, of multicultural constitutionalism, happened in the 1980s when countries like Guatemala,

---

20 Brazil adopted a new constitution in 1988, Colombia in 1991, Paraguay in 1992, Ecuador in 1998 and 2008, Peru in 1993, Venezuela in 1999, Bolivia in 2009. Other countries introduced major reforms to their existing constitutions, including Argentina in 1994, Mexico in 1992, and Costa Rica in 1989. Guatemala adopted a new constitution in 1995, still during civil war. J. F. Gonzalez-Bertomeu and R. Gargarella (eds.), *The Latin American Casebook: Courts, Constitutions, and Rights* (Abingdon, UK: Routledge, 2016).
21 R. Brañes, "El Acceso a La Justicia Ambiental en América Latina," UNEP Mexico, 2000.
22 D. R. Boyd, "The Constitutional Right to a Healthy Environment" (2012) 54 *Environment: Science and Policy for Sustainable Development* 3–15; S. Atapattu, "The Right to a Healthy Life or the Right to Die Polluted? The Emergence of a Human Right to a Healthy Environment Under International Law" (2002) 16 *Tulane Environmental Law Journal* 65 at 72–73.
23 J. Colon-Rios, "The Rights of Nature and the New Latin American Constitutionalism" (2015) 13 *NZ Journal Public International Law* 107.
24 This working definition of environmental rights builds on the definition proposed by Shelton in 2010: "the term 'environmental rights' . . . refers to any proclamation of a human right to environmental conditions of a specified quality." Descriptive terms for environmental quality referenced by Shelton included "safe, healthy, ecologically sound, adequate for development" (D. Shelton, "Developing Substantive Environmental Rights" (2010) 1 *Journal of Human Rights and the Environment* 89).
25 R. Verdum (ed.), *Povos indígenas: constituições e reformas políticas na América Latina/Indigenous Peoples: Constitutions and Political Reform in Latin America* (Portugal: INESC, 2009); G. B. G. de Oliveira Filho, "Novo Constitucionalism Latino-Americano: o Estado Moderno em Contextos Pluralistas/New Constitutionalism in Latin America: The Modern State in Pluralistic Contexts" (2014) 1 *Revista culturas jurídicas*; A. R. Ramos (ed.), *Constituciones nacionales y pueblos indígenas* (Colombia: Editorial Universidad del Cauca, 2014); F. S. Benavides Vanegas, "Movimientos Indígenas y Estado Plurinacional en América Latina" (2010) 27 *Pensamiento jurídico* 239–264.
26 Larsen, note 10.
27 R. Z. Yrigoyen Fajardo, "Aos 20 anos da Convenção 169 da OIT: balanço e desafios da implementação dos direitos dos Povos *Indígenas* na América Latina/On the 20th Anniversary of 160 ILO Convention: Balance and Challenges for Implementation of Indigenous Rights in Latin America," in Verdum, note 25, pp. 9, 31–32.

Nicaragua, and Brazil elevated cultural and ethnic diversity to the constitutional level, recognizing specific Indigenous rights like the right to cultural identity.[28]

The 1990s inaugurated the second phase, of pluricultural identity. Many Latin American constitutions[29] adopted during this decade have reinforced the right to cultural identity, while further developing the concept of "multiethnic nation" and "pluricultural state,"[30] by for example recognizing the collective dimension of cultural identity. During the second phase some constitutions also formally incorporated legal pluralism, recognizing certain autonomy rights like the authority of Indigenous peoples to create their own institutions based on their customs and legal traditions. The third phase, more recent, is reflected in the constitutions of Ecuador (2008) and Bolivia (2009). It includes the constitutional recognition of more transformative demands from Indigenous peoples proposing truly "pluricultural states." Here Indigenous peoples are not merely acknowledged as "diverse cultures" within a postcolonial state, but rather as original nations with rights to participate in the configuration of all state structures.[31]

The parallel development of human rights, Indigenous rights and environmental rights in Latin American constitutions illustrates the fact that concerns with environmental objectives and social justice have developed in tandem in the region.[32] Thus, the social dimension of sustainable development and environmental justice, discussed in the framing chapter of this book, have been at the center of the political agenda for social and environmental movements and Indigenous peoples organizations in Latin America for decades, even if not always clearly articulated as such. The constitutional recognition of rights is however just the first step in a long fight for social justice, and not necessarily the most difficult one. Looking at constitutional environmental rights, Gellers argues that the barriers to their adoption can be relatively low, as they are often aspirational, and worded broadly.[33] Constitutional environmental rights can encourage legislative action, but they offer no guarantees of comprehensive implementation. The same happens to constitutional recognition of human rights and Indigenous rights. Implementation depends on the strength of legislative and administrative institutions and judicial mechanisms that have often been lacking.

For politicians in a number of developing countries, constitutional rights offer a mechanism to score political points with domestic social movements and international donors, without necessarily leading to the costly (politically and financially) phase of implementation. This reality has led social groups in Latin America to invoke national courts and the Inter-American Human Rights System to give effect to constitutionally recognized environmental rights and Indigenous rights, as

---

[28] This move contrasted with earlier legal regimes that officially promoted assimilation and were influenced by global negotiations leading to the 1989 ILO Indigenous and Tribal Peoples Convention.

[29] For example Colombia 1991, Mexico 1992, Peru 1993, Bolivia 1994, 2004, Argentina 1994, Ecuador 1998, Venezuela 1999 (Verdum, note 25).

[30] Fajardo, note 27, p. 26.

[31] R. Uprimny, "The Recent Transformation of Constitutional Law in Latin America: Trends and Challenges" (2011) 89 *Texas Law Review* 1587.

[32] Some authors contrast Latin American environmentalism, which has since colonial times developed inextricable links to social justice struggles, to the history of environmentalism in settler colonial states like the USA, or in Western European colonial powers. Environmentalism in these latter countries only developed a closer link to social justice struggles at a later stage, with the advent of environmental justice movements (Carruters, note 11); J. T. Roberts, J. Timmons, and N. D. Thanos, *Trouble in Paradise: Globalization and Environmental Crisis in Latin America* (Abingdon, UK: Routledge, 2003); D. Faber, *Environment under Fire: Imperialism and the Ecological Crisis of Latin America* (New York: Monthly Review Press, 1993).

[33] J. C. Gellers, "Explaining the Emergence of Constitutional Environmental Rights: A Global Quantitative Analysis" (2015) 6 *Journal of Human Right and the Environment* 75.

well as to clarify their scope and application in the light of regional human rights obligations. At the national level, this movement has led to a number of important judicial decisions on complex environmental issues,[34] including on climate change,[35] that are contributing to the development of national and global environmental rights. The jurisprudence on Indigenous rights in national courts has not been as forthcoming.[36]

Latin American countries have officially embraced the mantra of balancing the three dimensions of sustainable development – the social, the economic, and the environmental – and they have incorporated important constitutional guarantees in relation to environmental rights and Indigenous rights in their national legal regimes. In practice, however, economic interests often continue to displace environmental goals and the rights, values, and interests of Indigenous peoples that have unequal political power vis-à-vis economic elites. A persistent gap between constitutional guarantees and the creation, implementation, and enforcement of effective laws and policies on environmental rights and Indigenous rights may explain why, despite these normative advances, violent environmental conflicts and severe environmental degradation continues to be a reality on the ground in Latin America, with Indigenous peoples being particularly affected.

In this context, many social movements and NGOs in the region have continued to resort to international regimes as additional legal and political tools to help in the domestic efforts to improve implementation of environmental rights in the region. In 1988, the Additional Protocol in the Area of Economic, Social and Cultural Rights (the Protocol of San Salvador)[37] officially recognized a substantive right to a healthy environment, adding this environmental right to the other treaty obligations under the American Convention of Human Rights.[38] The Inter-American Human Rights System has developed a significant body of jurisprudence on environmental rights[39] and Indigenous rights.[40]

---

[34] For example, in 2011, an Ecuadorian court ruled that the Vilcabamba River had a right to flow, a right that had been violated by road development, and ordered the restoration of the river and its flow. *Vilcabamba River v. Provincial Government of Loja, Provincial Justice Court of Loja*, No. 11121–2011–10 (Mar. 30, 2011). In 2006 Argentina's Supreme Court ordered a comprehensive environmental response, including cleanup and restoration of the Matanza–Riachuelo River basin, a heavily polluted area of Buenos Aires. UNEP, *Environmental Rule of Law: First Global Report* (2019), p. 160; see Organization of American States, *Environmental Rule of Law: Trends from the Americas* (Montego Bay, 2015); J. H. Knox and R. Pejan (eds.), *The Human Right to a Healthy Environment* (Cambridge, MA: Cambridge University Press, 2018).

[35] In 2018, the Colombian Supreme Court has recognized the Amazon River ecosystem as subject of rights. An earlier decision had already granted legal rights to the Atrato River (Rio Atrato) in 2016 (Paola Villavicencio Calzadilla, "A Paradigm Shift in Courts' View on Nature: The Atrato River and Amazon Basin Cases in Colombia" (2019) 15 *Law, Environment and Development Journal* 1–11).

[36] R. Sieder, "Indigenous Peoples' Rights and the Law in Latin America," in C. Lennox and D. Short (eds.), *Handbook of Indigenous Peoples' Rights* (Abingdon, UK: Routledge, 2016), p. 414; Economic Commission for Latin America and the Caribbean (ECLAC), "Indigenous Peoples in Latin America," Sept. 22, 2014.

[37] Article 11 states that "everyone shall have the right to live in a healthy environment and to have access to basic public services." It also states that "the state parties shall promote the protection, preservation and improvement of the environment" (Organization of American States (OAS), Additional Protocol to the American Convention on Human Rights in the Area of Economic, Social and Cultural Rights ("Protocol of San Salvador"), Nov. 16, 1999, A-5228 ILM 156 (1989)).

[38] Organization of American States (OAS), American Convention on Human Rights, "Pact of San Jose", Costa Rica, Nov. 22, 1969 [American Convention].

[39] M. A. Orellana, "Derechos Humanos y Ambiente: Desafíos para el Sistema Interamericano de Derechos Humanos," Conference on International Law of the Organization of American States/Organization of American States, Center for International Environmental Law, Nov. 2007; D. Shelton, "Legitimate and Necessary: Adjudicating Human Rights Violations Related to Activities Causing Environmental Harm or Risk" (2015) 6 *Journal of Human Rights and the Environmental* 139.

[40] The Indigenous rights jurisprudence of the IACtHR goes back to 2001, with the *Mayagna (Sumo) Awas Tingni v. Nicaragua* case. The IACtHR provided a good summary of the most relevant cases related to Indigenous rights in the context of environmental protection in Advisory Opinion 23 (IACtHR, "Environment and Human Rights," Advisory Opinion OC-23/17, Requested by the Republic of Colombia, Nov. 15, 2017 (in Spanish only) [Advisory Opinion 23]).

11.3 THE ESCAZÚ AGREEMENT: WHOSE ENVIRONMENTAL RIGHTS?

During the 2012 United Nations Conference on Sustainable Development (Rio + 20), Latin American and Caribbean (LAC)[41] countries launched negotiations for a regional treaty to operationalize Principle 10 of the 1992 Rio Declaration: access to information, public participation in decision-making, and access to justice.[42] These rights are part of international human rights law and have been recognized in regional human rights treaties and in national legal systems.[43] However, before Escazú, Principle 10 had only been operationalized at a regional level by European Countries under the UNECE Convention on Access to Information, Public Participation in Decision-Making and Access to Justice in Environmental Matters (the Aarhus Convention).[44]

During the negotiation of the agreement, Latin American countries drew lessons from the Aarhus Convention, but purposely created a regional instrument that would be more representative and responsive to the realities of the region.[45] Besides procedural rights, Escazú includes a clear enunciation of the substantive right to a healthy environment, which most countries in the region had already incorporated in their constitutions. The Agreement also adopts a novel provision focused on a problem that is particularly significant in the region: systemic violence against environmental defenders. However, Escazú does not reflect an equally salient regional issue: the environmental rights of Indigenous peoples. This omission is noteworthy because Latin America has been marked by serious environmental conflicts involving Indigenous peoples, the parallel development of substantive environmental rights and Indigenous rights in Latin American constitutions, and by the solid jurisprudence of the Inter-American Court of Human Rights (IACtHR) on Indigenous rights.

The "Regional Agreement on Access to Information, Public Participation and Justice in Environmental Matters"[46] was signed on March 4, 2018 in Escazú, in Costa Rica. The Escazú Agreement will enter into force after eleven ratifications.[47] This landmark treaty is the region's first treaty on procedural environmental rights.[48] Substantive environmental rights, like the right to a healthy environment, seek to guarantee the enjoyment of environmental conditions of a certain quality.[49] Procedural rights seek to ensure that the interests of individuals and groups potentially affected by decision-making that affects the environment will be taken into consideration in national or international procedures, and that environmental decisions are subject to accountability.[50]

---

[41] We use Latin American countries for short, although recognizing that Caribbean countries are often treated separately from other Latin American countries for their particularities, which we deem are not relevant to the topic of this chapter.

[42] Giupponi, note 4.

[43] Atapattu and Schapper, note 1, chs. 6 and 8; Kravchenko and Bonive, note 1, chs. 6–8.

[44] UN, Convention on Access to Information, Public Participation in Decision-Making and Access to Justice in Environmental Matters, 2161 UNTS 447; 38 ILM 517 (1999) [Aarhus Convention].

[45] Barritt, note 4.

[46] Escazú Agreement, note 2.

[47] Ibid., Art. 21. States decided for a meticulously negotiated agreement that admits no reservations (Art. 23). As of 20 August 2019, seventeen countries had signed the Escazú Agreement, with one country (Guyana) ratifying it (ECLAC, "Observatory on Principle 10 in Latin America and the Caribbean," https://observatoriop10.cepal .org/en/treaties/regional-agreement-access-information-public-participation-and-justice-environmental).

[48] Barritt, note 4.

[49] Shelton, note 39.

[50] B. Peters, "Unpacking the Diversity of Procedural Environmental Rights: The European Convention on Human Rights and the Aarhus Convention" (2017) 30 *Journal of Environmental Law* 1–27; J. Jendroska,

Escazú, much like the Aarhus Convention, is structured around three procedural rights. Articles 5 and 6, respectively, address access to environmental information and the generation and dissemination of this information. Guided by the principle of maximum disclosure, Article 5 imposes an obligation to create a legal regime to provide public access to all environmental information in a party's "possession, control or custody."[51] Article 5.6 provides a non-exhaustive list of exceptions that parties may adopt. Any other exception needs to be narrowly tailored and justified. Authorities denying access to environmental information in concrete cases must present reasons. Parties are also required to provide opportunities for applicants to challenge denials.

Unlike Aarhus, Escazú takes into account social and economic barriers to access to information, including provisions requiring parties to avoid prohibitive costs and to provide assistance, so that persons or groups in vulnerable situations are able to access environmental information.[52] Thus, Escazú is alert to the need to take into consideration the economic and political reality of many social groups in the region that may benefit the most from environmental access rights, but do not have the material means to obtain this information.

Article 6 presents a non-exhaustive list of types of information parties are mandated to generate, collect, publicize, and disseminate in a systematic, timely, and comprehensive manner. This list includes texts of international treaties and agreements, reports on the state of the environment, scientific reports and studies, and information on the use and conservation of natural resources and ecosystem services. Despite advances in the recognition of the importance of traditional Indigenous knowledge in international law, including agreements like the Convention on Biological Diversity, Article 6 does not explicitly require the generation, collection, and dissemination of information on traditional knowledge related to sustainable use and conservation of natural resources. Article 6 is equally silent on information on Indigenous alternative systems of environmental governance based on ecocentric cosmovisions.

Article 7 requires states to ensure the public's right to participate in environmental decision-making processes. States shall create open and inclusive mechanisms for public participation, based on domestic and international normative frameworks. The provision indicates which types of decision-making processes would require participation: projects and activities that could have a significant impact on the environment or the conservation, use, and management of natural resources, activities that are subject to environmental impact assessments, as well as activities that are subject to other environmental permitting processes.[53] The scope is limited to administrative decisions and does not encompass lawmaking processes. The Convention acknowledges socioeconomic barriers to participation in environmental decision-making, establishing that parties will provide support to enable the participation of vulnerable persons or groups that are directly affected or potentially affected by the decisions by, for example, providing information in various languages.

Participation includes explicit references to Indigenous peoples and local communities.[54] The requirement that parties shall comply with their national laws and international obligations

---

"Introduction Procedural Environmental Rights in Theory and Practice," in J. Jendroska and M. Bar (eds.), *Procedural Environmental Rights: Principle X in Theory and Practice* (Cambridge, MA: Intersentia, 2018)

[51] Escazú Agreement, note 2, Art. 5.

[52] Ibid., Arts. 5.3 and 5.17.

[53] Ibid., Art. 7.

[54] Ibid., Art. 7.15 for example "In the implementation of the present Agreement, each Party shall guarantee that its domestic legislation and international obligations in relation to the rights of Indigenous peoples and local communities are observed."

related to Indigenous peoples, though vague, is an important one. Most Latin American countries are parties to ILO Convention 169 and signatories to the United Nations Declaration on the Rights of Indigenous Peoples (UNDRIP) and the 2016 American Declaration on the Rights of Indigenous Peoples. UNDRIP and the 2016 American Declaration both establish the right of Indigenous Peoples to free, prior, and informed consent (FPIC) in relation to any project affecting their lands, territories, and natural resources.[55] There have been many debates over the actual meaning and scope of FPIC. Indigenous groups contend that many governments are failing to live up to their commitments to properly implement FPIC in concrete cases. Parties could have used Escazú as an opportunity to elaborate on the nature and scope of FPIC obligations in the context of environmental decision-making projects that affect Indigenous peoples, but they failed to do so.

Perhaps the most important provision of Escazú is Article 8, on access to justice in environmental matters. Many countries in Latin America had already adopted laws on access to environmental information and public participation, but those laws are not being fully implemented or enforced. Article 8 provides that parties shall ensure "judicial or administrative mechanisms to challenge and appeal, with respect to substance and procedure" matters related to access to environmental information and public participation in environmental decision-making. If parties fail to provide legal remedies for cases of lack of implementation of these rights, they may now be declared in breach of international obligations. That clarifies the jurisdiction of the Inter-American Commission and the Court to hear cases related to violations of the Escazú provisions, facilitating justiciability through the Inter-American system.[56] By elaborating on specific Indigenous rights like FPIC, Escazú would have improved access to justice for Indigenous peoples on this important right.

Article 9 of the Escazú Agreement is a Latin American innovation, responding to the reality in the region. The provision establishes that "Each Party shall guarantee a safe and enabling environment for persons, groups and organizations that promote and defend human rights in environmental matters, so that they are able to act free from threat, restriction and insecurity." Article 9 also includes measures to prevent, investigate, and punish any violence or threat of violence against environmental defenders. Under existing national and international human rights law, Latin American countries are already under the obligation to protect citizens exercising freedom of expression and freedom of association from all types of violence and threats related to their civil and political activities, and to impose liability on wrongdoers. The reality of persisting violation of these rights to the detriment of environmental defenders led Latin American countries to include this provision to offer additional tools to counter this trend.

By adopting a binding regional instrument on environmental access rights, Latin American countries have moved IEL forward, following the steps of the parties to the Aarhus Convention in Europe. But it would be wrong to consider Escazú merely as a treaty providing for procedural rights. The Agreement is important because it also guarantees "the right of every person to live in a healthy environment and any other universally-recognized human right related to the present Agreement."[57]

Many countries in Latin America had already included the right to a healthy environment in their constitutions. The right is mentioned in the Protocol of San Salvador and has also been articulated by

---

[55] M. Barelli, "Free, Prior and Informed Consent in the Aftermath of the UN Declaration on the Rights of Indigenous Peoples: Developments and Challenges Ahead" (2012) 16 *International Journal of Human Rights* 1–24

[56] Giupponi, note 4, p. 140.

[57] Escazú Agreement, note 2, Art. 4(1).

the Inter-American Court in several cases. Yet the clear reaffirmation of this substantive right to a healthy environment in a treaty brings coherence to the system, reinforces the embeddedness of this substantive environmental right in the region, grants more political power to those currently fighting for the implementation of this right in domestic courts, and discourages regressive legislation during a global moment of rising authoritarianism that did not spare Latin America.

However, parties failed to use Escazú as an opportunity to explicitly integrate existing international Indigenous rights to the environmental rights framework. The link between Indigenous peoples' rights, environmental stewardship, and sustainable development has been emphasized in Principle 22 of the 1992 Rio Declaration.[58] Article XIX of the 2016 American Declaration on Indigenous Rights articulates the intersection between Indigenous rights and the right to a healthy environment:

> Indigenous peoples have the right to live in harmony with nature and to a healthy, safe, and sustainable environment, essential conditions for the full enjoyment of the right to life, *to their spirituality, worldview and to collective* well-being. [emphasis added]

Article XIX also protects Indigenous peoples' rights to conserve, restore, and protect the environment and to manage their lands, their territories, and their resources in a sustainable way. It requires states to establish and to implement programs to assist Indigenous peoples with the conservation and protection of their territories, without discrimination. The articulation of a more specific version of an Indigenous right to a healthy environment that defines "healthy" to clearly include their cosmovision, spirituality, and attention to collective rights and concerns is important. It gives Indigenous peoples more leverage to have their relationship with the natural world and alternative ways of managing natural resources legally recognized and respected, and less prone to being overruled by dominant Western anthropocentric views of sustainable development when conflicts arise.

The IACtHR has also recognized the special link between Indigenous rights and environmental rights in a series of cases brought by Indigenous and tribal populations before the Inter-American System, following the failure of their countries to give effect to domestic Indigenous rights. The IACtHR revisited and expanded this jurisprudence when it issued its landmark Advisory Opinion 23 (Opinion) on *Environment and Human Rights* on November 15, 2017.[59] The context of the Opinion was the potential adverse transboundary environmental impacts of major new infrastructure projects by Nicaragua.

The opinion allowed the IACtHR to consider the scope of human rights obligations resulting from transboundary environmental harm at length, including an unequivocal recognition of the existence of an "autonomous" right to a healthy environment under the American Convention.[60] The court also took into consideration a petition that a group of Indigenous peoples had filed before the Inter-American Commission against Nicaragua, denouncing the

---

[58] UN General Assembly, *Report of the United Nations Conference on Environment and Development, Annex I: Rio Declaration on Environment and Development*, Aug. 12, 1992, UN Doc. A/CONF.151/26, vol. I, Principle 22.

[59] Advisory Opinion 23, note 40. For analyses of Advisory Opinion 23, see M. Feria-Tinta and S. C. Milnes, "International Environmental Law for the 21st Century: The Constitutionalization of the Right to a Healthy Environment in the Inter-American Court of Human Rights Advisory Opinion 23" (2019) 12 *Anuario Colombiano de Derecho Internacional* 43; C. Campbell-Duruflé and S. A. Atapattu, "The Inter-American Court's Environment and Human Rights Advisory Opinion: Implications for International Climate Law" (2018) 8 *Climate Law* 321–337; A. Papantoniou, "Advisory Opinion on the Environment and Human Rights" (2018) 112 *American Journal of International Law* 460–466; M. L. Banda, "Inter-American Court of Human Rights' Advisory Opinion on the Environment and Human Rights" (2018) *American Society International Law: Insights*.

[60] Advisory Opinion 23, note 40, paras. 32–38.

violations of their Indigenous rights due to the same infrastructure project.[61] The court reviewed its prior decisions on Indigenous peoples' land rights and the right to a healthy environment, reiterating the link. In the court's words:

> [I]n cases about territorial rights of Indigenous and tribal peoples, this Court has made references to the interrelation between a healthy environment and human rights protection, considering that Indigenous collective ownership is associated with the protection and access to resources located in [Indigenous] peoples' lands, as those natural resources are necessary for the very survival, the development and the continuity of the lifestyle of said peoples.[62]

Importantly, the IACtHR has taken a step toward an ecocentric approach to sustainable development advanced by many Indigenous peoples, as opposed to the prevailing anthropocentric approach, when it held that the right to a healthy environment includes the legal protection of components of nature (like rivers, forests, seas, and living organisms) per se. Under this interpretation, a state may breach international law if it causes significant harm to nature, even if there is no harm to individuals. The court emphasized the strong link between the right to a life with dignity and the protection of the ancestral lands and natural resources of Indigenous peoples. The Advisory Opinion established that states must adopt positive measures to ensure life with dignity to Indigenous peoples, including protection of their cosmovisions and the close relationship they maintain with land, both individually and collectively.[63]

When Latin American states were negotiating the Escazú Agreement, they were cognizant of both the international soft law and the IACtHR jurisprudence on the special link between Indigenous rights and environmental rights. Yet, Escazú includes very few specific references to Indigenous peoples' rights. This was not for lack of discussion. According to Giupponi, Ecuador proposed the inclusion of explicit references to the ILO Convention 169, the UNDRIP, and the 2016 American Declaration on Indigenous Rights, but it was rejected.[64] There was also a proposal to include an explicit reference to the various "cosmovisions of [Latin American] peoples which was dropped."[65] In contrast, the list of principles guiding the Agreement includes the *pro persona* principle, according to which treaty provisions must be "interpreted in favour of the individual, who is the object of international protection."[66]

Empirical research is needed to shed light on why this integration was rejected in Escazú. It may be due to lack of political agreement on the scope of binding international Indigenous rights, insufficient social pressure, trade-offs, or very likely a reflection of the uphill battle Indigenous peoples still face to have their alternative normative systems recognized in the face of hegemonic Western-based domestic and international legal orders. For whatever reason, Indigenous rights were integrated only marginally into Escazú in 2018, indicating that the dominant Western-centric view that emphasizes humans over nature and individual rights over collective rights still prevails, despite the gains by Indigenous peoples in other fronts.

---

[61] This petition was still pending by the time the IACtHR issued its Opinion. Centro de Asistencia Legal a Pueblos Indigenas (CALPI), "La CIDH abre el Caso de los Pueblos Indigenas y Afrodescendients en contra del Canadal Interoceanico de Nicaragua," June 30, 2018, https://kaosenlared.net/la-cidh-abre-el-caso-de-los-pueblos-indigenas-y-afrodescendientes-en-contra-del-canal-interoceanico-de-nicaragua/.

[62] Advisory Opinion 23, note 40, para. 48 (authors' translation from the official version in Spanish).

[63] Ibid.

[64] Giupponi, note 4.

[65] ECLAC, *Text Compiled by the Presiding Officers Incorporating the Language Proposals from the Countries on the Preliminary Document on the Regional Agreement on Access to Information, Participation and Justice in Environmental Matters in Latin America and the Caribbean, Sixth Version,* Apr. 13, 2017 UN Doc LC/L.4059/Rev.5, Preamble.

[66] Giupponi, note 4, p. 141.

To be clear, the absence of more explicit and clear articulations of Indigenous peoples' rights in Escazú does not exempt Latin American countries from complying with the commitments and obligations they already recognize under existing domestic and international law governing Indigenous peoples' rights. ILO Convention 169 applies to all Latin American countries that have ratified it. States are required to comply with domestic and international human rights obligations in the context of environmental protection and natural resources management, independent of explicit enunciation of this intersection. Yet, over time the need for clear and more explicit integration of human rights regimes and environmental law, with further elaboration of the meaning and scope of environmental rights, came to be recognized. This integration promotes legal coherence and certainty and empowers those fighting to give effect to these rights on the ground.

The meaning and scope of Indigenous environmental rights (both substantive and procedural) should also be clarified under environmental law. We argue, therefore, that Escazú missed an opportunity to consolidate this integration, between Indigenous rights and environmental law, failing to reflect the reality in the region that places Indigenous peoples at the center of environmental justice struggles.

In Section 11.4 we use the community-based water management system of Mayan Indigenous peoples in Totonicapán, Guatemala, to illustrate the importance of this integration in order to ensure the protection of alternative Indigenous cosmovisions of sustainable development in Latin America.

11.4 INDIGENOUS ENVIRONMENTAL RIGHTS: THE TOTONICAPÁN WATER GOVERNANCE EXPERIENCE

The Guatemalan legal framework for water is a tale of incomplete regulation, the formal adoption of a human right to water, and token commitments to consider the social dimension of sustainable development. [67] This framework fails to muster the political will to implement the necessary environmental regulations to make this right and commitments a reality on the ground. There are several water conflicts in Guatemala between Indigenous peoples and the Guatemalan postcolonial state that highlight the clash between different visions of sustainable water management. The gradual formal incorporation of water rights in the Guatemalan legal system has proved so far insufficient to mediate these conflicts anchored in very different cosmovisions related to water resources.

11.4.1 *Guatemala's Postcolonial Legal Framework*

The Guatemalan Civil Code, influenced by Franco-Roman law, has historically regulated all aspects of water governance in the country.[68] The current Civil Code was adopted

---

[67] This section is based on an analysis of Guatemala's legal framework for water resources management, as well as on a series of informal interviews with individuals with in-depth knowledge of Totonicapán's participatory water management systems. The interviews were conducted by coauthor Mario Mancilla (Dec. 13–16, 2018), with the following individuals: Santos Augusto Norato, former president of the forty-eight cantones; Roberto Chuc, expert in natural resources management and resident in a neighboring municipality, who has worked for several NGOs in the region; Robins López, community forestry expert from CARE, who works in partnership with the forty-eight cantones.

[68] B. S. Sanchez and T. Serebrisky, "Water and Sanitation in Latin America and the Caribbean: An Update on the State of the Sector," Robert Schuman Centre for Advanced Studies Research Paper No. RSCAS 10, 2018.

in 1963.[69] Unlike previous iterations, the current Civil Code creates two distinct legal regimes for water management: a private regime and a public regime. The current Civil Code creates a regulatory system for "private water." The 1963 Code established that a new law regulating public waters was to be adopted. More than five decades later, Guatemala lawmakers have yet to achieve consensus to approve a water law.[70] In the absence of a law regulating the management of public water, the provisions of the 1933 Civil Code apply.[71] These provisions treat water as an object or thing (res), subject to property rights. The legal treatment of water does not consider the resource as it relates to biodiversity, social organization, culture, and life more generally.

In other words, much like the system Spain imposed on Guatemala as a colony in the eighteenth century, the only value attached to water under the 1933 (and the 1963) Civil Code is an economic value. The Code does not recognize other values – social, moral, religious, ecosystemic – for people and nature. Water resources are legally treated as dissociated from the broader hydrological system or the biosphere. As a result, all water conflicts are to be resolved by deciding who has the legal property rights over the water resources. In the wake of the approval of more progressive new constitutions in Latin America in the 1980s, following democratic transitions away from dictatorships and civil conflicts, Guatemala's 1985 Constitution represented a seminal change in the legal treatment of water resources, away from the economic model.[72] Articles 127 and 128 of the Constitution provide as follows:

> All waters belong to the public domain and are inalienable and imprescriptible. Their exploitation, use, and enjoyment are granted in the form established by law in accordance with the social interest. A specific law will regulate this matter.

> The exploitation of the waters of lakes and rivers for agricultural, livestock, tourism, or any other purpose contributing to the development of the national economy is at the service of the community rather than of any specific individual, but the users are obliged to reforest the banks and corresponding trenches as well as to facilitate access roads.[73]

In principle, these constitutional provisions have abrogated the Civil Code's legal treatment of water as a mere object or economic commodity, introducing values such as social interest into the water regime, and giving priority to community interest over individual interest. Unfortunately, the Constitution delegates the development of a new water regime to a specific law, to be discussed and passed by the legislature. Thirty-four years after the Constitution was adopted, no specific water law has been approved. In practice, the Civil Code still regulates water rights as individual property rights, without reference to social interest and community rights.[74] In 2010, the UN General Assembly explicitly recognized a human right to water and

---

[69] The first iteration of the Civil Code was adopted in 1887 and modified in 1882 and 1926. The second iteration of the Civil Code was adopted in 1933.

[70] Several water bills have been presented since 1985, but none have been approved due to opposition from both civil society and the private sector, the former advocating for full recognition and respect of Indigenous rights, and the latter lobbying for less restrictive regulations to decrease business costs (A. D'Andrea, "Legal Pluralism and Customary Water Resources Management in Guatemala" (2012) 37 *Water International* 683–699).

[71] Chapters II–V of Title II; Chapters II and III of Title VI of the 1933 Civil Code.

[72] The Constitution was approved during the civil conflict, as the Peace Accords would be signed only in 1996 (J. L. Burrell, *Maya after War: Conflict, Power, and Politics in Guatemala* (Texas: University of Texas Press, 2013)).

[73] Authors' translation; 1985 Constitution of the Republic of Guatemala, with 1993 reforms (in Spanish), online: http://pdba.georgetown.edu/Constitutions/Guate/guate93.html.

[74] Guatemala's Constitutional Court has decided a few cases declaring the existence of a human right to water and sanitation, as essential elements to guarantee a life with dignity and the realization of other human rights. The social interest should prevail over individual private interests when there is a conflict." (Sentencia del

sanitation and acknowledged that clean drinking water and sanitation are essential to the realization of all human rights.[75] Guatemala has thus far not adopted national legislation providing for a human right to water, nor established clear priority of water use for domestic purposes over commercial or industrial uses.

In practice, Guatemala's policies and administrative decisions related to water give industry and agribusiness privileged access to water in the name of economic development. The confusing patchwork of progressive but unimplemented constitutional provisions, coupled with outdated or nonexistent legal regimes, coexist with alternative Indigenous or community water management systems that are more holistic and benefit from strong moral, cultural, and spiritual elements. In this context, opposing views related to water have generated constant conflicts between Guatemala's various social groups, in particular the largely poor Indigenous communities and the economic elites composed primarily of European descendants.

The most common types of conflict include:

- Use of water resources for commercial activities,[76] particularly sugar cane[77] and African palm crops,[78] as opposed to prioritizing communities' access to water in keeping with the human right to water and sanitation.
- Use of water for electricity generation (dams), for mining activities,[79] and for other industrial purposes, versus protecting water levels to maintain sustainable flows for rivers and lakes.
- Inequitable access to water. In urban zones, low-income families have less access to drinking water than higher-income families, despite paying the same overall taxes, because there is a monthly charge (*canon de agua* or *servicio de agua*) that many can't afford. Around three million Guatemalans lacked access to water in 2016.[80]
- Lack of sanitation systems and wastewater treatment.[81] Infant mortality rates in Guatemala, in great part due to lack of sanitation, are higher than the regional average.[82]
- Food security. Without adequate access to water, low-income communities cannot rely on subsistence farming or on family crops to ensure their food security. Nowadays many families rely on rainfall, which is becoming ever more unreliable due to climate change.

16–5–17 en el Expediente 308–2017). The lack of a water law gives space for private actors to act in disobedience of the constitutional mandate, as litigating for water rights is an expensive and cumbersome process that is often not accessible to Indigenous groups.

[75] UN General Assembly, Resolution adopted by the General Assembly on July 28, 2010 [without reference to a Main Committee (A/64/L.63/Rev.1 and Add.1)] 64/292. The human right to water sanitation, Aug. 3, 2010, UN Doc. A/RES/64/292.

[76] S. de León, "Crisis de agua y monocultivos en la costa sur de Guatemala," www.entremundos.org/revista/politica/crisis-de-agua-y-monocultivos-en-la-costa-sur-de-guatemala/.

[77] C. Salvatierra, "Guatemala: los amargos impactos de la caña de azúcar," June 30, 2009, https://wrm.org.uy/fr/les-articles-du-bulletin-wrm/section1/guatemala-los-amargos-impactos-de-la-cana-de-azucar/.

[78] C. Salcatierra, "Guatemala: monocultivos de palma y caña de azúcar lesionan a comunidades del río Coyolate," Dec. 30, 2010, https://wrm.org.uy/es/articulos-del-boletin-wrm/seccion2/guatemala-monocultivos-de-palma-y-cana-de-azucar-lesionan-a-comunidades-del-rio-coyolate/

[79] J. Menkos Zeissig, "La minería en Guatemala: realidad y desafíos frente a la democracia y el desarrollo," Guatemala: Instituto Centroamericano de Estudios Fiscales, 2014.

[80] E. Pitán, "Más de 500 mil vecinos sufren escasez de agua," May 20, 2016, www.prensalibre.com/guatemala/comunitario/mas-de-500-mil-vecinos-sufren-escasez-de-agua/

[81] "Situación del Recurso Hídrico en Guatemala: Documento Técnico del Perfil Ambiental de Guatemala," Universidad Rafael Landívar, Instituto de Incidencia Ambiental, Embajada Real de los Países Bajos, Nov. 2015.

[82] J. Elías, "Las Aguas sucias de Guatemala," June 24, 2015, https://elpais.com/internacional/2015/06/24/actualidad/1435177135_432060.html.

An example of the environmental and social impacts of the lack of a coherent system of water regulations is the pollution of Lake Atitlán. In 1996 the Guatemalan government created the Authority for the Sustainable Management of the Basin of Lake Atitlán, to help coordinate efforts to protect the lake watershed.[83] Despite the existence of this framework, the contamination of the waters – caused by growing population, agricultural runoff, and tourism in the lake basin – increased exponentially. In March 2016, a group of Mayan communities from Lake Atitlán, supported by local organizations, filed an official complaint against ten municipalities for the continued environmental pollution of the lake.[84]

The attempts to call attention to the water problems in Lake Atitlán were part of a broader movement by Indigenous communities throughout Guatemala to denounce the many instances where their water resources were being contaminated or undermined by monoculture farming, deforestation, plastic wastes,[85] mines, and hydroelectric projects. In April 2016, thousands of Indigenous groups and campesinos marched to Guatemala City to demand that the Guatemalan government respect their right to water.[86] At the time of writing this chapter, the government has taken no action to resolve these problems, and Indigenous peoples continue their fight to protect Lake Atitlán's water resources.

This situation contrasts with examples of Indigenous communities' successful management of scarce water resources in other watersheds, as in the case of Totonicapán. The Totonicapán experience illustrates some of the important particularities of Indigenous peoples' relation to nature and stewardship of natural resources based in ecovisions that Escazú failed to recognize.

11.4.2 *Ecocentric Water Regimes: the Totonicapán Experience*

Totonicapán is a Guatemalan region that covers an area of about 1,000 square kilometers in the country's western volcanic highlands. More than 95 percent of Totonicapán's approximately 491,000 inhabitants are K'iche', an Indigenous Maya population.[87] Totonicapán's climate is moderately dry, and the region has no large rivers or important permanent water bodies like lakes. This climate and topography mean that all significant water resources in Totonicapán come from a forest watershed.[88]

The Communal Forest of Totonicapán is recognized as the largest and most well-preserved coniferous forest in all of Central America.[89] Approximately 39,000 hectares of forests support a rich ecosystem that has been communally preserved for centuries in spite of extreme pressures

[83] Decreto 133–96 del Congreso. Similar authorities have been created to manage other national lakes: Decreto No. 64–96 (Lake Amatitlan); Acuerdo Gubernativo 697–2003 (Peten-Itza).

[84] J. Abbott, "Contamination of Sacred Lake Underscores Environmental Racism in Guatemala," May 28, 2016, https://truthout.org/articles/contamination-of-sacred-lake-underscores-environmental-racism-in-guatemala/.

[85] Sometimes even when municipal governments take the initiative to protect water resources private interests offer political or legal resistance. One example of municipal initiative resisted by the private sector is the one in San Pedro La Laguna in Lake Atitlán. In 2016 the municipal government approved a regulation prohibiting the commercialization of single-use plastics in the city's perimeter to counter plastic pollution. A group of private associations filed action in the Constitutional Court, questioning the legal authority of the municipality to issue such a prohibition. The court declared the regulation valid, within the powers of the municipal government. Yet this shows the difficulty of countering private interests. Sentencia del 5 de octubre de 2017, Expediente 5956–2016 Corte de Constitucionalidad.

[86] Abbott, note 84.

[87] "Tema/Indicadores," Instituto Nacional de Estadística, Guatemala, (National demographic projections), 2019, www.ine.gob.gt/ine/poblacion-menu/.

[88] T. T. Veblen, "Forest Preservation in Western Highlands of Guatemala" (1978) 68 *Geographical Review* 417.

[89] USAID Guatemala, "Scene Setter for the Visit to the Alcaldia Comunal of the 48 Cantones de Totonicapán," updated 2013, https://rmportal.net/groups/cbnrm/cbnrm-literature-for-review-discussion/48-cantones-de-totoni capan-1; S. E. Gramajo, *Autogestión comunitaria de recursos naturales: estudio de caso en Totonicapán* (Guatemala: Guatemala, 1997).

on the land resulting from the high rural population densities[90] and broader economic pressures of a national economy with a strong focus on exporting natural resources. The forest ecosystem functions as a sponge[91] which is possible because the surface of the volcanic soil consists of permeable material like sand and clay, while impermeable material is found in the subsoil. This is the only source of water for Totonicapán through the six months of the dry season. But the forest has a bigger role that transcends the municipality. The 1,200 water springs found in Totonicapán communal forest are the headwaters for five of Guatemala's major rivers – Samalá, Chixoy, Nahualate, Motagua, and Quiscab, with this last river draining into Lake Atitlán.[92]

The Maya K'iche' peoples of Totonicapán have sustainably managed this forest watershed for hundreds of years. They have adapted their systems along the way, in order to address natural and societal changes that threatened their water resources, considered sacred.[93] In order to protect the watershed, the Maya K'iche' have adopted participatory models of water governance. These communal water management systems function independently from Guatemalan water management systems and they are anchored in a distinct cosmovision.

11.4.3 *Conception of Water/Hydric Resources*

Totonicapán Maya communities consider water a special entity: it has physical characteristics and manifestations, but it also possesses a spiritual character. In fact, the Mayas in Totonicapán have recognized that water has its own Nahual – a form of guardian spirit possessed by each person and by certain natural entities.[94] The Nahual embodies the strength, the character, and the spirit of the person or entity, and it is often materialized as an animal that serves as guide and conscience.[95] The main value attached to water is life itself: water is life and this is one reason it is considered sacred. Water is not reduced to its chemical composition, in isolation from the rest of the ecology. On the contrary, water can only be understood and conceived in its intimate relationship with natural entities like mountains, hills, rivers, lakes, springs, and the forests.

Totonicapán Mayas believe that the long-term existence of water is compromised unless this ecological context is taken into account. According to their cosmovision, certain birds, animals, plants, and flowers are able to announce the arrival and the departure of water because they are part of water and water is part of them.[96] In this sense, water encompasses all: animals, plants, land, and people. Food security and good health (physical and spiritual) for all

---

[90] Totonicapán is the most densely populated department in Guatemala excluding the capital city.

[91] Totonicapán experiences a pronounced seasonality in precipitation, with more than 90 percent of annual rain falling between April and October (Veblen, note 88).

[92] USAID Guatemala, note 89.

[93] The water management systems have developed organically, as part of ancient cultural practices, with no formality, no legal personality associated Western legal systems. With population growth, the need to establish relations with Guatemala's colonial and postcolonial state institutions, which had embraced market economy, has gradually moved toward a formalization of the water systems, albeit under Indigenous rules. This formalization has helped in interactions with authorities at various levels of government – municipal, provincial, regional, national – as well as in relationships with neighboring communities. Despite the adoption of some written reports and documents, the Indigenous traditions of oral documentation and the values and beliefs related to water resources persist.

[94] The closest concept to a Nahual, from a Western Judeo-Christian cultural tradition, would be a guardian angel (R. Martínez González, "Las entidades anímicas en el pensamiento maya" (2007) 30 *Estudios de cultura maya* 153–174).

[95] Ibid.

[96] Interview conducted by Mario Mancilla in Quetzaltenango with Santos Augusto Norato (14–12–18).

living beings, including human communities, depend on the existence of sufficient water throughout the year.

Because water is life itself, it cannot be considered a material commodity. Water cannot be reduced to its monetary value, a commodity amenable to sale, exchange, or private ownership. Totonicapán Mayas do recognize that water has an economic value, but this is not the most important value. As water is considered a special entity (sacred, integral, and essential for life), it cannot belong to anyone. All community members have both the right to access water and the responsibility to protect it. This strong ancient Maya cosmovision that conceives water not as an economic or material element, but as sacred and integrated into broader ecological systems, is the basis of the governance system the communities have employed to manage water resources, borrowing some elements of the formal postcolonial system but transforming it to fit the Indigenous cosmovision.

11.4.4 *Water Governance System*

Totonicapán has an unusual model of participatory institutional organization. The forty-eight cantones[97] of Totonicapán are a conglomerate of distinct assemblies and their respective boards of directors (*junta directivas*). These assemblies are formed by a group of smaller administrative divisions distributed in all eight municipalities in the region of Totonicapán. These divisions are charged not only with building, managing, and protecting water systems and other collective natural resources and services, but also with addressing social conflicts and delinquency in Totonicapán. The divisions also provide other public services such as preserving traditions and historical documents.

Governance and power structures are based on the K'axk'ol[98] principle of charitable service to the community that entails responsibility and "suffering" with and for others.[99] Those given the honor of being elected to serve do not receive any economic or other monetary benefits. Under this conception, power is based and legitimated by service to others, and authority continues to rest with the community. Those receiving this power have to guide others to do collective work (K'amalb'e) so that the common good is achieved.[100] Leadership roles are based on three principles: (a) political power alternation; (b) unlimited possibilities for the community to withdraw authority; and (c) accountability to the community.

A water committee is delegated the task of building, managing, and maintaining water systems to distribute water for consumption by communities. Because water is considered a collective good, to be shared between all community members who have both the right to water and responsibilities to protect it, water cannot be owned individually.

The Totonicapán water management system has succeeded in promoting harmonious social relations and protecting water quality and water access. There is a clear absence of serious conflicts over water among community members but also with external actors, despite the many stressors along the centuries.

---

[97] For an explanation of the administrative structure of cantons and the history of this name dating back to colonial times, see B. Escobar and L. Eugenia, *Tras las huellas del poder local: la Alcaldía Indígena en Guatemala, del siglo XVI al siglo XX* (Guatemala: Universidad Rafael Landívar, 2001).

[98] Norato, Santos Augusto, Gobernanza del agua en Totonicapán (interview, 14–12–18).

[99] M. Garía and E. Hernándezs, *Una Oportunidad de Servir: Conociendo Nuestra Experiencia de Trabajo* (2017).

[100] Membership in the assembly or a board of directors of the forty-eight cantones of Totonicapán is a year-long service. A citizen is expected to complete no more than three terms as a member in a lifetime. This community work usually implies a significant economic burden, and therefore those that serve and the broader community do not take this service lightly (ibid.).

Any discussion on the creation of the much-needed overarching water law in Guatemala needs to include IEL principles such as sustainability, conservation, and participation, and constitutional principles such as social justice and public trust. It should not only reflect substantive and procedural environmental rights reflected in Escazú but go beyond them.

11.5 CONCLUSION

The process of integrating human rights and environmental law at the international level represents one important step toward the actualization of the social dimension of sustainable development. This integration should, however, be expansive enough to incorporate not only the universal set of environmental rights now being enshrined in international agreements like Escazú, but also the more specific Indigenous environmental rights that are based on alternative cosmovisions of the natural world and the place of human beings in it. By making only marginal references to Indigenous environmental rights, Escazú does not advance the growing recognition of Indigenous peoples' rights to alternative approaches to sustainable development that seek to better harmonize human relationships with the natural world. By failing to contribute to a more coherent international environmental rights regime that integrates the evolving body of Indigenous rights, Escazú reinforces the dominant Western approaches to international and national environmental law and policy and sustainable development.[101]

Escazú also represents a missed opportunity for Latin America to show leadership in steering IEL toward a more pluralistic, ecocentric, and biocentric approach, increasingly recognized by Latin American countries at the domestic level, as exemplified by the new constitutions of Ecuador and Bolivia. As Judge Weeramantry observed in 1997, international law needs to draw lessons from traditional societies and diverse cultures, including Indigenous peoples, in harmonizing the various dimensions of sustainable development.[102]

Securing more space for alternative legal systems based on different cosmovisions that place nature at the center and not at the margins of living beings' existence may generate more successful experiences of sustainable development like the one in Totonicapán. This is particularly important in countries with very high levels of violent environmental conflicts such as Guatemala.

---

[101] C. M. Kauffman and P. L. Martin, "Scaling up Buen Vivir: Globalizing Local Environmental Governance from Ecuador" (2014) 14 *Global Environmental Politics*.

[102] ICJ, *Gabčíkovo–Nagymaros Project*, Separate Opinion of Justice Weeramantry, Reports, 1997, p. 107.

Indigenous Ancestors

Recognizing Legal Personality of Nature as a Reconciliation Strategy for Connective Sustainable Governance

Jacinta Ruru

12.1 INTRODUCTION

On the world stage there is now a suite of laws that aspire to recognize Indigenous peoples' cultural environmental management philosophies and practices. Of international acclaim, on July 27, 2014, Te Urewera, a large forested national park in the North Island of Aotearoa New Zealand, became simply: Te Urewera "a legal entity" with "all the rights, powers, duties, and liabilities of a legal person."[1] Three years later, on March 20, 2017, Aotearoa New Zealand enacted legislation giving legal personality to the country's third longest river, the Whanganui River.[2] In December 2017, it was announced that law will be enacted in the near future to recognize Mount Taranaki as a legal person "effectively giving the mountain the same protections as a citizen."[3] Legal personality of this land, river, and mountain mark a significant positive transformation for Aotearoa New Zealand's environmental *and* constitutional laws. These laws provide a connective example of how western colonial law can positively forge a bridge to Indigenous laws. These resolutions are groundbreaking political solutions to constructively accept at a national level Māori Indigenous laws for knowing, caring for, and using lands and waters. In the Māori world, Te Urewera is the heart of the fish caught by *Maui* (a demi-god); Whanganui River is a *tupuna* (ancestor) as is Mount Taranaki/Egmont. These statutes endorse Māori visions for knowing and caring for lands and waters and reassert a founding place for *tikanga Māori* (Māori law) for guiding contemporary New Zealand regional environmental governance and management.

The Māori kinship base for law is aligned around the world with other Indigenous peoples' legal systems. The Indigenous ways of knowing and caring for the environment disrupt the Western myths that the environment is something apart from humanity, humanity's economy, and its social well-being.[4] New innovative nation-state law and policy, such as legal personality,

---

[1] Te Urewera Act, 2014 No. 51, s. 11(1).

[2] Te Awa Tupua (Whanganui River Claims Settlement) Act, 2017 No. 7.

[3] B. Smith, "Mt Taranaki to Become Legal Personality under Agreement between Iwi and Government," Dec. 21, 2017, www.stuff.co.nz/taranaki-daily-news/news/100085814/mt-taranaki-to-become-legal-personality-under-agreement-between-iwi-and-government?rm=m.

[4] See generally, I. Watson, "First Nations, Indigenous Peoples: Our Laws Have Always Been Here," in I. Watson (ed.), *Indigenous Peoples as Subjects of International Law* (Abingdon, UK: Routledge, 2018), p. 96; C. Jones, *New Treaty New Tradition: Reconciling New Zealand and Māori Law* (Vancouver: UBC Press, 2017); H. Friedland, *The Wetiko Legal Principles: Cree and Anishinek Responses to Violence and Victimization* (Toronto: University of Toronto Press, 2018); J. Borrows (Kegedonce), *Drawing out Law: A Spirit's Guide* (Toronto: University of Toronto Press 2010).

offer all citizens hope for more just and sustainable environmental futures couched in more respectful constitutional relationships. This chapter considers the ethics of sustainability as a continuing mainstay in Māori law, how sustainable development has fared in environmental law in Aotearoa New Zealand, and how the concept of legal personality of the environment, specifically the Te Urewera solution, advances connective commitments to sustainable governance for at least this one country.

12.2 MĀORI AND ENVIRONMENTAL LAWS IN AOTEAROA NEW ZEALAND

The legal history of Aotearoa New Zealand began when the first peoples – Māori – deliberately sailed the ocean expanse to make their home on the lands and waters lying far into the horizon of the South Pacific some centuries ago. They brought with them their cosmology, science, law, social organization, and systems of knowledge. At the heart of this culture was (and is):[5]

> [T]he defining principle of . . . kinship – the value through which [they] expressed relationships not only with each other but also with ancestors and with the physical and spiritual worlds. The sea, for example, was not an impersonal thing, but an ancestor deity. Kinship was a revolving door between the human, physical, and spiritual realms. This culture had its own creation theories, its own science and technology, its own bodies of sacred and profane knowledge. It emphasised individual responsibility to the collective at the expense of individual rights, yet greatly valued individual reputation and standing. It also enabled human exploitation of the environment, but through the kinship value (known in [the Māori world] as whanaungatanga) it also emphasised human responsibility to nurture and care for it (known in [the Māori world] as kaitiakitanga).

These peoples became literally, *tangata whenua* (the people of the land). Approximately forty distinct tribal federations continue today to practice this kinship system.[6] All Māori tribal federations have geographical identity markers linked to significant ancestral lands and waters. For instance, "Ko wai au?" asks who am I, but more literally translates as "Who are my waters?" Throughout the Māori language, these daily reminders of kinship abound. For instance, *iwi* means both 'tribe' and 'bone'; *hapū* means both 'sub-tribe' and 'to be pregnant,' *whānau* means both 'extended family' and 'to give birth'; *whenua* means 'land' and 'afterbirth'; and *wai* means 'water' but also 'memory,' and 'who.'[7] The Māori legal system reflects this kinship personified world view. It is predominantly values, not rules-based,[8] and centers on the notions of multiple relationships between people and the surrounding environment. Integral values in the Māori legal system include *whakapapa* (genealogy), *whanaungatanga* (family relationships), *mana* (authority), *mauri* (spiritual life principles/life force), *tapu* (sacredness), *rahui* (prohibition or conservation), and *manaaki* (hospitality).[9] The regulatory concept, *utu*, requires the

---

[5] T. T. Tuatahi, "Ko Aotearoa Tēnei: A Report into Claims Concerning New Zealand Law and Policy Affecting Māori Culture and Identity," Wai 262, Waitangi Tribunal Report, 2011, p. 13.

[6] See A. Anderson, J. Binney, and A. Harris, *Tangata Whenua: An Illustrated History* (Wellington: Bridget Williams Books, 2014); M. Reilly, S. Duncan, G. Leoni, et al. (eds.), *Te Kōparapara: An Introduction to the Māori World* (Auckland: Auckland University Press, 2018).

[7] See H. W. Williams, *A Dictionary of the Māori Language* (Wellington: Government Printer, 1971); H.M. Mead, *Tikanga Māori. Living by Māori Values* (rev. ed.) (Wellington: Huia Publishers, 2016).

[8] See E. T. Durie, "Te Hono ki Hawai'iki: The Bond with the Pacific," in M. Wilson and P. Hunt (eds.), *Culture, Rights, and Cultural Rights. Perspectives from the South Pacific* (Wellington: Huia Publishers, 2000), p. 47; E. T. Durie, "Will the Settlers Settle? Cultural Conciliation and Law" (1996) 8 *Otago Law Review* 449.

[9] R. Benton, A. Frame, and P. Meredith, *Te Mātāpunenga: A Compendium of References to the Concepts and Institutions of Māori Customary Law* (Wellington: Victoria University Press, 2013); New Zealand Law

maintenance of harmony and balance ensuring reciprocal acts of continued generosity. *Kaitiakitanga* (guardianship), as a further example, is about "more than managing relations between environmental resources and humans; it also involves managing relationships between people in the past, present and future."[10] A common Māori phrase for this law – *tikanga Māori* – involves an "obligation to do things in the 'right' way" or "way(s) of doing and thinking held by Māori to be just and correct."[11] To illustrate in a specific context, Māori legal contracts concern not the transfer of rights for a prescribed consideration or immediate return as is typical in Western transactions,[12] but the establishment of a permanent and personal relationship with reciprocal obligations where the main benefit to both sides would come in the course of time.

This legal system was significantly disrupted with the arrival of Europeans in the late 1700s who had developed their own specific world views about the environment that differently positioned people above nature, with prioritized responsibilities to tame the environment for human utilization. In 1840, the British Crown declared sovereignty over Aotearoa New Zealand. The English language version of the Treaty of Waitangi was partly relied on as proof of sovereignty. In English, it recorded Māori ceding their sovereignty to the British Crown but in the Māori language version, Māori were to retain their chieftainship over their own properties. While the Treaty is said to now represent an important component of our constitution, for the most part the colonial government dishonored the Treaty commitments. From 1840, Māori were purposively alienated from the management of significant natural features and resources.[13] Even significant ancestral treasures, such as the tallest mountain in the country, Aoraki/Mount Cook – the son of Raki (sky father)[14] – were not exempt from the exclusive 'take-all' stance of the Crown. The mountain came under assumed Crown ownership and management in the nineteenth century,[15] along with most of the lands and waters in the country.

Commission, "Study Paper 9: Māori Custom and Values in New Zealand Law, Mar. 2001; A. Frame, "A Few Simple Points about Customary Law" (2010–2011) 13–14 Yearbook of New Zealand Jurisprudence 20; R. Boast and A. Erueti, "Māori Customary Law and Land Tenure," in R. Boast, A. Erueti, D. McPhail, and N. F. Smith (eds.), *Māori Land Law* (2nd ed.) (Wellington: LexisNexis, 2004), p. 1; M. Jackson, "The Treaty and the Word: The Colonization of Māori Philosophy," in G. Oddie and R. Perrett (eds.), *Justice, Ethics, and New Zealand Society* (Auckland: Oxford University Press, 1992), p. 1; D. Hikuroa, "Mātauranga Māori – the Ukaipo of Knowledge in New Zealand" (2017) 41(1) *Journal of the Royal Society of New Zealand* 5; P. Tohe, "Māori Jurisprudence: The Neglect of Tapu" (1998) 8 *Auckland Universities Law Review* 884; J. Williams, "Lex Aotearoa: An Heroic Attempt to Map the Māori Dimension in Modern New Zealand Law" (2013) 21 *Waikato Law Review* 1; M. Stephens and M. Boyce, *He Papakupu Reo Ture: A Dictionary of Māori Legal Terms* (Wellington: LexisNexis, 2013).

10 M. Kawharu, "Kaitiakitanga: A Māori Anthropological Perspective of the Māori Socio-Environmental Ethic of Resource Management" (2000) 109 *Journal of the Polynesian Society* 349; J. Hutchings, J. Smith, N. Roskruge, C. Severne, J.P. Mika, and J. Panoho, "Enhancing Māori Agribusiness through Kaitiakitanga Tools," Our Land and Water National Science Challenge, July 2017.

11 NZ Law Commission, note 9, p. 16.

12 Although Western challenges certainly exist, for example, see G. K. Hadfield, "Problematic Relations: Franchising and the Law of Incomplete Contracts" (1990) 42 *Stanford Law Review* 927.

13 The best records are with the Waitangi Tribunal: for example, see Waitangi Tribunal, "The Ngai Tahu Report. Volume One: Summary of Grievances, Findings and Recommendations," Wai 27, 1991; Waitangi Tribunal, "The Taranaki Report. Kaupapa Tuatahi," Wai 143, 1996. Alienation by dubious means, including confiscation, is also documented, and apologized for, in Crown–Māori settlement legislation, commencing with the first contemporary settlements, see Waikato Raupatu Claims Settlement Act, 1995 No. 58; Ngai Tahu Claims Settlement Act, 1998 No. 97.

14 See Ngai Tahu Claims Settlement Act, 1998 No. 97, sch. 80, for an explanation of the Ngai Tahu cultural, spiritual, historic, and traditional values relating to Aoraki/Mount Cook.

15 For a detailed discussion of historical and current ownership and management issues concerning mountains in New Zealand, see J. Ruru, "Indigenous Peoples' Ownership and Management of Mountains: The Aotearoa/New Zealand Experience" (2004) 3 *Indigenous Law Journal* 111.

In 1984, the government formed a working party to consider major reform of the institutional management of natural and historic resources.[16] It acknowledged that the then existing colonial-inspired system had failed to "recognise either the conservation ethic practised by the Māori community or their rights guaranteed by the Treaty of Waitangi,"[17] and commented that:[18]

> The views of the Māori community deserve special mention. Whereas the philosophy of the pakeha [New Zealand European] community has evolved from one based on the values of development to a belief that conservation must be integrated with development, the Māori people have traditionally practised conservation and lived off sustainable resources. Their relationship to all physical and natural resources is a personal one, and their view of the environment as a context of cultural identity is important. They have seen themselves, for much longer than conservation groups, as poorly treated by development-oriented administrations. They see their rights to "o ratou taonga katoa" ("all things prized by them") guaranteed by the Treaty of Waitangi, and their partnership contract with the pakeha, ignored or overlooked.

A prominent catalyst for the working party's stance was the work of the Waitangi Tribunal. The Tribunal had been established in 1975 to make recommendations on claims relating to the practical application of the Treaty and to determine whether the activities of the Crown are inconsistent with the Treaty principles.[19] It released several prominent reports in the early-to-mid 1980s that criticized the government-sanctioned degradation of natural resources.[20] It classified the actions as breaches of the Treaty of Waitangi. Common themes emphasized in many of the reports included that existing structures were "unacceptably monocultural,"[21] and that any reform of the environmental system must take into account the concerns of Māori as rightful partners in the management of natural resources.[22] Even though the Tribunal's recommendations for change had no binding force, the government became acutely aware of the issues and accepted the working party's recommendations to establish two new institutions. The Ministry for the Environment and the Department of Conservation were established in 1986 and 1987, respectively. The Ministry was directed to take a full and balanced account of the principles of the Treaty; the Department was directed to give effect to the principles of the Treaty.[23]

All environmental legislation today requires some level of commitment to the Treaty principles. No exhaustive list of the Treaty principles has been developed, but generally they include commitments to partnership, reciprocity, autonomy, active protection, options, mutual benefit, equity, equal treatment, and redress.[24] However, as is explored below, these Treaty commitments are often demoted in favor of

---

[16] See Minister for the Environment, "Environment 1986. Report of the Post-Environment Forum Working Party," State Services Commission, 1985.

[17] As summarized by D. Fisher, "The New Environmental Management Regime in New Zealand" (1987) 4 *Environmental and Planning Law Journal* 33, p. 39.

[18] See Minister for the Environment, note 16, p. 17.

[19] See Treaty of Waitangi Act, 1975 No. 114.

[20] For example, see Waitangi Tribunal, "Report of the Waitangi Tribunal on the Motuni-Waitara Claim," Wai 6, 1983; Waitangi Tribunal, "Report of the Waitangi Tribunal of the Kaituna River Claim," Wai 4, 1984; Waitangi Tribunal, "Finding of the Waitangi Tribunal on the Manukau Claim," Wai 8, 1985.

[21] Parliamentary Commissioner for the Environment, "Environmental Management and the Principles of the Treaty of Waitangi. Report on Crown Response to the Recommendations of the Waitangi Tribunal 1983–1988," Nov. 1988, p. 4.

[22] For further discussion, see N. Wheen and J. Ruru, "The Environmental Reports," in J. Hayward and N. Wheen (eds.), *The Waitangi Tribunal: Te Roopu Whakamana i te Tiriti o Waitangi* (Wellington: Bridget Williams Books, 2004), p. 97.

[23] See Environment Act, 1986 No. 127; Conservation Act, 1987 No. 65, s. 4.

[24] For example, see Waitangi Tribunal, "Te Tau Ihu o te Waka a Maui: Report on Northern South Island Claims," Wai 785, 2008.

other priorities including couched in commitments to sustainability. Legislative directives are significant in Aotearoa New Zealand because its system of government prioritizes Parliament (the legislature) as supreme (rather than a constitution).[25] The courts are empowered to interpret and apply the law, which in recent decades has become inclusive of Treaty principles.

12.3 SUSTAINABLE PHILOSOPHIES UNDERPINNING ENVIRONMENTAL LAWS IN AOTEAROA NEW ZEALAND

The Department of Conservation has the governance responsibility for the most scenically spectacular "mountains, forests, sounds, seacoasts, lakes, and rivers" which lie in the conservation estate.[26] A variety of labels are used to protect this large estate, constituting more than 30 percent of the country's landmass, such as national parks, reserves, wildlife areas, and marine mammal sanctuaries. The Department has a singular mandate: conservation through the practice of preservation and protection. The Conservation Act 1987 defines 'conservation' as:[27]

> the preservation and protection of natural and historic resources for the purpose of maintaining their intrinsic values, providing for their appreciation and recreational enjoyment by the public, and safeguarding the options of future generations.

This management ethic of preservation and protection is not new; managers operating under the previous institutional system of protecting, for example, national parks, were already practicing preservation policies.[28] Despite a legislative requirement to give effect to the Treaty principles in administering the Conservation Act, the mismatch between Māori law (humans are an important part of the environment) and the Conservation's primary mandate of preservation (humans are separate from nature) has unsurprisingly warranted few significant shifts toward more holistically departmental inclusive practices toward Māori.[29]

Inclusive of the conservation estate, and more importantly beyond to all land, air, and water in the country, is the Resource Management Act 1991 (RMA). The purpose of the RMA is to promote the sustainable management of natural and physical resources.[30] "Sustainable management" is defined in the cornerstone section 5 of the RMA as:

> managing the use, development and protection of natural and physical resources in a way, or at a rate which enables people and their communities to provide for their social, economic and cultural well-being and for their health and safety while –
>
> (a) sustaining the potential of natural and physical resources (excluding minerals) to meet the reasonably foreseeable needs of future generations; and
> (b) safeguarding the life-supporting capacity of air, water, soil and ecosystems; and
> (c) avoiding, remedying or mitigating any adverse effects of activities on the environment.

[25] J. Ruru, P. Scott, and D. Webb, *The New Zealand Legal System. Structures and Processes* (6th ed.) (Wellington: LexisNexis NZ, 2016).

[26] See National Parks Act, 1980 No. 66, s. 4(2)(e).

[27] Conservation Act, note 23, s. 2 'Conservation.'

[28] See the now repealed National Parks Act, 1952 No. 54, s. 3(1), and the current National Parks Act, note 26, s. 4(1).

[29] Waitangi Tribunal, note 5; J. Ruru, P. O. Lyver, N. Scott, and D. Edmunds, "Reversing the Decline in New Zealand's Biodiversity: Empowering Māori within Reformed Conservation Law" (2017) 13 *Policy Quarterly* 65.

[30] Resource Management Act, 1991 No. 69, s. 5.

When the RMA was enacted, it was heralded globally as groundbreaking in moving a domestic jurisdiction toward sustainable development.[31] However, the RMA quickly came under fire for its shortcomings. The challenge, as once put by the Commissioner for the Environment, is "for New Zealand to maintain a real commitment to achieving sustainable management and make a commitment to move beyond sustainable management to sustainable development. New Zealand does not seem committed to sustainable development."[32] A substantial hindrance has been the ideological commitment to let market solutions and nonintervention by government practices address social, economic, and cultural well-being factors.[33]

Interpretation of section 5 of the RMA has itself been divisive. Much of the debate has focused on the interpretation of the word "while." Until recently, the courts preferred an "overall broad judgment approach," meaning they took into account all relevant considerations, their scale, degree, and relative significance in deciding whether a proposal reflects sustainable management.[34] Therefore, even if a development proposal failed to meet one of the requirements in section 5, it may still be considered sustainable management, especially if it could create substantial social and economic benefits. However, in 2014, the Supreme Court (Aotearoa New Zealand's final appeal court) substantially challenged this approach.[35] It held that the definition of sustainable management should not be read as two distinct parts linked by the word "while," but rather "as an integrated whole" and that "environmental protection is a core element of sustainable management."[36] The Supreme Court concluded that while section 5 does not give primacy to environmental protection, a particular planning document may give primacy to environmental protection in certain circumstances. The Supreme Court emphasized the importance of such planning documents, stating "the RMA envisages the formulation and promulgation of a cascade of planning documents, each intended, ultimately, to give effect to s 5."[37]

Interestingly, a whole suite of other statutes contain clear commitments to sustainable development. For example, the Local Government Act 2002 requires local authorities to make decisions by "taking a sustainable development approach" that is defined to take account of "the social, economic and cultural interests of people and communities; the need to maintain and enhance the quality of the environment; and the reasonably foreseeable needs of future generations."[38] The Preamble of the Environment Act 1986 states that it is an act to ensure that, in the management of natural and physical resources, full and balanced account is taken of: "the intrinsic value of ecosystems; all values which are placed by individuals and groups on the quality of the environment; the principles of the Treaty of Waitangi; the sustainability of natural and physical resources; and the needs of future generations."[39] The purpose of the

---

[31] S. Curran, "Sustainable Development v Sustainable Management: The Interface between the Local Government Act and the Resource Management Act" (2004) 8 *New Zealand Law Journal* 267, p. 276.

[32] Parliamentary Commissioner for the Environment, "Towards Sustainable Development: The Role of the Resource Management Act 1991. PCE Environmental Management Review No. 1," Aug. 1998, p. 3.

[33] Parliamentary Commissioner for the Environment, "Creating our Future: Sustainable Development for New Zealand," 2002, p. 15.

[34] For a good summary of environmental law, see Environment Foundation, "New Zealand Environment Guide," www.environmentguide.org.nz. See also, for example *North Shore CC v. Auckland RC* [1996] 2 ELRNZ 305, p. 346.

[35] *Environmental Defence Society v. the New Zealand King Salmon Company Ltd* [2014] 17 ELRNZ 442.

[36] Ibid., para. 24.

[37] Ibid., para. 31.

[38] Local Government Act, 2002 No. 84, s. 14(1)(h).

[39] Environment Act, note 23, Preamble.

Fisheries Act 1996 is to provide for the utilization of fisheries resources while ensuring sustainability.[40] Under the Hazardous Substances and New Organisms Act 1996 the commitment to sustainability requires consideration of: the sustainability of all native and valued introduced flora and fauna; the intrinsic value of ecosystems; public health; the relationship of Māori and their culture and traditions with their ancestral lands, water, sites, wahi tapu, valued flora and fauna, and other taonga; the economic and related benefits and costs of using a particular hazardous substance or new organism; and Aotearoa New Zealand's international obligations.[41] The sustainability principles under the Energy Efficiency and Conservation Act 2000 are broader including: the health and safety of people and communities and their social, economic, and cultural well-being; the need to maintain and enhance the quality of the environment; the reasonably foreseeable needs of future generations; and the principles of the Treaty of Waitangi.[42]

The varying definitions of sustainability are reflective of specific legislative focus. They each further reinforce the initial commitment made by the RMA in 1991. It is evident that a commitment to sustainability has been adopted by the government as a guiding principle of environmental management.[43] While these environmental statutes also reference the principles of the Treaty of Waitangi, there is little consideration for whether Māori ethics and laws of care and kinship (for example, kaitiakitanga and whanaungatanga) sit comfortably with commitments to sustainability. Lacking in these legislative definitions of sustainability is the inherent relational importance of humans *within* the environment. The definitions certainly value the environment for its ability to serve human well-being including future generations, but not specifically the positionality of humans and the environment as kin that necessitates two-way relational relationships. From a Māori perspective, humans are an integral welcomed part of the environment; they are relations, they are family. This view is shared by other Indigenous peoples and has some sympathy in international law instruments. For example, in 2000, the World Commission on Protected Areas, in conjunction with the International Union for Conservation of Nature and the World Wildlife Federation, committed to key principles including:[44]

> Indigenous and other traditional peoples have long associations with nature and a deep understanding of it. Often they have made significant contributions to the maintenance of many of the earth's most fragile ecosystems, through their traditional sustainable resource use practices and culture-based respect for nature. Therefore, there should be no inherent conflict between the objectives of protected areas and the existence, within and around their borders, of indigenous and other traditional peoples. Moreover, they should be recognised as rightful, equal partners in the development and implementation of conservation strategies that affect their lands, territories, waters, coastal seas, and other resources, and in particular in the establishment and management of protected areas.

---

[40] Fisheries Act, 1996 No. 88, s. 8.
[41] Hazardous Substances and New Organisms Act, 1996 No. 30, s. 6.
[42] Energy Efficiency and Conservation Act, 2000 No. 14, s. 6.
[43] See K. Bosselmann and D. Grinlinton (eds.), *Environmental Law for a Sustainable Society* (Auckland: New Zealand Centre for Environmental Law Monograph Series, 2002), vol. 1; K. Bosselmann, D. Grinlinton, and P. Taylor (eds.), *Environmental Law for a Sustainable Society* (2nd ed.) (Auckland: New Zealand Centre for Environmental Law Monograph Series, 2013), vol. 1; Hon. P. Salmon QC and D. Grinlinton (eds.), *Environmental Law in New Zealand* (2nd ed.) (Auckland: Thomson Reuters, 2018).
[44] J. Beltran and A. Phillips (eds.), "Indigenous and Traditional Peoples and Protected Areas. Principles Guidelines and Case Studies. Best Practice Protected Area Guidelines Series No. 4," ICUN World Commission on Protected Areas, Cardiff University, 2000, p. ix.

Other international instruments reinforce the rights of Indigenous peoples including importantly the United Nations Declaration on the Rights of Indigenous Peoples.[45]

In the midst of these domestic and international environmental laws relevant for Aotearoa New Zealand, legal personality of some parts of the environment has been recognized. Why, and do they take this country any further in this legislative journey of relational kinship sustainability?

12.4 THE NEW SCENARIO: TE UREWERA

In 2014, Aotearoa New Zealand significantly advanced its package of environmental laws (for constitutional reasons). Te Urewera, named a national park in 1954 and managed as Crown land by the Department of Conservation, was removed from the national park estate in 2014 to become simply Te Urewera: "a legal entity" with "all the rights, powers, duties, and liabilities of a legal person."[46] The negotiated agreement was between the Māori tribal federation of this area – Ngāi Tūhoe (who had never consented to their homeland being turned into a national park) and the Crown. This political solution was created not to progress environmental protection and preservation of the native forested expanse but to acknowledge the wrong done by the government in confiscating Tūhoe property that included deliberately denying Tūhoe their long experience of caring for and knowing Te Urewera.[47] The negotiated settlement was born from the brutal wrongs done by the Crown to the Indigenous nation.

In the companion Act to the Te Urewera Act, the Tūhoe Claims Settlement Act 2014 acknowledges some of this history with attached apologies from the Crown. For example, the Act records that in 1865 "the Crown confiscated much of their [Tūhoe] most productive land, even though they were not in rebellion."[48] After the land confiscation, "the Crown waged war in Te Urewera until 1871."[49] The Crown was responsible for the execution of unarmed Tūhoe prisoners and the killing of noncombatants. In 1870, Tūhoe were forced out of Te Urewera. As the Act states "The wars caused Tūhoe to suffer widespread starvation and extensive loss of life."[50] The atrocities continued. The government continued to use harsh tactics to acquire land. Of relevance to this chapter, the Act records:[51]

---

[45] UN General Assembly, United Nations Declaration on the Rights of Indigenous People, Sept. 13, 2007, UN Doc. A/RES/61/295, Art. 43. See: B. Saul, *Indigenous Peoples and Human Rights: International and Regional Jurisprudence* (Oxford: Hart, 2016); C. Charters and R. Stavenhagen (eds.), "Making the Declaration Work: The United Nations Declaration on the Rights of Indigenous Peoples," International Work Group for Indigenous Affairs, Dec. 2009; L. Heinamaki, "Protecting the Rights of Indigenous Peoples – Promoting the Sustainability of the Global Environment?" (2009) 11 *International Community Law Review* 3.

[46] Te Urewera Act, note 1, s. 11(1). See also the management plan: Te Kawa o Te Urewera (2017), www.ngaituhoe.iwi.nz/te-kawa-o-te-urewera; J. Ruru, "Tūhoe–Crown Settlement – Te Urewera Act 2014" (2014) *Māori Law Review* 16; J. Ruru, "Reimagining Governance for National Parks," in L. Elenius (ed.), *Indigenous Rights in Modern Landscapes: Nordic Conservation Regimes in Global Context* (Abingdon, UK: Routledge, 2017), p. 113; K. Saunders, "'Beyond Human Ownership'? Property, Power and Legal Personality for Nature in Aotearoa New Zealand" (2018) 30 *Journal of Environmental Law* 207; C. J. Iorns Magallanes, "Māori Cultural Rights in Aotearoa New Zealand: Protecting the Cosmology that Protects the Environment" (2015) 21 *Widener Law Review* 271.

[47] See Tūhoe Claims Settlement Act, 2014 No. 50. See also C. Jones "Tūhoe Claims Settlement Act 2014: Te Urewera Report of the Waitangi Tribunal" (Oct. 2014) *Māori Law Review* 13.

[48] Tūhoe Claims Settlement Act, note 47, s. 8(1).

[49] Ibid., s. 8(3).

[50] Ibid.

[51] Tūhoe Claims Settlement Act, note 47, s. 8(10).

In 1954, the Crown established Te Urewera National Park, which included most of Tūhoe's traditional lands. The Crown neither consulted Tūhoe about the establishment of the park nor about its 1957 expansion and did not recognise Tūhoe as having any special interest in the park or its governance. National Park policies led to restrictions on Tūhoe's customary use of Te Urewera and their own adjoining land.

The 2014 Act records the Crown's unreserved apology for not honoring Tūhoe, for the wrongful killings, and "for its unjust and excessive behavior and the burden carried by generations of Tūhoe who suffer greatly and carry the pain of their ancestors."[52]

Recognizing Te Urewera, not as a national park but as its own legal entity, enables the return of Māori law to the forefront of managing people's relationships with this place, and, importantly, the kinship relationship of law to once again become primary in caring for these lands. This intent is clear in the Te Urewera Act 2014:[53]

> Te Urewera should have legal recognition in its own right, with the responsibilities for its care and conservation set out in the law of New Zealand. To this end, Tūhoe and the Crown have together taken a unique approach, as set out in this Act, to protecting Te Urewera in a way that reflects New Zealand's culture and values.
>
> The Crown and Tūhoe intend this Act to contribute to resolving the grief of Tūhoe and to strengthening and maintaining the connection between Tūhoe and Te Urewera.

Te Urewera Act marks, for the first time in Aotearoa New Zealand's history, the permanent removal of a national park from the national park legislation. In 2014, Te Urewera ceased to be vested in the Crown, ceased to be Crown land, and ceased to be a national park.[54] Te Urewera is now freehold land with the fee simple estate vested in Te Urewera.[55] However, the land cannot be alienated by, for example, a mortgage which usually attaches to a fee simple estate.[56] Te Urewera is now managed by the new Te Urewera Board. This Board is responsible "to act on behalf of, and in the name of, Te Urewera."[57] Te Urewera will continue to have a management plan like other national parks in Aotearoa New Zealand. The Board, rather than the Department of Conservation, will approve these plans.[58] Initially the Board had a 50/50 membership of Tūhoe and Crown appointed persons (four persons each). The Board now has six persons Tūhoe appointed/three persons Crown appointed.[59] The Board, in contrast to nearly all other statutory bodies including the Department of Conservation, is directed to reflect customary values and law. Section 18(2) states that the Board needs to consider Tūhoe concepts of management and these are described in the legislation in the Māori language.[60] The Act mandates that the Board must strive to make some decisions by unanimous agreement (such as the approval of Te Urewera management plan) and some decisions by consensus.[61]

The Board must work with the chief executive of the Tūhoe tribal group and the Director-General of Conservation to develop an annual budget. Section 38(2) states that the chief

---

[52] Ibid., s. 10(3).
[53] Te Urewera Act, note 1, ss. 3(10) and (11).
[54] Ibid., s. 12.
[55] Ibid., s. 12.
[56] Ibid., s. 13.
[57] Ibid., s. 17(a).
[58] Ibid., s. 18.
[59] Ibid., s. 21.
[60] Aotearoa New Zealand recognized the Māori language as an official language in 1987: see the Māori Language Act, 2016 No. 176.
[61] Te Urewera Act, note 1, ss. 33 and 34.

executive and the Director-General "must contribute equally to the costs provided for in the budget, unless both agree to a different contribution." All revenue received by the Board must be paid into a bank account of the Board and used for achieving the purpose of this Act.[62] For the purposes of taxation, Te Urewera and the Board are deemed to be the same person.[63] The chief executive of Tūhoe and the Director-General of Conservation are responsible for the operational management of Te Urewera and must prepare an annual operational plan.[64]

Te Urewera Act stipulates what activities are permitted in Te Urewera and what activities require authorization and in what form.[65] The National Parks Act has similar provisions relating to national parks. Section 58 of Te Urewera Act lists activities that require a permit. These include: taking any plant; disturbing or hunting any animal (other than sports fish); possessing dead protected wildlife for any cultural or other purpose; entering specially protected areas; making a road; establishing accommodation; farming; and recreational hunting. This is a comprehensive list and demonstrates that tight rules for preserving national park land have been transported to Te Urewera. Still, throughout Te Urewera Act it makes it clear that Te Urewera may still be mined just as conservation land can potentially be. In the very unlikely situation where a mining activity is sought for within Te Urewera, the Board will have little power to stop this if it has been authorized by the Crown.[66] It is most unlikely that mining of any significant size would be permitted (except in dire circumstances relating to a national emergency) because this would certainly amount to an affront to the new Tūhoe–Crown constitutional relationship.

While there are similarities between Te Urewera Act and the National Parks Act (such as the requirement to have a management plan and to ensure these lands are available for public use and enjoyment) the purpose for setting aside the land is subtly but importantly different. This is significant. For example, section 4 of the National Parks Act 1980 preserves national parks for their scenery, recreation, and science. The National Parks Act does not recognize that national park lands can be of specific cultural and spiritual importance to Māori. The National Parks Act is a monocultural statute premised only on Western values for preserving land for protection and conservation values. Te Urewera Act, on the other hand, demonstrates a new bicultural way of articulating the importance of lands for multiple reasons incorporating both Western *and* Māori values. Section 3 of Te Urewera Act captures in law the importance of the place for itself and all peoples:

Section 3
Te Urewera

(1) Te Urewera is ancient and enduring, a fortress of nature, alive with history; its scenery is abundant with mystery, adventure, and remote beauty.
(2) Te Urewera is a place of spiritual value, with its own mana and mauri.
(3) Te Urewera has an identity in and of itself, inspiring people to commit to its care.
     Te Urewera and Tūhoe

---

[62] Ibid., s. 39(1).
[63] Ibid., s. 40(1).
[64] Ibid., ss. 50 and 53.
[65] Ibid., s. 55.
[66] See Ibid., ss. 64(1) and 56(b), where a mining activity authorized by the Crown Minerals Act can be undertaken without authorization from the Board. In the late 1800s and early 1900s, the Crown did permit some small private mining for gold in Te Urewera, see Waitangi Tribunal, "Te Urewera. Part III. From self-governing Native Reserve to National Park," Wai 894, 2012.

(4) For Tūhoe, Te Urewera is Te Manawa o te Ika a Māui; it is the heart of the great fish of Maui, its name being derived from Murakareke, the son of the ancestor Tūhoe.

(5) For Tūhoe, Te Urewera is their ewe whenua, their place of origin and return, their homeland.

(6) Te Urewera expresses and gives meaning to Tūhoe culture, language, customs, and identity. There Tūhoe hold mana by ahikāroa; they are tangata whenua and kaitiaki of Te Urewera.

Te Urewera and all New Zealanders

(7) Te Urewera is prized by other iwi and hapū who have acknowledged special associations with, and customary interests in, parts of Te Urewera.

(8) Te Urewera is also prized by all New Zealanders as a place of outstanding national value and intrinsic worth; it is treasured by all for the distinctive natural values of its vast and rugged primeval forest, and for the integrity of those values; for its indigenous ecological systems and biodiversity, its historical and cultural heritage, its scientific importance, and as a place for outdoor recreation and spiritual reflection.

Section 4 of Te Urewera Act explicitly positions the purpose of this Act in a unique manner to all other existing environmental legislation in Aotearoa New Zealand. It reads:

The purpose of this Act is to establish and preserve in perpetuity a legal identity and protected status for Te Urewera for its intrinsic worth, its distinctive natural and cultural values, the integrity of those values, and for its national importance, and in particular to –

(a) strengthen and maintain the connection between Tūhoe and Te Urewera; and

(b) preserve as far as possible the natural features and beauty of Te Urewera, the integrity of its indigenous ecological systems and biodiversity, and its historical and cultural heritage; and

(c) provide for Te Urewera as a place for public use and enjoyment, for recreation, learning, and spiritual reflection, and as an inspiration for all.

Te Urewera Act 2014, and the subsequent legislation in Aotearoa New Zealand that is advancing legal recognition of Māori ancestral knowledge of place, is enabling a new humanness within the paradigm of environmental justice and sustainability. It recognizes upfront the value in strengthening and maintaining the connection between people and place unlike other environmental legislation. The recognition of legal personality for the Whanganui River is similar to Te Urewera. In brief, the Te Awa Tupua (Whanganui River Claims Settlement) Act 2017 recenters the country's understanding of this river to be led by the Māori world view of knowing and caring for these waters. One important component of this repositioning is to value that specific Māori tribal federations have responsibilities for the health and well-being of the river because: "*Ko au te Awa, ko te Awa ko au*: I am the River and the River is me."[67] The Act recognizes that the face of the river – Te Awa Tupua – is "a legal person and has all the rights,

---

[67] This well-known belief is captured in Te Awa Tupua (Whanganui River Claims Settlement) Act, 2017 No. 7, s. 13(c). See also L. Te Aho, "Legislation – Te Awa Tupua (Whanganui River Claims Settlement) Bill – The Endless Quest for Justice" (Aug. 2016) *Māori Law Review* 1; L. Te Aho "Ngā Whakatunga Waimāori: Freshwater Settlements," in N. R. Wheen and J. Hayward (eds.), *Treaty of Waitangi Settlements* (Wellington: Bridget Williams Books, 2012), p. 102.

powers, duties, and liabilities of a legal person."[68] An office has been created to "be the human face of Te Awa Tupua and act in the name of Te Awa Tupua."[69]

Te Urewera and Te Awa Tupua read like no other environmental legislation in this country because the starting motivation was not to create law to further enhance the environmental protection of these places (as already strongly provided for in the Conservation Act and the Resource Management Act), but rather to acknowledge the Crown's violence of colonization and the cultural wrongs inherent in existing environmental legislation. The current scope of environmental legislation (including the Conservation Act 1987 and the Resource Management Act 1991) is premised on Crown government's control and authority of land and water without serious regard or recognition of Māori interests, values, or laws. The legal personality solutions do not simply give 'rights to nature' as such,[70] but instead reposition law to acknowledge the "enduring concept" of, in the case of the Whanganui River, "the inseparability of the people and the River,"[71] and in the case of Te Urewera, it gives meaning to Tūhoe identity as "their place of origin and return."[72] Both statutes are negotiated settlements that begin with a recognition that the government and its practices, policies and laws as implemented since 1840 onward have been in total disregard of Māori. Similar to the deep apologies contained in the Te Urewera Act, the Te Awa Tupua Act records that the Crown "acknowledges that it has failed to recognize, respect, and protect the special relationship of iwi and hapū of Whanganui with the Whanganui River."[73] The grounding in these Acts result in a new appreciation for how environmental law can be positioned more attuned to sustainability of place and of peoples for today and in the future. They do more than simply give a voice to nature (or an equal standing to nature as humans) to better enable them to defend themselves against forms of human development and degradation; they give a Māori Indigenous emphasis to place through kinship that is cognizant of the importance of Māori laws and colonial history.

12.5 CONCLUSION

Legal personality of the environment as used in Aotearoa New Zealand presents a significant shift toward a return to the first laws that were known in these lands. The Māori legal system, with its base in the knowledge of kinship between one another *and* with the physical and spiritual worlds, has been permitted by the state legal system to resurface for all to see. The politically negotiated agreements of legal personality of specific parts of the environment in this country all stem from Crown recognition of its breaching of the principles of the Treaty of

---

[68] Te Awa Tupua (Whanganui River Claims Settlement) Act, note 67, s. 14(1).

[69] Ibid., s. 18(2).

[70] See generally C. Stone, "Should Trees Have Standing? Towards Legal Rights for Material Agents" (1972) 45 *Southern California Law Review* 450; D. R. Boyd, *The Rights of Nature: A Legal Revolution That Could Save the World* (Toronto: ECW Press, 2017); M. Margil, "Building an International Movement for Rights of Nature," in M. Maloney and P. Burdon (eds.), *Wild Law – In Practice* (London: Routledge, 2014), p. 149; C. G. Gonzalez, "Bridging the North–South Divide: International Environmental Law in the Anthropocene" (2015) 32 *Pace Environmental Law Review* 407; M. Maloney and P. Siemen, "Responding to the Great Work: The Role of Earth Jurisprudence and Wild Law in the 21st Century" (2015) 5 *Environmental and Earth Law Journal* 6; E. L. O'Donnell, "At the Intersection of the Sacred and the Legal: Rights for Nature in Uttarakhand, India" (2018) 30 *Journal of Environmental Law* 135; P. V. Calzadilla and L. J. Kotze, "Living in Harmony with Nature? A Critical Appraisal of the Rights of Mother Earth in Bolivia" (2018) 7 *Transnational Environmental Law* 397.

[71] Te Awa Tupua (Whanganui River Claims Settlement) Act, note 67, s. 69(2).

[72] Te Urewera Act, note 1, s. 3(5).

[73] Te Awa Tupua (Whanganui River Claims Settlement) Act, note 67, s. 69(8).

Waitangi and an attempt to find a middle ground in negotiating new and just solutions for caring for land.

The negotiated settlements of legal personality of the environment in Aotearoa New Zealand demonstrate to the world that reconciliation between the Crown and an Indigenous group is possible even in scenarios where relationships have been strained and pained for a very long time. But even more so these new politically inspired reconciliatory legal arrangements reveal something more nuanced for environmental law more broadly: it is possible to stand the stool of sustainability upon a floor *and* that a more sturdy framework for environmental law is more apparent when the floor accepts humans are part of, rather than, separate from land and water.

13

Water Justice and the Social Pillar of Sustainable Development

The Case of Israel

Tamar Meshel

13.1 INTRODUCTION

This chapter explores the relationship between water[1] and the social pillar of sustainable development as embodied in the notions of water justice and the human right to water. In light of the unique social, environmental, and economic significance of water and its indispensability to human survival, water justice must be placed at the forefront of any sustainable development analysis. This chapter sets out to do so by critically examining water justice issues in Israel and the Palestinian Territories and identifying broader linkages between social and economic development in the water context.

Section 13.2 of the chapter will briefly introduce the concept of water justice and situate it within the sustainable development discourse and its social pillar. It will focus on the link between water justice and sustainable development as reflected in the evolving human right to water, which is designed to ensure equal access to and use of water for the basic human needs of all. Section 13.3 will examine the interplay between social development and water justice in Israel. While the human right to water has been affirmed in legislation as well as by the Israeli Supreme Court (ISC), its implementation in practice has been partial at best and the Israeli government has been infringing on the rights of vulnerable populations to equal access to and use of water. The negative social and economic effects of such water injustices will be discussed with regard to two local communities: the Bedouins in the south of Israel and the Palestinians in the West Bank and East Jerusalem.[2] Section 13.4 will conclude the chapter by suggesting a broader interpretation of the human right to water that ensures water justice and facilitates sustainable development by emphasizing nondiscrimination and prohibiting the use of water as a policy weapon against vulnerable communities.

---

[1] For present purposes, the term "water" refers to freshwater available for human use, as opposed to seas or oceans.

[2] While water injustice exists also in the Gaza Strip, the focus is on these two groups since they depend on water sources shared with or controlled by Israel, whereas 98 percent of Gaza's water supply comes from the Coastal Aquifer that traverses the border between Israel and the Gaza Strip but constitutes a hydrologically separate system. Furthermore, unlike the West Bank, the worst problem in the Gaza Strip is not the shortage or irregular supply of water but its poor quality (Y. Lein, "Thirsty for a Solution: The Water Crisis in the Occupied Territories and Its Resolution in the Final-Status Agreement," B'Tselem – Israeli Information Center for Human Rights in the Occupied Territories, July 2000, pp. 4, 18, 22, and 35). Nonetheless, it should be noted that Israel extracts water from the Gazan part of the Aquifer, thereby contributing to its "over-extraction," that is, extracting water in quantities greater than are naturally replenished, and thus to the ongoing water crisis in the Strip (ibid., pp. 24 and 47).

13.2 WATER JUSTICE AND SUSTAINABLE DEVELOPMENT: THE HUMAN RIGHT TO WATER

The interdependence between water and sustainable development is self-evident. The former is clearly vital to achieving the latter, as reflected in Sustainable Development Goal 6 which is designed to "ensure availability and sustainable management of water and sanitation for all."[3] By the same token, without sustainable development the fate of water as a finite natural resource will likely be dire, as we have already witnessed a 55 percent drop in globally available water per capita since 1960 while global demand for water is expected to grow by 50 percent by 2030.[4] A convergence point between water and sustainable development, explored in this chapter, is the notion of water justice, which links the hydrological availability of water and the social and legal determinants of its allocation.[5] One tool that has developed for the achievement of water justice is the human right to water. The human right to water features a "social" aspect of equal access to water,[6] an "environmental" aspect of protecting water as a natural resource for current and future human needs,[7] and an "economic" aspect of ensuring water facilities and services affordable for all.[8] Therefore, the notion of water justice, facilitated by the human right to water, relates to all three pillars of the sustainable development framework.[9]

With respect to the social pillar of sustainable development, the human right to water is particularly crucial since without it "other human rights become meaningless."[10] Its "social" aspect is chiefly understood as requiring states to "refrain from interfering directly or indirectly with the enjoyment of the right to water,"[11] take action to help secure water for individuals and communities, and provide it where people are unable to do so by themselves "for reasons beyond their control."[12] These obligations align with the World Health Organization's guidelines requiring access to water of an acceptable color, odor, and taste, and in the amount and quality sufficient to meet basic human needs, including drinking, personal sanitation, washing of clothes, food preparation, and personal and household hygiene.[13]

---

[3] UN Sustainable Development Knowledge Platform, "Sustainable Development Goal 6," https://sustainabledevelopment.un.org/sdg6.

[4] L. Guppy and K. Anderson, "Global Water Crisis: The Facts," United Nations University Institute for Water, Environment and Health, 2017, p. 3.

[5] M. Z. Zwarteveen and R. Boelens, "Defining, Researching and Struggling for Water Justice: Some Conceptual Building Blocks for Research and Action" (2014) 39 *Water International* 144.

[6] R. Boelens, J. Vos, and T. Perreault, "Introduction: The Multiple Challenges and Layers of Water Justice Struggles," in R. Boelens, J. Vos, and T. Perreault (eds.), *Water Justice* (Cambridge: Cambridge University Press, 2018), p. 1.

[7] Ibid., pp. 1–2.

[8] UN Economic and Social Council, "General Comment No. 15: The Right to Water (Arts. 11 and 12 of the Covenant," Jan. 20, 2003, UN Doc. E/C.12/2002/11, para. 12(c)(ii)).

[9] UN World Summit on Sustainable Development, Johannesburg Declaration on Sustainable Development, Sept. 4, 2002

[10] S. C. McCaffrey, "The Human Right to Water," in E. B. Weiss, L. Boisson de Chazournes, and N. Bernasconi-Osterwalder (eds.), *Fresh Water and International Economic Law* (Oxford: Oxford University Press, 2005), p. 95; T. Meshel, "Environmental Justice in the United States: The Human Right to Water" (2018) 8 *Washington Journal of Environmental Law and Policy* 264.

[11] ECOSOC, note 8, para. 21.

[12] Ibid., para. 25.

[13] Ibid., para. 12(a), (b). The WHO's minimum recommended daily allowance for these basic needs is between 50 and 100 liters of water per person per day: UN-Water Decade Programme on Advocacy and Communication and Water Supply and Sanitation Collaborative Council, "The Human Right to Water and Sanitation: Media Brief," p. 2.

The human right to water also serves to ensure "physical accessibility" to water (i.e. sufficient and continuous water for personal and domestic uses within safe physical reach).[14] Additional rights that arise from the human right to water and promote water justice include the right to information and due process, effective review mechanisms, including judicial review of decisions, and remedies.[15]

13.3 THE HUMAN RIGHT TO WATER AND SUSTAINABLE DEVELOPMENT IN ISRAEL

Israel has two main water sources. The first, which it shares with the West Bank, is the Mountain Aquifer, a system composed of three main basins: the Yarkon-Taninim on the west, the Nablus-Gilboa on the north, and the eastern basins between Jericho and Hebron.[16] The Aquifer is fed by rainfall on the mountains of the West Bank that seeps into it. The water then flows eastward and westward to the reservoir areas, from where it is drawn by wells.[17] The second main source of water is the Jordan River Basin system, which includes the Yarmouk River and its tributaries, the Sea of Galilee, and the Jordan River. While only the Jordan River is geographically shared between Israel, the West Bank, and Jordan, the water that Israel draws from the Sea of Galilee directly affects the amount of water available to Jordan.[18] These two sources – the Mountain Aquifer and the Jordan River Basin – supply more than two-thirds of the water consumed in Israel.[19]

Despite high water scarcity in the country,[20] Israel's technological and hydrological innovation has enabled it to supply adequate water to most of its citizens.[21] Examined from the perspective of water justice and the human right to water, however, Israel's accomplishments are far less impressive. As a result of its hydro-hegemonic status in the Jordan River Basin, which enables it "through various expressions of power to maintain a situation in [the] basin in which it receives more than its equitable share of the water,"[22] and its discriminatory policies, water injustices in Israel abound. In particular, the Israeli government has continuously failed to meaningfully implement the human right to water of Bedouin citizens as well as Palestinians residing in the West Bank. This failure has resulted in negative social and economic ramifications for these communities, illustrating the vital importance of water justice to sustainable development.

---

[14] ECOSOC, note 8, para. 12(c)(i).

[15] OHCHR "The Right to Water: Fact Sheet No. 35," UN Habitat, World Health Organization, Aug. 2010, pp. 40–42.

[16] Y. Lein, "Disputed Waters: Israel's Responsibility for the Water Shortage in the Occupied Territories," B'Tselem – Israeli Information Center for Human Rights in the Occupied Territories, Sept. 1998, p. 2.

[17] Ibid., pp. 2–3.

[18] Ibid., p. 3.

[19] Ibid.

[20] UN Food and Agriculture Organization, "Coping with Water Scarcity in Agriculture: A Global Framework Faction in a Changing Climate," 2016, p. 3.

[21] Such as desalination and wastewater reclamation (N. Becker and F. A. Ward, "Adaptive Water Management In Israel: Structure and Policy Options" (2015) 31 *International Journal of Water Resources Development* 540 at 548–549).

[22] "The hegemonic position is less related to riparian position than it is a reflection of the relative economic and political power in the basin" (A. Jägerskog, "Mena Water Overview: Transboundary Cooperation, IWRM and Opportunities for Swedish Engagement," Stockholm International Water Institute, June 2007, p. 17 (on file with author)).

13.3.1 *The Bedouins' Human Right to Water*

The human right to water has been recognized to some extent by the ISC[23] and in legislation providing that "each person is entitled to receive water and to use it."[24] However, this right is by no means safeguarded equally for all Israeli citizens. One of the groups most discriminated against in this regard is the Arab Bedouins in the southern Negev desert.[25] This tribal nomadic and semi-nomadic society, comprising approximately 240,000 people, has been engulfed in a prolonged land rights dispute with the State of Israel.[26] Nowadays, almost half of the Bedouins in the Negev live in government-created townships while the remainder live in thirty-six "unrecognized" villages, which the Israeli government considers to be in breach of construction and planning laws and to constitute trespass on government or private lands.[27]

The Indigenous status of the Bedouins in Israel is a contentious issue.[28] The Negev Bedouins self-identify as a population Indigenous to the area since the fifth century.[29] However, the ISC has recently rejected an application by members of a Bedouin tribe for recognition of their Indigenous land rights on the basis of both Israeli and international law.[30] In rejecting the application, the ISC noted that Israel has not joined the United Nations Declaration on the Rights of Indigenous Peoples[31] and has not adopted it domestically.[32] The ISC further found

---

[23] CA 9535/06 *Abdallah Abu Masad* v. *Water Commissioner* [2011], discussed further below. An English translation of the decision is available at www.adalah.org/uploads/oldfiles/upfiles/2012/Supreme%20Court%20Ruling,%20Civil%20Appeal%20No.%209535.06%20-%20Abu%20Masad,%20Right%20to%20Water%20-%20English.pdf.

[24] Water Law 1959, s. 3, available (in Hebrew) at www.nevo.co.il/law_html/Law01/235_001.htm.

[25] Another group that is discriminated against is the Arab population of the Golan Heights in the north of Israel, also known as the Occupied Syrian Golan. On this issue, see for example Al-Marsad – Arab Human Rights Centre in Golan Heights, "Parallel Report to the Committee on the Elimination of All Forms of Racial Discrimination on the Occasion of the Consideration of the Fourteenth to Sixteenth Periodic Report of Israel," Submission to the UN Committee on the Elimination of Racial Discrimination, Jan. 23, 2012; HIC–HLRN, "Implementation of Obligations under ICERD Article 5(E)(III) The Right to Housing," Parallel Report submitted to the UN Committee on Elimination of Racial Discrimination, Feb. 13–Mar. 9, 2012, pp. 20–21.

[26] A detailed discussion of this dispute and the history of the Bedouin people is beyond the scope of this chapter. In this regard, see for example A. Amara, I. Abu-Saad, and O. Yiftachel (eds.), *Indigenous (In)justice: Human Rights Law and Bedouin Arabs in the Naqab/Negev* (Cambridge, MA: Harvard University Press, 2012); H. Yahel, "Land Disputes between the Negev Bedouin and Israel" (2006) 11 *Israel Studies*; P. Jacquelin-Andersen (ed.), "The Indigenous World 2018," International Work Group for Indigenous Affairs, Apr. 2018; S. L. Murthy, M. Williams, and E. Baskin, "The Human Right to Water in Israel: A Case Study of the Unrecognised Bedouin Villages in the Negev" (2013) 46 *Israel Law Review* 25.

[27] Bimkom, "The Unrecognized Villages in the Negev – Facts and Figures," http://bimkom.org/2008/04/2487/ [in Hebrew].

[28] See for example S. J. Frantzman, H. Yahel, and R. Kark, "Contested Indigeneity: The Development of an Indigenous Discourse on the Bedouin of the Negev, Israel" (2012) 17 *Israel Studies* 78; I. Abu-Saad and A. Amara, "Introduction," in Amara et al., note 26, pp. 2–3; O. Yiftachel, B. Roded, and A. Kedar, "Between Rights and Denials: Bedouin Indigeneity in the Negev/Naqab" (2016) 48 *Environment and Planning* A2129; H. Yahel, R. Kark, and S. J. Frantzman, "Are the Negev Bedouin an Indigenous People?" (2012) 19 *Middle East Quarterly* 3.

[29] R. Stavenhagen and A. Amara, "International Law of Indigenous Peoples and the Naqab Bedouin Arabs," in Amara et al., note 26, p. 181.

[30] *Al Uqbi* v. *State of Israel*, 4220/12 (May 14, 2015), paras. 80–81, http://elyon1.court.gov.il/files/12/200/042/v29/12042200.v29.htm (in Hebrew).

[31] Israel was absent from the United Nations General Assembly vote adopting the UNDRIP: UN General Assembly, "General Assembly Adopts Declaration on Rights of Indigenous Peoples; 'Major Step Forward' towards Human Rights for All, Says President," Sept. 13, 2007, GA/10612, www.un.org/press/en/2007/ga10612.doc.htm.

[32] *Al Uqbi* v. *State of Israel*, note 30, para. 81.

that, in any event, the Declaration has no binding authority on states, there is no other international treaty that recognizes Indigenous rights to which Israel is a party, nor is Israel bound to recognize such rights under international customary law.[33] Finally, the ISC noted that the applicants in this case were seeking recognition of their private ownership of the land in question, rather than collective Indigenous ownership rights like those recognized in other countries.[34] In light of this private nature of the applicants' claim, the ISC found it unnecessary to decide on the broader question of the Indigenous status of the Bedouins.[35]

Regardless of their Indigenous status, the Bedouin citizens of Israel are entitled to equal access to water of the same quantity and quality as that provided to the Jewish population. The ISC affirmed in 2011 that access to water is a basic human right of Bedouin citizens, including those living in unrecognized villages.[36] In this case, dozens of Bedouin residents of such a village appealed the refusal of the Water Commissioner to connect them to the national water supply. The ISC noted that the human right to water has not only been recognized in Israeli legislation, but is also a constitutional right arising from the Basic Law: Human Dignity and Liberty.[37] This basic law is intended to protect individuals' "life, body, and dignity," and "dignity" includes the right to basic housing, food, water, and healthcare, which the state is required to provide.[38] Therefore, "access to water for basic human use," according to the ISC:

> [F]alls within the right to minimal human dignity. Water is an essential resource for humans, and without access to this resource in adequate quality humans cannot survive. Therefore, one must view the right to water as part and parcel of the human right to dignity, which is constitutionally protected under the Basic Law: Human Dignity and Liberty.[39]

While the Israeli government did not deny the right of the Bedouin citizens to water, it posited that the access to and quality of such water are impacted by the need to comply with legislation and government policies designed to incentivize the Bedouin communities to resettle in recognized townships. Therefore, the government claimed that until such resettlement occurs it was permitted to provide water to residents of unrecognized villages either in the form of water centers from which they independently transport water to the villages, or, in individual cases and for humanitarian reasons, by way of a permit for a private connection to the national water grid.[40]

The ISC agreed. It noted that, as with any constitutional right, the right to water is not absolute. It has limitations set out in the Water Law itself, which provides for specific permitted uses of water and requires payment for water services.[41] Other negating interests must also be considered, such as the fact that the unrecognized villages at issue were considered illegal and that the claimants were provided with alternative options for obtaining water from the national grid, specifically by relocating to government townships. Accordingly, while the government was obligated to supply water to unrecognized villages, as this constitutes an essential human need, the illegal nature of these villages could legitimately impact the degree of comfort in the

---

[33] Ibid.
[34] Ibid.
[35] Ibid.
[36] *Abdallah Abu Masad*, note 23.
[37] The Knesset, Basic Law: Human Dignity and Liberty, 1992, www.knesset.gov.il/laws/special/eng/basic3_eng .htm.
[38] *Abdallah Abu Masad*, note 23, paras. 21–22.
[39] Ibid., para. 23.
[40] Ibid., para. 40.
[41] Ibid., para. 24.

residents' access to water sources.[42] The ISC found that under the government's policy, what was impacted was not the Bedouins' fundamental access to water as such but rather the ease and potential additional cost associated with such access. This, the ISC held, was a proportional and reasonable violation of their human right to water, which violation was also directly relevant to the goal of preventing illegal villages and promoting recognized townships, and thus justified.[43]

Even in the recognized government townships, however, water discrimination seems to persist.[44] Some of these townships lack water infrastructure altogether and, even where such infrastructure exists, "there is considerable disparity in the standard of service between them and similar Jewish settlements."[45] For instance, Bedouin villages need at least ten families in order to apply for a water connection, some government-created townships only receive water for one to two hours per day, and most villages have only one access point to water that is intended to supply the whole village.[46] In contrast, Jewish family farms in the Negev are connected to the national water grid and receive continuous supply immediately after their establishment and regardless of the number of residents.[47]

As a result of these water inequalities, the Human Rights Committee responsible for monitoring states' compliance with the International Covenant on Civil and Political Rights (ICCPR)[48] has expressed its concern over "the discrimination faced by Bedouins . . . in settlements in the Negev which are not recognized by the Israeli Government and which are not provided with basic infrastructure and essential services."[49] Similarly, the Committee on the Economic, Social and Cultural Rights responsible for monitoring states' compliance with the International Covenant on Economic, Social and Cultural Rights (ICESCR)[50] has expressed its concern regarding the poor living conditions in the unrecognized Bedouin villages, including the lack of access to water.[51] The UN Committee on the Elimination of Racial Discrimination has also urged Israel to reconsider its planning and zoning policy in order to guarantee "Bedouin rights to property, access to land, access to housing and access to

---

[42] Ibid., para. 42.

[43] Ibid., para. 45. Ultimately, the ISC found that in the case of three of the six appellants the Water Commissioner did not clearly show that they had reasonable access to water absent private connections to the national grid. Therefore, while the government could in principle deny their applications on the basis of the illegality of their unrecognized villages, in order to do so it had to ensure their reasonable access to water and that there were no special humanitarian reasons that justified private connections in their particular cases. With regard to these appellants, the ISC ordered an additional examination by the Water Commissioner of the adequacy of their water access in order to ensure "minimal" access (paras. 49–50). The Water Commissioner reportedly concluded that the petitioners had no right to private water connections (I. E. Kornfeld, "Dignity and the Right to Water in Comparative Constitutional Law: Israel's Supreme Court Extends the Human Right to Water" (2013) 28 *Journal of Environmental Law and Litigation* 1 at 21).

[44] O. Bar-Meir, "Why Even Legal Bedouin Villages Are Not Connected to Water and Electricity in 2016?," Apr. 6, 2016, www.mynet.co.il/articles/0,7340,L-4787544,00.html [in Hebrew].

[45] Negev Coexistence Forum for Civil Equality (NCF), "Alternative Report Submitted to the Committee on the Elimination of Racial Discrimination on the Occasion of the Consideration of the 14th to 16th Periodic Reports of Israel," Jan. 30, 2012, pp. 18, 20, and 28.

[46] Ibid., p. 28.

[47] Ibid., pp. 18, 20, and 30.

[48] International Covenant on Civil and Political Rights (ICCPR), Mar. 23, 1976, 999 UNTS 171, Art. 6. Israel became a party in 1991.

[49] UN General Assembly, *Report of the Human Rights Committee, Concluding Observations: Israel*, Sept. 11, 1998, UN Doc. A/53/40, para. 310.

[50] International Covenant on Economic, Social and Cultural Rights (ICESCR), Jan. 3, 1976, 993 UNTS 3, Art. 11. Israel became a party in 1991.

[51] Committee on the Economic, Social and Cultural Rights, *Concluding Observations: Israel*, Apr. 27–May 15, 1998, Nov. 1–Dec. 4, 1998, UN Doc. E/1999/22, para. 254.

natural resources (especially water resources)."[52] In its 2017 Periodic Report to the Committee, Israel reported twenty-nine Bedouin localities with "approved outline plans" that included infrastructure for running water.[53]

However, unrecognized Bedouin villages remain detached from the national water grid, and residents continue to obtain their drinking water from water centers located several kilometers from their villages. In many instances this water supply is intermittent or stops entirely, and is of poor quality.[54] Therefore, although the ISC has affirmed the government's obligation to supply unrecognized villages with minimal access to water despite their illegal status, its narrow interpretation of the human right to water and the broad discretion it granted the government to limit the access to water of unrecognized villages have arguably turned the human right to water of these Bedouin citizens to a *de jure* right that is unprotected *de facto*. If Israel is to claim compliance with the human right to water, "the number of water centers and private access points for unrecognized villages needs to be increased"[55] and the government should not be allowed to use access to water as a political weapon for pressuring Bedouin communities to relocate to recognized townships.

13.3.2 *The Palestinians' Human Right to Water*

A detailed discussion of the Israeli–Palestinian dispute is beyond the scope of this chapter. It is worth noting, however, that the dispute has long had an important water dimension: Arab states created Palestinian commando units to carry out sabotage operations against Israeli water installations in the 1960s, and Israel has attacked dams erected by Syria and has been diverting water resources shared with Jordan, Syria, the West Bank, and Gaza since the 1950s.[56]

As in the case of the Negev Bedouins, Israel does not recognize the Palestinians in the West Bank as having Indigenous status,[57] even though the International Court of Justice (ICJ) has confirmed their right to self-determination.[58] Unlike the Bedouin citizens of Israel, the water supply of Palestinians in the West Bank is, at least in theory, the responsibility of the Palestinians National Authority, and specifically the Palestinians Water Authority, rather than the Israeli government.[59] However, in 1967 Israel obtained, and has since retained, exclusive control over all water resources located between the Jordan River and the Mediterranean Sea, with the exception of the section of

---

[52] UN Committee on the Elimination of Racial Discrimination, *Consideration of reports submitted by States parties under article 9 of the Convention: concluding observations of the Committee on the Elimination of Racial Discrimination: Israel*, Apr. 3, 2012, UN Doc. CERD/C/ISRCO/14–16, para. 25.

[53] UN Committee on the Elimination of Racial Discrimination, *Seventeenth to Nineteenth Periodic Reports of States Parties: Israel*, Mar. 14, 2017, UN Doc. CERD/C/ISR/17–19, paras. 201–202.

[54] M. Hussain (ed.), "Shadow Report: United Nations Committee against All Forms of Racial Discrimination: Suggested Issues for Consideration Regarding Israel's Combined 14th, 15th, and 16th Periodic Report to the UN Committee on the Elimination of All Forms of Racial Discrimination (CERD)," Mossawa Center, the Advocacy Center for Arab Citizens in Israel, Israel Religious Action Center, Hotline for Migrant Workers, Submitted on Behalf of Coalition against Racism in Israel, Jan. 2012, p. 42; HIC–HLRN, note 25, pp. 15–16.

[55] Murthy et al., note 26, p. 26.

[56] M. Tessler, A *History of the Israeli–Palestinian Conflict* (2nd ed.) (Bloomington: Indiana University Press, 2009), pp. 361–364, 373, 521, and 681.

[57] Yiftachel et al., note 28, p. 2137.

[58] ICJ, "Legal Consequences of the Construction of a Wall in the Occupied Palestinian Territory," Advisory Opinion of July 9, 2004.

[59] A. Abu-Eid, "Water as a Human Right: The Palestinian Occupied Territories as an Example," in A. K. Biswas, E. Rached, and C. Tortajada (eds.), *Water as a Human Right for the Middle East and North Africa* (Abingdon, UK: Routledge, 2008), p. 78.

the coastal aquifer where it runs under the Gaza Strip.[60] As a result, the Palestinians Water Authority has been left with practically no power over water management in the West Bank.[61] The Israeli–Palestinian bilateral peace talks have resulted in two agreements that relate to water in Israel and the West Bank[62] – the 1993 Declaration of Principles[63] and the 1995 Interim Agreement (Oslo II).[64] In these agreements, the parties established two principles for future negotiations over water: equitable division of the shared water sources and cooperation in their management.[65] In the Interim Agreement, Israel also recognized "the Palestinian water rights in the West Bank."[66] Notwithstanding these commitments, the Palestinian population of the West Bank has been continuously suffering from unequal distribution of, and access to, water.

The UN Committee on Economic, Social and Cultural Rights has expressed its concern regarding the "limited access to and distribution and availability of water for Palestinians in the occupied territories, as a result of inequitable management, extraction and distribution of shared water resources, which are predominantly under Israeli control."[67] The Committee has also noted the "destruction of the local civilians' wells, roof water tanks, and other water and irrigation facilities under military and settler operations since 1967."[68] The UN Committee on the Elimination of Racial Discrimination has denounced Israel's inconsistent policies toward the Palestinian population, on the one hand, and the Jewish settler population, on the other, in the West Bank. The separation of these two groups "who live on the same territory but do not enjoy . . . equal access to basic services and water resources," the Committee noted, amounted to "de facto segregation."[69]

Indeed, average water consumption for all domestic, commercial, and industrial uses in the West Bank in 2015 was 84.3 liters per person per day,[70] while Israeli settlers in Area C[71] of the West Bank enjoyed the same rate of domestic water consumption as the residents of Israel, who

---

[60] B'Tselem – Israeli Information Center for Human Rights in the Occupied Territories, "Water Crisis," Nov. 11, 2017, www.btselem.org/water#gaza.

[61] Abu-Eid, note 59, p. 78. TheCommittee on th eEconomic, Social and Cultural Rights has also noted that shared water resources are "predominantly under Israeli control" (UN Committee on Economic, Social and Cultural Rights (CESCR), *Concluding Observations: Israel*, June 26, 2003, UNDoc.E/C.12/1/Add.90, para. 25). However, the Palestinian Authority has also contributed to the insufficient and unsafe access to water of Palestinians in the West Bank by failing to repair pipelines and to ensure adequate water treatment facilities (B. Schlütter, "Water Rights in the West Bank and in Gaza" (2005) 18 *Leiden Journal of International Law* p. 633).

[62] Lein, note 16, p. 51.

[63] Israel Ministry of Foreign Affairs, "Declaration of Principles," Sept. 13, 1993, www.mfa.gov.il/mfa/foreign policy/peace/guide/pages/declaration%20of%20principles.aspx.

[64] Israel Ministry of Foreign Affairs, Israel–Palestine Interim Agreement, Sept. 28, 1995, www.mfa.gov.il/mfa/ foreignpolicy/peace/guide/pages/the%20israeli-palestinian%20interim%20agreement.aspx.

[65] Israel Ministry of Foreign Affairs, note 63, Annex 3, Art. 1. Under the Interim Agreement, however, 80 percent of water in the West Bank pumped from the Mountain Aquifer were allotted for Israeli use and the remaining 20 percent for Palestinian use (B'Tselem, note 60).

[66] Ibid., Art. 40(1).

[67] UN CESR (2003), note 61.

[68] UN Committee on the Economic, Social and Cultural Rights, *Concluding Observations: Israel*, June 26, 2003, UN Doc. E/C.12/1/Add.90, para. 229

[69] UN Committee on the Elimination of Racial Discrimination, note 51.

[70] B'Tselem, note 60.

[71] "Over 60 per cent of the West Bank is considered Area C, where Israel retains near exclusive control, including over law enforcement, planning and construction," and where the Israeli settlements are located: United Nations Office for the Coordination of Humanitarian Affairs, "Occupied Palestinian Territories: Area C," www.ochaopt.org/location/area-c.

average 300 liters per person per day.[72] This discrepancy is partially a result of the lack of a centralized water network in the West Bank,[73] which forces the Palestinian Authority to purchase water from Israel's national water company, Mekorot. Moreover, due to the poor state of the pipelines linking Palestinian communities in the West Bank to Mekorot's regional reservoirs located within Israeli settlements and of the water grids within Palestinian cities and villages, about one-third of all water supplied to the Palestinian Authority is lost to leakage.[74]

The water shortage in the West Bank is most severe in the summer, when many Palestinians suffer lengthy water outages ranging from a few days to a week, and at times water does not reach distant locations or those at high elevations.[75] There are further inequalities in water distribution within the West Bank, as cities and developed communities have a network that supplies running water to residents' homes for at least some time every day, as well as paved roads that make it easier to transport water from alternative sources when Israel cuts back on supply. Second in line are villages that have a water grid but are not easily accessible, making transportation of water from alternative sources costly and difficult. Worst off are 180 communities, home to some 30,000 Palestinians, located entirely or in part in Area C, that Israel has prevented from connecting to the water grid, forcing them to purchase costly water privately from tankers all year round. As a result, as well as due to the takeover of natural water resources by Israeli settlers and authorities and the destruction or blocking of cisterns and spring-fed pools, average water consumption in these communities can be as low as 20 liters a day per person.[76]

The situation is no better in the East Jerusalem section of the West Bank, where some 160,000 Palestinians residents "are not allowed under Israeli law to connect to the water network" and thus "lack access to adequate water and sanitation infrastructure and services."[77] This is mainly because the required housing permits have not been issued by the Jerusalem Municipality due to its strict housing and urban planning regime, which places stringent and unrealistic criteria for access to such services.[78] Moreover, parts of East Jerusalem that have been cut off by the construction of the Separation Wall have no access to municipal services, including water and sanitation.[79] As noted by the ICJ, citing the observation of the Special Rapporteur on the Right to Food of the United Nations Commission on Human Rights, the

---

[72] S. Koppelman and Z. Alshalalfeh, "Our Right to Water: The Human Right to Water in Palestine," Blue Planet Project, LifeSource, Mar. 2012, p. 4, www.researchgate.net/publication/320008804_Our_Right_to_Water_The_Human_Right_to_Water_in_Palestine.

[73] Ibid., p. 4.

[74] B'Tselem, note 60.

[75] Ibid.

[76] Ibid.

[77] Al-Haq, Addameer Prisoner Support and Human Rights Association, BADIL Resource Center for Palestinian Residency and Refugee Rights, and Women's Centre for Legal Aid and Counselling, "Joint Parallel Report," Submitted to the UN Committee on the Elimination of All Forms of Racial Discrimination (CERD) on the Occasion of the Consideration of Israel's 14th, 15th, and 16th Periodic Reports on the implementation of the International Convention on the Elimination of All Forms of Racial Discrimination," Jan. 30, 2012, paras. 104–105.

[78] Ibid. For instance, requirements related to proof of ownership of the land and its registration in the Land Registry Office, and high application fees (Bimkom, "Construction in the Planning Trap: Policy, Planning and Development in the Palestinian Neighborhoods of East Jerusalem," 2014, pp. 56 and 60 (in Hebrew)).

[79] Ibid., para. 106; David Pellow, *What Is Critical Environmental Justice?* (Cambridge: Polity, 2018), p. 89. The Separation Wall, or Security Barrier, was constructed by Israel in 2002 to separate most of the West Bank from Israel. In 2004, the ICJ found in its Advisory Opinion on the *Legal Consequences of the Construction of a Wall in the Occupied Palestinian Territory* that the Wall was illegal under international law. In 2005, the ISC in its decision in *Mara'abe et al. v. Prime Minister of Israel et al.*, HCJ 7957/04 rejected the Advisory Opinion.

Wall operates to "annex most of the western aquifer system (which provides 51 per cent of the West Bank's water resources)."[80]

13.3.3 *Water (In)justice and Sustainable Development in Israel*

The negative consequences of these water injustices experienced by Palestinians in the West Bank and by Bedouins in Israel include inadequate food, housing, and healthcare, as well as broader social, cultural, and economic impacts that disproportionately affect vulnerable segments of these populations such as women, farmers, and shepherds. In the West Bank, discriminatory restrictions on access to water and sanitation make the daily tasks of Palestinian women, who are typically responsible for household chores and childcare, more difficult.[81] Moreover, the economic, social, and cultural survival of herding communities in Area C depends to a large extent on access to water.[82] As a result, many Palestinian farmers and shepherds in the Jordan Valley who require large amounts of water for irrigation and for their cattle have been forced to abandon their work in agriculture or to sell their cattle as a result of the costs associated with access to water systems.[83] They are then "relegated to making a living from low-wage day jobs, and to a life of poverty next to Palestinian cities which are themselves impoverished."[84] Similarly, in the absence of sewage treatment systems in Palestinian communities in the West Bank, wastewater flows into the valleys and streams and pollutes water sources and grazing lands. As a result, there are areas where communities "avoid grazing because they fear for the health and safety of the flocks due to the sewage and pollution."[85]

Bedouin communities who are not connected to the main water grid in Israel are subject to expenses as much as ten times higher than the regular price of water as a result of the additional costs of purchasing water, purchasing or renting equipment to transport the water to their villages, or installing their own network of above-ground pipes. These expenses "are an additional burden on populations that are already severely disadvantaged and living under the poverty level,"[86] including those living in government townships. Since "there are no industries near the planned cities, the rates of unemployment are high and the townships are economically depressed."[87] Moreover, these recognized townships, which Israel established without consulting the Bedouin community, fail to accommodate the traditional livelihood and particular cultural needs of this community. As a result, "forced urbanization and prolaterezation [*sic*] obliterated the [Bedouins'] nomadic traditions and their rural way of life" and "those now living in these government-planned townships no longer have adequate space to maintain traditional practices such as agriculture and herding. The towns have disrupted the social fabric and hierarchies of Bedouin communities."[88] Indeed, research suggests that Israel's water policy designed to encourage Bedouins to resettle in recognized townships may be ineffective since

---

[80] ICJ, note 58, p. 191, citing E/CN.4/2004/10/Add.2 Oct. 31, 2003, para. 51.

[81] Ibid., paras. 29–30.

[82] A. Zuabi, S. Hartman, A. Cohen Lifshitz, "Access to Natural Resources: A Necessity for the Existence of the Herding Communities in Area C," Bimkom, 2017.

[83] Al-Haq et al., note 77, paras. 94.

[84] Zuabi et al., note 82.

[85] Ibid.

[86] NCF, note 45, pp. 18, 20, and 30.

[87] Murthy et al., note 26, p. 49.

[88] NCF, note 45, p.18; Murthy et al., note 26, p. 49.

"many Bedouins in unrecognized villages are not willing to relinquish their land claims and their traditional way of life simply to have better access to water and other municipal services."[89]

These far-reaching implications of water inequalities in Israel and the West Bank illustrate the indivisible linkages between water and sustainable development. They also reflect the limited ability of the human right to water as currently recognized and implemented in Israel to prevent water injustice. The next section will conclude by suggesting a broader understanding of the human right to water which calls for a nondiscriminatory and contextual application.

13.4 CONCLUSION: THE RIGHT TO WATER REVISITED

Israel does not have specific legislation that prohibits discrimination relating to land planning, allocation, and use, or that ensures equal water access and supply. Moreover, it has not recognized the Bedouin and Palestinian populations as having Indigenous status. Nevertheless, Israel is required to abide by human rights standards that bind it both as a matter of treaty law and customary international law.[90] These include the obligation to ensure equal rights "to public health . . . and social services,"[91] "to adequate food . . . and housing,"[92] and "to life."[93] The human right to water, which is derived from these obligations, further requires Israel to "ensure that any form of service provision guarantees equal access to affordable, sufficient, safe and acceptable water,"[94] as well as "non-discrimination" in water access and use in order to protect the most vulnerable or marginalized segments of the population "in law and fact."[95] Moreover, these obligations apply equally in times of conflict and therefore Israel, in exercising sovereign powers in the Palestinian Territories, is bound by them also with respect to the Palestinian residents of the West Bank.[96] However, Israel's treatment of the Bedouin and Palestinian populations evidences the disturbing ease with which these obligations can be disregarded.[97] Indeed, the *de jure* recognition of the human right to water in Israel has not translated into equal, or equitable, access to and supply of water *de facto*, which has in turn impaired the social and economic development of these vulnerable communities.

Bedouins living in the Negev suffer from discrimination that is excused by an unduly narrow interpretation of the human right to water by the Israeli government and courts as imposing a

---

[89] Murthy et al., note 26, p. 27.

[90] Schlütter, note 61, p. 632

[91] UN General Assembly, International Convention on the Elimination of All Forms of Race Discrimination, Jan. 4, 1969, 660 UNTS, 195, Art. 5. Israel became a party in 1979.

[92] In its General Comment 4, the Committee on Economic, Social and Cultural Rights held that the right to housing includes adequate basic infrastructure and sustainable access to safe drinking water (UN International Human Rights Instruments, *General Comment No. 4: The Right to Adequate Housing*, May 12, 2004, UN Doc. HRI/GEN/1/Rev.7, paras. 7–8).

[93] The human right to water is closely linked with the right to life since "a minimum amount of water is so essential for life that withholding it amounts to a deprivation of life" (S. L. Murthy, "A New Constitutive Commitment to Water" (2016) 36 *Boston College Journal of Law and Social Justice*, pp. 159 and 197).

[94] OHCHR, note 15, p. 35.

[95] UNESC, note 8, para. 12(c)(iii), (iv).

[96] Schlütter, note 61, p. 631.

[97] Human rights law can in fact be used as a tool of "social control" rather than as "a mechanism for enabling individuals to exercise greater agency in their everyday lives," and can "play an important role in maintaining the *status quo* of many aspects of social control in contemporary societies" (P. Johnson and S. Falcetta, "Human Rights Law as Social Control" (2019) *European Journal of Criminology* at 2–3, and 13). In the water context, projects that divert water from distant rural to urban areas around the world have been justified by reference to the human right to water, and the right has been used to represent such decisions as neutral even though they "generate very unequal outcomes for different groups" (Boelens et al., note 6, p. 10).

minimal obligation on the state to satisfy only the most basic water needs of its citizens, with little regard to equality in quality, quantity, or ease of access. Palestinians in the West Bank and East Jerusalem are not even guaranteed the most basic water needs, although they are just as dependent on water resources controlled by Israel as the Jewish settlers in Area C.[98] These water injustices are closely intertwined with historical displacement, land expropriation, and disruptions of traditional lifestyles suffered by Bedouins and Palestinians.[99] The Israeli government has used discriminatory land and water policies as a tool for eradicating the Bedouin and Palestinian way of life by denying them equal access to and use of water.[100] Such "weaponization" of water to coerce resettlement or control livelihood should be viewed as a violation of the human right to water, and states that use water as a tool for forced relocation of minority communities, whether of Indigenous status or otherwise, should not be allowed to claim compliance with this right.

In order to achieve truly equal water rights, the interpretation and application of the human right to water cannot be divorced from broader historical and socioeconomic conditions and from antidiscrimination obligations. It must be understood and implemented jointly with the basic right to life and to be free from discrimination in access to housing, food, social and health services, and basic infrastructure. Viewed in this way, the human right to water would obligate states such as Israel to ensure that all populations relying on water resources located within their territories or subject to their control have *equal* access to *equal* amounts of water of *equal* quality, regardless of ethnicity, religion, land and political claims, Indigenous status, or citizenship.

[98] UNCERD, note 52, para. 24.
[99] I. Abu-Saad and C. Creamer, "Socio-Political Upheaval and Current Conditions of the Naqab Bedouin Arabs," in Amara et al., note 26, p. 20.
[100] Ibid., p. 57.

14

Gender, Indigeneity, and the Search for Environmental Justice in Postcolonial Africa

Damilola S. Olawuyi

14.1 INTRODUCTION

This chapter examines legal and governance innovations for advancing gender equality in environmental decision-making processes in postcolonial Africa. First, it evaluates how inequitable colonial, cultural, legal, social, and power relationships continue to create interlocking structures of gender-based ecological vulnerabilities in Africa, paying specific attention to Nigeria as a case study. It then discusses the need for a human rights–based gender framework as a policy tool for addressing gender-based environmental inequalities in Africa.

Despite the conceptualization and promotion of the environmental justice paradigm globally, gender-based inequity in the distribution of environmental burdens and benefits, especially in Indigenous communities, remains a major threat to sustainable development in Africa.[1] Gender inequality refers to the unequal treatment or perception of individuals based on their gender.[2] Several studies have compiled the growing evidence of gender injustice and inequality in Africa.[3] The manifestations of gender inequality in Africa include: uneven education, training, and empowerment opportunities for girls and women;[4] unequal access of women to, and control of, important resources such as land, property, employment, and credit facilities;[5] prevalence of social and cultural norms that assign secondary and subordinate roles to women in household,

---

[1] A. Ademuson, "Women Domination and Oppression in Nigerian Society: Implications for Sustainable Development" (2016) 19 *African Journal for the Psychological Studies of Social Issues* 24–36; C. Ridgeway, *Framed by Gender: How Gender Inequality Persists in the Modern World* (Oxford: Oxford University Press, 2011), pp. 1–15; D. Olawuyi, *The Human Rights Based Approach to Carbon Finance* (Cambridge: Cambridge University Press, 2016), pp. 1–15.

[2] See United Nations Development Programme (UNDP), "Gender Inequality," in "Poverty Reduction – Humanity Divided: Confronting Inequality in Developing Countries," Bureau for Development Policy, November 2013, pp. 162–165.

[3] UNDP, "Africa Human Development Report 2016: Accelerating Gender Equality and Women's Empowerment in Africa," Regional Bureau for Africa, 2016, pp. 1–15, stating that: African women achieve only 87 percent of the human development outcomes of men; and that endemic gender gaps costs sub-Saharan Africa $US95 billion a year. See also J. Arbache, A. Kolev, and E. Filipiak (eds.), "Gender Disparities in Africa's Labour Market," Agence Française de Développement and the International Bank for Reconstruction and Development/World Bank, Africa Development Forum Series, 2010, pp. 1–10.

[4] UNDP, note 3.

[5] M. Benschop, *Rights and Reality: Are Women's Equal Rights to Land, Housing and Property Implemented in East Africa?* (Nairobi: UN-Habitat, 2002); UN, "2009 World Survey on the Role of Women in Development: Women's Control over Economic Resources and Access to Financial Resources, including Microfinance," Department of Economic and Social Affairs, Division for the Advancement of Women, 2009), pp. 1–5, noting that equal access to economic and financial resources is critical for gender equality and empowerment.

community, and national decision-making processes;[6] inadequate opportunities for women to hold government, and other senior leadership positions;[7] and the increased adoption of governmental policies and programs that suppress women's experiences, perceptions, and voices.[8] These problems have over the years impacted the abilities of African women to effectively take part in, and influence, decision-making processes on development activities and projects that may impact their health, subsistence, and livelihoods, even in times of environmental disasters.[9] According to a 2011 report of the United Nations, women in Africa and Asia are particularly vulnerable to the impacts of environmental disasters due to skewed power relations and inequitable cultural and social norms.[10] These concerns are more pronounced in Indigenous communities where systemic discrimination against women, coupled with predominant marginalization and forced displacements of native women from ancestral lands, have created 'double jeopardy' effects of intersecting alienation because they are both women and they belong to Indigenous communities.[11]

For several decades, international law instruments – ranging from the Universal Declaration of Human Rights (UDHR) of 1948, to Goal 3 of the Millennium Development Goals of 2000, and to Goal 5 of the Sustainable Development Goals (SDGs) of 2015 – have all advocated for new power relationships that respect, protect, and fulfil the rights of women to equality and nondiscrimination.[12] Yet, as this chapter illustrates, policy approaches aimed at strengthening adaptive capacity in several African countries still largely fail to properly recognize and integrate women's perspectives and experiences, especially women in Indigenous communities.[13] Without a gender-based perspective, the search for environmental justice in postcolonial Africa may remain stifled.[14]

---

[6] See C. Nellemann, R. Verma, and L. Hislop (eds.), "Women at the Frontline of Climate Change: Gender Risks and Hopes: A Rapid Response Assessment," United Nations Environment Programme, GRID-Arendal, ICIMOD, Center for International Climate and Environmental Research – Oslo, 2011, p. 6.

[7] S. Seguino, "Toward Gender Justice: Confronting Stratification and Power" (2013) 2 *Géneros* 1–36.

[8] See UNEP, note 6, p. 6; S. Lastarria-Cornhiel, "Impact of Privatization on Gender and Property Rights in Africa" (1997) 25 *World Development* 317–333.

[9] Olawuyi, note 1; UNEP, note 6; D. Scholsberg and L. Collins, "From Environmental to Climate Justice: Climate Change and the Discourse of Environmental Justice" (2014) 5 *Wires Climate Change Journal* 359–374.

[10] See UNEP, note 6, p. 6.

[11] Studies have recommended the need for an intersectional approach that takes into account how various grounds of discrimination, ranging from gender, indigeneity, to education and class, symbiotically reinforce one another to produce marginalized subjects. See L. Okolosie, "Beyond 'Talking' and 'Owning' Intersectionality" (2014) *Feminist Review* 108 *Gender Studies Database* 90; J. Bond, "International Intersectionality: A Theoretical and Pragmatic Exploration of Women's International Human Rights Violations" (2003) 52 *Emory Law Journal* 71, 76.

[12] UN General Assembly, *Transforming Our World: The 2030 Agenda for Sustainable Development*, Oct. 21, 2015, A/RES/70/l. For the MDGs, see UN General Assembly, *Keeping the Promise: United to Achieve the Millennium Development Goals*, Oct. 19, 2010, UN/A/RES/65/1.

[13] This chapter does not delve into debates as to whether Indigenous communities exist in Africa. Rather it adopts the definition of Indigenous peoples endorsed by the African Commission on Human and Peoples' Rights, which categorizes Indigenous peoples to include those communities in Africa whose survival depends on access and rights to traditional lands and natural resources thereon; who suffer from discrimination; live in inaccessible or geographically isolated regions; suffer from various forms of marginalization and are subjected to domination and oppression within national political and economic structures; and who self-identify as Indigenous. See African Commission on Human and Peoples' Rights, "Indigenous Peoples in Africa: The Forgotten Peoples? The African Commission's Work on Indigenous Peoples in Africa," International Work Group for Indigenous Affairs, 2006.

[14] M. O. Okome, "Domestic, Regional and International Protection of Nigeria Women against Discrimination: Constraints and Possibilities" (2002) 6 *African Studies Quarterly* 33–54; N. Rao, E. Lawson, W. Raditloaneng,

This chapter examines how institutions and programs on environmental justice in Africa may be revitalized and strengthened to address gender-based inequalities and vulnerabilities. Section 14.2 considers how gender inequality may worsen ecological vulnerabilities, drawing examples from climate mitigation and adaptation projects in Nigeria. Section 14.3 discusses the need for a human rights–based gender proofing framework as a policy tool for addressing gender-based environmental inequalities in Africa. Section 14.4 summarizes the chapter's recommendations and proposals.

14.2 DUAL VULNERABILITIES OF INDIGENOUS WOMEN TO CLIMATE CHANGE IN AFRICA: NIGERIAN EXAMPLES

14.2.1 *Methodology*

Drawing examples from Nigeria, this section demonstrates how climate change risks may be magnified by preexisting social marginalization, gender inequality, and uneven distribution of the burdens of adaptation and mitigation. It draws on a mixed method study (survey, in-depth interviews, and focus group discussions) conducted in Badia, Lagos, Nigeria; and a literature review of Indigenous peoples' experiences with a planned REDD+ project in Cross River State of Nigeria.[15] Despite the lack of formal legal recognition of Indigenous groups in Nigeria, and in several African countries, the Badia and Cross River communities fit within the categorizations of Indigenous peoples that has been endorsed by the African Commission on Human and Peoples Rights.[16] These case studies demonstrate how a confluence of preexisting marginalization against women due to retrograde customs and stereotypes, coupled with land grabbing of Indigenous peoples lands, expose Indigenous women in Africa to double vulnerability to climate change risks.

14.2.2 *Results and Analysis*

14.2.2.1 Climate Maladaptation in Badia Slum in Lagos, Nigeria

Lagos, in southwestern Nigeria, is one of the world's rapidly growing cities and, at the same time, one with extreme vulnerabilities to climate change. The city is bounded to the south by the

---

D. Solomon, and M. Angula, "Gendered Vulnerabilities to Climate Change: Insights from the Semi-Arid Regions of Africa and Asia" (2017) *Climate and Development* 1–10.

[15] I. Ajibade and D. Olawuyi, "Climate Change Impacts on Housing and Property Rights in Nigeria and Panama: Toward a Rights-Based Approach to Adaptation and Mitigation," in D. Stucker and E. Lopez-Gunn (eds.), *Adaptation to Climate Change through Water Resources Management: Capacity, Equity and Sustainability* (New York: Routledge 2014), pp. 264–284.

[16] Several African countries have so far failed to recognize the existence of Indigenous groups. For example, the Nigerian government and laws, do not specifically recognize, protect, or refer to any group as Indigenous. As a member of the UN Human Rights Council, Nigeria abstained from voting on the Declaration on the Rights of Indigenous Peoples and has failed to ratify ILO Convention No. 169 which deals specifically with the rights of Indigenous and tribal peoples. Central African Republic remains the only African country to ratify ILO Convention No. 169. Furthermore, Kenya in 2010 became the first African country to recognize 'minorities and historically marginalized groups' in its Constitution, while Republic of Congo in 2011 became the first African country to enact a specific legislation on the promotion and protection of the rights of Indigenous populations. See ACHPR, note 13: stating that one of the key challenges is the widespread misconception across African countries that the term 'indigenous' is not applicable in Africa as 'all Africans are indigenous.' See also NORMLEX, International Labour Organization, "Ratifications of C169 – Indigenous and Tribal Peoples Convention, 1989 (No. 169)," www.ilo.org/dyn/normlex/en/f?p=1000:11300:0::NO:11300:P11300_INSTRUMENT_ID:312314.

Atlantic Ocean and surrounded by wetlands, beaches, lagoons, and estuaries.[17] From a population of 252,000 in 1952, Lagos has grown to over 24.6 million people in 2015, of which 70 percent live in slums characterized by extreme poverty and poor water, energy, and food infrastructure systems.[18] Slum residents face a potential worsening of their situations due to climate-induced increases in storm surges, rainfall, and sea level.[19] In the last decade, excessive precipitation of more than 100mm/day has occurred from June through August, resulting in massive flooding and displacement of people in slum communities.[20]

Badia is one of Lagos's slum settlements with severe infrastructural deficits, poor housing conditions, and heightened exposure to the problem of flooding linked to heavy rains and groundwater intrusion from the Lagos Lagoon. It has a total land area of about 1.6km² and a population of 600,000 people.[21] Many of its current residents are victims of previous forcible eviction from Oluwole village, Iganmu Lagos, a land area acquired by the federal government of Nigeria for the purpose of constructing a massive development project – the National Arts Theatre – in celebration of the 1977 African Festival of Arts and Culture.[22] Due to persistent protest, some of the Oluwole evictees were awarded paltry sums as compensation while those that insisted on resettlement were allocated plots of land in the swampy area of Badia.[23] However, no further assistance was rendered to the resettled population in terms of material or financial support for proper land reclamation, construction of quality housing, solid waste disposal systems, and healthcare facilities.[24] A combination of these preexisting political inequalities and deprivations, mean that flooding continues to threaten the existence and survival of the historically marginalized people of Badia.[25]

For example, during the July 10, 2011 rainstorm, in which Lagos received over 264mm of rain in eighteen hours (a volume equivalent to what is usually recorded for the whole month), the

---

[17] UN-HABITAT, *The State of World's Cities, 2016/2017: Bridging Urban Divide* (London: Earthscan, 2016); Lagos State Government of Nigeria, "About Lagos," https://lagosstate.gov.ng/about-lagos/.

[18] Ibid.

[19] S. Mehrotra, C. E. Natenzon, A. Omojola, R. Folorunsho, J. Gilbride, and C. Rosenzweig, "Framework for City Climate Risk Assessment: Buenos Aires, Delhi, Lagos and New York," World Bank Commissioned Research: Fifth Urban Research Symposium Cities and Climate Change: Responding to an Urgent Agenda, 2009.

[20] S. Meikle, "The Urban Context and Poor People," in T. Lloyd-Jones and C. Rakodi (eds.), *Urban Livelihoods: A People Centred Approach to Reducing Poverty* (London: Earthscan, 2012); P. Milly, T. Wetherald, K. Dunne, and T. Delworth, "Increasing Risk of Great Floods in a Changing Climate" (2002) 415 *Nature* 514–517.

[21] F. Morka, "A Place to Live: Resisting Evictions in Ijora-Badia, Nigeria," in L. White and J. Perelman (eds.), *Stone of Hope: How African Activists Reclaim Human Rights Challenge Global Poverty* (Stanford: Stanford University Press, 2011), pp. 1–15.

[22] Ibid.

[23] F. C. Morka, "A Place to Live: A Case Study of the Ijora-Badia Community in Lagos, Nigeria," case study prepared for Enhancing Urban Safety and Security: Global Report on Human Settlements 2007.

[24] Ibid.

[25] The Badia community is a predominantly fishing settlement under the traditional rulership of the Ojora Chieftaincy Family. The Badia people share ancestral land, culture, tradition, and history that date back to precolonial era. However, years of marginalization by the Lagos state government, and alleged collusion by the Ojora Chieftaincy Family, have resulted in extreme poverty, persistent conditions of isolation, culturally inadequate social services, and human rights violations in the community. See "Joint Press Statement: Thousands of Evictees Suffer Homelessness & Loss of Livelihood after Ijora Badia Forced Evictions," Sept. 28, 2015, www.spacesforchange.org/2015/09/thousands-of-evictees-suffer-homelessness-loss-of-livelihood-after-ijora-badia-forced-evictions/.

entire Badia community was submerged in flood waters.[26] More than 90 percent of respondents recorded severe damages to household properties; 80 percent experienced direct structural damages to their shelters; 56 percent were displaced; 16.5 percent reported injuries of household members; and twenty-seven people were killed during the rainstorm.[27] Other reported impacts include restriction of movement, loss of income, increased transportation cost, loss of productive and family time, and health and psychological problems.[28] Based on a mixed survey conducted, petty traders, who are mostly women, were the most affected by the impacts of the flood.[29] Many of the affected traders lamented being forcibly removed from their homes for flood control efforts without any alternative housing provisions by the government.[30] Many of these petty traders, who rely on the proceeds of their sales to support their families, have been left with no source of subsistence.[31]

Impacts of the July 2011 rainstorm in Badia have been heightened by social and economic marginalization that prevent Badia residents from implementing effective adaptation to the regular flooding problem in their community.[32] Efforts by Badia residents to build resilience by themselves are consistently undermined by insecurity of land tenure and the forcible eviction by governments for different development projects.[33] According to a petition submitted to the World Bank, over one hundred structures in Badia have been demolished to make way for the construction of a drainage canal built as part of a World Bank funded development project, forcibly evicting more than 9,000 residents in the process.[34] Such forcible evictions deter people in Badia from implementing good environmental practices and structural measures against flood risks.[35] For example, many interview participants in Badia expressed a reluctance to invest in quality housing that could withstand heavy rain because they feared it might be demolished anytime. Similarly, only a few (10 percent) of the total survey respondents were willing to take part in communal action and projects to improve their local environment because of the threat of eviction.[36]

Forcible eviction of Badia residents by the government in the planning of development and climate adaptation projects violates the fundamental rights of the people of Badia and could have wider-ranging livelihood impacts, especially for women.[37] In the course of being moved to other locations, evicted households, especially petty traders, often lose access to key markets and

---

[26] National Emergency Management Agency (NEMA) "Flooding: 1 Million Nigerians May Die," *Nigerian Tribune*, Sept. 28, 2012; Nigeria Meteorological Agency (NIMET) (2011) "Nigeria: Flooding Will Continue – Nimet, Niomr," www.aidnews.org/nigeria-flooding-will-continue-nimet-niomr.

[27] See Ajibade and Olawuyi, note 15.

[28] Ibid.

[29] Ibid.

[30] M. Oladunjoye, "Nigeria: July 10 Flooding, Lagos Gives Relief Materials to Victims," www.allafrica.com/stories/201109080792.html.

[31] Joint Press Statement, note 25.

[32] Ibid.

[33] See Amnesty International, "Nigeria: The Human Cost of a Mega City: Forced Evictions of the Urban Poor in Lagos, Nigeria," Nov. 14, 2017, pp. 14–17, documenting how thousands of Badia residents have been forcibly ejected by the Lagos state government, without compensation or alternative housing, to make way for city development projects.

[34] See World Bank Inspection Panel (WBIP), "Request for Inspection Nigeria: Lagos Metropolitan Development and Governance Project (P071340)," paras. 3–5, noting that families living in the Badia have been forcibly ejected from their homes and lands by governments "without prior consultation, notice, compensation or resettlement."

[35] Ajibade and Olawuyi, note 15.

[36] Ibid.

[37] UN, International Covenant on Economic Social and Cultural Right, Dec. 16, 1966, 993 UNTS 3, Art. 11.

livelihood sources as well as significant social networks and capital.[38] The loss of these crucial resources can negatively affect the ability of women to contribute to household financial resources. Women's access to and control over financial resources have been associated with overall improvements in the ability of African households to cope or adapt to future risks including those related to climate change, child health, and nutrition.[39] Protecting the subsistence and income of women traders can prevent the exclusion of women in intra-household decision-making and have positive outcomes for overall sustainable development.[40]

Another major factor constraining adaptation in Badia is the unequal power relations, including legal and customary norms that prevent women from owning lands. The enactment of formal land allocation laws during colonial era which allocated lands to the state, coupled with patriarchal policies that limit the abilities of women to acquire land under formal structures without male sponsorship, combine to create interlocking structures of gender exclusion in Africa.[41] For example, in Badia, as is the case in several African countries, although women represent more than 70 percent of the agricultural labor, account for 60–80 percent of food production and are involved in 80–90 percent in food processing, storage, and transportation, only 15 percent of women farmers in Africa own their farmlands.[42] Large amounts of land historically jointly owned and controlled by the Badia community during the precolonial era, and accessible to women, have shifted into the hands of government agencies and private landowners during the colonial era.[43] For example, based on a mixed survey conducted in Badia community, only 5 percent of women in the community owned lands.[44] As a result, the amount and quality of land available to women food producers in Badia as well as across Nigeria is declining. Lack of land ownership or title is also tied to the inability of women farmers to access bank loans, credit facilities, technologies, and seeds on which commercial agriculture is heavily dependent, resulting in a cycle of perpetual subjugation and dependence on men.[45]

---

[38] See WBIP, note 34.

[39] Joint Press Statement, note 25; see Nelleman et al., note 6.

[40] African societies are largely patriarchal. Most of the household decision in sub-Saharan African countries are made by men who are the de facto house heads and main income providers. On the importance of increasing women income generation, see D. Angel-Urdinola and Q. Wodon, "Income Generation and Intra-Household Decision Making: A Gender Analysis for Nigeria," in J. S. Arbache, A. Kolev, and E. Filipiak (eds.), *Gender Disparities in Africa's Labor Markets* (Washington, DC: World Bank, 2010), pp. 381–406; UN, note 5.

[41] See A. Torkelsson and F. Onditti, "Addressing Gender Gaps in Agricultural Productivity in Africa: Comparative Case Studies from Tanzania, Malawi and Uganda" (2018) 9 *Afe Babalola University Journal of Sustainable Development Law and Policy* 35–57; A. Ilumoka, "Globalization and the Re-establishment of Women's Land Rights in Nigeria: The Role of Legal History" (2012) 87 *Chicago-Kent Law Review* 423–430.

[42] See Food and Agriculture Organization (FAO), "Gender and Land Rights Database: Nigeria Country Profile," www.fao.org/gender-landrights-database/country-profiles/countries-list/general-introduction/en/?country_iso3=NGA: stating that 90 percent of registered land and properties are in men's names; less than 14 percent of females have land in their name; and that only 15 percent of beneficiaries of government programs are women.

[43] For example, in 1863, about a year and half after the British colony of Lagos, Nigeria was officially established, the colonial government initiated a set of land reforms which recognized a few private claims to land, and then transferred the absolute control of all lands to the state. First, the Land Registration Ordinance No. 9 of 1863 established a land allocation commission with powers to grant title certificates to private owners with valid land claims made within one year. In 1869, Land Registration Ordinance No. 9 of 1869, which grants the state absolute jurisdiction over lands in Lagos, was passed. In 1883, the Land Registration Ordinance No. 8 of 1883 was passed which established a land registry in Lagos and required all land titles to be registered within thirty days. See T. O. Elias, *Nigerian Land Law and Custom* (London: Routledge & Kegan Paul, 1951), p. 361; F. Anunobi, "Women and Development in Africa: From Marginalization to Gender Inequality" (2002) 2 *African Social Science Review* 57.

[44] Ajibade and Olawuyi, note 15.

[45] UN, note 5.

Such cycle of dependence also impacts the abilities of married women to make unilateral decisions to migrate to less dangerous locations even in times of environmental disasters, floods, and climate induced natural disasters.[46]

The Lagos, Nigeria example mirrors the situations in Burundi, Namibia, Lesotho, Liberia, Mali, Ghana, Togo, Benin, Kenya, Mali, Burkina Faso, and Senegal, where women still face three major challenges: inequitable access to land, limited legal protection for women's land rights, and weak safeguards and protection for businesses and investments by women.[47] These systemic inequalities against women, coupled with preexisting vulnerabilities of women in Indigenous communities, such as Badia, have created double marginalization for Indigenous African women. According to a UN study, such lopsided and inequitable practices alone double the vulnerabilities of African women to the direct and indirect impacts of climate change.[48]

14.2.2.2 REDD+ Project in Calabar, Cross River State of Nigeria

The international climate change regime has promoted efforts aimed at Reducing Emissions from Deforestation and Forest Degradation, sustainable management of forests and conservation, and enhancement of forest carbon stocks (REDD+) as a prominent potential emission mitigation strategy.[49] REDD+ schemes allow industrialized countries to gain emission reduction credits by engaging in forest conservation efforts and efforts that protect trees from being cut down.[50] Nigeria was among the first few African countries to indicate an early willingness to execute REDD+ projects.[51] Nigeria's first REDD+ project is financed by Shell Canada and Gazprom and is situated in Calabar, Cross River State of Nigeria.[52]

However, the design and implementation of this REDD+ project has been fraught with several challenges. The first problem is the failure by Nigerian authorities to properly engage with tribal communities in Calabar who depend on lands and forests for their economic, social, and cultural survival.[53] In preparation for the REDD+ project, the government unilaterally

---

[46] Nelleman et al., note 6; Ajibade and Olawuyi, note 15.

[47] Women ownership of land in Africa ranges from 0 percent in Burundi, Liberia, Lesotho, and Namibia, to 3 percent in Mali, 5 percent in Kenya, 35 percent in countries such as Botswana and Malawi, and more than 50 percent in Cape Verde and South Africa. See Food and Agriculture Organization (FAO), "Gender and Land Rights Database," www.fao.org/gender-landrights-database/country-profiles/countries-list/en/. In Lesotho for example, a woman is considered a legal minor and therefore cannot own property or enter into any binding contract without the consent of her husband.

[48] See Nelleman et al., note 6; G. Terry, "No Climate Justice without Gender Justice: An Overview of the Issues" (2009) 17 *Gender & Development* 5–18; G. Terry, Climate Change and Gender Justice (Oxford: Practical Action Publishing with Oxfam, 2009), p. 3.

[49] See UN Framework Convention on Climate Change, *Decision 1/CP.13: Bali Action Plan*, Mar. 14, 2008, FCCC/CP/2007/6/Add.1.

[50] See A. Angelsen, S. Brown, C. Loisel, L. Paskett, C. Streck, and D. Zarin "Reducing Emissions from Deforestation and Forest Degradation (REDD): An Options Assessment Report," prepared for the government of Norway, Mar. 2009, pp. 3–4.

[51] S. Ogidan, "Nigeria to Earn N 34.44 Billion Yearly in Tree Planting" *Nigerian Compass* (Lagos, Feb. 14, 2011).

[52] D. Forgarty, "Shell Bankrolls REDD Project in Nigeria," Sept. 7, 2010, http://climatevoices.wordpress.com/2010/09/07/shell-bankrolls-redd/.

[53] It has been described as 'perverse incentives' to convert natural forests into monoculture tree plantations and to actually increase deforestation. According to Nigeria's environmental group: "Most of the forests of the world are found in Indigenous Peoples' land. REDD-type projects have already resulted in land grabs, violations of human rights, threats to cultural survival, militarization, scams and servitude." See R. Osarogiagbon, "REDD & Its Implication on Community People" presentation made at Cross River State stakeholders' forum on Climate change, REDD & Forest Dependent Community Rights, Mar. 1, 2011; C. Lang, "'Our Forest Is Not for Sale!' NGO Statement on REDD in Nigeria," Sept. 1, 2010, https://redd-monitor.org/2010/09/01/our-forest-is-not-for-sale-ngo-statement-on-redd-in-nigeria/.

declared a logging ban in certain forests in Calabar, and created a militarized Anti-deforestation Task Force to enforce the ban.[54] According to Nigeria's main environmental group, the Environmental Rights Action, communities in Cross River State whose forests are targeted for the REDD+ project were not consulted by the Nigerian government, and only woke up to hear of the logging ban in the news.[55] Consequently, local communities have opposed the project as "the largest land grab of all time and genocide against Indigenous Peoples."[56] Confiscating traditionally inhabited lands for "overriding public purpose" not only dismantles the culture and identity of local communities in Calabar, it particularly deprives women of access to farmlands and livelihoods.

Equally problematic is the absence of a framework for compensating or providing alternatives for women farmers who have been deprived access to forests by the project. In Calabar, over 70 percent of women identify themselves as farmers who rely on forests for food, wood, medicines, and subsistence, and are actively involved in the food supply value chain.[57] While REDD+ projects could contribute to climate change mitigation, confiscating a large proportion of land by military force, without providing compensation or settlement options for these women farmers is a major human rights concern.[58]

Another concern is the lack of a transparent environmental impact assessment (EIA) and human rights impact assessment (HRIA) of REDD+ projects on the inhabitants of these areas.[59] A transparent assessment process allows governments to measure, and the local communities to understand the immediate and long-term environmental and human rights implications of a project on local communities.[60] However, the process leading to the approval of the REDD+ project in Cross River State did not indicate the conduct of a public impact assessment process of any kind by Shell. While REDD+ projects would contribute to climate change mitigation, confiscating a large proportion of land from Indigenous communities with brute military force, and without transparently analyzing and communicating the environmental and human rights implications of the project on the forest dependent communities is a threat to the attainment of sustainable development.

14.2.3 *Drivers of Gender Injustice in Postcolonial Africa*

The Nigerian case studies illustrate and reveal four key drivers of gender injustice and vulnerabilities in the design and implementation of development projects and programs in Africa. They are colonialism and restrictive property regimes; lack of legal recognition of Indigenous rights; ineffective enforcement or implementation of human rights instruments (to housing, land and forests, and equal access to decision-making forums in project planning processes); and lack of institutional capacity and coordination.

---

[54] C. Lang, "REDD in Cross River, Nigeria: Property Rights, Militarized Protectionism, and Carbonized Exclusion," Jan. 20, 2017, https://redd-monitor.org/2017/01/20/redd-in-cross-river-nigeria-property-rights-militarised-protectionism-and-carbonised-exclusion/.

[55] See C. Lang, "Shell Project Slammed in Nigeria," Sept. 8, 2010, www.redd-monitor.org/2010/09/08/indigenous-environmental-network-and-friends-of-the-earth-nigeria-denounce-shell-redd-project/.

[56] Ibid.

[57] See Lang, note 54.

[58] UN, note 37, Arts. 26 and 27: rights of minority and Indigenous communities to enjoy their culture.

[59] Ibid; A. Asiyanbi, "A Political Ecology of REDD+: Property Rights, Militarised Protectionism and Carbonised Exclusion in Cross River" (2016) *Geoforum* 146–156.

[60] Asiyanbi, note 59.

14.2.3.1 Colonialism and Restrictive Property Regimes

One of the enduring negative legacies of colonialism in Africa is that it upended and replaced customary African practices on land ownership, with state-centric formal structures that eroded and weakened the rights of women to own and access land.[61] In precolonial Africa, land was owned and controlled by customary leaders who allocated land for the equal use of members of the community. This allowed both men and women to farm on family lands on an equal and complementary basis.[62] However, the adoption of formal land registration and tenure laws during the colonial regime replaced the authority of customary leaders with state control over land tenure and imposed a uniform, nationwide land tenure system. This system of state control over land tenure has continued to date and has resulted in the transfer of formal land titles from communities and individuals to the state.[63]

In Nigeria for example, the Nigerian Land Use Act 1979 vests absolute ownership, management, and control of land in the state governor, leaving individuals with "rights of occupancy."[64] Second, the Act fails to recognize any right of control or administration by community leaders or tribal chiefs. Furthermore, section 28 of the Act provides that land may be appropriated by the state at any time for "overriding public interests."[65] The arbitrary provisions of this Act, coupled with other societal factors such as low level literacy of women, uneven employment opportunities, poor income, exclusion of women from important meetings where decisions on projects or policies are taken, among others, mean that women in Nigeria are typically unable to afford or access land ownership without the support of men.[66] Consequently, while the precolonial Nigerian woman contributed to the production and distribution of food and goods, postcolonial Nigerian women are caught up in a cycle of perpetual dependence on men for accessing land as well as financial and technical resources needed to participate in cash crop schemes.

Without reversing and addressing the lopsided legislative regimes on land allocation and ownership in Africa, it will be difficult to achieve gender justice in the design and implementation of sustainable development programs.[67]

14.2.3.2 Lack of Legal Recognition of Indigenous Rights

As earlier noted, while communities in Badia and Calabar self-identify as "Indigenous communities," this nomenclature remains unrecognized in the laws of Nigeria, as is the case in several

---

[61] See Benschop, note 5; S. Pierce, "Pointing to Property: Colonialism and Knowledge about Land Tenure in Northern Nigeria" (2013) 83 *Africa Bibliography* 142–163.

[62] Pierce, note 61.

[63] See A. Njoh, "Indigenous Peoples and Ancestral Lands; Implications of the Bekweri Case in Cameroon," in R. Home (ed.), *Essays in African Land Law* (Pretoria: Pretoria University Law Press, 2011), pp. 69–90 discussing how Indigenous land rights of Bekweri people of Cameroon were forcibly expropriated by German colonial authorities; R. T. Ako, "Nigeria's Land Use Act: An Anti-Thesis to Environmental Justice" (2009) 53 *Journal of African Law* 289.

[64] Land Use Act, Laws of the Federation of Nigeria 1990, ch. 202, s. 1.

[65] Ibid; *Abioye* v. *Yakub*, 5 NWLR (pt 190) 130, 223, paras. (d)–(g) (1991).

[66] See also L. Onyango, A. Omollo, and E. Ayo, "Gender Perspectives of Property Rights in Rural Kenya," in Home, note 63, pp. 146–153 discussing how retrograde cultural practices in Kenya mean that women can only have access to farmlands through their husbands.

[67] M. O'Sullivan, A. Rao, R. Baberjee, K. Gulati, and M. Vinez, *Levelling the Field: Improving Opportunities for Women Farmers in Africa* (Washington, DC: World Bank, 2014), pp. 1–20; A. Njoh, "Development Implications of Colonial Land and Human Settlement Policies in Cameroon" (2002) 26 *Habitat International* 399–415.

African countries.[68] For example, the Nigerian Constitution does not specifically recognize any group as Indigenous, rather it contains human rights provisions that apply equally to all Nigerians.[69] Furthermore, all African countries, except Central African Republic, have failed to ratify the ILO Convention 169, while Kenya, Republic of Congo, and Cameroon are the only African countries to have adopted domestic legislation that mention or recognize minority or Indigenous groups.[70] This lack of formal recognition means that any notion of extreme vulnerability of Indigenous women remains debated and unrecognized by several African governments.[71] As far back as 2006, the African Commission's Working Group on Indigenous Populations/ Communities called on all African countries to formally recognize the existence and critical human rights situations of Indigenous groups in Africa.[72] Despite this and many other declarations at international and regional levels, on the need to protect Indigenous communities and highly vulnerable groups such as women through robust human rights safeguards, lack of domestication and enforcement at national levels remains a key hinderance to environmental justice in Indigenous communities in Africa.

African countries can no longer afford to continue to deny, or remain ambiguous on, the existence of Indigenous groups. Without recognizing and identifying the critical human rights situations of Indigenous peoples across Africa, it will be difficult to formulate effective legal approaches and strategies that address double discrimination and extreme vulnerabilities of Indigenous women in Africa to environmental harm. A good starting point is for African countries to reflect the human rights–based definition of Indigenous peoples, that has been provided by the African Commission, in domestic legislation.[73]

14.2.3.3 Ineffective Enforcement or Implementation of Human Rights Instruments

As illustrated by the case studies, one of the key limitations to environmental justice in Africa is the ineffective enforcement and implementation of procedural human rights safeguards on participation, access to information, nondiscrimination, and accountability in the design and implementation of development projects. While several African countries are signatories to international human rights instruments that guarantee these procedural rights, the level of domestic implementation vary and are often less robust across Africa.[74] In Nigeria for example, although the Nigerian Constitution, as well as several other human rights instruments, recognize the rights of women to participate in public life, and own property, the practical reality is that such rights are hardly protected and fulfilled.[75] Furthermore, social and cultural barriers

---

[68] See note 16.

[69] Chapter IV of the Nigerian Constitution fails to recognize distinct rights of minority, tribal, or Indigenous groups. Section 21 refers to the protection of 'Nigerian culture,' while s. 10 emphasizes that Nigeria is a secular state. Also, in a country of about 250 ethnic groups and languages, s. 55 officially recognizes only the three ethnic languages of the majority tribes: Yoruba, Hausa, and Igbo. See Constitution of the Federal Republic of Nigeria 1999 Cap C-23, LFN 2004.

[70] See note 16.

[71] See International Labour Organization and African Commission on Human and Peoples' Rights, "Overview Report of the Research Project by the International Labour Organization and the African Commission on Human and Peoples' Rights on the Constitutional and Legislative Protection of the Rights of Indigenous Peoples in 24 African Countries," Centre for Human Rights, University of Pretoria, 2009; ACHPR, note 13.

[72] See ACHPR, note 13.

[73] Ibid.

[74] Okome, note 14.

[75] J. Dada, "Impediments to Human Rights Protection in Nigeria" (2012) 18 *Annual Survey of International and Comparative Law* 67–90.

such as low level of literacy, high cost of litigation, low income by women, and procedural delays in finalizing cases often leave women, such as the petty traders in Badia, with little or no recourse even in clear cases of human rights violations.[76]

The importance of effective domestic legal frameworks in addressing local manifestations of environmental injustice cannot be overemphasized.[77] For example, one key requirement in the approval of international climate projects, such as REDD+, is that such projects receive host country approval.[78] This requirement places great responsibilities on national authorities to approve climate actions and projects as meeting national sustainability criteria before their implementation nationally or under existing international climate project mechanisms. Without a legal framework that defines a country's sustainability criteria or basis for implementing and approving climate projects, many of the key issues of exclusion, lack of participation, and discrimination in climate actions and responses identified in the case studies are either left unaddressed or unprotected under local laws.[79] Failure to effectively enforce and implement legal frameworks on women and property rights in a systematic and committed manner often leaves victims of environmental injustices without robust legal protection or remedy.

14.2.3.4 Lack of Institutional Capacity and Coordination

A common thread in the case studies is the failure by development and environmental agencies and ministries to adequately mainstream or integrate human rights safeguards and norms into their operations and work. Several African countries lack robust institutional capacity to coordinate and implement human rights programs.[80] Similarly, environment and human rights institutions continue to function separately without adequate coordination and consideration of the intersections and linkages of how environmental projects may affect human rights and vice versa. In Nigeria for example, one of the key problems with the Nigerian Climate Change Unit (CCU), within the Ministry of Environment, is its composition. Largely comprised of environmentalists and planners, with little or no expertise on justice and human rights, the CCU has been unable to develop coherent rights-based policy responses to several human rights issues identified in adaptation and mitigation projects.

Environmental justice can be enhanced at national levels by restructuring human rights and environment institutions to foster coordination, coherence, and systemic integration.[81] The gap between environment and human rights institutions is fueled by the tendency of actors to remain within the formal confines of their areas of mandate (i.e. of human rights ministries or

---

[76] Ibid.

[77] See UN Environment Programme (UNEP), "Guidelines for the Development of National Legislation on Access to Information, Public Participation and Access to Justice in Environmental Matters: Adopted by the Governing Council of the United Nations Environment Programme in decision SS. XI/5," Feb. 26, 2010.

[78] UN, Kyoto Protocol to the UN Framework Convention on Climate Change, 1998, Art. 12, para. 2: CDM modalities and procedures requires host countries to confirm that project activity assists in achieving sustainable development"; UNFCCC, *Decision 3/CMP 1 2005, Modalities and Procedures for the Clean Development Mechanism as Defined in Article 12 of the Kyoto Protocol,* Mar. 30, 2006, FCCC/KP/CMP/2005/8/Add.1.

[79] UNFCCC, note 78.

[80] M. Manrique Gil and A. Bandone, "Policy Briefing: Human Rights Protection Mechanisms in Africa: Strong Potential, Weak Capacity," European Parliament, Policy Department, Directorate-General for External Policies, Feb. 2013, pp. 3–12, identifying weak institutional capacity as a key reason for the violation of human rights across Africa.

[81] See Olawuyi, note 1.

within environment departments).[82] This is due to the absence of a formal agenda or obligations to collaborate between actors; the lack of fluid programmatic activity between human rights ministries and environment ministries and departments; lack of a coherent agenda between human rights and environmental interest groups; and personal unwillingness by actors to collaborate across sectors and agendas spurred by the absence of training and capacity to do so.[83] As such, human rights have no place, visibility, or political support in development or environmental actions, while environmental protection is not a priority issue in the everyday affairs of human rights institutions.

Fostering institutional coordination and constructive engagement between human rights and environment, such that programs and projects to address vulnerability are designed, financed, and implemented together by both communities is a holistic way of improving capacity at national levels. Appointing human rights experts into environment ministries, and vice versa, could ensure that human rights and human rights instruments are understood, internalized, implemented, and enforced in environmental actions; and that environmental actions do not violate human rights.

It is also pertinent for countries to provide human rights education and training for environmental leaders and institutions. For example, though not legally binding, the United Nations Declaration on Human Rights Education and Training emphasizes that human rights education and training is essential for the "promotion of universal respect for and observance of all human rights and fundamental freedoms for all."[84] Article 7(4) provides that states should ensure adequate training in human rights of state officials.[85] A robust implementation of this declaration at national levels will educate security agents on how to prevent concerns of forced relocations and human rights repression that have trailed adaptation and REDD+ projects.

Revitalizing environmental institutions to achieve environmental justice will come with considerable costs. This would include the cost of achieving wider public participation, establishing new institutions, expanding current institutions, staffing, training, and program funding.[86] To reduce the cost of a human rights–based approach, the United Nations emphasizes the importance of eliminating institutional overlaps and fragmentation; improving institutional coordination; and building on existing capacities and resources.[87]

The above problems underscore the need for national governments to reassess and revitalize the architecture for delivering sustainable development programs to avoid placing disproportionate burdens of development on women. A needed step forward is to holistically address existing gender inequalities and unequal power relations through robust rights-based frameworks.

---

[82] See J. Knox, "Linking Human Rights and Climate Change at the United Nations" (2009) 33 *Harvard Environmental Law Review* 477.

[83] Ibid.

[84] UN General Assembly, Declaration on Human Rights Education and Training, Dec. 19, 2011, UN Doc. A/RES/66/137.

[85] Ibid.

[86] See J. McCrudden, "Mainstreaming Human Rights," in Colin Harvey (ed.), *Human Rights in the Community: Rights as Agents for Change* (Oxford: Hart, 2005), pp. 9–26.

[87] United Nations Population Fund, "A Human Rights–Based Approach to Programming: Practical Implementation Manual and Training Materials," Program on International Health and Human Rights, Harvard School of Public Health and the Gender, Human Rights and Culture Branch of the UNFPA Technical Division (GHRCB), 2014, p. 165.

14.3 TOWARD A RIGHTS-BASED APPROACH TO GENDER VULNERABILITY REDUCTION AND DEVELOPMENT

Existing inequalities and unequal power relations among government and marginalized groups such as women, can deepen vulnerability and undermine adaptive capacity, producing a vicious spiral of maladaptation and environmental degradation. Addressing these often-neglected social dimensions of sustainability, through rights-based approaches, is critical to achieving environmental justice and just adaptation.[88]

The duty of states to harmonize development programs with human rights safeguards is well entrenched in the international law.[89] The principle of systemic integration of international law, as outlined in Article 31(3)(c) of the Vienna Convention on the Law of Treaties speaks of a presumption that states, when designing rules, measures, and action plans under one treaty obligation, should not violate their obligations under other preexisting treaties.[90] As such, when countries design development and climate response projects and plans in line with Goal 13 of the SDGs, due care must be taken not to set aside or violate other international human rights obligations relating to gender equality and nondiscrimination, including Goal 5 of the SDGs which calls for gender equality and the empowerment of all women and girls.[91]

Furthermore, the Paris Agreement, in its Preamble, recognizes that parties should, "when taking action to address climate change, respect, promote and consider their respective obligations on human rights."[92] This includes the rights of Indigenous peoples, local communities, people in vulnerable situations, as well as gender equality, empowerment of women, and intergenerational equity.[93] Similarly, the Conference of Parties to the United Nations Framework Convention on Climate Change (COP16) in Cancun recognized gender equality and the effective participation of women and Indigenous peoples as very important for effective action on all aspects of climate change.[94]

Notably, several human rights treaties recognize equality and nondiscrimination as core pillars of international law. Articles 1, 2, and 7 of the UDHR recognize that all humans are equal before the law and are entitled without any discrimination to equal protection of the law.[95] Article 26 of the ICCPR guarantees to all persons equal and effective protection against discrimination on any ground such as gender.[96] Article 2(3) and 3 of the ICESCR also contain similar provisions on nondiscrimination.[97] Finally, Article 7 of the Convention on the Elimination of All forms of Discrimination against Women (CEDAW) provides for the elimination of discrimination against women in political and public life, and Article 5 encourages states to take measures to eliminate prejudices and stereotyping against women.[98]

---

[88] See D. McCauley and R. Heffron, "Just Transition: Integrating Climate, Energy and Environmental Justice" (2018) *Energy Policy* 1–7.

[89] Olawuyi, note 1.

[90] Vienna Convention on the Law of Treaties (VCLT), May 22, 1969, 1155 UNTS 331.

[91] See Terry, "No Climate Justice without Gender Justice," note 48; Olawuyi, note 1.

[92] See UNFCCC, Adoption of the Paris Agreement, Dec. 12, 2015, FCCC/CP/2015/L.9.

[93] Ibid.

[94] UNFCCC, "Outcome of the Work of the Ad Hoc Working Group on Long-term Cooperative Action under the Convention," Dec. 10, 2010, Draft decision/CP.16, para. 7.

[95] UN General Assembly, Universal Declaration on Human and Peoples Rights, Dec. 10, 1948, UN Doc. A/810, p. 71.

[96] UN, International Covenant on Civil and Political Rights, Mar. 23, 1976, 999 UNTS 171.

[97] UN, note 37.

[98] See UN General Assembly, Optional Protocol to the Convention on the Elimination of Discrimination Against Women (CEDAW), Oct. 15, 1999, UN Doc. A/RES/54/4.

The critical intersections between climate and human rights obligations show that we cannot enjoy human rights without effectively addressing ecological problems such as climate change. Conversely, sustainable development and climate adaptation plans can only be effective when underpinned by respect for the human rights of the public, particularly vulnerable individuals and groups.[99] The human rights–based approach (HBRA) to development therefore underscores the need for equal treatment of men and women in sustainable development efforts and projects.[100]

Equality and nondiscrimination can be achieved if national authorities reflect three fundamental elements in project planning: equality of opportunity and treatment, burden sharing, and gender vulnerability assessment and proofing.

14.3.1 *Equality of Opportunity and Treatment*

To fulfil the nondiscrimination norms of international law, African countries need to ensure that marginalized groups, particularly women and Indigenous groups, have equal rights to participate effectively in public life, and that decisions directly affecting their rights and interests are not taken without their free, prior, and informed consent (FPIC).[101] FPIC underlines the idea that consent to a development activity or project must be freely given by all relevant stakeholders, including vulnerable members of the society, obtained prior to implementation of activities, and be founded upon an understanding of the full range of benefits and challenges resulting from the activity or decision in question.[102]

Equality of opportunity entails the idea of inclusivity, which focuses on the need to provide a fair opportunity for stakeholders and representatives of diverse societal groups or interests to attend decision-making processes.[103] For example, it is not enough to invite all members of the public to decision-making meetings; inclusivity includes taking proactive measures to remove preexisting barriers to effective participation by women in such meetings. Women in Africa face preexisting hindrances to effective participation, such as high levels of illiteracy, low level of income, limited childcare facilities and support, and lack of information, among others which render participatory rights merely academic if not backed by proactive inclusivity measures. Furthermore, Indigenous women may face greater challenges to participation because they live in less accessible areas, or because public consultation forums are not adapted to their language or cultural preferences.[104] Inclusivity will mean choosing accessible venues for meetings or scheduling meeting in different areas of the community that are close to day care or school centers; providing childcare facilities; providing free transportation; hiring language interpreters;

---

[99] See McCauley and Heffron, note 88.

[100] UN Development Group Human Rights Working Group, "The Human Rights Based Approach to Development Cooperation towards a Common Understanding among UN Agencies," 2003.

[101] See UN General Assembly, Promotion and Protection of All Human Rights, Civil, Political, Economic, Social and Cultural Rights, Including the Right to Development: Report of the Special Rapporteur on the Situation of Human Rights and Fundamental Freedoms of Indigenous People, James Anaya, July 15, 2009, UN Doc. A/HRC/12/34.

[102] M. Colchester and F. MacKay, "In Search of Middle Ground: Indigenous Peoples, Collective Representation and the Right to Free, Prior and Informed Consent," paper presented to the 10th Conference of the International Association for the Study of Common Property Oaxaca, Oct. 2004, pp. 8–14.

[103] Olawuyi, note 1.

[104] For example, retrograde customs in several parts of Central Africa require women to dress in certain ways or exclude them from public consultations. See Forest Peoples Programme, "Indigenous Women in Central Africa 'Increasingly Vulnerable' When It Comes to Access to Land," Oct. 31, 2016, www.forestpeoples.org/en/topics/african-human-rights-system/news/2016/10/indigenous-women-central-africa-increasingly-vulnera.

and reducing technicalities in discussions. It will include utilizing technology to provide an opportunity for online participation through webinars, online surveys, and questionnaires. Also, patriarchal practices and policies that prevent girls from going to school, or women from attending public meetings should be dismantled to address systemic exclusivity.[105]

14.3.2 *Burden Sharing*

A human rights–based approach (HRBA) to development emphasizes the need to avoid governmental decisions or projects that disproportionately imperil the life, safety, and health of a section of the society. For example, targeting minority or Indigenous communities as locations for development projects is a discriminatory practice as it subjects the poor to greater harm due to their societal status. As shown in the Lagos case study, forced relocation of Indigenous families due to development or environmental projects unduly imperil the abilities of women to work and contribute to household income. Furthermore, land grabbing and forced relocations in Indigenous communities in Cross River, Nigeria, as well as in Indigenous communities across Central Africa, elevate the vulnerabilities of Indigenous women farmers in Africa.[106]

An HRBA to planning seeks to ensure that the burdens of development are spread across every segment of the society and shared equally. Implementing nondiscriminatory policies would include laying down clear criteria for selecting project locations, conducting environmental and human rights impact assessments on the effects of a project at that location, and providing public information on the outcome of these assessments. If the assessments show that the inhabitants of the specific location would be harmed by that project, then the project should be discontinued irrespective of the volume of emission reductions the project would generate.

14.3.3 *Vulnerability Assessment and Proofing*

To protect and fulfil the nondiscrimination norm of international law in environmental action and programs, national authorities need to incorporate vulnerability assessment and proofing as part of the wider human rights assessment of all development laws, policies, programs, and projects.[107] Gender vulnerability assessment is an active process of assessing and measuring the implications of a project or policy on a specific category of people or gender, most especially marginalized and vulnerable groups such as Indigenous women.[108] By establishing an effective process for assessing risks on the basis of gender, national authorities can better understand and assess legal and customary constraints operating against the effective participation of women in

---

[105] See G. Atta, "Education Inequality: How Patriarchy and Policy Collide in Ghana" (2015) 5 *International Journal of Humanities and Social Science* 11–19: discussing how placing greater value on male child education, lack of women teachers as role models, forced and early marriages, child labor, and endemic sexual harassment silence the voices of women in national dialogue in Ghana; T. Alabi, M. Bahah, and S. Alabi, "The Girl-Child: A Sociological View on the Problems of Girl-Child Education in Nigeria" (2013) 3 *Global Research Journal of Education* 57–65.

[106] See Forest Peoples Programme, note 104.

[107] See P. Tschakert, B. Van Oort, A. Lera St. Clair, and A. LaMadrid, "Inequality and Transformation Analyses: A Complementary Lens for Addressing Vulnerability to Climate Change" (2013) 5 *Climate and Development* 340–350.

[108] M. Crawley and L. O'Meara, "The Gender Proofing Handbook," National Development Plan, Gender Equality Unit, Department of Justice, Equality and Law Reform, Dublin, May 2002, pp. 1–5; F. Mackay and K. Bilton, "Equality Proofing Procedures in Drafting Legislation: International Comparisons," Governance of Scotland Forum, University of Edinburgh, Scottish Executive Central Research Unit 2001, Apr. 2, 2002, pp. 5–8.

project approval and decision-making processes. Furthermore, analyzing gender-based assessments from the lens of specific impacts on Indigenous women can help governments to understand the multiple forms of human rights violations that Indigenous women face. For example, even though women generally face considerable vulnerability to climate change, Indigenous women in Badia, Cross River, as well as in other Africa countries, who face involuntary displacements are exposed to double or greater vulnerability. Indigeneity vulnerability assessment can help governments and project planners to better anticipate and address such dual vulnerabilities.

While general EIA studies focus on overall environmental implications of projects, they mostly fail to reveal how such projects may disproportionately disadvantage women. There is therefore a need for countries to develop human rights impact assessment (HRIA) procedures that analyze and assess the human rights vulnerabilities of women, especially women in Indigenous communities, in the design, approval, finance, and implementation of development projects.[109]

After measuring the unique vulnerabilities of women to specific projects and policies, gender proofing is required to proactively ensure equality of outcome for men and women in development processes.[110] Gender proofing is the process of ensuring that knowledge, experiences, and perceptions of both women and men are given equal weight in the final planning and approval processes. For example, where a specific group is identified as disadvantaged or vulnerable, project proponents ought to be mandated to implement differentiated measures so that adverse impacts do not fall disproportionately on a particular gender or group. Furthermore, there is the need to provide equal and inclusive opportunities for women to take part in and influence final decision-making processes.

14.4 CONCLUSION

Despite the emergence of several international law instruments designed to respect, protect, and fulfil gender equality and nondiscrimination in the quest for sustainable development, the realization of gender justice in Africa is incomplete. A confluence of several preexisting colonial, customary, legal, and social norms continue to stifle the abilities of African women to play active roles in environmental policy formation; access educational, financial, and land resources needed to break free from the cycle of dependence and oppression; and maintain the sources of income and subsistence required to contribute to household welfare and income. Women in Indigenous communities in Africa, whose lands are often targeted for large-scale development projects, face double vulnerabilities because they are women and because they are Indigenous.

Gender equality is not only a fundamental human right, but an indispensable foundation for attaining sustainable development. Without a gender justice perspective, development projects, especially climate mitigation and adaptation projects, risk exacerbating gender-based marginalization in Africa. The HRBA provides a procedural framework through which countries can holistically address gender inequality by integrating human rights norms into the design, approval, finance, and implementation of environmental projects.

---

[109] Nordic Trust Fund, "Human Rights Impact Assessment: A Review of the Literature, Differences with other Forms of Assessments and Relevance for Development," World Bank, Feb. 2013.

[110] Ibid.

To ensure that the HRBA moves from theory to successful practical implementation, logistical concerns that stifle the utility and relevance of the HRBA at local levels, must be carefully reviewed and addressed. Barriers to the implementation and adoption of the HRBA can be holistically addressed by: invigorating national sustainable development programs, policies, and legislation with human rights safeguards; harmonizing environment and human rights institutions; updating postcolonial laws that stifle the realization of human rights; and promoting human rights awareness at all levels of governance. Ultimately, the aim for African countries must be to ensure that development projects that threaten human rights are not approved.

Colombo International Financial City

An Example of Unsustainability and Injustice?

Sumudu A. Atapattu, Joshua C. Gellers, and Lakshman Guruswamy

15.1 INTRODUCTION: SRI LANKA'S COUNTRY PROFILE AND ITS COLONIAL LEGACY

Sri Lanka recently graduated to an upper middle-income country with a GDP per capita of US$4,102 (2018) and a total population of 21.7 million people.[1] Located in South Asia, its recent history is marred by a violent three decades-long ethnic conflict,[2] and the Indian Ocean tsunami that affected many parts of the country killing over 35,000 people and displacing over 500,000.[3] Political in-fighting, corruption, and nepotism have almost undone its achievements since it gained independence from the British in 1948. From 1983 to 2009, the nation was ravaged by a brutal civil war between its military and the Liberation Tigers of Tamil Eelam (LTTE), of the ethnic minority Tamils. By the end of the conflict, close to 100,000 people had been killed or disappeared[4] and the country had spent over US$200 billion on war costs.[5] Its human rights record has had a roller-coaster ride, especially in the context of the armed conflict and its brutal ending.[6]

Despite these challenges, Sri Lanka ranks among the countries with the world's highest literacy rates,[7] and has been able to continue to provide universal healthcare[8] and universal

---

[1] World Bank, "The World Bank in Sri Lanka," Oct. 15, 2019, www.worldbank.org/en/country/srilanka/over view. Other World Bank documents refer to Sri Lanka as a "lower" middle-income country (O. Smith, "Sri Lanka: Achieving Pro-Poor Universal Health Coverage without Health Financing Reforms," Universal Health Coverage Study Series No. 38, World Bank Group, Washington, DC, 2018; World Bank Group, "Sri Lanka: Ending Poverty and Promoting Prosperity: A Systematic Country Diagnostic," Oct. 2015.

[2] For an overview of the ethnic conflict and its aftermath, see J. Uyangoda, "Civil War, War Ending, and Dilemmas of Peace Building in Sri Lanka, 1983-2017," in S. Atapattu (ed.), *Sri Lanka: State of Human Rights* (Colombo: Law and Society Trust, 2019).

[3] See World Bank, "Lessons Learned from Sri Lanka's Tsunami Reconstruction," Dec. 23, 2014, www .worldbank.org/en/news/feature/2014/12/23/lessons-learned-sri-lanka-tsunami-reconstruction; A. Sathkunanathan, "Overview of the State of Human Rights 2005 in Sri Lanka: State of Human Rights" (Colombo: Law and Society Trust, 2006), p. 23.

[4] There are differing accounts of the total number of casualties. Some claim as many as 40,000 may have died during the last major offensive that killed the LTTE leader, Prabhakaran. See Uyangoda, note 2.

[5] A. Bendix, "Sri Lanka Is Building a $15 Billion Metropolis Meant to Rival Cities Like Hong Kong and Dubai," Sept. 15, 2018, www.businessinsider.com/sri-lanka-port-city-dubai-2018-9.

[6] See Atapattu, note 2; Uyangoda, note 2.

[7] See World Bank, note 1.

[8] Smith, note 1. The study points to the well-organized network of preventive healthcare services provided across the country as contributing to this success and that few low- or middle-income countries have been able to achieve strong health outcomes, good financial protection, and low cost.

education[9] that were started during the colonial era. Its social and health indicators are on par with those of developed countries.[10] Called the "Pearl of the Indian Ocean," Sri Lanka has beautiful beaches, an ancient civilization dating back 2,500 years, rainforests, mountains, and wildlife, as well as a multi-ethnic, multi-religious culture. A popular tourist destination, Sri Lanka was named No. 1 travel destination by Lonely Planet in 2019.[11]

Although extreme poverty is rare in the country, many subsist just above the poverty line.[12] Economic growth during 2010–2017 (after the war ended in 2009) was around 5.8 percent but has since declined to 3.2 percent.[13] The country has transitioned from a predominantly rural agricultural economy to a more urbanized manufacturing and service-based economy,[14] exporting, inter alia, apparel, cash crops (mainly tea), and software products and services.[15] The majority of the people still live in rural areas, and urban–rural disparities are notable in education and health services.[16]

Sri Lanka came under colonial rule when its coastal areas were conquered by the Portuguese in 1592. The Dutch ruled the country (except the central province) from 1658 until 1796 when the British captured the coastal areas. The whole country came under British rule in 1815. Ceylon, as it was then known, gained independence in 1948 and became a republic in 1972 at which point it changed the name to "Sri Lanka."[17] Its colonial past is still visible today especially in relation to the legal system.

While colonialism may be a thing of the past, another form of domination by a world giant is visible in Sri Lanka today. In this chapter, we tell the story of the Colombo Financial City, popularly known as the "Port City," that is being constructed with a loan from the Chinese government and with Chinese workforce. The sheer magnitude of the project with its far-reaching economic, environmental, and social consequences, as described below, is a grave concern.

This chapter proceeds in five sections. Section 15.2 examines sustainable development and environmental justice concerns of the project and discusses the affected communities. Section 15.3 describes the project, its myriad and complex legal agreements, lack of public consultations, and the litigation that is currently pending. Section 15.4 discusses the environmental implications of the project, its financial viability, geopolitical ramifications, and impacts on the livelihoods of people. Section 15.5 concludes with some thoughts on the justice implications of the project. We argue that a project of this magnitude can undermine Sri Lanka's commitment to sustainable development and the Sustainable Development Goals.[18]

---

[9] Free education in Sri Lanka came into effect in 1945. While it was introduced to cover ages 5–16 years initially, Sri Lanka provides free education at the tertiary level as well (https://lk.one.un.org/7060/en/free-education-policy-in-sri-lanka).

[10] See Smith, note 1.

[11] A Wilson, "Sri Lanka Ranked Top Country for Travel in 2009 by Lonely Planet," Oct. 23, 2018, www .theguardian.com/travel/2018/oct/23/sri-lanka-ranked-top-country-for-travel-in-2019-by-lonely-planet.

[12] World Bank, note 1. Sri Lanka reduced its poverty level from 22 percent in 2002 to 6.7 percent in 2015 (Asian Development Bank, "Poverty in Sri Lanka," www.adb.org/countries/sri-lanka/poverty).

[13] World Bank, note 1

[14] Ibid.

[15] "Sri Lanka – Market Overview," July 22, 2019, www.export.gov/article?series=aoptooooooooGteAAE andtype= Country_Commercial__kav. The USA is the single largest market for Sri Lanka's exports.

[16] See Smith, note 1.

[17] From 1948 to 1972, Ceylon was a dominion of the British Empire, similar to Canada and Australia.

[18] UN General Assembly, *Transforming Our World: The 2030 Agenda for Sustainable Development*, Oct. 21, 2015, UN Doc. A/RES/70/1 and which Sri Lanka signed in 2015. See Government of the Democratic Socialist Republic of Sri Lanka, "Voluntary National Review on the Status of Implementing the Sustainable Development Goals," Ministry of Sustainable Development, Wildlife and Regional Development, June 2018.

15.2 SUSTAINABLE DEVELOPMENT AND ENVIRONMENTAL
JUSTICE IN SRI LANKA

After the ethnic conflict ended militarily in 2009, President Rajapaksa's government concentrated effort on developing the country especially in the North and East, the site of the armed conflict. It undertook many infrastructure projects and engaged in "beautifying" the capital city, Colombo.[19] Environmental laws were disregarded and those who were in the beautification path were forcibly evicted, without notice, compensation, or alternative accommodation. No information or opportunity to be heard was provided.[20] These actions raised serious concerns about Sri Lanka's obligations under international human rights law and international environmental law,[21] as well as compliance with national laws.[22] Moreover, they disproportionately affected the poor and vulnerable, raising environmental justice concerns.[23]

This chapter applies Agyeman's "just sustainability" framework[24] together with Kuehn's fourfold categorization of environmental justice comprising distributive, procedural, corrective, and social justice[25] to the Port City Project, discussed next. "Just sustainability" is defined as: "the need to ensure a better quality of life for all, now, and into the future, in a just and equitable manner, while living within the limits of supporting ecosystems."[26] This chapter argues that the Port City project contravenes both frameworks for several reasons. First, no credible environment impact assessment (EIA) was carried out for the expanded project as required by the National Environmental Act and, therefore, the expanded project did not go through public participation as required by law. This, coupled with the fact that the public was not consulted about the project initially, resulted in procedural injustice. Moreover, no EIA was done for the sand mining or the transportation of sand by trucks multiple times a day leading to noise, air, and water pollution. Second, the disproportionate impact on fisherfolk who depend on a reliable fish catch to earn a living resulted in distributive injustice. Additionally, no compensation was offered to these fisherfolk thereby resulting in corrective injustice. Third, the project, when completed, will cater to the rich and the elite and exclude ordinary Sri Lankans, and will exacerbate social inequities in society, raising distributive justice and social justice concerns. Finally, the project is contrary to the just sustainabilities framework as it is neither environmentally, economically, nor socially sustainable, enmeshing current and future generations in a vicious cycle of financial and ecological debt.

Because Sri Lanka is an island nation, marine fisheries around the country's coastline have socioeconomic significance as important sources of export revenues, animal protein, and

---

[19] "Beautifying" essentially referred to improving roads and sidewalks, building luxury hotels and mega department stores, and evicting poor people in slums. See B. Sirimanna, "Major Changes in Colombo to Beautify and Develop the Capital," Mar. 25, 2012, www.sundaytimes.lk/120325/BusinessTimes/bt10.html.

[20] See V. Peiris, "Colombo's 'Fastest Growing Tourism' Status Obtained at the Poor's Expense," July 4, 2015, www.wsws.org/en/articles/2015/07/04/cmbo-j04.html.

[21] Sri Lanka has ratified most major human rights treaties and environmental treaties (Atapattu, note 2).

[22] Fundamental rights are enshrined in the 1978 Constitution of Sri Lanka. While these are essentially civil and political rights, its Supreme Court has interpreted these rights broadly to include socioeconomic rights and environmental rights (C. Guneratne, "Using Constitutions Provisions to Advance Environmental Justice – Some Reflections on Sri Lanka" (2015) 11 *Law, Environment and Development Journal* 1).

[23] Sri Lanka enacted the National Environmental Act in 1980, EIA laws in 1988 and a Sustainable Development Act in 2017. It has adopted legislation to give effect to many of its human rights obligations.

[24] See J. Agyeman, R. D. Bullard, and B. Evans (eds.), *Just Sustainabilities: Development in an Unequal World* (Boston: MIT Press, 2003), p. 7

[25] See R. Kuehn, "A Taxonomy of Environmental Justice" (2000) 30 *Environmental Law Reporter* 10681.

[26] Agyeman et al., note 24, p. 2.

livelihoods. According to the Food and Agriculture Organization country profile, the fisheries sector contributes about 2 percent to the GDP.[27] The fisheries sector consists of three subsectors – coastal; offshore and deep sea; and inland and aquaculture – and employs around 250,000 active fishers and another 100,000 in support services.[28] The 2004 Tsunami had a devastating impact on the fisheries sector with 80 percent of active fishers affected and 75 percent of fishing fleets destroyed or damaged. Many fishing families along the Eastern and Southern coasts lost their loved ones, their homes, and their life possessions. Moreover, about 610 species of fish inhabit the coastal waters, and many commercially important species are abundant in its exclusive economic zone. In recent years, fisheries have become an important source of foreign exchange through the export of fish varieties including tuna, shrimp, lobsters, shark fins, and sea cucumber.[29] According to 2017 data, there are 183,650 fishing households, 220,870 active fishers (both men and women), and a total population of 802,340 people dependent on the fisheries sector.[30] A total of 582,000 people are directly and indirectly employed in the fisheries sector.

The Port City Project will have a direct impact on subsistence coastal fisherfolk. While there are a few affluent fish merchants in the country, subsistence fisherfolk comprise the majority of active fishers. As discussed later in the chapter, sand mining for the project may jeopardize the livelihood of 15,000 fishermen.[31] The area is also rich in biodiversity, including coral reefs, fish, and other marine species.[32] Moreover, there are signs that this project is already having adverse impacts downstream (south of Colombo city), likely to affect fisherfolk in those areas as well.[33]

15.3 COLOMBO INTERNATIONAL FINANCIAL CITY PROJECT

15.3.1 *The Project*

The concept of a "port city," to rival mega-cities like Hong Kong, was originally envisioned in the early 2000s by President Rajapaksa's government, but the idea had to be shelved because of the ongoing armed conflict.[34] It was originally proposed as a government-funded project to be undertaken by the Sri Lanka Ports Authority (SLPA) with the main objective of creating jobs and bringing economic opportunities to the capital city, Colombo.[35]

Interest in the project resurfaced when an unsolicited proposal was submitted by China Harbour Engineering Company (CHEC) in 2011.[36] In mid-2012, SLPA announced that construction would commence in September 2014 with an estimated budget of US$1.5 billion.[37] There is no indication that the public was ever consulted at the planning stage.[38] While strategic environmental assessment

---

[27] FAO, "Fishery Country Profile, Sri Lanka," Jan. 2006. According to the 2017 data, this number is 1.3 percent, down from 1.6 percent in 2014 (Ministry of Fisheries and Aquatic Resources Development and Rural Economy, "Fisheries Statistics 2018").

[28] FAO, note 27.

[29] Ibid.

[30] Ministry of Fisheries and Aquatic Resources Development and Rural Economy, note 27.

[31] Petition submitted to the Court of Appeal, discussed in Section 15.3.4.

[32] Ibid.

[33] Ibid.

[34] Bendix, note 5.

[35] Ibid.

[36] D. Jayawardane, "Critical Analyses of Colombo Port City Project," Feb. 16, 2015, www.dailymirror.lk/63749/critical-analysis-of-colombo-port-city-project.

[37] S. Aneez, "Sri Lanka Takes Next Step to Opening Strategic China-Built Port," Mar. 4, 2013, www.reuters.com/article/us-srilanka-port-china-idUSBRE92312Y20130304.

[38] The National Environmental Act (NEA) does not require public participation at the planning stage.

(SEA) is not mandatory in Sri Lanka, the Cabinet of Ministers has approved implementation of SEA for policies, programs, and plans in Sri Lanka, and all ministries and departments are expected to carry out an SEA prior to the implementation of a new policy, plan, or program.[39] Given its magnitude and reach, it is not clear why a SEA was not required for the Port City Project.

The Port City project is a Sino-Sri Lankan enterprise with national and international ramifications. This joint venture between the government of Sri Lanka and China Communications Construction Company (CCCC), a Chinese multinational corporation, is a monumental land reclamation and sea appropriation project[40] of 269 hectares (664 acres), consisting of five separate sub-projects: a Financial District; Central Park Living; Island Living; a Marina; and an International Island.[41] As presently envisioned, the Port City will be a nonindustrial complex aimed at making Colombo *the* most livable city in South Asia. The project aims to create over 80,000 jobs, filled by both Sri Lankans and foreigners, and hopes to attract foreign direct investment to make Sri Lanka the main tourist and regional business hub in South Asia between Dubai and Singapore.[42]

The project seeks to accommodate an expansive range of nonindustrial commercial entities, including banks, offices and retail, hotels and restaurants, diplomatic missions, residential facilities, apartment buildings, serviced apartments, healthcare facilities, educational and research and development institutions, entertainment centers and theaters, indoor amusement parks, recreational spaces, art galleries, community centers, tourism, businesses, and convention and event facilities.[43] Some of these facilities will offer open access to locals, but others will be restricted to owners (who are likely to be mostly foreigners), and entry to amusement parks will be restricted to those who are able to pay admission fees. While, in theory, many of these amenities will be open to everybody, in reality they will be accessible only to affluent locals and foreigners while excluding ordinary Sri Lankans who cannot afford them.

Construction was officially launched on September 17, 2014[44] but was suspended after the defeat of President Rajapaksa in 2014. However, when the Chinese company threatened to sue for millions of dollars, the Sirisena–Wickremesinghe government conceded, despite their election promise to scrap it.[45]

---

[39] Sri Lanka's Central Environmental Authority defines Strategic Environmental Assessment (SEA) as the systematic and comprehensive process of evaluating the environmental effects of a policy, plan, or program including significant economic and social effects to promote integrated decision making. See Central Environmental Authority, "Simple Guide to Strategic Environmental Assessment."

[40] Land reclamation is the process of creating new land from the sea mainly as a way to address shortage of land. The simplest method of land reclamation involves filling the area with large amounts of heavy rock and/or cement, then filling with clay and soil until the desired height is reached. See J. L. Stauber, A. Chariton, and S. Apte, "Chapter 10 – Global Change" in J. Blasco, P. Chapman, O. Campana, and M. Hampel (eds.), *Marine Ecotoxicology: Current Knowledge and Future Issues*, (Cambridge, MA: Academic Press, 2016), pp. 288–289.

[41] J. Narin and W. Wuthmann, "Port City Where Are We Now?" Jan. 12, 2018, www.dailynews.lk/2018/01/12/features/139663/port-city-where-are-we-now.

[42] According to the website of the Ministry of National Policies and Economic Affairs, 15,000 jobs will be created during phase I of the project ("Colombo Port City to be transformed into an International Financial Centre," www.mnpea.gov.lk/web/index.php/en/news-events/150-colombo-port-city-to-be-transformed-into-an-international-financial-centre.html).

[43] Narin and Wuthmann, note 41.

[44] ANI, "Sri Lanka, China Presidents Inaugurate Colombo Port City Project," Sept. 17, 2014, www.business-standard.com/article/news-ani/sri-lanka-china-presidents-inaugurate-colombo-port-city-project-114091700458_1.html.

[45] Narin and Wuthmann, note 41.

15.3.2 *Legal Agreements*

The plethora of legal agreements and their parties are complex, and only those that are necessary for the discussion are highlighted. These agreements are best understood, if placed within the framework of the three phases of the project. In total, the project envisages three interrelated but separate projects: (a) reclamation of the ocean to create land for the Port City Project; (b) construction of the Port City itself with the sub-projects described above; and (c) an underground tunnel connecting the Port City with the mainland's road network.

In April 2011, CCCC submitted a proposal for the Colombo Port City for the reclamation of land of 200 hectares (ha) and for the entire financial investment to be foreign direct investment. A Review Committee (SCARC) appointed by the Cabinet recommended that a detailed proposal be requested, and the two parties – CCCC and the Urban Development Authority (UDA) – signed a memorandum of understanding (MOU) in November of 2011.[46]

The Cabinet of Ministers identified the Port City Project as a Strategic Development Project[47] which exempted it from certain laws, such as tax laws, and made it eligible for financial concessions. The 2014 agreement was replaced by the Tripartite Agreement of 2016 signed by (a) the Secretary to the Ministry of Megapolis & Western Development (a new ministry), on behalf of the Government of Sri Lanka (b) the UDA, and (c) the CHEC.[48] This agreement granted the CHEC Project Company a 99-year lease, and authorized the Sri Lanka government to carry out infrastructure development through public–private partnerships. Under the Tripartite Agreement more land was allocated for public purposes and entrusted a third party with maintaining the reclaimed area.[49] While new legislation to govern the Financial City and make it an international financial zone was proposed, it had not been enacted at the time of writing this chapter.

In addition, an underground tunnel called the Marine Drive Tunnel is proposed to link the Port City with Colombo's road network. Two MOUs[50] were signed in January of 2018 by the China Harbour Engineering Company and Sri Lankan authorities.[51] One MOU was for the tunnel to be constructed under a public–private partnership model.[52] The other MOU was for a building complex that will be made up of three towers in the Port City that will be about

---

[46] A Technical Evaluation Committee (TEC) made up of members from SLPA, Department of Coast Conservation (CCD), UDA, Board of Investment (BOI), and the Central Bank was also set up under SCARC's recommendation.

[47] Declared under Strategic Developments Act No. 14 of 2008. It defines these as projects which are in the national interest and are likely to bring economic and social benefit to the country (s. 6).

[48] Ministry of Urban Development, Water Supply and Housing Facilities, "Government Signs Tripartite Agreement for Colombo International Financial City (Formerly Colombo Port City)," http://megapolismin .gov.lk/web/index.php?option=com_content&view=article andid=88:government-signs-tripartite-agreement-for-colombo-international-financial-city-formerly-colombo-port-city&catid=9&Itemid=229&lang=en.

[49] Ibid.

[50] "Sri Lanka Signs Two MOUs with China for Building Complex in Port City, Underground Marine Drive," Jan. 24, 2018, www.ft.lk/business/Sri-Lanka-signs-two-MOUs-with-China-for-building-complex-in-Port-City–underground-Marine-Drive/34-647937.

[51] They included Megapolis and Western Development Minister Champika Ranawaka, Ambassador of Sri Lanka to China Dr Karunasena Kodituwakku, Senior Adviser to the Minister Vidya Amarapala, Project Director of the Port City Project Nihal Fernando and CHEC Port City Colombo Ltd. Managing Director Jiang Houliang.

[52] Lanka Business Online, "CHEC to Kick off Port City Project with Billion Dollars Towers: Minister," Jan. 26, 2018, www.lankabusinessonline.com/chec-to-kick-off-port-city-project-with-billion-dollar-towers-minister/.

45 meters tall.[53] Because the roof of the tunnel will be at the level of Galle Face Green – a popular open, free recreational area overlooking the ocean which is enjoyed by people from all walks of life[54] – many fear that this open space will be adversely affected by the construction of the tunnel.[55]

There is a paucity of information about the status and cost of this underground tunnel. According to news reports, the original cost estimate of the first phase of the Port City was US$1.4 billion.[56] However, the cost has increased to US$1.9 billion, because of interest charges during the first phase of the project.[57] It is likely that the tunnel will cost millions of dollars, bringing the total cost of the development to around US$2.5 billion. It is not clear what the rate of return will be and much depends on who invests in it, who can afford to buy property there, and pay for its amenities, the geopolitical situation of the region, and the global economic situation. Thus, not only the social and environmental viability of the project is questionable, but also its long-term economic feasibility.

15.3.3 *Environmental Concerns*

The overall project attracted several objections from various sources, most significantly from environmental groups and local fisherfolk who experienced the greatest adverse impacts. They raised objections about the government's failure to consider the project's adverse environmental impacts. These related to added sewage and waste disposal from a massive port city that will exacerbate the lack of proper sewage treatment in the city of Colombo, as well as inadequate waste disposal facilities. The massive amount of sand (approximately 200 million cubic feet) that will be mined from the ocean floor for the reclamation could lead to coastal erosion and to the destruction of coral reefs in the vicinity of the excavations. Sand mining also impacts the feeding and breeding ground of fish which much of the Sri Lankan population rely on as a source of protein. The excavation of the ocean floor for sand could lead to the alteration of currents between the coast and the coral reefs leading to still waters that could aggravate coastal pollution by preventing the dilution of pollution. Finally, the project will also require large quantities of granite, which will be quarried from other parts of the country using explosives – an activity that

---

[53] The government will enter into an agreement with the developer, CHEC Port City Colombo (Pvt.) Ltd, a subsidiary of China Harbour Engineering Company, which is part of China Communication Construction Company Limited (CCCC) group ("Sri Lanka Approves PPP for Port City Tunnel Link," Dec. 13, 2017, https://economynext.com/Sri_Lanka_approves_PPP_for_%E2%80%98Port_City%E2%80%99_tunnel_link-3-9347-4.html).

[54] The Galle Face Green, currently a 5-hectare ribbon strip of land between Galle Road and the Indian Ocean, is the largest open space in Colombo. This is a popular recreation destination for people of all ages, especially, children, kite flyers, merrymakers and joggers enjoying the sea breeze. During weekends, Galle Face Green is particularly busy, bustling with day trippers, picnickers and food vendors ("Galle Face Green," https://lanka .com/about/attractions/galle-face-green/).

[55] Previous attempts to "develop" the Galle Face Green failed. In *Environmental Foundation Ltd.* v. *Urban Development Authority and others* (2009) 1 SRI LR 123, the Supreme Court directed the UDA to refrain from handing over the management and control of the 14-acre seaside promenade of Colombo, "the Galle Face Green," to a private company to build a mega leisure complex. The court stated: "We make this order on the basis that Galle Face Green has been open to the public, established and maintained as a public utility for the past 150 years" (p. 125). No development plans were divulged to the public and the court held that the refusal to provide access to official information amounts to an infringement of the fundamental right under Article 14 (l)(a) (on freedom of speech and expression) and the arbitrary refusal of information is an infringement of the fundamental right guaranteed by Article 12(1) of the Constitution (on equality).

[56] Aneez, note 37.

[57] D. N. R. Samaranayaka, "The Economic of Port City Colombo," Mar. 17, 2015, www.colombotelegraph.com/index.php/the-economics-of-the-colombo-port-city-project/.

could lead to mudslides and landslides, cause noise pollution, and constitute a nuisance to the people living in the vicinity.

EIAs became part of the National Environmental Act[58] in 1988,[59] and regulations to give effect to the EIA provisions were promulgated in 1993.[60] Since then, EIAs have been mandatory for projects likely to have a significant impact on the environment.[61] Given the magnitude of the project's geographic and environmental footprint, the project animated concerns about potential environmental impacts. As such, an EIA was required before proceeding with the project. It is not clear why an SEA was not required for the entire plan.

However, jurisdictional issues and attributes of the Port City resulted in an EIA process that was fraught with controversy from the start. Because the project involved both sand extraction and reclamation, government agencies charged with regulating development on coasts and in surrounding ocean waters needed to be consulted. This meant that both the Coast Conservation and Coastal Resources Management Department (CC & CRMD) and the Central Environmental Authority (CEA) would need to be designated as the appropriate Project Approving Agencies (PAAs) given that they possess jurisdiction over coastal and offshore activities, respectively. However, the CEA directed the CC & CRMD to issue the terms of reference which serve as the guidelines for the structure and content of the eventual EIA.

In 2010, the SLPA commissioned the University of Moratuwa to produce an Initial Technical Feasibility Study and Environmental Impact Assessment Study for the Port City Development Project. In April 2011, the study was published. Importantly, because burrow areas for sand extraction had not been identified during the planning stage, the EIA did not include an assessment of the impact of this activity. This was an important oversight, as studies show that sand extraction poses serious risks to the health of waterways and coastlines as extraction of large quantities of sand leads to coastal erosion.[62] Instead, the CC & CRMD awarded preliminary clearance based only on an assessment of impacts from reclamation, and the developer sought to provide an addendum to the EIA without seeking new terms of reference from the PAA. This was unusual because while submitting an addendum to an approved EIA is not without precedent, it must be subject to supplemental terms of reference issued by the PAA that reflect changes to the proposed project. In addition, the CEA, the government agency responsible for regulating offshore activities, was not consulted on conversations regarding the addendum, which was intended to address environmental issues squarely within its legal purview.[63] Ultimately the CEA sought to address the sand extraction issue by issuing terms of reference for a separate initial environmental examination (IEE), which is a "preliminary screening tool" used to determine whether an EIA is necessary.[64]

Due to identifiable weaknesses in the IEE, the CEA rejected the report submitted by the developer. An addendum to the EIA was submitted in September 2013 and by November 2013,

---

[58] National Environment Act No. 47 of 1980.

[59] National Environmental (Amendment) Act No. 56 of 1988.

[60] Regulation 772/22, National Environment Act No. 47 of 1980.

[61] National Environmental Act, note 58, s. 23AA. These are called "prescribed projects." See L. Zubair, "Challenges for Environmental Impact Assessment in Sri Lanka" (2001) 21 *Environmental Impact Assessment Review* 469 at 472. Current law does not require human rights impact assessments.

[62] S. Sreebha and D. Padmalal, "Environmental Impact Assessment of Sand Mining from the Small Catchment Rivers in the Southwestern Coast of India: A Case Study" (2011) 47 *Environmental Management* 130.

[63] C. Fernando, "To Sink or Swim with Colombo Port City?" Apr. 5, 2015, www.sundaytimes.lk/150405/news/to-sink-or-swim-with-colombo-port-city-143604.html.

[64] M. Samarakoon and J. S. Rowan, "A Critical Review of Environmental Impact Statements in Sri Lanka with Particular Reference to Ecological Impact Assessment" (2008) 41 *Environmental Management* 44 at 441.

the entire EIA received a no-objection letter from the Coast Conservation Department. In October of 2014 final approval for the project was given.[65] Construction officially began in September 2014 at a ceremony attended by both then President Mahinda Rajapaksa and Chinese President Xi Jinping.[66]

Despite the relative ease with which the EIA secured approval from the CC & CRMD, the document did not enjoy widespread support among members of Sri Lankan civil society. In particular, Environmental Foundation Limited (EFL), the oldest public interest environmental law organization in Sri Lanka, identified many critical shortcomings in the report. EFL argued that the EIA failed to describe specific activities associated with the project, neglected environmental and socioeconomic impacts,[67] did not consult all relevant government authorities, and was written by a team that lacked the expertise required to properly evaluate a project of this magnitude.[68] In addition, some Sri Lankans alleged that, from its inception, the Port City project was developed in a secretive manner that left the public largely "in the dark."[69] This is contrary to the jurisprudence of the Supreme Court.[70] As the Court held in *Environmental Foundation Ltd.* v. *Urban Development Authority and others*:

> Although the right to information is not specifically guaranteed under the Constitution as a fundamental right, the freedom of speech and expression including publication guaranteed by Article 14(1)(a), to be meaningful and effective should carry within its scope an implicit right of a person to secure relevant information from a public authority in respect of a matter that should be in the public domain. It should necessarily be so where the public interest in the matter outweighs the confidentiality that attaches to affairs of State and official communications.[71]

Although a combination of controversy and politics frustrated efforts to realize the Port City project, the project gained official sanction during the tenure of President Rajapaksa at the end of 2014. However, the national elections of January 2015 ushered in new leadership under President Maithripala Sirisena and Prime Minister Ranil Wickremesinghe, who promised to "review all projects to ensure they were environmentally viable and corruption-free."[72] In line

---

[65] C. Nathaniel, "Controversy Surrounds Colombo Port City," Feb. 15, 2015, www.thesundayleader.lk/2015/02/15/controversy-surrounds-colombo-port-city/.

[66] W. Shepard, "Sri Lanka's Colombo Port City: The Frontline of China and India's Geopolitical Showdown," Aug. 12, 2016, www.forbes.com/sites/wadeshepard/2016/08/12/a-look-at-colombo-port-city-the-frontline-of-china-and-indias-geopolitical-showdown/.

[67] As noted, while the EIA process is confined to environmental impacts under the National Environmental Act (as amended) as well as that under the Coast Conservation Act, EIAs have regularly included social impacts such as relocation and livelihoods. Cost benefit analysis is a requirement under the law as well as the need to discuss alternatives. EIAs are public documents subject to public participation. Many have, however, noted the flaws in the system, such as the technical nature of the reports and the fact that it comes too late in the decision-making process to make much of an impact. See Zubair, note 61. The new Sustainable Development Law will go a long way in redressing this situation.

[68] Environmental Foundation Ltd, "Why the Port City EIA Needs to Be Reassessed: Concerns on the Port City Development," 2015.

[69] Jayawardane, note 36.

[70] And also contrary to the New Freedom of Information Act and the fundamental right included in the Constitution. See S. Gunaratne, "The Right to Information in Sri Lanka," in D. Samararatne (ed.), *Sri Lanka: State of Human Rights 2017* (Colombo: Law and Society Trust), 2017, p. 227.

[71] *Environmental Foundation Ltd.* v. *Urban Development Authority and others*, note 55.

[72] "Protest in Colombo Against Chinese Funded Port City Project," Apr. 4, 2016, http://beta.sundaytimes.lk/news-online/protest-against-chinese-funded-port-city-project/2-99862.

with his campaign promise, PM Wickremesinghe directed an Evaluation Committee to determine whether the project should proceed as planned.[73] In March 2015, the Committee rendered its decision and the Cabinet of Ministers opted to halt construction.[74] By this time, approximately 13 percent of the project had already been completed.[75] During this suspension, Central Engineering Consultancy Bureau (along with a number of associate consultants) conducted a supplemental EIA (SEIA) designed to address deficiencies in the 2011 EIA on behalf of the project proponent, Ministry of Megapolis and Western Development. The SEIA was completed in December 2015.

Although more extensive than its predecessor, the SEIA did not allay concerns about the impacts of the Port City project. In their report on the SEIA, EFL concluded that the "previous shortfalls and deficiencies identified in the original EIA have not been addressed adequately. This study contains the same anomalies in terms of technical/scientific and social aspects."[76] In particular, EFL maintained that the SEIA failed to address impacts due to climate change, provided an inaccurate assessment of how the Port City project would affect fisheries, offered only vague mitigation measures, and neglected to analyze impacts on terrestrial fauna located near the project.

Under Sri Lankan law, the public has thirty days to comment on an EIA after it has been published.[77] Although provisions for public participation in the EIA process vary considerably across the world,[78] only affording the public the opportunity to comment on an EIA after it has already been completed is viewed as a critical weakness of the EIA process in Sri Lanka.[79] While the law provides for public hearings, it appears that no public hearing was held for this project. Following publication of the SEIA, a flurry of public comments from members of civil society were sent to the Director General of Coast Conservation and Coastal Management.[80] Led by the founder of the People's Movement Against Port City, Sri Lankans raised a number of concerns about the SEIA, including the excessive use of technical jargon, the inappropriateness of soliciting comments during an important religious event, and the inattention given to impacts caused to the people in the area by rock extraction.[81] In addition, a study of public opinion on the Port City project found that common reasons for opposing the project included "[l]ack of transparency, environmental concerns, doubts about the motive of the project and its feasibility, and concerns regarding Sri Lanka's sovereignty."[82] However, despite its campaign promise to kill

---

[73] M. M. Perera, "Police Charge Peaceful Protesters, Including Nuns, Who Oppose a Port City Project," May 3, 2015, www.asianews.it/news-en/Police-charge-peaceful-protesters,-including-nuns,-who-oppose-a-port-project-33635.html.

[74] S. Naleer, "Colombo Port City: What You Need to Know in a Nutshell and More," Aug. 22, 2016, www.adaderana.lk/news/36607/colombo-port-city-what-you-need-to-know-in-a-nutshell-and-more.

[75] Fernando, note 63.

[76] Environmental Foundation Ltd, "Comments Sent by Environmental Foundation Limited on SEIA on Colombo Port City Project," 2016, p. 2.

[77] World Bank, "Democratic Socialist Republic of Sri Lanka: Review of the Environmental Impact Assessment System," 2012, p. 18.

[78] A. Morrison-Saunders, *Advanced Introduction to Environmental Impact Assessment* (Cheltenham, UK: Edward Elgar, 2018), pp. 110–111.

[79] World Bank, note 77, p. 32.

[80] S. Iddamalgoda, "EIA Report on the Environmental Impact of the Colombo Port City," Jan. 5, 2016, www.colombotelegraph.com/index.php/eia-report-on-the-environmental-impact-of-the-colombo-port-city/.

[81] Ibid.

[82] D. L. Thoradeniya, "Public–Private Partnerships: The Case Study of the Colombo Port City," master's thesis, University of Moratuwa, 2016, http://dl.lib.mrt.ac.lk/handle/123/12784, p. 129.

the project[83] and against a wave of public criticism, the Sirisena administration decided to move forward with the controversial mega-project in January 2016.[84]

15.3.4 *Litigation*

The Centre for Environmental Justice, a Colombo-based NGO, whose mission is to protect the environment and environmental rights of people, and promote ecological sustainability,[85] filed action in the Court of Appeal for writs of certiorari and mandamus under Article 140 of the Constitution[86] against the SLPA, CEA, Coast Conservation Department, and several others in November 2016. The salient points of the petitioner's objections are summarized here.

15.3.4.1 Deficiencies of the SEIA with regard to the Reclamation Phase

The petitioner pointed to several deficiencies in the SEIA. It argued that first, according to the SEIA, the project would reclaim an area of 269 ha, which is 36 ha in excess of the original proposal. Second, when the waterway and two canals are included, the total footprint of the project will be 485 ha (1,200 acres) of the ocean. Third, increase in rock blasting requires a proper environmental study as it is negatively impacting local communities in the area, biodiversity, archeological sites, and other infrastructure. Fourth, according to the SEIA, 65 million cubic meters of dredged sand will be required. However, taking into account wastage during dredging, the total sand requirement will likely exceed 90 million cubic meters. Fifth, rocks and boulders will be transported by using 300 trucks twice a day which will amount to 1,200 round trips. This will add to the traffic considerably but is not considered in the SEIA.

The petitioner also pointed to procedural flaws and inconsistencies. For example, a new company named CHEC Port City Colombo (PVT) Ltd with the same address as the CCCC had emerged as the developer. EIAs done by different project proponents do not constitute a single EIA within the meaning of the law. There are discrepancies in the documents about the amount of sand needed for the project. While the SLPA refers to a total of 65 million cubic meters of sand, the National Aquatic Resources Research and Development Agency (NARA) states that the project will require only 30 million cubic meters. Given this discrepancy, both documents should be treated as invalid. In any event, sand mining of this scale will result in severe environmental degradation.

15.3.4.2 Environmental Justice Concerns and the Affected Public

The petitioner expressed concern about the communities that are affected by various components of the project. The project requires 2.83 million cubic meters of quarry material. This

[83] E. Barry, "New President in Sri Lanka Puts China's Plans in Check," Jan. 9, 2015, www.nytimes.com/2015/01/ 10/world/asia/new-president-in-sri-lanka-puts-chinas-plans-in-check.html.

[84] S. Aneez and R. Sirilal, "Sri Lanka to Allow Chinese Port City Project after Delay," Jan. 12, 2016, www.reuters .com/article/sri-lanka-china-portcity-idUSL3N14W42G20160112.

[85] There are two main NGOs in Sri Lanka that use the law to promote environmental justice – the Environmental Foundation (the oldest) and the Centre for Environmental Justice. Both organizations have been successful in getting standing to bring cases in the public interest (https://ejustice.lk/).

[86] CA Writ Application No. 112/2015, filed in November 2016. On file with authors. The information in this section is from the writ application.

material will be taken from eleven existing metal quarries, which are currently causing a public nuisance due to noise and traffic. Any increase in rock blasting will exacerbate the nuisance. In addition, the sand mining required for the project will likely disrupt the livelihoods of 15,000 fishers, and harm biodiversity, including coral reefs, fish, and other marine species. Local fishers feared that extensive sand mining for this project will accelerate slipping and erode the very small sandy strip between the ocean and the Negombo lagoon destroying the lagoon and the marine life as well as their livelihoods. The SEIA did not consider these potential impacts.

15.3.4.3 Impact of the Construction Phase and Resources Needed

The project consists of two main components: (a) filling up of an area of 269 ha of the Indian Ocean adjacent to the Colombo harbor; and (b) construction of an iconic business district consisting of high-rise buildings, water sports areas, shopping malls, a mini golf course, hotels, apartments, recreation areas, and a luxury yacht marina. Neither the EIA nor the SEIA considered component (b). The petitioner argued that the project cannot be compartmentalized in this manner. Component (b) will require more sand, rock materials, and other natural resources. Moreover, it will require electricity, water supply, garbage and sewage disposal, and flood protection mechanisms which can only be evaluated by the relevant authorities after a comprehensive EIA for the *entire project*.

The quantity of water required for the construction phase alone amounts to around 1,000 cubic meters per day. It is not clear how this quantity of water will be provided, and this issue has not been addressed. Given that sewage disposal system in Colombo is already overburdened, this project will lead to severe stress on the system. The increased demand for electricity will lead to the emission of more greenhouse gases.

15.3.4.4 Laws Invoked

The petitioner averred that the entire Port City project lacks credibility, and that the discrepancy in the documents raises serious questions about the extent of the land to be reclaimed. Moreover, allegations of bias and conflict of interest raise questions about the credibility of the EIA and SEIA and other documents. The petitioner expressed concern about the adverse impacts of the project on the environment and on the fundamental rights of the people, and sought to uphold the principles of good governance enshrined in the directive principles chapter of the Constitution. The petitioner further argued that the respondents have failed to perform their statutory duties, and that the agreements entered into are contrary to the laws of the country. The petition also noted that the project proponent had failed to carry out a comprehensive EIA for the entire project and prepared only a supplementary EIA, violating the provisions of the Coast Conservation Act and the National Environment Act.

The petitioner relied on directive principles of state policy, especially Article 27(14) which requires the state to protect, preserve, and improve the environment for the benefit of the community; the public trust doctrine as articulated by the Supreme Court in cases such as *Bulankulama and others* v. *Secretary, Ministry of Industrial Development and others* (2000)[87] and

---

[87] *Bulankulama and others* v. *Secretary, Ministry of Industrial Development and others*, 3 Sri LR (2000) 243, referred to in Chapter 9 in this volume. See also, M. de Silva, "Environmental Rights," in *Sri Lanka: State of Human Rights 2009–2010* (Colombo: Law and Society Trust, 2011), p. 465.

Wattegedera Wijebanda v. *Conservator General of Forests* (2009);[88] and international environmental treaties and declarations that the state has signed or ratified.[89] In sum, they argued the EIA and SEIA are flawed, violate existing law, and do not address the entire project. The petitioner concluded that:

> The petitioner states that grave and irreparable loss and harm will be caused to its rights, as well as to the rights of the public at large unless the implementation of the said project and its validity is quashed by way of a writ of certiorari and an order in the nature of Mandamus is issued to the respondents to perform their statutory obligations.[90]

Although the case was taken up for hearing, the court decided in October 2017 to postpone the final decision and considered that the appearance of the Attorney General was necessary given the importance of the case. There have been no further hearings as of the time of writing.

15.4 IMPLICATIONS OF THE PROJECT

This project raises several issues of concern. As noted, the most significant concern relates to the environmental impacts of reclaiming and appropriating a large area of the ocean. The adverse environmental impacts of land reclamation from the sea have been documented in many parts of the world. It is important, therefore, to evaluate the EIAs prepared for the project to ascertain if they systematically and comprehensively consider the adverse environmental impacts for the entire project.[91] Reclamation projects around the world have demonstrated a continuing need for remedial actions to combat their ecological impacts, and intrusion of salt water into reclaimed areas which can be costly.[92] It is not clear whether the costs of these remedial actions have been included in calculating the true costs of the project and how a developing country like Sri Lanka can afford such costs.

Second, concerns were raised regarding the actual costs and benefits of the venture itself. The reclamation costs alone are more than US$2.5 billion, and they will be financed with loans from China. In addition, the actual cost of building on this reclaimed land, and transforming it into the grand tourist and business center of the kind anticipated will cost billions of dollars more, and the Chinese company is planning to spend an additional US$3 billion.[93] Will Sri Lanka be able to borrow such a large sum of money for the reclamation and for its section of the Port City, and repay these debts? Is it prudent or fair to enmesh future generations of Sri Lankans in a vicious cycle of financial and ecological debt, over which they had no say? Is it not a violation of the public trust doctrine, principles of sustainable development, intergenerational equity principle, prudent use of natural resources, and the precautionary principle?

A third cluster of questions relates to the project's geopolitical ramifications. The Port City project is located in close proximity to India and lies close to strategic sea routes that the United States has pledged to protect. Neither country can be happy about such a large Chinese presence in Sri Lanka. Is a 99-year lease conceding a major part of the Port City to China, a

---

[88] *Wattegedera Wijebanda* v. *Conservator General of Forests*, 1 Sri LR (2009) 337
[89] Sri Lanka has ratified, inter alia, the Convention on Biological Diversity, UN Law of the Sea Convention, UN Framework Convention on Climate Change, the Paris Agreement, and signed the Stockholm and Rio Declarations.
[90] CA Writ Application No. 112/2015, note 86, para. 73.
[91] H. Duan, H. Zhang, Q. Huang, et al., "Characterization and Impacts of Environmental Impact Analysis of Sea Land Reclamation Activities in China" (2016) 130 *Ocean and Coastal Management* 128–137.
[92] Ibid.
[93] Ibid.

result of the debt owed to China? The investment in this project is part of China's Belt and Road Initiative, one of the most ambitious infrastructure projects ever conceived connecting the continents of Asia, Africa, and Europe.[94] This attempt to revive the original Silk Road is seen by many as an unsettling extension of China's rising power.[95] The Center for Strategic and International Studies summarizes China's ambitious plans as follows:

> China's leaders have mapped out an ambitious plan, the Maritime Silk Road Initiative (MSRI), to establish three "blue economic passages" that will connect Beijing with economic hubs around the world. It is the maritime dimension of President Xi Jinping's Belt and Road Initiative (BRI), which could include $1–4 trillion in new roads, railways, ports, and other infrastructure. Within this broad and ever-expanding construct, Chinese investments have been especially active in the Indo-Pacific region, raising questions about whether it is China's economic or strategic interests that are driving major port investments.[96]

The precedent set by the 99-year lease of the Southern seaport and harbor (in Hambantota) to China is not reassuring.[97] Sri Lanka was unsuccessful in obtaining financing for this project and turned to China which gave loans at a high interest rate. President Sirisena sought to renegotiate Colombo's repayment schedule in 2017, but China requested a long lease in return for debt forgiveness.[98] Sri Lanka had no option but to agree to this and in 2017, Sri Lanka gave China a controlling equity stake in the port and a 99-year lease for operating it[99] effectively giving China a strategic foothold just 100 miles from its rival India.[100] Will Sri Lanka be able to stop China from using Hambantota port and the Port City for military purposes? This future possibility could draw Sri Lanka into an Indian Ocean power struggle.

The final cluster of concerns relates to the livelihood of fisherfolk and their families who will be adversely affected by this project. The number of those who will be affected is significant. In addition to coastal erosion and the impact on coral reefs, this project will likely affect the breeding grounds of fish and other aquatic species leading to diminished fish catch and undermining the biodiversity of the area. Moreover, there could be other unforeseen consequences as a project of this magnitude has never been attempted in Sri Lanka.

15.5 CONCLUDING THOUGHTS: A JUSTICE CONUNDRUM?

As discussed, the Port City project is disconcerting on several grounds. The project raises issues of sustainability, economic viability, and justice. A project of this magnitude has to be executed with extreme caution if it is to be undertaken at all. Large-scale reclamation projects can cause irreparable damage to the marine environment, and affect marine life and the livelihoods of thousands of fisherfolk. Sand mining is another area of concern and from documents available to us, it seems that no EIA was done of sand mining. The project also envisages an underground tunnel. No environmental assessment appears to have been done for that either. The project site

---

[94] A. Chatzky and J. McBride, "China's Massive Belt and Road Initiative," May 21, 2019, www.cfr.org/backgrounder/chinas-massive-belt-and-road-initiative.

[95] Ibid.

[96] M. P. Funaiole and J. E. Hillman, "China's Maritime Silk Road Initiative: Economic Drivers and Challenges," Mar. 2018.

[97] M. Abi-Habib, "How China Got Sri Lanka to Cough up a Port," June 25, 2018, www.nytimes.com/2018/06/25/world/asia/china-sri-lanka-port.html.

[98] J. Hillman, "Game of Loans: How China Bought Hambantota," Mar. 2018.

[99] Ibid.

[100] T. Fernholz, "China's 'Debt Trap' Is Even Worse than We Thought," June 28, 2018. https://qz.com/1317234/chinas-debt-trap-in-sri-lanka-is-even-worse-than-we-thought/.

is in close proximity to a congested area with hotels and many old buildings, some dating back to the colonial era. Digging a tunnel is bound to cause damage to these buildings and the environment. Moreover, nobody has even raised the climate change implications of this project (except in the writ petition discussed above), from its inception through construction phase to the final implementation. It could cause a significant dent in the commitments that Sri Lanka made under the Paris Agreement.[101]

Similarly, the economic viability of the project is a grave concern.[102] There is no indication that people were consulted on this massive project. It seems to have been done at the whim of the Rajapaksa administration. If this is done in the name of "development," then surely people should have a say in the matter? What about public participation? What about divulging correct information to the people? What about soliciting the opinion of people on whether they want this project in the first place in the exercise of the Sri Lankans' right to self-determination? Do people want to create such a massive debt for their children and grandchildren? What about the poor fisherfolk whose livelihoods are affected? Have alternative forms of employment been created for them?

Politicians will come and go, but it is the general public and future generations that have to bear the brunt of the decisions made by the politicians. Given the negative consequences of this project and the public outcry against it, the project raises questions about transparency and accountability of the government officials involved and whether any of them are illegally profiting from this venture.

Signs of imperialism and neocolonialism by China are troubling. The terms of the project are extremely favorable to China, and Sri Lanka will be in China's debt for decades. Its strategic location is causing geopolitical tension in the region as India is eyeing this project with concern. By giving the reclaimed land on a 99-year lease to the Chinese government, is Sri Lanka not ceding part of its sovereignty to a foreign power?[103]

Even more disconcerting is those who will be left out of the project. The project will create a divide between the rich and the poor as ordinary Sri Lankans will not be able to afford the amenities generated by this "development," essentially excluding them from the financial city. At the same time, they will be bound by the economic debt created by this project. A project that provides benefits for a handful of people while imposing a massive burden on everybody else is contrary to principles of environmental justice,[104] especially the distributive justice component. The project has also violated the procedural justice component as Sri Lankans were not consulted about the project and even the EIAs that were prepared are flawed and incomplete and do not look at the project in its entirety. No compensation has been forthcoming for the fishers whose livelihoods are affected, thereby infringing the corrective justice component. In addition, this project could exacerbate social inequities in Sri Lankan society, thereby affecting the social justice component.

The Sustainable Development Act was enacted in 2017 to improve institutional coherence in implementing the SDGs.[105] Its objectives are laudable:

---

[101] Ministry of Mahaweli Development and Environment, Sri Lanka, "Nationally Determined Contribution," Sept. 2016.

[102] The petition noted that no reliable cost–benefit analysis was carried out.

[103] There is much literature on land grabs. See generally, S. Sassen "Land Grabs Today: Feeding the Disassembling of National Territory" (2013) 10 *Globalization* 25–46 at 25.

[104] See discussion in Section 15.2.

[105] G. Tilakaratna, "Sri Lanka's Sustainable Development Act: Improving Institutional Coherence for SDGs," July 17, 2018, www.ips.lk/talkingeconomics/2018/07/17/sri-lankas-sustainable-development-act-improving-institutional-coherence-for-sdgs/.

The Act provides for the establishment of a Sustainable Development Council as the national coordinating body for implementing the SDGs. The Council is tasked with preparing the National Policy and Strategy for Sustainable Development . . . All government entities are required to prepare Sustainable Development Strategies in line with the national strategy. The Council monitors the implementation of the national strategy.[106]

EIAs under the National Environmental Act have sometimes included social impacts such as relocation of people and impacts on livelihoods, but this is not mandatory. The Sustainable Development Act, if implemented properly, is a major step forward in addressing environmental and social impacts of new development projects. Interestingly, this law adopts the same definition of sustainable development as that proposed by the Brundtland Commission.[107]

Sri Lanka is heading in the right direction toward adopting sustainability impact assessments under its Sustainable Development Act, similar to countries such as Canada that have enacted such impact assessment legislation.[108] However, the Port City Project makes us seriously question whether any attempt was made by decision makers to balance the three dimensions of sustainable development (economic, environmental, and social)[109] or whether, as in the past, economic development is given primacy over other concerns. In this instance, however, even the project's economic viability is in question.

Sri Lanka has excellent laws on paper, and its judiciary has developed an impressive body of jurisprudence on environmental rights.[110] Moreover, Sri Lanka has ratified all major human rights and environmental treaties and has adopted enabling legislation to give effect to these obligations. Sri Lanka's commitment to achieving the SDGs is reflected in the adoption of the Sustainable Development Act. However, the implementation of laws and compliance with judicial decisions leaves much to be desired. A project that caters to the elite, is neither environmentally nor financially sustainable, and exacerbates social inequities, is contrary to Sri Lanka's national laws, international obligations, and sustainable development objectives. Indeed, it can undermine the realization of the SDGs. At the heart of this injustice is the imposition of economic and ecological burdens on the Sri Lankan people in total disregard of their concerns. As the People's Movement Against the Port City questioned: "Where is the space for People's participation, which is a hallmark of democracy and good governance?"[111]

---

[106] Sustainable Development Act, No. 19 of 2017, Preamble.

[107] See UN World Commission on Environmental and Development, *Report of the World Commission on Environment and Development: Our Common Future* (Oxford: Oxford University Press, 1987), p. 43.

[108] See Impact Assessment Act, SC 2019, c. 28, s. 1; Federal Sustainable Development Act, SC 2008, c. 33. See R. B. Gibson, M. Doelle, and A. J. Sinclair, "Fulfilling the Promise: Basic Components of Next Generation Environmental Assessment" (2015) *Journal of Environmental Law and Practice* 251.

[109] See World Summit on Sustainable Development, *Johannesburg Declaration on Sustainable Development and Plan of Implementation of the World Summit on Sustainable Development: The Final Text of Agreements Negotiated by Governments at the World Summit on Sustainable Development, 26 August–4 September 2002, Johannesburg, South Africa.* New York: United Nations Department of Public Information.

[110] de Silva, note 87.

[111] "Port City Is Detrimental to Sri Lanka: People's Movement against Port City," Apr. 14, 2016, www.colombotelegraph.com/index.php/port-city-is-detrimental-to-sri-lanka-peoples-movement-against-port-city/.

Toxic Substances and Hazardous Wastes

16

Chemical Pollution and the Role of International Law in a Future Detoxified

Sabaa A. Khan

16.1 INTRODUCTION

This chapter explores the environmental justice dimensions of international trade in hazardous chemicals and waste. It considers the central argument of the environmental justice movement – according to which, marginalized populations have unwillingly assumed a disproportionate share of the toxic hazards produced throughout society[1] – in the context of the global chemicals industry. Building on environmental sociological analyses of the international hazardous waste trade,[2] the notion of environmental justice is conceptualized in the language of human and labor rights. This chapter aims to strengthen understanding of how the existing international legal regimes for regulating transboundary flows of toxic chemical substances influence the disproportionate impact of chemical pollution on vulnerable populations and ecosystems that is evidenced across the globe.[3]

The chapter interrogates whether the existing legal complex for international chemicals and waste management corresponds with the contemporary global objectives of a "Pollution-free Planet" and a "Future Detoxified," the respective themes of the third United Nations Environment Assembly and the 2017 Conference of the Parties to the Basel, Rotterdam, and Stockholm Conventions (BRS).[4] These three treaties are the primary international legal

---

[1] R. Bullard, "Environmental Justice for All," in R. Bullard (ed.), *Unequal Protection: Environmental Justice & Communities of Color* (San Francisco: Sierra Club, 1994).

[2] See D. N. Pellow, *Resisting Global Toxics: Transnational Movements for Environmental Justice* (Cambridge: MIT Press, 2007); D. N. Pellow, "The Global Waste Trade and Environmental Justice Struggles," in K. P. Gallagher (ed.), *Handbook on Trade and the Environment* (Cheltenham, UK: Edward Elgar, 2009); J. Clapp, *Toxic Exports: The Transfer of Hazardous Wastes from Rich to Poor Countries* (Ithaca, NY : Cornell University Press, 2001); T. Smith, D. Sonnenfeld, and D. Pellow (eds.), *Challenging the Chip: Labor Rights and Environmental Justice in the Global Electronics Industry* (Philadelphia: Temple University Press, 2006).

[3] UNEP, *Report of the Executive Director to the 3rd United Nations Environment Assembly: Towards a Pollution Free planet*, Oct. 15, 2017, UNEP/EA.3/25; World Health Organization, "Public Health Impacts of Chemicals Knowns and Unknowns," International Programme on Chemical Society, Geneva, 2016; World Health Organization, "Ambient Air Pollution: A Global Assessment of Exposure and Burden of Disease," Geneva, 2016.

[4] Basel Convention on the Control of Transboundary Movements of Hazardous Wastes and Their Disposal, Basel, Switzerland, Mar. 22, 1989, UN Doc. UNEP/WG. 190/4; Stockholm Convention on Persistent Organic Pollutants, Stockholm, Sweden, May 22, 2001, UNTS, vol. 2256, p. 119; Rotterdam Convention on the Prior Informed Consent Procedure for Certain Hazardous Chemicals and Pesticides in International Trade, Rotterdam, Netherlands, Sept. 10, 1998, UNTS, vol. 2244, p. 337.

instruments regulating global transfers of chemicals and waste, and together they form the international minimum standard for chemicals control. In examining the operational mechanisms of these treaties and their implementation and interrelations, this work seeks to uncover the philosophy of technology that is embedded in our international chemicals and waste law, and questions whether the underlying legal ontologies[5] of hazardous chemicals and waste compromise the overarching common aim of these treaties, which is the protection of human health and the environment from toxics in global trade.[6]

16.2 CONTEMPORARY CHEMICALS FLOWS AND ENVIRONMENTAL JUSTICE CONCERNS

There is nothing quite like the synthetic chemical that shows how deeply intertwined social, economic, and environmental ecosystems are, and how their concurrence and dissonance critically determine planetary health from the molecular to global level. The pervasion of chemically manufactured plastic – a seemingly never-ending material,[7] ubiquitous throughout land and water ecosystems in both visible and invisible form,[8] infiltrating food webs,[9] and human bodies[10] – provides one of the most visible manifestations of the liberally toxic way society has used, produced, and disposed of chemically based products since their widespread availability in global markets beginning in the 1950s.

Plastic is not the only material fueling a constantly rising wave of global chemical contamination. The harmful chemical effects of pesticides, first brought to global attention over half a century ago,[11] continue to proliferate across the globe. Pesticide-heavy agriculture dominates world food production, with the effect of decimating biodiversity across regions.[12] Highly toxic crop protectants that were formerly in widespread use have been replaced by newer generation

---

[5] Ontology here is understood as describing "how some domain is 'committed' to a particular view: not so much by the collection of the terms involved in but in particular by the way these terms are structured and defined. This structure tells us 'what a domain is about'" (J. Breuker, A. Valente, and R. Winkels, "Legal Ontologies in Knowledge Engineering and Information Management (2004) 12 *Artificial Intelligence and Law* 241 at 242).

[6] Stockholm Convention, note 4, Art. 1; Rotterdam Convention, note 4, Art. 1; Basel Convention, note 4, Preamble.

[7] "The longevity of plastic is estimated to be hundreds to thousands of years but is likely to be far longer in deep sea and non-surface polar environments" (D. K. A. Barnes, F. Galgani, R. C. Thompson, and M. Barlaz, "Accumulation and Fragmentation of Plastic Debris in Global Environments" (2009) 364 *Philosophical Transactions of the Royal Society* 1985 at 1985).

[8] J. Boucher and D. Friot, *Primary Microplastics in the Oceans: A Global Evaluation of Sources* (Gland: International Union for the Conservation of Nature, 2017).

[9] See C. J. Foley, Z. S. Feiner, T. D. Malnich, and T. O. Hook, "A Meta-Analysis of the Effects of Exposure to Microplastics on Fish and Aquatic Invertebrates" (2018) 631–632 *Science of the Total Environment* 550.

[10] On the presence of microplastics, nanoplastics, and plastic additives in human bodies, see T. Galloway "Micro- and Nano- Plastics and Human Health," in M. Bergmann, L. Gutow, and M. Klages (eds.), *Marine Anthropogenic Litter*, (London: SpringerOpen, 2015), pp. 343–366.

[11] R. Carson, *Silent Spring* (Boston: Houghton Mifflin, 1962).

[12] S. G. Potts, V. L. Imperatriz-Fonseca, H. T. Ngo, et al. (eds.), "Summary for Policymakers of the Assessment Report on Pollinators, Pollination and Food Production," Inter-governmental Science Policy Platform on Biodiversity and Ecosystem Services (IPBES), Jan. 2016; R. L. Stanton, C. A. Morrissey, and R. G. Clark, "Analysis of Trends and Agricultural Drivers of Farmland Bird Declines in North America: A Review" (2018) 254 *Agriculture, Ecosystems and Environment* 244; F. Sanchez-Bayo "Impacts of Agricultural Pesticides on Terrestrial Ecosystems," in F. Sánchez-Bayo, P. J. van den Brink, R. M. Mann (eds.), *Ecological Impacts of Toxic Chemicals* (UAE: Bentham, 2011); Muséum National d'histoire naturelle, "Le printemps 2018 s'annonce silencieux dans les campagnes françaises," Mar. 20, 2018, www.mnhn.fr/fr/recherche-expertise/actualites/printemps-2018-s-annonce-silencieux-campagnes-francaises.

pesticides whose repercussions upon workers and ecosystems are, in some cases, just as lethal, with the full extent of their damage still unknown.[13]

Another major source of global chemical contamination is the world's fastest growing toxic waste stream composed of defunct technological products (e-waste), up to "90% of which is illegally traded or dumped."[14] E-waste generally flows along the global recycling chain from developed to developing countries,[15] where it may leach toxins into agricultural fields[16] and mangroves,[17] poison aquatic species,[18] and cover school yards with toxic dust.[19] It is widely recognized that the harshest negative externalities of the high-tech Anthropocene are shouldered by a predominantly informal e-waste workforce and their communities.[20]

Problems of chemical pollution do not end with plastics, pesticides, pharmaceuticals,[21] or e-waste – virtually all manufactured products including cosmetics[22] and cash register receipts[23] contain harmful chemicals that pose hazards to human and ecosystem health at various phases in their life cycles. In fact, the intensification of air, water, and soil pollution that has characterized world production and consumption patterns since the dawn of industrialization[24] – and come sporadically to the global public forefront through massive disasters, such as the Bhopal

---

[13] See HRC, *Report of the Special Rapporteur on the Right to Food Hilal Elver*, Jan. 24, 2017, UN Doc. A/HRC/34/38 at 3: "pesticides are responsible for an estimated 200,000 acute poisoning deaths each year, 99 percent of which occur in developing countries." See also E. C. Marquez and K. S. Schafer, *Kids on the Frontline: How Pesticides Are Harming the Health of Rural Children* (Oakland: Pesticide Action Network North America, 2016).

[14] I. Rucevska, C. Nellemann, N. Isarin, et al., "Waste Crime – Waste Risks: Gaps in Meeting the Global Waste Challenge" (Nairobi: United Nations Environment Programme and GRID–Arendal, 2015).

[15] C. P. Baldé, F. Wang, and R. Kuehr, "Transboundary Movements of Used and Waste Electronic and Electrical Equipment," United Nations University Vice Rectorate in Europe – Sustainable Cycles Programme (SCYCLE), 2016.

[16] J. Fu, Q. Zhou, and J. Liu, "High Levels of Heavy Metals in Rice (oryza sativa L.) from Typical E-waste Recycling Are in Southeast China and Its Potential Risk to Human Health" (2009) 31 *Chemosphere* 1269.

[17] S. Umair and S. Anderberg, *E-waste Imports and Informal Recycling in Pakistan – A Multidimensional Governance Challenge* (Stockholm: KTH Royal Institute of Technology, 2011).

[18] J. P. Wu, X. J. Luo, Y. Zhang, et al., "Bioaccumulation of Polybrominated Diphenyl Ethers (PBDEs) and Polychlorinated Biphenyls (PCBs) in Wild Aquatic Species from an Electronic Waste (E-waste) Recycling Site in South China" (2008) 34 *Environment International* 1109.

[19] S. M. Atiemo, F. G. Ofosu, I. J. Kwame Aboh, and H. Kuranchie-Mensah "Assessing the Heavy Metals Contamination of Surface Dust from Waste Electrical and Electronic Equipment (E-waste) Recycling Site in Accra, Ghana" (2012) 4 *Research Journal of Environmental and Earth Sciences* 605; A. O. W. Leung, N. S. Duzgoren-Aydin, K. C. Cheung, and M. H. Wong, "Heavy Metals Concentrations of Surface Dust from E-waste Recycling and Its Human Health Implications in Southeast China" (2008) 42 *Environmental Science and Technology* 2674.

[20] International Labour Office, "Tackling Informality in E-waste Management: The Potential of Cooperative Enterprises," International Labour Office, Sectoral Activities Department, Cooperatives Unit, Geneva, 2014; K. Lundgren, "The Global Impact of E-waste: Addressing the Challenge," International Labour Office, Sectoral Activities Departments, SafeWork Programme on Safety and Health at Work and the Environment, Geneva, 2012 at 11: "Of the e-waste in developed countries that is sent for recycling, 80 per cent ends up being shipped (often illegally) to developing countries to be recycled by hundreds of thousands of informal workers."

[21] T. aus der Beek, F. Weber, and A. Bergmann, "Pharmaceuticals in the Environment: Global Occurrence and Potential Cooperative Action under the Strategic Approach to International Chemicals Management (SAICM)," German Environment Agency, Nov. 2015.

[22] WHO, "Preventing Disease through Healthy Environments: Mercury in Skin Lightening Products," Public Health and Environment, WHO, Geneva, 2011.

[23] G. Zaharias Miller and L. Olsen, *More than You Bargained for: BPS and BPA in Receipts* (Ann Arbor, MI: Ecology Center, 2018); J. Liu and J. W. Martin "Prolonged Exposure to Bisphenol A from Single Dermal Contact Events" (2017) 51 *Environmental Science and Technology* 9940.

[24] See E. A. Wrigley, *Energy and the English Industrial Revolution* (Cambridge: Cambridge University Press, 2010); E. Homburg, A. S. Travis, and H. G. Schroter (eds.), *The Chemical Industry in Europe, 1850–1914: Industrial Growth, Pollution and Professionalization* (Dordrecht: Springer Netherlands, 1998).

gas tragedy (1984), the Abidjan toxic waste dumping (2006), and the Tianjin chemicals ware-house explosion (2015) – persistently threatens fundamental human rights all over the world, to an unprecedented degree.[25] There is substantial evidence that illegal pesticides are also being used as chemical warfare.[26]

Despite the ubiquity of chemicals in global manufacturing and agri-food systems, there exist profound health and environmental uncertainties (data gaps) related to a vast number of contemporary chemicals in global production and use. A 2012 UNEP report highlights that out of a set of 95,000 industrial chemicals screened, only 1,000 had data on the extent of their buildup in the environment and only 220 had data on their biodegradation half-lives.[27] Out of approximately 143,000 chemicals on the global market, only a "fraction"[28] have been rigorously evaluated to determine their effects on human and environmental health. Among the 5,000 most heavily produced and globally dispersed pesticides and chemicals, less than half have been through any testing for toxicity, safety, or rigorous premarket evaluation.[29] Even in the case of the European Union, where a comprehensive regulatory regime for chemicals based on the principles of precaution and "no data, no market"[30] has been in force since 2007, significant data gaps on chemicals registered in the EU are a systemic problem; a recent evaluation conducted by the European Chemicals Agency found over 50 percent of chemicals registration dossiers failed to comply with information requirements imposed by the REACH regulation.[31]

16.2.1 *Shifting Sites of Chemical Production and Deepening Health Inequities*

Even though our knowledge of the long-range, deep-sea, and intergenerational impacts of chemicals in prevalent use remains embryonic, scientific evidence consistently reveals to us

---

[25] WHO, note 3; UN Human Rights Council, *Report of the Special Rapporteur on the implications for human rights of the environmentally sound management and disposal of hazardous substances and wastes Baskut Tuncak: Impact of Toxics and Pollution on Children's Rights*, Aug. 2, 2016, UN Doc. A/HRC/33/41; UN Human Rights Council, *Report of the Special Rapporteur on the implications for human rights of the environmentally sound management and disposal of hazardous substances and wastes Baskut Tuncak: Right to Information on Hazardous Substances and Waste*, July 8, 2015, UN Doc. A/HRC/30/40; UN Human Rights Council, *Report of the Special Rapporteur on the human rights obligations related to environmentally sound management and disposal of hazardous substances and waste, Calin Georgescu: Human Rights and Extractive Industries*, July 2, 2012, UN Doc. A/HRC/21/48.

[26] See M. Watts, T. Lee, and H. Aidy, "Pesticides and Agroecology in the Occupied West Bank: Conclusions from a Joint APN–PANAP Mission in Palestine," PAN Asia Pacific and Arab Group for the Protection of Nature, Penang, May 2016; UN Human Rights Council, *Human rights situation in Palestine and other occupied Arab territories*, UN Doc. A/HRC/31/L.39; H. Salah, "Gaza Farmers Denounce Israel Pesticide Use along Border," Mar. 20, 2018, www.al-monitor.com/pulse/originals/2018/03/israel-fights-agriculture-near-gaza-border-through-pesticide.html.

[27] UNEP, "Background Report: Towards a Pollution-free Planet," Nairobi, Kenya, Sept. 2017 at 28 citing S. Strempel, M. Scheringer, C. A. Ng, and K. Hungerbuhler, "Screening for PBT Chemicals among the 'Existing' and 'New' Chemicals of the EU" (2012) 46 *Environmental Science and Technology* 5680.

[28] UNEP, "The Global Chemicals Outlook: Synthesis Report for Decision-Makers," UNEP and WHO, 2012 at 20.

[29] P. J. Landrigan et al. "The Lancet Commission on Pollution and Health, Executive Summary" (2018) 391 *Lancet* 462 at 462.

[30] Regulation (EC) No. 1907/2006 of the European Parliament and of the Council of 18 December 2006 concerning the Registration, Evaluation, Authorisation and Restriction of Chemicals (REACH) (2006) *Official Journal of the European Union* L 396 at Art. 5. The Regulation requires industry to provide safety information on substances prior to placing them on the market.

[31] European Commission, "Commission Staff Working Document, Accompanying the Document: Communication from the Commission to the European Parliament, the Council and the European Economic and Social Committee, Commission General Report on the operation of REACH and review of certain elements, Conclusions and Actions," Brussels, May 3, 2018, p. 31.

the effects of this dependency have been disastrous for the ecosystem and for human health, particularly in developing countries. Global trade flows of hazardous chemicals and waste present patterns of toxic colonialism[32] and a multitude of other environmental justice concerns linked to the unequal burden of toxic chemicals on children,[33] women,[34] and informal workers.[35] In fact, environmental pollution from chemicals and waste is recognized as one of the most prominent causes of illness and death in developing countries, in particular, "rapidly developing and industrializing lower-middle-income countries."[36] This is especially alarming considering that chemicals production for the global market is expected to continue surging in the developing world.

In the last decades, global chemicals manufacturing has risen considerably in non-OECD countries (in particular, BRIICS)[37] and declined in the OECD region, due to the combined factors of cost-efficiency, less stringent chemicals regulatory frameworks, expanding consumer markets, and increasingly globalized corporate structures (e.g. joint ventures and mergers) that have allowed emerging economies to assume a greater role in global manufacturing.[38] By 2050, BRIICS are expected to dominate the world chemicals industry.[39] Currently, 75 percent[40] of chemicals production within BRIICS takes place in China, the world's largest chemicals producer.[41]

This geographical shift in global chemicals production from developed to developing countries is cause for concern due to the large-scale human health and environmental deterioration it is associated with. In China, growth of the chemical industries has led to the emergence of an estimated 500[42] "cancer villages" – communities where cancer rates are extraordinarily high due to their proximity to chemicals-producing factories. Specific industrial sectors responsible include "first and foremost . . . chemical industries, and secondly . . . paper factories, resource extraction and processing, downstream pollution (particularly from industry and mining), and heavy metals (caused by the above forms of pollution)."[43] While formally acknowledging the problem in 2013,[44] governmental authorities denied the existence of cancer villages for over a

---

[32] Pellow, *Resisting Global Toxics*, note 2, p. 11; J. Puckett, S. Westervelt, R. Gutierrez, and Y. Takamiya, "The Digital Dump: Exporting Re-use and Abuse to Africa," Basel Action Network, Seattle, Oct. 24, 2005.

[33] HRC (2016), note 25.

[34] International POPs Elimination Network, "IPEN a Toxics-Free Future: A Focus on Women and Chemicals," July–Dec. 2017, https://mailchi.mp/ea159f73f438/ipen-global-newsletter-women-and-chemicals-july-december-2017; OHCHR, "Vietnam: UN Experts Concerned by Threats against Factory Workers and Labour Activists," Mar. 20, 2018, www.ohchr.org/EN/NewsEvents/Pages/DisplayNews.aspx?NewsID=22852&LangID=E.

[35] S. A. Khan, "Struggles and Actions for Legal Space in the Urban World: The Case of Informal Economy E-waste Workers" (2018) 33 *Canadian Journal of Law and Society, Special Issue on Transnational Labour Law* 115.

[36] Landrigan, note 29, p. 462.

[37] Brazil, Russia, India, Indonesia, China, South Africa.

[38] *Environmental Outlook to 2050: The Consequences of Inaction* (OECD, 2012) at p. 310.

[39] Ibid., at p. 312.

[40] Ibid.

[41] European Chemical Industry Council (CEFIC), "Facts and Figures of the European Chemical Industry," 2017.

[42] J. Huang, J. Macbeath, and Q. Tian, "Environmental Pollution, Cancer Villages and the State's Response", presented at the Annual Meeting of the American Association for Chines Studies, Arlington, VA, Oct. 10–12, 2014.

[43] A. Lora-Wainwright, *Resigned Activism: Living with Pollution in Rural China* (Cambridge, MA: MIT Press, 2017), p. 38.

[44] Ministry of Environmental Protection of the People's Republic of China, "Guard against and Control Risks Presented by Chemicals to the Environment During the 12th Five-Year Plan (2011–2015)," in A. Lora-Wainwright, *Resigned Activism: Living with Pollution in Rural China* (Cambridge, MA: MIT Press, 2017), pp. 1–36.

decade and actively suppressed dissemination of scientific information on chemical pollution, going so far as to declare soil samples a "national secret."[45]

It is important to note that cancer villages linked to industrialization are not exclusive to China, but also affect other countries that manufacture chemicals and chemically based products for worldwide consumption. Cancer villages in India[46] and Vietnam,[47] along with multiple other sites of manufacturing (such as globally spread clusters of electronics assembly and disassembly)[48] are concrete manifestations of how the contemporary international division of labor along global commodity chains leaves the heaviest toxic burdens of global consumption on poor workers and communities in developing nations.

16.2.2 *Chemicals and Waste on the Global Governance Agenda*

At the international level, the environmental justice dimension of the global chemicals and waste trade has gained attention through the advocacy and investigative work of international environmental NGOs and UN human rights mechanisms.[49] Moreover, Agenda 2030 has swept in an unprecedented opportunity for the mainstreaming and integration of sound chemicals and waste management into the global sustainable development agenda. All Sustainable Development Goals (SDGs) are linked in one or several dimensions to the issue of chemicals and waste management.[50] For example, at the inaugural UN Ocean Conference to support implementation of SDG 14: Life Below Water, governments recognized the urgent need to "halt and reverse"[51] the cycle of decline that has been cast upon the oceans through, inter alia, the diffusion of hazardous substances, plastics, microplastics, and waste discharges. The resolution that was adopted on this occasion explicitly brings to the sustainable development forefront the regulation of chemicals and waste,[52] an area of international environmental law that generally receives minimal political attention at all levels of governance.

As for discussions under multilateral environmental agreements (MEAs), the 2017 joint Conference of the Parties (COP) of the BRS treaties highlighted the important human rights implications of global chemicals use. At the meeting venue, civil society participants and

---

[45] Huang, note 42, p. 6.

[46] High cancer rates affect villages in India's cotton belt of Punjab where pesticides are excessively used. See S. Mittal, G. Kaur, and G. S. Vishwakarma, "Effects of Environmental Pesticides on the Health of Rural Communities in the Malwa Region of Punjab, India: A Review" (2014) 20 *Human and Ecological Risk Assessment* 366–387.

[47] At least thirty-seven cancer villages have been identified by Vietnamese environmental protection authorities. See S. Ortmann, *Environmental Governance in Vietnam: Institutional Reforms and Failures* (London: Palgrave Macmillan, 2017); T. Thuy, "Cancer Deaths in the 'Cancer Villages' around Ho Chi Minh City," July 29, 2015, www.asianews.it/news-en/Countless-deaths-in-the-cancer-villages-around-Ho-Chi-Minh-City-34902.html.

[48] A. Waterson and S. Chang, "Environmental Justice and Labour Rights," in T. Smith, D. Sonnenfeld, and D. Pellow (eds.), *Challenging the Chip: Labor Rights and Environmental Justice in the Global Electronics Industry* (Philadelphia: Temple University Press, 2006), p. 107; BBC News, "Samsung Pledges Compensation for Cancer Sufferers," May 14, 2014, www.bbc.com/news/technology-27407493.

[49] In particular, the Basel Action Network and the International POPs Elimination Network (accredited as observers to the Basel Convention) and the UN Special Rapporteurship on the implications for human rights of the environmentally sound management and disposal of hazardous substances and wastes.

[50] For a detailed discussion of SDGs in relation to chemicals and waste, see T. Honkonen and S. A. Khan, *Chemicals and Waste Governance beyond 2020: Exploring Pathways for a Coherent Global Regime* (Copenhagen: Nordic Council of Ministers, 2017), p. 30.

[51] UNGA, Ocean Conference, Resolution Adopted by the General Assembly on 6 July 2017: Our Ocean, Our Future: Call to Action, July 14, 2017, UN Doc. A/RES/71/312 at para. 5.

[52] Ibid., Art. 13(g)(h)(i).

asbestos survivors held a demonstration against global trade in asbestos, with the Global Asbestos Alliance Action presenting a petition in this regard to the president of the Rotterdam COP.[53] During plenary discussions on chrysotile asbestos, the World Health Organization underlined the irrefutable carcinogenicity of the substance, while the Rotterdam Chrysotile Alliance and global union IndustriALL stressed how asbestos threatens fundamental labor rights.[54] In a high-level segment, the UN Deputy High Commissioner for Human Rights emphasized the linkage between exposure to toxics and poverty, and the protective role of the state.[55]

These global discourses and the scientific evidence they are based on clearly demonstrate the urgent need for transformational change in the way chemicals are produced, used, and disposed of. The experience of chemical pollution and human suffering from unsustainable chemical production is historical, pervasive, and ongoing, knowing no political or legal boundaries. Given the globalized life of chemical products and waste, as well as the long-range transport of chemical pollution through air, water, and migratory wildlife, unilateral regulatory action is not sufficient to protect citizens from chemical pollution in any state; international law has a critical role to play in forging a detoxified future. At the same time, there is a need to reconceptualize traditional approaches to international chemicals and waste law.

The existing chemicals and waste treaties were not originally formulated from the perspective of human rights, or with the aim of protecting the integrity of the natural ecosystem. While their common overarching objective of human health protection evokes the sense that these MEAs are intended to strengthen government obligations toward the protection of human rights threatened by global flows of hazardous substances, their legal and institutional frameworks fail to provide inclusive deliberative or rule-making spaces. Organizations representing vulnerable groups that suffer the most severe burdens of global chemical pollution remain "observers" in what are essentially state-driven decision-making processes. In treating the human rights and ecological impacts of toxic substances as indeterminate concerns and aiming instead to impose the lowest possible barriers on the international chemicals and waste trade, these MEAs have neglected the social dimension of sustainable development to the detriment of the health of future generations and the integrity of the planetary ecosystem. Current impasses in controlling certain highly hazardous substances under this cluster of treaties suggest that strengthening their connection to human rights is imperative.

16.3 GLOBAL AGREEMENTS ON CHEMICALS AND WASTE

An extensive body of international law on chemicals and waste has developed since the problem of chemical pollution was identified as a global concern at the 1972 UN Conference on the Human Environment.[56] However, a juxtaposition of the experiences of early chemical production in the developed world and current chemicals manufacturing in the developing world casts doubt on the advances we have made in protecting human health from one period of chemical industrialization to another. An overview of the current international regulatory framework for

[53] IISD, "2017 Meetings of the Conference of the Parties to the Basel, Rotterdam and Stockholm Conventions," May 2, 2017, http://enb.iisd.org/chemical/cops/2017/2may.html.

[54] J. Allan J. Templeton, J. Jones, T. Kantai, and Y. Sun, "Summary of the Meetings of the Conference of the Parties to the Basel, Rotterdam and Stockholm Conventions April 24–May 5, 2017," IISD Reporting Services, Earth Negotiations Bulletin, A Reporting Service for Environment and Development Negotiations, New York, May 8, 2017, p. 27.

[55] Ibid., p. 8.

[56] A. Daniel, "Canadian Contributions to International Law on Chemicals and Wastes: The Stockholm Convention as a Model," Centre for International Governance Innovation, Waterloo, ON, 2018.

hazardous chemicals and waste shows that existing agreements ignore systemic injustices of the globalized chemicals and waste economy, even though the fundamental purpose of this body of international law is to protect human health from international movements of toxics in global trade.

The BRS treaties have played a facilitative role in the rise of the chemical world. Their coverage is extremely narrow in scope and their controls are sporadic, limited to specific points of the chemical or hazardous waste life cycle. We have yet to adopt international regulatory frameworks that encapsulate the entire life cycle of hazardous substances in global use and that define, clearly, stakeholder responsibilities at every life-cycle phase.[57] The only global treaty that adopts a life-cycle approach is the Minamata Convention[58] which controls virtually all anthropogenic releases of mercury. While it is certainly the most comprehensive MEA in this regard, it applies exclusively to *one* toxic substance. Considering there are tens of thousands of chemicals on the global market, adopting a substance-by-substance treaty approach would be a profoundly ineffective way to comprehensively address all sources of global chemical pollution.

In addition to the BRS treaties, a voluntary global policy framework for chemicals and waste management known as the Strategic Approach to Chemicals and Waste Management (SAICM) was adopted in 2006. SAICM operationalizes commitments made by the global community with regard to the worldwide chemicals and waste sector at the 2002 World Summit on Sustainable Development held in Johannesburg. Specifically, the key commitment is "to achieve, by 2020, that chemicals are used and produced in ways that lead to the minimization of significant adverse effects on human health and the environment."[59] SAICM provides practical guidance to governments, chemical manufacturers, and other relevant stakeholders on the legal and non-legal measures required to reach the Johannesburg 2020 goal.[60]

Since the adoption of SAICM and of the BRS treaties before it, global cooperation and knowledge generation on chemicals and waste management have significantly evolved.[61] At the same time, it is widely acknowledged that the pace of progress toward the Johannesburg 2020 goal has been inadequate, and the problems linked to chemical pollution have only intensified with the rising production of chemicals and wastes.[62] Part of the problem is that neither the existing international legal agreements, nor the overarching global policy framework allow for a complete vision of the chemical life cycle, in which substances travel from mine to manufacturer, into chemical mixtures and product components, and then to waste or recyclable material before simply degrading or persisting in the environment.

16.3.1 *Basel Convention (1989)*

The Basel Convention was adopted as a response to toxic trading patterns that emerged in the 1970s whereby developed countries were found to be exporting hazardous wastes to developing countries.

---

[57] In the context of technological products and e-waste, see S. A. Khan, "E-products, E-waste and the Basel Convention: Regulatory Challenges and Impossibilities of International Environmental Law" (2016) 25 *Review of European, Comparative & International Environmental Law* 248.

[58] United Nations, *Minamata Convention on Mercury*, 10 Oct. 10, 2013, UN Doc. CN.560.2014.TREATIES-XXVII.17.

[59] UN, *Report of the World Summit on Sustainable Development*, Sept. 4, 2002, UN Doc. A/CONF.199/20 at para. 23.

[60] UNEP, "Strategic Approach to International Chemicals Management: SAICM Texts and Resolutions of the International Conference on Chemicals Management," UNEP, Geneva, 2006.

[61] See Honkonen and Khan, note 50.

[62] UNEP, *The Global Chemicals Outlook* (Geneva: UNEP, 2012).

The Convention restricts trade in wastes categorized as "hazardous waste" under the Convention itself or under Basel parties' national legal definitions for hazardous wastes.[63] It prohibits hazardous waste exports for the purpose of disposal, from developed to developing countries.[64] While an amendment[65] to the Convention that would prohibit transfers of hazardous waste intended for recycling or recovery operations from developed to developing countries has yet to enter into force at the international level, it has been implemented by some parties at regional and national levels.

The Basel Convention does not regulate non-waste chemicals or any other type of "product," nor do its controls apply to all transboundary movements of wastes. The strict mechanism it establishes (the procedure of prior informed consent (PIC)), is applicable only to transboundary movements of hazardous wastes. The PIC is essentially a human health and environmental protection measure based on the principles of prevention and transparency. Under this system, parties are prohibited from exporting hazardous wastes unless the state of import has consented to the shipment beforehand, in writing.[66]

Fluctuating definitions of hazardous waste across borders have made it difficult to apply the Basel PIC procedure to used electronic equipment and other used and end-of-life goods.[67] Various used goods are exported between countries as regular commodities rather than waste, even though they may pose environmental and human health hazards and even contain waste components. Lack of consensus between Basel parties over the distinction between wastes and non-wastes is regarded as a "particular problem in relation to cross-border transports of used substances or objects intended for re-use."[68] Terms such as hazardous waste, nonhazardous waste, goods, products, used goods, reuse, direct reuse, recycling, refurbishment, recovery, and disposal are interpreted differently by individual Basel parties, resulting in a lack of legal clarity over critical definitional concepts used to determine whether the PIC procedure applies to a specific shipment.[69]

In essence, there remain significant definitional loopholes regarding the distinction between wastes and non-wastes, as well as the distinction between hazardous wastes and nonhazardous wastes, which create the possibility for a wide range of hazardous shipments to evade the Convention's stringent controls.[70] Nevertheless, remarkable progress was made at the 2019 COP, at which Basel parties amended the Convention by introducing a legally binding framework to regulate and enhance transparency in the global trading of certain plastic waste streams. Widely hailed as a monumental success, the extension of the Basel Convention to plastic waste demonstrates its contemporary relevance and potential to play a leading, catalytic role in responding to emerging global environmental health issues.

16.3.2 *Rotterdam Convention* (1999)

The Rotterdam Convention is narrower in scope than the Basel Convention. Currently, its regulatory controls (a legally binding PIC procedure and an information exchange mechanism)

---

[63] The Convention's definition of "hazardous waste" extends to those wastes listed in Annexes I and VIII of the Convention, unless they do not exhibit one of the characteristics listed in Annex III. Basel Convention, note 4, Art. 1(a).

[64] Ibid., Art. 4(A).

[65] UNEP, *Decision III/1 Amendment to the Basel Convention*, Nov. 28, 1995, UNEP/CHW.3/35.

[66] Basel Convention, note 4, Art. 4.1(c).

[67] For a discussion of the Convention's limitations in controlling e-waste, see Khan, note 57.

[68] Secretariat of the Basel Convention, "Basel Convention: Glossary of Terms," UNEP, Dec. 2017, p. 7.

[69] See UNEP, Basel Convention, Study on used and End-of-Life Goods, Feb. 1, 2013, UN Doc. UNEP/CHW.11/INF/3.

[70] Khan, note 57.

apply to only fifty-two hazardous chemicals in international trade. The Convention regulates hazardous chemicals and pesticides that have been banned or severely restricted for use due to environmental or human health considerations in at least two of the seven PIC regions established under the Convention, and have subsequently been listed under Annex III of the Convention by the COP, following a recommendation in this regard by the Chemical Review Committee ((CRC) a subsidiary body of the COP). Once a chemical has been listed in Annex III, all Rotterdam parties have an obligation to notify other parties whether they wish to continue receiving future imports of the hazardous chemical in question.

Listing of a chemical to Annex III requires a recommendation by the CRC *and* the subsequent consensus of all parties to the Convention. As such, the opposition of even one party can block the listing of an almost universally banned or restricted hazardous chemical. This is precisely the case with chrysotile asbestos, a carcinogenic substance banned or restricted in an overwhelming number of countries and recommended for listing by the CRC, but blocked at the last COP due to requests for more scientific data by Zimbabwe, India, Kyrgyzstan, and Belarus, and opposition by Kazakhstan and Syria.[71] Paraquat dichloride is another substance that has been recommended for listing by the CRC, but continued opposition by Indonesia, Guatemala, India, and Chile has stalled progress on the issue. At the 2019 COP, Rotterdam parties were unable to reach consensus on the listing of five out of the seven chemicals recommended for listing by the CRC. What is perhaps most striking about certain parties' continued opposition to Annex III's listing of these substances is that listing under Annex III does not result in an export ban or change the legality of trade of the chemical in question; it simply triggers the PIC procedure and ensures the regular exchange of information between parties on the substance.

16.3.3 *Stockholm Convention (2001)*

The Stockholm Convention aims to protect human and environmental health from pesticides and industrial chemicals that are persistent organic pollutants (POPs).[72]

Parties are required to either prohibit, eliminate, or restrict the production, use, import, and export of a number of intentionally and unintentionally released POPs that are listed in Annexes A, B, or C to the Convention. Stockpiles of POPs and POPs-contaminated wastes must be managed in an environmentally sound manner. The Convention initially covered twelve POPs, and since then an additional eighteen POPs have been listed for control. Any party can propose a new chemical for listing, which is then reviewed by the POPs Review Committee, a subsidiary body of the COP. Following a rigorous and comprehensive assessment of each new chemical proposed, the POPRC makes a recommendation and listing of the chemical is put to vote at the COP. The limitations of the Stockholm Convention lie in the wide scope of exemptions that are sometimes attached to a listing, which often veer away from POPRC recommendations and can render the listing futile. For instance, the listing of decaBDE was attached to exemptions under which it may be used for another twenty years in certain products and up to 2100 in aircraft.[73] Similarly, the listing of short-chained chlorinated paraffins (SCCPs) was attached to several exemptions, none of which were recommended by the POPRC.[74]

---

[71] Allan et al., note 54, p. 27.
[72] Stockholm Convention, note 4, Preamble.
[73] See J. DiGangi, "Stockholm Convention Problem is in the Details, NGO Says," July/Aug. 2017, https://chemicalwatch.com/57822/stockholm-convention-problem-is-in-the-details-ngo-says; IPEN, "Loopholes for DecaBDE and SCCPs Undercut Treaty Additions," May 7, 2017, www.ipen.org/news/press-release-loopholes-decabde-and-sccps-undercut-treaty-additions.
[74] Ibid.

16.4 PHILOSOPHIES OF TECHNOLOGY IN THE GLOBAL GOVERNANCE
OF CHEMICALS AND WASTE

Collectively, the BRS Conventions currently cover transboundary movements of hazardous wastes, fifty-two hazardous chemicals and pesticides in international trade, and twenty POPs. If we examine closely the philosophy of technology that underlies our chemicals and waste MEAs, we see that while the existing agreements seek to protect human health and the environment from toxic hazards, their procedural decision-making elements ultimately support a liberalized international trade in hazardous chemicals and waste. Minimization of the social and environmental effects of chemical pollution may provide the overarching objectives for international chemicals and waste law, yet the latter's mechanisms have been structured to minimize interventions on global transfers of hazardous chemicals. None of the existing MEAs can be said to include the human rights impacts of the global production and consumption of hazardous substances among their primary concerns. In each of these spheres of global negotiation, science does not appear to be translating into effective decision-making for the protection of the environment and human rights. Governmental decisions to ban, phase out, or restrict use or trade in hazardous chemicals and waste are rarely, if ever, based on impact assessments on children's, women's, or workers' rights. Rather, as evidenced by the ongoing trade and use of chrysotile asbestos, the economic interests of industry stakeholders take precedence over human rights and ecosystem health concerns.

16.4.1 *Reasserting the Social Pillar of Sustainable Development: Centralizing Human Rights in International Chemicals and Waste Law*

How could we reimagine the existing international chemicals and waste regime so as to centralize human rights? At the very least, decision-making rules and compliance mechanisms under the BRS treaties cannot remain exclusively state driven. One transformative way to think about how to make international law more inclusive, is to consider how to break out of the deadlock of "observer status" of non-state entities and integrate models of permanent participation[75] or transboundary representation of vulnerable groups in negotiating bodies, as well as in informal and intersessional working groups established by the COPs.

Critical problems with the current voting systems of the Stockholm and Rotterdam Conventions must also be addressed. The Stockholm COP has not yet been able to establish mechanisms and procedures for noncompliance due to the requirement of consensus decision-making under the Convention, and continued opposition to existing proposals by a small number of parties.[76] In the case of the Rotterdam Convention, after several years of failing to reach consensus, parties finally voted to establish a compliance committee at the 2019 COP, under a newly adopted Annex VII to the Convention. While the compliance mechanism is optional, party-driven, and nonbinding, its adoption was a strenuous and long-awaited

---

[75] The concept of permanent participation is drawn from the Arctic Council, an intergovernmental forum that has centralized the participation of Arctic Indigenous peoples, by granting six Arctic Indigenous groups active participation and full consultation rights in all aspects of the Council's work. Permanent participants do not have voting power, but they have been described as holding a "de facto power of veto," and exercising an extraordinary influence in the Arctic Council, due to the AC's consensus decision-making approach. See T. Koivurova and L. Heinämäki, "The Participation of Indigenous Peoples in International Norm-making in the Arctic" (2006) 42 *Polar Record* 101.

[76] See Daniel, note 56.

development. It is imperative to note that the critical enabling element that allowed parties to advance on stalled compliance negotiations was the possibility (outlined in Article 21(3) of the Convention) to hold a vote when efforts to reach consensus regarding the adoption or amendment of an Annex have failed. Regrettably, voting is not a last resort option with respect to amendments to Annex III chemicals listings, as it is for other Annexes. Evidently, consensus decision-making relating to chemicals listing creates barriers to the protection of environmental human rights, as seen with the inability of Rotterdam parties to control chrysotile asbestos under the Convention.

Apart from these instrumental changes to the deliberation and decision-making structures of the BRS treaties, connection between the latter and human rights could further be strengthened by establishing complaint mechanisms accessible to civil society actors and adopting guidelines for parties on how to address children's rights, women's rights, and fundamental labor rights in chemicals impact assessments and in regulatory decisions regarding the prohibition or restriction of hazardous substances. The nexus of human rights and chemicals and waste governance is well established, having already been a focal point of concern of the UN OHCHR since the establishment of the Special Rapporteurship on the human rights implications of hazardous substances and wastes in 1995.[77] The recent program of work of the current Special Rapporteur on children's rights, business and human rights in the chemicals industry, and on workers' rights and toxic chemical exposures, provide valuable insight on the multiple ways human rights are connected to and directly impacted by decision-making under the BRS treaties. The closer collaboration that is emerging between the BRS regime and the Special Rapporteurship[78] will certainly contribute to bringing human rights to the forefront of international chemicals and waste law.

One of the most profound impediments to achieving human health and environmental protection goals outlined in the BRS Conventions and SAICM is how we have problematized chemical pollution in the language of international law, that is, with a regulatory focus on "hazardous chemicals" and "hazardous waste," consequently dismissing a broad range of hazardous substances and materials in their product, or "non-hazardous waste" phases. This categorization has made it impossible to comprehensively map chemicals throughout their life-cycle and global trajectories. For example, even though certain streams of plastic waste are now regulated under the Basel Convention, there is an overwhelming lack of transparency on hazardous chemical substances released in the manufacturing of plastics, and on the identity and quantity of hazardous chemical substances contained in plastic products, whether they are intentionally added (such as plasticizers and solvents) or non-intentionally added (such as impurities and by-products).[79]

Our inability to see transparently through our globalized commodity chains gravely limits our capacity to ensure the protection of human and ecosystem health from toxic commercial

---

[77] OHCHR, "Special Rapporteur on the Implications for Human Rights of the Environmentally Sound Management and Disposal of Hazardous Substances and Wastes," www.ohchr.org/EN/Issues/Environment/ ToxicWastes/Pages/SRToxicWastesIndex.aspx.

[78] See for instance, M. A. Taoufiq-Cailliau and M. Simon, Secretariat of the Basel, Rotterdam, and Stockholm Conventions, "The Rights of Children, the Environment and the Basel, Rotterdam and Stockholm (BRS) Conventions on Hazardous Chemicals and Wastes," SBRS, UNEP, June 1, 2016.

[79] D. Azoulay, P. Villa, Y. Arellano, et al., "Plastic and Health : The Hidden Costs of a Plastic Planet," Centre for International Environmental Law, Earthworks, Global Alliance for Incinerator Alternatives, Healthy Babies Bright Futures, IPEN, Texas Environmental Justice Advocacy Services, UPSTREAM, #breakfreefromplastic, Feb. 2019; K. J. Groh, T. Backhaus, B. Carney-Almroth, et al., "Overview of Known Plastic Packaging-Associated Chemicals and Their Hazards" (2019) 651 *Science of the Total Environment* 3253.

substances and waste. The legal visibility that is required to effectively protect our global communities and common resources from the toxic hazards of chemicals and waste must cut across entire global chains of production, consumption, and reproduction. Most importantly, this legal visibility must incorporate the legal perspectives and voices of those stakeholders that suffer the deepest burdens of chemical pollution, and yet are consistently marginalized in global and local decision-making over chemicals and waste: workers (informal and formal), Indigenous peoples, women, and children.

In this regard, international chemicals and waste law could extend its lens toward mapping responsibility and accountability linkages along chemicals-based global value chains by seeking clarification on the regulation of, and relationships between, relevant actors along these chains. This includes upstream chemicals designers and manufacturers, downstream industries, workers, distributors, retailers, consumers, as well as recycling and waste collection stakeholders. Framing chemical pollution problems from this angle would resolve the life-cycle-blind approach of the existing international legal regime and introduce the possibility to link regulatory efforts more closely to the real way in which chemical pollutants are socially produced, used, disposed, and environmentally dispersed. The life-cycle approach highlights the connected nature of globally spread environmental justice struggles that may otherwise appear distinct and unrelated. For example, the life cycle of plastic involves environmental justice struggles at the fossil fuel extraction, refining, and production phases, with local communities, workers, and ecosystems exposed to substantial air and water pollution.[80] These struggles multiply at the consumption phase, with the public lacking access to information on health hazards of chemicals commonly contained in plastic products in global commercial circulation. They subsequently extend to the end-of-life phase, at which point the hazards of globally consumed plastics are assumed by vulnerable populations and recycling workers in low-income countries that are prime destinations for the plastic waste trade. A final burden is cast upon the world's marine ecosystems which have become global plastic pollutant sinks in which the toxic materials break down over hundreds of years.

On a broader level, the international community needs to reconsider the fragmented methodology of conventional international lawmaking as an effective approach to the protection of human and ecosystem health from hazardous substances in global trade. In this regard, recent initiatives under the UN toward a "Global Pact for the Environment," specifically, the establishment of an ad hoc working group to "address gaps in international environmental law and environment-related instruments"[81] is expected to provide some clarity on how to surpass the limitations of international environmental legal fragmentation. The UN Special Rapporteur on Human Rights and Toxics has already issued practical guidelines that bring to the forefront the human rights dimension of chemicals and waste management, in clearly delineating the duties of states to protect, and responsibilities of businesses to respect, human rights in the context of toxic substances and pollution.[82] These guidelines draw on and build upon the UN Guiding Principles on Business and Human Rights, with both instruments elucidating the imperative role of private sector actors in the realization of human rights. Other ongoing UN initiatives that may provide concomitant pathways to address the injustice of chemical and waste globalization include efforts to draft a legally binding instrument on transnational corporations with respect to

---

[80] For a comprehensive discussion of the global health and environmental impacts of the plastic life cycle, see Azoulay et al., note 79.

[81] UNGA, *Towards a Global Pact for the Environment*, May 7, 2018, UN Doc. A/72/L.51.

[82] UN Special Rapporteur, *Report of the Special Rapporteur on the implications for human rights of the environmentally sound management and disposal of hazardous substances and wastes*, July 20, 2017, UN Doc. A/HRC/36/41.

human rights[83] and the International Law Commission's work relating to the progressive development and codification of international law on the protection of the atmosphere.[84]

16.5 CONCLUSION

Thoughtlessness toward the end-of-life of chemical products pervades the global manufacturing economy. The ubiquity of e-waste pollution, abundant toxic debris in oceans, and chemically polluted air in almost all regions of the world are global trends signaling to us that our current systems of chemical production and consumption are rapidly and irreversibly changing the ecosystem and human health; we are deep in the language of tipping points.[85] Evidently, states are failing at their obligation to prevent the exposure of children and workers to toxic chemicals. In many countries, basic legislative protections are missing or unenforced, further reinforcing a "silent pandemic of disability and disease."[86]

Chemical pollution on the rise forces us to acknowledge that we have missed the ambitious Johannesburg deadline. The success of our efforts toward soundly managing chemicals and waste beyond 2020 will depend largely on how we raise global awareness of the human rights and ecological impacts of chemicals-based value chains, and of the transboundary causes and consequences of chemical pollution. Above all, there is a need to incite governments and society to care about chemicals from the molecular to global level, and to demand that responsibility and accountability for toxic substances be assumed across all globalized production systems and recycling chains, across all borders. A common-sense step that can be taken immediately is for countries that have banned the use of certain chemicals in their own jurisdictions to concomitantly prohibit within their jurisdictions the production of those chemicals for export.

Given the continuous worsening of chemical pollution worldwide, a deeper interrogation of the global legal regime for chemicals and waste management, encompassing an assessment of its past and prospects for its future is urgently required. In particular, understanding global chemicals regulation from an environmental justice perspective, meaning, from the point of view of bridging ideas of law together with an understanding of the latter's concrete impacts on space, equity, and environmental and human health, is critical in order to bring an end to the disproportionate impacts of toxic chemical exposures experienced by vulnerable populations and fragile ecosystems.

---

[83] UNGA, *Elaboration of an international legally binding instrument on transnational corporations and other business enterprises with respect to human rights*, July 14, 2014, UN Doc. A/HRC/RES/26/9. See also Chairmanship of the OEIGWG established by HRC Res. A/HRC/RES/26/9, *Elements for the draft legally binding instrument on transnational corporations and other business enterprises with respect to human rights*, Sept. 29, 2017.

[84] International Law Commission, "Summaries of the Work of the International Law Commission," Nov. 20, 2018, http://legal.un.org/ilc/summaries/8_8.shtml

[85] OECD, note 36, p. 28: "There is compelling scientific evidence that natural systems have 'tipping points' or biophysical boundaries beyond which rapid and damaging change becomes irreversible."

[86] UNHRC (2016), note 25, p. 3.

17

China's Cancer Villages

Quoc Nguyen, Linda Tsang, and Tseming Yang[*]

17.1 INTRODUCTION

For some decades now, China's environmental problems have been well known. Ranging from headline-grabbing instances of life-threatening air pollution in the country's major cities, to horrendous industrial accidents that claim shocking numbers of lives, to water pollution that make the rivers run black, the world has come to know China's pollution problems as systemic and serious in nature. For decades, the government has taken the position that pollution was an unavoidable by-product of the nation's need to industrialize and develop economically. Nevertheless, concern about pollution has now become so widespread among ordinary citizens that an investigative documentary on China's air pollution issues, "Under the Dome,"[1] garnered tens of millions of views on YouTube before the government shut it down.[2] Across China, public protests and activism related to environmental issues are now commonplace.

Yet, pollution burdens have not been evenly distributed across the country. As in many places over the world, the marginalized and the poor tend to suffer more from the adverse side effects of economic development than others. The most palpable illustrations of these inequities are China's cancer villages. So-called because they constitute cancer clusters that are mainly found in the rural areas, the cancer villages show that even China, with its socialist past and rhetoric of egalitarianism, has not been immune from environmental inequity and injustice. Among the best known of these are the Wengyuan County Cancer Villages in Guangdong Province.

[*] The authors wish to thank Eric Hagle, Shuyang Shawn Chou, Lei Kang, and Monshuan Phoebe Wu for their valuable research assistance. The research for this chapter was generously supported by the Lingnan Foundation and by Santa Clara University Law School.

[1] For a full-length version of the documentary with English subtitles, see www.youtube.com/watch?v=V5bHb3ljjbc.
[2] S. Mufson, "This Documentary Went Viral in China. Then It Was Censored. It Won't Be Forgotten," Mar. 16, 2015, www.washingtonpost.com/news/energy-environment/wp/2015/03/16/this-documentary-went-viral-in-china-then-it-was-censored-it-wont-be-forgotten/?noredirect=on&utm_term=.8b598c8f93f8.

17.2 THE STORY OF THE WENGYUAN COUNTY CANCER VILLAGES

Nestled on the banks of the Hengshi River sits Liangqiao Village, a sleepy little hamlet of just a few hundred people in Guangdong's rural countryside. We arrive here in December 2006 after a two- and half-hour van-ride from the City of Guangzhou, China's southern manufacturing hub. Our driver negotiated not only heavy truck traffic on country roads but also a martial arts movie playing on his portable DVD player to get us to a community of plain single-story brick dwellings, widely spaced along the state road running through the village, and an empty Sinopec gas station. A festive red banner draped across an overhead road sign greets us with a special welcome, though its characters just urge safe driving.

A short walk from the gas station, a small side road crosses the river. From the bridge, rust-orange-colored mud covering the riverbed and banks is visible. It stretches as far as the eyes can see, both upstream and downstream. Some forty years ago, the Hengshi River was healthy and clear, depositing fertile soil as it wound through villages like Shangba and Liangqiao. Now, it is known as the "dead river," without a trace of any fish and shrimp.[3] It is severely polluted with heavy metals and acid drainage from the operations of the Dabaoshan Mining Company up toward the top of the Dabao mountain (or "Dabaoshan" in Chinese) and other smaller private mining operations, many illegal, that have sprung up in the area.

Later, two village leaders, including the head of the local communist party committee, tell us that their community used to prosper, and that fish were abundant for centuries. Springs from the mountain fed the Hengshi, which was used to irrigate the village's crops and replenish the local fishponds. However, everything changed once valuable mineral deposits were discovered on Dabao Mountain. The state-owned Dabaoshan Mining Co. began to engage in open surface mining for the rich mineral deposits. As the mountain was denuded of vegetation and cover and mining debris began to accumulate, run-off laden with eroded soil and heavy metals leached from the overburden began to flow into the Hengshi River.

Then the really bad things started to happen. First, the fish in the ponds by the river died. Soon thereafter, the harvests began to diminish. Finally, the people became sick from cancer. Now, the farmland by the riverbanks produces little in crops. The fishponds have been abandoned because nothing survives in the water.

To support their accounts of rampant cancer deaths, the village leaders show us a brown paper-covered notebook that is the village's "death log." It shows the causes of deaths over the last two decades, many listed as some form of cancer. Over the years, the high rate of cancer deaths in Liangqiao Village, nearby Shangba Village and several other surrounding communities in Wengyuan County has sparked the interest of researcher and the media and has drawn attention to similar cancer clusters across China. With the highest number of cancer deaths among the five villages, Shangba was dubbed the "Village of Death" by a CCTV [China Central Television] program in 2005. As a group, Liangqiao, Shangba and the other three have come to be known less prosaically as the Wengyuan County "Cancer Villages."[4]

* * * * *

Originating in the springs of the Dabao Mountain in Shaoguan City, Wengyuan County, is the Hengshi River, a third-order tributary of the Beijiang River, which eventually empties into Guangdong Province's prosperous Pearl River Delta.[5] Traveling downstream, one encounters

---

[3] Y. Chuanmin and F. Qiahua, "A Village of Death and Its Hopes for the Future" (2006) 1 *China Rights Forum* 25.

[4] D. Griffiths, "Chinese Village with Deadly Story," Jan. 25, 2007, http://news.bbc.co.uk/2/hi/programmes/from_our_own_correspondent/6295915.stm; Chuanmin and Qiahua, note 3.

[5] C. Lin, X. Tong, W. Lu, et al., "Environmental Impacts of Surface Mining on Mined Lands, Affected Streams and Agricultural Lands in the Dabaoshan Mine Region, Southern China" (2005) 16 *Land Degradation and Development* 463 at 463.

first Liangqiao Village, and then, in order, Tangxin, Yanghe, Shangba, and Xiaozhen villages. All have depended for centuries on the waters of the Hengshi River for drinking and agricultural irrigation needs.[6]

In 1966, the central government established the state-owned facility, Dabaoshan Mining Co. ("Dabao Mining"), to exploit the mineral resources discovered there, mainly copper and iron.[7] Soon after, other private mining enterprises began to operate, mostly illegally, in the Guangdong Dabao Mountain region. Production drastically increased in the late 1990s to meet China's growing demand for iron ore.[8]

As resource exploitation proceeded, pollution and environmental damage followed. The mining operations on Dabao Mountain and other companies stripped parts of the mountain bare, resulting in significant erosion, and leaving exposed mining debris that leached large volumes of runoff containing high concentrations of sulfuric acid, cadmium, and lead into the Hengshi River.[9] A study led by the College of Resources and Environment at the South China Agricultural University in Guanzhou, China, found concentrations of zinc, copper, lead, and cadmium up to sixteen times higher than permitted by national standards.[10] Moreover, the aquatic ecosystem was severely degraded.[11] Another study in 2003 found manganese, known to cause neurological diseases, at ten times the national permitted levels.[12]

With respect to aquatic organisms, fish and shrimp in the Hengshi River gradually disappeared in the 1980s. Villagers recounted that when ducks swam in the riverbeds, they tended to die soon after.[13] Other scientific studies demonstrated that no aquatic life could survive in the polluted waters for more than twenty-four hours, even after the water had been diluted by a factor of 10,000.[14]

As a result of the contaminated river water, the soils became contaminated by heavy metals, which in turn enhanced the uptake of these heavy metal contaminants by crop plants.[15] For example, the concentration of cadmium, a probable human carcinogen,[16] in bananas grown in the region was 187 times greater than the Chinese national limit.[17]

Exposure to the toxic waters of the Hengshi River for more than thirty years has taken an enormous toll on public health.[18] Scientists and villagers in Shangba, Liangqiao, and Tangxin have blamed the contamination for high cancer rates, and neighboring communities started referring to them as the Wengyuan "cancer villages." One scientist from Guangdong Province Soil and Ecology Research Center believes that the mining situation on Dabao Mountain is

---

[6]   Chuanmin and Qiahua, note 3.
[7]   C. Simons, "Water Pollution Takes a Toll in China," Feb. 18, 2007, *Atlanta Journal and Constitution*, at E1; Lin et al., note 5, p. 464.
[8]   Ibid.
[9]   Chuanmin and Qiahua, note 3, p. 27; J. Ma, "Bickering Mars Bid to Control," Dec. 7, 2000, *South China Morning Post*, p. 9 (article on file with author); Q. Chuan, "Joint Mine Review Seeks Compliance," Sept. 2, 2004, www.chinadaily.com.cn/english/doc/2004-09/03/content_371371.htm.
[10] See Lin, note 5, p. 472.
[11] Ibid., p. 473.
[12] See Simons, note 7.
[13] "A Great Wall of Waste – China's Environment," Aug. 21, 2004, www.economist.com/special-report/2004/08/19/a-great-wall-of-waste ["A Great Wall of Waste"].
[14] Chuanmin and Qiahua, note 3, p. 25.
[15] Ibid.
[16] US Environmental Protection Agency, "Cadmium Compounds: Hazard Summary," Sept. 2016.
[17] Ibid. Among the metal found in the local crops of Shangba, cadmium was the most prominent contamination among the heavy metal (ibid., at 472).
[18] Chuanmin and Qiahua, note 3, p. 25.

"a textbook case of environmentally-caused cancer."[19] In Shangba Village, the most populous of the five villages, more than 250 of about 3,000 total villagers died from cancer between 1987 and 2005.[20]

Besides the alarming rates of cancer, the pollution destroyed the economies of the downstream villages.[21] Since the irrigation water was filled with toxic heavy metals, the output of crops decreased, farmland became unusable, and fishponds were abandoned. In Liangqiao, nothing grows on fields irrigated with river water.[22] Fish raised in ponds died.[23] Doctors warned the villagers not to eat their own crops but many subsistence farmers had no other choice.[24] In other villages like Shangba, rice yields are one-third the national average.[25] Even though many villagers in Shangba did not eat the contaminated rice they grow, they would still sell it at the market to maintain an income for their families, though there were few buyers.[26] Others decided to plant sugarcane as an alternative to rice crops, not knowing that the sugarcane would also become contaminated with cadmium at concentration of up to 149 times greater than Chinese national public health limit.[27] With the loss of their agricultural livelihood and unable to feed themselves or pay their medical bills, some cancer victims left a legacy of debt upon their death.[28] In Liangqiao, only the elderly remained in a dismally bleak village, while their children joined China's mass of migrant workers seeking work in urban areas.

Though Dabao Mining denied responsibility for the water and soil pollution, it constructed a kilometer-long mud embankment in an effort to divert mine drainage water and prevent soil erosion from polluting the Hengshi River.[29] Unfortunately, because of heavy siltation, the mud embankment reached its capacity quickly, and by 2005, untreated mine water started overflowing continuously and pouring sulfuric acid into the Hengshi River at concentrations 1,000 times greater than national limits.[30] Dabao Mining planned to raise the height of the mud embankment at the time of our visit in 2006, but any additional height would just be a temporary fix because of siltation.[31]

Villagers initially approached Dabao Mining directly for compensation. However, when no agreement was reached by 1979, and as health effects grew more severe and the contamination adversely affected their livelihoods, Shangba Village petitioned the central government for assistance. Intervention by the former Metallurgy Ministry resulted in instructions to Dabao Mining to build a reservoir for drinking and irrigation water, but for reasons that remain unclear, the dam project was never completed.[32] Subsequent intervention by local and provincial

---

[19] Ibid., p. 26.

[20] Ibid., pp. 25, 26, and 28. In 2003, fourteen of thirty-one deaths in the village were attributable to cancer ("Great Wall of Waste," note 13). In 2004, about half were attributable to cancer; and in 2005, only two of the eleven people died from natural causes or from an accident; the remaining died from cancer. The proportion of deaths between Shangba and Liangqiao are approximately the same.

[21] "Great Wall of Waste," note 13.

[22] Chuanmin and Qiahua, note 3, p. 28.

[23] Simons, note 7.

[24] Ibid.

[25] "Great Wall of Waste," note 13.

[26] Chuanmin and Qiahua, note 3, p. 28.

[27] Lin et al., note 5, pp. 472–473. Among the metal found in the local crops of Shangba, cadmium was the most prominent heavy metal contaminant.

[28] Chuanmin and Qiahua, note 3, p. 26.

[29] Ibid; Lin et al., note 5, p. 464.

[30] Chuanmin and Qiahua, note 3, p. 28; Lin et al., note 5, p. 464.

[31] Chuanmin and Qiahua, note 3, p. 27.

[32] C. You, "Areas Flowing with Milk and Honey Are Turning into Cancer Villages and Poor Villages," May 2001, www.legaldaily.com.cn/gb/content/2001-05/11/content_17414.htm.

officials resulted in a mediated settlement agreement[33] under which Liangqiao Village, closest to the Dabao Mining facility, received 1,288 yuan annually (about US$800 at the time) for its 300 residents. Downstream Tangxin Village received 9,800 yuan annually (approximately US$6,000 at the time) for over 1,000 residents; farthest downstream, Shangba Village, with about 3,000 residents, was compensated 33,000 yuan (approximately US$22,000 at the time).[34]

Then, in 2005, the provincial government agreed to build a reservoir to provide potable water for Shangba,[35] though villagers still had to pay out of their own pocket for the significant cost of laying pipes to bring water from the reservoir to their homes. At the time, it was unclear whether the reservoir's capacity would be sufficient to irrigate all of Shangba's farmlands.[36] Liangqiao and other villages upstream from Shangba did not benefit from the Shangba reservoir because it sat too low.[37] Instead, families in Liangqiao took to paying thousands of yuan of their own to lay plastic pipes for clean water from Dabao Mountain's Yangmei Cavern.[38]

Tangxin Village took a more aggressive path. After repeated attempts to obtain greater compensation from Dabao Mining failed, Tangxin villagers filed a tort action in the local courts in 2006, seeking about 500,000 yuan in compensation for polluted farmland and 123,000 yuan for a polluted pond.[39] It is unclear what came of the lawsuit, though one might infer from the lack of information in media reports that it was not successful. As of this writing, Dabao Mining continues its mining operations.

17.3 CHINA'S CANCER VILLAGES

Cancer villages have largely been associated with China's extraordinary economic growth. When the first *OECD Economic Survey: China* was published in 2005, its economy had averaged a 9.5 percent annual growth in the previous two decades.[40] Since then, growth has moderated to just above 6 percent as of 2017, though it soared to a high of more than 14 percent in 2007.[41] China continues to maintain a trade surplus of US$275 billion with the United States[42] and was in

[33] According to a 1995 Shaoguan City government document, Dabao Mining was to pay a total amount of 80,000 yuan per year (US$53,000 per year at the time) to the Wengyuan County environmental protection bureau government which was to allocate the funds to the villages downstream (Chuanmin and Qiahua, note 3, p. 28).

[34] Ibid.

[35] Ibid. The 14.29 million yuan (about US$9.5 million at the time and about US$1.8 million at 2018 exchange rates) project, completed in 2006, was funded jointly by the provincial government (4.29 million yuan), the Shaoguan city government (5 million) and Dabaoshan Mining Co. (5 million) yuan. Based on subsequent complaints that water was still not clean enough for drinking, a Western company, Siemens, installed an additional water filtration system in 2008. "Guangdong Shaoguan Municipal Government Reported that the Incidence of 'Cancer Village' Is Not Specific," Apr. 10, 2013, http://politics.people.com.cn/n/2013/0410/c14562–21083711.html. However, the cost of electricity to run the filtration system was so high that villagers ended up shutting it down. See "Chen Xiaojian, Xu Hui Huang, Liang Dong Wei, Revisit 'Cancer Village' in Wengyuan County, Guangdong Province, Xinhuanet," June 26, 2005, http://news.sohu.com/20050626/n226087071.shtml.

[36] Chuanmin and Qiahua, note 3, p. 28.

[37] Ibid.

[38] Ibid.

[39] Complaint, *Tangxin Villagers Committee* v. *Dabaoshan*, No. 310 (Shaoguan City, Qujiang Dist. People's Ct., Jun. 18, 2006). See also Simons, note 7.

[40] Organisation for Economic Co-operation and Development, "Economic Surveys: China 2005," https://read.oecd-ilibrary.org/economics/oecd-economic-surveys-china-2005_eco_surveys-chn-2005-en#page17, pp. 16–17.

[41] OECD, "Economic Surveys: China 2017," p. 12, https://read.oecd-ilibrary.org/economics/oecd-economic-surveys-china-2017_eco_surveys-chn-2017-en#page12.

[42] E. Rosenfeld, "China's Trade Surplus with the US Hit a Record High in 2017," Jan. 11, 2018, www.cnbc.com/2018/01/11/chinas-trade-surplus-with-the-us-hit-a-record-high-in-2017.html.

possession of foreign exchange reserves in excess of US$3 trillion.[43] All the while, it has been able to reduce "the share of the rural population living below the poverty line . . . from 30% in 2005 to 5.7% in 2015, [with the aim of lifting] the remaining 43.3 million rural poor out of poverty by 2020."[44]

However, economic development has come at a price of unmanageable pollution and tragic environmental and public health consequences.[45] Using satellite images, the Chinese Academy of Sciences estimated that by the early 1990s, approximately 375 million hectares, about 40 percent of the country, showed moderate or severe signs of erosion.[46] Yale University's 2018 Environmental Performance Index study ranked China 120 out of 180 countries in a cross-country comparison of environmental pollution control and natural resources management.[47] And in 2006, China overtook the United States to become the world's largest greenhouse gas emitter.[48]

The World Bank has estimated that pollution and environmental degradation cost China's economy 3.5 percent to 8 percent of its GDP.[49] As part of the same research report, it had also found that approximately 460,000 deaths in China were attributable to air pollution, though that estimate was left out of the report's final version because it was deemed too politically sensitive.[50] Of course, the citizenry has not been ignorant of the country's serious environmental issues and they have increasingly taken to the streets in protest in thousands of "mass incidents," the government's term for demonstrations or other unsanctioned public activism.[51]

Unfortunately, the rising levels of pollution have not affected urban and rural populations equally. Although the government dedicated significant resources to alleviating urban pollution issues, it largely ignored the rural areas until the late 1990s.[52] Cancer villages have been the result of this neglect.

China's cancer villages appear to have no ready analog in wealthy developed nations, where cancer clusters are relatively uncommon. Nor is there a universally agreed-upon definition of what a cancer village is. Rather, the term has been used to describe rural communities in China that have experienced cancer clusters and unusually high rates of cancer deaths. The term itself first appeared in the media in 1998 in reporting by China Central Television (CCTV) and *Shenghuo Shibao* (*Life Times*) on industrial pollution of the Hai River in the City of Tianjin.[53]

---

[43] OECD, note 41, p. 17.

[44] Ibid., p. 47.

[45] E. C. Economy, *The River Runs Black: The Environmental Challenge to China's Future* (Ithaca, MY: Cornell University Press, 2004), pp. 60–90.

[46] World Bank, China, "Air, Land and Water – Environmental Priorities for a New Millennium," Aug. 2001, p. 17.

[47] Environmental Performance Index, "2018 EPI Report," https://epi.envirocenter.yale.edu/2018/report/category/hlt; D. C. Esty, M. A. Levy, T. Srebotnjak, A. de Sherbinin, C. H. Kim, and B. Anderson, "Pilot 2006 Environmental Performance Indicator," Yale Center for Environmental Law and Policy, Center for International Earth Science Information Network, World Economic Forum, Joint Research Centre of the European Commission, 2006, p. 139.

[48] "China Overtakes U.S. in Greenhouse Gas Emissions," June 20, 2007, www.nytimes.com/2007/06/20/business/worldbusiness/20iht-emit.1.6227564.html.

[49] World Bank and State Environmental Protection Administration P.R. China, "Cost of Pollution in China: Economic Estimates of Physical Damages," Feb. 2007, p. ix.

[50] "Pollution Kills 460,000 Chinese a year: World Bank," July 3, 2007, www.reuters.com/article/us-china-environment-worldbank/pollution-kills-460000-chinese-a-year-world-bank-idUSPEK9105920070703.

[51] A. Taylor, "Rising Protests in China," Feb. 17, 2012, www.theatlantic.com/photo/2012/02/rising-protests-in-china/100247/.

[52] World Bank, China, note 46, p. 108.

[53] CCTV, "Hai River Pollution Control Gratitude and Grievance," Nov. 9, 1998, www.gmw.cn/01shsb/1998-11/09/gb/793%5ESH12-911.htm.

There, government records showed that cancer rates were 1.3 percent and 2.1 percent (in two cancer villages), and 0.12 percent in the large City of Tianjin, significantly higher than the national average of 0.07 percent.[54]

Reporting on cancer villages across the country proliferated thereafter, though the government has largely ignored or even suppressed public attention to them.[55] It was not until 2013 that the central government, in a report by the then Ministry of Environmental Protection, officially acknowledged their existence across the country.[56]

A review by Lee Liu of government reports, public media stories, and internet and other private accounts of "cancer villages" and cancer hot spots identified at least 459 such cancer villages in 2009.[57] The epidemiological connection between the observed prevalence of various types of cancers in a community to a common cause or to specific industrial pollution and contamination is usually difficult to prove with certainty. However, according to Liu, "water contamination from industrial pollution is believed to be the main cause of cancer villages, [since many] cancer villages tend to cluster along the major rivers and their branches."[58] For example, along one tributary of the Huai River, approximately twenty cancer villages have been identified.[59]

17.4 UNDERSTANDING THE CANCER VILLAGE PHENOMENON

Fundamentally, the environmental and public health disaster experienced by the Wengyuan County Cancer Villages, and its counterparts across the country, are attributable to China's rampant pollution. They are the product of an incessant push for rapid industrial growth as a national priority unconcerned with protection of the environment and a corresponding failure of regulators to keep the excesses of industry and other polluters in check. Insofar that these dynamics have not been unique to China, other places have now found themselves with similar rashes of cancer clusters.[60]

It is true that environmental protection and sustainability has become a much greater priority across the world, including in China. In fact, China is among the countries that have made the greatest strides in developing its environmental regulatory system. In the last three decades, it has enacted between twenty and fifty major pieces of legislation creating new environmental laws or adopting significant amendments, significantly upgraded the status of its environment agency, facilitated the creation of specialized environmental courts, including a specialized Adjudication Tribunal for Environment and Natural Resources in the Supreme People's

[54] China Quality Ten-Thousand-Li Journey, "Undercover Investigation in Xiditou Township in Tianjin: Over 120 Cancer Victims from Industrial Pollution," Mar. 1, 2005, http://news.china.com/zh_cn/domestic/945/20050301/12139378.html.

[55] Ibid.

[56] E. Kao, "Environmental Watchdog Admits to 'Cancer Village' Phenomenon," Feb. 21, 2013, www.scmp.com/news/china/article/1155528/environmental-watchdog-admits-cancer-village-phenomenon.

[57] L. Liu, "Made in China: Cancer Villages" (2010) 52 *Environment: Science and Policy for Sustainable Development* 8–21.

[58] Ibid.

[59] J. Ma, "Terminal Debt and Despair Hit Cancer Villages," Oct. 3, 2005, www.scmp.com/article/518817/terminal-debt-and-despair-hit-cancer-villages.

[60] See B. Adak, "Cancer Lords over 5 Greater Noida Villages," Oct. 7, 2014, www.indiatoday.in/india/story/big-c-hepatitis-c-cancer-greater-noida-224640-2014-10-27; H. Tao, "Cancer Haunts Village in Central Vietnam after Claiming 40 Lives," Apr. 27, 2017, https://e.vnexpress.net/news/news/cancer-haunts-village-in-central-vietnam-after-claiming-40-lives-3577086.html.

Court, and accorded formal legal recognition to public interest litigation.[61] Most recently, the National People's Congress (NPC), China's national legislative body, empowered the country's prosecutorial authority, the Supreme People's Procuratorate, to bring environmental public interest cases against local environmental regulators.[62]

It is too early to evaluate the impact of the procuratorate's new role in enhancing the effectiveness of China's environmental governance system, but it is clear that previous reform efforts have not been sufficient to stem the deterioration of environmental quality in China. In fact, the results of reforms in the past have fallen far short of their often far-reaching promise.

The root causes are both simple and complex. At one level, the poor record of China's environmental regulatory system is "simply" the result of insufficient implementation and enforcement of existing laws. On the books, China's laws and regulations are full of promise. However, in their real-world application, their operation falls far short of what one might expect in comparison to well-developed and effective environmental regulatory systems in other countries.

At the same time, the root causes are complex if one enquires into the specific reasons for the implementation and enforcement failures. The problems are diverse in origin, though they are all related to the failure of China's system of environmental governance, its formal policy priorities, and institutional arrangements, to keep up with the legal requirements and mechanisms put in place by the legislative reforms. A detailed discussion of these issues is beyond the scope of this chapter, though a brief recap is useful here.

First, one of the primary reasons for the historic disconnect between the mandates set out in environmental legislation and the actions of regulators and polluters, was the explicit priority accorded by the nation's top leaders to economic growth and development over environmental protection. With such a clear set of national priorities, resources and official attention were focused primarily on economic growth as a national objective, and as a preferred choice over environmental protection when they were in conflict.[63] It was not until the 11th Five-year plan (2006–2011) that China's central government for the first time included environmental requirements among the compulsory plan targets for the bureaucracy and thus elevated the national importance of environmental protection. Major pollutants and pollutant measures, specifically COD (chemical oxygen demand) for water pollution and sulfur dioxide for air pollution, were to be reduced by 10 percent. Energy efficiency for each unit of the country's GDP was to be improved by 20 percent. In the following cycle – the 12th Five-year plan – the central government imposed requirements to cut COD and sulfur dioxide by another 8 percent each and energy intensity (energy per unit of GDP) by an additional 16 percent.[64]

Reorientation of government priorities through the inclusion of environmental protection targets has been critical to progress on China's environmental quality. However, repeated wintertime "airpocalypse" events in Beijing and other major cities[65] demonstrate that decades

---

[61] D. Carpenter-Gold, "Castles Made of Sand: Public-Interest Litigation and China's New Environmental Protection Law" (2015) 39 *Harvard Environmental Law Review* 241 at 256 and 270.

[62] Civil Procedure Law of the People's Republic of China (2017 Revision), Art. 55(2).

[63] P. Howlett, "Striking the Right Balance: The Contrasting Ways in which the United States and China Implement National Projects Affecting the Environment" (2004) 12 *Missouri Environmental Law and Policy Review* 27.

[64] "China's 12th Five-Year Plan: Overview," Mar. 2011, https://climateobserver.org/wp-content/uploads/2014/10/China-12th-Five-Year-Plan-Overview-2011041.pdf., p. 3.

[65] On such occasions, air pollution is not only extremely hazardous for public health but also persists for extended periods of times, sometimes many days on end. Oliver Wainwright, "Inside Beijing's Airpocalypse – A City Made 'Almost Uninhabitable' by Pollution," Dec. 16, 2014, www.theguardian.com/

of uncontrolled growth have created conditions where a 10 percent pollution reduction goal over five years does little to ameliorate profound and pressing public health hazards. In other words, without more ambitious measures on many different fronts, the path toward environmental improvement by this governance mechanism alone, though important in the context of China's traditional governance mechanisms, will remain a long and arduous one.

A second reason for the failure of environmental governance in China is the structure of China's environmental regulatory system.[66] Many of the functions of China's Ministry of Environmental Protection, recently renamed the Ministry of Ecology and Environment (MEE), reflect the regulatory functions of other national environmental agencies. However, its staff is small, by some counts fewer than 400 employees.[67] The recent restructuring of the central government bureaucracy in Beijing suggests that this number may go up, as high as 500.[68] However, compared to the size of the US Environmental Protection Agency, for example, with its 15,000 employees,[69] China's environmental ministry lacks the personnel required to provide effective regulatory oversight for a country with a population more than four times the size of the United States and with far more serious pollution problems. An exacerbating circumstance that undercuts the Ministry's authority and effectiveness is the weakness of the rule of law, as described more below. There is little formal documentation, but it is commonly accepted that more influential ministries, especially those charged with advancing economic growth, are able to overrule or constrain the actions of MEP on a routine basis.

Substantive implementation and enforcement of environmental laws and regulations are also advanced by some 180,000 staff working in the environmental agencies at the provincial and local government levels, usually referred to as the environmental protection bureaus (EPBs).[70] Unfortunately, that number does not make up for the central government's regulatory and enforcement staffing shortage because of the tricky institutional relationship between provincial/local regulatory staff and the environment ministry. Even though local staff must follow central government mandates, ministry officials have very limited practical control over local and provincial EPB staff. Local and provincial government leaders usually control the operational budgets and are in charge of hiring and promotion decisions, giving them day-to-day operational control over local environmental regulators.[71]

These local and provincial governments (or the officials themselves) often either directly own or have significant financial interest in some of the large polluting industries that are subject to environmental regulation. Even if local governments do not have a direct financial stake in a regulated industry, there may be an indirect interest. Since performance evaluations of local officials and party cadres for promotion and year-end bonus purposes have long been based on the

---

cities/2014/dec/16/beijing-airpocalypse-city-almost-uninhabitable-pollution-china; H. Agerholm, "Chinese 'Airpocalypse' Affects Half-a-Billion People as Smog Crisis Worsens," Dec. 20, 2016, www.independent.co .uk/news/world/asia/china-airpocalypse-smog-air-pollution-levels-red-alert-beijing-a7487261.html.

[66] For a broader explanation of these structural issues, see T. Yang, "Mysteries, Myths, and Misunderstandings: Ten Things that Every American Environmental Professional Should Know about China before Engaging with the World's Second-Largest Economy" (2016) 33 *The Environmental Forum* at 36.

[67] M. I. Kahn and Y. C. Chang, "Environmental Challenges and Current Practices in China – A Thorough Analysis" (2018) 10 *Sustainability* 2547.

[68] Ibid.

[69] E. Walsh, "EPA Workforce Shrinking to Reagan-Era Levels – Agency Official," Sept. 27, 2017, www.reuters .com/article/us-usa-epa/epa-workforce-shrinking-to-reagan-era-levels-agency-official-idUSKCN1BH1LY.

[70] T. Yang and X. Zhang, "Public Participation in Environmental Enforcement with Chinese Characteristics: A Comparative Assessment of China's Environmental Complaint Mechanism" (2012) 24 *Georgetown International Environmental Law Review* 333.

[71] Ibid.

achievement of economic growth targets set by Beijing, there has been an incentive for local officials to ensure that local industries operate with few constraints.[72] To complicate things further, in the past, significant portions of local EPB operational budgets have been underwritten by pollution discharge fees paid by industry. Strict enforcement of pollution limits could effectively deprive EPBs of significant portions of their financial resources. The overall effect of these tangled relationships is that the incentives and direct pressures local regulators face daily are oftentimes in direct conflict with their environmental protection mission.[73]

A final set of obstacles can be found in the weakness of the rule of law and of civil society. China's courts generally have not been able to exercise their authority independent of political influence.[74] In fact, virtually all of China's governmental apparatus is subject to the practical control of the communist party and its hierarchy. Corruption within the bureaucracy as well as the influence of *guanxi*, the web of personal relationship and connections relied upon extensively by business people, is still prevalent, especially in the rural areas.[75] Civil society institutions, including environmental nongovernmental organizations, are tightly controlled by the government and have largely been unable to effectively hold regulators or polluters accountable for failing in their responsibility under the law.[76] And at present, the number of environmental lawyers, attorneys competent and sufficiently expert in China's environmental law system, is still very small.[77]

These institutional deficiencies have undercut the promise of China's environmental law reforms. But they only begin to explain the underlying causes of the cancer villages. Those go deeper. Cancer villages are the result of deeply embedded and remaining structural societal inequities: poverty and government policies that have marginalized rural communities.[78] These influences magnify the environmental and public health impacts of pollution and environmental degradation and have left such communities with few effective remedies.[79]

First, cancer villages tend to be "found in poorer parts of the provinces."[80] The plight of residents of Liangqiao Village illustrates the issue in concrete detail. There, villagers had to spend thousands of yuan to build a system of pipes that would provide them with potable water. There are also more insidious effects. When poverty is coupled with lower levels of education, the poor may suffer more harmful consequences because of their lack of understanding of health risks of polluted water and contaminated soils. Another effect of rural poverty is diminished access to healthcare. As Lee Liu notes, "villagers have no healthcare and rarely do physical exams, so cancer is usually found at a late stage, and they are too poor to pay for treatments, leading to the high death rate."[81] The effect is to

---

[72] A. L. Wang, "The Search for Sustainable Legitimacy: Environmental Law and Bureaucracy in China" (2013) 37 *Harvard Environmental Law Review* 387.

[73] This is oftentimes referred to as local protectionism.

[74] J. Liu, "Overview of the Chinese Legal System, Environmental Law Reporter" (2013) 1 *Environmental Law Review* at 4.

[75] M. Szto, "Chinese Gift-Giving, Anti-Corruption Law, and the Rule of Law and Virtue" (2016) 39 *Fordham International Law Journal* 621–623.

[76] A. Chodorow, "Charity with Chinese Characteristics" (2012) 30 *UCLA Pacific Basin Law Journal* 13.

[77] A. Moser and T. Yang, "Environmental Tort Litigation in China" (2011) 41 *Environmental Law Reporter News & Analysis* 10898.

[78] J. Liu, "Environmental Justice with Chinese Characteristics: Recent Developments in Using Environmental Public Interest Litigation to Strengthen Access to Environmental Justice" (2012) 7 *Florida A and M University Law Review* 236.

[79] Ibid., p. 237.

[80] Liu, note 57.

[81] Ibid.; L. Nguyen, "Cancer Villages in China," in F. Gemenne, C. Zickgraf, and D. Ionesco (eds.), "The State of Environmental Migration 2015 – A Review of 2014," International Organization for Migration, SciencesPo, 2015, p. 82.

make communities both more vulnerable and less resilient to the health risks of contaminated water and soil. They simply have far fewer resources and thus diminished capacity to reduce the impact of pollution by obtaining water or food from other sources, seeking medical care, or moving to a less polluted area.

Second, cancer villages tend to be marginalized communities, its inhabitants formally excluded from valuable government benefits by virtue of their assigned status as residents of rural villages.[82] That is the practical reality of China's household registration (*hukou*) system, however counterintuitive in light of the egalitarian ideology of China's socialist system. The *hukou* system was created in its modern form in the 1950s to advance the government's economic development policies. Those policies called for subsidies to China's industrial development by providing those with a nonagricultural registration status, that is urban populations, with preferential welfare benefits, such as "state-provided housing, employment, grain rations, education, and access to medical care."[83] To maintain those subsidies, the *hukou* system required each individual to be registered in their place of birth and attached non-transferable social and economic benefits to the place of registration. Because household registration could only be changed with great difficulty, the *hukou* system sharply limited geographic mobility of individuals from the countryside to the cities. Moreover, because *hukou* registration was practically unalterable for most rural dwellers, and since important rights and benefits were tied to that registration, some scholars have noted the analogies to South Africa's system of apartheid[84] and the US system of Jim Crow laws prior to the civil rights movement.[85]

Some of China's major cities have sought to reform or abolish the applicability of the *hukou* system within their jurisdiction, and the system is generally not as strictly administered as in the past.[86] Nevertheless, as a practical matter it continues to limit the geographic mobility and economic opportunities of rural populations across China. Over the decades, economic development has focused on urban areas and has created an income gap where per capita income of urban households is about two and a half times that of rural households.[87] Thus, the *hukou* system has effectively locked in the economic marginalization of rural populations.

Finally, their economic and social marginalization has also made it more difficult to mobilize other resources, especially higher-level government attention, to provide assistance with their problems. In a society where *guanxi* and the web of personal relationships can be critical to mobilizing resources, public attention, and assistance of government officials, their marginalization means also that they have much less *guanxi* than other communities to help with their problems. In fact, case studies by Anna Lora-Wainwright and Ajiang Chen of cancer villages suggest that when such marginalized communities *are able* to gain attention from the media and support by outside activists, their success in obtaining remedies is dramatically enhanced.[88]

---

[82] OECD, "Economic Survey: China 94," 2013, https://read.oecd-ilibrary.org/economics/oecd-economic-surveys-china-2013_eco_surveys-chn-2013-en#page95.

[83] K. W. Chan, "The Chinese *Hukou* System at 50" (2009) 50 *Eurasian Geography and Economics* 197.

[84] P. Alexander and A. Chan, "Does China Have an Apartheid Pass System?" (2004) 30 *Journal of Ethnic and Migration Studies* 610.

[85] H. K. Josephs, "Residence and Nationality as Determinants of Status in Modern China" (2011) 46 *Texas International Law Journal* 298.

[86] OECD, note 82, p.94.

[87] OECD, note 41, p. 47.

[88] A. Lora-Wainwright and A. Chen, "China's Cancer Villages: Contested Evidence and the Politics of Pollution in a Companion to the Anthropology of Environmental Health" (2016) *Merrill Singer Edition* 408.

17.5 LEGAL REMEDIES TO ADDRESS ENVIRONMENTAL AND PUBLIC HEALTH RISKS

Leading environmental lawyers, such as Professor Wang Canfa of the Center for Legal Assistance to Pollution Victims, have had remarkable success in winning environmental tort cases.[89] However, proving causation and other evidentiary issues, the limited availability of trained environmental lawyers, attorney fees and other costs of bringing such cases make such lawsuits an uphill battle.[90] As a new litigation remedy, public interest lawsuits have received a lot of public attention in recent years. Formally authorized by the National People's Congress legislation only over the course of the last decade, such lawsuits can also be used to stop pollution.[91] However, the plaintiff will still have to find trained environmental lawyers as well as face the cost of litigation. And if defendants are local polluting enterprises, local protectionism may still influence the impartiality of the presiding judge.[92]

An alternative to litigation that villagers frequently pursue is China's "letters and visits" system (*xinfang*). This is a process by which Chinese citizens can petition high-ranking government officials for assistance with virtually anything.[93] The letters and visits system is essentially an institutionalized and highly regulated process for imploring government officials for discretionary help. As part of the process, citizens submit a letter or pay an in-person visit to *xinfang* offices to plead their grievance. The annual number of *xinfang* petitions reportedly exceeds the annual number of cases filed with China's judiciary.[94] With respect to the environment, the central and local government agencies have actually converted this process, with some success, into an environmental complaint mechanism for the reporting of violations and pollution problems, akin to a crimes "tip" line.[95]

Citizens of the Wengyuan County Cancer Villages have taken advantage of this channel to get official attention to their concerns ever since the mid-1980s.[96] And, at first blush, the 1995 compensation agreement as well as the reservoir built for Shangba Village in 2006, both achieved through the intervention of government officials, seem to suggest the success of this approach.

However, characterizing these outcomes as success may be too generous. It took decades to achieve these outcomes. In the interim, villager after villager fell ill and passed away. And the villagers themselves have complained that the compensation was grossly inadequate for the loss of livelihoods, deteriorating health, and pain and suffering from the death of loved ones. For example, the compensation for Shangba villagers under the 1995 arrangement was 11 yuan per villager per year (approximately US$7 at the time; about US$2 at 2018 exchange rates) with no inflation adjustments.[97] Furthermore, the 2006 reservoir, while an important remedy for Shangba

---

[89] Moser and Yang, note 77, p. 10899.

[90] Ibid., p. 10898.

[91] Ibid., p. 10899.

[92] Ibid.

[93] For a general overview of the *Xinfang* system, see C. F. Minzner, "Xinfang: An Alternative to Formal Chinese Legal Institutions" (2006) 42 *Stanford Journal of International Law* 103.

[94] Ibid., pp. 3–4. Ironically, even the courts have *Xinfang* offices.

[95] For a detailed description and analysis of China's environmental complaint mechanism, see Yang and Zhang, note 70.

[96] See C. Xiaojian, "Xu Hui Huang, Liang Dong Wei, Revisit 'Cancer Village' in Wengyuan County, Guangdong Province, Xinhuanet," June 26, 2005, http://news.sohu.com/20050626/n226087071.shtml.

[97] Moreover, according to one report, the annual income of villagers for the decade preceding 2004 stood at only 1,500 *yuan* per person (about US$188), almost three times less than the average income in the Guangdong province ("Great Wall of Waste," note 13).

villagers, was of no help to Liangqiao and the other higher-lying villages. In fact, given the time and resources invested in the petitioning process, including a 1979 visit to Beijing, the limited success was a source of considerable frustration to village leaders.[98] Ultimately, careful examination of the environmental complaint process suggests that the system is rarely an effective channel for addressing substantive environmental problems, such as the serious public health issues here.[99]

17.6 ENVIRONMENTAL JUSTICE, THE CANCER VILLAGES, AND THE SOCIAL PILLAR OF SUSTAINABLE DEVELOPMENT

Cancer villages would not exist if China's environmental regulatory system functioned effectively. Unfortunately, that failure is compounded by a variety factors, many of which directly implicate aspects of injustice that legal scholars usually associated with the environmental justice movement: distributive, procedural, corrective, and social injustice.[100] They are a manifestation of traditional distributive injustice because the provincial government and other owners of Dabao Mining have benefited financially for decades from the extraction of the rich mineral resources of Dabao Mountain, while the villagers have not. Instead, the villagers have been saddled with the resulting burdens of a polluted river, a contaminated food supply, and a high rate of cancer. Villagers face issues of procedural injustice in their inability to obtain relief from the government authorities because of their marginalization. And when they have been successful in obtaining some attention and action, the corrective justice effects of remedies have been inadequate in terms of financial compensation as well as practical assistance (such as providing villagers with potable water). In fact, some of the villages have had to pay for portions of the water purification systems out of their own pockets.

Most importantly, however, cancer villages are a manifestation of the broader problems of social injustice in China, a plight that is a direct result of their social and economic marginalization. Even though China has made enormous strides in building its economy and alleviating poverty, these advances have not occurred evenly across the country. Some segments of the society and geographical regions, especially the urban areas have benefited far more than rural regions, exacerbated by the hukou system. Cancer clusters are in that sense a manifestation of economic inequality and marginalization of poor rural communities that have been exposed more severely to pollution and contaminated water and soil. They are unable to protect themselves against the risks and consequences of such environmental hazards and ultimately face significant barriers to removing themselves from such exposures. These are, of course, the same types of challenges that communities fighting environmental injustice experience everywhere.

There is one further important point that the cancer villages illustrate. For decades, those advocating uncontrolled development sought to minimize the significance of environmental protection and sustainable development by arguing that the developing world should grow their economies first, without regard to attendant environmental harm, and then clean up later, once they had grown wealthy. Under that logic, rapid economic growth was necessary to lift hundreds of millions of people out of abject poverty, maybe even rescue millions more from hunger and

---

[98] Xiaojian, note 96.

[99] Yang and Zhang, note 70, pp. 347–351. In fact, Carl Minzner has argued that the *Xinfang* system generally is "fundamentally a multipurpose tool of governance for an authoritarian state, rather than an institution of particularized justice" (Minzner, note 93, p. 6).

[100] See, for example, R. R. Kuehn, "A Taxonomy of Environmental Justice" (2000) 30 *Environmental Law Reporter* 10681.

starvation. It confronted environmental advocates with the stark dilemma of environment versus livelihoods, containing the implicit proposition that a pristine environment and beautiful scenery was a luxury of little use to a starving person.

However compelling that argument might have been, it also advanced a false choice. China's cancer villages demonstrate in concrete detail the fallacy. A clean and healthy environment is not a luxury, but a necessity of life. Economic development alone is not sufficient for human survival when the food consumed is poisoned because of contaminated agricultural fields, when the drinking water comes from polluted streams and lakes, and when the air is unbreathable because of uncontrolled air pollution. In the end, the proposition that the environment needs to be sacrificed for the sake of rapid (and uncontrolled) economic growth neglects to mention that the sacrifice includes mainly the poor and marginalized. It completely ignores the social development pillar of sustainable development that calls not only for creating more economic opportunity but also addresses other basic human needs such as access to food, clean water, healthcare, shelter, and education.[101]

17.7 CONCLUSION

The Wengyuan County Cancer Villages and their cousins across the country are a vivid reminder that the cost of unchecked economic development must be measured not only in environmental terms but also in human health and lives. Prioritizing economic growth over human well-being is a calculus that most ordinary Chinese citizens have come to understand and reject.[102] Ironically, the ostensible beneficiaries of rapid economic growth have paid the highest price: exposed to greater amounts of pollution even though they possess fewer resources than wealthier communities to protect themselves from environmental hazards. Their economic and social marginalization has made them less resilient to the adverse health and environmental consequences and less well equipped to pursue legal remedies.

Ultimately, cancer villages demonstrate the fallacy of the development *versus* environment choice. Trade-offs are a necessity of life. However, economic policy decisions must fairly consider the effects on human health and the environment rather than pursuing GDP growth at any cost. After all, a just and sustainable society is impossible without a clean and healthy environment.

---

[101] UN World Summit for Social Development, Copenhagen Declaration on Social Development, Mar. 14, 1995, UN Doc. A/CONF.166/9.

[102] A 2011 Gallup Poll of Chinese adults showed that 57 percent prioritized environmental protection over economic growth. D. Yu and A. Pugliese, "Majority of Chinese Prioritize Environment Over Economy," June 8, 2012, https://news.gallup.com/poll/155102/majority-chinese-prioritize-environment-economy.aspx.

18

Colonialism, Environmental Injustice, and Sustainable Development

Nuclear Testing in the Marshall Islands

Antoni Pigrau

18.1 INTRODUCTION

The Republic of Marshall Islands (RMI) is an archipelagic state in the Pacific Ocean consisting of five islands and twenty-nine atolls. These islands are inhabited by approximately 53,000 people.[1] The islands were under the administration of different countries: Germany from 1885;[2] Japan between 1919 and 1944;[3] and the United States from 1944, during the final phase of World War II.[4]

In 1947, they were listed by the United Nations (UN) in the Trust Territory of the Pacific Islands,[5] under the administration of the United States. However, the United States prioritized the military use of the territory, with little attention to investment to meet the needs of its inhabitants, despite the commitments formally made before the UN.[6]

This chapter examines the social and environmental impacts of the nuclear testing program carried out by the United States in the Marshall Islands for twelve years. It analyzes the mechanisms used by the victims of nuclear testing to seek compensation for the resulting harms, including the relevant provisions of the agreement between the United States and the Marshall Islands that laid the groundwork for the formal decolonization of the territory. The chapter briefly discusses the complaints filed by the RMI before the International Court of Justice (ICJ) in 2014 against all nuclear weapons states. Finally, it draws on some of the lessons from the Marshall Islands case study to critique the sustainable development paradigm through the framework of environmental justice.

This work is part of the research project, funded by the Spanish Ministry of Economy and Competitiveness, titled "Global climate constitution: Governance and Law in a Complex Context" (DER2016–80011-P). It is based on one of the themes dealt with in A. Pigrau, "El caso de las Islas Marshall: Colonialismo, armas nucleares y justicia ambiental" (2018) 34 *Anuario Español de Derecho Internacional* 443.

[1] UNFCCC, "The Republic of the Marshall Islands: Nationally Determined Contribution," Nov. 22, 2018, p. 6.
[2] The islands were delivered by Spain to Germany following papal mediation, in exchange for economic compensation. See G. Petersen "Differences, Connections, and the Colonial Carousel in Micronesian History" (2011) 2 *Pacific Asia Inquiry* 9 at 11–12
[3] On December 17, 1920, the islands were included by the Council of the League of Nations in the South Pacific Mandate under the administration of Japan.
[4] During World War II, the United States captured the islands from Japan. The military campaign ended on February 27, 1944.
[5] UN Security Council, *Trusteeship of Strategic Areas*, Apr. 2, 1947, UN Doc. S/RES/21. The territories included in the Mandate of the League of Nations and in the Trusteeship Agreement are the present-day Palau, the Northern Mariana Islands, the Federated States of Micronesia, and the Marshall Islands.
[6] See United Nations, Charter of the United Nations, Oct. 24, 1945, 1 UNTS XVI, Art. 76.

18.2 NUCLEAR TESTS AND ENVIRONMENTAL AND SOCIAL IMPACTS IN THE MARSHALL ISLANDS

The United States conducted 1,032 nuclear tests between 1945 and 1992.[7] After the first test in the desert of New Mexico, it decided to move part of its nuclear testing to the Pacific, to the Marshall Islands. An estimated 14,000 individuals were displaced during the era of US nuclear testing from 1947 to 1958 to facilitate the testing program. Some were relocated to the United States, but most stayed within the Marshall Islands.[8] Between July 1946 and August 1958, sixty-seven nuclear tests were performed on the atolls of Bikini and Enewetak, including the most powerful ever carried out, the Bravo bomb in 1954.[9] Many of these were atmospheric tests while others were under water. The nuclear tests had a combined explosive yield of 108,000 kilotons, equivalent to over 7,200 Hiroshima bombs[10] or 1.6 Hiroshima bombs each day over the twelve years that the tests were carried out.[11] In 1958, the United States ended the nuclear testing program in the Marshall Islands.[12]

The nuclear tests caused long-lasting, serious environmental damage, and resulted in the physical disappearance of some small islands, which were pulverized by the atomic explosions and submerged by seawater.[13] Forced displacement severed the inhabitants' bond with their land and destroyed their self-sufficient economy.[14] The islands' inhabitants also suffer "unusually high rates of thyroid disorders, birth defects, and cancer."[15]

The UN Special Rapporteur on hazardous substances and wastes, Mr. Calin Georgescu, visited the RMI and the United States in 2012. His report stated that "the effects of radiation have been exacerbated by near-irreversible environmental contamination, leading to the loss of livelihoods and lands."[16] In assessing the most negative impacts of the nuclear testing on the

---

[7]   Another twenty-four tests were conducted jointly with the United Kingdom. Stockholm International Peace Research Institute, *SIPRI Yearbook 2018: Armaments, Disarmament and International Security* (Oxford: Oxford University Press, 2018), pp. 300–301.

[8]   International Organization for Migration (IOM), *Republic of the Marshall Islands IOM Country Strategy 2017–2020*, 2017, p. 5.

[9]   The second North American test of a hydrogen bomb ("Bravo," 15 Mt yield), on Mar. 1, 1954 on Bikini Atoll, caused nuclear fallout over an area of 11,000 km², exposing approximately 665 island residents to high doses of ionizing radiation and requiring the evacuation of several atolls. It also affected the crew of a Japanese fishing boat, the *Daigo Fukuryu Maru*; Pacific Islands: Congress of Micronesia, "Compensation for the People of Rongelap and Utirik: A Report by the Special Joint Committee Concerning Rongelap and Utirik Atolls to the Fifth Congress of Micronesia," Feb. 28, 1974, p. 6; T. Kunkle and B. Ristvet, "Castle Bravo: Fifty Years of Legend and Lore: A Guide to Off-site Radiation Exposures," Defense Threat Reduction Agency, Defense Threat Reduction Information Agency Center SR-12–001, Jan. 2013.

[10] Senate Report No. 111–268, Republic of the Marshall Islands Supplemental Nuclear Compensation Act, US 111th Congress, 2nd Session, Aug. 5, 2010.

[11] T. A. Ruff, "The Human Cost of Nuclear Weapons" (2015) 97 *International Review of the Red Cross* 775 at 794.

[12] In 1963, the Treaty Banning Nuclear Weapon Tests in the Atmosphere, in Outer Space and Under Water was signed by the governments of the USSR, the UK, and the USA (UNTS, vol. 480, p. 43, No 6964).

[13] A chronology of the facts together with a complete list of the tests performed and their scale is available at www .rmiembassyus.org/Nuclear%20Issues.htm#History.

[14] See the Bikinian lawsuit against the US government in the US Court of Federal Claims: *The People of Bikini, by and through the Kili/Bikini/Ejit Local Government Council, Plaintiffs* v. *United States of America; Complaint*, US Court of Federal Claims No. 06–288C, Aug. 2, 2007; International Atomic Energy Agency, "Radiological Conditions at Bikini Atoll: Prospects for Resettlement," Radiological Assessment Reports Series, Mar. 1998.

[15] IOM, note 8. For the effects of the nuclear tests, see Z. D. Ishtar, "Poisoned Lives, Contaminated Lands: Marshall Islanders Are Paying a High Price for the United States Nuclear Arsenal" (2003) 2 *Seattle Journal for Social Justice* 287 at 288–293.

[16] UN General Assembly (UNGA), *Report of the Special Rapporteur on the implications for human rights of the environmentally sound management and disposal of hazardous substances and waste, Calin Georgescu:*

inhabitants, the report focused on two aspects: impacts associated with health; and those triggered by the displacement of the population.[17] Regarding the health impacts, the Special Rapporteur noted the lack of scientific consensus on the causal link between the US nuclear testing and incidence of cancer, and the limited availability of data due to the lack of thorough studies.[18] In relation to the population displacement, the report emphasized that US nuclear testing "has created nomads who are disconnected from their lands and their cultural and indigenous way of life."[19] The report specifically referred to the humiliating way in which women were treated by American authorities, while at the same time reiterating the need to respect the Guiding Principles on Internal Displacement:[20]

> The Special Rapporteur heard the accounts of women survivors of the shame that they had experienced during the relocation process, when they were subjected to examinations with Geiger counters while naked and hosed down with liquid in the presence of their male relatives, as well as enduring on-site analysis of their pubic hair by American male personnel. In this context, many women, in particular those from Rongelap Atoll, were stigmatized, which affected their prospects for marriage and motherhood.[21]

The report concluded with some recommendations. Among the ones addressed to the government of the United States[22] are exhortations to grant the RMI full access to United States information and records regarding the environmental and human health impacts of the United States' military use of the islands, as well as full access to US medical and other related records on the Marshallese.

The Special Rapporteur also recommended that the United States:

> [g]uarantee the right to effective remedy for the Marshallese people, including by providing full funding for the Nuclear Claims Tribunal to award adequate compensation for past and future claims, and exploring other forms of reparation, where appropriate, such as restitution, rehabilitation and measures of satisfaction (for example, public apologies, public memorials and guarantees of non-repetition).[23]

18.3 DENIAL OF ACCESS TO JUST REPARATION FOR RMI INHABITANTS

Negotiations for the decolonization of the Marshall Islands led to a Compact of Free Association, signed in 1983, approved by the people of the Marshall Islands by plebiscite that same year,[24] and endorsed by the US Congress in 1985 with the enactment of Public Law

---

Missions to the Marshall Islands (27–30 March 2012) and the United States of America (24–27 April 2012), Sept. 3 2012, UN Doc. A/HRC/21/48/Add.1, para.19.

[17] The Rapporteur notes that consent for medical tests appears to have been neither sought nor obtained (ibid, para. 49).

[18] Ibid., paras. 22–24.

[19] Ibid., paras. 33–34.

[20] UN Economic and Social Council, *Report of the Representative of the Secretary-General, Mr. Francis M. Deng, submitted pursuant to Commission resolution 1997/39. Addendum: Guiding Principles on Internal Displacement,* Feb. 11, 1998, UN Doc. E/CN.4/1998/53/Add.2.

[21] UNGA, note 16, para. 32.

[22] Ibid., pp. 16–19.

[23] Ibid., para. 64, subpara. f.

[24] With 58 percent of voters in favor: UN, *Rapport de la mission de visite des Nations Unies chargée d'observer le referendum dans les Iles Marshall, Territoire sous tutelle des Iles du Pacifique, en Septembre 1983,* Conseil de Tutelle. Documents officiels: Cinquante-unième session (mai–juin 1984); Supplement No. 2, UN Doc. T/186S.

99–239.[25] The Compact came into effect in 1986. The trusteeship of the United States was formally terminated pursuant to Security Council Resolution 683 of December 22, 1990, and the RMI was admitted to the United Nations on September 17, 1991.[26] Nevertheless, the Compact of Free Association limited the sovereignty of the RMI in several respects, including giving the United States full authority and responsibility for security and defense matters.[27] Using these powers, the United States prevented the RMI from signing the 1985 South Pacific Nuclear Free Zone Treaty.[28]

Section 177 of the 1985 Compact states:

> (a) The Government of the United States accepts the responsibility for compensation owing to citizens of the Marshall Islands . . . for loss or damage to property and person of the citizens of the Marshall Islands . . . resulting from the Nuclear Testing Programme . . .

> (b) The Government of the United States and the Government of the Marshall Islands shall set forth in a separate agreement provisions for the just and adequate settlement of all such claims which have arisen in regard to the Marshall Islands and its citizens . . . or which in the future may arise . . .

> (c) The Government of the United States shall provide the Government of the Marshall Islands, on a grant basis, with the amount of $150 million to be paid and distributed in accordance with the separate agreement referred to in this Section . . .[29]

The separate agreement referred to here was signed on June 25, 1983.[30] Among other provisions, the Agreement included the following:

> (1) The Government of the Marshall Islands shall establish a Claims Tribunal which shall have jurisdiction to render final determination upon all claims past, present and future, of the Government, citizens and nationals of the Marshall Islands which are related to the Nuclear Testing Program.
>
> (Art. IV, s. 1)

> (2) A fund of US$150 million[31] is created to finance a series of social programs (Health, Food, Agricultural Maintenance and Radiological Surveillance) for 15 years, as well as the payment of claims for loss or damage to property and personal injury sustained by the

---

[25] Compact of Free Association Act of 1985, US Public Law 99–239, 99th Congress, Jan. 14, 1986.

[26] UN Security Council, *Resolution 683 [Pacific Islands (Trust Territory)]*, Dec. 22, 1990, UN Doc. S/RES/683.

[27] Compact of Free Association Act, note 25.

[28] South Pacific Bureau for Economic Co-operation, South Pacific Nuclear Free Zone Treaty, Aug. 6, 1985, UNTS vol. 1445, p. 177, No. 24592.

[29] Compact of Free Association Act, note 25

[30] Agreement between the Government of the United States and the Government of the Marshall Islands for the Implementation of Section 177 of the Compact of Free Association, available at: www.nuclearclaimstribunal .com/177text.htm until at least the end of March 2014. The website has since been disabled.

[31] The intention was for the Fund's capital to be invested so as to produce average annual proceeds of at least US$18 million for each year of the Fund's existence: "The investment returns on the Fund were expected to generate $270 million over the 15 years of the first Compact term while the original $150 million would remain as principal" (T. Lum, K. Thomas, C. S. Redhead, D. Bearden, M. Holt, and S. Lazzari, "Republic of the Marshall Islands *Changed Circumstances Petition* to Congress," CRS Report for Congress, Order Code RL32811, May 16, 2005, p. 7).

people of Bikini, Enewetak, Rongelap and Utrik,[32] the creation and operation of the Tribunal,[33] and the compensations awarded by the Claims Tribunal.

(Arts. 1–8)

(3) A change of circumstances clause (Article IX) provides as follows:

If loss or damage to property and person of the citizens of the Marshall Islands, resulting from the Nuclear Testing Program, arises or is discovered after the effective date of this Agreement, and such injuries were not and could not reasonably have been identified as of the effective date of this Agreement, and if such injuries render the provisions of this Agreement manifestly inadequate, the Government of the Marshall Islands may request that the Government of the United States provide for such injuries by submitting such a request to the Congress of the United States for its consideration. . . .

(4) The Agreement forecloses other redress options (Article X):

This Agreement constitutes the full settlement of all claims, past, present and future, of the Government, citizens and nationals of the Marshall Islands which are based upon, arise out of, or are in any way related to the Nuclear Testing Program, and which are against the United States, its agents, employees, contractors and citizens and nationals.[34]

The inhabitants of the Marshall Islands, either privately or with government backing, have tried to obtain compensation for the damages suffered due to US nuclear testing via the Nuclear Claims Tribunal and on several occasions before US federal courts. The government of the Marshall Islands also attempted to do so by political means alleging the "changed circumstances" clause before the US Congress. But these attempts have delivered only limited results.

18.3.1 *The Marshall Islands Nuclear Claims Tribunal*

In 1987, pursuant to Agreement implementing section 177 of the Compact, the Marshall Islands passed the Nuclear Claims Tribunal Act. The Tribunal commenced operations in 1992.[35] The Tribunal received personal injury claims from individuals[36] and several group claims concerning property damage[37] from the communities of Rongelap (1991), Enewetak (1992), Bikini (1993), and Utrik (1998). In principle, the Tribunal had a fund of US$45.75 million to resolve

---

[32] In accordance with a previously established allocation of the following amounts, to be distributed equally over fifteen years: US$75,000,000 (Bikini); US$48,750,000 (Enewetak), US$37,500,000 (Rongelap); and US$22,500,000 (Utrik). Note that these figures already far exceeded US$150 million.

[33] There was US$500,000 allocated for the establishment of the Claims Tribunal and US$500,000 annually for its operation.

[34] This provision includes "any legal proceedings in the courts of the Marshall Islands . . . arising out of the Nuclear Testing Program" and any proceedings in the courts of the United States.

[35] All information on the activity of the court was available on their website: www.nuclearclaimstribunal.com/, until at least the end of March 2014 (see note 30). A part of the information can be recovered in https://web .archive.org/web/20140517172030/http://nuclearclaimstribunal.com/.

[36] The estimate for damages by the Tribunal was based on the US Radiation Exposure Compensation Act 42 USC §2210.

[37] The estimated damages have included three categories: the loss of use of their property; the costs to restore and remediate their property; and the hardships suffered during their period of forced relocation. In the case of Bikini, the inhabitants have not been able to return to their place of origin yet. D. Thornburgh, G. Reichardt, J. Stanley, and Kirkpatrick and Lockhart LLP, "The Nuclear Claims Tribunal of the Republic of the Marshall Islands: An Independent Examination and Assessment of its Decision-Making Processes," Washington, DC, Jan. 2003, pp. 42–45.

these claims, to be paid out over a fifteen-year period.[38] However, the inadequacy of this fund soon became evident.

On April 13, 2000, the Tribunal awarded the People of Enewetak, US$385,894,500.[39] On March 5, 2001, the Tribunal awarded the People of Bikini US$563,315,500.[40] On December 15, 2006, the Tribunal awarded the People of Utrik US$307,356,398.91.[41] Finally, on April 17, 2007, the Tribunal determined that the amount of compensation due to the People of Rongelap was US$1,031,231,200.[42] Because the damages awarded far exceeded the US$45.75 million allocated when the compensation fund was created and because the Fund failed to achieve its projected growth,[43] the Tribunal's resources were completely depleted in 2007. The Tribunal has been unable to make any payments to the communities of Utrik and Rongelap and paid only a fraction of the amounts awarded to the communities of Enewetak and Bikini.[44]

18.3.2 *Appeal to the US Congress*

Based on the "changed circumstances" clause of the Agreement implementing section 177 of the Compact, the RMI government submitted a petition to the US Congress on September 11, 2000.[45] The petition specifically requested that Congress authorize the additional funds needed to cover the unpaid part of the compensation award issued by the Nuclear Claims Tribunal.[46]

According to the petition, injuries and damages resulting from the United States Nuclear Testing Program have arisen, been discovered, or have been adjudicated in the Marshall Islands since the Compact took effect; and these injuries and damages could not reasonably have been discovered, or could not have been determined, prior to the effective date of the Compact. Thus, the terms of section 177 of the Compact have turned out to be "manifestly inadequate to provide just and adequate compensation for injuries to Marshallese people and for damage to or loss of land resulting from the U.S. Nuclear Testing Programme."[47]

---

[38] Agreement between the Government of the United States and the Government of the Marshall Islands for the Implementation of Section 177 of the Compact of Free Association (Art. II, s. 6(c)).

[39] Before the Nuclear Claims Tribunal Republic of the Marshall Islands, *In the Matter of the People of Enewetak, et al.*, Claimants for Compensation, NCT No. 23–0902, Apr. 13, 2000.

[40] Before the Nuclear Claims Tribunal Republic of the Marshall Islands, *In the Matter of the People of Bikini, et al.*, Claimants for Compensation, NCT No. 23–04134, Memorandum of Decision and Order, of Mar. 5, 2001.

[41] Before the Nuclear Claims Tribunal Republic of the Marshall, *Islands in the Matter of the People of Utrik, et al.*, Claimants for Compensation, NCT No. 23–06103, Memorandum of Decision and Order, of Dec. 15, 2006.

[42] Before the Nuclear Claims Tribunal Republic of The Marshall Islands, *In the Matter of the Alabs of Rongelap, et al.*, Claimants for Compensation, *Rongelap Atoll Local Government/Rongelap Local Distribution Authority, Intervener*, NCT No. 23–02440, *In the Matter of Jabon on Rongelap Atolli*, NCT No. 23–05443-B and *In the Matter of Rongerik Atoll, Ronglap Atoll, by Iroij Anjua Loeak, et al.*, Claimants for Compensation, NCT No. 23–05445-B, *In the Matter of Iroij Imata Jabro Kabua, Ronglap Atoll*, Claimant for Compensation, NCT No. 23–00501. Memorandum of Decision and Order, of Apr. 17, 2007.

[43] "According to the Tribunal, the Fund earned approximately $160 million rather than $270 million (1986–2001) as projected when the Compact was negotiated" (Lum et al., note 31, p. 15).

[44] *Ismael John v. United States*, No. 06–289L (Fed. Cl. filed Apr. 12, 2006), pp. 26–28; K. Thomas and D. Bearden, "Republic of the Marshall Islands *Changed Circumstances Petition* to Congress," CRS Report for Congress, Order Code RL32811, Aug. 30, 2005.

[45] Petition presented to the congress of the United States of America regarding changed circumstances arising from US nuclear testing in the Marshall Islands, Submitted by the Government of the Republic of the Marshall Islands (RMI) pursuant to Article IX of the Nuclear Claims Settlement Approved by Congress in Public Law 99–239, Sept. 11, 1990, www.bikiniatoll.com/petition.html.

[46] Lum et al., note 31, pp. 18–19.

[47] Agreement between the Government of the United States and the Government of the Marshall Islands for the Implementation of Section 177 of the Compact of Free Association (Art. IX).

Two particular areas of "changed circumstances" were noted in the petition: the increased scientific understanding of the biological effects of radiation, and the evolution of maximum permissible exposure levels. The exposure levels sustained by people living on nearly every atoll in the Marshall Islands in 1954 exceeded US maximum permissible levels established in 1957. Although much of the data on the radiation present in the different atolls was held by the US Atomic Energy Commission, these documents were classified for forty years and were never made known to the negotiators of the 1983 Agreement.[48]

In 2002, the government of the RMI commissioned the former US Attorney General, Richard Thornburgh, to conduct an independent evaluation of the processes used by the Nuclear Claims Tribunal. This report, submitted in January 2003, found that the Tribunal had been staffed by qualified people with access to adequate resources; that the Tribunal's procedures were reasonable; that the Tribunal's independence had not been compromised; and that the Tribunal had not mismanaged the Trust Fund or acted improperly by making cumulative awards that greatly exceeded the dollar amounts available from the Trust Fund.[49]

The report concluded:

> it is our view that the $150 million initially provided by the U.S. Government for the Trust Fund has proven to be manifestly inadequate to fairly compensate the inhabitants of the Marshall Islands for the damages they suffered as a result of the U.S. Nuclear Testing Program.[50]

In the same year, the US government and the RMI adopted an amended version of the Compact of Free Association that modified provisions relating to economic assistance.[51] The issue of compensation for damage resulting from the nuclear program was left out of the negotiation at the insistence of the United States, which claimed that the matter was already subject to an act of Congress.[52] The compensation program derived from section 177 ended in December 2003.

However, in November 2004, the US Department of State presented a report to Congress on the petition, which concluded that the facts did not support a funding request under the "changed circumstances" provision.[53] The matter was debated in various committees.[54] In 2007 and 2010, the president and the minister of foreign affairs of the RMI appeared before the US Senate to report, among other matters, that the RMI's health programs were no longer covered by US economic assistance and that monitoring was needed at the subterranean site used to store radioactive waste that is located on the island of Runit on Enewetak Atoll. On Runit, a crater caused by one of the nuclear tests had been filled to create an above-ground

---

[48] Lum et al., note 31, p. 19.

[49] Thornburgh et al., note 37.

[50] Ibid., pp. 72–73.

[51] Compact of Free Association Amendments Act of 2003, US Public Law 108–188, 108th Congress, Dec. 17, 2003. It entered into force on May 1, 2004 for a twenty-year period.

[52] *People of Bikini*, note 14.

[53] US Department of State, "Report Evaluating the Request of the Government of the Republic of the Marshall Islands Presented to the Congress of the United States of America," Nov. 2004, https://2001–2009.state.gov/p/eap/rls/rpt/40422.htm. Against, see Harvard Law Student Advocates for Human Rights, "Keeping The Promise. An Evaluation of Continuing U.S. Obligations Arising out of the U.S. Nuclear Testing Program in the Marshall Islands," Apr. 2006.

[54] On May 25, 2005, the House Committee on Resources and the Subcommittee on Asia and the Pacific of the House Committee on International Relations held a joint hearing; and on July 19, 2005, the Senate Committee on Energy and Natural Resources held a hearing on the effects of the US nuclear testing program on the Marshall Islands. S. Lazzari, "Loss-of-Use Damages from U.S. Nuclear Testing in the Marshall Islands: Technical Analysis of the Nuclear Claims Tribunal's Methodology and Alternative Estimates," Order Code RL33029, Aug. 12, 2005, p. 9.

nuclear waste storage site that houses 110,000 cubic yards of radioactively contaminated soil from the Enewetak Atoll, including plutonium-239, whose estimated active life is 24,000 years.[55] As the RMI minister of foreign affairs stated, "[T]his type of nuclear waste storage facility would not have been permitted in the US because it would not have been considered to be adequately protective of human health and the environment."[56]

On July 10, 2007 various senators submitted a draft bill to address the RMI's concerns.[57] The bill met with opposition from the executive branch of the US government,[58] and was submitted again on January 20, 2010. Finally, on August 5, 2010, the Senate Committee on Energy and Natural Resources issued a favorable report on the bill. The bill included a provision for monitoring the radiological conditions on Runit Island. It also made some RMI citizens eligible to receive compensation under the Energy Employees Occupational Illness Compensation Program, allocated US$4.5 million annually to the Four Atoll Health Care Program, and requested an assessment of RMI's medical needs by the National Academy of Sciences. The bill was introduced in the 112th Congress, on February 14, 2011, but was not enacted.[59] Only the provision for monitoring the radiological conditions on Runit Island was included in a new text passed by the Senate on December 16, 2011,[60] approved by the House of Representatives on Jul 19, 2012,[61] and signed into law by the president on July 26, 2012, as US Public Law 112–149.[62]

18.3.3 *Claims before the Federal Courts*

The first attempt to seek redress before the US federal courts coincided with the negotiation of the legal instrument that would end the United States' trusteeship over the Marshall Islands. In March 1981, the inhabitants of Bikini filed a claim before the US Court of Claims requesting compensation under the Fifth Amendment of the US Constitution for the confiscation of their land and for breach of fiduciary obligations by the United States.[63] On October 5, 1984, the court denied the motion to dismiss filed by the United States, concluding that the court had jurisdiction to hear the case, and deemed the Fifth Amendment applicable to the plaintiffs' claims. However, after the Compact of Free Association was negotiated and approved, the Court of Claims dismissed the case on the grounds that the Agreement terminated the court's jurisdiction over the matter, despite the fact that the United Nations Security Council had not yet declared the end of the trust.[64]

---

[55] See M. B. Gerrard, "America's Forgotten Nuclear Waste Dump in the Pacific" (2015) 35 *SAIS Review of International Affairs* 87; UNGA, note 16, para. 60.

[56] Statement of the Honorable John M. Silk, Minister of Foreign Affairs, Republic of the Marshall Islands before the United States Senate Committee on Energy and Natural Resources, May 19, 2010; Gerrard, note 56, pp. 90–91.

[57] GovTrack, "S. 1756 (110th): Republic of the Marshall Islands Supplemental Nuclear Compensation Act of 2008," 2007, www.govtrack.us/congress/bills/110/s1756.

[58] Marshall Islands Nuclear Testing Compensation, Statement of Thomas Bussanich, Acting Director Office of Insular Affairs, Department of the Interior Before the Senate Committee on Energy and Natural Resources, Subcommittee on Insular Affairs Regarding the Implementation of the Compact of Free Association with the Republic of the Marshall Islands, Sept. 25, 2007, www.doi.gov/ocl/hearings/110/S1756_092507.

[59] The bill was introduced as GovTrack, "S. 342 (112th): Republic of the Marshall Islands Supplemental Nuclear Compensation Act of 2008," www.govtrack.us/congress/bills/112/s342.

[60] GovTrack, "S. 2009 (112th): Insular Areas Act of 2011," July 19, 2012, www.govtrack.us/congress/bills/112/s2009/text/es.

[61] Ibid.

[62] Insular Areas Act of 201, 48 USC 1901, US Public Law 112–149, July 26, 2012.

[63] *Juda v. United States*, 6 Cl. Ct. 441, 444 (1984).

[64] *Juda v. United States*, 13 Cl. Ct. 667 (1987), appeal dismissed, People of Bikini, 859 F.2d 1482 (Fed. Cir. 1988). See J. J. Whittle, "*Juda v. United States*: An Atoll's Legal Odyssey" (1989) 4 *American University International Law Review* 655.

The second attempt to seek redress arose from the failure of the US Congress to respond to the RMI petition based on the changed circumstances. In April 2006, the inhabitants of Bikini Atoll filed a lawsuit against the US government in the US Court of Federal Claims (formerly known as the US Court of Claims). The plaintiffs sought to recover the difference between the amount of compensation awarded by the Nuclear Claims Tribunal and the amount actually paid, namely US$561,036,320 plus interest as required by law, for a total of US$724,560,902.[65] The inhabitants of Enewetak Atoll also filed a related lawsuit[66] seeking payment of US$386 million in accordance with the judgment issued by the Nuclear Claims Tribunal.

On August 2, 2007, the court granted the US government's motion to dismiss the lawsuits for lack of jurisdiction, finding that the plaintiffs' claims impinged on the conduct of foreign affairs which the Constitution delegates to the executive and legislative branches.[67] In January 2009, the Court of Appeals decided that the 1983 Compact between the government of RMI and the United States precluded such claims.[68] The court also noted that the Compact itself provided a course of action in the event that "such injuries render the provisions of this Agreement manifestly inadequate" through the changed circumstances petition to Congress. Thus, the Compact relegated compensation for nuclear testing "to a procedure outside the reach of judicial remedy."[69] Finally, the plaintiffs unsuccessfully petitioned for US Supreme Court review. On April 5, 2010, the Supreme Court declined to hear the case.[70] With this decision, the judicial proceedings in the United States for the claims filed by victims of the damage caused by the use of the Marshall Islands as a nuclear test site between 1946 and 1958 were closed definitively without the victims obtaining any relief for the damage they suffered.

18.4 THE MARSHALL ISLANDS BEFORE THE ICJ

In addition to its efforts to secure justice for the victims of nuclear testing, the RMI brought an action before the ICJ to stop the proliferation of nuclear weapons. On April 24, 2014, the government of the RMI simultaneously filed in the ICJ separate applications against the nine nuclear weapons states (NWS) for their alleged failure to comply with their obligation to halt the nuclear arms race, and to pursue nuclear disarmament, as required by Article VI of the Treaty on the Non-Proliferation of Nuclear Weapons (NPT), of July 1968.[71]

Arguing that Article VI of the NPT had become part of customary international law, the RMI alleged that the non-NPT parties violated customary international law and that the NPT parties

---

[65] *People of Bikini*, note 14.

[66] *Ismael John* v. *United States*, note 45.

[67] *People of Bikini* v. *United States* 554 F 3d 996 (2009), Brief for Plaintiffs-Appellants People of Bikini, Dec. 21, 2007.

[68] By its own terms, the Compact constitutes "the full settlement of all claims, past, present and future, of the Government, citizens and nationals of the Marshall Islands which are based upon, arise out of, or are in any way related to the Nuclear Testing Program" (ibid.).

[69] Ibid.

[70] Ibid.

[71] UN Office for Disarmament Affairs, Treaty on the Non-Proliferation of Nuclear Weapons, 729 UNTS 161. On April 24, 2014, a federal lawsuit was filed against the United States for breach of the NPT (S. Neuman, "Pacific Island Nation Sues US, Others for Violating Nuclear Treaty," Apr. 24, 2014, www.npr.org/sections/thetwo-way/2014/04/24/306540808/pacific-islands-sue-u-s-others-for-violating-nuclear-treaty). The lawsuit was rejected by the District Court on February 3, 2015, for lack of standing and under the political question doctrine (Republic of the *Marshall Islands* v. *United States*, 79 F. Supp. 3d 1068, 1072 (ND Cal. 2015)). The decision was affirmed by Court of Appeals. United States Court of Appeals for the Ninth Circuit, No. 15–15636, Submitted Mar. 15, 2017, Filed July 31, 2017.

violated both the NPT and customary international law.[72] The six NWS that had not accepted the jurisdiction of the ICJ (China, North Korea, France, Israel, Russian Federation, USA) continued to do so, thereby evading ICJ review.[73] The three states that had historically accepted ICJ jurisdiction (UK, India, Pakistan)[74] objected to the ICJ's jurisdiction in this particular case for a variety of reasons.[75]

On October 5, 2016, the ICJ issued three brief judgments declining to assert jurisdiction over the claims against India, Pakistan, and the United Kingdom, on the ground that no dispute existed between the Parties prior to the filing of the application.[76] The UN General Assembly responded to the controversy engendered by this case by resolving "to convene in 2017 a United Nations conference to negotiate a legally binding instrument to prohibit nuclear weapons, leading towards their total elimination."[77] The Treaty on the Prohibition of Nuclear Weapons was adopted at this Conference on July 7, 2017.[78] In addition, the RMI applications coincided with a review of the NPT, which resulted in three international conferences on the humanitarian impact of nuclear weapons: in Oslo, Norway (March 2013), Nayarit, Mexico (February 2014), and Vienna, Austria (December 2014).[79] In this regard, by submitting its claims to the ICJ, the RMI, a state that has been disproportionately affected by nuclear weapons, gave voice to the concerns of many nonnuclear weapons states.

---

[72] *Obligations concerning Negotiations relating to Cessation of the Nuclear Arms Race and to Nuclear Disarmament (Marshall Islands v. India)*, [2016] ICJ Rep 255; *Obligations concerning Negotiations relating to Cessation of the Nuclear Arms Race and to Nuclear Disarmament (Marshall Islands v. Pakistan)*, [2016] ICJ Rep 552.

[73] A. Poskakukhin, B. Heim, J. Moore, and G. Madurga, "The Republic of the Marshall Islands files Applications against nine States for their alleged failure to fulfil their obligations with respect to the cessation of the nuclear arms race at an early date and to nuclear disarmament," International Court of Justice, April 25, 2014.

[74] The Marshall Islands has based the court's jurisdiction on its own declaration of acceptance made on April 24, 2013, and those of the respondent states, made by Pakistan on September 13, 1960, India on September 18, 1974, and the United Kingdom on July 5, 2004.

[75] *Obligations concerning Negotiations relating to Cessation of the Nuclear Arms Race and to Nuclear Disarmament (Marshall Islands v. United Kingdom)*, Preliminary Objections, [2015] ICJ Rep 1; *Obligations concerning Negotiations relating to Cessation of the Nuclear Arms Race and to Nuclear Disarmament (Marshall Islands v. India)*, Counter-Memorial of India, [2015] ICJ Rep 1; *Obligations Concerning Negotiations Relating to Cessation of the Nuclear Arms Race and to Nuclear Disarmament (Marshall Islands v. Pakistan)*, Counter-Memorial of Pakistan (Jurisdiction and Admissibility), [2015] ICJ Rep 1..

[76] International Court of Justice, *Reports of Judgments, Advisory opinions and Orders: Obligations Concerning Negotiations Relating to Cessation of the Nuclear Arms Race and to Nuclear Disarmament: (Marshall Islands v. India)judgment of 5 October 2016* (New York: United Nations, 2016); International Court of Justice, *Reports of Judgments, Advisory opinions and Orders: Obligations Concerning Negotiations Relating to Cessation of the Nuclear Arms Race and to Nuclear Disarmament (Marshall Islands v. Pakistan)* (New York: United Nations, 2016); International Court of Justice, Reports of Judgments, Advisory opinions and Orders: Obligations Concerning Negotiations Relating to Cessation of the Nuclear Arms Race and to Nuclear Disarmament (Marshall Islands v. United Kingdom)(New York: United Nations, 2016).

[77] UN General Assembly, *Resolution 71/258: Taking forward multilateral nuclear disarmament negotiations*, Jan. 11, 2017, UN Doc. A/RES/71/258, para. 8. States voted in favor, with thirty-five against and thirteen abstaining.

[78] UN Conference to negotiate a legally binding instrument to prohibit nuclear weapons, leading towards their total elimination: UN General Assembly, *Treaty on the Prohibition of Nuclear Weapons*, July 7, 2017, UN Doc. A/CONF.299/2017/8; 122 states voted in favor, one voted against (Netherlands) and one abstained (Singapore); sixty-nine nations did not vote, including all of the NWS.

[79] Europe Integration Foreign Affairs – Federal Ministry Republic of Austria, "Report and Summary of Findings of the Conference presented under the sole responsibility of Austria," Vienna Conference on the Humanitarian Impact of Nuclear Weapons, Dec. 8–9, 2014; H. Williams, P. Lewis, and S. Aghlani, "The Humanitarian Impacts of Nuclear Weapons Initiative: The 'Big Tent' in Disarmament," research paper, Chatham House, Royal Institute of International Affairs, 2015.

18.5 THE MARSHALL ISLANDS CASE IN THE GLOBAL CONTEXT

The story of Marshall Islands provides yet another example of a colonial power using the territory of the colonized for its own ends, regardless of the impact on the local populations and the environment.

The impact of colonialism has been particularly severe in the case of small, sparsely populated island territories. Nauru and the Chagos archipelago, each with its own distinct characteristics, are examples of cases where colonial powers ruthlessly pursued their own interests without considering the needs of the local population. In Nauru, colonial powers, particularly Australia, exploited the island's extensive phosphate reserves, creating an environmental disaster which the new state, following the island's independence, did not know how to reverse. This served as an impediment to sustainable development.[80] In the Chagos archipelago, the United Kingdom expelled all of the archipelago's inhabitants in order to hand over the Island of Diego Garcia to the United States for use as a military base.[81]

Similarly, the Marshall Islands have been subject to colonial domination by successive powerful states, but always with minimal regard for the rights of their inhabitants. RMI's current political and economic dependency on the United States is just the latest iteration of a long-standing pattern. While payments by the United States under the 1983 Compact,[82] conditioned on maintaining the strategic military bases on Kwajalein Atoll and the Ronald Reagan Ballistic Missile Defense Test Site,[83] have contributed an estimated 50–70 percent of RMI's GDP since 1986, "the RMI economy has failed to grow in any sustained manner and trends in social indicators are worrying," including indicators relating to poverty eradication, health, and education.[84]

The inhabitants of the Marshall Islands did not benefit from the nuclear tests, did not ask for them, and were never consulted about the use of their territory, or informed about the consequences of the nuclear program in clear violation of international human rights principles.[85] The intensive nuclear testing destroyed Marshallese way of life, displaced them from their lands, and continues to have a significant, irreversible and long-term impact on their health and the environment.

---

[80] A. Anghie, "'The Heart of My Home': Colonialism, Environmental Damage, and the Nauru Case" (1993) 34 *Harvard International Law Journal* 445 at 461–491.

[81] D. Vine, *Island of Shame: The Secret History of the U.S. Military Base on Diego Garcia* (Princeton, NJ: Princeton University Press, 2009), chs. 5–7; P. H. Sand, "Diego Garcia: British–American Legal Black Hole in the Indian Ocean?" (2009) 21 *Journal of Environmental Law* 113–137. See also, UN General Assembly, *Resolution 71/292. Request for an advisory opinion of the International Court of Justice on the legal consequences of the separation of the Chagos Archipelago from Mauritius in 1965 Statement of financial implications*, June 22, 2017, UN Doc. A/RES/71/292.

[82] Ishtar, note 15, p. 300.

[83] Compact of Free Association Act of 1985, note 25. The Ronald Reagan Ballistic Missile Defense Test Site covers about 750,000 square miles and includes rocket launch sites at the Kwajalein Atoll (on multiple islands), Wake Island, and Aur Atoll.

[84] Republic of the Marshall Islands Ministry of Foreign Affairs, "Republic of the Marshall Islands: National Report," Prepared for the Third International Conference on Small Islands States in Apia, Samoa, May 2013; UNICEF, "United Nations Pacific Strategy 2018–2022: A Multi-Country Sustainable Development Framework in the Pacific Region," United Nations in the Pacific, 2017, pp. 11–14.

[85] K. Skoog, "U.S. Nuclear Testing on the Marshall Islands: 1946 to 1958" (2003) 3 *Teaching Ethics* 67 at 72; R. Tsosie, "Indigenous Peoples and the Ethics of Remediation: Redressing the Legacy of Radioactive Contamination for Native Peoples and Native Lands" (2015) 13 *Santa Clara Journal of International Law* 203 at 271. However, the practice has not been exclusive to the United States (Ruff, note 11, pp. 777–778).

Under Article 76 of the UN Charter, the United States, as trustee was under an obligation to protect the islanders' interests but failed to do so.[86] Moreover, the United Nations declined to implement effective monitoring to ensure said obligations were fulfilled.[87] As a practical matter, at least until 1960, the international community accepted and tacitly endorsed the right of administrative powers to take over the natural resources of their colonial possessions.[88] This case clearly shows how the legal instruments that purport to promote decolonization – the mandate and trusteeship systems – have historically allowed trustees to develop by exploiting trust territory's land and resources in total disregard of the impact on the local populations while externalizing the environmental costs.[89]

Furthermore, the people of the Marshall Islands have been denied access to any form of justice. The rulings issued by the Nuclear Claims Tribunal have not been enforced due to lack of funds. When the islanders brought suit in the US federal courts, their claims were denied on the basis of the 1983 Compact that laid the groundwork for decolonization. And when they sought congressional review and amendment of this agreement, the application was opposed by the executive branch of the US government. Ultimately, congressional action resulted in the award of only minimal compensation for harms caused by the nuclear testing program.

The UN Charter was insufficient to protect the Marshall Islands from US abuse of the trusteeship regime. The 1983 Compact that ultimately resulted in independence for the RMI was violated by the United States through its refusal to correctly apply the clause relating to the changed circumstances. Moreover, the matter is not actionable before US federal courts as judicial review would interfere with the conduct of foreign relations. The end result is denial of justice for Marshallese people. Therefore, the Special Rapporteur, Calin Georgescu, urged the international community and the United Nations to: "Recall that the Marshall Islands were placed under the trusteeship of the United States of America by the international community, which therefore has an ongoing obligation to encourage a final and just resolution for the Marshallese people."[90]

The Marshall Islands case study also illustrates the violation of all four components of environmental justice – distributive, procedural, corrective, and social.[91] Furthermore, the United States has incurred an ecological debt toward the state and peoples of the Marshall

[86] According to Article 76 of the United Nations Charter: "The basic objectives of the trusteeship system, in accordance with the Purposes of the United Nations laid down in Article 1 of the present Charter, shall be . . . b. to promote the political, economic, social, and educational advancement of the inhabitants of the trust territories, and their progressive development towards self-government or independence as may be appropriate to the particular circumstances of each territory and its peoples and the freely expressed wishes of the peoples concerned, and as may be provided by the terms of each trusteeship agreement" (UN, note 6, Art. 76).

[87] The same colonial powers controlled the decisions made by the UN Trusteeship Council. On May 28, 1986, the Trusteeship Council, adopted Resolution 2183 (LIII) in favor of ending the regime, having considered that the United States, as Administering Authority of the Trust Territory of the Pacific Islands, had "satisfactorily discharged its obligations under the terms of the Trusteeship Agreement."

[88] UN General Assembly, *Resolution 1514 (XV) Declaration on the Granting of Independence to Colonial Countries and Peoples*, Dec. 14, 1960, UN Doc. A/RES/1514(XV).

[89] See A. Anghie, *Imperialism, Sovereignty and the Making if International Law* (New York: Cambridge University Press, 2004), p. 192; A. Pigrau, "Conceptual Background," in A. Pigrau, S. Borràs, A. Cardesa-Salzmann, and J. Jaria i Manzano, "International Law and Ecological Debt: International Claims, Debates and Struggles for Environmental Justice," EJOLT Report No. 11, Jan. 2014, pp. 10–11.

[90] UNGA, note 16, para. 66(a).

[91] A. Nollkaemper, "Sovereignty and Environmental Justice in International Law," in J. Ebbesson and P. Okowa (eds.), *Environmental Law and Justice in Context* (New York: Cambridge University Press, 2009), p. 253; C. G. Gonzalez, "Environmental Justice, Human Rights, and the Global South" (2015) 13 *Santa Clara Journal of International Law* 151 at 155.

Islands for having deliberately caused serious and long-lasting ecological harm, which has a direct impact on inhabitants, and for preventing the state and its inhabitants from benefiting from the ecosystems that exist in their territory.[92]

Adding insult to injury, there is further injustice caused to Marshall Islands by climate change. The RMI faces existential threats from the impacts of climate change, such as rising sea levels that will devastate its low-lying islands and atolls. The RMI contributes less than 0.00001 percent of annual global greenhouse gas emissions.[93] Its cumulative carbon dioxide (CO_2) emissions from 1751 to 2016 consists of 2.14 million tons, which represents 0.0054 percent of US emissions over the same period.[94] Despite the RMI's minimal greenhouse gas emissions, climate change could lead to the total annihilation of the islands. As the world's second largest emitter of greenhouse gases, the United States has refused to take measures to reduce its emissions and its recent withdrawal from the Paris Agreement shows its determination not to change its profligate way of life.[95] This constitutes yet another example of the ecological debt owed by the United States to the RMI and another manifestation of environmental injustice. The Marshall Islands case study illustrates that environmental and social injustice are inextricably intertwined. While the nuclear dimension makes this an extreme case, RMI shares the consequences of colonial and postcolonial domination (and resulting economic vulnerability) with many other countries.

In an attempt to address some of these disparities in the global community, especially poverty, the international community adopted Agenda 2030 and the Sustainable Development Goals (SDGs) in 2015.[96] The SDGs aim to balance the economic, social, and environmental dimensions of sustainable development. However, they treat poverty and environmental degradation as if they were natural disasters rather than drawing an explicit causal link between the prevailing global economic system and such challenges. The SDGs' focus on supposedly independent national policymaking fails to take into account the impact on SDG implementation of the global economic system, including the international legal frameworks for trade, investment, and intellectual property; the ways that these international frameworks constrain national decision-making; and the lack of accountability of powerful countries and multinational corporations for practices that violate the SDGs.[97] Without questioning the foundations of the global economic order with its roots in colonialism, and the legal instruments that sustain that order, achieving these

---

[92] See E. Paredis, J. Lambrecht, G. Goeminne, and W. Vanhove, "VLIR-BVO Project 2003: 'Elaboration of the concept of ecological debt,'" Centre for Sustainable Development – Ghent University, Sept. 1, 2004, p. 50; J. Jaria i Manzano, A. Cardesa-Salzmann, A. Pigrau, and S. Borras, "Measuring Environmental Injustice: How Ecological Debt Defines a Radical Change in the International Legal System" (2016) 23 *Journal of Political Ecology* 381.

[93] UNFCCC, note 1.

[94] H. Ritchie and M. Roser, "CO_2 and other Greenhouse Gas Emissions," 2019, https://ourworldindata.org/co2-and-other-greenhouse-gas-emissions.

[95] B.R. Johnston, "Atomic Times in the Pacific" (2009) 1 *Anthropology NOW* 1–10 at 9. Hence the support the RMI receives from other countries in the region that are particularly vulnerable to climate change: Pacific Islands Forum Secretariat, "Forty-Fourth Pacific Islands Forum, Majuro, Republic of the Marshall Islands, 3–5 September 2013: Forum Communiqué," paras. 49–51. See IOM, note 8, p. 9.

[96] UN General Assembly, *Resolution 70/1. Transforming our world: the 2030 Agenda for Sustainable Development*, Oct. 21, 2015, UN Doc. A/RES/70/1.

[97] UN General Assembly, *Right to Development: Report of the Secretary-General and the UN High Commissioner for Human Rights*, July 26, 2017, UN. Doc. A/HRC/36/23, para. 51; S. Deva, "Human Rights Violations by Multinational Corporations and International Law: Where from Here?" (2003) 19 *Connecticut Journal of International Law* 1; P. Simons, "International Law's Invisible Hand and the Future of Corporate Accountability for Violations of Human Rights" (2012) 3 *Journal of Human Rights and Environment* 5 at 40.

goals is not feasible.[98] With sparse funding committed by the Global North to achieve SDGs, the Global North will continue to impose the financial burden of SDG implementation on the Global South. Ignoring the underlying economic system is the main reason for the current predicament over the very concept of sustainable development.[99] Sustainable development, which requires the protection of the environment and the people to be an integral part of the development process, and which was consolidated as a conceptual matrix[100] of international environmental law, has turned out to be a weak and malleable concept in practice. Sustainable development has been incorporated into the hegemonic development discourse in ways that maintain the unfair allocation of resources and their irrational and ultimately unsustainable use. Therefore, the influence of this kind of sustainable development on national and international law constitutes an inadequate response to achieving intragenerational justice.[101] The UN reports that evaluate progress on the integration of the three pillars of sustainable development have highlighted the weakness of the social and environmental pillars in the face of the economic pillar.[102]

The concept of sustainable development needs to be reclaimed from hegemonic development discourse by placing the emphasis on its social justice component, in line with the binding framework of human rights,[103] (which must also be reconceptualized),[104] in order to place ecological sustainability at its core – as the foundation for both social and economic pillars. A healthy environment makes it possible for present and future generations to enjoy an adequate standard of living in accordance with the social pillar of sustainable development, irrespective of when and where they were born. Environmental justice requires that the costs and benefits of economic and social development be shared fairly, in such a way that those who are least fortunate not only aspire to improving their situation, but are also protected against unfair distribution of costs and have the opportunity to receive reparations when they have had to assume disproportionate burdens.

Projecting the concept of environmental justice into the international arena requires strengthening the concepts of differential treatment and compensatory equity used in the debate

---

[98] R. Goodland and H. Daly, "Environmental Sustainability: Universal and Non-Negotiable" (1996) 6 *Ecological Applications* 1002 at 1004; A. Cardesa-Salzmann and A. Pigrau, "La agenda 2030 y los objetivos para el desarrollo sostenible. Una mirada crítica sobre su aportación a la gobernanza global en términos de justicia distributiva y sostenibilidad ambiental" (2017) 69 *Revista Española de Derecho Internacional* 1 at 279–285.

[99] J. E. Viñuales, "The Rise and Fall of Sustainable Development" (2013) 22 *Review of European, Comparative and International Environmental Law* 1 at 3–13.

[100] P. M. Dupuy, "Où en est le droit international de l'environnement à la fin du siècle?" (1997) 101 *Revue générale de droit international public*, 873 at 878.

[101] A. Pigrau, "España, la Unión Europea, el Derecho internacional y el desarrollo insostenible," in J. Alcaide Fernández and E. W. Petit de Gabriel (eds.), *España y la Unión Europea en el orden internacional* (Valencia: Tirant lo Blanch, 2017), pp. 1253–1288.

[102] See UN General Assembly, *Progress to date and remaining gaps in the implementation of the outcomes of the major summits in the area of sustainable development, as well as an analysis of the themes of the Conference: Report of the Secretary-General*, Apr. 1, 210 UN. Doc. A/CONF.216/PC/2.

[103] S. Atapattu, "The Paris Agreement and Human Rights: Is Sustainable Development the 'New Human Right'?" (2018) 9 *Journal of Human Rights and the Environment* 68 at 80–82, 84–86; J. H. Knox, "Human Rights, Environmental Protection, and the Sustainable Development Goals" (2015) 24 *Washington International Law Journal* 3 at 517–536; see UN General Assembly, *Report of the Special Rapporteur on the issue of human rights obligations relating to the enjoyment of a safe, clean, healthy and sustainable environment*, Jan. 24, 2018 UN, Doc. A/HRC/37/59.

[104] J. Jaria i Manzano, "Si fuera sólo una cuestión de fe. Una crítica sobre el sentido y la utilidad del reconocimiento de derechos a la naturaleza en la Constitución del Ecuador" (2013) 4 *Revista Chilena de Derecho Y Ciencia Política* 43; L. J. Kotzé, "Human Rights and the Environment in the Anthropocene" (2014) 1 *Anthropocene Review* 252; Gonzalez, note 96, pp. 172–193.

over development[105] (including the concept of common but differentiated responsibilities),[106] as well as reaffirming the right of all states and peoples to participate in decision-making processes.[107] Environmental justice also requires taking into account and confronting inequality within states. Hence it must pierce the veil of the state in order to meet people's needs and must promote the substantive goals of intragenerational[108] and intergenerational[109] equity as well as the environmental procedural rights of access to information, participation in decision-making and access to justice in environmental matters.[110]

In 2014, the government of RMI, which had been supporting victims' claims, changed its strategy by simultaneously adopting two lines of action that focused on the violation of the NPT, by states that possess nuclear weapons.[111] The debate shifted from personal injury and environmental damage to the global question of the very existence of nuclear weapons and the NPT, the key instrument of the nuclear weapons regime. The multiple actions brought before the ICJ could have enabled it to deliver a ruling on the unsustainability of the nuclear nonproliferation regime in its current form. Regrettably, given the disappointing judgments delivered in October 2016,[112] it seems this was not to be.

---

[105] UN General Assembly, *Declaration for the Establishment of a New International Economic Order*, May 1, 1974, UN Doc. A/RES/S-6/3201; UN General Assembly, *Charter of Economic Rights and Duties of States*, Dec. 12, 1974, UN Doc. A/RES/3281 (XXIX).

[106] UN General Assembly, *Report of the United Nations Conference on Environment and Development*, Aug. 12, 1992, UN Doc. A/CONF.151/26 (Vol. I), Principle 7. See K. Mickelson, "South, North, International Environmental Law, and International Environmental Lawyers" (2000) 11 *Yearbook of International Environmental Law* 58 at 69–78; P. Cullet, "Differential Treatment in International Law: Towards a New Paradigm of Inter-state Relations" (1999) 10 *European Journal of International Law* 549; L. Rajamani, *Differential Treatment in International Environmental Law* (Oxford: Oxford University Press, 2006), esp. ch. 7; UNGA, note 105, para. 56.

[107] A. Pigrau Solé, *Subdesarrollo y adopción de decisiones en la economía mundial* (Madrid: Tecnos, 1990), pp. 185–260.

[108] C. G. Gonzalez, "Bridging the North–South Divide: International Environmental Law in the Anthropocene" (2015) 32 *Pace Environmental Law Review* 407 at 426–429.

[109] UNGA, note 103; International Law Association, *Report of the Seventieth Conference Held in New Delhi 2–6 April 2002* (London: Cambrian Printers, 2002), pp. 22–29; E. Brown Weiss, "In Fairness to Future Generations and Sustainable Development" (1992) 8 *American University Journal of International Law and Policy* 19.

[110] UNGA, note 102; UNGA, note 103; UN ECE, Convention on Access to Information, Public Participation in Decision-Making and Access to Justice in Environmental Matters, June 28, 1998 2161 UNTS 447; A. Barcena, "Regional Agreement on Access to Information, Public Participation and Justice in Environmental Matters in Latin America and the Caribbean," United Nations ECLAC, Mar. 4, 2018.

[111] UN Office for Disarmament Affairs, note 71. The Republic of the Marshall Islands acceded to the Treaty on Jan. 30, 1995.

[112] See ICJ judgments, note 75.

Resource Extraction

19

The Vedanta (Niyamgiri) Case

Promoting Environmental Justice and Sustainable Development

Stellina Jolly

19.1 INTRODUCTION

On April 18, 2013, in the case of *Orissa Mining Corporation v. Ministry of Environment and Forest and Others*[1] (Vedanta mining) the Supreme Court of India decreed that the 'Gram Sabha'[2] has authority to determine whether the proposed project would affect individual or community rights including cultural and religious rights under the Scheduled Tribes and Other Traditional Forest Dwellers (Recognition of Forest Rights) Act, 2006 and that this is a precondition before the mining process in 'Niyamgiri' hills can proceed. The judgment is a significant victory for the 'Dongria Kondh,' a small tribal Adivasi community,[3] residing in the Niyamgiri hills, who have been involved in an organic, grassroots resistance movement for decades against the corporate giant Vedanta. Following the judgment, the first environmental referendum was conducted in all the twelve 'Gram Sabhas' located in the Niyamgiri hills in July 2013.[4] In a scintillating process that has been unprecedented in the Indian legal context, the Dongria Kondh demonstrated the unity and resistance of the marginalized, and all the twelve 'Gram Sabhas' unequivocally rejected the project. This chapter explores the innovative interpretation adopted by the Supreme Court of the free and prior informed consent (FPIC) principle and discusses its potential reimagination in shaping the contemporary environmental justice discourse by considering the development narrative and the experience of marginalized communities.

Section 19.2 of the chapter contextualizes the Vedanta project and the struggle by the Dongria Kondh by considering the rise of environmental movements as part of the evolution of environmental justice in India and interlinkages with sustainable development. Section 19.3 explores

---

[1] *Orissa Mining Corporation v. Ministry of Environment and Forests and Others*, 2013 6 SCR 881, p. 3 [Vedanta].

[2] According to s. 2(g) of the Forest Rights Act, 2006 (FRA) (India), 'Grama Sabha' "means a village assembly which shall consist of all adult members of a village and in case of States having no Panchayats, Padas, Tolas and other traditional village institutions and elected village committees, with full and unrestricted participation of women."

[3] The Adivasi communities are generally equated with the tribal communities. The word 'Adivasi' is a Hindi term meaning descendants of the original inhabitants. From that perspective, Adivasis can be equated with the Indigenous population. See D. J. Rycroft and S. Dasgupta (eds.), *Indigenous Pasts and the Politics of Belonging, in The Politics of Belonging in India: Becoming Adivasi* (Abingdon, UK: Taylor & Francis, 2011), p. 1; M. R. Krishna, *First Citizens: Studies on Adivasis, Tribals, and Indigenous Peoples in India* (Oxford: Oxford University Press, 2016), p. 12.

[4] S. P. Raut, "Land Law and Resistance Legal Pluralism and Tribal Conflicts over Land Alienation in Orissa," in M. Bavinck and A. Jyotishi (eds.), *Conflict, in Negotiations and Natural Resource Management: A Legal Pluralism Perspective from India* (Abingdon, UK: Routledge, 2014), p. 88.

the essential components and settings of the environmental justice movement and assesses how the social pillar of sustainable development has been perceived and interpreted by the judiciary to promote environmental justice and human rights. Section 19.4 addresses the evolution of FPIC with a special focus on the Indian legal and judicial context. Section 19.5 examines the innovative interpretation of FPIC in the Vedanta judgment. Section 19.6 concludes by drawing out the implications of the Vedanta judgment for environmental justice and sustainable development in India.

19.2 CONTEXTUALIZING THE VEDANTA PROJECT AND STRUGGLE OF DONGRIA KONDH

The unexplored lush green Niyamgiri mountains in the eastern ghats of India is a storehouse of minerals and home to rich biodiversity.[5] The Dongria Kondh, regarded as an endangered tribe, has been part of the landscape for many generations.[6] The community shares a symbiotic, traditional, customary, and sacred relationship with the area embedded through their cultural and religious beliefs.[7]

In 2003, M/s Sterlite Industries (India) Limited (SIIL), fully owned and controlled by Vedanta Resources, proposed to set up an alumina refinery and bauxite mining from the area adjoining Lanjigarh in Kalahandi district, based on a memorandum of understanding (MoU) signed with the government of Orissa.[8] On August, 2004, M/s Sterlite filed a separate forest clearance application for the construction of a refinery and a conveyor belt to connect the refinery and the mine.[9] In September 2004, environment clearance for the construction of an alumina refinery was granted by the Ministry of Environment and Forests (MoEF) with the condition that the Sterlite industries should obtain separate clearance for bauxite mining from MoEF and on the understanding that no forest land be cleared by the project.[10] The State of Orissa forwarded the proposal to MoEF for diversion of forest land for mining bauxite ore in favor of Orissa Mining Corporation and SIIL.[11] Writ petitions were filed at the High Court in Orissa and in the Supreme Court of India challenging the proposed bauxite mining on the grounds that it violated India's constitutional provisions under Schedule V.[12] The Supreme Court's Centre

[5] "A brief report on Biodiversity and Ecological Significance of Niyamgiri Hill and Implications of Bauxite Mining," p. 5.

[6] S. Marshall and S. Balaton-Chrimes, "Tribal Claims against the Vedanta Bauxite Mine in Niyamgiri, India What Role Did the UK OECD National Contact Point Play in Instigating Free, Prior and Informed Consent?" Non-Judicial Redress Mechanisms Report Series 9, Corporate Accountability Research, 2016, p. 14.

[7] M. Tatpati, A. Kothari, and R. Mishra, "The Niyamgiri Story: Challenging the Idea of Growth without Limits?" Kalpavriksh, Oxfam-India, July 2016, p. 5; N. C. Saxena, S. Parasuraman, P. Kant, and A. Baviskar, "Report of the Four Member Committee for Investigation into the Proposal Submitted by the Orissa Mining Company for Bauxite Mining in Niyamgiri," Ministry of Environment and Forests, Government of India, Aug. 16 , 2010, pp. 25–26.

[8] Saxena et al., note 7, p. 14. As per the MoU, a certain quantity of bauxite for the plant was to be supplied by the Orissa Mining Corporation, a government undertaking. See B. K. Sidhu, "The Niyamgiri Hills Bauxite Project-Balancing Resource Extraction and Environment Protection" (2011) 41 *Environment Policy and Law* 166 at 167.

[9] Sidhu, note 8, p. 166.

[10] Ibid.

[11] Vedanta, note 1, para. 4.

[12] Saxena et al., note 7, p. 14. The legal system in India follows a hierarchy in judicial structure with the Supreme Court as the apex body followed by High Courts and District Courts. Schedule V pertains to the administration and control of Scheduled Areas and Scheduled Tribes. The 'Dongria Tribe' occupying the Niyamgiri are notified Scheduled Tribes.

Empowered Committee (CEC), an advisory body set up to advise the court on environmental issues, investigated aspects of the case,[13] highlighted violations of constitutional and statutory provisions, and recommended that the mining operations should not be granted forest clearance.[14] However, the recommendations of the CEC were disregarded by the Supreme Court which approved the clearance of the forest in the Niyamgiri Hills in August 2008.[15] Allegations of instances of violation of environmental laws by the company following approval of the clearances prompted MoEF to establish a committee (hereafter, Saxena Committee) to look into the issue of forest diversion.[16]

In the face of fierce protests and resistance exhibited by the Dongria community, and the report of the Saxena Committee, the MoEF rejected the forest clearance for the proposed bauxite mining project at Niyamgiri.[17] It has also been suggested that the decision of the MoEF may have been bolstered by a finding of the UK National Contact Point (UK NPC), a nonjudicial human rights mechanism created in accordance with the Organisation for Economic Co-operation and Development (OECD) Guidelines for Multinational Enterprises.[18] However, the decision of the MoEF was challenged by the Orissa Mining Corporation and in a landmark 2013 judgment, the Supreme Court of India held that mining could proceed only with the consent of the Dongria Kondh communities.[19] In August 2013, all twelve tribal villages through their 'Gram Sabha' voted against Vedanta's project in the Niyamgiri Hills.[20] The Orissa Mining Corporation again challenged the decision of the 'Gram Sabhas' in the Supreme Court in early 2016. On May 6, 2016, the Supreme Court rejected the petition of the Corporation.[21] The Dongria Kondh struggle is a powerful illustration of community resistance for the inalienable right to existence, preservation of cultural rights, accessibility to natural resources, and sustainable management of resources. The next section discusses the evolution of environmental justice and the incorporation of the concept of sustainable development in India that gave rise to this result.

19.3 EVOLUTION OF ENVIRONMENTAL JUSTICE AND INCORPORATION OF SUSTAINABLE DEVELOPMENT IN INDIA

19.3.1 *Environmental Justice in the Global Context*

The environmental justice movement originated formally as a reaction to the disproportionate impact of the dumping of toxic industrial wastes on marginalized communities in the USA.[22]

---

[13] Supreme Court of India in its order dated 09/05/2002 in Writ Petitions (Civil) Nos. 202/95 & 171/96 ordered to constitute a Centre Empowered Committee (CEC) "for monitoring of the implementation of Hon'ble Court's orders and to place the non-compliance of cases before it."

[14] Saxena et al., note 7, p.14.

[15] Ibid., p. 15.

[16] Ibid., p. 14.

[17] A. Bindal, "Resurrecting the Other of Modern Law: Investigating Niyamgiri Judgment & Legal Epistemology" (2014) 5 *NUJS Journal of Indian Law and Society* 237–248 at 240. See also Vedanta, note 1, para. 1.

[18] Marshall et al., note 6, p. 6; R. Bass, D. Dio, and S. Moreno, "Final Statement by the UK National Contact Point for the OECD Guidelines for Multinational Enterprises: Complaint from Survival International against Vedanta Resource plc," Sept. 25, 2009; see generally S. L. Seck, "Indigenous Rights, Environmental Rights, or Stakeholder Engagement? Comparing IFC and OECD Approaches to Implementation of the Business Responsibility to Respect Human Rights" (2016) 12 *JSDLP – RDPDD* 51–88.

[19] Vedanta, note 1, para. 63.

[20] Raut, note 4, p. 88.

[21] Marshall et al., note 6, p. 7.

[22] R. L. Turner and D. P. Wu, "Environmental Justice and Environmental Racism: An Annotated Bibliography and General Overview, Focusing on U.S. Literature, 1996–2002," Berkeley Workshop on Environmental

From a narrow focus on land use management in the urban setting, the environmental justice movement has made substantial progress in expanding its coverage[23] in relation to multiple issues, jurisdictions, and localities through grassroots resistance, litigation, and legislative reforms.[24]

In spite of the broad and general acceptance of environmental justice, ambiguities persist regarding its definition and scope. The concept of environmental justice encompasses the crucial components of distributive, procedural, corrective, and social justice.[25] At the global level, these core components of environmental justice were ameliorated through incorporation of procedural human rights[26] and the subsuming of environmental justice into the foundation for the conceptualization of sustainable development.[27]

19.3.2 *Environmental Justice in Indian Context*

Environmental justice discourse in India did not begin with a mere focus on the disproportionate impacts on the marginalized communities and population. It was broadly based, to begin with, and has taken multi-pluralistic forms and languages.[28] The Indian environmental justice movement, for the most part, has ingrained the broad concept of social justice with development at the core. The emblematic Chipko movement[29] with its rural context and all-encompassing nature became popularized as the environmentalism of the poor and raised concerns of justice and sustainability.[30]

Environmental justice terminology emerged in India in the aftermath of the Bhopal industrial tragedy which highlighted the hollowness of the environmental laws operating in the country.[31]

Politics, Institute of International Studies, University of California, Berkeley, 2002; R. D. Bullard (ed.), *Dumping in Dixie: Race, Class and Environmental Quality* (3rd ed.) (Abingdon, UK: Routledge, 2000), p. 16.

[23] A. Kaswan, "Environmental Justice and Environmental Law" (2003) 24 *Fordham Environmental Law Review* 149–179; A. Dobson, *Justice and the Environment: Conceptions of Environmental Sustainability and Theories of Distributive Justice* (Oxford: Oxford University Press, 1998), p. 33.

[24] S. Foster, "Justice from the Ground up: Distributive Inequities, Grassroots Resistance, and the Transformative Politics of the Environmental Justice Movement" (1998) 86 *California Law Review* 4 at 776; C. Rechtschaf, "Strategies for Implementing the Environmental Justice" (2008) 1 *Golden Gate Environmental Law Journal* 321.

[25] C. Gonzalez, "Environmental Justice, Human Rights, and the Global South" (2015) 13 *Santa Clara Journal of International Law* 151–195 at 155; see S. Foster, "Environmental Justice in an Era of Devolved Collaboration" (2002) 26 *Harvard Environmental Law Review* 459–498.

[26] A. Boyle, "Human Rights and the Environment: Where Next?" (2012) 23 *European Journal of International Law* 3 at 613–642; J. H. Knox, "Human Rights, Environmental Protection, and the Sustainable Development Goals" (2015) 24 *Washington International Law Journal* at 517–536.

[27] D. McGoldrick, "Sustainable Development and Human Rights: An Integrated Conception" (1996) 45 *International and Comparative Law Quarterly* 796–818 at 796; E. B. Weiss, "In Fairness to Future Generations and Sustainable Development" (1992) 8 *American University Journal of International Law and Policy* 19–26; J. B. Ruhl, "The Co-Evolution of Sustainable Development and Environmental Justice: Cooperation, Then Competition, Then Conflict" (1999) 9 *Duke Environmental Law & Policy Forum* 161–186 at 182.

[28] S. C. Shastri, *Environmental Law* (Lucknow: Eastern Book Company, 2002); J. M. Alier, *The Environmentalism of the Poor* (New Delhi: Oxford University Press, 2005); R. Guha, *Environmentalism: A Global History* (New Delhi: Oxford University Press, 2000); R. Guha and J. M. Alier, *Varieties of Environmentalism: Essays North and South* (New Delhi: Oxford University Press, 1998).

[29] Chipko movement was a forest conservation movement where people embraced the trees to prevent them being cut. See V. Shiva, *Staying Alive: Women, Ecology and Survival in India* (Delhi: Kali for Women, 1998), p. 63.

[30] R. Guha, "Social–Ecological Research in India: A Status Report" (1997) 32 *Economic and Political Weekly* 345–352; Guha and Alier, note 28.

[31] C. M. Jariwala, "The Directions of Environmental Justice: An Overview Critical Appraisal of 1987 Law" (1993) 35 *Journal of Indian Law Institute* 92–114.

The long legal battle and the inordinate delay in receiving compensation, highlighted the distributive and corrective injustices caused to the marginalized sections of society.[32] As far as the terminology and language of the environmental justice movement are concerned, there exist divergent views with legal academics concentrating more on the access and delivery of environmental justice through the legal system.[33] Experts from other subject disciplines have employed a more holistic approach and analysis with Guha and Agarwal employing the term environmentalism of the poor.[34] According to Guha, "Crusading Gandhians, Appropriate Technologists and Ecological Marxists represent the three most forceful strands in the environment-development debate in India."[35] However, regarding the actual language used by the communities at the grassroots level, one does not see environmental justice as a leading discourse, but rather references to philosophical, cultural, religious, political, and moral debates.[36] For instance, the movement against the construction of Tehri dam resorted to religious arguments with the river 'Ganga' being the mother.[37] In the case of Vedanta, the tribal resistance was based on the perceived threat brought by the project to the Niyamgiri, the spiritual abode of the Dongria Kondh. Further, the undercurrent of historical injustices, characterized mainly in the form of the caste system, has always been important.[38]

Environmental justice activism flourished through the mechanisms of environmental litigation and the grassroots civil society movement. However, in most of the cases, these strategies were combined with litigation being the major component. In 2010, the National Green Tribunal was established with an explicit reference to administering environmental justice.[39] Though judgments have referred to 'environmental justice' as a significant object of the legal framework,[40] they have not explored a general theory on environmental justice. The same pattern can be seen in other South Asian jurisdictions where an absence of a conceptual definition of environmental justice can be observed.[41]

In the case of *Asghar Leghari*,[42] the Lahore High Court observed "The existing environmental jurisprudence has to be fashioned to meet the needs of something more urgent and overpowering (i.e. climate change). From environmental justice, which was largely localized and limited to our ecosystems and biodiversity, we need to move to climate justice. Fundamental rights lay at the foundation of these two overlapping justice systems."[43] In the case of *S. P. Sharma Dhungel*

---

[32] J. Cassels, "The Uncertain Promise of Law: Lessons from Bhopal" (1991) 29 *Osgoode Hall Law Journal* 6–8.

[33] M. K. Ramesh, "Environmental Justice: Courts and Beyond" (2002) 3 *Indian Journal of Environmental Law* 32; G. N. Gill, *Environmental Justice in India: The National Green Tribunal* (Abingdon, UK: Routledge Explorations in Environmental Studies, 2016).

[34] R. Guha, "Anil Agarwal and the Environmentalism of the Poor" (2002) 13 *Capitalism Nature Socialism* 147–155.

[35] R. Guha, "Ideological Trends in Indian Environmentalism" (1988) 23 *Economic and Political Weekly* 49 at 2578–2581.

[36] M. Sharma, "Passages from Nature to Nationalism: Sunderlal Bahuguna and Tehri Dam Opposition in Garhwal" (2009) 44 *Economic & Political Weekly* at 35–42.

[37] Ibid.

[38] *Kailas and Others v. State of Maharashtra Tr. Taluka P.S.*, SLP (Crl) No. 10367 of 2010.

[39] Gill, note 33; S. Shrotria, "Environmental Justice Is the National Green Tribunal of India effective" (2015) 17 *Environmental Law Review* at 169–188.

[40] *Kalpavriksh Others v. Union of India Others*, July 17, 2014, Application No. 116 (Thc) of 2013.

[41] P. Basu, "Environmental Justice in South and South East Asia: Inequalities and Struggles in Rural and Urban Context," in R. Holifield, J. Chakraborty, and G. Walker (eds.), *Routledge Handbook of Environmental Justice* (Abingdon, UK: Routledge, 2017), pp. 603–614.

[42] *Asghar Leghari v. Federation of Pakistan*, WP No. 25501/2015.

[43] Ibid.

v. *Godavari Marble Industries*[44] involving the health and environmental hazards of marble indus-tries in Nepal, the Supreme Court of Nepal seemed to have equated environmental justice with the right to a healthy environment by expanding the scope of the right to life in the Constitution.

19.4 PROMOTION OF ENVIRONMENTAL JUSTICE THROUGH SUSTAINABLE DEVELOPMENT AND HUMAN/CONSTITUTIONAL RIGHTS

Environmental protection in India was advanced through the creative expansionist interpret-ation of the right to life guaranteed under Article 21,[45] directive principles under Articles 48[46] and 51(a)(g) of the Indian Constitution[47] and the incorporation of the principle of sustainable development. Various judgments have emphasized facets of the fundamental right to a healthy environment and established substantive and procedural obligations to make environmental decision-making more transparent, better informed, and more responsive to the public. The result has been to promote environmental justice even though the cases did not specifically refer to environmental justice.[48] Second, the concept of sustainable development as developed under international instruments was also incorporated into judicial decisions to balance environmental protection and economic development for a just and sustainable future.[49] Yet, although the courts in India have adopted sustainable development as the overarching goal, there has not been any comprehensive discussion of its definition and parameters. The court in *Vellore Citizens Welfare Forum* v. *Union of India and Others*,[50] the first case which articulated the concept of sustainable development, traced its legal development to the precautionary principle and the polluter pays principle.[51]

At the global level, the social pillar of sustainable development incorporates human rights[52] which has influenced similar incorporation at the domestic level. In the case of *N D Jayal* v. *Union of India*[53] the Supreme Court of India proactively pronounced that sustainable development is part of Article 21 as a fundamental right. The court stated that the "right to environment is a fundamental right. On the other hand right to development is also one. Here the right to 'sustainable development' cannot be singled out. Therefore, the concept of sustain-able development is to be treated as an integral part of 'life' under Article 21."[54]

---

[44] *Suray Prasad Sharma Dhungel* v. *Godavari Marble Industries and Others*, WP 35/1992 (Oct. 31, 1995); S. P. Subedi, "Environmental Inputs into the Planning Process and Access to Justice" (1998) 28 *Environmental Policy and Law* 96–103; S. Ghimire, "Concept of Environmental Justice in Nepal: Environmentalism of Poor for Sustainable Livelihood" (2003) 1 *Himalayan Journal of Sciences* 47–50.

[45] Constitution of India 1949, Art. 21.

[46] Ibid., Arts. 48 and 53.

[47] A. Rhuks, *Environmental Justice in Developing Countries: Perspectives from Africa and Asia-Pacific* (Abingdon, UK: Routledge, 2013), p. 61; *Damodhar Rao* v. *Municipal Corporation, Hyderabad*, AIR 1987 AP 170; L. K. Koolwal v. State of Rajasthan, AIR 1988 Raj 2; *Attakoya Thangal* v. *Union of India*, 1990 KLT 580.

[48] S. Dam, "Polluting Environment, Polluting Constitution: Is a 'Polluted' Constitution Worse than a Polluted Environment?" (2005) 17 *Journal of Environmental Law* 383; M. R. Anderson, "Individual Rights to Environmental Protection in India," in A. Boyle and M. Anderson (eds.), *Human Right Approaches to Environmental Protection* (Oxford: Clarendon Press), pp. 199–225, 201.

[49] A. Basu, "Balancing of Competing Rights through Sustainable Development: Role of Indian Judiciary" (2015) 6 *Jindal Global Law Review* 61–72 at 69.

[50] *Vellore Citizens Welfare Forum* v. *Union of India & Others*, AIR 1996 SC647.

[51] R. Ramalogum, *Sustainable Development: Towards a Judicial Interpretation* (Leiden: Nijhoff, 2010), p. 112.

[52] K. Arts, "Inclusive Sustainable Development: A Human Rights Perspective" (2017) 24 *Current Opinion in Environmental Sustainability* 58–62; United Nations, *Copenhagen Declaration on Social Development*, Mar. 14, 1995, UN Doc. A/CONF.166/9.

[53] *N D Jayal* v. *Union of India*, AIR, 2004 SC 867.

[54] Ibid.

Studies reveal that environmental movements spearheaded by marginalized communities against multinational corporations especially involving Indigenous peoples' right of access to resources in the face of the deliberate denial of rights became an important area of development–environment conflict.[55] In this context, self-determination expressed through the concept of FPIC is significant and serves to integrate principles of environmental justice and sustainability in order to provide a stronger moral and legal force to Indigenous rights.

19.5 CONCERNS OF ENVIRONMENTAL JUSTICE WITH A SPECIFIC FOCUS ON FPIC

19.5.1 *Legal Framework on FPIC*

Environmental justice in the Indian context revolves around the development–environment conflict. The development paradigm dominated by a surge in demand for natural resources leads to resource extraction on Indigenous lands as an inevitable eventuality. The concept of FPIC, rooted in human rights law and drawing inspiration from the collective right of self-determination[56] is an important safeguard mechanism for Indigenous rights protection.[57] The concept, though lacking an accepted definition, is entrenched through the normative framework of the International Labour Organization's Convention on Indigenous and Tribal Peoples in Independent Countries 1989 (ILO 169)[58] and the 2007 United Nations Declaration on the Rights of Indigenous Peoples (UNDRIP).[59] However it is important to point out that the UN Declaration which adopts FPIC is a soft law instrument whereas ILO 169 which refers to consultation with the Indigenous and tribal populations creates binding obligations for state parties regarding Indigenous people.[60] However India is not a state party to ILO 169.

The FPIC has its origins in the struggles by Indigenous population across the world in the 1980s.[61] The ILO Convention concerning the Protection and Integration of Indigenous and Other Tribal and Semi-Tribal Populations in Independent Countries 1957 (ILO 107), which covers the rights of not only Indigenous populations but also tribal populations, contains certain limited obligations of collaboration and participation regarding Indigenous people.[62] The ILO

---

[55] M. S. Vani and R. Asthana, "Environmental Justice and Rural Communities, India," in P. Moore and F. Pastakia (eds.), *Environmental Justice and Rural Communities, Studies from India and Nepal* (Bangkok: IUCN, 2007), p. 48.

[56] *International Covenant on Civil and Political Rights*, Dec. 19, 1966, 999 UNTS 171 (1978), Art. 1; *International Covenant on Economic, Social and Cultural Rights*, Dec. 16, 1966, 993 UNTS 3 (1967); E. Cirkovic , "Self-Determination and Indigenous Peoples in International Law" (2006/2007) 31 *American Indian Law Review* at 375–399.

[57] B. Clavero, "The Indigenous Rights of Participation and International Development Policies" (2005) 22 *Arizona Journal of International and Comparative Law* at 42; J. Gilbert, *Indigenous Peoples' Land Rights under International Law: From Victims to Actors* (Leiden: Brill, 2016); J. S. Phillips, "The Rights of Indigenous Peoples under International Law" (2015) 26 *Global Bioethics* at 120–127.

[58] International Labour Organization (ILO), *Indigenous and Tribal Peoples Convention*, C169, June 27, 1989, 28 ILM 1382 [ILO 169].

[59] United Nations General Assembly, *United Nations Declaration on the Rights of Indigenous Peoples*, Oct. 2, 2007, UN Doc. A/RES/61/295 [UNDRIP].

[60] T. Ward, "The Right to Free, Prior, and Informed Consent: Indigenous Peoples' Participation Rights within International Law" (2011) 10 *North Western Journal of International Human Rights* at 59.

[61] P. Hanna and F. Vanclay, "Human Rights, Indigenous Peoples and the Concept of Free, Prior and Informed Consent" (2013) 31 *Impact Assessment and Project Appraisal* at 146–157, 148.

[62] International Labour Organization (ILO), *Indigenous and Tribal Populations Convention*, C107, June 26, 1957, 328 UNTS 24 [ILO 107]. In the context of India, Article 366(25) of the Constitution of India, states that Scheduled Tribes "are the tribes or tribal communities or part of or groups within these tribes and tribal

169, an improvement over ILO 107, incorporated participation and consultation under its ambit which is reflected in many of its provisions.[63] However, the term 'free and informed consent' (FIC), a precursor to the concept of FPIC, first appeared under Article 16 of ILO 169.[64] Further Article 7(1) of the ILO 169 articulates the right to self-determination by providing for the right to decide and exercise control over economic, social, and cultural development. Since the FIC is intrinsically linked to the right to self-determination, this provision could be construed as being a right to FIC.[65]

The idea of FPIC was adopted in several places under the UNDRIP. Negotiations leading to the concretization of FPIC was highly contested regarding its meaning and scope.[66] Articles 10 and 29 of the Declaration provide for FPIC of Indigenous peoples in case of relocation and the disposal of hazardous waste.[67] Articles 19 and 32 emphasize consultation for the approval of any project affecting Indigenous lands or territories and other resources, particularly in connection with the development, utilization, or exploitation of minerals, water, or other resources.[68] The Declaration emphasizes the full and active participation, and consultation with and consent of Indigenous populations, before any action that may affect them.[69] Many authors have evaluated the normative significance of UNDRIP and have argued that the Declaration at least in part reflects customary international law.[70]

FPIC as a safety net mechanism for Indigenous autonomy is not only context-specific but its meaning and scope are also highly contested by states and Indigenous communities.[71] The legal instruments[72] and institutions[73] employ different standards ranging from meaningful consultation to participation and consent in the case of Indigenous people's land and protection.[74]

communities which have been declared as such by the President through a public notification." However, the term 'Scheduled Tribes' (STs) is not coterminous with the term 'Indigenous.' Neither the Constitution nor other statutes define the term 'Indigenous.' The term Scheduled Tribes is an administrative term used for conferring certain specific constitutional benefits for specific sections of peoples considered historically disadvantaged and 'backward.'

[63] ILO 169, note 58. ILO 107 is no longer open for ratification, but remains in force for eighteen countries including India which ratified the Convention on September 29, 1958. See generally, ILO and Indigenous and Tribal Peoples, Newsletter, International Labour Organization (2007), www.ilo.org/wcmsp5/groups/public/@ed_norm/@normes/documents/publication/wcms_100542.pdf; Hanna and Vanclay, note 61, p. 150.

[64] Hanna and Vanclay, note 61, p. 150.

[65] Ibid.

[66] C. M. Doyle, *Indigenous Peoples, Title to Territory, Rights and Resources: The Transformative Role of Free Prior and Informed Consent* (Abingdon, UK: Routledge 2014), p. 53.

[67] UNDRIP, note 59, Arts. 10 and 29.

[68] Ibid.

[69] M. Barelli "Free, Prior and Informed Consent in the Aftermath of the UN Declaration on the Rights of Indigenous Peoples: Developments and Challenges Ahead" (2012) 16 *International Journal of Human Rights* at 1–24.

[70] S. G. Barnabas, "The Legal Status of the United Nations Declaration on the Rights of Indigenous Peoples (2007) in Contemporary International Human Rights Law" 6 *International Human Rights Law Review* at 242–261; S. Wiessner, "The Cultural Rights of Indigenous Peoples: Achievements and Continuing Challenges" (2011) 22 *European Journal of International Law* at 121–140.

[71] R. Shrinkhal, "Free Prior Informed Consent as a Right of Indigenous Peoples" (2014) 2 *Journal of National Law University Delhi* at 54–65, 54.

[72] ILO 107, note 62; ILO 169, note 58; UNDRIP, note 59.

[73] The Inter-American Commission on Human Rights and the Inter-American Court of Human Rights have recognized the right to FPIC (Hanna and Vanclay, note 61, p. 151). The World Bank adopted FPIC in development projects (F. Mackay, "The Draft World Bank Operational Policy 4.10 on Indigenous Peoples: Progress or More of the Same?" (2005) 22 *Arizona Journal of International & Comparative Law* at 65–98).

[74] P. Alex, "Indigenous Peoples' Free Prior and Informed Consent in the Inter-American Human Rights System" (2004) *Sustainable Development Law and Policy* 16–20 at 19; S. J. Anaya, "Indigenous Peoples' Participatory Rights in Relation to Decisions about Natural Resource Extraction: The More Fundamental Issue of What

As the concept is still evolving, it is premature to reach a fixed understanding about its contours.[75] However, despite this, the implementation of the principle is extremely important in stewarding the rights of Indigenous communities.

India has ratified the ILO 107 but is yet to ratify the ILO 169. India voted in favor of UNDRIP but stated that it does not consider any specific section of its people to be 'indigenous peoples', rather, all its peoples are Indigenous.[76] In May 2012, India's National Commission for Scheduled Tribes highlighted the objections raised by government agencies about ILO 169, emphasizing that the concept of 'indigenous peoples' is not relevant to India and that ILO 169 violates state ownership of sub-surface resources in existing laws of the country that provides fair compensation for lands.[77] It needs to be highlighted that treaties or customary international laws are not considered to be binding on Indian courts unless they have been incorporated into domestic law.[78] However, in recent times the courts have referred to and relied on international law where there is no apparent conflict of domestic law with the international law.[79]

Specific to the application of international treaties on the rights of Indigenous peoples to Scheduled Tribes and Scheduled Areas, the court has taken divergent positions. In the *Samatha v. State of Andhra Pradesh & Others*[80] the court observed:

> India is an active participant in the successful declaration of the Convention on the Right to Development, it is its duty to formulate its policies, legislative or executive, accord equal attention to the promotion of, and to protect the right to social, economic, civil and cultural rights of the people, in particular, the poor, the Dalits and Tribes as guaranteed by Article 21 of the Constitution of India.[81]

In the case of *Narmada Bachao Andolan* v. *Union of India and Others*[82] the court interpreted the right to life under Article 21 of the Constitution in accordance with Article 12 of ILO 107.[83] The court observed "The displacement of the tribals and other persons would not per se result in the violation of their fundamental or other rights. The effect is to see that on their rehabilitation at new locations they are better off than what they were. The gradual assimilation in the mainstream of the society will lead to betterment and progress."[84] However in the case of

Rights Indigenous Peoples Have in Lands and Resources" (2005) 22 *Arizona Journal International and Comparative Law* 7–17.

[75] *Report of the International Workshop on Methodologies Regarding Free, Prior and Informed Consent and Indigenous Peoples*, Feb. 17, 2005, UN Doc. E/C.19/2005/3, para. 47; Shrinkhal, note 71, p. 55.

[76] C. R Bijoy, S. Gopalakrishnan, and S. Khanna, *India and the Rights of Indigenous Peoples Constitutional, Legislative and Administrative Provisions Concerning Indigenous and Tribal Peoples in India and Their Relation to International Law on Indigenous Peoples* (Thailand: Asia Indigenous Peoples Pact (AIPP) Foundation, 2010), p. 10.

[77] Ibid., p. 13. See Ministry of Tribal Affairs, "National Commission for Scheduled Tribes: Special Report Good Governance for Tribal Development and Administration," May 2012, pp. 9–12.

[78] S. Jolly, "A Legal Analysis of Linking Human Right Approach to Access to Water and Sharing of Trans-Boundary Rivers in South Asia" in J. L. Kaul and A. Jha (eds.), *Shifting Horizons of Public International Law* (New York: Springer, 2018), pp. 135–158; *Gramophone Company of India Ltd* v. *Birendra Bahadur Pandey and Others*, 1984 AIR 667.

[79] *Vishaka and Others* v. *State of Rajasthan and Others*, AIR 1997 SC 3011; *Vellore Citizens Welfare Forum* v. *Union of India and Others*, note 50.

[80] *Samatha* v. *State of Andhra Pradesh and Others*, 1997 8 SCC 191.

[81] Ibid., para 75.

[82] *Narmada Bachao Andolan* v. *Union of India and Others*, SCC 2000, p. 10.

[83] ILO 107, note 62, Article 12 prohibits the removal of populates from the habitats except on grounds relating to national security, or in the interest of national economic development, or of the health of the said populations.

[84] The observation is contrary to the UNDRIP provisions. However, the decision was in 2000, prior to the adoption of UNDRIP and the parties in the instant case only relied on ILO 107 to which India is a party.

M. Mohan Kumar v. *P. Nalla Thampy Thera and Another*,[85] a case relating to the restoration of tribal lands, the court observed while examining Article 21 of the Constitution, ILO 107 and 169, and the UNDRIP, that:

> It is now accepted that the Panchsheel doctrine which provided that the tribes could flourish only if the State interfered minimally and functioned chiefly as a support system in view of passage of time is no longer valid. Even the notion of autonomy contained in the 1989 convention[86] has been rejected by India. However, India appears to have softened its stand against autonomy for tribal people, and voted in favour of UNDRIP which affirms various rights to autonomy that are inherent in tribal peoples.[87]

The court did not go into the discussion of what notion of autonomy has been rejected by India. The National Commission for Scheduled Tribes highlighted the stand of the Ministry of Home Affairs about ILO 169.[88] The Commission observed that the self-determination provided under Article 7 of ILO 169 would create administrative problems in the formulation of development plans and may distort the planning process in the country.[89]

The term 'Indigenous people'[90] is not referenced under India's Constitution or its official position. For the operational part, the Constitution uses the term Scheduled Tribes[91] to indicate the original inhabitants locally referred to as Adivasi. Constitutional and statutory provisions have articulated certain rights recognized under international law to the tribal communities. Schedule V of the Constitution directs the state governments to frame laws to "prohibit or restrict the transfer of land by or among members of the Scheduled Tribes in Scheduled Areas."[92] Through the Panchayats (Extension to the Scheduled Areas) Act 1996 (PESA) the decentralized local self-government system established through the 73rd constitutional amendment with panchayats as the grassroots level of administration was extended to scheduled areas.[93] Section 4(d) of PESA authorizes 'Gram Sabha' as the competent authority to safeguard and preserve the traditions and customs of the tribes[94] Consultation with the 'Gram Sabha' before the acquisition of land and the decisions of the competent authority has to be in consonance with the wishes of 'Gram Sabha.'[95] The National Advisory Council has recommended that PESA should be amended to provide for mandatory consent of the affected population before the acquisition of their land. The Forest Rights Act was a response to the

---

[85] *M. Mohan Kumar* v. *P. NallaThampy Thera and Another*, July 21, 2009.

[86] ILO 169, note 58.

[87] *M. Mohan Kumar* v. *P. NallaThampy Thera and Another*, note 85. India's position on UNDRIP is that self-determination applies only to peoples under foreign domination and not to sovereign independent states or to a section of people or a nation. Further the autonomy provided under UNDRIP is in terms of internal and local affairs. It was on this basis that India had voted in favor of the adoption of the Declaration.

[88] Ministry of Tribal Affairs, note 77, pp. 9–12.

[89] Ibid.

[90] The concept of 'Indigenous people' lacks a clear definition under international law. Legal instruments have applied different yardsticks to articulate the concept of Indigenous people. While accepting the heterogeneity of the Indigenous societies, authors have highlighted common characteristics including historical continuity, territorial connection lack of statehood, economic and political marginalization, and cultural and racial discrimination. See C. W. Chen, *Indigenous Rights in international Law* (Oxford: Oxford University Press, 2014).

[91] See note 62 for the definition of Scheduled Tribes.

[92] Constitution of India, 1949, Schedule V.

[93] The Provisions of the Panchayats (Extension to the Scheduled Areas) Act, 1996 (PESA).

[94] Ibid., s. 4(d).

[95] Ibid., s. 4(i) and 4(k).

prolonged intense struggle of the communities to address historical injustices experienced by tribes.[96] The Act specifically vests in the 'Gram Sabha' the sole responsibility for settling the forest rights and provides that the free informed consent of the 'Gram Sabha' should be obtained regarding the settlement in case of the diversion of forest lands for listed purposes.[97] However, this critical component is often not adhered to in the implementation of the Act.[98]

19.5.2 *Vedanta: a Shift in Stance and Incorporation of Social and Cultural Aspects*

The judgment in Vedanta marks a watershed in India's environmental jurisprudence in furthering environmental justice for the poor and marginalized.[99] The judgment gave a new interpretation to the FPIC process, enunciated the socioeconomic and cultural components of sustainable development, and integrated these into the fundamental rights paradigm.

The judgment upheld the FPIC of the Indigenous peoples without actually using the phrase by observing that 'Gram Sabhas' have the authority to determine whether the proposed project would affect any of the individual or community rights including cultural and religious rights, particularly under the Forest Rights Act.[100] The court analyzed the rights of Indigenous peoples under the Indian Constitution and referred to international conventions including ILO 107, ILO 169, and UNDRIP to reinforce the importance of Indigenous rights.[101] The judgment sought support from UNDRIP which articulates the necessity to respect and promote the inherent economic, cultural, and spiritual traditions of Indigenous peoples and observed "The State has got a duty to recognize and duly support their [Indigenous peoples] identity, culture and interest so that they can effectively participate in achieving sustainable development."[102] The court recognized the intimate and sacred relationship the tribal communities have with the forest and observed that the Forest Rights Act aims to protect the right of tribal and traditional forest dwelling communities for sustainable use, conservation of biodiversity, and maintenance of the ecological balance of the forests while ensuring their livelihood and food security.[103]

The court recognized Indigenous peoples' inherent right to determine their political status freely and to pursue their economic, social, and cultural development. The court held that the 'Gram Sabha' has an obligation under the Panchayats (Extension to the Scheduled Areas) Act, when read with the Forest Rights Act, to safeguard and preserve the traditions and customs of the Schedueld Tribes and other forest dwellers, their cultural identity, and their community

---

[96] The Scheduled Tribes and Other Traditional Forest Dwellers (Recognition of Forest Rights) Act, 2006. The Forest Act attempts to recognize, restore, and vest forest rights in forest dwelling Scheduled Tribes and other traditional forest dwellers. The Act defines the "forest dwelling Scheduled Tribes" as the members or community of the Scheduled Tribes who primarily reside in and who depend on the forests or forest lands for bona fide livelihood needs and includes the Scheduled Tribe pastoralist communities. The Act defines the "other traditional forest dweller" as any member or community who has for at least three generations prior to the 13th day of December, 2005 primarily resided in and who depend on the forest or forests land for bona fide livelihood need. See L. Bhullar, "The Indian Forest Rights Act 2006: A Critical Appraisal" (2008) 4 *Law, Environment and Development Journal* 394–408.

[97] The Scheduled Tribes and Other Traditional Forest Dwellers (Recognition of Forest Rights) Act, 2006, s. 4.

[98] "Observations on the State of Indigenous Human Rights in India," prepared for United Nations Human Rights Council Universal Periodic Review 2016, 27th Session Third Cycle, Cultural Survival, 2005.

[99] Doyle, note 66, p. 199.

[100] Vedanta, note 1, paras. 58–59, 60.

[101] Ibid., para. 37.

[102] Ibid., para. 39.

[103] Ibid., para. 41.

resources.[104] It is of immense significance that the court held that the tribals' right to worship the Niyamgiri hills is to be preserved and protected under Articles 25 and 26 of the Indian Constitution which guarantee the right to practice and propagate not only matters of faith or belief, but all those rituals and observations which are regarded as an integral part of their religion.[105] The court authorized 'Gram Sabha' to consider all individual and community, cultural, and religious claims.[106]

Following the judgment, the first environmental referendum was conducted in all the twelve 'Gram Sabhas' located in the Niyamgiri hills in July 2013 and all twelve 'Gram Sabhas' unequivocally rejected the project.[107]

19.6 VEDANTA JUDGMENT: A NEW PARADIGM OF ENVIRONMENTAL JUSTICE AND SUSTAINABLE DEVELOPMENT

The Vedanta judgment pronounced on April 18, 2013 strengthened the social pillar of sustainable development and incorporated the participatory principles of good governance.[108] The judgment stressed that recognizing and duly supporting the identity, culture, religion, and interests of tribal people is necesary so that they can effectively participate in achieving sustainable development.[109] The Vedanta judgment did not consider the issue from the perspective of balancing development and environmental protection. By granting 'Gram Sabha' which consists of all adult members of a village including women[110] the authority to determine how the identity and culture of the tribal communities are to be maintained, the verdict articulated tribal rights as an integral component of sustainable development.

The judgment is revolutionary, and gives communities the right to decide on the process and mode of development, and is a clear indication that the principle of sustainable development could be used to address the issue of deprivation, marginalization, poverty, and discrimination by emphasizing inclusive governance, participation, awareness, and information.[111] The principles propounded in the judgment could be a precursor to restructure the future course of environmental jurisprudence in the country.[112]

This judgment should also be appreciated from a social justice perspective intrinsically linked to sustainable development and environmental justice. The court referred to the Forest Rights Act as a social welfare or remedial statute because land is the most important and valuable asset of the tribals from which they derive social status and economic and social equality. Scheduled Tribes and Traditional Forest Dwelling Communities (TFDs) have a right to maintain distinctive spiritual relationship with their land. Therefore, constitutional and statutory provisions must

---

[104] Vedanta, note 1, para. 56.

[105] Ibid., para. 55.

[106] Ibid., para. 59.

[107] Raut, note 4, p. 88.

[108] See T. S. Doabia J and I. P. S. Doabia, *Environmental & Pollution Laws* (Nagpur: Wadhwa, 2005) p. 451; I. Chaturvedi, "A Critical Study of Free, Prior and Informed Consent in the Context of the Right to Development – Can Consent Be Withheld" (2014) 5 *Journal of Indian Law and Society* 37 at 52.

[109] S. Jolly and Z. A. Makuch, "Procedural and Substantive Innovations Propounded by the Indian Judiciary in Balancing Protection of Environment and Development: A Legal Analysis," in C. Voigt and Z. A. Makuch (eds.), *Courts and the Environment* (Cheltenham, UK: Edward Elgar, 2018), pp. 142–168.

[110] Article 243 Constitution of India defines 'Gram Sabha' as a body consisting of persons registered in the electoral rolls relating to a village comprised within the area of Panchayat at the village level (see note 2).

[111] See S. Torjman, "The Social Dimension of Sustainable Development," Caledon Institute of Social Policy, May 2000.

[112] Basu, note 49, p. 72.

be read widely to encompass the dignity of Scheduled Tribes and distributive justice: "State has a duty to recognize and duly support their identity, culture, and interest so that they can effectively participate in sustainable development." These are all expressions of social justice.[113]

Many scholars recognize FPIC as an integral part of social justice and sustainable development. Dr. Hossain observes "Projects undertaken without extensive prior consultation with the people affected cannot qualify as projects which would achieve sustainable development and social justice."[114] FPIC is related to environmental justice as justice is undermined when people are deprived of participation in decision-making affecting their rights. The decision elevates FPIC as a central tenet of development policies as it has the innate ability to deepen democracy by encouraging people's participation and taking into account the voice of the people in determining the kind of development preferred by the community. As a bottom-up approach, FPIC attempts to incorporate the interests and aspirations of the affected Indigenous population fundamental to the concept of environmental justice.

By referring to international law as persuasive authority to emphasize the customary and cultural rights of tribal populations, the court has indirectly articulated that there is no apparent conflict between the international law on the protection of Indigenous peoples' rights and Indian domestic law. The case is already having a ripple effect. In 2016 Tribal villages of Raigarh Chhattisgarh, unanimously voted against the mining of their forests.[115] The Kamanda 'Gram Sabha' articulated a similar position in Orissa.[116] The Vedanta decision resulted in endorsing the right of self-determination for tribal people exercised through 'Gram Sabhas' which is underwritten by Indian constitutional law. The referendum process undertaken by 'Gram Sabha' could serve as an international model for a democratic means of obtaining FPIC.

However, the judgment is not without criticism. By giving 'Gram Sabha' the ultimate authority to decide on mining, it was contended that the court has abdicated and diluted state sovereignty over natural resources.[117] The case also opens up the question of balancing development, Indigenous rights, and environmental protection especially when the government and Indigenous communities have different takes on a particular development project. The decision has given primacy to 'Gram Sabha' to choose the kind of development that disregards the government perspective. The question is raised on the future of mining in India, as 'Gram Sabha' could easily preempt developmental projects through the right to rejection following the process of FPIC. Though the court cited several international documents as persuasive authority to emphasize the customary and cultural rights of Indigenous people,[118] the way it used them

---

[113] The objective of the Fifth Schedule of the Constitution, observed the SC, is to preserve the culture, autonomy of tribals, and for their economic empowerment to ensure social, economic, and political justice for the preservation of peace and good governance in scheduled area.

[114] K. Hossain, "Human Rights, Environment and Sustainable Development: An Integrated Approach to Achieve a Just Balance in the Emerging Normative Framework," in M. Rahman (ed.), *Human Rights and Environment* (Bangladesh: ELCOP, 2011).

[115] A. Chandrasekhar, "How Chhattisgarh Adivasis taught the State a lesson," Apr. 12, 2016, www.dailyo.in/politics/chhattisgarh-land-acquisition-dalit-forest-rights-act-adivasi-coal-india-secl-bharat-mata/story/1/10037.html.

[116] "Odisha-Kamanda Village Gram Sabha Rejects Mining," May 4, 2016, https://kractivist.org/odisha-kamanda-village-gram-sabha-rejects-mining/.

[117] See generally J. C. Dernbach, "Sustainable Development as a Framework for National Governance" (1998) 49 *Case Western Reserve Law* 3–103.

[118] The judgment refers to ILO 107, ILO 169 and UNDRIP to showcase the international law developments for the protection of social, political, and cultural rights of Indigenous people without elaborating the ambit of those rights. However, the court went onto detail the rights granted to STs and TFDs under the Forest Rights Act (FRA) which include the right to hold and live in the forest land under the individual or common occupation, individual or community rights. Under s. 6 of the FRA, 'Gram Sabha' shall be the authority to initiate the process for determining the nature and extent of individual or community forest rights.

makes one question the court's understanding of those instruments. For example, the court stated that "ILO convention No. 107. . . emphasized the necessity for the protection of social, political and cultural rights of indigenous people."[119] Yet, this Convention is criticized for its state-centered view of development and for recognizing Indigenous people's participation only during their relocation.[120] Preferably, the court could have cited documents and ICJ cases relating to the right to self-determination, which can also be used to uphold the FPIC.[121] Unfortunately, the court never used the term FPIC in spite of the emphasis in the Saxena Committee report on its violation.[122] The court could have helped in clarifying the boundaries of FPIC, as the question of whether FPIC includes the right of affected people to veto the project is still unclear.[123]

19.7 CONCLUSION

The Vedanta judgment upheld the overriding power of the 'Gram Sabha' about decisions regarding the tribal rights over their habitats including religious and cultural rights. The case is a historic precedent that could potentially determine the course of similar developments in other tribal areas in India. The case and its unique unfolding are rooted in the context of the country's multifaceted environmental justice movement and represents the main strands of environmental justice identified through grassroots movement and litigation.

In its decision, the Supreme Court evaluated, contextualized, and reassessed the fundamental premises of environmental law, human rights law, sustainable development, and the essential core of social justice as the foundation of the legal process. Specifically, through the interlinking of Indigenous/tribal rights, constitutional provisions on the protection of scheduled tribes, religious rights, and the Forest Act, the court gave a new interpretation to the concept of FPIC in the Indian context, marking a turning point in the pursuit of environmental justice and sustainable development. By granting 'Gram Sabha' the authority to determine how the identity and culture of the tribal communities are to be maintained, the decision articulated tribal rights as an integral component of sustainable development and strengthened the social pillar of sustainable development.

Through the emphasis on the FPIC of the local 'Gram Sabhas,' the Supreme Court illustrated the significance of inclusive democratic process. The judgment is a good precedent for all projects that have environmental and social consequences. The judgment while emphasizing that the right to development is a fundamental right, noted as equally important the right of tribal communities to freely determine what constitutes 'development' and how such development will be undertaken. Herein lies the significance of Niyamgiri, which underscores its importance for future iterations of environmental justice.

---

[119] Vedanta, note 1, para. 37.
[120] Ward, note 60, pp. 54–59.
[121] Right to self-determination is considered to be the foundation of Indigenous rights (ibid.). Also for discussions regarding FPIC from right to development perspective, see also Chaturvedi, note 108.
[122] Saxena et al., note 7, p. 4.
[123] Chaturvedi, note 108, p. 52.

Demarginalizing the Intersection of Ecological and Social Disadvantage in South Africa

A Critique of Current Approaches to Dealing with Historical Injustice – the Tudor Shaft Case Study

Jackie Dugard*

20.1 INTRODUCTION

We are writing this letter to ask for help with the place we're living in. We live in a dangerous place which has dust and radioactive [material] . . . which gets inside our place . . . Our children are sick [from] asthma and sinuses. Adults have skin infections. [The] municipality is relocating people with the same problem . . . but we were left out. We don't know why, so we are asking for your help.[1]

South Africa's commercial capital, Johannesburg, owes its existence to the discovery of a gold-bearing reef on a farm in the Witwatersrand basin in 1886. Over time, gold-mining on the Witwatersrand reef developed to sustain a "minerals–energy complex" that formed the basis of apartheid's racialized capital accumulation model.[2] While many of the major gold-mining houses have long-since decamped due to the depletion of gold reserves and declining profitability of these mines since the early 1990s, the landscape is still emblematically littered with numerous gold-colored mine dumps, or tailings dams, which provide a very visible reminder of the history of gold-mining in the area.[3]

* I am grateful to Nkosinathi Sithole, attorney at the Socio-Economic Rights Institute of South Africa (SERI) for generously spending time with me in February 2017 to discuss the Tudor Shaft litigation, and for responding to further questions by email during May 2017. I am also grateful to Anna Alcaro (now back in the USA) who, as a SERI intern in 2012, wrote useful background notes on the preliminary stages of the litigation. I am indebted to the Chr. Michelsen Institute in Bergen, Norway, along with the Research Council of Norway, for funding some initial social research in Tudor Shaft in 2011 (before any litigation had commenced), which became the impetus for further research involvement over the years. Thanks also go to the Law and Society Association, which provided a scholarship to attend the annual meeting in June 2017 in Mexico City at which an early draft of this chapter was presented. Finally, I would like to warmly thank Carmen Gonzalez and Sumudu Atapattu for suggesting the Kimberlé Crenshaw angle of analysis for this chapter. I have deliberately echoed the phrasing of the title of her seminal 1989 article ("Demarginalizing the Intersection of Race and Sex: A Black Feminist Critique of Antidiscrimination Doctrine, Feminist Theory and Antiracist Politics") in my title.
1. S. Bega, "Down in the (Radioactive) Dumps without Hope," Oct. 29, 2016, www.pressreader.com/.
2. B. Fine and Z. Rustomjee, *The Political Economy of South Africa: From Minerals–Energy Complex to Industrialisation* (London: Hurst & Co., 1996).
3. There are some 270 tailings dams scattered around Johannesburg, comprising large mounds of residue (collectively weighing over 6 billion tons) from the decades of deep-level gold-mining along the Witwatersrand reef (M. Liefferink, "Assessing the Past and the Present Role of the National Nuclear Regulator as Public Protector against Potential Health Injuries: The Witwatersrand as Case Study" (2011) 62 *New Contree* 125.

Notwithstanding the latter-day wealth created for its (White) owners (largely based on the exploitation of Black miners), the natural environment and the surrounding poor, Black communities have been badly impacted by the decades of exploitative gold-mining operations. As with all aspects of apartheid life, "black communities were disproportionately affected by the unchecked environmental damage," either because of having to work in exploitative conditions in the mines or having to live in areas subjected to intense mining pollution.[4] Among the forms of harm bequeathed by the mining companies is the considerable ecological hazard posed by the tailings, which contain large amounts of radioactive uranium (a by-product of the processes for extracting gold from the rock). The mining houses that were responsible were not held accountable at the time of the damage and left behind many unrehabilitated tailings dams when they discontinued their mining operations.[5]

In contemporary South Africa, apartheid's enduring legacy of racialized exclusion has meant that poor, Black communities have often had no choice but to settle close to the tailings dams in their search for land to occupy informally. Caught in the quagmire of cross-cutting social and ecological injustice, such communities continue to live in informal shacks perilously close to, or even on top of, radioactive tailings as they attempt to engage in survivalist economic activities on the margins of the cities and the formal economy. One such community[6] was Tudor Shaft informal settlement, located alongside the Tudor Shaft tailings dam on Johannesburg's West Rand, near the town of Krugersdorp.

As the chapters in this book emphasize, sustainable development demands close linking of economic, social, and environmental systems while at the same time ensuring that marginalized, poor communities are not disproportionately affected. As such, "sustainable development" equates to the concept of environmental justice advocated by Jacklyn Cock, who explains that, in seeking to bridge ecological and social justice issues, environmental justice is "located at the confluence of three of our greatest challenges: the struggle against racism, the struggle against poverty and inequality and the struggle to protect the [natural] environment."[7] But how does this requirement for the close linking of ecological and social systems play out in practice in South Africa, with its "troubled history of de-linking among social systems and between these and natural systems"?[8] Seeking to contribute toward an understanding of the challenges for environmental justice in the South African context, this chapter examines the formal government responses to the predicament of Tudor Shaft residents, which resulted between 2012 and 2016

---

[4] J. Dugard, J. MacLeod, and A. Alcaro, "A Rights-Based Examination of Residents' Engagement with Acute Environmental Harm across Four Sites on South Africa's Witwatersrand Basin" (2012) 79 *Social Research* 931–956 at 936.

[5] Auditor-General South Africa, "Report of the Auditor-General to Parliament on a Performance Audit of the Rehabilitation of Abandoned Mines at the Department of Minerals and Energy," Oct. 2009. See also R. Adler, M. Claassen, L. Godfrey, and A. Turton, "Water, Mining and Waste: An Historical and Economic Perspective on Conflict Management in South Africa" (2007) 2 *Economics of Peace and Security Journal* 32–41.

[6] By using the term 'community' I do not suggest a romanticized notion of unity or cohesion. Indeed, as indicated below, efforts to address their problems resulted in significant tensions and divisions among the residents of Tudor Shaft, specifically as related to their relocation.

[7] J. Cock, "Connecting the Red, Brown and Green: The Environmental Justice Movement in South Africa," Globalisation, Marginalisation and New Social Movements in Post-Apartheid South Africa, a joint project between the Centre for Civil Society and the School of Development Studies, University of KwaZulu-Natal, 2004.

[8] J. Dugard and A. Alcaro, "Let's Work Together: Environmental and Socio-Economic Rights in the Courts" (2013) 29 *South African Journal on Human Rights* 191–207.

in the case of *Federation for a Sustainable Environment* v. *National Nuclear Regulator and Others (FSE v. NNR and Others)*[9] and culminated in their relocation in 2016 away from Tudor Shaft but not from their position of social marginalization. Using evidence from legal papers to highlight the shortcomings of fragmented regulatory frameworks, responses, and remedies, the chapter proposes an intersectional approach to understanding and addressing ecological and social disadvantage in South Africa.

In 1989, Kimberlé Crenshaw coined the term "intersectionality" to describe the complex, multifaceted and aggregated discrimination experienced by Black women in the USA.[10] Crenshaw's seminal article highlighted how the USA's antidiscrimination approaches failed Black women due to the tendency of these approaches "to treat race and gender as mutually exclusive categories of experience and analysis."[11] Demonstrating how, by focusing on only race- or only gender-related discrimination, antidiscrimination efforts privileged the more empowered among these two groupings (Black men and White women respectively) and served to overlook and continually marginalize Black women, Crenshaw persuasively argued that approaching disadvantage as though it occurred along a single categorical axis effectively undermined the ability to identify and remedy intersectional discrimination.[12]

Inspired by Crenshaw, I argue that, like the intersectional discrimination faced by Black women in the USA, the intersectional disadvantage experienced by poor Black communities[13] in South Africa cannot be understood or remedied through any single categorical axis. In this chapter, I first identify Tudor Shaft as a case study of intersectional disadvantage. Examining the legal papers filed in the course of the *FSE v. NNR and Others*, I then critique the fragmented ("marginalizing") responses by government, which, although alleviating some of the relatively less intractable axes of disadvantage, have failed to address either the underlying ecological damage or the residents' profound and multifaceted social exclusion. I conclude by highlighting the need for an alternative, integrated approach to identifying and resolving historical injustice in South Africa.

20.2 TUDOR SHAFT AS A CASE STUDY OF INTERSECTIONAL DISADVANTAGE

First occupied in 1995, during the first year of South Africa's democratic dispensation, Tudor Shaft was initially established in the shadow of the decamping of the large mining houses, as a transit camp for communities affected by the mining houses folding their operations and no longer needing miners.[14] Two decades later, by 2015, Tudor Shaft had grown to comprise 500 shacks housing approximately 1,800 people unlawfully occupying the land. Like all of South Africa's informal settlements, Tudor Shaft is overwhelmingly (if not exclusively) Black

---

[9] *Federation for a Sustainable Environment* v. *National Nuclear Regulator and Others* [2012] ZAGPHC 24611/12 [*FSE v. NNR and Others*].

[10] K. Crenshaw, "Demarginalizing the Intersection of Race and Sex: A Black Feminist Critique of Antidiscrimination Doctrine, Feminist Theory and Antiracist Politics" (1989) 1989 *University of Chicago Legal Forum* 139.

[11] Ibid.

[12] Ibid., 140.

[13] I have not engaged in a direct race/gender identity-based application of Crenshaw's critique for two reasons. First, my entry point into the Tudor Shaft case study came through the lens of ecological and social disadvantage rather than identity-based discrimination. Second, I have not undertaken any identity-based inquiry in Tudor Shaft and, specifically, I have not focused on gender. Instead, I have taken as a starting point the objective reality that all the residents are poor and Black (this is not to suggest that there are not degrees of poverty among the residents) and face the intersectional ecological and social disadvantages outlined here.

[14] www.mogalecity.gov.za/news-archive/2015-news/218-september/833-tudor-shaft-residents-relocate.

and entirely poor, with most households relying on meager social grants and/or survivalist informal activities to make ends meet.[15] As explained by Phumla Patience Mjadu, a poor, Black former resident of Tudor Shaft: "I am unemployed, but I do sometimes obtain temporary work as a domestic worker in and around Krugersdorp. My income is approximately R200[16] per month."[17]

From the outset, Tudor Shaft's residents experienced four considerable ecological- and social development-related problems. The most acute problem was the hazard posed by the tailings (the *ecological axis*). Because of the proximity of the settlement's flimsy shacks to the dam, with some shacks only 5 meters away, residents were continuously exposed to radioactive matter in the airborne dust and water runoff from the tailings.[18] Following a sustained campaign initiated by environmental campaigner Mariette Lieferrink of the Federation for a Sustainable Environment (FSE), in July 2010 the National Nuclear Regulator (NNR) undertook a radiological survey of the tailings material at Tudor Shaft informal settlement. This report found that the potential dose of radiation the residents were exposed to was four times the statutory limit.[19] As detailed below, although the ecological axis was the catalyst for government intervention, this axis was subsequently abandoned in the ensuing litigation after efforts to address the radioactive hazard became bogged down in intergovernmental disagreement over responsibility for the remediation. At the time of writing, the Tudor Shaft tailings dam had not been rehabilitated and continued to pose an ongoing ecological threat to air, water, and non-human animals, as well as a latent threat to other poor communities that might settle there with no alternative access to land.

Beyond the ecological problem, Tudor Shaft residents faced three interwoven social development-related challenges. First was the unsatisfactory nature of the housing and municipal services in the settlement (the *housing axis*). Residents lived in rudimentary shacks with inadequate water and sanitation supply (three communal standpipe taps and seven communal chemical toilets for the entire settlement to share) and no electricity apart from high-mast lighting on the edges of the settlement, meaning that residents had to use dangerous and unhealthy paraffin stoves for heating and cooking, and candles for lighting.[20] Following the collapse of attempts to resolve the ecological axis, efforts in Tudor Shaft refocused on the housing axis. This resulted in 2016 in the relocation of the Tudor Shaft residents away from the immediate radioactive threat, to several nearby locations, where some community members received formal government housing in the new locations.[21] However, notwithstanding these improvements, in key respects, the relocation has entrenched the residents' disadvantage. This is because, like the Tudor Shaft locale, the new locations are on the urban periphery, with few

---

[15] Approximately 8.9 percent of South Africa's 16,122,000 households live in informal settlements. All such households are low- or no-income households and, apart from a statistically insignificant number, all of these households are Black (South African Institute of Race Relations, "South Africa Survey 2017," Centre for Risk Analysis, pp. 692–695).

[16] Approximately US$15.

[17] *FSE v. NNR and Others*, note 9 (Founding affidavit (July 27, 2012), Phumla Patience Mjadu (Tudor Shaft resident at para. 1)).

[18] V. Tshivhase, "The Radiation Level at the Tudor Shaft in Krugersdorp South Africa," Council for GeoScience Report to the Department of Mineral Resources, June 4, 2014.

[19] *FSE v. NNR and Others*, note 9 (Annexure 'ML4,' letter from Fourth Respondent dated Sept. 5, 2011 at p. 2 and answering affidavit (July 4, 2012), Dan Metlana Mashitisho (MCLM Municipal Manager)), *FSE v. NNR and Others*.

[20] See for example Dugard et al., note 4, p. 942; *FSE v. NNR and Others*, note 9 (Founding affidavit (July 27, 2012), Phumla Patience Mjadu (Tudor Shaft resident at para. 14)).

[21] "Residents to Be Moved from Radioactive Areas," Oct. 23, 2015, https://krugersdorpnews.co.za/279028/residents-to-be-moved-from-radioactive-area/.

social and economic opportunities, thereby perpetuating a second axis of social development-related disadvantage (the *spatial apartheid axis*).[22] Moreover, the relocation process itself was highly contested and resulted in debilitating conflict and deep divisions among the residents over the formal qualification criteria for receiving a new house under the government's housing program. This meant that, instead of receiving a house, some residents were merely allocated land on which to reconstruct their shacks.[23]

The third social development-related problem was the entrenched poverty and high levels of unemployment among Tudor Shaft's residents (the *poverty axis*).[24] Like the spatial apartheid axis, the poverty axis of disadvantage was not addressed and persists in their relocation despite some alleviation for those who received formal houses.

[22] As pointed out by commentators such as Marie Huchzermeyer, the government's focus on using public funds to provide individual privately owned houses is inherently contradictory in that it results in "expansive, peripherally located, segregated housing schemes" for the poor that perpetuate apartheid's spatial inequalities and entrench social exclusion (M. Huchzermeyer, "Housing for the Poor? Negotiated Housing Policy in South Africa" (2001) 25 *Habitat International* 303–331 at 317 and 325). Regarding how the government's housing program reproduces apartheid geography through providing housing "far from economic centers and jobs, with tiny houses on separate plots and in communities that mostly lack facilities for shopping, recreation or economic activity" (N. Makgetla, "Innovative Systems Needed to Revamp Service Delivery: The Discussion on Way of Improving Public Services for Everyone Should Be Reopened," May 3, 2018, www .businesslive.co.za/bd/opinion/columnists/2018-05-08-neva-makgetla-innovative-systems-needed-to-revamp-ser vice-delivery/).

[23] The two main reasons for failing to qualify for formal housing are that many of the residents are foreign nationals and, among the South African applicants, some had already received a housing subsidy at some previous point – both which disqualify any applicant in terms of the government's housing program (discussion with Nkosinathi Sithole, Johannesburg, Feb. 6, 2017). A group of residents who rejected the relocation plans because they did not qualify for formal government housing caused significant delays to the project. For a description of how 'a group of rowdy' residents of Tudor Shaft disrupted a meeting that was being held to discuss the relocation plans: "Residents Choose Shacks over Houses," June 2, 2016, www.mogalecity.gov.za/ news-archive/2016-news/224-january/849-residents-choose-shacks-over-houses. In addition, because the government pursued a phased approach to moving residents into formal housing as this became ready for occupation, there was heightened anxiety among the residents who remained left behind during each phase, resulting in at least one attempted unlawful occupation of identified houses by desperate residents, along with several incidents of civil disobedience and ongoing conflict among the residents (discussion with Nkosinathi Sithole, Johannesburg, Feb. 6, 2017).

[24] While South Africa made some progress in alleviating poverty between 1994 and 2011 (largely through a social welfare system that provides minimal monthly pension, disability and child-support grants to qualifying poor households – notably, there is no basic income grant for unemployed persons), since 2011 poverty has again been increasing and social inequality is rising (both between and within race groups) (see for example W. Hurlburt (ed.), "Overcoming Poverty and Inequality in South Africa: An Assessment of Drivers, Constraints and Opportunities," Department: Planning, Monitoring and Evaluation Republic of South Africa, Statistics South Africa, 2030 NDP, World Bank, 2018). One of the main determinants of the increasing poverty and rising inequality is that unemployment is very high: 26.6 percent if you exclude people who have been looking for work in the past thirty days, and 36.4 percent by the expanded definition, which includes such recent jobseekers. And, as with all other social indices in South Africa, the unemployment (and, concomitantly, poverty) statistics remain highly racialized across the various racial groups. It should be noted that, largely for affirmative action reasons, South Africa retains the same racial classifications used under apartheid in terms of which 'black' refers to a differentiated grouping of Africans, Coloureds, and Indians/ Asians (the term Coloured is a formal term used to describe a particular multiracial ethnic group with mixed ancestry including from Austronesia and South Asia; it does not have the same pejorative connotation that it does in other countries). Taking the expanded definition of unemployment of 36.4 percent, the rate of unemployment across the race groups is: Africans, 40.9 percent; Coloureds, 28 percent; Indian/Asians, 16.7 percent; and whites, 8.6 percent (SAIRR, note 15, p. 291). Thus, while whites have an unemployment rate of 8.6 percent, Africans have an unemployment rate of 40.9 percent. As testament to the enduring legacy of apartheid, these figures coincide with the relative advantage/disadvantage of each group under apartheid, with whites being the most privileged, and with a spectrum of disadvantage ranging from Indians/Asians, through Coloureds, to Africans, who were most severely disadvantaged by apartheid's social and legal order.

Exposing but failing to resolve these various axes of exclusion, the legal papers filed by the various parties in *FSE* v. *NNR and Others* provide a useful lens through which to view the fragmentation of regulatory frameworks and approaches for dealing with the intersectional disadvantage of poor, Black communities and especially those living in ecologically compromised locations. An examination of the formal exchanges between the relevant government agencies – chiefly the Department of Environmental Affairs (DEA), Department of Mineral Resources (DMR), and Mogale City Local Municipality (MCLM), along with NNR – reveals an alarming degree of finger-pointing, avoidance of responsibility, and fragmentation of functions among government agencies. It also highlights the inadequacies of single axis, marginalizing approaches to intersectional ecological and social disadvantage.

20.3 FRAGMENTED MARGINALIZATION IN ACTION

Following years of campaigning initiated by FSE, the entry point for government intervention in Tudor Shaft initially came by way of the ecological axis. That Tudor Shaft informal settlement was too dangerous for human habitation was first flagged by the relevant local municipality (MCLM) in 2010.[25] At the time, MCLM's view was that, since the harm related to environmental radioactivity, NNR should be dealing with the matter.[26] However, following a heated exchange with DEA between September 2011 and March 2012 (detailed below), MCLM reluctantly agreed with the arguably even more reluctant NNR to deal with Tudor Shaft.[27]

On September 5, 2011, responding to worrying results from several radiological surveys of Tudor Shaft informal settlement, the Deputy Director-General of DEA, Ishaam Abader, wrote to the City Manager of MCLM issuing a "Notice of intention to issue a Directive" in terms of, inter alia, section 28(4) of the National Environmental Management Act 107 of 1998 (NEMA)[28] for having failed to "take reasonable measures to prevent significant pollution or environmental degradation" as the owner of the Tudor Shaft land.[29] On this basis, the notice invited MCLM within seven days to make representations as to why DEA should not issue a directive requiring MCLM as a matter of urgency to resettle people living within 10 meters of the tailings dam and submit a report containing a detailed radiological assessment to determine the extent of the contamination by the radioactive material and to provide options on "how this may be managed in situ or whether other disposal technologies are available to safely deal with this material."[30]

Almost a month later, on October 3, 2011, MCLM Municipal Manager, Dan Mashitisho, responded in writing to the Deputy-Director General's Notice. In his letter, Mr. Mashitisho

---

[25] *FSE* v. *NNR and Others*, note 9 (answering affidavit (July 4, 2012), Dan Metlana Mashitisho (MCLM Municipal Manager) at para. 16.)

[26] Ibid. (answering affidavit (July 4, 2012), Dan Metlana Mashitisho (MCLM Municipal Manager) at para. 23).

[27] Ibid. (answering affidavit (July 4, 2012), Dan Metlana Mashitisho (MCLM Municipal Manager) at para. 16).

[28] Section 28(4) of NEMA provides that DEA may "direct any person who fails to take the measures required under subsection (1)" to inter alia "commence taking specific reasonable measures before a given date." Section 28(1) of NEMA establishes that "every person who causes, has caused or may cause significant pollution or degradation of the environment must take reasonable measures to prevent such pollution or degradation from occurring, continuing or recurring, or, in so far as the harm to the environment is authorized by law or cannot reasonably be avoided or stopped, to minimize and rectify such pollution or degradation of the environment" (National Environmental Management Act 107 of 1998 (South Africa) [NEMA]).

[29] *FSE* v. *NNR and Others*, note 9 (Annexure 'ML4,' letter from Fourth Respondent dated Sept. 5, 2011 at pp. 2–3 and answering affidavit (July 4, 2012), Dan Metlana Mashitisho (MCLM Municipal Manager)).

[30] Ibid. (Annexure 'ML4,' letter from Fourth Respondent dated Sept. 5, 2011 at p. 6 and answering affidavit (July 4, 2012), Dan Metlana Mashitisho (MCLM Municipal Manager at p. 6)).

accepts the municipality's responsibility to handle the relocation of affected households.[31] However, in the remainder of the letter Mr. Mashitisho disputes DEA's assertions that, as the owner of the property, MCLM is responsible for having caused the environmental damage and/or for remedying it. Acknowledging that MCLM is the owner of the property on which Tudor Shaft is situated, Mr. Mashitisho "confirms in the strongest terms possible" that MCLM "was never involved or conducted mining operations on the said portion and is therefore not responsible for any mining rehabilitation and or mitigation measures . . . caused by historic and/or current mining activities."[32] Pointing out that while MCLM owns the land, it does not own any mineral rights,[33] Mr. Mashitisho argued that DMR is responsible for all aspects of mine safety, including mine-related damage.[34]

On October 25, 2011, Frances Craigie, Grade 1 Environmental Management Inspector at DEA, responded to MCLM's letter, writing that DEA "does not share your view" that MCLM is "exempt from the requirements" of NEMA simply because MCLM does not hold any mining rights for the property in question. Pointing out that "the duty of care" contemplated in section 28(1) of NEMA applies to the owner of the land "on which or in which" "any activity or process is or was performed or undertaken; or any other situation exists, which causes, has caused or is likely to cause significant pollution or degradation of the environment."[35] Mr. Craigie concluded that MCLM as the landowner has a responsibility under NEMA.[36]

Not having received a response to this letter, on 30 March 2012, DEA issued MCLM with a final warning Notice in which Sonny Bapela, Acting Deputy Director-General: Environmental Quality and Protection wrote:

> Irrespective of the attempts by the DEA to give effect to co-operative governance and achieve an amicable resolution of the matter for the benefit of the residents of Mogale City . . . DEA has been met with silence and inaction on the part of the Mogale City . . . In light of the above, I am granting you a final opportunity of five (5) working days . . . to provide a plan of action . . . to achieve compliance to the instructions given in the Notices of Intent . . . Should you fail to act swiftly and in an appropriate manner to address the problems identified . . . this Department will have to conclude that all attempts at a co-operative solution have been exhausted. The consequence of your failure to act accordingly will leave me with no other alternative but to issue a final Compliance Notice. In the event of failing to comply with Instructions set down in the Compliance Notice I will not hesitate to institute criminal sanction against the accounting

---

[31] Ibid. (Annexure 'ML5,' letter from Second Respondent dated Oct. 3, 2011 at p. 2 and answering affidavit (July 4, 2012), Dan Metlana Mashitisho (MCLM Municipal Manager)).

[32] Ibid. (Annexure 'ML5,' letter from Second Respondent dated Oct. 3, 2011 at p. 2, answering affidavit (July 4, 2012), Dan Metlana Mashitisho (MCLM Municipal Manager)).

[33] In South Africa, there is a distinction between the ownership of land and the ownership of mineral rights, meaning that the owner of the land is not automatically the owner of any mineral rights on the land.

[34] *FSE v. NNR and Others*, note 17 (Annexure 'ML5,' letter from Second Respondent dated Oct. 3, 2011 at p. 2 and answering affidavit (July 4, 2012), Dan Metlana Mashitisho (MCLM Municipal Manager)).

[35] NEMA, note 28, s. 28(2).

[36] *FSE v. NNR and Others*, note 17 Annexure 'ML6' (letter from Fourth Respondent dated Nov. 29, 2011 at p. 1 and answering affidavit (July 4, 2012), Dan Metlana Mashitisho (MCLM Municipal Manager)). Regarding authority specifically to make any decision to move a tailings dam, DEA argued in its subsequent court papers that because inter alia of the high levels of radiation measured in Tudor Shaft, the NNR, rather than DEA "ought to be the lead authority to grant the necessary authorisation for the for the removal of the tailings" (*FSE v. NNR and Others*, note 17 (answering affidavit (Oct. 31, 2012), Sonnyboy Bapela (Chief Director: Compliance, DEA) at para. 13)). The NNR, for its part, disagreed with this interpretation, arguing that it is not NNR's function to "remove mine residue after mining operations have been concluded" and that the responsibility lay with MCLM "as the registered owner of the land" (*FSE v. NNR and Others*, note 17 (answering affidavit (Oct. 31, 2012), Boyce Mackeson Mkhize (Chief Executive Officer, NNR) at para. 3.3)).

officer of the Mogale City Local Municipality in terms of the National Environmental Management: Waste Act 59 of 2008 ('the NEM:WA') *Please note that the State is not excluded from criminal liability as far as offences in terms of the NEM:WA is concerned.*[37]

Evidently galvanized by this final warning and threat of criminal sanction, on April 17, 2012, Mr. Mashitisho of MCLM wrote to Mr. Bapela of DEA, wishing "to report on progress on the Tudor Shaft Informal Settlement, with special reference to the relocation of affected families from land contaminated by elevated levels of radiation, and the rehabilitation of a slimes dam in close proximity to the said settlement."[38] Reporting that it had liaised with NNR to obtain a list of technical experts to conduct a radiological survey at Tudor Shaft settlement and with the Provincial Department of Human Settlement to identify suitable land for the resettlement of affected families in the Tudor Shaft area,[39] Mr. Mashitisho requested "DEA to withdraw its intention to issue a final compliance notice,"[40] which DEA apparently did.

On June 8, 2012, MCLM and NNR met, together with private mining company, Mogale Gold (Pty) Ltd. (Mogale Gold),[41] which had agreed to help to "resolve the challenges in relation to the Tudor Shaft community" as "part of their social and labour plan initiative."[42] According to this joint venture, the plan was for NNR to oversee Mogale Gold's removal of the tailings and MCLM to identify sites for the relocation of affected households.[43] Thus, on the afternoon of Wednesday June 27, 2012, without any impact or risk assessment having been undertaken, operations commenced to remove the tailings dam, entailing the tailings being scooped up by digging machines and loaded onto trucks, which drove away in a dust cloud.[44] Concerned that the operation was exposing residents to an even higher radioactive threat than usual, FSE filed *FSE v. NNR and Others* as an urgent application in the South Gauteng High Court on June 29, 2012 against inter alia NNR (first respondent), MCLM (second respondent), and the Minister of Environmental Affairs (fourth respondent), in which it sought to interdict the mine residue removal operations until they complied with legal requirements.

On Friday June 29, 2012, following an undertaking from MCLM to immediately cease the removal operations, the High Court granted an interim injunction to cease the removal operations at Tudor Shaft pending a substantive hearing on the matter, set down for July 10, 2012, and later postponed by successive court orders to July 31 and October 23, 2012, and then until further notice.[45] On July 27, 2012, 292 residents from Tudor Shaft applied to intervene as

---

[37] *FSE v. NNR and Others*, note 17 (Annexure 'ML7,' letter from Fourth Respondent dated Mar. 30, 2012 at p. 2 and answering affidavit (July 4, 2012), Dan Metlana Mashitisho (MCLM Municipal Manager)) (emphasis added).

[38] Ibid. (Annexure 'ML8,' letter from Second Respondent dated Apr. 17, 2012 at p. 1 and answering affidavit (July 4, 2012), Dan Metlana Mashitisho (MCLM Municipal Manager)).

[39] Ibid. (Annexure 'ML8' (letter from Second Respondent dated Apr. 17, 2012 at pp. 1–2 and answering affidavit (July 4, 2012), Dan Metlana Mashitisho (MCLM Municipal Manager)).

[40] Ibid. (Annexure 'ML8,' letter from Second Respondent dated Apr. 17, 2012 at p. 3 and answering affidavit (July 4, 2012), Dan Metlana Mashitisho (MCLM Municipal Manager)).

[41] Sometimes referred to as Mintails.

[42] Under the post-apartheid Minerals and Petroleum Resources Development Act 28 of 2002 (South Africa) [MPRDA], as a condition of being allocated mining rights, mining companies have to undertake various social and labor-related activities.

[43] *FSE v. NNR and Others*, note 17 (answering affidavit (July 4, 2012), Dan Metlana Mashitisho (MCLM Municipal Manager) at para. 37).

[44] Research notes taken during the operations of 27 June 2012 by Anna Alcaro, former intern at the Socio-Economic Rights Institute of South Africa, who while conducting ongoing research in the settlement witnessed the operation.

[45] In the light of subsequent developments, the interdict has never been made final, essentially leaving the radioactive tailings as they were.

co-applicants (with FSE) in the application based on their direct interest in the matter, and were granted leave to intervene on September 11, 2012. On November 20, 2013 – having in March and April 2013 undertaken their own preliminary health risk assessment, which found "all of the soil at Tudor Shaft" to be "dangerously contaminated"[46] – the residents filed a further application, in two parts. Part A was an application for the joinder of the Minister of Mineral Resources to the proceedings.[47] Part B was an application seeking to stop the respondents from any further mine residue removal operations pending the respondents producing an appropriate risk assessment report and, based on this report, providing a suitable implementation plan for dealing with the problem.[48] On December 18, 2013, the court granted the Part A application for joinder.

In its application for joinder of DMR (and Interdict Application as Part B), filed on November 20, 2013, Tudor Shaft residents note that although more than a year had passed since the last court appearance in the matter, and despite the removal operations having long-since ceased, none of the government respondents had produced the risk assessment report called for by FSE, sought to engage the residents on the health risks posed by the tailings dam, proposed measures to reduce and/or eliminate any of the risks, or sought to consult the residents about possible relocation to a safer site. Instead, "all that" the parties had done "is file a set of answering affidavits" in which they:

> seek to avoid responsibility for commissioning and issuing the report called for or otherwise addressing the health and environmental risks posed by the tailings dam. Each of these respondents alleges that someone else is required to address the risk and mitigate the health and environmental consequences of doing so. This is inexplicable, given the significant involvement and engagement by all three of them in relation to this matter prior to the launch of this application. The practical consequence of this abandonment of responsibility by them all is that notwithstanding the recognized serious health and safety risks posed by the contaminated tailings dam (and all their prior engagement in the matter), no government body is doing *anything* anymore to address the situation.[49]

Having been admitted to the legal proceedings, and in the context of the failure of the other respondents to furnish risk assessment reports as sought by FSE, DMR commissioned an independent report, which was submitted on June 4, 2014. Based on thirty-one tests of the soil in and around the settlement, the report found that "the radiation levels at the Tudor Shaft mine are above the public limits."[50] It concluded that, because Tudor Shaft residents "are continuously exposed to high levels of radiation, the ways to protect the public from the radiation in situ – namely keeping a safe distance from the source, minimizing the amount of time spent

---

[46] *FSE v. NNR and Others*, note 17 (Annexure 'PM9,' Tudor Shaft Informal Settlement Preliminary Health Risk Assessment, supplementary affidavit (Nov. 20, 2013), Phumla Patience Mjadu (Tudor Shaft resident) and paras. 33–39 of supplementary affidavit).

[47] The joinder of DMR was necessary since ss. 45–46 of the MPRDA, over which DMR has primary jurisdiction, provide that where any prospecting or mining causes ecological degradation, pollution or environmental damage which might be harmful to the health or wellbeing of anyone requires urgent remedial measures, the minister may direct the holder of the relevant right, permit, or permission to investigate and take remedial measures.

[48] As with the main FSE application, in the light of subsequent developments, Part B of this application was never heard.

[49] *FSE v. NNR and Others*, note 17 (Supplementary affidavit (Nov. 20, 2013), Phumla Patience Mjadu (Tudor Shaft resident) at paras. 13–14) (emphasis added).

[50] Tshivhase, note 18, p. 4.

close to the source, and shielding the source – would be difficult to implement and instead recommended that "the residents be relocated to an alternative safe habitable area."[51]

This recommendation, although not accepted by other government agencies such as DEA, had the effect of diverting all subsequent interventions toward an attempt to identify an alternative accommodation solution[52] and away from the ecological harm question, leaving the tailings dams where they were as undisturbed since the interim injunction of July 29, 2012. In November 2015, DEA produced its own independent report, but this was submitted to the legal proceedings only in May 2016. The report concluded that there were ways to remove the tailings without harming the residents.[53] By this time, however, the parallel process of relocating Tudor Shaft residents was substantially underway, effectively halting any further remedial efforts by the government.

20.4 CONCLUSION

In 2013, writing with a colleague when the Tudor Shaft litigation process had just begun, I optimistically concluded: "it is possible that [this case] might signal a new approach to environmental cases that seeks to combine environmental and socioeconomic rights and infuse an expansive and holistic approach to environmental [justice]."[54] Unfortunately, this initial observation proved overly optimistic. At the time of writing the chapter for this book, although the residents of Tudor Shaft had finally been relocated to an ecologically safer location and some had received formal housing, the radioactive hazard of the Tudor Shaft tailings had still not been addressed. In addition, critical aspects of the residents' intersectional social disadvantage persist, albeit in a new location. Moving the Tudor Shaft residents from one socially marginalized location to another has produced a bleak vortex that David Dickinson refers to as the "Dismal Merry Go Round of Never Enough."[55]

Kimberlé Crenshaw's 1989 article highlighted how, in the US context, single axis antidiscrimination efforts tended to benefit the more empowered among racial and gender groups (benefiting Black men and White women respectively) leaving the more intractable dimensions (as affecting Black women) intact. Similarly, the Tudor Shaft case study illustrates how the South African government's fragmented approach to dealing with intersectional ecological and social disadvantage has addressed only the most acute aspects, leaving the more complex dimensions of disadvantage unresolved. It also underscores the clear need to develop and implement an environmental justice/integrated sustainable development approach to dealing with the intersectional disadvantage of communities such as Tudor Shaft that would identify the dimensions of social and ecological disadvantage, and address these in a holistic, balanced way. Using rights- and justice-based as well as Sustainable Development Goal-related frameworks,

---

[51] Ibid.

[52] This process proved highly volatile, with conflict among residents about who would qualify for new houses (for example, foreign nationals do not qualify for households) and the negotiated process took over two years, from mid-2014 to the end of 2016, when the final households were relocated.

[53] South African Council of Scientific and Industrial Research, "Report on Human Health Risk Assessment of Exposure to Particulate Matter and Metals in Soil at Tudor Shaft Informal Settlement, Mogale City," Nov. 2015 (copy with author).

[54] Dugard and Alcaro, note 8, 207.

[55] D. Dickinson, "A Contested Commons: Land, Class and Race within and around a Township in the Eastern Free State, South Africa," paper presented at the Centre for Applied Legal Studies (CALS)/South African Journal on Human Rights Colloquium on Property and Land in a Contested Terrain, University of the Witwatersrand, July 2, 2018, p. 12.

pursuing the kind of approach advocated in this book would entail a context-specific and nuanced engagement between the affected communities and within and between the relevant government agencies (to ensure procedural and corrective justice) to properly understand the intersectional nature of their disadvantage, as well as to find integrated and sustainable remedies to comprehensively address their socioecological insecurity and exclusion (to ensure distributive and social justice).

Sustainable Mining, Environmental Justice, and the Human Rights of Women and Girls

Canada as Home and Host State

Sara L. Seck and Penelope Simons

21.1 INTRODUCTION

Resource extraction of minerals and metals is often touted as a pathway to sustainable development, especially for poor countries and communities of the Global South.[1] While large-scale mining projects can bring with them certain benefits, and opportunities, they can also have significant detrimental impacts, particularly for Indigenous communities, who "often rely on natural resources that mining activities disrupt, threaten, or poison, and [who] have cultural and spiritual relationships to landscapes that may be destroyed or degraded."[2] For industrial mining to meet accepted understandings of sustainable development, it must be responsive to the concerns of local communities, including Indigenous peoples, and women, who must all have the opportunity to choose to actively participate in, and benefit from, mining development.[3] Yet, as will be explored in this chapter, even in rich settler states of the Global North, like Canada, there are few, if any, sustainable mining practices that are truly respectful of the environmental and other human rights of women and girls. Consequently, it is not surprising that there is also a failure to ensure that mining companies based in Canada respect these rights when operating transnationally outside of Canada especially in developing countries.

---

[1] S. L. Seck, "Transnational Corporations and Extractive Industries," in S. Alam, S. Atapattu, C. G. Gonzalez, and J. Razzaque (eds.), *International Environmental Law and the Global South* (New York: Cambridge University Press, 2015), pp. 380–398; S. K. Lodhia (ed.), *Mining and Sustainable Development: Current Issues* (Abingdon, UK: Routledge, 2018). This chapter will focus on sustainable mining of minerals and metals and will exclude consideration of fossil fuel extraction, including oil, gas, and coal, due to climate change. The authors take the position that due to the imperative of green energy transition, it is no longer possible to claim that the exploitation of future fossil fuel reserves can be undertaken while respecting human rights. See further D. Chimisso dos Santos and S. L. Seck, "Human Rights Due Diligence and Extractive Industries," in S. Deva (ed.), *Research Handbook on Human Rights and Business* (Cheltenham: Edward Elgar, 2020).

[2] L. S. Horowitz, A. Keeling, F. Lévesque, T. Rodon, S. Schott, and S. Thériault, "Indigenous Peoples' Relationships to Large-scale Mining in Post/Colonial Contexts: Toward Multidisciplinary Comparative Perspectives" (2018) 5 *The Extractive Industries and Society* 404 at 411.

[3] Seck, note 1, p. 385, citing UN, *Report of the World Summit on Sustainable Development*, August 26–September 4, 2002, A/CONF.199/20, p. 29. See further Columbia Center on Sustainable Investment, Sustainable Solutions Network, UNDP, World Economic Forum, "White Paper: Mapping Mining to the Sustainable Development Goals: An Atlas," July 2016; K. Lahiri-Dutt, "Do Women Have a Right to Mine?" (2019) 31 *Canadian Journal Women and the Law* 1.

From an environmental justice perspective, it is common for scholars to identify four interrelated aspects that together lead to injustice.[4] First, a distributive justice approach foregrounds inadequate access to environmental goods as well as differential exposures to environmental harms. A procedural justice approach highlights the unfairness that arises when underrepresented groups are excluded from governmental decision-making. Corrective justice draws attention to the inadequacy of enforcement of environmental laws, leaving those who cause or contribute to environmental degradation free to operate with impunity while those who suffer harm lack redress. Finally, a social justice perspective shines a spotlight on the broader context in which social ills, such as poverty and racism, are closely linked with environmental degradation.[5] Each of these interrelated aspects of environmental justice may manifest in relation to proposed or actual mining exploration and development, and concern that environmental justice issues will not be addressed may lead to local community resistance to resource extraction.[6]

Whether what local communities seek is responsibly managed mineral development, or none at all,[7] international human rights law serves as a tool through which resistance can be legally expressed, and environmental injustice challenged.[8] Importantly, the environmental injustices of mining development have gendered impacts with implications for the enjoyment by women and girls of their environmental and other human rights.[9] Moreover, when women resist environmentally destructive extractive projects, they may experience intersectional vulnerability, being targeted both for challenging gender norms, and for their role as defenders of land and natural resources.[10] The human rights of women and children are recognized under international treaties and customary international law,[11] and have been endorsed by the international

---

4   R. R. Kuehn, "A Taxonomy of Environmental Justice" (2000) 30 *Environmental Law Reporter* 10681; C. G. Gonzalez, "Environmental Justice, Human Rights, and the Global South" (2015) 13 *Santa Clara Journal of International Law* 151 at 155.

5   Kuehn, note 4, p. 10681; Gonzalez, note 4, p. 155.

6   See, for example, D. Zillman, A. Lucas, and G. R. Pring (eds.), *Human Rights in Natural Resource Development: Public Participation in Sustainable Development of Mining and Energy Resources* (Oxford: Oxford University Press, 2001); Seck, note 1, pp. 388–393; K. Deonandan and C. Bell, "Discipline and Punish: Gendered Dimensions of Violence in Extractive Development" (2019) 31 *Canadian Journal of Women and the Law* 24; S. Morales, "Digging for Rights: How Can International Human Rights Law Better Protect Indigenous Women from Extractive Industries?" (2019) 31 *Canadian Journal of Women and the Law* 58.

7   Compare "First Nations Women Advocating Responsible Mining": http://fnwarm.com, with "WoMin African Women Unite against Destructive Resource Extraction": https://womin.org.za, including WoMin, "Extractives Assembly, World Social Forum, Political Declaration": https://womin.org.za/images/the-alterna tives/fighting-destructive-extractivism/World%20Social%20Forum%20Declaration%20on%20Extractives%202013 .pdf, *with* A. Valencia, ALTERNAUTAS, "Women in Defense of Mother Earth," Oct. 14, 2014, www.alternautas .net/blog/2015/1/28/women-defense-mother-earth.

8   Gonzalez, note 4, p. 193; Zillman et al., note 6; Seck, note 1, pp. 391–393; S. L. Seck, "Human Rights and Extractive Industries: Environmental Law and Standards," prepared for the Rocky Mountain Mineral Law Foundation: special Institute on Human Rights Law and the Extractive Industries, Paper No. 12, Feb. 2016, pp. 12-1–12-42.

9   K. Jenkins, "Review Article: Women, Mining and Development: An Emerging Research Agenda" (2014) 1 *Extractive Industries and Society* 329 at 333–335; K. Koutouki, K. Lofts, and Gisselle Davidian, "A Rights-Based Approach to Indigenous Women and Gender Inequities in Resource Development in Northern Canada" (2018) 27 *Review of European, Comparative and International Environmental Law* 63–74 at 64–67.

10 See for example I. Barcia, "Women Human Rights Defenders Confronting Extractive Industries: An Overview of Critical Risks and Human Rights Obligations," Association for Women's Rights in Development (AWID) and Women Human Rights Defenders International Coalition (WHRDIC), 2017.

11 UN General Assembly, *Convention on the Elimination of All Forms of Discrimination against Women (CEDAW)*, Dec. 18, 1979, UN Doc. A/34/46 [CEDAW]; UN, *Beijing Declaration and Platform for Action, Report of the Fourth World Conference on Women*, Oct. 17, 1995, UN Doc. A/CONF. 177/20 and A/CONF. 177/20/Add.1; UN Convention on the Rights of the Child, *Committee on the Rights of the Child,*

community in the Sustainable Development Goals (SDGs).[12] Yet, as will be seen in this chapter, implementation of these rights in domestic law and policy as well as in international guidance tools for responsible business conduct is lacking, resulting in a failure to prevent and respond to gendered environmental injustice in the context of mining activity.

There is sometimes a tendency to assume that all is well in the Global North, while environmental justice problems that have an impact on vulnerable communities and the women and girls within them, arise only in the Global South.[13] The two case studies presented in this chapter will consider some of the similarities and differences in the experiences of women and girls within the context of large-scale minerals and metals extraction in both Global North and Global South, and will assess the extent to which current guidelines and regulatory mechanisms address gendered impacts and benefits of such activity. We use Canada for both case studies given the prominent role that Canada plays in the global mining industry,[14] as well as the importance of domestic natural resource extraction, such as mining development, within Canada.[15]

We will first briefly discuss the nature of environmental and other human rights violations of women and girls in the mining context with attention to the extent to which such violations contribute to environmental injustice. We will then examine Canadian legal and policy responses first from the perspective of Canada as a home state, and then from the perspective of Canada as a host state. Ultimately, we will consider how these perspectives reveal common problems for which there may be common solutions.

21.2 ENVIRONMENTAL JUSTICE AND THE HUMAN RIGHTS OF WOMEN AND GIRLS IN GLOBAL MINING

The nature of large-scale mining inevitably means that it will often have impacts on the land and resources of local communities. These impacts implicate a wide range of environmental and other human rights including the right to a healthy environment.[16] For example, improper disposal of toxic wastes and hazardous substances from extractive operations threaten the rights to health and water.[17] Pollution and habitat loss more generally threaten the right to food.[18] Procedural environmental rights may be violated, including rights of access to information, participation, and access to justice, as well as the related but distinct Indigenous and local community rights to free, prior, and informed consent (FPIC).[19] Due to the "extraordinary risks"

General Comment No. 16 on State Obligations regarding the Impact of the Business Sector on Children's Rights, Apr. 17, 2013, UN Doc. CRC/C/GC/16.

[12] UN General Assembly, *Draft Outcome Document of the United Nations Summit for the Adoption of the Post-2015 Development Agenda*, Aug. 12, 2015, UN Doc. A/69/L.85.

[13] Seck, note 1, p. 390.

[14] Mining Association of Canada, "Facts and Figures 2017," Mar. 5, 2018.

[15] Natural Resources Canada, "10 Key Facts on Canada's Minerals Sector," Aug. 2017.

[16] UN General Assembly, *Report of the Independent Expert on the Issue of Human Rights Obligations Relating to the Enjoyment of a Safe, Clean, Healthy and Sustainable Environment, John H. Knox*, Dec. 30, 2013, A/HRC/25/53, para. 18.

[17] Ibid., p. 7, paras. 20–21.

[18] Ibid., p. 7, para. 21.

[19] On the differences and similarities between Indigenous rights to FPIC and local non-Indigenous community participatory rights, see S. L. Seck, "Indigenous Rights, Environmental Rights, or Stakeholder Engagement? Comparing IFC and OECD Approaches to the Implementation of the Business Responsibility to Respect Human Rights" (2016) 12 *McGill Journal of Sustainable Development Law* 51 at 57–65. See also UNGA, note 16, p. 8. para. 29, observing the "striking" "agreement among sources" that states have procedural obligations including "duties (a) to assess environmental impacts and make environmental information public; (b) to

facing human rights defenders (HRDs) who work to protect the environment, land, and natural resources, it is essential to safeguard the exercise of participation rights on which sustainable mining depends, including rights of freedom of expression, association, peaceful protest, and the rights to protection of life, liberty, and security of person.[20] Moreover, as will be explored in this section, women and children are often included among those who are most "vulnerable to, or at particular risk from, environmental harm" in the large-scale mining context.[21]

Neither the Convention on the Elimination of Discrimination against Women (CEDAW)[22] nor the Convention on the Rights of the Child (CRC)[23] includes an explicit right to a healthy environment. However, the Committee on the Elimination of Discrimination against Women has recognized the links between environmental harm and many of the rights protected under CEDAW.[24] These include the right to nondiscrimination in the field of healthcare (Article 12); the right to equal enjoyment of adequate living conditions (Article 14(2)(h)); the right to equal treatment in land and agrarian reform as well as in land resettlement schemes (Article 14(2)(g)); the equal right to freedom of movement (Article 15(4)); and, the equal right to development (Articles 3 and 14(2)(a)).[25] The Committee, in construing CEDAW, has concluded that states should ensure that women's concerns and participation are incorporated into public participation in environmental decision-making, and that this includes climate policy.[26] The CRC, on the other hand, in Article 6 obliges states to respect the inherent right of children to life and to ensure their survival and development.[27] Article 24 requires states to ensure the enjoyment of the

---

facilitate public participation in environmental decision-making, including by protecting the rights of expression and association; and (c) to provide access to remedies for harm." See further paras. 30–35 (duties to assess environmental impacts and make information public); pp. 9–12, paras. 36–40 (duties to facilitate public participation in environmental decision-making); and paras 41–43 (duty to provide access to legal remedies).

[20] UNGA, note 16, p. 11, para. 39, referring to the work of the Special Rapporteur on the situation of HRDs. See UNGA, *Report of the Special Rapporteur on the Situation of Human Rights Defenders*, Aug. 5, 2013, UN Doc. A/68/262, paras. 15–20; UNGA, *Report of the Special Rapporteur on the Situation of Human Rights Defenders, Margaret Sekaggya*, Dec. 21, 2011, UN Doc. A/HRC/19/55, paras. 60–87, 124–126.

[21] UN Human Rights Council, *Report of the Special Rapporteur on the issue of human rights obligations relating to the enjoyment of a safe, clean, healthy and sustainable environment: Framework principles, John Knox*, Jan. 24, 2018, A/HRC/37/59, paras. 40–41; UNGA, note 16, pp. 7–8, paras. 23–25. See further paras. 69–78 (obligations relating to members of groups in vulnerable situations, women, children, Indigenous peoples).

[22] CEDAW, note 11.

[23] UN General Assembly, Convention on the Rights of the Child, Nov. 20, 1989, UN Doc. A/44/49 (1989) [CRC].

[24] UNHCR, *Mapping Human Rights Obligations Relating to the Enjoyment of a Safe, Clean, Healthy and Sustainable Environment: Individual Report on the United Nations Convention on the Elimination of All Forms of Discrimination against Women, Report No. 4*, Dec. 30, 2013, para. 16, www.ohchr.org/Documents/Issues/Environment/Mappingreport/4.CEDAW-25-Feb.doc; *Report of the Committee on the Elimination of Discrimination against Women for the Forty-fourth & Forty-fifth sessions, Statement of the Committee on the Elimination of Discrimination against Women on gender and climate change*, July 20–Aug. 7, 2009, UN Doc. A/65/38 (SUPP), Annex II, para. 3 (on discrimination with regard to women's rights to an adequate standard of living in the context of natural disaster related conflicts).

[25] UNHCR, note 24, paras. 16, 21, 26, 32, 36.

[26] Ibid., paras. 42–48; UNGA note 16, para 70. Similar observations have been made by the Special Rapporteur on the right to health, observing that "even though women bear a disproportionate burden in the collection of water and disposal of family wastewater, they are often excluded from relevant decision-making processes. States should therefore take measures to ensure that women are not excluded from decision-making processes concerning water and sanitation management" (ibid., citing A/62/214, para. 84).

[27] This includes an obligation on both home and host states to take steps through regulation and monitoring of business activities (such as mining) to prevent "environmental degradation and contamination [that] can compromise children's rights to health, food security and access to safe drinking water and sanitation" or to ensure that transferring land rights to investors does not "deprive local populations of access to natural resources linked to their subsistence and cultural heritage." UN CRC, note 11, para. 19. For a discussion of state obligations with respect to children's human rights in the context of mining activity, see M. Paré and

highest attainable standard of health and to take appropriate measures to fully implement this right by combatting disease and malnutrition "through the provision of adequate nutritious foods and clean drinking-water, taking into consideration the dangers and risks of environmental pollution."[28]

Globally, the extractive industries are highly gendered and deeply masculine, and women's relationship to mining activity is "under-recognised and under-theorised" especially in terms of development benefits for "poor communities in the global south."[29] Women face significant discrimination in seeking employment within the mining industry in the Global South,[30] whether in the context of large-scale mining, the focus of this chapter, or artisanal and small-scale mining sector (ASM).[31] Women face analogous gendered discrimination in accessing employment (particularly more lucrative skilled employment) and promotion opportunities in the mining industry in Canada,[32] and Indigenous women experience intersecting forms of gender and racial discrimination.[33]

Environmental pollution arising from extractive industries can have major deleterious impacts on women working within the industry as employees of mining companies, as well as on women living in and around the extraction project, and their families,[34] and a growing number of reports on resource extraction in countries in the Global South testify to this continuing problem.[35] Toxic pollution of water and the environment may have a greater impact on women in the Global South due to their traditional roles as collectors of water and preparers of food, and as small-scale farmers with responsibilities for subsistence agriculture.[36] In addition, mining may also have harmful effects on the health of women that differ from those on men. When family members fall ill from contamination to land or water sources caused by a mining

---

T. Chong, "Human Rights Violations and Canadian Mining Companies: Exploring Access to Justice in Relation to Children's Rights" (2017) 21 *International Journal of Human Rights* 908 at 914–918.

[28] CRC, note 23, Art. 24(2)(c).

[29] Jenkins, note 9, p. 330. According to Jenkins, women "should be recognised as important actors in communities affected by mining" in four key areas: as mine workers, in relation to the gendered impacts of mining, with regard to the impact of mining on gender relations and identifies, and with regard to access to the benefits from mining.

[30] Lahiri-Dutt, note 3, 4–6.

[31] Ibid., 2–3. The role of women in the ASM sector around the world is very important, and the environmental impacts overlap with large-scale mining. See generally K. Lahiri-Dutt (ed.), *Between the Plough and the Pick: Informal, Artisanal and Small-Scale Mining in the Contemporary World* (Canberra: Australian National University Press, 2018); A. Eftimie, K. Heller, J. Strongman, J. Hinton, K. Lahiri-Dutt, and N. Mutemeri "Gender Dimensions of Artisanal and Small-Scale Mining: A Rapid Assessment Toolkit," World Bank Gender Action Plan, 2012.

[32] U. R. Ozkan and C. Beckton, "The Pathway Forward: Creating Gender Inclusive Leadership in Mining and Resources," Carleton University, Centre for Women in Politics and Public Leadership, Nov. 2012, pp. 13, 25; E. Nightingale, K. Czyzewski, F. Tester, and N. Aaruaq, "The Effects of Resource Extraction on Inuit Women and Their Families: Evidence from Canada" (2017) 25 *Gender and Development* 367 at 371.

[33] R. Deonandan, K. Deonandan, and B. Field, "Mining the Gap: Aboriginal Women and the Mining Industry," SSHRC Report, 2016, p. 8; Amnesty International Canada, "Out of Sight, Out of Mind: Gender, Indigenous Rights, and Energy Development in Northeast British Columbia, Canada," Nov. 3, 2016; Nightingale et al., note 25, pp. 375–376, where they note that employment in mining can provide a variety of benefits, including helping women gain financial independence, skills and confidence. However, the three most common reasons for Inuit women leaving mine employment relate to gender discrimination: a nonpermanent contract; no access to childcare; and sexual harassment and assault.

[34] Jenkins, note 9, pp. 332–334.

[35] See for example, WoMin, "Land and Food Sovereignty Undermined: Impacts on Peasant Women," p. 13–16; WoMin, "'No longer a Life Worth Living': Mining Impacted Women Speak through Participatory Action Research in Somkhele and Fuleni Communities, Northern Kawazulu Natal, South Africa," Feb. 24, 2017.

[36] Jenkins, note 9, p. 333.

project, women may have increased responsibilities in caring for them, which can take such women away from paid and unpaid work that supports the family, and which can take girls away from school.[37]

There is a dearth of social research on the impacts of mining on Indigenous communities in Canada.[38] Nonetheless, Tara Joly and Clinton Westman note that the toxic contamination of land and water by mining activity has been well documented in the natural science literature, and such environmental effects have "easily-inferable impacts on Indigenous communities' abilities to maintain their ways of life."[39] There are a small but increasing number of studies that suggest that such pollution to land and waterways can have differentiated impacts on Indigenous women living in remote and isolated places where Indigenous communities often depend on access to "country food," such as wildlife, fish, and flora for their sustenance. In some Indigenous communities "hunting and fishing are traditionally seen as men's domain [while] women are frequently responsible for harvesting plants and other wild products,"[40] including medicinal plants for their own and their families' well-being.[41] Women may also sell harvested wild products to generate extra income.[42] Thus contamination from, or an inability to access lands and water sources due to, mining activity can violate their rights to food, health, livelihood, and their culture including "the ability to teach or pass on Traditional Ecological Knowledge to the next generation."[43] Mining activity may also violate Indigenous women's rights to property, religion, improvement of economic and social conditions, and participation in decision-making.[44] The unique experiences of Indigenous women in relation to ecological harms arises in part from the cultural connection to the land that many Indigenous women feel, with the environmental destruction of land destroying "both their cultural and personal well-being" and experienced as violence.[45] For this reason it is particularly crucial that these women are represented in environmental impact assessment processes and in negotiations over

---

[37] Ibid. See also A. Eftimie, K. Heller, and J. Strongman, "Gender Dimensions of the Extractive Industries: Mining for Equity," World Bank, Extractive Industries and Development Series No. 8, Aug. 2009, p. 17. These gendered environmental impacts of extractive industries have also been identified by the former and current Special Rapporteurs on the Disposal of Hazardous Wastes and Substances. See UN General Assembly, *Report of the Special Rapporteur on the implications for human rights of the environmentally sound management and disposal of hazardous substances and waste*, July 20, 2017, UN Doc. A/HRC/36/41, paras. 16, 24, 37–38; UN General Assembly, *Report of the Special Rapporteur on the human rights obligations related to environmentally sound management and disposal of hazardous substances and waste, Calin Georgescu*, July 2, 2012, A/HRC/21/48, paras. 31–33.

[38] T. L. Joly and C. N. Westman, "Taking Research off the Shelf: Impacts, Benefits, and Participatory Process around the Oil Sands Industry in Northern Alberta," Final Report for the SSHRC Imagining Canada's Future Initiative, Knowledge Synthesis Grants: Aboriginal Peoples, Sept. 11, 2017, p. 7.

[39] Ibid.

[40] Koutouki et al., note 9, p. 67.

[41] T. Kunkel, "Aboriginal Values and Resource Development in Native Space: Lessons from British Columbia" (2017) 4 *Extractive Industries and Society* 6 at 12.

[42] Ibid.

[43] Ibid. See also Morales, note 6, pp. 63–77; Koutouki et al., note 9. Although see S. Manning, P. Nash, L. Levac, D. Stienstra, and J. Stinson "A Literature Synthesis Report on the Impacts of Resource Extraction for Indigenous Women," Canadian Research Institute for the Advancement of Women, Canada Environmental Assessment Agency, Aug. 17, 2018, p. 14 where they note that for some Indigenous communities employment income from resource extraction can improve food security by helping to finance hunting expeditions or to pay for groceries, among other things.

[44] Morales, note 6.

[45] Ibid., p. 68. This is equally true for Indigenous women in the Global South. See Jenkins, note 9, p. 334. See also Inter-American Commission on Human Rights, "Inter-American Commission on Human Rights: Indigenous Peoples, Afro-Descendent Communities, and Natural Resources: Human Rights Protection in the Context of Extraction and Development Activities," Dec. 31, 2015, OEA/Ser.L/V/IL Doc.47/15, paras.

community–company agreements once it has been decided that mining will take place, so as to avoid gendered inequalities in relation to benefits.[46] Yet, in Canada, socioeconomic impact assessments that are part of environmental reviews of extractive projects vary with jurisdiction and do not systematically, comprehensively, or consistently take into account potential gendered impacts.[47] Some research suggests that women often do participate either directly or indirectly in the negotiation of impact benefit agreements (IBAs).[48] However, as Deborah Stienstra et al. note, there is little evidence on the extent to which, if at all, gendered and intersectional analyses are used in developing such agreements or on how these agreements "interact with public regulatory mechanisms."[49]

Large-scale mining also brings with it increased violence against women, including sexual violence within the workplace and the community as well as increased instances of domestic violence. Although women's experiences of violence are intersectional and unique depending on their race, socioeconomic status, and many other factors, "there appear to be some notable similarities in the causes and the multi-faceted nature of gendered violence associated with mining and oil and gas projects across the globe."[50] It is beyond the scope of this chapter to discuss each of these causes, but we consider a few of them below.

First, studies have shown that large-scale mining projects and their large, transient, principally male workforce significantly escalates the risk of sexual and other gender-based violence for women and girls in the local community. For example, Isabel Cane, Amgalan Terbish, and Onon Bymbasuren reported increased incidences of gender-based violence and increased sex work, among other things, associated with the workers at three gold mines in the South Gobi desert.[51] Similarly, Canadian women, particularly Indigenous women, face a high risk of violence, including sexual violence, associated with resource extraction projects.[52] Indeed, according to the Firelight Group, there is a direct link "between the highly paid shadow populations at industrial camps, the hyper-masculine culture, and a rise in crime, sexual violence, and trafficking of Indigenous women" in Canada.[53]

Second, there is a particular environmental justice dimension to this harm. The Special Rapporteur on the Situation of Human Rights Defenders has noted that women environmental HRDs "who may oppose large-scale development projects" may also "challenge the systemic power inequality and discrimination deeply rooted in societies," including in their own communities. They are more likely than other environmental HRDs to "face gender-specific

---

319–321, where it states that "largescale mining activities leave deep impacts on the lives and . . . the bodies of women."

[46] Jenkins, note 9, pp. 336–337; J. Keenan, D. Kemp, and R. Ramsay, "Company–Community Agreements, Gender and Development" (2014) 135 *Journal of Business Ethics* 607 at 613.

[47] D. Stienstra, L. Levac, G. Baikie, J. Stinson, B. Clow, and S. Manning, "Gendered and Intersectional Implications of Energy and Resource Extraction in Resource-Based Communities in Canada's North," CRIAW ICREF, Feminist Northern Network, May 13, 2016, p. 12.

[48] See C. O'Faircheallaigh, "Women's Absence, Women's Power: Indigenous Women and Negotiations with Mining Companies in Australia and Canada" (2013) 36 *Ethnic and Racial Studies* 1789.

[49] Stienstra et al., note 47, pp. 12–13.

[50] P. Simons and M. Handl, "Relations of Ruling: The United Nations Guiding Principles on Business and Human Rights, Gender, Resource Extraction and Violence against Women" (2018) 31 *Canadian Journal of Women and the Law* 113 at 122.

[51] I. Cane, A. Terbish, and O. Bymbasuren, "Mapping Gender Based Violence and Mining Infrastructure in Mongolian Mining Communities," International Mining for Development Centre, May 2014, pp. 26–32.

[52] Morales, note 6, pp. 64–66.

[53] G. Gibson, K. Yung, L. Chisholm, and H. Quinn, with Lake Babine Nation and Nak'azdli Whut'en, "Indigenous Communities and Industrial Camps: Promoting Healthy Communities in Settings of Industrial Change," Firelight Group, Feb. 2017, at p. 22.

violence" to silence them.[54] In the context of transnational extractive projects, security forces engaged to protect the infrastructure may also engage in sexual violence against women and girls as an intimidation tactic.[55] In Latin America, where many Canadian extractive companies operate, the Special Rapporteur notes that "women defenders are among the most threatened environmental human rights defenders."[56]

21.3 CANADA AS A HOME STATE

Much has been written about Canadian extractive companies operating internationally, and associated violations of human and environmental rights.[57] It has also been the subject of intense advocacy by Canadian human rights groups,[58] complaints brought to nonjudicial dispute resolution mechanisms,[59] litigation in Canadian courts,[60] and federal government

---

[54] UN General Assembly, *Report of the Special Rapporteur on the situation of human rights defenders*, Aug. 3, 2016, UN Doc. A/71/281, para. 54.

[55] Three Canadian companies, Talisman Energy Inc., HudBay Minerals Inc., and Barrick Gold Corporation have been implicated in rape, including gang-rape, perpetrated by their security providers. See J. Harker, "Human Security in Sudan: The Report of a Canadian Assessment Mission," Department of Foreign Affairs and International Trade, Ottawa, Canada, Jan. 2000; G. Gagnon and J. Ryle, "Report of an Investigation into Oil Development, Conflict and Displacement in Western Upper Nile, Sudan," Canadian Auto Workers Union, Steelworkers Humanity Fund, Simons Foundation, United Church of Canada, Division of World Outreach, World Vision Canada, Oct. 2001; *Choc v. HudBay Minerals Inc.*, 2013 ONSC 1414; Human Rights Watch, "Canada: Events of 2017," www.hrw.org/world-report/2018/country-chapters/canada; Columbia Law School Human Rights Clinic and Harvard Law School International Human Rights Clinic, "Righting Wrongs? Barrick Gold's Remedy Mechanism for Sexual Violence in Papua N.G.: Key Concerns and Lessons Learned," Columbia Law School, Harvard Law School, Nov. 2015.

[56] UNGA, note 54.

[57] See P. Simons and A. Macklin, *The Governance Gap: Extractive Industries, Human Rights and the Home State Advantage* (New York: Routledge, 2014); P. Simons, "Canada's Enhanced CSR Strategy: Human Rights Due Diligence and Access to Justice for Victims of Extraterritorial Corporate Human Rights Abuses" (2015) 56 *Canadian Business Law Journal* 167; S. L. Seck, "Business, Human Rights, and Canadian Mining Lawyers" (2015) 56 *Canadian Business Law Journal* 208–237; S. L. Seck "Canadian Mining Internationally and the UN Guiding Principles for Business and Human Rights" (2011) 49 *Canadian Yearbook of International Law* 51; S. L. Seck, "Home State Responsibility and Local Communities: The Case of Global Mining" (2008) 11 *Yale Human Rights and Development Law Journal* 177; S. Imai, L. Gardner, and S. Weinberger, "The 'Canada Brand': Violence and Canadian Mining Companies in Latin America" (2017) *Osgoode Legal Studies Research Paper No. 17/2017* 1; V. Crystal, S. Imai, and B. Maheandiran, "Access to Justice and Corporate Accountability: A Legal Case Study of Hudbay in Guatemala" (2014) 35 *Canadian Journal of Development Studies* 286.

[58] See MiningWatch Canada, "A Policy Framework for the Regulation of Canadian Mining Companies Operating Internationally," Nov. 9, 2005; Canadian Network on Corporate Accountability, "Government Policy," http://cnca-rcrce.ca/resources/due-diligence-csr-mining/; Above Ground, "Frequently Asked Questions (FAQs): Corporate Accountability," July 3, 2015.

[59] See Global Affairs Canada, "Office of the Extractive Sector Corporate Social Responsibility (CSR) Counsellor," June 26, 2018, http://international.gc.ca/csr_counsellor-conseiller_rse/index.aspx?lang=eng; Global Affairs Canada, "Canada's National Contact Point for the Organisation for Economic Cooperation and Development Guidelines for Multinational Enterprises," Dec. 11, 2017, www.international.gc.ca/trade-agreements-accords-commerciaux/ncp-pcn/index.aspx?lang=eng&menu_id=1&menu=R.

[60] See *Araya v. Nevsun Resources Ltd.*, 2017 BCCA 401 1856, appeal heard by the Supreme Court of Canada, Jan. 23, 2019, judgment reserved; *Choc v. HudBay Minerals Inc.*, 2013 ONSC 1414; *Recherches Internationales Québec v. Cambior Inc.*, [1998] QJ No. 2554 (QL) (QC CS); *Piedra v. Copper Mesa Mining Corp*, 2011 ONCA 91; *Association canadienne contre l'impunité (ACCI) c Anvil Mining Ltd*, 2011 QCCS 1966, overturned [2012] JQ No. 368 (QCCA), leave to appeal to SCC refused [2012] SCCA No. 128; *Garcia v. Tahoe Resources Inc.*, 2017 BCCA 39. The case settled in July 2019. See G. Friedman, "Big Win for Foreign Plaintiffs as Panamerican Silver Settles Guatemala Mine Case," July 31, 2019, https://business.financialpost.com/commodities/mining/big-win-for-foreign-plaintiffs-as-pan-american-settles-guatemala-mine-case.

policy.[61] Yet, to date, the Canadian government has not developed a coherent set of effective policies and/or law addressing the overseas environmental and human rights impacts of extractive companies headquartered in Canada or extractive companies listed on the Canadian stock exchanges. Indeed the federal government has only taken tentative steps in this regard. For example, Canada's 2014 enhanced policy for the extractive sector, "Doing Business the Canadian Way: A Strategy to Advance Corporate Social Responsibility in Canada's Extractive Sector Abroad" only mentions women in the context of listing the potential impacts of extractive operations.[62] The policy does encourage corporations to "align their [business] practices as applicable" to the Organisation for Economic Co-operation and Development (OECD) Guidelines for Multinational Enterprises (OECD MNE Guidelines),[63] the International Finance Corporation's Performance Standards on Social and Environmental Sustainability (IFC Performance Standards),[64] the Voluntary Principles on Security and Human Rights (Voluntary Principles),[65] the UN Guiding Principles on Business and Human Rights,[66] as well as the OECD Due Diligence Guidance on Responsible Supply Chains of Minerals from Conflict Affected and High-Risk Areas,[67] and the Global Reporting Initiative (GRI).[68] However, a number of these initiatives ignore gender entirely[69] or simply include a few references to women or gender,[70] while integration of local community and Indigenous rights is more common, although it is not consistent.[71] For example, while the GRI Standards contain a substantial number of references to gender and women in the reporting guidance and indicators, the majority relate to nondiscrimination and equality in relation to employment.[72]

---

[61] See Global Affairs Canada, "Building the Canadian Advantage: A CSR Strategy for the Canadian International Extractive Sector," Mar. 2009, www.international.gc.ca/trade-agreements-accords-commer ciaux/topics-domaines/other-autre/csr-strat-rse-2009.aspx?lang=eng; Global Affairs Canada, "Doing Business the Canadian Way: A Strategy to Advance Corporate Social Responsibility in Canada's Extractive Sector Abroad," Nov. 14, 2014; Global Affairs Canada, "Canada's Enhanced Corporate Social Responsibility Strategy to Strengthen Canada's Extractive Sector Abroad," Jan. 17, 2018, www.international.gc.ca/trade-agreements-accords-commerciaux/topics-domaines/other-autre/csr-strat-rse.aspx?lang=eng.

[62] Global Affairs Canada (2018), note 61, p. 8.

[63] OECD, "OECD Guidelines for Multinational Enterprises," 2011. The OECD MNE Guidelines are a set of "principles and standards of good practice" and include norms on taxation, corruption, environment, and human rights.

[64] International Finance Corporation, World Bank Group, "IFC Performance Standards on Environmental and Social Sustainability," Jan. 1, 2012. These standards are discussed below.

[65] Voluntary Principles on Security and Human Rights, "What Are the Voluntary Principles?" 2000. The Voluntary Principles provide guidelines for companies in dealing with public and private security companies in order to ensure respect for human rights in the course of protecting business assets.

[66] UN Human Rights Council, *Report of the Special Representative of the Secretary-General on the issue of human rights and transnational corporations and other business enterprises, John Ruggie: Guiding Principles on Business and Human Rights: Implementing the United Nations "Protect, Respect and Remedy" Framework*, Mar. 21, 2011, UN Doc. A/HRC/17/31.

[67] OECD, "OECD Due Diligence Guidance for Responsible Supply Chains of Minerals from Conflict-Affected and High-Risk Areas, Third Edition," 2016. These guidelines provide companies with recommendations to respect human rights and avoid conflict through mineral purchasing and practice decisions.

[68] Global Reporting Initiative, "GRI Standards," 2016, www.globalreporting.org/standards. The GRI has developed guidelines and indicators for sustainability reporting by organizations, including human rights indicators and industry supplements.

[69] See Voluntary Principles, note 65.

[70] See UNHCR, note 66; OECD, note 63. For a feminist critique of the UN Guiding Principles (and by reference the OECD MNE Guidelines), see Simons et al., note 50.

[71] Seck, note 19.

[72] GRI, note 68. Sector specific standards have also been developed including mining and oil and gas supplements.

The IFC Performance Standards have a dedicated standard for Indigenous rights,[73] and integrate gender as part of a World Bank gender mainstreaming approach,[74] but a more fulsome feminist analysis of these standards is required to understand the strengths and shortcomings of such references. On the other hand, the more recently adopted OECD's 2017 Due Diligence Guidance for Meaningful Stakeholder Engagement in the Extractive Sector does include Annexes on engaging with Indigenous peoples and with women.[75] This guidance is subject to the dispute resolution process available under the highly criticized National Contact Point (NCP) mechanism.[76] However, the fundamental problem with the CSR Strategy is that each of these various initiatives, "differs in focus and in prescription for action" and the prescription for extractive corporations to align their practices to such initiatives "as applicable" could be interpreted to "suggest that companies can pick and choose among these initiatives . . . and still meet the policy's standard of expected conduct."[77]

The Canadian government's January 2018 announcement that it would establish the Canadian Ombudsperson for Responsible Enterprise (CORE) for the extractive and garment sectors was seen as a welcome step forward in terms of establishing a more effective nonjudicial grievance mechanism for complaints about Canadian extractive companies.[78] Model legislation developed by the Canadian Network on Corporate Accountability (CNCA) on the ombudsperson office included some references to environmental harm,[79] and references to gender-sensitive investigation and international best practices for the investigation of sexual violence.[80] However,

---

73 IFC Standards, note 64, Performance Standard 7; See also, Seck, note 19. However, this standard has been criticized as having been narrowly conceived as a risk management tool and therefore does not provide Indigenous communities with any real power "to change the trajectory" of IFC financed projects but only to "consultation plus." See S. H. Baker, "Why the IFC's Free, Prior, and Informed Consent Policy Doesn't Matter (Yet) to Indigenous Communities Affected by Development Projects" (2013) 30 *Wisconsin International Law Journal* 668. See also A. Dunlap, "'A Bureaucratic Trap:' Free, Prior and Informed Consent (FPIC) and Wind Energy Development in Juchitán, Mexico" (2017) 29 *Capitalism Nature Socialism* 88 at 91, who argues that concept of FPIC in IFC Performance Standard 7, has been captured by the IFC and other market actors and "reinforces state-corporate power . . . constructing the illusion of real dialogue, negotiation and, by extension, democratic decision-making."

74 World Bank, "Integrating Gender into the World Bank's Work: A Strategy for Action" (Jan. 2002), http://siteresources.worldbank.org/INTGENDER/Resources/strategypaper.pdf.

75 OECD, "OECD Due Diligence Guidance for Meaningful Stakeholder Engagement in the Extractive Sector," 2017, p. 100: Annex B. Engaging with Indigenous Peoples; Annex C. Engaging with Women.

76 Global Affairs Canada, "Closed National Contact Point Specific Instances," June 13, 2019, www.international.gc.ca/trade-agreements-accords-commerciaux/ncp-pcn/specific-specifique.aspx?lang=eng; OECD Guidelines for Multinational Enterprises, "Frequently Asked Questions: National Contact Points for the OECD Guidelines for Multinational Enterprises," OECD, 2017; OECD, "National Contact Points," http://mneguidelines.oecd.org/ncps/; see MiningWatch Canada, "Peer Review of the Canadian National Contact Point on the OECD Guidelines for Multinational Enterprises," Jan. 23, 2018, Appendix I for "specific concerns related to the Canadian NCPs handling of ten specific Instance cases."

77 Simons (2015), note 57, p. 181; see Seck (2015), note 57, for an alternate reading of the legal relevance of these standards.

78 Global Affairs Canada, "The Government of Canada brings leadership to responsible business conduct abroad," Jan. 17, 2018, www.canada.ca/en/global-affairs/news/2018/01/the_government_ofcanadabrings leadershiptoresponsiblebusinesscond.html. The CORE replaces the mandate of the CSR counsellor's office which ended on May 18, 2018. See generally Global Affairs Canada, "Office of the Extractive Sector Corporate Social Responsibility (CSR) Counsellor," June 26, 2018, www.international.gc.ca/csr_counsellor-conseiller_rse/index.aspx?lang=eng.

79 Canadian Network on Corporate Accountability, "The Global Leadership in Business and Human Rights Act: An Act to Create an Independent Human Rights Ombudsperson for the International Extractive Sector," Nov. 2, 2016, ss. 3.20, 13.2. "Harm" which could be the subject of a complaint was defined as "infringement(s) of the international instruments listed in Schedule 1." Schedule 1 does not reference international environmental instruments.

80 Ibid., ss. 3.9, 3.20, 8.1, 11.7(i).

the Order in Council (OIC) that establishes the office and appoints the ombudsperson, released in April 2019 and amended in September 2019, does not specify any powers of the office to compel witnesses and documents.[81] In addition, the definition of human rights abuse only includes human rights that are referenced in the International Bill of Human Rights.[82] No mention is made of CEDAW, the CRC, or the International Convention on the Elimination of All Forms of Racial Discrimination,[83] nor is there mention of UNDRIP or ILO 169, among others that are specifically relevant to the protection of women's human rights and the rights of Indigenous peoples.[84] Nor does the OIC mention gender or women, or Indigenous peoples in the text.[85] These limitations have been the subject of intense civil society critique.[86] Therefore, the effectiveness of this mechanism in terms of providing access to justice for women and girls harmed by mining activity abroad may depend on the personal tenacity and focus of the new ombudsperson. A multi-stakeholder advisory body was established in 2018 to advise the government on effective implementation of responsible business conduct policies for companies operating internationally including the CORE and its relationship with the OECD NCP[87] but has yet to develop any advice or guidance. In July 2019, all the civil society and labor union representatives on the advisory body resigned in protest of the failure on the part of the government to give the CORE the necessary investigatory powers.[88]

The Canadian government has recently adopted a revised set of guidelines for Canadian diplomatic missions on supporting HRDs.[89] These guidelines recognize the "multiple and

---

[81] Government of Canada, "Canadian Ombudsperson for Responsible Enterprise," Order in Council, PC Number 2019–1323, Sept. 6, 2019.

[82] Ibid., s. 1(1). The International Bill of Rights consists of the Universal Declaration of Human Rights, Dec. 10, 1948, UN Doc A/810, p. 71; International Covenant on Civil and Political Rights, Dec. 16, 1966, 999 UNTS 171 (entered into force Mar. 23, 1976); International Covenant on Economic, Social, and Cultural Rights, Dec. 16, 1966, 993 UNTS 3 (entered into force Jan. 3, 1976).

[83] 660 UNTS 195 (entered into force Jan. 4, 1969).

[84] United Nations, Declaration on the Rights of Indigenous Peoples, Sept. 13, 2007, UN Doc. A/RES/61/295; ILO, Convention Concerning Indigenous and Tribal Peoples in Independent Countries (ILO Doc. 169), adopted June 27, 1989, entered into force Sept. 5, 1991, 28 ILM 1382. As many countries in which Canadian mining companies operate are party to ILO 169, this is a notable omission.

[85] The OIC does state that the ombudsperson is to be guided by the UN Guiding Principles on Business and Human Rights and the OECD MNE Guidelines in discharging her mandate (OIC, s. 5). However, there is no mention of other OECD instruments such as the 2017 Stakeholder Engagement Guidance, which, unlike the OECD MNE Guidelines, provide specific guidance on the rights of Indigenous peoples, as well as engagement with women.

[86] Canadian Network on Corporate Accountability, "Canadian Government Reneges on Promise to Create Independent Corporate Human Rights Watchdog," Apr. 8, 2019, http://cnca-rcrce.ca/recent-works/canadian-government-reneges-on-promise-to-create-independent-corporate-human-rights-watchdog/; M. Blanchfield, "UN Official Criticizes Canadian Delays Setting up Corporate Ethics Watchdog," Apr. 30, 2019, www.cbc.ca/news/politics/un-watchdog-carr-corporate-ethics-1.5116399. See also, P. Simons, "Trudeau Government's Global Reputation at Risk Due to Poor Corporate Accountability" *Globe and Mail Report on Business*, June 5, 2019, www.theglobeandmail.com/business/commentary/article-trudeau-governments-global-reputation-at-risk-due-to-poor-corporate/.

[87] Global Affairs Canada, "Responsible Business Conduct Abroad," Nov. 26, 2018, www.international.gc.ca/trade-agreements-accords-commerciaux/topics-domaines/other-autre/csr-rse.aspx?lang=eng; Global Affairs Canada, "Advisory Body on Responsible Business Conduct," Dec. 20, 2018, www.international.gc.ca/trade-agreements-accords-commerciaux/topics-domaines/other-autre/advisory_body-groupe_consultatif.aspx?lang=eng; Global Affairs Canada, "Multi-stakeholder Advisory Body on Responsible Business Conduct – Minutes," Apr. 23, 2018, www.international.gc.ca/trade-agreements-accords-commerciaux/topics-domaines/other-autre/advisory_body-groupe_meeting_april_2018.aspx?lang=eng.

[88] J. Lim, "Civil Society, Labour Groups Resign in Protest from Federal Panel on Corporate Responsibility Abroad," July 11, 2019, https://ipolitics.ca/2019/07/11/civil-society-labour-groups-resign-in-protest-from-federal-panel-on-corporate-responsibility-abroad/.

[89] Global Affairs Canada, "Voices at Risk: Canada's Guidelines on Supporting Human Rights Defenders," 2019.

intersecting identities" of HRDs, including the particular and intersectional vulnerability of women HRDs.[90] They also outline best practices for diplomatic missions with respect to supporting women, Indigenous, LGBTI,[91] youth, among other HRDs. Missions are required to "consider links to Canada's development priorities and programming contexts, trade program contexts such as the intersection of business and human rights, and the identification of Canadian entity involvement in alleged or apparent human rights violations or abuses."[92] Where a Canadian business is allegedly involved in human rights abuses against an HRD, including where the business in question "receives support from the Trade Commissioner Service," missions are directed to consult the Canada's Enhanced CSR Strategy and provide support for, and protection to, the HRD. The guidelines note that in such cases "there may be an impact on the support that the mission offers to the Canadian company in question, including denying or withdrawing individualized trade advocacy support."[93] These policies and guidelines, however, cannot be used to hold Canadian diplomatic missions accountable for actions or failure to act. A recent decision of the Federal Court (confirming the decision of the Public Service Integrity Commissioner not to investigate the alleged actions or inactions of the Canadian Embassy in Mexico with respect to the murder of an HRD) noted that Canada's 2009 CSR Strategy and other "aspirational documents and policies" did not impose legal obligations on diplomatic missions.[94]

Under the CSR Strategy for the extractive industry (which is currently under review), companies that do not collaborate in good faith with the NCP or CORE may be denied trade advocacy support by the Canadian government when operating in host countries abroad.[95] Export Development Canada (EDC), Canada's export credit agency which supports direct investment abroad by Canadian companies, may consider such uncooperative corporate conduct in providing support to its clients.[96] However, EDC has been accused of supporting extractive companies that have violated environmental and other human rights[97] despite the existence of a human rights policy and an Environmental and Social and Social Risk Management Framework, all of which were subject to review in 2018.[98] Similar to the other frameworks discussed above, EDC's policies and review frameworks have so far failed to integrate a gender perspective, including a requirement for its client companies to respect the environmental and other human rights of women and girls.[99]

---

[90] Ibid., pp. 2, 12.

[91] Ibid., p. 28. LGBTI HRDs are defined as "people who act to promote or protect the human rights of lesbian, gay, bisexual, transgender and intersex (LGBTI) persons" (ibid., p. 27).

[92] Ibid., p. 13.

[93] Ibid., p. 21. The government of Canada also provides some brief guidance to Canadian corporations on how to reduce the likelihood of becoming involved in human rights violations against HRDs and how to respond if they do become involved. See Global Affairs Canada, "Responsible Business Conduct Abroad: CSR Snapshot #7 – Private Sector Support for Human Rights Defenders: A Primer for Canadian Businesses," Mar. 4, 2019, www.international.gc.ca/trade-agreements-accords-commerciaux/topics-domaines/other-autre/csr-snapshot-7 .aspx?lang=eng.

[94] *Gordillo v. Canada (Attorney General)* 2019 FC 950, para. 66.

[95] Global Affairs Canada (2018), note 87, "Current Voluntary Dispute Resolution Mechanisms."

[96] Ibid.

[97] Above Ground, "Bringing Accountability and Transparency to Export Development Canada's Practices: A Submission for Parliament's Review of the *Export Development Act*," Nov. 9, 2018.

[98] Export Development Canada (EDC), "Review of Environmental & Social Risk Management Policies – Discussion Paper," May 2018. For a history of the first review process adopted by EDC, the Environmental Review Framework, see S. L. Seck, "Strengthening Environmental Assessment of Canadian Supported Mining Ventures in Developing Countries" (2001) 11 *Journal of Environmental Law and Practice* 1–82.

[99] S. L. Seck, P. Simons, and K. MacMaster, "Submissions RE: 2018 Legislative Review of Export Development Canada (EDC)," Nov. 9, 2018.

Access to judicial remedy for environmental and other human rights harms arising from the conduct of Canadian-based transnational mining companies has also proved elusive to date, although this may be changing. Not so long ago all cases brought in Canadian courts against Canadian-based mining companies for harms arising from operations abroad were routinely dismissed at the pleadings stage, often as an exercise of the discretion to decline to hear actions under private international law doctrines such as *forum non conveniens* (FNC),[100] or procedural motions, including alleging a failure to establish a reasonable cause of action.[101] There are now several cases against Canadian extractives in Canadian courts that are proceeding to the merits. This includes the case of *Caal v. Hudbay*[102] in which the plaintiffs, eleven Mayan Q'eqchi' women, are seeking damages for gang-rape allegedly perpetrated by the security forces working for the Fenix mining project in Guatemala formerly owned by Hudbay. In that case and the two others against Hudbay, the motion for dismissal based on FNC was dropped two weeks before the hearing. In two other cases, the British Columbia Court of Appeal held that to overcome a motion for FNC, the plaintiffs need to demonstrate "a real risk that the alternate forum will not provide justice."[103]

Although Canadian courts now appear to be more willing to hear these types of claims, motions for FNC, act of state, international comity, or failure to disclose a cause of action remain significant obstacles for plaintiffs. Mounting a defense to such motions and the fact that decisions may (have to) be appealed all the way up the court system is onerous and costly for the plaintiffs. As such women and girls who have suffered environmental and other human rights harms related to Canadian transnational extractive activity, including women environmental HRDs, face these and other practical hurdles in obtaining justice through the courts.[104]

The Canadian federal government has articulated a commitment to the promotion and protection of women's rights and gender equality both as a human rights issue and as an essential component of sustainable development, peace, and security, in relation to international development assistance.[105] Its Feminist International Assistance Policy (FIAP) commits the government to supporting and taking action on a range of areas in order to meet Sustainable Development Goal 5 of achieving equality and empowering women and girls.[106] The FIAP provides a range of action areas addressing gender inequality and empowerment, among other things. However, in its current form, it overlooks the gendered impacts of resource extraction, as well as the environmental and humanitarian implications of

---

[100] S. L. Seck, "Environmental Harm in Developing Countries Caused by Subsidiaries of Canadian Mining Corporations: The Interface of Public and Private International Law" (2000) 37 *Canadian Yearbook of International Law* 139–221 at 174 (see detailed analysis of first case, environmental harms arising from a transnational mining company's tailings dam spill); see cases, note 60.

[101] See for eg *Piedra* v. *Copper* Mesa, note 60.

[102] This is one of the three cases against HudBay. See *Choc v. HudBay Minerals Inc.*, note 55.

[103] *Garcia v. Tahoe*, note 60, para. 124; *Araya v. Nevsun* note 60, paras. 199–120.

[104] See Amnesty International, "Injustice Incorporated: Corporate Abuses and the Human Right to Remedy," 2014, p. 84. While Australian courts took jurisdiction over environmental harms arising from mining at Ok Tedi, justice has remained elusive for other reasons. See analysis in S. L. Seck, "Lessons for the Treaty Process from the International Law Commission and International Environmental Law," in Jernej Letnar Černič and Nicolás Carrillo-Santarelli (eds.), *The Future of Business and Human Rights: Theoretical and Practical Considerations for a UN Treaty* (Cambridge: Intersentia, 2018), pp. 273–298.

[105] See Government of Canada, "Policy on Gender Equality," June 7, 2017, http://international.gc.ca/world-monde/funding-financement/policy-politique.aspx?lang=eng; Global Affairs Canada, "Canada's Feminist International Assistance Policy," 2017.

[106] Global Affairs Canada, note 105, p. 5.

Canadian extractives and other extractives listed on Canadian stock exchanges operating in the countries to which Canada provides international assistance.[107]

Canada is a member of the Intergovernmental Forum (IGF) on Mining, Minerals, Metals and Sustainable Development.[108] The IGF is a consultative and advisory initiative designed to bring governments together to consider key issues of policy and governance in sustainable mineral development.[109] Since 2015, the Canadian-based NGO, International Institute for Sustainable Development (IISD) has served as the Secretariat for the IGF, with the Government of Canada providing financial support.[110] The IGF drafted its Mining Policy Framework in 2010 with the participation of forty-three (mostly) developing and emerging market states, and it was updated in 2013.[111] This Policy Framework is designed to serve as guidance for the over seventy IGF member states from around the world[112] and is said to represent a commitment to both poverty reduction and sustainable development.[113]

The IGF claims that the Framework represents "best practices for good environmental, social and economic governance of the mining sector and the generation and equitable sharing of benefits."[114] It is said to have "universal application" that is "as ambitious as it is necessary, particularly for developing countries."[115] The Framework highlights the need for clear, modern legislation that is essential for good governance and sustainable development.[116] However, the Framework is essentially silent on the rights of women and girls, with reference to women only in relation to the ASM sector,[117] and in a discussion on gender equality in optimizing employment opportunities in large-scale mining.[118] The Framework also encourages governments and "mining entities" to be "guided in their actions by international norms," including the IFC Performance Standards, the Voluntary Principles on Security and Human Rights, and the OECD MNE Guidelines.[119] Yet, as noted above, to date, few of these normative guidance tools provide meaningful, if any, guidance on the environmental and other human rights of women and girls, and their treatment of Indigenous rights is inconsistent.

---

[107] S. Seck and P. Simons, "Resource Extraction and the Human Rights of Women and Girls: Policy Recommendations Associated with the Feminist International Assistance Policy," June 2018, www .researchgate.net/publication/334204007_Resource_Extraction_and_the_Human_Rights_of_Women_and_ Girls_Policy_Recommendations_Associated_with_the_Feminist_International_Assistance_Policy.

[108] Intergovernmental Forum on Mining, Minerals, Metals and Sustainable Development, "About IGF," http:// igfmining.org/about/.

[109] Ibid.

[110] Ibid.

[111] Intergovernmental Forum on Mining, Minerals, Metals and Sustainable Development, "IGF Mining Policy Framework: Mining and Sustainable Development," Oct. 2013.

[112] Intergovernmental Forum on Mining, Minerals, Metals and Sustainable Development, "Members," www .igfmining.org/member/. Founding member states include Canada and South Africa, a large number of African states, as well as Bolivia, Dominican Republic, Romania, the Philippines, and the United Kingdom. More recent members include (in no particular order) Brazil, the Russian Federation, Egypt, Germany, Guatemala, Peru, Sierra Leone, Papua New Guinea, Myanmar, Kazakhstan, India, and Iran. Neither China nor the USA are currently members.

[113] IGF, note 111, p. 6.

[114] Ibid.

[115] Ibid.

[116] Ibid., pp. 6–7.

[117] Ibid., p. 44.

[118] Ibid., p. 33. "An appropriately structured mine operation will allow direct and indirect employment that increases the likelihood of educational opportunity for children, advances in gender equality, general improvement in quality of life, and diversity in economic activity. It also increases the tax base for local, regional and national governments."

[119] Ibid., pp. 11, 13, 34–35.

21.4 CANADA AS HOST STATE

As discussed above, concerns have also been raised over violations of environmental and other human rights, within Canada, including the human rights impacts of environmental harm and violence against women and girls, and a failure to seek FPIC of Indigenous communities.[120] The IGF Mining Policy Framework is designed for all host states, and, as noted above, for the most part does not address gender considerations related to resource extraction. Neither does Canada have a coherent set of laws and policies to address the environmental and other human rights impacts of resource extraction. In the laws that do exist there has been a tendency to ignore the gendered dimensions of resource extraction. For example, while some provincial mining laws now mandate that mining companies engage in consultation with Indigenous peoples early on during exploration,[121] these provisions make no reference to gender, and so there is no guarantee that women have appropriate input into these consultation processes.

Although the environmental assessment (EA) process in theory provides an opportunity for input from communities who will be affected by resource extraction, the history of EA in Canada has been fraught with controversy over the constitutional relationship between federal and provincial assessment processes, as well as the relationship between the federal processes and EA provisions in select land claims agreements.[122] Opportunities for public participation have tended to be greater in the federal process, when it applies, and the social dimensions of assessment have increasingly become integrated into EA, including the importance of Indigenous knowledge and consultation, if not consent. However, the process has not reached the level of a full sustainability assessment which would evaluate whether a project makes a positive contribution to sustainability, rather than simply asking whether a project causes significant adverse effects that can be adequately mitigated.[123] Most recently, new federal impact assessment legislation was introduced in the form of Bill C-69,[124] which for the first time integrates reference to gender.[125] Section 22(1) specifies a list of factors to be taken into account

---

[120] See for example R. Ariss with J. Cutfeet, *Keeping the Land: Kitchenuhmaykoosib Inninuwug, Reconciliation and Canadian Law* (Black Point: Fernwood, 2012); Morales, note 6; UN General Assembly, *Report of the Working Group on the issue of human rights and transnational corporations and other business enterprises on its mission to Canada*, Apr. 23, 2018, UN Doc. A/HRC/38/48/Add.1; Human Rights Watch, note 55.

[121] P. Simons and L. Collins, "Participatory Rights in the Ontario Mining Sector: An International Human Rights Perspective" (2010) 6 *McGill Journal of Sustainable Development Law* 179; S. Theriault, "Aboriginal Peoples' Consultations in the Mining Sector: A Critical Assessment of Recent Mining Reforms in Québec and Ontario," in A. Bélanger and M. Papillon (eds.), *Aboriginal Multilevel Governance* (Ottawa: McGill-Queen's Press, 2015).

[122] *Quebec (Attorney General)* v. *Moses*, 2010 SCC 17; *Mikisew Cree First Nation* v. *Canada (Governor General in Council)*, 2018 SCC 40; M. Doelle, "Reflecting on Federal Jurisdiction for Upcoming Federal EA Reform," June 21, 2016, https://blogs.dal.ca/melaw/2016/06/21/ea-jurisdiction/.

[123] M. Doelle and A. J. Sinclair, "EA Expert Panel Report: Reflections on Canada's Proposed Next Generation Assessment Process" (2017) *SSRN Electronic Journal*; R. B. Gibson, M. Doelle, and A. J. Sinclair, "Fulfilling the Promise: Basic Components of Next Generation Environmental Assessment" (2016) 29 *Journal of Environmental Law and Practice* 251; University of Waterloo, "Next Generation Environmental Assessment Project: Published Papers," https://uwaterloo.ca/next-generation-environmental-assessment/research-contributions/published-papers.

[124] Bill C-69, An Act to enact the Impact Assessment Act and the Canadian Energy Regulator Act, to amend the Navigation Protection Act and to make consequential amendments to other Acts, 1st Session, 42nd Parl., 2015–Present (royal assent granted June 21, 2019).

[125] Ibid. The original version of the Preamble, subsequently omitted, stated: "Preamble: And whereas the Government of Canada is committed to assessing how groups of women, men and gender-diverse people may experience policies, programs and projects and to taking actions that contribute to an inclusive and democratic society and allow all Canadians to participate fully in all spheres of their lives."

in the assessment of a designated project.[126] This list includes Indigenous traditional knowledge and other Indigenous cultural considerations with respect to the project, as well as community knowledge and public comments.[127] In section 22(1)(s) it is specified that consideration is to be given to "the intersection of sex and gender with other identity factors."[128] The precise meaning of this provision is open to interpretation, but will certainly be informed by the Canadian government's commitment to the integration of Gender-Based Analysis Plus (GBA+) into decision making,[129] in part to assist in meeting Canada's obligations under CEDAW.[130]

An as yet unused opportunity to draw attention to gender in the early stages of consultation with Indigenous peoples, and women in particular, is available through the OECD NCP process which recently confirmed that the OECD MNE Guidelines and related responsible business conduct guidance, including the Stakeholder Engagement Guidance for Extractive Industries with the annex on gender, are equally relevant to projects developed in Canada as to those involving Canadian companies outside of Canada.[131] While this is clearly not equivalent to a legislated requirement, it does suggest a normative expectation that gender be considered in stakeholder engagement processes. However, one challenge is the separate treatment of gender and Indigeneity in the Guidance. While the annex on Indigenous peoples notes the importance of FPIC as an international legal expectation for Indigenous peoples, there is no reference to international law or human rights in the annex on engaging with women, including Indigenous women.[132]

Another issue relates to the gendered nature of royalty distributions. For example, a 2015 report provided evidence that resource-based economies such as Alberta's lead to greater income inequality among men and women.[133] Also in 2015, the United Nations Human Rights Committee noted its continuing concerns about gendered income inequality in Canada,

---

[126] Ibid., s22(1).

[127] Ibid., s22(1) (g), (l), (m), (n).

[128] Ibid., s22(1)(s). See further J. Koshan, "Bills C-68 and C-69 and the Consideration of Sex, Gender and Other Identity Factors," May 2, 2018, https://ablawg.ca/2018/05/02/bills-c-68-and-c-69-and-the-consideration-of-sex-gender-and-other-identity-factors/.

[129] Status of Women Canada, "Action Plan on Gender-based Analysis (2016–2020)," May 12, 2016, http://cfc-swc.gc.ca/gba-acs/plan-action-2016-en.html; Government of Canada, "Gender Based Analysis," Oct. 25, 2016, www.canada.ca/en/treasury-board-secretariat/services/treasury-board-submissions/gender-based-analysis-plus.html: GBA+ is described by the government as a "process by which a policy, program, initiative or service can be examined for its impacts on various groups of women and men. GBA provides a snapshot that captures the realities of women and men affected by a particular issue at a specific time. This means that analysts, researchers, evaluators, and decision makers are able to continually improve their work and attain better results for Canadian men and women by being more responsive to their specific needs and circumstances." See also Office of the Auditor General of Canada, "2015 Fall Reports of the Auditor General of Canada: Report 1 – Implementing Gender-Based Analysis," www.oag-bvg.gc.ca/internet/English/parl_oag_201602_01_e_41058.html. See further Senate GRO, "Setting the Record Straight on Legislation to Strengthen Project Reviews," Nov. 10, 2018, https://senate-gro.ca/news/setting-the-record-straight-on-legislation-to-strengthen-project-reviews/.

[130] Office of the Auditor General of Canada, note 129, para. 1.21.

[131] Global Affairs Canada, "Canada's National Contact Point's Final Statement – Seabridge Gold and Southeast Alaska Conservation Council," Nov. 13, 2017, www.international.gc.ca/trade-agreements-accords-commerciaux/ncp-pcn/final_stat-seabridge-comm_finale.aspx?lang=eng, paras. 31–33. Specifically, the NCP states in paragraph 33: "The Guidelines and this associated due diligence guidance are relevant and applicable to all mining companies and in all countries, not just developing countries. In particular, the NCP wishes to clarify with the Company that the Guidelines apply to Canadian companies regarding their Canadian projects or operations, and not just their activities in foreign countries."

[132] The importance of intersectional consideration of gender and Indigeneity is evident in Morales, note 6, p. 78.

[133] K. A. Lahey, "The Alberta Disadvantage: Gender Disadvantage: Gender Taxation and Income Inequality," Parkland Institute, Mar. 2015, at pp. 85–86.

including in Alberta, and especially with respect to Indigenous and other visible minority women.[134] Lessons to remedy this problem could be drawn from international studies that provide guidance on how to actively seek to understand and incorporate into project planning and development the differential impacts of extractive development on men and women.[135] Beyond this, as suggested by Indigenous legal scholar, Sarah Morales, there is a need to better respect how Indigenous laws and practices can themselves provide answers to these challenges, through implementation of UNDRIP.[136]

A further question is whether access to justice for environmental and other human rights harms involving extractive industries is readily available through Canadian courts, something that is often assumed to be the case in the Global North. The failure of attempts to seek an effective remedy for the significant harms arising from the tailings dam spill at the Mount Polley mine in British Columbia provides clear evidence of a systemic failure in Canadian law.[137] The collapse of the tailings pond in August 2014 is often described as one of Canada's worst environmental disasters, and led to the contamination of the pristine Quesnel Lake, upon which local Indigenous peoples depended for water and food, including sockeye salmon, and related cultural practices. Despite the persistence of Indigenous women activists, the British Columbia Prosecution Service has stated that it will not be filing regulatory charges against the mining company.[138]

A commonality between North and South is that industrial mining, and especially mining company leadership, remains disproportionately White and male, and legal reform to address this problem has been very slow.[139] While gender diversity is increasingly evident in corporate

---

[134] UN Human Rights Committee, *Concluding observations on the sixth periodic report of Canada*, Aug. 13, 2015, UN Doc. CCPR/C/CAN/CO/6, para. 7. Nova Scotia was also singled out in this report. Note that Alberta's economy is highly dependent on fossil fuel extraction, which is inherently unsustainable, yet the correlation between gendered income inequality and resource extraction more broadly appears to be a widespread issue. See I. Hussey and E. Jackson, "Gendering the Downturn: Is the NDP Doing Enough for Alberta Women?" May 4, 2017, www.parklandinstitute.ca/gendering_the_downturn; T. T. Onifade, "Alberta, Canada, Royalty Review and Its Lessons for Resource Economies" (2017) 35 *Journal of Energy and Natural Resources Law* 171–196.

[135] See for example A. Eftimie, K. Heller, and J. Strongman, "Mainstreaming Gender into Extractive Industries Projects: Guidance Note for Task Team Leaders," World Bank, Extractive Industries and Development Series No. 9, Aug. 2009, tables 1–4. For example, when in control of financial resources, women are more likely to devote resources to food and children's healthcare and education (ibid., pp. 18–19).

[136] Morales, note 6, at 77ff.

[137] J. Marshall, "Tailings Dam Spills at Mount Polley and Mariana: Chronicles of Disasters Foretold," Canadian Centre for Policy Alternatives – BC office, Corporate Mapping Project, PoEMAS, Wilderness Committee, Aug. 2018; C. Linnitt, "No Charges, No Fines for Mount Polley Mine Disaster as Three-Year Legal Deadline Approaches," July 23, 2017, https://thenarwhal.ca/no-charges-no-fines-mount-polley-mine-disaster-three-year-legal-deadline-approaches/; C. Pollon, "What's Changed on the Ground Since the Mount Polley Mine Disaster?" Apr. 12, 2017, https://thetyee.ca/News/2017/04/12/Mount-Polley-Disaster-Changes/; Environmental Law Centre, University of Victoria, "Fixing Systemic Failures in BC's Mining Regulation: The Urgent Need for a Judicial Inquiry," Prepared for the Fair Mining Collaborative, Mar. 2017; Amnesty International, "Mining and Human Rights in BC: Mount Polley Disaster," www.amnesty.ca/our-work/issues/business-and-human-rights/human-rights-at-mt-polley-mine.

[138] C. Linnitt, "Jacinda Mack Wants to Get Real about What that Mine Is Actually Going to Do to Your Community," June 21, 2018, https://thenarwhal.ca/jacinda-mack-wants-to-get-real-about-what-that-mine-is-actually-going-to-do-to-your-community/; "Province Halts Private Prosecution against Mount Polley Tailings Spill," Jan. 30, 2018, www.cbc.ca/news/canada/british-columbia/bev-sellars-private-charges-mount-polley-stay-of-proceedings-1.4511305.

[139] Global Mining Guidelines Group, "Women in Mining: Steps, Strategies and Best Practices for Gender Diversity," Mar. 18, 2014, http://gmggroup.org/women-mining-steps-strategies-best-practices-gender-diversity/; UN Women, "Promoting Women's Participation in the Extractive Industries Sector: Examples of Emerging Good Practices," 2016.

boards globally,[140] the underrepresentation of women in positions of leadership in the Canadian private sector was noted by the UN Human Rights Committee in 2015.[141] Canadian extractive firms have been found to lag even further behind.[142] As a result, many mining companies may be fundamentally incapable of understanding the concerns of women and girls and their environmental justice dimensions. This intuitive conclusion is supported by literature that suggests an increased number of women on corporate boards of directors is associated with greater firm commitment to corporate social responsibility and environmental sustainability, as well as improved decision-making more generally.[143]

Corporate board diversity has been the subject of recent discussion and modest legislative action in Canada as part of the regulatory review of federal corporate law known as the Canada Business Corporations Act (CBCA).[144] Businesses may choose to incorporate under the federal CBCA or under provincial or territorial corporate law. Regulatory amendments to the CBCA were passed in the form of Bill C-25 in May 2018,[145] imposing new disclosure requirements on CBCA companies that go beyond reporting on gender diversity to include reporting on the inclusion on boards of members of visible minorities, Aboriginal peoples, and persons with disabilities ("designated persons").[146] CBCA companies are now required to disclose the number of designated persons on the board, the percentage of the board that they comprise, whether the company has a written policy on board diversity, and whether the company has any identified targets for diversity representation.[147] However, the CBCA changes are merely consistent with the approach that has been taken under existing securities law that implements a "comply or explain" regime for gender diversity on corporate boards.[148] The CBCA amendments do not require the board to change any policies or to adopt specific targets (the "comply" provision) but if they do not have these policies, they need to include a note as to why (the "explain"). Moreover, only publicly traded companies incorporated under the CBCA are subject to these

---

[140] A. Dhir, *Challenging Boardroom Homogeneity: Corporate Law, Governance, and Diversity* (New York: Cambridge University Press, 2015), p. 3. See further on why an initial focus on corporate board diversity is a useful strategy for changing firm composition and culture more generally (ibid., pp. 3–8, 24–35).

[141] UN Human Rights Committee on Canada, note 134, para. 7.

[142] A. MacDougall and J. Valley, "2018 Diversity Disclosure Practices: Women in Leadership Roles at TSX-Listed Companies," Osler, 2018, pp. 19, 25 (number of women directors by industry). See further K. MacMaster and S. L. Seck, "Mining for Equality: Soft Targets and Hard Floors for Boards of Directors" (draft, June 2019, on file with authors).

[143] See for example D. Setó-Pamies, "The Relationship between Women Directors and Corporate Social Responsibility" (2015) 22 *Corporate Social Responsibility and Environmental Management* 334; C. Post, N. Rahman, and C. McQuillen, "From Board Composition to Corporate Environmental Performance through Sustainability-Themed Alliances" (2015) 130 *Journal of Business Ethics* 423; L. Liao, L. Luo, and Q. Tang, "Gender Diversity, Board Independence, Environmental Committee and Greenhouse Gas Disclosure" (2015) 47 *British Accounting Review* 409. See further Dhir, note 140, pp. 118–128 (noting improvements in decision-making processes and risk mitigation with increased corporate board gender diversity).

[144] *Canada Business Corporations Act*, RSC 1985, c C-44.

[145] Bill C-25, *An Act to amend the Canada Business Corporations Act, the Canada Cooperatives Act, the Canada Not-for-profit Corporations Act and the Competition Act*, 1st Sess., 42nd Parl., 2018 (assented to May 1, 2018) SC 2018, c. 8.

[146] These designated groups will have the same definition as under the *Employment Equity Act*, SC 1995, c. 44, s. 3. See Government of Canada, "Explanatory Note on Proposed Regulatory Amendments," Dec. 13, 2016, amended Jan. 19, 2018, www.ic.gc.ca/eic/siTe/cd-dgc.nsf/eng/cs07274.html.

[147] Bill C-25 note 145, s. 172.1. The information to be disclosed will be the same as under provincial securities law rules of Form 58–101F1 (*Disclosure of Corporate Governance Practices*) with "members of designated groups" replacing "women" in items 11–15 (ibid., GOC "Explanatory note").

[148] *Disclosure of Corporate Governance Practices*, OSC NI 58–101 (Dec. 31, 2016); *Corporate Governance Disclosure*, Form 58–101F1.

new disclosure requirements.[149] While not onerous, there is still the possibility of corporate forum-shopping by Canadian-incorporated companies wishing to avoid these disclosures, as provincial corporate laws to date have not adopted even these modest disclosure requirements, nor do all provinces follow similar gender-focused disclosure requirements implemented through securities law.[150]

21.5 CONCLUSIONS

This chapter has considered some of the similarities in the impacts of mining activity, in Canada and by Canadian companies operating abroad, on the environmental and other human rights of women and girls, with attention to intersectional complexities particularly evident in the experience of Indigenous women and girls. The similarities include distributive injustice through disproportionate exposures to environmental harms and contamination of lands and resources on which women depend; procedural injustice where women both in Canada and outside of Canada are excluded from decision-making with respect to mining activity; corrective injustice in the failure to develop and implement adequate laws, policies, and remedial mechanisms to protect women's environmental and other human rights in the context of domestic and transnational mining activity; and the social injustices that result.

States like Canada with substantial mining sectors must take steps to develop a coherent set of laws and policies for domestic and transnational mining by companies within their jurisdiction in order to prevent and remedy the environmental injustice disproportionately faced by women and girls, and particularly those who experience intersecting forms of discrimination based on race, gender, sexuality, socioeconomic status, geographical location, among others. While legal and policy reform is only one facet, it can help to prompt systemic changes.

Domestically, more research must be funded and undertaken, on the impacts of mining on Indigenous communities, particularly with respect to Indigenous women, and must be carried out by or with the participation of Indigenous women. Such research must include providing sex-disaggregated data on the adverse effects of environmental contamination.[151] Since the use of toxic substances in mining may have harmful effects on the female reproductive function, international human rights law requires that Canada, at the very least, implement preventive measures to protect women of childbearing age as well as children, including the girl child, from exposure to such substances.[152]

Additionally, environmental and human rights impact assessments undertaken in the context of an environmental review must integrate gender considerations in a more comprehensive and consistent way across federal and provincial jurisdictions. Women in communities that will be affected by the mining project must be provided with a meaningful opportunity to participate in such reviews, including by giving input into the design and scope of such reviews as well as by ensuring their access to relevant information in a timely manner. Similarly, IBAs should be required through laws and regulations to include gender considerations and meaningful input

---

[149] Unlike NI 58–101, venture issuers will not be exempt (R. Ramchandani and G. R. Johnson, "CBCA Reforms Receive Royal Assent," May 3, 2018, www.torys.com/insights/publications/2018/05/cbca-reforms-receive-royal-assent).

[150] *Disclosure of Corporate Governance Practices*, OSC NI 58–101 (Dec. 11, 2014).

[151] UNGA, note 16, para. 71.

[152] Ibid.; UN General Assembly, *Report of the Special Rapporteur on the implications for human rights of the environmentally sound management and disposal of hazardous substances and wastes*, Aug. 2, 2016, UN Doc. A/HRC/33/41, paras. 18, 56, 70, and 110(a).

and participation by women, providing them with equal benefits to mining activity, including access to more lucrative and stable employment opportunities, safe workplaces, and royalties. Moreover, federal, provincial, and territorial governments, mining-affected communities and industry must work together to reimagine how sustainable mining can be undertaken in a manner that reduces the risk of violence against women, including sexual violence. Where such violence occurs, perpetrators must be investigated, charged, and prosecuted, while victims must be provided with legal, social, psychological, medical, and other necessary support.

Beyond this, it is crucial that Canadian law evolves to ensure respect for Indigenous legal orders so that when decisions are made as to whether, and if so, how, to undertake mining development, the resulting projects proceed respectfully and in keeping with Indigenous laws and the consent of Indigenous communities. Canadian regulatory systems at federal, provincial, and territorial levels must also ensure that those experiencing harm, particularly gendered harm, caused by mining activity, have access to judicial and administrative remedies through civil and criminal (including regulatory) laws, or as appropriate through Indigenous legal orders. The federal and provincial governments should also consider establishing a domestic mining ombudsperson within their jurisdictions with appropriate powers to compel witnesses and documents in order to investigate complaints of environmental and other human rights violations, to complement the existing but underutilized and, so far ineffective, OECD NCP mechanism.

Canada needs to regulate the conduct of Canadian mining companies operating abroad to ensure that such companies engage in comprehensive preventative environmental and human rights due diligence that includes a gender impact assessment. Access to government support, such as from Export Development Canada, should require such due diligence and assessment. Corporations that have been involved in violations of environmental and other human rights abroad, or at home, within five years should not be eligible for EDC or other government support or procurement opportunities. The FIAP should also be modified to ensure that the potential gendered impacts of Canadian private sector activity, which is often funded as development assistance, is explicitly addressed, particularly in the case of mining activity.

Canada must also take steps, along with provincial and territorial governments to ensure that victims of environmental and other human rights violations allegedly perpetrated by or with the complicity of Canadian extractive companies have access to justice in Canadian courts. Canadian courts should be considered the appropriate forum to hear such claims and the number of motions that can be brought to have a claim dismissed at the pleadings stage in these types of cases should be minimized. Where such claims are successful, the courts should ensure that it provides appropriate gender transformative remedies in order to both address the harm done and, as much as possible, to reduce the risk of future harm by encouraging change to underlying patriarchal laws and policies, as well as unequal power relations responsible for gender stereotyping, violence, and discrimination.[153] Moreover, the Canadian Ombudsperson for Responsible Enterprise (CORE) must be given appropriate powers to allow her independently and effectively to investigate complaints, and her mandate should reference CEDAW, the ICERD, the CRC, customary international human rights law, as well as applicable international legal instruments on the rights of Indigenous peoples, such as UNDRIP and ILO 169. Moreover, it should require her to engage in gender-sensitive investigation.

---

[153] UN Human Rights Council, *Gender dimensions of the Guiding Principles on Business and Human Rights – Report of the Working Group on the issue of human rights and transnational corporations and other business enterprises*, May 23, 2019, UN Doc. A/HRC/41/31, paras. 5, 39–40.

The Canadian government should also use its influence in international forums such as the IGF to implement a comprehensive set of gender considerations into the IGF Mining Policy Framework. Similarly, Canada should use its influence to ensure that responsible business conduct guidance tools aimed at implementing business responsibilities for human rights are responsive to the rights of women and girls, as well as local and Indigenous communities.[154] Finally, more work needs to be done to ensure the diversity of corporate boards and senior management in the mining sector, to better enable responsive and responsible business conduct including respect for the environmental and other human rights of women and girls.

---

[154] Interestingly, a key Canadian industry association is already taking steps in this direction. See Prospectors and Developers Association of Canada (PDAC), "Gender Diversity and Inclusion: A Guide for Explorers," July 2019.

Energy

22

Environmental Justice, Sustainable Development, and the Fight to Shut the Poletti Power Plant

Rebecca M. Bratspies

When the power authority needs to construct new generators that could foul the air with dangerous toxins, the state immediately looks to black and Hispanic neighborhoods in the outer boroughs.[1]

I firmly believe that this State does not need to abuse its most vulnerable citizens to keep the lights on.[2]

22.1 INTRODUCTION

The campaign to shut the Charles A. Poletti Power Plant in New York City involved remarkably successful environmental advocacy. It also created one of those rare moments when the larger public can actually "see" the structural nature of environmental racism[3] at the core of the environmental justice movement in the United States. Indeed, the Poletti saga offers an environmental justice primer of sorts, revealing the remorseless logic that views placing further environmental burdens on already-overburdened community as inevitable and natural. The successful campaign to shut the Poletti Plant also offers a ray of hope – it was a victory that dramatically improved environmental quality in an overburdened community. There is much to learn from a close examination of just how that happened – from what the successful advocates/activists did on the ground, and how they invoked ideas of justice and sustainability in pursuit of their environmental objectives. Yet, the Poletti campaign's victory has largely faded into history.

This chapter seeks to revive those fading memories by using the campaign to shut the Poletti Power Plant as a case study to interrogate the complex relationship between sustainable development and environmental justice. Section 22.1 provides a brief introduction to the environmental justice movement in the United States, and the parallel rise of sustainable development as a principle of international law. Section 22.2 introduces the Poletti case study with some key background information about the neighborhood of Astoria and the Poletti Plant. Section 22.3 outlines the victorious campaign to shutter the Poletti Plant. Section 22.4 gleans some lessons from the campaign that are salient for environmental justice and sustainable development advocates. Finally, Section 22.5 raises some difficult questions about the

---

[1] J. C. McKinley Jr. and D. Cardwell, "Court Clears Plan to Build Power Plants," Apr. 7, 2001, www.nytimes.com/2001/04/07/nyregion/court-clears-plan-to-build-power-plants.html.

[2] Public Hearing on Issues Involving Decisions Made by the Power Authority of New York State to Site Gas Turbine Generators in the City of New York, Opening Remarks of Assembly-member Paul Tanko at 9–10 (Mar. 22, 2001) [hereafter Hearing Transcript].

[3] For a thorough discussion of what this means, see J. C. Scott, *Seeing Like a State* (New Haven, CT: Yale University Press, 1999).

relationship between core problems of racism and the discourse of environmental justice or sustainable development. By highlighting some lingering questions about how issues of race and class influenced the Poletti victory, this last section elucidates the need to explicitly articulate a racial justice imperative as integral to the social pillar of sustainable development.

22.2 WHAT IS ENVIRONMENTAL JUSTICE?

The United States has an extensive body of environmental laws and regulations. For many key environmental decisions made within this governance system, policy choices are influenced by assumptions about the kinds of risks that are acceptable. These typically unstated and unexamined assumptions too often ensure that new decisions merely replicate existing power and economic dynamics. The resulting environmental standards often systematically fail to protect poor and minority communities.

The environmental justice movement emerged from the recognition that poverty, racism, and pollution are inextricably linked.[4] Not only are poor and minority communities disproportionately exposed to pollutants of all kinds,[5] they are also more likely to be selected to house hazardous waste facilities, power plants, and contaminated industrial sites.[6]

Scholars like Robert Bullard[7] and activists like Peggy Shepard[8] have laid bare the profound structural and systemic racial inequality in environmental decision-making in the United States. Their work shows how institutionalized racism poses a barrier to achieving the kind of cooperation that was successful in the Poletti campaign. De facto segregation and racialized voting can leave poor and minority communities isolated in their battles against pollution and environmental degradation. The environment in those communities can deteriorate even as overall

---

[4] For example, the majority of wastes generated from the cleanup of the BP oil spill were disposed of in communities of color. K. Thompson, "Waste from BP Oil Spill Cleanup Has Gulf Residents Near Landfills Concerned," Aug. 16, 2010, www.business-humanrights.org/en/waste-from-bp-oil-spill-cleanup-has-gulf-residents-near-landfills-concerned-usa; D. Hernandez, "Here Is Where BP Is Dumping Its Oil Spill Waste," Aug. 4, 2010, www.colorlines.com/content/heres-where-bp-dumping-its-oil-spill-waste. See generally, R. D. Bullard, "Anatomy of Environmental Racism and the Environmental Justice Movement," in R. D. Bullard (ed.), *Confronting environmental racism: voices from the grassroots* (Boston: South End Press, 1993), pp. 98–100.

[5] See National Advisory Council for Environmental Policy and Technology (NACEPT), "Report of the Title IV Implementation Advisory Committee: Next Steps for EPA, State and Local Environmental Justice Programs," US Environmental Protection Agency, Mar. 1, 1999; US Environmental Protection Agency, "Environmental Justice in the Permitting Process: A Report from the Public Meeting on Environmental Permitting Convened by the National Environmental Justice Advisory Council," Office of Environmental Justice, Nov. 30–Dec. 2, 1999; National Environmental Justice Advisory Council, "Executive Summary of the 2000 NEJAC Meeting," Dec. 11–14, 2000; A. Kaswan, "Distributive Justice and the Environment" (2003) 81 *North Carolina Law Review* 1031 at 1069–1077; S. Lerner, *Diamond: A Struggle for Environmental Justice in Louisiana's Chemical Corridor (Urban and Industrial Environments)* (Cambridge: MIT Press, 2006); R. D. Bullard, *Dumping in Dixie: Race, Class, and Environmental Quality, Third Edition* (Boulder, CO: Westview Press, 2000).

[6] See US Government Accounting Office (GAO), *Siting of Hazardous Waste Landfills and Their Correlation with Racial and Economic Status of Surrounding Communities*, June 1, 1983, GAO/RCED-83–168; Commission for Racial Justice, *Toxic Waste and Race in the United States: A National Report on the Racial and Socioeconomic Characteristics of Communities with Hazardous Wastes Site*, United Church of Christ, 1987 (documenting that race was the most significant factor in determining the location of commercial hazardous waste facilities).

[7] Robert Bullard is a prolific scholar, author of many key environmental justice books, including his seminal work *Dumping in Dixie: Race, Class and Environmental Quality* (1990) and more recently, *The Wrong Complexion for Protection* (2012).

[8] Peggy Shepard is co-founder and executive director of WEACT for Environmental Justice, an environmental justice organization that has changed the face of New York City

environmental quality improves. Environmental justice rejects this racialized, unequal status quo and demands that we do things differently. In particular, environmental justice demands that decisions be based on "mutual respect and justice for all people, free from any form of discrimination or bias";[9] that decision makers recognize the universal right "to participate as equal partners at every level of decision-making";[10] and that decision makers prioritize "a sustainable planet for humans and other living things."[11]

While the environmental justice movement was surfacing bias and discrimination in US domestic environmental policy, similar questions were emerging on a more globalized scale. Decolonization forced questions of equity and racism onto the international governance agenda. As a result, the post–World War II era saw a profound transformation of traditional notions of state sovereignty. Emerging principles of human rights and sustainable development revolutionized thinking about the responsibilities that states have within their own territories. Sovereignty in its Westphalian sense – based on principles of nonintervention – gave way to a more nuanced vision of the state holding duties toward individuals and their environment.[12] Thick layers of international theory began shaping the state duty to progressively realize human rights, including the right to development[13] and the right to a healthy environment.[14] In 1987, the Brundtland Commission report *Our Common Future*[15] introduced the concept of sustainable development, which was supposed to be the apotheosis of this process – the means of integrating economic, environmental, and social drivers of state action. The Brundtland Commission identified the "links between poverty, inequality, and environmental degradation" as its major thesis.[16] Unfortunately, sustainable development's ambitious integration project rapidly found itself falling under the sway of neoliberal economic theory,[17] which prioritized economic growth and gave short shrift to environmental and social concerns.

22.3 BACKGROUND ON THE POLETTI CAMPAIGN

In 2013, the New York Power Authority (NYPA) dismantled the Charles A. Poletti Power Plant in Astoria, Queens.[18] In doing so, NYPA removed what one local elected official characterized as a "symbol of pollution that haunted [the] neighborhood for too long."[19] This characterization was

---

9 "Principles of Environmental Justice," First People of Color Environmental Leadership Summit, Washington, DC, Oct. 24–27, 1991, Principle 2.

10 Ibid., Principle 7.

11 Ibid., Principle 3.

12 The International Commission on Intervention and State Sovereignty (ICISS), "Report: The Responsibility to Protect," International Development Research Centre, December 2001, para. 1.35.

13 UNGA, Declaration on the Right to Development, Dec. 4, 1986, A/Res/41/128.

14 UNGA, *Report of the Special Rapporteur on the issue of human rights obligations relating to the enjoyment of a safe, clean, healthy and sustainable environment*, Jan. 24, 2018, A/HRC/37/59.

15 UN General Assembly, *Annex: Report of the World Commission on Environment and Development: Our Common Future*, Aug. 4, 1987, UN Doc. A/42/427.

16 Ibid., p. 7.

17 O. M. Fiss, "The Autonomy of Law" (2001) 26 *Yale Journal of International Law* 517 at 518.

18 Queens is widely recognized as one of the most diverse places on earth: G. Lubin, "Queens Has More Languages than Anywhere in the World – Here's Where They Are Found," February 15, 2017, www.businessinsider.com/queens-languages-map-2017-2, with more residents than fifteen states; World Population Review, "US States Ranked by Population 2018," http://worldpopulationreview.com/states/; US Census Bureau, "Table PL-P5 NTA: Total Population and Persons Per Acre, New York City Neighborhood Tabulation Areas, 2010," Population Division – New York City Department of City Planning, Feb. 2012.

19 M. Florio, "Charles Poletti Power Plant Loses a Smokestack as Deconstruction Is in Sight," May 7, 2014, https://astoriapost.com/charles-poletti-power-plant-loses-a-smoke-stack-as-deconstruction-is-in-sight.

an apt one – the 825 MW Poletti Plant was one of the dirtiest energy facilities in the United States.[20] For years, it had been the single-biggest polluter in New York City, emitting more pollution than all sources in Brooklyn, Manhattan, Staten Island, and the Bronx combined.[21]

The Poletti Plant was one of a cluster of major power plants all sited in Astoria. Together these plants supplied 60 percent of New York City's power needs, generating the power that kept wealthier (whiter) Manhattan cool and illuminated.[22] The toll of hosting all those plants was immense. In 2000, when this story began, Astoria's air quality violated the national, health-based standards for carbon monoxide, PM_{10}, and ozone promulgated by the US Environmental Protection Agency (EPA).[23] Indeed, the air was among the worst 10 percent in the entire country.[24] One local leader claimed that "the pollution is so bad, no birds will nest [in Astoria]."[25] The health effects from all this pollution were unmistakable – Astoria suffered from skyrocketing child asthma hospitalization rates,[26] and significantly higher cardiopulmonary deaths than the rest of the city and state.[27] The Poletti Plant posed a particular risk to the thousands of children in Astoria's three major public housing projects, including Queensbridge Houses – the largest public housing project in the United States.[28] None of this prevented the NYPA from proposing a new 500 MW facility directly adjacent to the Poletti Plant.[29]

One of the pollutants raising the greatest concerns was particulate matter. The EPA had been regulating PM_{10} (large particulate matter) since the 1970s.[30] However, clear and growing

[20] Scorecard: The Pollution Information Site, "Facility: Poletti Power Project," http://scorecard.goodguide.com/env-releases/cap/ranking.tcl?facility_id=36081-PANY. The Poletti facility was "the largest source of toxic air, ground or water emissions in New York City, at more than 250,000 pounds per year – more than all reported sources in Brooklyn, Manhattan and the Bronx combined" (R. Pérez-Peña, "State to Close Queens Plant That Is Biggest Polluter in the City," Sept. 5, 2002, www.nytimes.com/2002/09/05/nyregion/state-to-close-queens-plant-that-is-biggest-polluter-in-city.html).

[21] Ibid.

[22] For a visual representation of power consumption across New York City, see Advanced Energy Intelligence, LLC, "An Interactive Energy Map of the City of New York," Mar. 2017, www.aeintelligence.com/news/140-an-interactive-energy-map-of-the-city-of-new-york. This dynamic was obvious at the time of the Poletti campaign. For example, the New York State Comptroller noted that the Poletti Plant's importance rests on the fact that it has a "direct transmission link to Manhattan" (A. G. Hevesi, Comptroller, "A Report by the New York State Office of the Comptroller: New York Power Authority: Power Generation in the New York City Area, 2001-S-64 3, May 12, 2004).

[23] Power Authority of the State of New York, Combined Cycle Project in Astoria, Queens: Application for Certification of a Major Electric Generating Facility under Article X of the New York State Public Service Law 5.2.3 (Jan. 1, 2001) [hereafter Article X Application].

[24] Scorecard: The Pollution Information Site, "Air Pollutant Report: Queens County NY," http://scorecard.goodguide.com/env-releases/cap/county.tcl?fips_county_code=36081#maps.

[25] J. D. Antos, "Poletti Plant Closes," Feb. 3, 2010, www.qgazette.com/articles/poletti-plant-closes/.

[26] C. Kilgannon, "Neighborhood Report: Northwest Queens; Plans for New Power Plants Spur Fears in Asthma Alley," Oct. 24, 1999, www.nytimes.com/1999/10/24/nyregion/neighborhood-report-northwest-queens-plans-for-new-power-plants-spur-fears.html. See also Hearing Testimony at 467 (Testimony of Representative Joe Crowley).

[27] T. Woolf, G. Keith, D. White, et al., "Air Quality in Queens County: Opportunities for Cleaning up the Air in Queens County and Neighboring Regions: Executive Summary," Synapse Energy Economics, Inc., May 2003, pp. 18–19.

[28] The average family in NYCHA housing has an annual income of US$24,336 (F. Menton, "Are the Residents of New York City Public Housing 'Poor'?," June 3, 2018, www.manhattancontrarian.com/blog/2018-6-3-are-the-residents-of-new-york-city-public-housing-poor). Just over 90 percent of current NYCHA residents are Black or Latino, 62.1 percent of residents are women, and 35.7 percent of households are headed by individuals over 62 years of age. In 2012, 26 percent of working age residents were unemployed (M. Jacobson, "The Land that Time and Money Forgot," Sept. 7, 2012, http://nymag.com/news/features/housing-projects-2012-9/).

[29] Article X Application, note 23.

[30] US Environmental Protection Agency, "National Primary and Secondary Ambient Air Quality Standards," Federal Register, Apr. 30, 1971.

evidence of the hazards posed by smaller $PM_{2.5}$ emissions[31] illuminated the shortcomings of this regulatory approach. As multiple studies identified $PM_{2.5}$ as a major public health threat,[32] the EPA responded by promulgating a National Ambient Air Quality Standard for $PM_{2.5}$.[33] The EPA predicted that Astoria, along with most of Queens, would not be able to meet that standard, and would therefore be a $PM_{2.5}$ nonattainment zone.[34] However, during most of the Poletti dispute, the $PM_{2.5}$ standard was tied up in court.[35] Taking advantage of the regulatory confusion, the NYPA made no mention of $PM_{2.5}$ in its application, and offered no assessment of the $PM_{2.5}$ emissions associated with its proposed 500 MW facility.

22.4 THE CAMPAIGN TO SHUT POLETTI

The Poletti campaign offers a model for broad coalition-building, effective advocacy, and social organization around a rights-based message that everyone is entitled to clean air. The campaign involved a coalition between the Natural Resources Defense Council (NRDC – a national environmental group), New York Public Interest Research Group (NYPIRG – a state-level organization), and a local organization called the Coalition Helping Organize a Kleaner Environment (CHOKE).[36] These advocates pursued a two-pronged strategy – challenging the NYPA in state court and before its licensing agency. At all stages of the campaign, the coalition maintained a three-point position: (1) the NYPA must prove that New York City actually needs new power before building more plants; (2) if new plants are built, there must be a system for retiring or cleaning older, dirtier plants; and (3) plants must be dispersed fairly across the city so that no neighborhood has undue burden.[37] Interestingly, the campaign did not explicitly invoke environmental justice. Nevertheless, the campaign's goals clearly resonate with that framework. Similarly, the campaign's goals of fairness and equity are clearly consonant with the equitable and socially just development at the heart of sustainable development.[38]

The CHOKE coalition intervened in the administrative permitting process for the new 500 MW facility.[39] As intervenors, the coalition had a platform to challenge the NYPA's

---

[31] Abt Associates Inc., "The Particulate-Related Health Benefits of Reducing Power Plant Emissions," prepared for Clean Air Task Force, Oct. 2000 concluding that more than half of those deaths could be avoided through better pollution control. A more recent study concluded that reduced $PM_{2.5}$ concentrations accounted for approximately 15 percent of the overall increase in life expectancy during the 1980s and 1990s (C. A. Pope, M. Ezzati, and D. W. Dockery, "Fine-Particulate Air Pollution and Life Expectancy in the United States" (2009) 360 *New England Journal of Medicine* 376–386).

[32] N. Fann, A. D. Lamson, S. C. Anenberg, K. Wesson, D. Risley, and B. J. Hubbell, "Estimating the National Public Health Burden Associated with Exposure to Ambient $PM_{2.5}$ and Ozone" (2012) 32 *Risk Analysis* 81 asserting that 10 percent of deaths in Los Angeles are attributable to $PM_{2.5}$.

[33] US Environmental Protection Agency, "National Ambient Air Quality Standards for Particulate Matter," Federal Register, July 18, 1997.

[34] Woolf et al., note 27, S-5.

[35] The Supreme Court eventually ruled unanimously for EPA: *Whitman v. American Trucking Association*, 531 US 457 (2001).

[36] For convenience, I will refer to this coalition as the CHOKE coalition.

[37] Hearing Transcript, note 2, p. 475.

[38] UN World Summit for Social Development, *Copenhagen Declaration on Social Development*, Mar. 14, 1995, A.CONF.166/9.

[39] New York State Department of Public Service, "Application of New York Power Authority for a Certificate of Environmental Compatibility and Public Need to Construct and Operate a 500 Megawatt Electric Generation Facility in the Astoria Section of Queens County," Exhibits 212, 213, and 214, Sept. 29, 27 and 5, 2000, http://documents.dps.ny.gov/public/MatterManagement/CaseMaster.aspx?MatterCaseNo=99-F-1627.

application for a "certificate of environmental compatibility and public need"[40] – a prerequisite for the new facility. Importantly, New York law guaranteed public intervenors access to funding. This leveled the playing field somewhat, allowing CHOKE to conduct discovery and hire independent experts.[41] With both funding and official status as an intervenor, CHOKE had the opportunity to submit briefs,[42] and expert testimony.[43] The coalition made the case that Astoria was already overburdened with polluting facilities, and that pollution from the new 500 MW plant would jeopardize public health and environmental safety.[44]

While this intervention in the permitting proceeding was ongoing, the CHOKE coalition also joined forces with other environmental justice and community groups challenging the NYPA on another front, this time in state court.[45] These lawsuits challenged the NYPA's Power Now! plan, which proposed installing eleven natural gas turbines around New York City. In late 2000, warning of a possible "summer of calamity,"[46] the NYPA announced that these turbines would be installed on an expedited basis, with little or no environmental review. All the turbines were slated for poor communities of color, and most were located near public housing. At the time, state law required extensive environmental analyses for siting "major electric generating facilities," which was defined as any facility capable of generating at least 80 MW.[47] Each of the proposed turbines could generate 44 MW, and the turbines were to be placed in pairs. The paired units could together generate 88 MW and should have triggered an extensive review. However, in their quest for speed, the NYPA elected to take a shortcut. By promising that each paired unit would be configured to generate only 79.9 MW of electricity (0.1 MW below the 80 MW threshold) the NYPA convinced regulators that the turbines were not major facilities.[48] In reaching this conclusion, the Siting Board permitted the public only ten days to offer comment and feedback.

The NYPA then conducted a cursory review under New York's State Environmental Quality Review Act (SEQRA).[49] Offering the public yet another abbreviated comment period, this time over Thanksgiving, the NYPA rapidly concluded that the turbines would have no negative

---

[40] Re: Case 99-F-1627, In the Matter of the Application of the Power Authority of the State of New York for Certification of a Major Electric Generating Facility Under Article X of the New York State Public Service Law, New York Power Authority, Aug. 18, 2000.

[41] New York State Board on Electric Generation Siting and the Environment, "Ruling Granting Queens and CHOKE Additional Funds to Analyze Issues," Department of Public Service, Department of Environmental Conservation, June 12, 2001.

[42] See for example New York State Department of Public Service, note 39, Exhibit 86, Apr. 15, 2002.

[43] See for example Testimony of Dr. George Thurston, Daniel Gutman and David Schissel submitted on behalf of CHOKE, NRDC, and NYPIRG, (Mar. 13, 2002) [hereafter CHOKE testimony]; Rebuttal Testimony of Dr. George Thurston and Daniel Gutman, submitted on behalf of CHOKE, NRDC, and NYPIRG (Mar. 27, 2002). The funding for hiring these experts came from NYPA pursuant to s. 164(6(a)(b) of the then existing Public Service Act.

[44] CHOKE Testimony at 1; New York State Department of Public Service, note 43, p. 1.

[45] *Matter of UPROSE v. NYPA*, 285 AD2d 603, 606–607, 729 NYS2d 42, 46 (2nd Dep., July 23, 2001); *Matter of Silvercup v. NYPA*, 285 AD2nd 598, 729 NYS 2d 47 (2nd Dept., July 23, 2001).

[46] E. W. Zeltmann, "Power in New York City," Mar. 22, 2001, www.nytimes.com/2001/03/22/opinion/l-power-in-new-york-city-499676.html?mtrref=www.google.com&gwh=B6550163CDCC98835BB5AA298406A6E1&gwt=pay.

[47] "PBS s160. Definitions," New York Consolidated Laws, Public Service Law, https://codes.findlaw.com/ny/public-service-law/pbs-sect-160.html.

[48] State of New York Board on Electric Generation Siting and the Environment, "Case 00-F-1934, Declaratory Ruling Concerning Standards for Defining Generating Capacity," Nov. 16, 2000.

[49] "New State Environmental Quality Review Act (SEQR) Title 6 NYCRR Part 617 Regulations," Jan. 1, 2019, www.dec.ny.gov/permits/357.html.

environmental impacts, and only insignificant cumulative impacts.[50] With this self-generated conclusion, the NYPA prepared to move forward immediately with the Power Now! plan.

The public backlash was immediate.[51] Legislators accused the NYPA of cutting regulatory corners and dodging environmental review,[52] subverting the spirit and letter of the law in a "mad rush" to install the turbines.[53] Indeed, internal agency documents explicitly discussed looking for "loopholes" to avoid a full siting review.[54] The *New York Times* criticized the project as having been "complicated by the secrecy, speed and dubious tactics used to pursue it."[55] Community concerns proved prescient – the Staten Island turbine violated its permitted emissions limits every time it started up or shut down for nearly two years, without any disclosure to the community.[56] In response to these violations, in January 2003, the State Department of Environmental Quality relaxed the environmental stringency of the operating requirements via a consent order with the NYPA.[57]

The Power Authority's primary response to the backlash involved reminding the public of California's rolling blackouts in the summer of 2000. The NYPA asserted (incorrectly) that California's blackouts were due to a failure to build power plants,[58] and accused those opposing its turbine plan of short-sighted NIMBYism[59] that put New York City at risk.[60] Indeed, the NYPA's mantra was that every day's delay in the Power Now! plan brought New York one day closer to California.[61] Critics called the NYPA's claims a scare tactic[62] and a

---

[50] See J. Sze, *Noxious New York: The Racial Politics of Urban Health and Environmental Justice* (Cambridge: MIT Press, 2006) describing the process and the community outrage it sparked. These findings, called a negative declaration and determination of non-significance, allowed construction to move forward without further environmental review (ibid., s. 617.7(a)(2)).

[51] The turbines required Air Permits. DEC held an eight-day public comment period. Despite the abbreviated window for participation, hundreds of people attended public hearings, with 130 people providing oral comments and over 600 submitting written comments; *Silvercup Studios, Inc.* v. *Power Authority of the State of New York*, No. 2858/01 at 5 (J. Golia, Mar. 29, 2001).

[52] "The Turbine Mess," Mar. 20, 2001, www.nytimes.com/2001/03/20/opinion/the-turbine-mess.html?mtrref=www.google.com&gwh=412E9EAAA9D3642C7C3936B852E4D218&gwt=pay.

[53] Hearing Transcript, note 2, pp. 9–10.

[54] Ibid., pp. 50–53.

[55] Pérez-Peña.

[56] Letter from Staten Island Borough President James P. Molinaro to Erin M. Crotty, Commissioner of the NY Department of Environmental Conservation, May 20, 2004, p. 27.

[57] Ibid. There was no explanation for this reduced stringency.

[58] See "Fordham Environmental Law Journal Symposium: Featured Address of Michael N. Gianaris" (2002) 13 *Fordham Environmental Law Journal* 445 at 447–448 (refuting this claim.).

[59] NIMBY is an acronym of "not in my backyard," a derogatory term for "opposition to the locating of something considered undesirable (such as a prison or incinerator) in one's neighborhood" (www.merriam-webster.com/dictionary/NIMBY). In other words, NIMBYism is shorthand for a selfish parochialism that impedes the attainment of societal goals. While NIMBYism certainly exists, the term is intended as a label for the phenomenon of wealthy, often suburban communities, resisting their fair share of social burdens based on racist or classist motivations. See F. Santos, "Mixed Success in Yonkers," May 28, 2006, www.nytimes.com/2006/05/28/nyregion/28yonkers.html?mtrref=www.google.com&gwh=0502F6347934E40FEFC38F510BBB5CE7&gwt=pay; E. Jaffe, "New York's Double Standard on NIMBYism," June 25, 2013, www.citylab.com/transportation/2013/06/new-yorks-double-standard-nimbyism/6012/. Nevertheless, accusations of NIMBYism are frequently deployed as a weapon against environmental justice communities to obscure the very real justice and equity issues embedded in the siting of projects like the turbines.

[60] See for example K. Johnson, "Critics of Power Generators Sue, Citing Threat to Environment," Feb. 8, 2001, www.nytimes.com/2001/02/08/nyregion/critics-of-power-generators-sue-citing-threat-to-environment.html?mtrref=www.google.com&gwh=5C91D18F49625CF57349E185AF993D50&gwt=pay.

[61] Ibid; McKinley et al., note 1. See also, Gianaris, note 58, p. 450 (decrying this tactic). Then Mayor Rudy Giuliani seconded this tactic, using a radio address to accuse turbine opponents of risking people's lives.

[62] Hearing Transcript, note 2, p. 21.

"smokescreen,"[63] pointing instead to credible allegations, later proven to be true, that California's blackouts were due to market manipulation, not lack of generating power.[64]

CHOKE joined forces with the legendary Brooklyn-based environmental justice organization UPROSE[65] to attack the NYPA's Power Now! plan. The New York Court Appellate Division sided with the coalition, unanimously ruling that NYPA's turbine plan illegally bypassed environmental rules.[66] As a result, the court ordered the NYPA to prepare a full environmental impact statement, including an assessment of $PM_{2.5}$.[67]

CHOKE then used these court decisions to its advantage in the ongoing administrative proceeding over the NYPA's Poletti proposal, persuading regulators to order an evidentiary hearing on the public health impacts of $PM_{2.5}$[68] associated with the Poletti facility. At the three-day hearing, the CHOKE coalition presented briefing, testimony, and exhibits about the health effects of adding more pollution to Astoria's already compromised airshed.[69] This hearing gave CHOKE new leverage to strike a deal with the NYPA. In exchange for the coalition withdrawing its objections to the new 500 MW plant, the NYPA agreed to "cease operation of the existing Poletti Facility permanently by January 31, 2010."[70] The NYPA also committed to burning cleaner fuel at the facility in the interim, investing US$10 million annually in energy efficiency programs, and spending US$2 million on community-based air improvements in Astoria.[71] With these caveats, the NYPA received a permit for the new 500 MW facility.[72] Describing the settlement in terms that resonate strongly with environmental justice and the social pillar of sustainable development, the Public Service Commission stated:

> The construction of a new state-of-the-art power plant will contribute to the long-term energy needs of the area, and it will be operated in a manner that considers the environmental and public health as well as safety of the community. In addition, the process yielded additional benefits regarding improved air quality from modifications in the operation of the existing facility as well as the provision for funding energy efficiency, public health and air quality improvements in the community.[73]

---

[63] Ibid., p. 8.

[64] Ibid., p. 172.

[65] UPROSE is the oldest Latinx community-based group in Brooklyn. It has been a leader in the fight for environmental justice and social justice for decades. For more information, see www.uprose.org/. UPROSE led the litigation, but many other environmental justice groups, including Poletti Coalition member NYPIRG joined as co-plaintiffs.

[66] *Matter of UPROSE* v. NYPA, 285 AD2d 603, 606–607, 729 NYS2d 42, 46 (2nd Dep., July 23, 2001); *Matter of Silvercup* v. NYPA, 285 AD 2nd 598, 729 NYS 2d 47 (2nd Dept., July 23, 2001).

[67] UPROSE at 607.

[68] New York State Board on Electric Generation Siting and the Environment, "Case 99-F-1627: Order Concerning Interlocutory Appeals from Article X Issues Ruling," Jan. 24, 2002.

[69] New York State Board on Electric Generation Siting and the Environment, "Brief on $PM_{2.5}$ of the Staff of the New York State Department of Public Service," Apr. 12, 2002.

[70] New York State Board on Electric Generation Siting and the Environment, "Additional Certificate conditions," Supplemental Joint Stipulation, Sept. 12, 2002, s. 7(c).

[71] Ibid., ss. 1(a), 1(b), 5, and 6. In a separate settlement with New York City, the NYPA agreed to conduct a cumulative air impact analysis (ibid.).

[72] New York State Board on Electric Generation Siting and the Environment, "Opinion and Order Granting a Certificate of Environmental Compatibility and Public Need Subject to Conditions," Oct. 2, 2002.

[73] State of New York Public Service Commission, "Press Release: State Siting Board Votes to Approve Application for NYPA 500MW Power Project – Existing 25-Year Old Charles Poletti Generating Plant to Be Shut Down," Oct. 1, 2002.

At 11:59 PM on January 31, 2010, the NYPA permanently ceased operations at the Poletti Plant.[74] Two years later, the plant was dismantled, thus ensuring it would never be restarted.[75] Shutting the Poletti Plant was a big victory for ordinary New Yorkers. Across the city, and most specifically within Astoria, neighbors united around the proposition that they were all entitled to cleaner air, and to a fairer distribution of environmental burdens.

22.5 LEARNING FROM POLETTI: LESSONS FOR SUSTAINABLE DEVELOPMENT ADVOCACY

The campaign to shut the Poletti Plant unquestionably improved the quality of life for Astoria residents. It replaced the dirtiest power plant in New York City with one of the cleanest in the nation.[76] Air pollution levels fell dramatically.[77] By 2015, the American Lung Association awarded the entire borough of Queens a passing grade for particulate pollution.[78] That alone was an accomplishment. But, if we let it, lessons from the Poletti campaign can pay dividends besides the obvious environmental one. Specifically, by examining this victory through an environmental justice lens, we can find principles for advancing the social and environmental pillars of sustainable development. Below are two key insights about successful environmental advocacy gleaned from the Poletti campaign that might resonate in other such struggles: the first is about constructing narratives, and the second about forming coalitions.

22.5.1 *Using Sustainable Development Narratives to Advance the Needs of Overburdening Environmental Justice Communities*

Access for all to affordable, reliable, sustainable energy is one of the Sustainable Development Goals (SDGs).[79] The Poletti fight reveals a potentially profound contradiction between the social, environmental, and economic imperatives embedded in this goal. The NYPA latched onto the need for affordable and reliable energy, which is undeniably a core sustainable development goal. To that end, the NYPA repeatedly warned of looming blackouts,[80] cautioning that "every day's delay will push New York City one day closer to California.[81] Invoking President Lincoln, the NYPA characterized its turbine plan as "New York's 'last, best hope' to keep the lights on this summer."[82] With this narrative, the NYPA sought to claim the mantle of a

---

[74] Antos, note 25.

[75] Florio, note 19; C. Constantinides, "Dismantle Poletti," Apr. 25, 2012, www.qgazette.com/articles/dismantle-poletti/.

[76] Antos, note 25.

[77] Ibid.

[78] American Lung Association, "State of the Air: New York 2015." However, Queens still received an F for ozone pollution.

[79] UN General Assembly, *Transforming Our World: The 2030 Agenda for Sustainable Development*, Oct. 21, 2015, UN Doc. A/RES/70/1, Goal 7.

[80] Letter from Staten Island Borough President James P. Molinaro to Stephen L. Johnson, Administrator of the US Environmental Protection Agency, October 26, 2005, Attachment #2: New York Power Authority, PowerNow! In-City Generation Projects Newsletter.

[81] Johnson, note 60.

[82] Hearing Transcript, note 2, p. 171 (testimony of Zeltmann). New York has certainly experienced blackouts. Indeed, in 2006, despite generating a majority of New York City's power, the neighborhoods of Astoria and Long Island City suffered a nine-day blackout. K. Belson, "Con Ed Apologizes for 2006 Blackout," Aug. 21, 2008, https://cityroom.blogs.nytimes.com/2008/08/21/con-ed-apologizes-for-2006-blackout/?mtrref=www .google.com&gwh=A9E130A2D7806701C9F838C31A54B856&gwt=pay; Queens Power Outage Task Force, "Report of the Queens Power Outage Task Force: Concerning the July 2006 Power Outage in Consolidated

public-interested actor and to position CHOKE and their allies as NIMBYs willing to sacrifice the public's well-being for their own narrow interest.[83]

The CHOKE coalition met this narrative head on, with an argument that highlighted how the NYPA's approach ignored the social dimensions of energy policy. They characterized the NYPA's rhetoric, which emphasized the urgent need for additional power at the expense of community-based pollution concerns as a "misinformation campaign intended to scare the daylights out of New Yorkers."[84] In making this case, CHOKE offered an equally compelling counter-narrative that echoed the Brundtland Commission's call for an "energy efficiency revolution."[85] The CHOKE coalition also presaged the SDGs with its demands for a transparent and inclusive siting process,[86] and its focus on making New York City a resilient, sustainable community,[87] improving energy production and consumption,[88] and decoupling economic growth from environmental degradation.[89]

First, the coalition pushed back hard on the claim that there was a looming power shortage,[90] and instead painted the portrait of an agency manipulating facts and figures to serve its own ends.[91] CHOKE made the case that the NYPA not only failed to demonstrate a need for additional power, but also ignored possibilities for reducing demand through conservation.[92] A New York State Comptroller audit offered support for CHOKE's alternative narrative when it expressed concern that the NYPA's plans risked generating 1000 MW *more* power than its New York City customers required.[93] The Comptroller also concluded that the NYPA "relied on information that was unreliable and incomplete"[94] and had failed to consider all reasonable alternatives before deciding to build new facilities.[95] In response to legislative questioning, the NYPA was forced to acknowledge that it had not seriously considered conservation measures as an alternative to building new facilities,[96] nor had it thoroughly vetted the data it used to conclude that New York faced an imminent power shortage.[97] This approach ran directly contrary to the Brundtland Commission's strictures that sustainable development required states to look beyond the short term and to prioritize conservation and energy efficiency.[98]

Edison's Service Territory," Jan. 30, 2007. However, those outages were all due to a failing power distribution system rather than an actual power shortage.

[83] "Groups File Lawsuit over Power Plants," Associated Press (Feb. 8, 2001) (quoting NYPA as characterizing the lawsuits as "a dangerous step" and adding that "[e]very day's delay will push New York City one day closer to California").

[84] Gianaris, note 58, p. 450.

[85] UNGA, note 15, ch. 7, para. 9.

[86] UNGA, note 79, Goal 16, targets 6 and 7.

[87] Ibid., Goal 11.

[88] Ibid., Goal 8, target 4.

[89] Ibid.

[90] See Fordham Environmental, "Panel III: Electric Generators In New York City: Balancing the Energy and Environmental Needs of the Community" (2002) 13 *Fordham Environmental Law Review* 531 at 534. "CHOKE's position is very simple . . . Number one, prove we need new power. As Assemblyman [sic] Gianaris said, that has not even been proved." See also Hearing Transcript, note 2, p. 475 (testimony of Peter Vallone Jr. on behalf of CHOKE).

[91] Ibid.

[92] Gianaris, note 58, p. 449 (asserting "there was really never a real scare in the summer of 2001 that the lights were going to go out in New York. That was just a fiction that was promulgated mostly by the various authorities that run energy policy in this state. I think it was a travesty").

[93] Hevesi, Comptroller, note 22.

[94] Ibid., p. 14.

[95] Ibid., pp. 12–14.

[96] Hearing Transcript, note 2, pp. 60–66 (testimony of Maureen Helmer and Howard Tarler on behalf of the Public Service Commission).

[97] Ibid., pp. 85–92 (questioning of Helmer and Tarler by Assembly Member Gianaris).

[98] UNGA, note 15, para. 201.

Second, the CHOKE coalition argued that even if new power generation was necessary, the burden of producing it needed to be shared across the city as a whole. This core environmental justice principle resonated not only in the Poletti fight, but also in the parallel fight against the turbines. Moreover, waging the two battles together allowed advocates to shine a spotlight on the absence of social welfare considerations in the planning process. By continually cross-referencing the two campaigns, CHOKE was able to call into question the efficiency-based arguments behind both plans – highlighting the utter incompatibility with sustainable development of the NYPA's process which gave no weight to equitable distribution of burdens,[99] to community participation,[100] or to empowering poor and minority communities through development that leaves no one behind.[101] In short, by emphasizing the right of everyone to breathe clean air and the imperative of shared environmental burdens, CHOKE forced basic principles of social development into the urban planning and decisional matrix for energy production in New York City.[102]

The NYPA found itself called to account for its disregard of sustainable development's stricture that inclusive development requires equitable sharing of both the benefits and the burdens of development.[103] For example, the NYPA claimed that its proposed facilities were all to be placed in industrial areas.[104] Indeed, with regard to the turbines, the NYPA went so far as to claim that they "were not looking in residential neighborhoods for any of these sites for reasons that are perfectly obvious."[105] However, the NYPA's definition of a 'residential neighborhood' apparently did not encompass the places where poor people of color lived in New York City. For example, the two turbines slated for Long Island City were roughly one block from Queensbridge Houses, a public housing complex with 3,300 apartments.[106] The Williamsburg site was next to a park, and around the corner from a school,[107] and the Staten Island site was across the street from homes.[108] By contrast, the NYPA's special counsel explained, in all earnestness, that there was no possible spot for power generation in the wealthier parts of Manhattan.[109]

The NYPA's own internal analysis concluded that all the turbines were being placed in environmental justice communities. Yet, the NYPA justified these placements as "consistent with the nature of the surrounding area." In other words, siting of one noxious industrial facility

---

[99] UNGA, note 79, Goal 10, Targets 2, 3.

[100] UNGA, note 79, Goal 16, Target 7.

[101] The EU Consensus on Development explicitly adopts this goal (New European Consensus on Development 'Our World, Our Dignity, Our Future,' "Joint Statement by the Council and the Representatives of the Governments of the Member States Meeting within the Council, the European Parliament and the European Commission," para. 16).

[102] S. D. Campbell, "Sustainable Development and Social Justice: Conflicting Urgencies and the Search for Common Ground in Urban and Regional Planning" (2013) 1 *Michigan Journal of Sustainability* 75.

[103] UNGA, note 79, Goal 11, Targets 3, 5, and 7.

[104] M. L. Wald, "Power Agency Details Plans for Electric Turbines in City," Nov. 22, 2000, www.nytimes.com/ 2000/11/22/nyregion/power-agency-details-plans-for-electric-turbines-in-city.html?mtrref=www.google.com& gwh=49BBA6C67F34305B299754EFB788CDC5&gwt=pay; Hearing Transcript, note 2, p. 114 (testimony of PSC Chair.)

[105] Hearing Transcript, note 2, p. 264 (testimony of Kass).

[106] Ibid., p. 126. NYPA's special counsel claimed that Queensbridge Houses were separated from the turbine site by the 59th Street bridge (ibid., p. 256). This statement was remarkably deceptive. While the housing project is on the north side of the Bridge and the turbine site on the south side, the bridge runs east–west, not north–south. Queensbridge Houses were only separated from the turbine by the width of the bridge, not its length.

[107] Hearing Transcript, note 2, p. 148 (remarks of Assembly member Lentol); pp. 310–3014 (remarks of Stephen Kass).

[108] Molinari, note 80, Attachment No. 1: December 20, 2001, testimony of then-borough president Guy Molinari on the Rosebank facility's court mandated EIS.

[109] Fordham Environmental, note 90, pp. 550–551.

in a community laid the groundwork for adding the next such facility.[110] This reasoning raised profound environmental justice concerns. As Astoria/Long Island City's then Assembly Member Michael Gianaris pointed out, the NYPA's rationale for siting turbines there rested on the fact that "there are already power plants located there across the street from a residential use."[111] Williamsburg's Assembly Member Joseph Lentol pushed even further, highlighting the structural choices that turned poor communities into industrial zones.[112] Similarly, Staten Island Borough President Guy Molinari accused the NYPA of "ignoring" and "demeaning" the residents living directly across the street from the turbines when it concluded they were "less likely to be significantly affected by the development of a power plant"[113] because there were already other industrial uses nearby.

All three politicians put their fingers on the way that the NYPA's reasoning discounted the social pillar of sustainable development and perpetuated environmental injustice. Channeling undesirable land uses like turbines into neighborhoods *because* they already have noxious uses sited there ensures that already-burdened communities will become ever-more burdened. Past environmental injustice not only creates a path dependency, it becomes the justification for further injustice.

Changing this pattern involves rejecting modes of thinking that assume the status quo as a neutral starting point and instead taking sustainable development's stricture to put people, especially those living in poverty, at the center of development.[114] The CHOKE coalition showed us how to do this. By talking about the need to share the burden of power-generating facilities across the city, the CHOKE coalition embraced the social dimensions of sustainable development. Justice became a counterweight to efficiency. In the process, the CHOKE coalition offered an alternative narrative for siting power plants; one that sought to highlight the interdependence of economic, social, and environmental concerns.[115]

22.5.2 *Broad Coalitions are Key to Sustainable Development*

The Brundtland Commission called for civil society to take the lead in sustainable development. The CHOKE coalition modeled an important lesson about how to do that – teaching us that the most successful advocacy is bottom-up and focuses on demands that originate from, and resonate within, affected communities. Local leadership that represented the full diversity of the community was key to the campaign's success. The CHOKE coalition brought together groups that rarely manage to unite under the same banner. It included New York City Housing Authority (NYCHA) Tenant Association leaders,[116] representatives from local private housing cooperatives, as well as local homeowners and residents.[117] CHOKE effectively united this diverse community

---

[110] Hearing Transcript, note 2, pp. 254–255 (remarks by Assembly member Gianaris). Many of the areas NYPA selected were actually zoned for light industry, and it was only NYPA's status as a state agency exempt from local control that allowed the plan to go forward. A private actor would not have been able to obtain the necessary zoning approvals. See Molinari, note 108, pp. 3–5.

[111] Hearing Transcript, note 2, pp. 254–255 (remarks by Assembly member Gianaris).

[112] Hearing Transcript, note 2, pp. 114–115 (remarks of Assembly member Lentol noting that "[w]e understand these are industrial zones. My community has been under development for so many years and this is the type of development we are getting").

[113] Molinari, note 108, pp. 3–4.

[114] UN WSSD, note 38, paras. 8 and 9.

[115] Ibid., para. 6.

[116] Queensbridge Houses was represented by Queensbridge Tenants Association President Rita Normandeau and by activist Areathia Winns.

[117] Rose Marie Poveromo, President of the United Community Civic Association, represented homeowners and businesses.

around the proposition that clean air belonged to all of them. By deploying environmental justice concepts without using the phrase environmental justice, CHOKE managed to pull together an unusually broad-based, locally driven coalition. With (mostly White) homeowners and (mostly Black) public housing residents united under one banner, hundreds of angry citizens turned out for rallies and meetings.[118] This public unity built a vocal local contingent in support of change.[119] Neighbors showed up at public meetings,[120] wrote letters, passed out leaflets and generally worked to achieve their shared goal of cleaner air for the entire Astoria community.

Community pressure prompted the New York State Assembly to hold a hearing on NYCHA's siting practices. The CHOKE coalition also reached beyond the local community to make common cause with other environmental organizations and with local businesses. While CHOKE's effective advocacy in the litigation and administrative proceedings was instrumental in getting the Poletti Plant shut, those proceedings occurred within the broader context of this social mobilization.

The inclusive and politically active CHOKE coalition demanded more effective citizen participation in decision-making. Local politicians took note. Indeed, the area's elected officials lined up to demand more equitable sharing of environmental burdens, and more effective public participation. The New York Assembly held a special hearing on the NYPA's siting process. CHOKE, and its allies, figured prominently in that hearing. Ultimately, New York State rewrote its electric generation siting rules, requiring environmental justice assessments as part of the licensing process, and reducing the threshold for a major facility to 25 MW.[121]

The CHOKE coalition's internal organization also offers lessons for what sustainable development advocacy looks like. In true environmental justice fashion, the coalition explicitly valued local practical knowledge[122] on par with more formally recognized expertise.[123] To that end, local community leaders were the face of the movement in the press and in court, with state-wide and national legal advocacy groups offering resources and support. This coalition also reached deep into civil society, collaborating with less traditional partners like academics. For example, in 2002, *Fordham Environmental Law Journal* hosted a daylong symposium titled "Energy and the Environment in New York State: Balancing Society's Need for Energy While Protecting and Preserving the Environment." Speakers included: local politicians, the NYPA and other energy company representatives, and many of CHOKE's lawyers.[124] The symposium, which took place during the pendency of the litigation, gave the Poletti antagonists a respite from politics and litigation, allowing for a fuller airing of ideas. The act of convening – of bringing industry representatives, politicians, and activists together for dialogue with academics –

---

[118] J. Warren, "Residents Oppose New Power Plants in LIC," Dec. 21, 2000, https://qns.com/story/2000/12/21/residents-oppose-new-power-plants-in-lic/; J. Kaufman, "Does Power Kill? Balancing the Energy Environment," Apr. 20, 2000, http://queenstribune.com/does-the-power-kill-balancing-the-energy-environment/.

[119] Indeed, community pressure prompted the State Assembly to hold a hearing on the matter. At the Hearing, these community voices were highly visible. Hearing Transcript, note 2.

[120] E. E. Lippincott, "Locals, Pols & Shulman Declare War on NYPA Plan at LIC Rally," Jan. 11, 2001, www.qchron.com/editions/western/locals-pols-shulman-declare-war-on-nypa-plan-at-lic/article_b193c23e-f52b-5e0e-9175-612ca45ede5c.html.

[121] PBS, note 47, s. 160(2).

[122] The generally recognized leader of CHOKE was Anthony Gigantelle, the long-time president of North Queensview Homes Cooperative, a private middle-income housing development located midway between the Poletti and Ravenswood Power Plants.

[123] Scott, note 3.

[124] Fordham Environmental, note 90.

helped put the dispute into a broader context, and in the process explained its importance and its trajectory. This is a role that the academy can play more broadly – promoting awareness, mobilization, capacity building, and collaboration for sustainable development.[125] The CHOKE coalition's activist/academic partnership can be a model for critical academic engagement with local concerns, promoting dialogue and enhancing public discourse around making all development sustainable development.

The Poletti campaign can also serve as a window into the Brundtland Commission's prediction that sustainable development requires profound institutional transformation. The CHOKE coalition forever changed the make-up and focus of local government in Astoria. Peter Vallone, Jr., ran for office while acting as CHOKE's pro bono counsel – winning the City Council seat representing Astoria.[126] Later, Aravella Simotas, the *Fordham Environmental Law Review* editor who organized Fordham's Poletti Symposium and wrote her law review comment on the fight,[127] also ran for office. Since 2011, Simotas has represented Astoria in the New York State Assembly. As chair of the Smart Power coalition, Simotas carries the campaign onward, advocating that Astoria's remaining dirty power plants be replaced by cleaner ones.[128] Astoria's current City Councilmember, Costa Constantinides, chairs the City Council Environmental Committee.[129] He has made environmental justice the centerpiece of his tenure,[130] with clean energy a particular focus of concern.[131] These political outcomes offer an important reminder that sustainable development requires political, as well as social, change. Institutional transformation must be part of any effective environmental advocacy strategy.

22.6 ENVIRONMENTAL JUSTICE AND SUSTAINABLE DEVELOPMENT: LESSONS FROM THE POLETTI STRUGGLE

The Poletti Plant has been shut for almost a decade,[132] and was fully demolished in 2015.[133] The CHOKE campaign to shut the Poletti was an unambiguous environmental success. By 2017, air

---

[125] InterAcademy Partnership, "Supporting the Sustainable Development Goals: A Guide for Merit-Based Academies," 2017.

[126] Vallone served twelve years in that position before being elected to a judgeship. J. V. Milowski and D. Miller, "Vallone Jr. Sworn in as Civil Court Judge," Jan. 13, 2016, www.qgazette.com/articles/vallone-jr-sworn-in-as-civil-court-judge/.

[127] A. Simotas, "Can Community Residents Use Class Action and Public Nuisance Suits to Gain Power against Local Power Producers and Encourage State Officials to Initiate the Development of Responsible Energy Policy?" (2002) 13 *Fordham Environmental Law Journal* 605.

[128] C. Trepasso, "Coalition Forms to Support Astoria Energy Plant's Bid to Repower," May 8, 2012, www.nydailynews.com/new-york/queens/coalition-forms-support-astoria-energy-plant-bid-repower-article-1.1074623.

[129] New York City Council, "District 22: Costa Constantinides," https://council.nyc.gov/district-22/.

[130] New York City Council, "City Council Passes Most Comprehensive Environmental Justice Legislation in Nation," Apr. 5, 2017, https://council.nyc.gov/costa-constantinides/2017/04/05/230/. Specifically, Constantinides sponsored Int. 359, A Local Law to Amend the Administrative Code of New York, in Relation to Requiring a Study of Environmental Justice Areas and the Establishment of an Environmental Justice Portal, which was signed into law on April 25, 2017. He also worked to support the companion bill Int. 886, A Local Law to Amend the Administrative Code of New York, in Relation to Identifying and Addressing Environmental Justice Issues. Both bills can be accessed at http://legistar.council.nyc.gov/Legislation.aspx.

[131] In 2018, Constantinides sponsored two wind energy bills and an energy efficiency bill. He also shepherded through a series of bills promoting solar energy, increased energy efficiency, more stringent fuel standards for buildings and power plants, and energy auditing. All these bills are all available from http://legistar.council.nyc.gov/Legislation.aspx.

[132] New York Power Authority, "NYPA Press Release: NYPA to Cease Operations of Queens Power Plant on January 31st," Jan. 29, 2010, www.nypa.gov/news/press-releases/2010/20100129-queens-power-plant-cease-operations.

[133] C. Tepasso, "State to Dismantle on of City's Dirtiest Former Power Plants," Dec. 18, 2012, www.nydailynews.com/new-york/queens/state-dismantle-dirty-poletti-power-plant-article-1.1223010.

pollution in Astoria was at an all-time low. Particulate matter pollution had fallen 18 percent in under a decade, and sulfur dioxides levels had plummeted 84 percent.[134] Asthma deaths fell significantly.[135] The tale of the campaign to shut the Poletti lives on in *Bina's Plant*, a graphic novel which tells a fictionalized version of the campaign. Published by the CUNY Center for Urban Environmental Reform, *Bina's Plant* is used in environmental justice education, to inspire a new generation to fight for sustainable development.[136]

Shutting the Poletti Power Plant made a real environmental and political difference. By explicitly connecting human health, energy, environmental protection, public participation, and equitable burden-sharing across the City, the Poletti campaign made a major contribution. Yet, in doing so, the CHOKE coalition made a deliberate choice to eschew formally invoking environmental justice and to elide the many ways in which race and class intersect with environmental inequality. The coalition sought to challenge the distributional inequality in how New York City sited its power plant, while simultaneously sidestepping a direct conversation about the racial dynamics that undergird so much of that disparity.

As a result, the cleaner environment has taken a different kind of toll on the community. Astoria and Long Island City are living proof of the intimate relationship between environmental improvement and gentrification. In the years since the Poletti Plant shut, property values in Astoria have soared by over 75 percent,[137] and rents have skyrocketed.[138] The increases in Long Island City have been even more dramatic. Indeed, Long Island City "emerged from the gentrification funnel"[139] with an abundance of shiny glass towers filled with expensive luxury apartments. Long-time residents suddenly found themselves priced out of the neighborhood they fought to improve.[140] At the same time, the area's public housing stock continues to deteriorate,[141] exacerbating the disparities.

This part of the Poletti story needs to be told as well – as a cautionary tale what happens when social mobilization does not expressly grapple with the embedded legacy of racism in the United States. The explicitly racist history of housing in the United States[142] has produced segregated

---

[134] E. Durkin, "Exclusive: New York City Air Pollution at All-Time Low, Data Reveals," Apr. 20, 2017, www.nydailynews.com/new-york/new-york-city-air-pollution-all-time-data-reveals-article-1.3077440.

[135] T. P. DiNapoli, New York State Comptroller's Office, "The Prevalence and Cost of Asthma in New York State," Office of the State Comptroller, Apr. 2014.

[136] Copies of *Bina's Plant* can be obtained by contacting the author. In the near future, the book will be available online at www.https://cuer.law.cuny.edu/?page_id=70.

[137] "Home Pricing in Astoria," *New York Times* (June 2018); NYCEDC Economic Research and Analysis, "Neighborhood Trends & Insights: Exploring New York City Communities: Astoria, Queens," Center for Economic Transformation, Apr. 2014.

[138] M. Quintana, "Neighborhood Profile: Astoria, the Sum of All Parts," May 12, 2015, https://streeteasy.com/blog/neighborhood-profile-astoria-the-sum-of-all-parts/.

[139] A. Murson, "Long Island City Real Estate: Old Is Cool; New Is Better," Aug. 2, 2016, www.propertyshark.com/Real-Estate-Reports/2016/08/02/long-island-city-real-estate-old-is-cool-new-is-better/: this article characterizes Long Island City as "fashionably artistic, diverse and still relatively affordable neighborhood," pointing to the two NYCA facilities (Queensbridge Houses and Ravenswood Houses) as evidence that the market still includes affordable options.

[140] The average rental cost in Long Island City is the highest in Queens. Studio apartments rent for US$2,513/month; with one-bedrooms going for more than US$3,000/month and two-bedrooms over US$4,000/month. MNS, "Queens Rental Market Report, Mar. 2019.

[141] Indeed, as of this writing, Queensbridge Houses residents are contemplating a rent strike protesting lack of heat and repairs. J. Jorgensen, K. Burke, and L. Greene, "Heat Is on: Freezing NYCHA Tenants Threaten Rent Strike over Broken Boilers and Other Problems," Jan. 30, 2019, www.nydailynews.com/new-york/ny-metro-nycha-rent-strike-takeover-20190130-story.html.

[142] For a description of how the United States government intentionally created housing segregation through its funding and policy choices, see R. Rothstein, *The Color of Law: A Forgotten History of How Our Government Segregated America* (1st ed.) (New York: Liveright, 2017).

neighborhoods in which race, poverty, and pollution exposure are closely linked. Reducing one of those variables – pollution – can drive subsequent changes in the race and wealth of a neighborhood through gentrification. The CHOKE coalition had the opportunity to make this phenomenon legible – to highlight the link between pollution, poverty, and racism. Instead, the coalition came together and stayed united by focusing on shared air quality concerns while bracketing the broader issue of racism.

This choice to remain silent about structural racial inequality blunted the transformative power of the Poletti victory. For example, even though New York City now has the cleanest air since monitoring began,[143] asthma rates are still unacceptably high in many parts of the Bronx[144] and Harlem,[145] with Black and Latina/o children hardest hit. Had the CHOKE coalition instead invoked a more explicitly racialized, environmental justice-oriented critique, the coalition might have leveraged its victory into a wholesale reevaluation of both power generation and residential segregation in New York City.[146] Instead, shutting the Poletti Plant paved the way for gentrification. The biggest lesson from the Poletti campaign may be the necessity of articulating a more intersectional conception of sustainable development – one in which its deeply racialized distribution of polluting facilities is fully recognized.[147]

There is no question that creating a diverse coalition is difficult. Institutionalized racism often prevents communities from achieving the kind of cooperation that was successful in the Poletti campaign. To be truly sustainable, decision makers must confront this racist legacy squarely. The UN SDGs take an important step in this direction by emphasizing the need for social inclusion and eradication of discrimination. The European Union went even further, explicitly recognizing the synergistic role that "multiple discriminations" can play in creating and perpetuating unequal, unsustainable development.[148] Addressing this intersectionality may also help respond to another threat to sustainable development – gentrification. The SDGs identify "mak[ing] cities and human settlements safe, inclusive, resilient and sustainable" as a priority.[149] Gentrification, which squeezes residents out of their communities in the name of economic profit, poses a significant threat to that goal.[150] Indeed, the United Nations Special Rapporteur on adequate housing has characterized the lack of affordable housing as not only unsustainable but an "assault on dignity and life."[151]

---

[143] "New York City's Air Is Cleaner than It Has Ever Been Since Monitoring Began," Apr. 19, 2018, www1.nyc .gov/office-of-the-mayor/news/204-18/new-york-city-s-air-cleaner-it-has-ever-been-since-monitoring-began.

[144] NYC Health, "Community Health Profiles 2015: East Harlem," 2015.

[145] Ibid.

[146] The good news is that this broader conversation is currently happening now, under the leadership of Astoria's City Councilmember Costa Constantinides. S. Colón, "Constantinides Bill Seeks to Do Away with Gas-Fired Power Plants," Jan. 8, 2019, https://queenscountypolitics.com/2019/01/08/constantinides-bill-seeks-to-do-away-with-gas-fired-power-plants/; New York City Council, "City Council Passes Most Comprehensive Environmental Justice Legislation in Nation," Apr. 5, 2017, https://council.nyc.gov/costa-constantinides/2017/04/05/230/. Perhaps this is a delayed legacy of the Poletti fight after all.

[147] L. Pulido, "Flint, Environmental Racism, and Racial Capitalism" (2016) 27 *Capitalism Nature Socialism* 1–16.

[148] New European Consensus on Development, note 101. Specifically, in this statement, the EU recognizes the "multiple discriminations faced by vulnerable people and marginalized groups" and commits to a rights-based approach geared to ensuring that "no-one is left behind."

[149] UNGA, note 79, Goal 11.

[150] Proponents of Henri Lefebvre's right to the city have fleshed out this gentrification problem in human rights and sustainability terms. See for example S. R. Foster and C. Iaione, "The City as a Commons" (2016) 34 *Yale Law and Policy Review* 281. This view of gentrification as a human rights challenge is gaining traction in New York. See for example W. Engel, "City Agency Imagines Gentrification as Human Rights Issue," June 30, 2017, www.kingscountypolitics.com/city-agency-imagines-gentrification-human-rights-issue/.

[151] UN General Assembly, *Report of the Special Rapporteur on adequate housing as a component of the right to an adequate standard of living, and on the right to non-discrimination in this context*, Jan. 15, 2018, A/HRC/37/53.

It is vital that the benefits of environmental victories, like Poletti, redound to everyone. That means reclaiming sustainable development from neoliberalism's efficiency-based economic determinism.[152] Those seeking to give social and environmental concerns equal weight in decision-making must seize the initiative – truly sustainable development will be "claimed not granted."[153] Indeed, the Brundtland Commission directed its appeal to citizens groups and ordinary people, calling for "a common endeavour and for new norms of behaviour at all levels and in the interests of all."[154] The message is clear: things will change only if ordinary people demand it. Learning from what the Poletti campaign did, and what it failed to do, can offer guidance for what a successful claiming of sustainable development might entail.

[152] M. T. McCluskey, "Efficiency and Social Citizenship: Challenging the Neoliberal Attack on the Welfare State" (2002) 78 *Indiana Law Journal* 783; M. T. McCluskey, "Subsidized Lives and the Ideology of Efficiency" (2000) 8 *American University Journal of Gender, Social Policy and Law* 115, 122–123.

[153] R. Bratspies, "Claimed Not Granted: Finding a Human Right to a Healthy Environment" (2017) 26 *Transnational Law and Contemporary Problems* 263.

[154] UNGA, note 15, pp. 8–9.

23

The Indigeneity of Environmental Justice

A Dakota Access Pipeline Case Study

Elizabeth Ann Kronk Warner

23.1 INTRODUCTION

Imagine a scenario where thousands of Indigenous people gather for months in makeshift camps to protest the construction of an oil pipeline that will almost assuredly have profound negative impacts on their Indigenous way of life for generations to come. The people are so steadfast in their convictions that most remain encamped through a brutally harsh and cold winter. Their efforts gain international attention, and they succeed in convincing the government to halt construction. That is until a new US president is elected and directs the newly formed government to move forward with the pipeline, and, after approximately seven months of encampment, the people are forced to leave their camps. This is the story of the Dakota Access Pipeline and the efforts lead by tribes and water protectors[1] to halt its construction. The Dakota Access controversy highlights the intersection of the social pillar of sustainability with environmental justice movements. At its heart, the protests constituted an environmental justice movement to stop a pipeline from negatively burdening a community of color. However, the protests erupted because the community's basic needs – food, water, and the right to engage in the community's traditional and spiritual practices – were threatened. The threat to their environment also constituted a threat to their basic human rights, rights protected by the social pillar of sustainability.

Sustainable development seeks to balance environmental protection, economic development, and social development. The social pillar of sustainability is generally expressed in the language of human rights, including the rights to food, water, housing, healthcare, and education.[2] The

---

[1] Most of the people engaged in the fight to stop the Dakota Access pipeline preferred to be called water protectors instead of protesters. This chapter attempts to respect that preference where possible. The term "water protector" has many layers. Many water protectors were working to protect the water of the Standing Rock Tribe from imminent contamination following an oil spill from the pipeline. As one water protector, Alexander Howland, explained, "We are water. That's why a lot of us are here. That's what water means to us: it means life, it means unity, it means one people." For many water protectors, the term has additional meanings. Water is connected to Mother Earth, who is a living being. As Rachelle Figueroa explained, "Mother Earth is our mother . . . The water flows through her creeks, the lakes, sacred places. This is why we're here." Daphne Singingtree sees the water protectors' work at Standing Rock as the start of a movement, "It's more than this pipeline, on this land, at this time. I see this movement continuing on." For some tribes, water plays an important part of their creation story, so the water protectors defend the origins of their tribes. A. Zambelich and C. Alexandra, "In Their Own Words: The 'Water Protectors' of Standing Rock," Dec. 11, 2016, www.npr.org/2016/12/11/505147166/in-their-own-words-the-water-protectors-of-standing-rock.
[2] See J. Knox, "Human Rights, Environmental Protection and Sustainable Development Goals" (2015) 24 *Washington International Law Journal* 517 at 518 who argues that while (draft) Sustainable Development

Copenhagen Declaration on Social Development explained that the social pillar includes: "[e]quitable social development [and] . . . recognizes [that] empowering the poor to utilize environmental resources sustainably is a necessary foundation for sustainable development."[3] Although under theorized, the social pillar seems to include the basic needs of people, such as food, water, and shelter.[4] The Copenhagen Declaration explains that social justice cannot be obtained without respect for human rights. Components of social development are included in the UN Sustainable Development Goals (SDGs). Absent from the SDGs, however, is a discussion of Indigenous rights. Environmental justice adds to these components of social development by considering the equality of development. For example, as with the Dakota Access Pipeline, vulnerable communities, such as tribal communities, will frame their demands for environmental justice in the rhetoric of human rights.

By examining the controversy surrounding the Dakota Access Pipeline, this chapter explores environmental justice concerns from an Indigenous perspective while also suggesting that application of the SDGs without consideration of Indigenous rights potentially leads to culturally blind and unjust results. The Dakota Access Pipeline example also highlights one of the critiques of sustainable development; that it places humanity outside of the environment.[5] This critique posits that such a view perpetuates the myth that the environment is apart from social well-being. Many Indigenous people would likely support such a critique. As for many tribal communities, the connection to the environment and location is intimately linked to the cultural and spiritual survival of the community. Indeed, during the Dakota Access Pipeline protests, water protectors spoke of clean water as necessary not only for people's survival, but also for the survival of Mother Earth and their spiritual connection with her.

To explore the connection between the social pillar of sustainability and environmental justice from an Indigenous perspective, this chapter begins with an in-depth examination of the protests over the Dakota Access Pipeline. Following this case study, the chapter then considers unique factors applicable to environmental justice claims brought by Indigenous communities. This section begins by considering commonalities among Indigenous peoples, such as international Indigenous law and a connection to land and the environment that many Indigenous communities possess, and then focuses on legal requirements applicable specifically to Indigenous peoples within the United States. In conclusion, the chapter suggests that environmental justice claims arising in Indigenous communities may differ from claims arising in other communities, but there are still significant interconnections between these claims and the social pillar of sustainable development.

23.2 CASE STUDY: PROTEST OF THE DAKOTA ACCESS PIPELINE

In 2016,[6] Indigenous peoples and their supporters, the water protectors, gathered in historic proportions near the Standing Rock Sioux Reservation in North Dakota[7] to protest the

---

Goals (SDGs) set out many worthwhile goals, "the targets often do not contain language that is concrete and focused enough to effectively promote human rights or environmental protection."

3 United Nations, *Report of the World Summit for Social Development, Copenhagen*, Mar. 6–12, 1995, UN Doc. A/CONF.166/9 [Copenhagen Declaration].

4 Ibid.

5 See N. Dawe and K. Ryan, "The Faulty Three-Legged-Stool Model of Sustainable Development" (2003) 17 *Conservation Biology* 1458–1460.

6 Portions of this chapter are taken from the author's previous article, E. A. Kronk Warner, "Environmental Justice: A Necessary Lens to Effectively View Environmental Threats to Indigenous Survival" (2017) 26 *Transnational Law and Contemporary Problems* 343.

7 S. Von Oldershausen, "Standing Rock Pipeline Fight Draws Hundreds to North Dakota Plains," Oc. 14, 2016, www .nbcnews.com/storyline/dakota-pipeline-protests/standing-rock-pipeline-fight-draws-hundreds-north-dakota-plains-n665956.

construction of the Dakota Access Pipeline.[8] The water protectors challenged the construction of the pipeline and related pollution that will occur when it leaks. Broadly, they argued that the Standing Rock Sioux Tribe was not adequately included in consultations leading to the pipeline approval, that the Religious Freedom Restoration Act (RFRA)[9] prohibited construction, and that the Army Corps of Engineers failed to meet the requirements of the National Environmental Policy Act (NEPA)[10] in approving the required permit.[11] Although the proposed pipeline does not cross existing tribal lands,[12] it would threaten Lake Oahe, and potentially the Missouri River, which are sources of water vital to the Tribe's survival.[13] Further, significant sites of tribal cultural, religious, and spiritual importance are located along the pipeline's route.[14]

Many tribal water protectors were troubled that the federal government considered and rejected a proposed route for the pipeline that would have crossed the Missouri River 10 miles north of Bismarck, North Dakota.[15] This Bismarck route was rejected, in part, because of concerns about protecting municipal water supply wells from potential pipeline spills.[16] Due in large part to factors related to the size of Bismarck and the location of that community's water resources, the pipeline's route was moved from close proximity to the nondiverse Bismarck community – where 90 percent of the population is White – to almost adjacent to the Standing Rock Sioux Reservation, where only 13.9 percent of the population is White.[17] It may be argued that this decision – to move the pipeline away from non-Native communities and toward a Native community – is evidence of the federal government's discriminatory intent toward Indigenous people. From an environmental justice perspective, such decisions are unjust because they disproportionately impact people of color regardless of the subjective intent of federal government officials.[18]

To fully understand this controversy, it must be put in its proper historical context. The Lakota/Dakota/Sioux people have long suffered at the hands of the federal government. For example, the federal government abrogated treaties with the Great Sioux Nation after gold was found in the Black Hills. Additionally, after the Sioux gave up the lands in question, the federal

---

[8] Ibid.
[9] Religious Freedom Restoration Act of 1993, Pub. L. No. 103–141, 107 Stat. 1488 (Nov. 16, 1993).
[10] National Environmental Policy Act of 1969, Pub. L. 91–190, 83 Stat. 852 (Jan. 1, 1970) [NEPA].
[11] K. A. Carpenter and A. R. Riley, "Standing Tall: The Sioux's Battle Against a Dakota Oil Pipeline Is a Galvanizing Social Justice Movement for Native Americans," Sept. 23, 2016, www.slate.com/articles/news_and_politics/jurisprudence/2016/09/why_the_sioux_battle_against_the_dakota_access_pipeline_is_such_a_big_deal.html.
[12] Ibid. (stating that portions of the Pipeline are located within traditional tribal lands that were guaranteed to the Tribe in prior treaties).
[13] A. Dalrymple, "Confused about Dakota Access Controversy? This Primer Will Get You Up to Speed," Sept. 24, 2016, www.inforum.com/news/4122538-confused-about-dakota-access-controversy-primer-will-get-you-speed.
[14] Carpenter and Riley, note 11.
[15] Dalrymple, note 13.
[16] Ibid.
[17] Compare Bismarck, North Dakota, www.city-data.com/city/Bismarck-North-Dakota.html (showing that 90 percent of the residents of Bismarck, North Dakota identify as White, and 4.1 percent identify as Indian alone), with Sioux County Demographics, www.northdakota-demographics.com/sioux-county-demographics (showing that Sioux County, North Dakota, where the majority of the Standing Rock Sioux Reservation is located, is only 13.9 percent White and 79.4 percent Indian).
[18] US antidiscrimination law has limited the scope of protection available to racial and ethnic minorities by requiring proof of intentional discrimination. Consequently, environmental justice claims based on disparate impact have generally failed. By contrast, international law on the right to equality recognizes the right to be free from intentional discrimination as well as practices that have a discriminatory impact (C. G. Gonzalez, "Environmental Racism, American Exceptionalism, and Cold War Human Rights" (2017) 26 Transnational Law and Contemporary Problems 28 at 303–305, 307–309).

government tried to starve them by overhunting buffalo and denying rations guaranteed by treaty.[19] In 1890, approximately 200 Sioux people were shot and killed by the federal government while they prayed during a ceremony called a Ghost Dance.[20] Fifty years ago, the federal government seized individual homes on the Standing Rock Reservation to build the Oahe hydroelectric dam project, and today, many descendants of the Great Sioux Nation live in some of the poorest reservations and counties within the United States.[21] For many of the water protectors, federal approval of the Dakota Access Pipeline offers another example in a long history of the federal government acting to the detriment of Indigenous people.

Initially, the legal controversy related to the pipeline focused on the Tribe's efforts to secure an emergency injunction to halt construction of the pipeline around the Lake Oahe area. The Tribe argued that an injunction was appropriate because the federal government failed to participate in adequate tribal consultations under the National Historic Preservation Act (NHPA)[22] prior to approval of the pipeline near tribal lands.[23] "The Tribe fears that construction of the pipeline . . . will destroy sites of cultural and historical significance. [The Tribe asserts] principally that the [Army Corps of Engineers] flouted its duty to engage in tribal consultations under the National Historic Preservation Act and that irreparable harm will ensue."[24] The US District Court for the District of Columbia denied the Tribe's motion for preliminary injunction, finding that the Corps complied with NHPA and the Tribe failed to demonstrate irreparable harm.[25]

The Departments of Justice, the Army, and the Interior, however, released a joint statement regarding the case.[26] While these departments acknowledged the district court's decision, they also recognized that important issues raised by the Tribe remained unresolved.[27] The joint statement noted that concerns about the consultation process exist and that there may be a need for reform.[28] The departments announced that "[t]he Army will not authorize constructing the Dakota Access Pipeline on Corps land bordering or under Lake Oahe until it can determine

---

[19] Carpenter and Riley, note 11.

[20] Ibid.

[21] Ibid.

[22] National Historic Preservation Act of 1966, Public Law 89–665, 54 USC 300101 (Oct. 15, 1966) [NHPA].

[23] As mentioned above, the Dakota Access Pipeline is not located within the Tribe's borders. As a result, tribal environmental law does not apply in this case, and, therefore, this chapter focuses on American federal law and the potential impact of international law. Such a focus, however, is not meant to suggest that tribes lack robust environmental legal schemes. In fact, for many tribes, quite the opposite is true. For a discussion of tribal environmental law enacted by tribes within the United States under their inherent sovereignty, see E. A. Kronk Warner, "Returning to the Tribal Environmental 'Laboratory': An Examination of Environmental Enforcement Techniques in Indian Country" (2017) 6 *Michigan Journal of Environmental and Administrative Law* 34; E. A. Kronk Warner, "Looking to the Third Sovereign: Tribal Environmental Ethics as an Alternative Paradigm" (2016) 33 *Pace Environmental Law Review* 397; E. A. Kronk Warner, "Justice Brandeis and Indian Country: Lessons from the Tribal Environmental Laboratory" (2015) 47 *Arizona State Law Journal* 857; E. A. Kronk Warner, "Tribes as Innovative Environmental 'Laboratories'" (2015) 86 *University of Colorado Law Review* 789; E. A. Kronk Warner, "Examining Tribal Environmental Law" (2014) 39 *Columbia Journal of Environmental Law* 42.

[24] *Standing Rock Sioux Tribe* v. *US Army Corps of Engineers*, No. 16–1534, 2016 US Dist. LEXIS 121997 at *2 (DDC 2016).

[25] Ibid.

[26] The United States Department of Justice, Office of Public Affairs, "Joint Statement from the Department of Justice, the Department of the Army, and the Department of the Interior Regarding DC circuit Court of Appeals in *Standing Rock Sioux Tribe* v. *US Army Corps of Engineers*," Oct. 10, 2016, www.justice.gov/opa/pr/joint-statement-department-justice-department-army-and-department-interior-regarding-standing.

[27] Ibid.

[28] Ibid.

whether it will need to reconsider any of its previous decisions regarding the Lake Oahe site under the National Environmental Policy Act (NEPA) or other federal laws."[29]

Meanwhile, the Tribe appealed the district court's decision.[30] On October 9, 2016, the US Court of Appeals for the District of Columbia Circuit denied the emergency injunction request, finding, as the district court had, that the Tribe failed to meet its burden demonstrating that such an extraordinary remedy was appropriate.[31]

On December 4, 2016, the Army Corps of Engineers announced that it would not grant the easement for the Dakota Access Pipeline to cross Lake Oahe.[32] This victory for the Tribe, however, was short-lived. On January 24, 2017, newly installed President Trump issued a presidential memorandum on the pipeline calling on the Secretary of the Army to direct the appropriate assistant secretary to review and approve the pipeline on an expedited schedule, subject to applicable laws.[33] On February 7, 2017, the Army Corps of Engineers announced its intention to approve the easement for the Dakota Access Pipeline under Lake Oahe.[34] The water protectors' camps were ultimately cleared and closed on February 23, 2017. On March 7, 2017, the district court also rejected a claim brought by the Tribe that the presence of oil in the pipeline desecrated the Tribe's sacred water, making it impossible for the Tribe to exercise its religious beliefs, and therefore violating the RFRA.[35]

In addition to claims based on the NHPA and RFRA, the Tribe also separately claimed that the Corps failed to comply with the NEPA.[36] The Tribe argued that the Corps failed to adequately consider the pipeline's environmental effects before granting the permits to construct and operate the pipeline under Lake Oahe. The majority of the Tribe's NEPA claims were unsuccessful. However, the court did find that the Corps failed to adequately consider the impacts of the pipeline on the Tribe's usufructuary rights, how highly controversial the impacts would be, and the pipeline's environmental justice implications.[37] With regard to environmental justice, the Tribe argued that that Corps's environmental justice analysis was arbitrary and capricious.[38] A 1994 executive order requires agencies to take into consideration achieving environmental justice when considering certain projects.[39] Although the order does not create a private right to judicial review, the US Court of Appeals for the District of Columbia has allowed environmental justice challenges through either NEPA or the Administrative Procedure Act.[40] Accordingly, the Tribe could bring its environmental justice claim as part of its NEPA claims.

---

[29] Ibid.

[30] Emergency Motion for Injunction Pending Appeal, *Standing Rock Sioux Tribe* v. *US Army Corps of Engineers* (2016) (No. 16–5259).

[31] Court Order, *Standing Rock Sioux Tribe* v. *US Army Corps of Engineers* (2016) (No. 16–5259).

[32] Stand with Standing Rock, "Standing Rock Sioux Tribe's Statement on US Army Corps of Engineers Decision to Not Grant Easement," Dec. 4, 2016, http://standwithstandingrock.net/standing-rock-sioux-tribes-statement-u-s-army-corps-engineers-decision-not-grant-easement/.

[33] The White House, Office of the Press Secretary, "Memorandum for the Secretary of the Army. Subject: Construction of the Dakota Access Pipeline," Jan. 24, 2017, www.npr.org/assets/news/2017/01/DakotaAccessConstruction.pdf.

[34] Letter from Paul D. Cramer, Deputy Assistant Secretary of the Army, to Honorable Raul Grijalva, Ranking Member of the US House of Representatives Committee on Natural Resources, Feb. 7, 2017, https://turtletalk.files.wordpress.com/2017/02/dakota-access-pipeline-notification-grijalva.pdf.

[35] *Standing Rock Sioux Tribe* v. *US Army Corps of Engineers*, No. 16–1534, 2017 WL 908538 (DDC Mar. 7, 2017).

[36] *Standing Rock Sioux Tribe* v. *US Army Corps of Engineers*, No. 16–1534 (DDC June 14, 2017).

[37] Ibid., p. 2.

[38] Ibid., p. 47.

[39] Exec. Order 12898, "Federal Actions to Address Environmental Justice in Minority Populations and Low-Income Populations," (1994) 59 Fed. Reg. 7629.

[40] *Communities against Railway Expansion, Inc.* v. *FAA*, 355 F.3d 678, 689 (DC Cir 2004).

The Corps did do an environmental justice analysis of the pipeline. However, it limited its analysis to a 0.5 mile radius around the pipeline crossing of the lake; the Tribe is 0.55 miles away from the crossing.[41] As a result of this decision, the county where the Tribe is located was excluded from the environmental justice analysis. Also, the two counties considered in the analysis were upstream from the potential impact of a spill. The Corps defended its choice of a 0.5 mile area by arguing that transportation projects and natural gas pipeline projects regularly use a 0.5 mile radius.[42] However, because the Corps failed to supply an example of an oil pipeline using such a radius, the court declined to conclude that the 0.5 mile radius excluding the Tribe was reasonable.[43] Also, although the Corps did consider the Tribe's interests, it did not include a discussion of the impacts of a potential oil spill on the Tribe, but rather focused on the impacts of the construction.[44] Ultimately, the court concluded that while the Corps did take some steps in meeting its requirements related to environmental justice, it failed to fully consider the environmental justice implications of the pipeline.[45]

In addition to these environmental justice issues, the Tribe raised concerns about the lack of effective consultation surrounding approval of the Dakota Access Pipeline. Given Indigenous peoples' human right to free, prior, and informed consent (FPIC), the concerns regarding consultation also relate to the social pillar of sustainable development. Section 106 of the NHPA requires the federal government to consult with tribes prior to issuing permits that might affect resources of historical significance to tribes.[46] Under the tribal consultation processes of the NHPA, the consultation regulations require that consultations occur "early in the planning process" in a "sensitive manner respectful of tribal sovereignty" and that the consultations recognize "the government-to-government relationship between the Federal Government and Indian tribes."[47]

The Tribe's legal arguments concerned whether the Corps adequately consulted it for a nationwide permit, as required under the NHPA. In its appeal to the US Court of Appeals for the District of Columbia, the Tribe focused its argument on two issues: a nationwide permit approved in 2012 that did not consider impacts on the Tribe's sacred sites and the Corps's focus on its narrow area of jurisdiction under the Clean Water Act, rather than impacts just beyond this narrow area and within the Tribe's territory.[48]

In responding to the district court's finding that the Corps contacted the Tribe on numerous occasions for consultation,[49] the Tribe contended that "those discussions were fundamentally impaired by the Corps's rigid approach to the scope of its review."[50] Therefore, at the heart of the Tribe's argument requesting an emergency injunction to halt construction near Lake Oahe, was the concern that there was inadequate consultation in regards to the siting of the pipeline.

Additionally, the joint statement released by the Departments of Justice, the Army, and the Interior recognized that the consultation process used by the Corps in this matter may be flawed.

[41] *Standing Rock Sioux Tribe* v. *US Army Corps of Engineers*, note 36, p. 48.
[42] Ibid., p. 50.
[43] Ibid.
[44] Ibid., pp. 50–51.
[45] Ibid., p. 54.
[46] NHPA, note 22, 54 USC §§ 306108, 302706(b), 300320.
[47] Ibid., 36 CFR § 800.2(c)(2)(ii)(A)–(C).
[48] Emergency Motion for Injunction Pending Appeal at 4, *Standing Rock Sioux Tribe* v. *US Army Corps of Engineers* (No. 16–5259) (DC Cir Sept. 12, 2016); Federal Water Pollution Control Act, 33 USC §1251 (1972) [Clean Water Act].
[49] Ibid.
[50] Ibid.

The statement explained that the pipeline controversy highlighted the need for nationwide reform related to consideration of tribal views of infrastructure projects.[51] At the very least, the federal government can be said to have recognized that a problem of effective consultation exists.

Beyond domestic law, concerns also exist regarding whether the federal government engaged in appropriate consultation with the Tribe under international law. The Chairman of the Standing Rock Sioux Tribe, David Archambault, represented the Tribe in front of the UN Human Rights Council[52] and argued that "[t]his pipeline violates our treaty rights and our human rights, and it violates the UN's own Declaration on the Rights of Indigenous Peoples."[53] Several provisions of the Declaration (UNDRIP) have direct bearing on the controversy at the Standing Rock Sioux Reservation. For example, Article 8 provides that states shall ensure effective mechanisms to protect tribal lands and resources.[54] In addition, UNDRIP recognizes Indigenous peoples' right to FPIC.[55] FPIC suggests that Indigenous communities be included early in any discussions potentially affecting them.[56] Such participation should be absent of "coercion, intimidation or manipulation," and "'consent' should be intended as a process of which consultation and participation represent central pillars."[57] Accordingly, under international law, the Tribe could argue that the Corps's failure to engage in meaningful consultation as to the permits means that the Tribe did not give its FPIC to the construction of the pipeline.

Many of the provisions of UNDRIP reflect general human rights law, and to the extent it follows general human rights law, it is binding. Some scholars have argued that UNDRIP is evidence of customary international law.[58] The Tribe has also raised claims related to the abrogation of its treaties with the United States, as the land at issue was reserved to the Tribe under the first Treaty of Fort Laramie between the United States and the Great Sioux Nation, which was a predecessor of the Standing Rock Sioux Tribe.[59] UNDRIP calls on domestic states to honor their treaties with Indigenous nations.[60]

Further, environmental justice claims arising within Indian territories often involve the federal trust responsibility. In the United States, the federal government is said to owe tribes a federal trust responsibility under certain circumstances. In general, federal courts recognize a moral responsibility on the part of the federal government to act in the best interests of tribes given the fact that tribes rely on the federal government for external protection and have lost considerable property to the federal government.[61] But, the federal trust responsibility is only legally binding against the federal government where the government has affirmatively agreed to take on a responsibility.[62] For example, where the federal government was seen to have undertaken the management and control of Fort Apache on the White Mountain Apache reservation, the US Supreme Court held that the federal government was bound by its trust

---

[51] The United States Department of Justice, Office of Public Affairs, note 26.

[52] Carpenter and Riley, note 11.

[53] Ibid. (quoting David Archambault).

[54] United Nations, Declaration on the Rights of Indigenous Peoples, Sept. 13, 2007, UN Doc. A/RES/61/295, Art. 8 [UNDRIP].

[55] Ibid., Arts. 10, 11(2), 19, 28, and 29.

[56] S. Baez, "The "Right" REDD Framework: National Laws that Best Protect Indigenous Rights in a Global REDD Regime" (2011) 80 *Fordham Law Review* 821 at 842.

[57] Ibid., p. 842.

[58] S. J. Anaya, *International Human Rights and Indigenous Peoples* (New York: Aspen, 2009), p. 185.

[59] Carpenter and Riley, note 11.

[60] UNDRIP, note 54, Art. 10.

[61] N. J. Newton, F. Cohen, and R. Anderson, *Cohen's Handbook of Federal Indian Law* (San Francisco: LEXISNEXIS, 2012), ch. 5.

[62] *United States v. Jicarilla Apache Nation* (2011) 564 US 162.

responsibility to repair the Fort.[63] Conversely, the Supreme Court held that the United States did not have a federal trust responsibility to act in the best interests of the Navajo Nation when the United States Secretary of the Interior acted in a way that ultimately led the Nation to accept a lower royalty rate for coal extraction. The court determined that the federal trust responsibility did not exist in this case because the federal government was not responsible for the actual management of the mining under the applicable statute.[64]

The challenges to the Dakota Access Pipeline present issues related to the federal government's trust responsibility to tribes. The Army Corps arguably breached its federal trust responsibility by failing to consider the best interests of the Tribe when it ultimately decided to issue the permit allowing for construction of the pipeline across federal lands. The federal trust responsibility helps inform the discussion of whether the Tribe receives justice in consideration of its claims.

Even though this case study focuses on the efforts to stop the Dakota Access Pipeline, the environmental justice and international human rights law issues raised in relation to this matter have potentially far-reaching application. For example, in 2015, many individual Natives and tribes joined to protest construction of the Keystone Pipeline.[65] As oil pipelines continue to be proposed for construction near or through the territories of Indigenous communities, such communities increasingly may be at the forefront of efforts to halt construction, and will likely base their claims, at least in part, on environmental justice and international human rights law. Clearly, environmental justice and human rights are inextricably intertwined with the social pillar of sustainable development.

23.3 ENVIRONMENTAL JUSTICE AND INDIGENOUS COMMUNITIES

With the Dakota Access Pipeline case study in mind, it is helpful to examine how domestic and international Indigenous law potentially informs environmental justice claims raised by Indigenous communities.[66] Although there are many similarities among environmental justice struggles in Indigenous communities all over the world, environmental justice claims arising in Indian country within the United States may differ from struggles elsewhere in the world due to unique features of US law, including tribal sovereignty (where applicable), and the trust obligations owed to the tribes by the federal government. This section discusses commonalities among Indigenous communities' relations to land and environment, the international legal rights and obligations applicable to all Indigenous communities, and finally the legal considerations specific to Indigenous communities in the United States.

23.3.1 *Unique Connection to the Land and Environment*

Many Indigenous communities around the world (although certainly not all) possess strong connections to land and environment.[67] These connections to the environment and the land

---

[63] *United States* v. *White Mountain Apache Tribe* (2003) 537 US 465.

[64] *United States* v. *Navajo Nation* (2003) 537 US 488.

[65] R. Boos, "Native American Tribes Unite to Fight the Keystone Pipeline and Government 'Disrespect,'" Feb. 19, 2015, www.pri.org/stories/2015-02-19/native-american-tribes-unite-fight-keystone-pipeline-and-government-disrespect.

[66] Portions of this Part of the Article are excerpted from E. A. Kronk Warner, "Application of Environmental Justice to Climate Change-Related Claims Brought by Native Nations," in S. Krakoff and E. Rosser (eds.), *Tribes, Land, and the Environment* (London: Routledge, 2012), pp. 75–102.

[67] The author recognizes that each Indigenous community has a different relationship with its environment and is hesitant to stereotype a common "Indigenous experience," recognizing that there is a broad diversity of thought and experience related to one's relationship with land and the environment. See R. Tsosie, "Tribal

stem from the fact that many Indigenous cultures are "land-based,"[68] meaning that they are physically and culturally connected to a certain location or area. Many individual Indigenous people and communities also possess a spiritual connection with land and the environment.[69] The spiritual connection between many tribes and their surrounding environment is crucial to the self-determination of these communities.[70]

Therefore, many communities facing environmental challenges may also encounter devastating impacts to their culture, spirituality, and traditions. Such spiritual, cultural, and historical connections to the affected land play an important role in any environmental justice claim arising in Indigenous territory as land, identity, and sovereignty/self-determination are uniquely connected within Indigenous communities. Failure to consider these interconnections will negatively impact the quality of the Indigenous community's participation in the legal process.

Further, how an Indigenous community determines whether justice has been achieved may be defined in part by its connection to land and the environment, which buttresses the point that the SDGs must be informed by Indigenous rights. For example, one of the central reasons the Tribe fought so hard against the Dakota Access Pipeline was because of concerns that its presence would have detrimental impacts on the Tribe's water, hunting, and fishing resources – resources central to the Tribe's survival and spirituality. In addition, there is concern that the pipeline will have devastating impacts for generations to come, which is inconsistent with sustainable development's recognition of intergenerational rights.

23.3.2 *Indigenous Rights under International Law*

Indigenous rights under international law should be considered when evaluating environmental justice matters impacting Indigenous communities. As a starting point, there are some principles under international law applicable to all people, which are helpful when discussing Indigenous rights from an environmental justice perspective. For example, states have an obligation to respect the human rights of individuals subject to their authority.[71] Moreover, members of the

---

Environmental Policy in an Era of Self-Determination: The Role of Ethics, Economics, and Traditional Ecological Knowledge" (1996) 21 *Vermont Law Review* 225 at 271.

[68] Ibid., p. 274.

[69] Ibid., pp. 282–283 ("American Indian tribal religions . . . are located 'spatially,' often around the natural features of a sacred universe. Thus, while indigenous people often do not care when the particular event of significance in their religious tradition occurred, they care very much about where it occurred" (citation omitted)).

[70] M. C. Wood and Z. Welcker, "Tribes as Trustees Again (Part I): The Emerging Tribal Role in the Conservation Trust Movement" (2008) 32 *Harvard Environmental Law Review* 373 at 424 ("Trust concepts therefore help to provide tribes with two essential tools of traditional Native self-determination: access to sacred lands and the ability to sustainably use the natural resources on those lands. These were, and remain today, vital tools of nation-building").

[71] Organization of American States, American Convention on Human Rights, Nov. 22, 1969, OASTS. No. 36, 1144 UNTS 123, Art. 1; Organization of American States, Additional Protocol to the American Convention on Human Rights in the Area of Economic, Social and Cultural Rights, Nov. 17, 1988, OASTS No. 69, Art. 1; United Nations, Charter of the United Nations, Art. 55; United Nations, Universal Declaration of Human Rights, Dec. 10, 1948, GA Res. 217 (III), UN Doc. A/810, preamble; United Nations Office of the High Commissioner Human Rights, International Covenant on Civil and Political Rights, Mar. 23, 1976, GA Res. 2200 (XXI), UN Doc. A/6316, Arts. 2(1)–2(2); United Nations Office of the High Commissioner Human Rights, International Covenant on Economic, Social and Cultural Rights, Dec. 16, 1966, GA Res. 2200 (XXI), UN Doc. A/6316, Art. 2(2); United Nations Office of the High Commissioner Human Rights, International Convention on the Protection of the Rights of All Migrant Workers and Members of their Families, Dec. 18, 1990, GA Res. 45/158, UN Doc. A/45/49, Art. 7; United Nations Office of the High Commissioner Human Rights, International Convention on the Elimination of All Forms of Racial Discrimination, Dec. 21, 1965, GA

Organization of American States (OAS) recognize the right to hold property as a human right under both Article 21 of the American Convention on Human Rights and Article 23 of the American Declaration of the Rights and Duties of Man.[72] The right to property is also recognized in Article 17 of the Universal Declaration of Human Rights.[73] These rights are significant to Indigenous peoples because, as demonstrated by the Dakota Access Pipeline controversy, it is not uncommon for disputes between states and Indigenous communities to center on the appropriation or misuse of land. For example, the Inter-American Commission on Human Rights found that the United States violated the right to property of the Dann sisters (citizens of the Western Shoshone Tribe), when the United States denied the sisters their right to graze horses on pastures the sisters claimed were Shoshone lands.[74]

Although the United States is not a party, international law also contains provisions that are specific to Indigenous peoples. Adopted in 1989, the International Labour Organization's Convention Concerning Indigenous and Tribal Peoples in Independent Countries (ILO 169) is a foundational document on the rights of Indigenous peoples. Notably, ILO 169 recognizes the right of Indigenous peoples to "exercise control . . . over their own economic, social and cultural development" and participate in development that "may affect them directly."[75] Furthermore, Article 14 guarantees that Indigenous peoples' "rights of ownership and possession . . . over the lands which they traditionally occupy shall be recognized," and Article 16 states that Indigenous peoples "shall not be removed from the lands which they occupy."[76]

UNDRIP was adopted by the United Nations General Assembly in 2007 and supports and reaffirms the rights of Indigenous peoples.[77] Although the United States initially voted against the Declaration, it later reversed its position, officially endorsing the Declaration in 2011.[78] UNDRIP Article 3 states that "Indigenous peoples have the right to self-determination."[79] Article 8 provides a right against "forced assimilation or destruction of [Indigenous] culture."[80] Article 10 specifies that Indigenous peoples shall not be forcibly removed from their territories and any relocation must occur with FPIC.[81] Article 26 recognizes Indigenous peoples should have rights to land traditionally occupied.[82] Finally, Article 28 provides that Indigenous peoples should have redress for lands and territories taken from them.[83] All of the aforementioned UNDRIP rights, as

Res. 2106 (XX), 660 UNTS 195; European Court of Human Rights, European Convention for the Protection of the Human Rights and Fundamental Freedoms, Nov. 4, 1950, 213 UNTS 221, Art. 1; Council of Europe, European Social Charter, Oct. 18, 1961, 529 UNTS 89, preamble; African Commission on Human and Peoples' Rights, African Charter of Human and Peoples' Rights, June 27, 1981, 1520 UNTS 217, Art. 1; Council of the League of Arab States, Arab Charter of Human Rights, Sept. 15, 1994, Res. 5437, 102nd Sess., Art. 2.

[72] Organization of American States (1969), note 71; Organization of American States, American Declaration of the Rights and Duties of Man, May 2, 1948, OEA/Ser. LN/I.4Rev. The USA is not a party to the Convention but is nevertheless bound by the Declaration. For a discussion how of the USA came to be bound by the Declaration, see C. M. Cerna, "Reflections on the Normative Status of the American Declaration of the Rights and Duties of Man" (2008–2009) 30 *University of Pennsylvania Journal of International Law* 1211.

[73] Baez, note 56.

[74] Inter-American Commission on Human Rights (2002) Report No. 75/02, Case 11.140, Mary and Carrie Dann.

[75] International Labour Organization, Indigenous and Tribal Peoples Convention, June 27, 1989, Art. 7.

[76] Ibid., Art. 14, cl. 1–Art. 16, cl. 1.

[77] At the time of writing, 148 countries endorsed the UNDRIP, and apparently nine countries abstained from voting on the Declaration (UNDRIP, note 54).

[78] US Department of State, "Announcement of U.S. Support for the United Nations Declaration on the Rights of Indigenous Peoples," Jan. 12, 2011, https://2009-2017.state.gov/s/srgia/154553.htm.

[79] UNDRIP, note 54.

[80] Ibid., Art. 8, cl. 1.

[81] Ibid., Art. 10.

[82] Ibid., Art. 26, cl. 1, 3.

[83] Ibid., Art. 28, cl. 1.

well as many other rights contained within the UNDRIP, are directly implicated by the Dakota Access controversy. As discussed previously, the controversy implicates questions related to the enforcement of a treaty between the federal government and a tribe, the Tribe's cultural resources, and the ability of the Tribe to have access to processes to assert its claims related to resources and treaties. As to the first point, although the pipeline is not located within the reservation of a Tribe, it is located on land that was historically granted to the Tribes through a treaty between the United States and the Tribes. As to cultural resources, the water protectors sought to protect the water not only because it is necessary to support life, but also because of the important spiritual role it plays in the community. Additionally, construction of the pipeline purportedly destroyed locations of cultural significance. And, finally, as demonstrated by the Tribes' legal claims, the Tribes asserted that the federal government, in its consultation with the Tribe, failed to obtain FPIC for the pipeline.

Further, the FPIC requirement of UNDRIP has become an important tool for enforcing Indigenous rights as Indigenous communities must be included early in any discussions potentially affecting Indigenous peoples.[84] In terms of Indigenous communities, FPIC means that such communities have the right to participate in decisions based on both adequate notice of opportunities to participate and adequate information to allow full participation from Indigenous parties.[85] "[C]oercion, intimidation or manipulation" should also be absent from that participation, and "'consent' should be intended as a process of which consultation and participation represent central pillars."[86] Indigenous peoples should be consulted in the early stages of the project when it is still possible to influence the development of the project. Relatedly, Indigenous decision-making processes should be respected. In this regard, the consultation process should be carried out in ways that are consistent with the norms of the Indigenous community.[87]

Notably, the FPIC requirement of the UNDRIP also relates to the social inclusion aspect of the social pillar of sustainability, as social inclusion requires adequate participation. As discussed above, the Standing Rock Sioux Tribe's challenge to the Dakota Access Pipeline includes arguments suggesting that the Tribe did not give its FPIC to construction of the pipeline, as the approval process was not carried out in a manner consistent with the tribal community's norms. The social pillar of sustainable development is generally interpreted to recognize the human rights obligations of states, which presumably includes obligations toward Indigenous communities under ILO 169 and UNDRIP. The SDGs, however, do not explicitly refer to Indigenous sovereignty and self-determination. As the Dakota Access examples demonstrates, the SDGs must be interpreted through a human rights lens, including from an Indigenous rights perspective, in order to avoid culturally blind or biased implementation.[88]

---

[84] "Both UNDRIP and ILO 169 explicitly recognize that indigenous peoples have a right to 'free, prior and informed consent' (FPIC) regarding activities that directly or indirectly affect them. FPIC is crucial to the protection of indigenous peoples' right to self-determination" (Baez, note 56, p. 842).

[85] M. Berelli, "Free, Prior, and Informed Consent in the Aftermath of the UN Declaration on the Rights of Indigenous Peoples: Developments and Challenges Ahead" (2012) 16 *International Journal of Human Rights* 1 at 2 (citing UN Economic and Social Council, *Report of the International Workshop on Methodologies regarding Free, Prior and Informed Consent and Indigenous Peoples*, Jan. 17–19, 2005 UN Doc. E/C.19/2005/3, para. 45).

[86] Ibid.

[87] See for example S. Baker, "Emerging Challenges in the Global Energy Transition: A View from the Frontlines," in R. Salter, C. G. Gonzalez, and E. Kronk Warner (eds.), *Energy Justice: US and International Perspectives* (forthcoming).

[88] UN Sustainable Development Knowledge Platform, "Indigenous Peoples," https://sustainabledevelopment.un .org/majorgroups/indigenouspeoples.

23.4 INDIGENOUS RIGHTS UNDER US LAW

Having examined some of the commonalities among Indigenous communities, such as Indigenous rights under international law and Indigenous peoples' strong connection to the environment and land, the chapter now considers how environmental justice claims involving Indigenous communities within the United States might differ from the claims of other communities. Within the United States, Indigenous communities recognized by the federal government are said to be sovereign. While other environmental justice communities typically come together as informal groups whose legal rights flow from environmental laws, the legal rights of Indigenous communities, with sovereign status, flow from their sovereignty and their related historical management of the land and resources.[89] In the United States, tribes exist as entities separate from state and federal governments.[90] American Indian tribes are extra-constitutional, meaning that tribes exist apart from the US Constitution as tribal governments existed prior to the formation of the United States and neither the US Constitution nor the federal government created such governments.[91] In the early nineteenth century, the US Supreme Court affirmed the separateness of tribes.[92] Although the federal government's perception of tribal sovereignty has ebbed and flowed significantly, today, a government-to-government relationship exists between federally recognized tribes and the federal government.[93]

Accordingly, environmental justice claims affecting tribes within the United States differ from claims arising elsewhere given the inherent sovereignty still possessed by tribes. The additional consideration of tribal sovereignty is crucial to any discussion of such environmental justice claims. Specifically, an environmental injustice occurs if courts fail to recognize the sovereignty of tribes, as tribes cannot meaningfully participate in the legal process absent such recognition. Therefore, courts must consider tribes' sovereignty when evaluating claims in order to ensure an environmentally just result.

23.4.1 *Federal Trust Relationship with Native Nations*

Beyond the consideration of tribal sovereignty, courts must also take into account special obligations owed by the United States to the tribes in evaluating environmental justice claims. For example, Indigenous communities within the United States have a unique trust relationship with the federal

---

[89] Newton et al., note 61.

[90] Ibid.

[91] A. E. Tweedy, "Connecting the Dots between the Constitution, the Marshall Trilogy, and *United States v. Lara*: Notes toward a Blueprint for the Next Legislative Restoration of Tribal Sovereignty" (2009) 42 *University of Michigan Journal of Law Reform* 651 at 656 (citing G. Valencia-Weber, "The Supreme Court's Indian Law Decisions: Deviations from Constitutional Principles and the Crafting of Judicial Smallpox Blankets" (2003) 5 *University of Pennsylvania Journal of Constitutional Law* 405 at 417). Although the federal government certainly has the ability to impact tribes as the US Congress possesses plenary authority over tribes, tribes and their governments exist because of their inherent tribal sovereignty and not because of a federal delegation of authority. Further, citizens of tribes are also citizens of the United States, as Indians were granted citizenship within the United States in 1924. For a discussion of the complicated relationship between tribal sovereignty and federal plenary power, see Newton et al., note 61.

[92] *The Cherokee Nation* v. *State of Ga.*, 30 US 1, p. 17 (1831).

[93] D. Cordalis and D. B. Suagee, "The Effects of Climate Change on American Indian and Alaska Native Tribes" (2008) 22 *Natural Resources and Environment* 45 (citing Exec. Order No. 13,175, 2, 65 Fed. Reg. 67, p. 249 (Nov. 6, 2000)); see also 25 USC § 3601(1) (2012) ("there is a government-to-government relationship between the United States and each Indian tribe").

government.[94] The trust relationship between the tribes and the federal government emerged from the many cessions of both land and external sovereignty.[95] The US government owes federally recognized tribes fiduciary obligations related to the management of tribal trust lands and resources.[96]

The federal trust responsibility doctrine has been the subject of many court decisions related to Indian country over the past two centuries. In the twentieth century, the court used the federal trust responsibility doctrine to define the scope of review of congressional legislation related to Indian country. Specifically, "because of the trust responsibility, it is well settled that statutes affecting Indians 'are to be construed liberally in favor of the Indians, with ambiguous provisions interpreted to their benefit.'"[97] Any Indian environmental justice claim should be considered under the federal trust responsibility doctrine.[98] Failure to include consideration of this responsibility again results in tribes being deprived of meaningful participation in the consideration of claims. For example, if the federal government has undertaken a mandatory duty to engage in government-to-government consultation with tribes under the NHPA, then the failure to engage in that type of consultation leading up to the Dakota Access controversy could be seen as a breach of the federal government's trust responsibility, in addition to breach of the international law obligations discussed above.

In conclusion, environmental justice requires consideration of the unique aspects of Indigenous communities to ensure adequate access to substantive and procedural justice. Environmental justice claims arising in Indigenous communities often raise issues that differ from claims arising in other environmental justice communities, including tribal sovereignty and federal trust responsibility.

23.5 CONCLUSION

Any comprehensive discussion of justice for Indigenous communities facing the disproportionate effects of environmental pollution must necessarily include environmental justice. In turn, it is not at all uncommon, as demonstrated by the Dakota Access case study, for claims involving environmental justice to also touch on elements protected by the social pillar of sustainable development – human rights and the basic needs of people. This chapter contends that both environmental justice and the social pillar of sustainable development (including the SDGs) must be interpreted through an Indigenous rights lens. Accordingly, decision-making bodies evaluating environmental conflicts in Indian territories must consider traditional environmental

---

[94] R. P. Chambers, "Compatibility of the Federal Trust Responsibility with Self-Determination of Indian Tribes: Reflections on Development of the Federal Trust Responsibility in the Twenty-First Century" (2005) *Rocky Mountain Law Institute* 13A-2 (relating to the federal trust responsibility doctrine is the concept that the federal government is morally obligated to act in the best interests of Native nations given the historical trauma heaped upon these governments by the federal government). However, a complete discussion of potential moral responsibility of the federal government to Native nations is beyond the scope of this chapter.

[95] Wood and Welcker, note 70, pp. 387–388.

[96] Cordalis and Suagee, note 93; Chambers, note 94, 13A-9.

[97] Chambers, note 94, 13A-13.

[98] This argument, that the federal government owes certain duties and obligations to Native nations under the federal trust responsibility doctrine, may be seen as contrary to the previous assertion that decision makers must also take into consideration tribal sovereignty when evaluating environmental justice claims arising in Indian country. However, both tribal sovereignty and the federal trust responsibility do exist within the current legal scheme applicable to modern-day Indian country. Resolution of the apparent tension between these two legal concepts is beyond the scope of this chapter.

justice concerns as well as issues unique to Indigenous communities – such as applicable international law, Indigenous peoples' connection to land and the environment, and, in the United States, tribal sovereignty and the federal trust responsibility. It is only through the robust evaluation of these many-layered factors that Indigenous communities facing such challenges can truly obtain justice.

24

Energy Poverty, Justice, and Women

Lakshman Guruswamy

24.1 INTRODUCTION

The phenomenon of energy poverty, found among the poorest people in the world, profoundly and disproportionately affects women. Principles of law and justice call on governments and civil society to address this phenomenon. This chapter first discusses the importance of energy to development; it then discusses specific dimensions of energy poverty and its inordinate impacts on women; the chapter then explores the phenomenon of energy poverty as it applies to the use of traditional biofuels for cooking through three case studies spanning the globe. The next section examines the predicament of women through the lens of justice as articulated by John Rawls. This is followed by an examination of the implementation of the Sustainable Development Goals (SDGs), and relevant international legal provisions as they relate to the predicament of women. It concludes by asserting that the SDGs and international law have not been satisfactorily implemented, and this failure points to the importance of employing a Rawlsian sense of justice in the implementation of international law and the SDGs.

24.2 THE IMPORTANCE OF ENERGY

The presence and impact of energy in the human and social world is essentially ubiquitous.[1,2] Energy is a fundamental human need and the driving determinant of human progress.[3] Humans must constantly engage in energy conversions – processes that transform one form of energy into another more useful form. Moreover, the inability to access energy can both cause and perpetuate poverty.

A rich stream of writers and thinkers considered below, spanning the life sciences, mathematics, sociology, anthropology, engineering, and philosophy have explained the central role played by energy in the development of society. They have illustrated how societies have used energy and have elucidated the interface between the physical or natural phenomena of exosmotic energy, and how technology was used to convert natural resources to energy, as well as the impact of energy on human social systems.

---

[1] This section is based on L. Guruswamy (ed.), *International Energy and Poverty: Emerging Contours* (Abingdon, UK: Routledge, 2016).

[2] E. A. Rosa, G. E. Machlis, and K. M. Keating, "Energy and Society" (1988) 14 *Annual Review of Sociology* 149.

[3] L. A. White, *The Evolution of Culture: The Development of Civilization to the Fall of Rome* (New York: McGraw-Hill, 1959), pp. 33–57.

Herbert Spencer (1820–1903) initially articulated that a society's ability to harness energy defines what it can produce, and that the ability to control and use energy is the basis of both social progress and disparities among societies. "Human progress," he explained, "is measured by the degree to which simple acquisition is replaced by production – achieved first by manual power, then by animal power, and finally by machine power."[4] Even though he did not pursue the fuller implications of using resources such as fossil fuels as energy, his thesis that energy was a central component of social organization set the stage for a fuller understanding of the role of energy in society.[5]

In the 1950s, the anthropologist Leslie White refined Spencer's ideas by conceptualizing cultural evolution as movement along a continuum, where progress is defined in terms of a linear path from "poor" to "advanced" energy use. White posited that societies' ability to exploit new, better forms of energy drives development and that access to energy dictates the progress of peoples: "Culture evolves as the amount of energy harnessed per capita per year is increased, or as the efficiency of the instrumental means, or the efficiency of conversions which put the energy to work, is improved."[6] He concluded there was little cultural growth until the nineteenth century and the discovery of fossil fuels, and he argued that the invention of fuel-powered engines inaugurated a new era in culture history,[7] tremendously increasing the amount of energy under human control and at his disposal for culture-building.[8] White further believed that energy is inextricably linked with development based on who has access to energy and control over its production.[9]

The sociologist Fred Cottrell further developed and built upon the theories of Spencer and White by considering energy as a limiting factor. According to him, the ability (or inability) to harness energy equates to human capacity for growth.[10] But, unlike White, he recognized that the natural world places a limit, articulated in the second law of thermodynamics, on the amount of energy that can ultimately be harnessed for human use.[11]

More recently, the economists Nicholas Georgescu-Roegen[12] and Herman Daly,[13] advanced this theme and challenged economic orthodoxy by emphasizing that the second law of thermodynamics dictates limits to economic growth. The physicist Amory Lovins has suggested that this necessitates shifting to a "soft energy path" emphasizing energy efficiency and renewable energy resources.[14] Moreover, modern empirical studies have demonstrated that the relationship between energy consumption and well-being is not, as White postulated, entirely linear. Rather, "while a threshold level of high energy consumption is probably necessary for a society to achieve industrialization and modernity, once achieved, there is wide latitude in the amount of energy needed to sustain a high standard of living."[15]

---

[4] H. Spencer, *The Principles of Sociology* (New York: Appleton, 1898), p. 356.

[5] A. McKinnon, "Energy and Society: Herbert Spencer's Energetic Sociology of Social Evolution and Beyond" (2010) 10 *Journal of Classical Sociology* at 439.

[6] White, note 3.

[7] Ibid., pp. 344–345.

[8] Ibid.

[9] Ibid.

[10] F. Cottrell, *Energy and Society (Revised): The Relation between Energy, Social Change, and Economic Development* (Bloomington: AuthorHouse, 2009), p. 7.

[11] Rosa et al., note 2.

[12] N. Georgescu-Roegen, *The Entropy Law and the Economic Process* (Bloomington: iUniverse, 1999).

[13] H. E. Daly, *Beyond Growth: The Economics of Sustainable Development* (Boston: Beacon Press, 1997).

[14] Rosa et al., note 2, pp. 153–154, citing A. B. Lovins, *Soft Energy Paths: Toward a Durable Peace* (London: Penguin, 1977).

[15] Rosa et al., note 2, p. 159.

Applying these insights within a modern milieu reveals that access to energy is essential to development and that the inability to access energy can both cause and perpetuate poverty. This occurs where those without access to modern forms of energy are forced to rely on the inefficient conversion of biomass and human muscle power to complete the daily tasks necessary for their well-being.

24.3 ENERGY POVERTY AND ITS INORDINATE IMPACTS ON WOMEN

A general lack of access to energy plays an enormous role in both creating and promulgating the condition of the least developed countries (LDCs), perpetuating the phenomenon of energy poverty.[16] Globally, around 1 billion people (the "Other Third" or "Energy Poor") have little or no access to beneficial energy to meet their basic needs.[17] More than 95 percent of the energy poor (EP) live either in sub-Saharan Africa or developing Asia, predominantly 84 percent in rural areas. The burdens arising from absence of energy fall predominantly on women. This section explores four major areas in which energy poverty impacts the EP, generally, and the specific impacts on women: cooking, lighting, drinking water, and sanitation.

24.3.1 *Cooking*

24.3.1.1 Effects of Cooking with Biomass on the EP, Generally

A large swath of humanity, specifically 715 million people in the LDCs, is caught in a time warp, relying on biomass-generated fire as their principal source of energy.[18] These fires are made by burning animal dung, waste, crop residues, rotted wood, other forms of harmful biomass, or raw coal. The lack of access to modern fuels and overwhelming reliance on biomass for cooking is greatly inefficient and presents adverse consequences on human health.

The EP who rely on biomass for their fuel for cooking generally cook over an open fire or with some other form of a traditional stove. This process is exceedingly inefficient, as only about 18 percent of the energy from the fire transfers to the pot,[19] and indoor air pollution can contain a variety of dangerous pollutants, such as carbon monoxide, nitrous oxides, sulfur oxides, formaldehyde, carcinogens (such as benzene), and small particulate matter.[20] According to the World Health Organization, exposure to high concentrations of indoor air pollution presents one of the most important threats to public health worldwide, resulting in diseases such as pneumonia, chronic pulmonary disease, lung cancer, asthma, and acute respiratory infections.[21]

24.3.1.2 Effects of Cooking with Biomass on Women among the EP

Energy poverty as it relates to energy access for cooking disproportionately affects women due to health risk exposure and time spent collecting fuel and cooking. Using biomass for cooking

---

[16] This section draws from L. Guruswamy, "Energy Poverty" (2011) 36 *Annual Review of Environment and Resources* 139.
[17] IEA, "World Energy Outlook 2019", IEA, Paris, Nov. 2019, www.iea.org/reports/world-energy-outlook-2019.
[18] G. Legros, I. Havet, N. Bruce, and S. Bonjour, "The Energy Access Situation in Developing Countries: A Review Focusing on Least Developed Countries and Sub Saharan Africa," United Nations Development Programme, World Health Organization, Nov. 2009.
[19] H. Warwick and A. Doig, *Smoke – The Killer in the Kitchen* (Warwickshire: Practical Action, 2004).
[20] World Health Organization, *Fuel for Life: Household Energy and Health* (2006), p. 10.
[21] World Health Organization, "Indoor Air Pollution Takes Heavy Toll on Health," Apr. 30, 2007, www.who.int/mediacentre/news/notes/2007/np20/en/.

results in 3.5 million premature deaths per year (mortality) and the illness of many millions more (morbidity).[22] This mortality and morbidity primarily affects women and children. Women are disproportionately affected by the use of biomass for cooking because they are traditionally responsible for cooking and childcare in the home, and they spend more time inhaling the polluted air that is trapped indoors. Thus, women and children have the highest exposure to indoor air pollution and suffer more than anyone from these negative health effects.[23] Specifically, women are about twice as likely to be afflicted with chronic pulmonary disease than men in homes using solid fuels.[24] In Africa, where around 730 million people rely on biomass for cooking, women and girls are mainly responsible for procuring and using cooking fuels.[25]

In conflict zones, the search for cooking fuels exposes women and girls to physical and sexual violence.[26] For example, in the refugee camps of Darfur, the work of women venturing to collect fuel presented increased risks of being raped.[27] This is equally the case in other refugee camps, such as those in Somalia.[28]

Additionally, lack of access to cooking fuel forces women and children to spend many hours gathering fuel or to spend significant household income purchasing fuel. Women provide 91 percent of households' total efforts in collecting fuel and water in the LDCs, and women have an average working day of eleven to fourteen hours compared to ten hours on average for men.[29] A reduction in time spent collecting fuel and cooking enables women to spend more time with their children, tend to other responsibilities, enhance existing economic opportunities; pursue income-generating, educational, and leisure activities; as well as rest – all of which contribute to poverty alleviation.

24.3.2 *Lighting*

24.3.2.1 Lighting-Related Effects on the EP, Generally

The EP also lack access to modern energy solutions for lighting. Lighting is essential to human progress, and, without it, humans would be comparatively inactive for about half of their lifetimes.[30] This lack of access to modern energy solutions for lighting hinders productivity, causes health and physical hazards, and tremendous financial waste.

As many of the LDCs have extremely hot climates, productivity, such as agricultural productivity, is hindered during the daytime, thus rendering it problematic that the absence of artificial

[22] Bioenergy Insight, "IEA: Biomass Fuels Linked to 3.5 Million Deaths Annually," July 18, 2016, www .bioenergy-news.com/news/iea-biomass-fuels-linked-to-3-5-million-deaths-annually/.

[23] Global Alliance for Clean Cookstoves, "Clean Cookstoves Can Save Lives and Empower Women," www .cleancookingalliance.org/resources/266.html.

[24] Legros et al., note 18.

[25] S. A. Ngum, African Development Bank Group, "Empowering Women and Girls in the Quest for Universal Energy Access for All," Apr. 25, 2016, https://blogs.afdb.org/fr/investing-in-gender-equality-for-africas-transform ation/post/empowering-women-and-girls-in-the-quest-for-universal-energy-access-for-all-15625.

[26] Ibid.

[27] Berkeley Lab, "Cookstoves: Our Story," http://cookstoves.lbl.gov.

[28] L. Shannon, "The Rape of Somalia's Women Is Being Ignored," Oct. 11, 2011, www.theguardian.com/ commentisfree/2011/oct/11/rape-somalia-women-famine.

[29] Clean Cooking Alliance, "Women and Gender," http://cleancookstoves.org/impact-areas/women-gender/ index.html.

[30] M. Luckiesh, *Artificial Light: Its Influence upon Civilization* (New York: Century Co., 1920).

light severely impedes working at night. The absence of lighting also creates physical insecurity while venturing out in the darkness and almost entirely prevents commercial activity after dark.

Almost 500 million of the EP rely on kerosene for illumination,[31] which has several associated risks. The hazards of kerosene, such as fires, explosions, and poisonings resulting from children ingesting it, are extensively documented.[32] There is evidence implicating kerosene in ailments including the impairment of lung function, asthma, and cancer.[33] The use of kerosene and candles is also costly. Households often spend 10 to 25 percent of their income on kerosene.[34] Over US$36 billion is spent on kerosene annually, US$10 billion of which is spent in sub-Saharan Africa.[35]

24.3.2.2 Lighting-Related Effects on Women among the EP

The lack of lighting has particularly adverse impacts on women and children. The lack of lighting at home leads to an inability to undertake homework or studies.[36] This affects the ability of women to break out of their unpaid domestic labor as wives or women in the home by educating themselves and obtaining paid jobs or becoming entrepreneurs.[37] The absence of street lighting leads to molestation and rape of women and prevents them from venturing outside their homes.[38] Moreover, the expense of paying for kerosene might prevent them from purchasing food or other household necessities.[39] Finally, due to the disproportionate time spent indoors by women, women are often more prone to accidents caused by kerosene lamps.[40]

24.3.3 *Drinking Water and Sanitation*

24.3.3.1 The Effects of Energy Poverty on Drinking Water and Sanitation Access, Generally

Lack of access to clean drinking water and sanitation are two interconnected, deadly issues facing the EP. Worldwide, approximately one in eight people – 884 million in total – lack access to safe water supplies.[41] In preventing diseases such as diarrhea, tuberculosis, cholera, and other waterborne diseases, basic sanitation is just as important as fresh drinking water.[42] There are 2.5 billion people who lack access to improved sanitation, including 1.2 billion who have no facilities at all.[43] As a

---

[31] N. Lam, K. Smith, A. Gautier, and M. Bates, "Kerosene: A Review of Household Uses and Their Hazards in Low- and Middle-Income Countries" (2012) 15 *Journal of Toxicology and Environmental Health* 396.

[32] Ibid., p. 423.

[33] Ibid., pp. 399–401, 412–423.

[34] "Lighting the Way," Aug. 30, 2012, www.economist.com/technology-quarterly/2012/08/30/lighting-the-way.

[35] Ibid.

[36] This subsection relies on the author's "Introduction to Model Laws on Lighting" (2016) 44 *Denver Journal of International Law and Policy* 324.

[37] Ibid., p. 325.

[38] Ibid.

[39] Ibid.

[40] Ibid.

[41] World Health Organization and UNICEF, "Progress on Drinking Water and Sanitation: Special Focus on Sanitation," 2008.

[42] Office of the High Commissioner for Human Rights, "Special Rapporteur on the Human Right to Safe Drinking Water and Sanitation," 2015, http://ohchr.org/EN/Issues/WaterAndSanitation/SRWater/Pages/SRWaterIndex.aspx.

[43] Ibid.

result, 3.4 million people die from water-related disease each year.[44] As with many other issues faced by the EP, children are intensely affected by lack of access to clean drinking water and sanitation facilities. Nearly one in five child deaths – about 1.5 million each year – is due to diarrhea, which is often caused by unclean drinking water and inadequate sanitation facilities.[45] Other consequences of the lack of clean drinking water and basic sanitation include crop failure in irrigated fields, livestock death, and environmental damage.[46] Energy is necessary to alleviate these problems of collecting, transporting, and distributing clean water, powering water treatment facilities, facilitating in-home water treatment (through boiling, for example), and constructing and powering sanitation facilities.[47]

24.3.3.2 The Effects of Unsafe Drinking Water and Sanitation on Women among the EP

In most developing societies, women have primary responsibility for management of household water supply, sanitation, and health. Accordingly, they disproportionately experience the effects of insufficient safe drinking water, and vis-à-vis the expenditure of significant time collecting water, women disproportionately experience the health, safety, educational, and professional effects of lack of access to basic sanitation.

Women and children among the EP have to walk many miles in the LDCs, including the poorest parts of sub-Saharan Africa and semi-desert regions of Asia, to obtain water. Research in sub-Saharan Africa suggests that women and girls in low-income countries spend forty billion hours a year collecting water – the equivalent of a year's worth of labor by the entire workforce in France.[48] The same study found that women and girls spend up to six hours every day collecting water in sub-Saharan Africa.[49]

Most women without access to basic sanitation, such as a latrine, must wait for nightfall and an empty field to defecate in private, a practice which has serious side effects for many women. Waiting so long to defecate leads to increased chances for urinary tract infections, chronic constipation, and psychological stress.[50] Many women going out alone at night are also at an increased risk of physical and sexual assault.[51] The symptoms of menstruation, pregnancy, and the postnatal period also become problematic if there are no adequate facilities to properly deal with them. Many girls are forced to leave school once they reach puberty and menstruate simply because there are no facilities or supplies accessible to them, and those who choose to stay often miss class during their menstrual cycle, making it harder for them to succeed in school.[52] Furthermore, adult female professionals without access to nearby facilities must choose between the indignity and health risks of caring for themselves in the open or leaving work.[53]

---

[44] A. Prüss-Üstün, R. Bos, F. Gore, and J. Bartram, "Safer Water, Better Health: Costs, Benefits and Sustainability of Interventions to Protect and Promote Health," World Health Organization, 2008, p. 12, table 1.

[45] Ibid.

[46] Ibid.

[47] International Energy Agency, "Water–Energy Nexus," www.iea.org/weo/water/#.

[48] United Nations, "Gender and Water," Oct. 23, 2014, http://un.org/waterforlifedecade/gender.shtml.

[49] Ibid.

[50] Ibid.

[51] UN Water, Interagency Task Force on Gender and Water (GWTF), "Gender, Water and Sanitation: A Policy Brief," June 2006, p. 5.

[52] Ibid.

[53] Ibid.

24.4 CASE STUDIES

The following case studies illustrate issues connected to the use of biofuels, such as wood, for cooking among the EP in India, Nicaragua, and Ghana. Spanning three continents and countries with differing levels of development, the case studies illustrate commonalities in the challenges faced by affected women. The studies additionally discuss potential solutions to these challenges, including the implementation of affordable sustainable energy technologies (ASETs).

The current era of globalization is driven by modern innovation and advanced technologies that occur in industrialized countries. These technologies are not necessarily affordable, appropriate, or accessible for the EP. However, traditional uses of energy, and the technologies surrounding them, are frequently harmful, inefficient, and unproductive. ASETs seek to bridge the gap between the capital-intensive advanced technologies of the developed world and the traditional subsistence technologies of the EP. The purpose of ASETs is to free the EP from the oppressive impacts of unhealthy and unreliable energy access and to facilitate sustainable development in the LDCs. The case studies discuss ASETs as one avenue to alleviate the burdens associated with the use of biofuels for cooking.

24.4.1 *India*

A case study carried out by Jyoti Parikh for Integrated Research and Action for Development in the Himalayan State of Himachal Pradesh in India explores the interlinkages of gender, energy use, health, and hardships with regard to the use of traditional biofuels for cooking. The study, based on a survey with questionnaires covering 4,296 individuals in 729 households where biomass fuels meet 70 percent of household fuel needs, examined fuel consumption, fuelwood collection, and health problems related to the use of biofuels.[54]

The study highlights the tremendous time and effort spent, distances traveled, and difficulties encountered in the collection of wood. The reported average distance to collect fuelwood is about 2 kilometers, which "means that women in [Himachal Pradesh] travel at 15 trips per household, a 30 kilometer distance per month in a mountainous, climatically cruel high altitude environment to gather the required quantity of fuel wood."[55] As for time, the study found that the average amount for a typical household is 40.8 hours per month, which amounts to households in Himachal Pradesh "losing 4–7 work days in a month" to collect wood.[56] Finally, the difficulties reported regarding the collection of wood were most prominently time taken, followed by the physical stress from carrying the heavy load, followed by searching and gathering.[57]

The health problems reported from collecting wood included neck ache, headache, backache, bruises, wild animal and snake encounters, burning eyes, and coughing.[58] The results suggested that "hardships and health impacts of fuel wood collection, transportation, and processing may be as serious – if not more serious – than the health impacts of smoke for the women in Himachal Pradesh."[59] Regarding the burning of fuelwood, the study concluded that girls below the age of

---

[54] J. Parikh, "Hardships and Health Impacts on Women due to Traditional Cooking Fuels: A Case Study of Himachal Pradesh, India" (2011) 39 *Energy Policy* 7587.

[55] Ibid., p. 7590.

[56] Ibid., pp. 7590–7591.

[57] Ibid., p. 7591.

[58] Ibid., p. 7592.

[59] Ibid.

5 and females in the 30–60 age group (who are usually the chief cooks in the family) are at higher risks of smoke-related disease than males in the same age groups.[60]

The case study concludes by stating that "[a] paradigm shift in thinking of policy makers is needed along with the knowledge of dissemination and awareness generation[.]"[61] Among the specific suggestions are: enabling access to transportation solutions such as wheelbarrows, better pathways, and small-motorized transport to "reduce the efforts needed for searching and gathering [of fuel]"; and, on the cooking side, improved stoves, solar cookers, biogas, and more LPG and kerosene.[62] These suggestions constitute ASETs, as they are technologies available and appropriate to the affected population and endeavor specifically to address the issues of transportation and indoor pollution connected to the use of biofuels for cooking. The case study concludes: "Women, who provide 30% of [India's] national energy, need to be supported through management, investment, and technology so as to manage their household cooking systems in a sustainable manner and with minimum hardship."[63]

24.4.2 *Ghana*

A second case study, conducted by Richard Arthur, Martina Francisca Baidoo, and Edward Antwi explores several aspects of biogas plants, which generate biogas from organic materials under anaerobic conditions, as a potential sustainable energy source in Ghana.[64] The economy of Ghana has been traditionally predominantly agricultural, though the country now has thriving gold and timber industries; thus, while Ghana overall has a "medium" United Nations Human Development Index, much of its rural population faces a quality of life similar to that of the LDCs, particularly where energy is concerned.[65] Of particular interest to this chapter, the case study examines women's empowerment and workload reduction as potential benefits to the implementation of biogas plants.

As with many of the EP, "men and women have different demands on energy due to the existing socio-cultural and traditional roles"; specifically, Ghanaian women mostly do the cooking, are heavily involved in fuelwood collection, and expend significant time in fuelwood collection.[66] It is estimated that a minimum of two to three mornings a week are spent by rural Ghanaian women collecting fuelwood. The authors state that time saved while not fetching firewood could be used for educational or other productive activities, which "consequently will improve the standard of living, provide additional income, and enhance the nutritional and health status of the household."[67] This time cost is significant given that Ghanaian male literacy is 20 to 30 percent higher than that of females.[68] The authors thus conclude that the installation of biogas plants will allow female children to attend school who have formerly been too busy looking for firewood, thus endeavoring to bridge the literacy gap between males and females. The authors, however, envisage several challenges to the implementation of biogas plants,

---

[60] Ibid.

[61] Ibid., p. 7593.

[62] Ibid.

[63] Ibid.

[64] R. Arthur, M. F. Baidoo, and E. Antwi, "Biogas as a Potential Renewable Energy Source: A Ghanaian Case Study" (2011) 36 *Renewable Energy* 1510.

[65] Ibid., pp. 1510–1511.

[66] Ibid., pp. 1515.

[67] Ibid.

[68] Ibid.

namely affordability, sociocultural barriers, poor monitoring, and issues with maintenance.[69] The authors recommend government infrastructure, soft loans, and subsidies as potential ways to overcome these barriers.[70]

24.4.3 *Nicaragua*

A third case study describes an ASET in action. Carried out in Nicaragua by Asociación Fénix Programme for Improved Stoves, the case study describes a program that installed improved biomass stoves (IBS) as substitutions for traditional cookstoves. Nicaragua has the lowest electrification rate in Central America (73.7 percent),[71] and 62 percent of the country's population uses firewood or charcoal to cook.[72] In rural areas, over 95 percent of poor households – approximately 3.2 million people – do not have access to efficient cooking technologies and utilize open fires, posing a massive public health problem.[73] This case study saw positive impacts on the 258 participant families' health and women's empowerment with regard to economic empowerment, decision-making, and the experiencing of nontraditional gender roles.

Following the implementation of the IBS, families, and "especially women, children, and older adults, began to report better eyesight and health in general."[74] For example, data collected in late 2014 for the project Municipality of Teustepe reflected that 96 percent of the seventy-five families noted improvements in health, particularly in respiratory health and eyesight.[75]

The IBS program additionally made a reported impact on women's empowerment vis-à-vis economic empowerment, the expression of nontraditional roles around food preparation, and decision-making power. Among the families studied, a group of women studied as bakers, thus utilizing their IBSs as work tools to prepare food products to sell. The families that used their IBS to sell corn tortillas and food reported a nearly 50 percent savings in purchasing firewood.[76] In one in five of the studied homes, men – including husbands, brothers, or sons – cooked and/or helped with cleaning and maintaining the IBS. Finally, the IBS program ensured that the women were the ones who made the ultimate decision regarding which stove they wished to acquire, providing the women with decision-making power over household expenditure – a role traditionally assigned to men in the studied population.

This case study highlights specific benefits of the implementation of this ASET and concludes by sharing some lessons learned by the experiment. Among these, of note, the organization states that "the factors that drive families' attachment to the rudimentary stoves should be considered, including their habits, customs, and livelihoods."[77] Specifically, the studied families tended to accept the traditional cook stoves because they play a role in other domestic and productive functions, for example drying cheeses, meats, and grains, and repelling flies.[78] This

---

[69] Ibid.
[70] Ibid.
[71] Asociación Fénix Programme for Improved Stoves, "Healthy Stoves in Rural and Urban Homes and Family Businesses in Nicaragua," ENERGIA and IUCN, 2015, p. 8.
[72] Ibid., p. 7
[73] Ibid., p. 9
[74] Ibid., p. 22.
[75] Ibid., p. 20.
[76] Ibid., p. 25.
[77] Ibid., pp. 25–26.
[78] Ibid.

lesson – as well as all discussed above – highlights the fact that ASET implementation must be approached holistically, considering all factors relevant to the affected population.

24.5 JUSTICE AND WOMEN

Justice requires that the predicament of women be addressed through law in addition to action through nongovernmental and intergovernmental organizations, such as that discussed in Section 24.3.[79] Law is inextricably related to the concept of justice. Defining the concept of justice requires moral reasoning. That is to say, in a society without a differentiation between morality and immorality, there is no such thing as a just or unjust decision. This is vitally important in understanding the very real and apparent differences in which legal outcomes are considered just among varying jurisprudential theories. Thus, a consideration of justice in a global sense must also consider theories of morality. The importance of doing what is fair and right based on principles of justice is established by a variety of global jurisprudential lineages emanating from Western, Islamic, Buddhist, and Confucian traditions.[80]

In discussing law and justice, it is unfortunate that Western theorizing on global justice is found within political and moral philosophy and not what Steven Ratner calls the "thin justice" of international law or jurisprudence.[81] Moral philosophy and justice have been treated as falling outside the compass of law and generally ignored.[82] Contemporary international law needs to fill in the lacunae between law and justice. This chapter, mindful of the enormity of this task, does not presume to take more than an incremental step toward this objective. It will do so by reviewing salient concepts of justice articulated by John Rawls and consider how Rawls may offer the philosophical foundation of laws addressing the plight of EP women.

John Rawls's theory of justice is predicated on what society "ought" to be. He makes the normative case for a society based on justice as fairness; a necessary corollary of his theory is that laws must reflect justice, and they cannot just express the will of the sovereign or lawmaker.

In "The Law of Peoples,"[83] John Rawls lays the foundations for his concept of international justice based on a "realistic utopia" grounded in sociopolitical, institutional, and psychological reality.[84] Rawls expands on his "original position," a thought experiment expounded in "A Theory of Justice,"[85] and developed in numerous other works. In "A Theory of Justice," Rawls envisioned a collection of negotiators from liberal democratic societies assembled behind a veil of ignorance, shorn of any knowledge that might be the basis of self-interested bias – such as knowledge of their gender, wealth, race, ethnicity, abilities, and general social circumstances. Rawls explains that the purpose of such a negotiation was to arrive at legitimate principles of justice under fair conditions – hence "justice as fairness."[86]

In "The Law of Peoples," Rawls addresses justice in the international context. In doing so, he extends his theories from liberal democratic states to "decent" peoples living in nondemocratic international societies. Rawls envisions such "well-ordered hierarchical societies" to be "nonliberal societies whose basic institutions meet specified conditions of political right and justice

---

[79] This section relies on and reproduces parts of the author's *Global Energy Justice: Law and Policy* (Eagan: West Academic Publishing, 2016).

[80] Ibid., pp. 31–41.

[81] S. Ratner, *The Thin Justice of International Law* (Oxford: Oxford University Press, 2015), pp. 1–2, 27–28.

[82] Ibid.

[83] J. Rawls, "The Law of Peoples" (1993) 20 *Critical Inquiry* 36–68.

[84] Ibid.

[85] Ibid., n. 21.

[86] Ibid., n. 59.

(including the right of citizens to play a substantial role, such as participating in associations and groups making political decisions) and lead their citizens to honor a reasonably just law for the Society of Peoples."[87] Well-ordered societies must satisfy a number of criteria: they must eschew aggressive aims as a means of achieving their objectives, honor basic human rights dealing with life, liberty, and freedom, and possess a system of law imposing bona fide moral duties and obligations, as distinct from human rights. Moreover, they must have law and judges to uphold common ideas of justice.[88]

Rawls demonstrated how the law of peoples may be developed out of liberal ideas of justice similar to, but more general than, the idea of "justice as fairness" presented in "A Theory of Justice."[89] Just as individuals in the first original position were shorn of knowledge about their attributes and placed behind a veil of ignorance to create principles for a just domestic society, the bargainers in the so-called second original position are representatives of peoples who are shorn of knowledge about their people's resources, wealth, power, and the like. Behind the veil of ignorance, the representatives of peoples – not states, as states lack moral capacity – develop the principles of justice that will govern relations between them: "the law of peoples."

Rawls seeks to determine the principles of cooperation for such "well-ordered peoples." Rawls posits that nonideal conditions cannot adequately be addressed unless principles of justice are determined for ideal conditions. Otherwise, it is impossible to know what kind of just society to aim to establish and the necessary means to do so.[90] A "realistic utopia," as Rawls prefers to call his theory, is an aspiration that does not reflect the existing reality of international law and relations.

Rawls emphasizes the crucial importance of peoples rather than states because of a people's capacity for "moral motives" that is lacking in the bureaucratic machinery of a state.[91] Noah Feldman correctly observes that a "people" for Rawls is a philosophical construct. It is an abstract conception needed to work out principles of justice for a particular subject – in this case, relations among different, well-ordered liberal and "decent" societies.[92] The assumption that states lack moral motives is partially refuted by their acceptance of sustainable development. Nonetheless, Rawls remains trenchant when it comes to the application of sustainable development. Rawls is not talking then about a people regarded as an ethnic or religious group (e.g. Slavs, Jews, Kurds) who are not members of the same society. Rather, a "people" consists of members of the same well-ordered society who are united under, and whose relations are governed by, a political constitution and basic structure. Comprised of members of a well-ordered society, a people is envisioned as having effective political control over a territory that its members govern and within which their basic social institutions take root. In contrast to a state, however, a people possesses a "moral nature" that stems from the effective sense of justice for its individual members. A people's members may have "common sympathies" for any number of nonrequisite reasons, including shared language, ethnic roots, or religion. The most basic reason for members' common sympathies, however, lies in their shared history as members of the same society and consequent shared conception of justice and the common good.

---

[87] Ibid., p. 106.
[88] Ibid., p. 3.
[89] Ibid.
[90] Ibid., n. 59.
[91] Ibid.
[92] N. Feldman, "Cosmopolitan Law?" (2007) 116 *Yale Law Journal* 1038.

24.6 SDGS, INTERNATIONAL LAW, AND JUSTICE

This section offers a brief synopsis relevant to the remit of this chapter, of the concept of sustainable development (SD) embodied in international law and policy.[93] It will also deal with the Convention on the Elimination of All Forms of Discrimination against Women (CEDAW), adopted in 1979 by the UN General Assembly, and the relevance of justice.

SD, a three-dimensional concept made up of economic development, social development, and environmental protection, has evolved over a period of fifty years. The first seeds were laid by the 1972 Stockholm Conference on the Human Environment[94] (Stockholm) culminating in the adoption of SDGs in 2015.

The conflict between the two competing concepts of economic development and environmental protection was resolved, by way of a compromise, in which the definition of environment included the human environment, which extends environmental protection to energy poverty. The essence of that understanding was summed up in the preamble to the Stockholm Declaration of the UN Conference on the Human Environment (Stockholm Declaration):[95] "[i]n the developing countries most of the environmental problems are caused by under-development" and that industrialized countries must "direct their efforts to development, bearing in mind their priorities and the need to safeguard and improve the environment."[96] Similarly, the industrialized countries were exhorted to make efforts to reduce the developmental gap between themselves and the developing countries.

Whatever the relative tension among the three dimensions of economic and social development and environmental protection, there is little doubt that the EP and particularly the predicament of women and children are the concern of all three dimensions of SD. While it is perhaps more obvious that social and economic development are directly applicable to the EP, the definition of environment to include the human environment as accepted at Stockholm, clearly extends environmental protection to energy poverty.

CEDAW is often described as an international bill of rights for women. Consisting of a preamble and thirty articles, it defines what constitutes discrimination against women and sets up an agenda for national action to end such discrimination. CEDAW's definition of discrimination is broad in that it encompasses the exclusion women face in their recognition, marital status, and basic equality in human rights and fundamental freedoms. Over 187 countries have ratified CEDAW making it one of the most highly ratified human rights treaties.[97]

While it is impressive that so many countries have ratified this international bill of rights for women, the reservations made by countries to Articles 2[98] and 16[99] have emasculated the true purpose of the treaty.[100] The CEDAW Committee considers these two articles to be "core

---

[93] For a fuller discussion of the evolution of SD, see generally, L. Guruswamy and M. Zebrowski Leach, *International Environmental Law in a Nutshell* (5th ed.) (St. Paul, MN: West Academic Publishing, 2017).

[94] UN, *Report of the United Nations Conference on the Human Environment, Stockholm*, June 5–16, 1972, UN Doc. A/CONF.48/14/Rev.1

[95] Ibid.

[96] Ibid., para. 4.

[97] UN, Convention on the Elimination of All Forms of Discrimination Against Women, Sept. 3, 1981, 1249 UNTS 13.

[98] Ibid., Article 2 requires states to adopt legislation and other measures to ensure equality between men and women, including abolishing discriminatory laws.

[99] Ibid., Article 16 relates to ensuring equality in marriage and family relations.

[100] L. M. Keller, "The Impact of States Parties' Reservations to the Convention on the Elimination of All Forms of Discrimination against Women" (2014) *Michigan State Law Review* 309 at 312.

provisions of the Convention"[101] and "inextricably linked with all other substantive provisions of the convention."[102] Additionally, CEDAW's scope of discrimination might not even extend to the EP. Article 1 defines discrimination against women as "any distinction, exclusion or restriction made on the basis of sex." This implies that for CEDAW, there must be an active form of discrimination against women, with explicit laws or policies. For the EP, this is not the case. Countries do not have laws on the books that aim to create harm from lack of energy. The socioeconomic conditions which give rise to the burdens on women are very much a reality.

Assuming that CEDAW does apply to EP women, the implementation of the treaty and therefore its effectiveness in improving the status of women, has not been thoroughly researched. Empirical data are essential to prove a treaty does have a positive impact and fixes the problem it was supposed to address.[103] One of the few studies that has been done noted that CEDAW had a greater impact in transition countries rather than stable democracies or autocracies.[104] However, other UN initiatives since CEDAW have solidified the UN's commitment to women's human rights, including the 1995 Beijing Conference on Women, and, in 2010, the creation of a new UN body dedicated to gender equality and the empowerment of women, known as UN Women.[105]

The SDGs of 2015[106] include a cluster of SDGs dealing with the condition of women, that should address their claim for access to energy. They include SDG 3 on health, SDG 4 on education, SDG 5 on gender equality, SDG 6 on clean water and sanitation, SDG 7 on access to energy, SDG 10 on reducing inequalities, and SDG 16 on peace, justice, and strong institutions.

An examination of these SDGs, however, reveals the extent to which access to energy for women has been overlooked or diminished not only in the SDGs themselves, but also their targets and indicators. Targets specify the goals, indicators represent the metrics by which the world aims to track whether these targets are achieved.[107] The UN has defined nine targets and fourteen indicators for SDG 5. Despite overwhelming evidence, discussed above, that lack of energy adversely impacts women, there are no targets or indicators relating to harms caused to women by lack of access to energy. SDG 7 on access to affordable, reliable, sustainable, and modern energy for all has five targets and six indicators. SDG 7, similar to SDG 5, overlooks or glosses over the dire plight of women. The targets and indicators are global or general, and there are no specific targets or goals relating to women.

---

[101] Amnesty International, "Reservations to the Convention on the Elimination of All Forms of Discrimination against Women Weakening the Protection of Women from Violence in the Middle East and North Africa Region," Nov. 3, 2004, p. 13.

[102] UN Committee on the Elimination of Discrimination Against Women (CEDAW), *General Recommendation No. 28 on the core obligations of States parties under article 2 of the Convention on the Elimination of All Forms of Discrimination against Women*, Dec. 16, 2010, UN Doc. CEDAW/C/GC/28.

[103] Guruswamy and Zebrowski Leach, note 93, p. 90.

[104] A. C. Brynes and M. Freeman, "The Impact of the CEDAW Convention: Paths to Equality" (2012) *UNSW Law Research Paper No. 2012–7* at 53.

[105] UN, "Gender Equality," www.un.org/en/sections/issues-depth/gender-equality/index.html. See further UN Women, www.unwomen.org/en; UN Women, "UN Created New Structure for Empowerment of Women," July 2, 2010, www.unwomen.org/en/news/stories/2010/7/un-creates-new-structure-for-empower ment-of-women.

[106] UN General Assembly, *Transforming Our world: The 2030 Agenda for Sustainable Development*, Oct. 12, 2015, UN Doc. A/RES/70/1.

[107] SDG Tracker "Achieve Gender Equality and Empower All Women and Girls," https://sdg-tracker.org/gender-equality.

Given the reality of the special hardships suffered by women, it was important for global targets and indicators in SDG 7 to have progressed from the hortatory realm of broad generality to specific realities. Consequently, it was reasonable to expect that targets actually enumerated priorities, and draw up an agenda for action, that acknowledged the importance of addressing the worst cases first. Instead, the first target in SDG 7 simply mirrors the generality of the objective of affordable and clean energy in SDG 7, by calling for universal access to affordable, reliable, and modern energy services by 2030. The other targets and indicators are similarly shorn of specificity. It would have been far more meaningful, consequential, and constructive if the specific plight of women were identified, and targets were directed toward women as a high priority.

SDG 16 addresses peace, justice, and strong institutions, and seeks to promote just, peaceful, and inclusive societies. The UN has defined twelve targets and twenty-three indicators for SDG 16. Target 16.3 that promotes the rule of law and ensures equal access to justice, merits mention. According to the UN, justice referred to in 16.3 should promote the rule of law at the national and international levels and ensure equal access to justice for all.[108] Pursuant to this interpretation, 16.3 has been applied to the reduction of violence, such as murders by avoiding conflict-related deaths, and preventing physical, psychological, and sexual violence against vulnerable children.[109] But, as we have seen, the concept of justice has a wider meaning. At its core, justice incorporates a social dimension based on fairness. Unfortunately, this essential social and humanitarian dimension of justice has been ignored or overlooked in SDG 16, and its targets. As promoting gender equality and empowerment of women underlies Agenda 2030, an enriched understanding of justice is essential to address the challenges facing women and children with poor access to energy.

Despite this seemingly bleak conclusion, it is important to note the work of UN Women in relation to the SDGs, including SDG 7. For example, in 2018 UN Women published a report detailing how gender equality is fundamental to the achievement of the 2030 Agenda and all seventeen SDGs.[110] UN Women is also working to draw attention to the gender dimensions of SDG 7 and to support related implementation initiatives.[111]

24.7 CONCLUSIONS

The conclusion most pertinent to our discussion of justice is that Rawls elucidates the duty of liberal democratic and decent hierarchical peoples to assist "burdened societies" to the point where burdened societies are enabled to join the "Society of Peoples." It is of particular pertinence that Rawls's duty of assistance does not absolve developing country governments of their obligation to take appropriate action. Based on our discussion of the plight of EP women, they fall within Rawls's rubric of burdened peoples. The SDGs, as we have seen, do not give expression to a Rawlsian sense of justice, and it is important that concepts of justice should illuminate any discussion on sustainable

---

[108] Ibid.

[109] Ibid.

[110] UN Women, "Turning Promises into Action: Gender Equality in the 2030 Agenda for Sustainable Development," 2018. See further UN Women, "Infographic: Why Gender Equality Matters to Achieving All 17 SDGs," July 5, 2018, www.unwomen.org/en/digital-library/multimedia/2018/7/infographic-why-gender-equality-matters-to-achieving-all-17-sdgs.

[111] UN Women, "SDG 7: Ensure Access to Affordable, Reliable, Sustainable and Modern Energy for All," www.unwomen.org/en/news/in-focus/women-and-the-sdgs/sdg-7-affordable-clean-energy; see case studies as examples of UN Women supported implementation initiatives.

development. Given that the SDGs have generally failed to do so, there are a number of compelling reasons for embedding SD within the vortex of justice.

First, the inability to access energy both causes poverty and disables impoverished people from developing. The connection between energy and poverty is fundamental to the discourse on sustainable development. Second, the plight of the EP cannot be remedied by relying solely on the states within which they reside. The EP have been glossed over by their identification only as national problems falling within the sovereign jurisdiction of the developing countries within which they reside. They are treated as internal problems of developing countries, and not perceived as a call for international action, sometimes independent of those countries. It would be a great step forward if those international intergovernmental and civil society organizations, that appear to be solely preoccupied with climate change, began to focus on the tragedy of the EP.

Second, allowing the EP to languish in their current state violates fundamental concepts of international justice and SD. Because Rawls's concepts of duty and distributive justice are not explicitly articulated in the concept of SD, or in the SDGs, justice can only be achieved if they are interpreted according to Rawlsian principles or other similar principles of justice.

Third, access to energy through electricity remains the ultimate objective. Unfortunately, it is a cost-prohibitive and protracted remedy that will take decades to implement and does not offer any interim solutions. During the long wait for electricity, large segments of the EP will remain energy-deprived for many decades unless they are offered intermediate solutions based on affordable/appropriate sustainable energy technologies (ASETs). Employing ASETs can begin the journey out of energy poverty.

Finally, despite the reservations expressed above, there is no doubt that the UN's recognition of the need for universal access to energy in SDG 7 is a significant step forward. SDG 7 acknowledges the connection between energy and poverty and charts a new path for SD. Though the targets and indicators do not refer specifically to women, recognition of universal access to energy offers a new space for formulating appropriate sustainable energy solutions. Such measures, based on Rawlsian principles of justice, could address the needs of EP women by providing timely, sustainable, and affordable ways to satisfy their energy need.

25

Energy without Injustice?

Indigenous Participation in Renewable Energy Generation

Adrian A. Smith and Dayna Nadine Scott

25.1 INTRODUCTION

There is growing involvement of Indigenous communities in renewable energy development across their traditional territories in what is now called Canada.[1] Here, we explore Indigenous participation in large-scale "green" energy generation as a response to encroachment, displacement, and dispossession wrought by the extractivist orientation of contemporary settler capitalism.[2] We consider the potential of these experiments in renewable energy generation and governance in terms of environmental justice and related conceptions of climate and energy justice.[3] We understand all of these concepts as entailing a fair distribution of the benefits and costs associated with environmental, climate, or energy policies, and requiring equitable access and meaningful participation. The central concern with fairness and equity across a broad swath of policy areas is what makes this body of scholarship so relevant to any discussion of the "social pillar" of sustainable development. In addressing the social pillar, scholars are urged to focus on deepening social inclusion which, as we contend, demands a commitment to Indigenous rights of self-determination, as well as gender equality and full participation.[4]

Taking the case of the Chinodin Chigumi Nodin Kitagan (Bow Lake Wind Farm), an initiative of the Batchewana First Nation in Ontario Canada, the chapter explores the potential of Indigenous participation in energy generation to promote a wider distribution of economic, social, and political power in society. It identifies opportunities to promote environmental

---

[1] See, for example, M. Bargh, "Indigenous Peoples' Energy Projects" (2010) 28 *Australasian Canadian Studies Journal* 37–57; C. Henderson, *Aboriginal Power: Clean Energy and the Future of Canada's First Peoples* (Erin, Canada: Rainforest Editions, 2013); G. Lowan-Trudeau, "Indigenous Environmental Education: The Case of Renewable Energy Projects" (2017) 53 *Educational Studies: A Journal of the American Educational Studies Association* 601–613.

[2] This chapter draws on and expands a case study initially published in D. N. Scott and A. A. Smith, "Transforming Relations in the Green Energy Economy: Control of Lands and Livelihoods," in R. Salter, C. G. Gonzalez, and E. A. Kronk Warner (eds.), *Energy Justice: U.S. and International Perspectives* (Cheltenham, UK: Edward Elgar, 2018).

[3] Ibid.; see also D. Schlosberg and L. B. Collins, "From Environmental to Climate Justice: Climate Change and the Discourse of Environmental Justice" (2014) 5 *Wires Climate Change* 359; J. Agyeman, R. D. Bullard, and B. Evans (eds.), *Just Sustainabilities: Development in an Unequal World* (Cambridge, MA: MIT Press, 2003); P. Mohai, D. Pellow, and J. Timmons Roberts, "Environmental Justice" (2009) 34 *Annual Review of Environment and Resources* 405; D. Schlosberg, "Reconceiving Environmental Justice: Global Movements and Political Theories" (2004) 13 *Environmental Politics* 517; B. K. Sovacool and M. Dworkin, "Energy justice: Conceptual Insights and Practical Applications" (2015) 142 *Applied Energy* 435.

[4] See Chapter 1 in this volume.

stewardship, the fulfillment of duties to future generations and less hierarchical governance compatible with Indigenous legal orders. Fundamentally, however, we confront a tension between, on one side, the project's crafting with careful attention to equity, environmental, and energy justice, and as an expression of the Anishinaabe community's inherent jurisdiction and, on the other, measured questions raised within the community about ecological impacts and the risks associated with operating within the parameters of dominant settler state economic and legal frameworks. Ultimately, it is our contention that real promise exists in transforming energy generation/power relations through Indigenous participation in renewable energy generation insofar as Indigenous communities initiate and control those projects, govern them, and benefit from them collectively, and operate them, without state interference, according to their own legal and political orders.

25.2 RESEARCH CONTEXT

A transition to a more just and sustainable energy future will require not just a more equitable distribution of political and economic power but also enhanced participation and empowerment.[5] Here we investigate the possibility that Indigenous participation in renewable energy generation may offer interesting prospects for furthering both of these goals. In particular, there is scope for these projects to provide examples or models for more sustainable and democratic forms of energy generation, distribution, and governance.[6] Further, an increase in the proportion of Indigenous-owned energy assets may counter a troubling trend ushered in by the green economy – that it is resulting in a greater proportion of energy generation assets under private control. Most new wind and solar generation is privately owned, whereas coal-fired or nuclear power plants have tended to be controlled by large publicly owned utilities.[7] In other words, the rise in renewable power has not necessarily resulted in more "community power," a concept described in more detail below.

That the growth in renewables may be fueling the trend toward private control is one of the factors that gives rise to the worry that the environmental injustices of the fossil era might carry forward into the green energy economy. Private investor-owned energy projects, even though renewable, continue to rely on "profit-based incentive structures and a lack of local participatory engagement in governance . . . [which] often leads to socially and environmentally damaging outcomes."[8] Thus, while some environmental advocates have supported the restructuring of the electricity sector in the hopes that a growth in renewables will lead to "distributed generation," according to analysts there is little reason to believe that this will *necessarily* be so.[9] On the other

---

[5] J. L. MacArthur, *Empowering Electricity: Co-operatives, Sustainability, and Power Sector Reform in Canada* (Vancouver: UBC Press, 2016).

[6] See, for example, C. E. Hoicka and J. L. MacArthur, "From Tip to Toes: Mapping Community Energy in Canada and New Zealand" (2018) 121 *Energy Policy* 162–174; J. Lipp and S. Bale, "Growing Indigenous Power: A Review of Indigenous Involvement and Resources to Further Renewable Energy Development Across Canada," TREC Renewable Energy Co-op, People, Power, Planet Partnership, Feb. 2018; Leap Manifesto, "A Call for Canada Based on Caring for the Earth and One Another," 2015, https://leapmanifesto.org/en/the-leap-manifesto; written by a coalition of social and environmental justice activists in Canada in 2015: "The time for energy democracy has come: we believe not just in changes to our energy sources, but that wherever possible communities should collectively control these new energy systems . . . we can create innovative ownership structures: democratically run, paying living wages and keeping much-needed revenue in communities. And Indigenous Peoples should be first to receive public support for their own clean energy projects."

[7] MacArthur, note 5.

[8] Ibid., p. 10.

[9] Ibid.

hand, we agree that these new technologies may indeed "open up the possibilities of an alternative energy future."[10] It is in this spirit that we bring forward the *Chinodin Chigumi Nodin Kitagan* project as an example of an innovative experiment in renewable energy generation and governance and highlight its promise for enhancing Indigenous self-determination aims as well as sustainability goals.

Methodologically, the core research for this chapter included fourteen in-depth comprehensive interviews with community leaders and residents, as well as current and former Batchewana First Nation councilors, staff, and consultants.[11] We spoke to community residents who were involved in the development of this project or have been impacted by it, to residents who have experience or views of relevance to how communities can own or control renewable energy projects, and to residents and community leaders who wished to share their views about the community's values, approach to self-determination, and exercise of inherent jurisdiction.

25.3 RENEWING INDIGENOUS POWER: EQUITY STAKES IN ENERGY RESOURCES

Energy generation in Canada, as elsewhere, has tended to privilege economic priorities over ecological ones and to disempower and distance most people from decision-making.[12] But a major effort is afoot to transform how energy is generated and distributed. Alternative players are emerging with the hopes of ultimately dislodging the traditional power sector. The involvement of First Nations in various degrees of ownership and control of large-scale renewable energy projects, as well as the emergence of community-based energy cooperatives, holds out the promise of "democratization" of energy generation, distribution, and governance.[13]

First Nations have demonstrated a growing interest in pursuing non-extractivist, renewable-driven development, based primarily on solar, wind, and geothermal energy generation.[14] Several hundred such projects are said to already exist or are at various stages of planning and

---

[10] Ibid., p. 11. In making this argument, we are accepting that a part Indigenous-owned project like Bow Lake falls more easily under the category of "public" rather than "private." We acknowledge that this is not obviously the case, given the complex corporate structure described later and the private equity partner. As Julie MacArthur says, partnerships with private sector actors, while they allow for "larger, more lucrative projects and often a more streamlined process," also "dilute the community control and return" (ibid., p. 161). In this particular case, while we feel there is a need for further analysis on this point, we would also wish to emphasize that conventional conceptions of "public" utilities under settler colonialism, have certainly not been inclusive of Indigenous peoples.

[11] The interviews were conducted from March 2016 to April 2017, with approval of the First Nation granted by Band Council Resolution in July 2016. The researchers also toured the Bow Lake wind farm site in July 2016 and reviewed all relevant publicly available documents.

[12] Ibid.

[13] Ibid.

[14] Of course, one must remember that the construction of renewable energy projects, including wind turbines, relies on the extraction of rare earth minerals, which highlights the potential trade-offs rather than synergies between struggles for environmental justice, energy justice, and climate justice, as we discuss elsewhere (D. N. Scott and A. A. Smith, "'Sacrifice Zones' in the Green Energy Economy: Towards an Environmental Justice Framework" (2017) 62 *McGill Law Journal* 861). We maintain, however, that "extractivism" is about more than simply whether materials must be extracted from the earth; it is a specific mode of accumulation that is nonreciprocal, organized around "taking" and oriented toward profit for distant parties at the expense of local peoples (see H. Veltmeyer, "The Natural Resource Dynamics of Post Neoliberalism in Latin America: New Developmentalism or Extractivist Imperialism?" (2012) 90 *Studies in Political Economy* 57–86 at 72). Further, of course, all viable modes of generating energy entail some social and environmental costs; that said, when the benefits and costs of undertaking any such development are borne by different people, it raises environmental justice considerations.

implementation across the country.[15] In southwestern Ontario, for instance, the Six Nations of the Grand River, through its Grand River Development Corporation, holds a 50 percent equity interest in the Niagara Regional Wind Farm, a 77-turbine project generating 230 MW.[16] M'Chigeeng First Nation on Manitoulin Island is the sole owner of a 4 MW wind farm through its Mother Earth Renewable Energy Wind Project. The aims of this project included stimulating a green economy, as well as increasing the standard of living and quality of life of band members. The profits made by the wind project were expected to benefit band members through social and development activities.[17]

There is of course an entrenched history of Indigenous resistance to the Canadian state's agenda of extractive capitalist development.[18] Recent flashpoints have emerged around the expansion of the tar sands and oil pipeline infrastructure, and hydraulic fracturing. But to the list of oppositional efforts Indigenous communities are taking to resist extractive capitalism, we should add the pursuit of a renewable energy agenda.[19] The "embrace" of renewables by Indigenous communities, as Métis scholar and community educator Lowan-Trudeau recently argued, should be taken as "a potential source of political and economic sovereignty" amounting to "a type of reclamation of land and environmental rights."[20] It is, according to Lowan-Trudeau, "a manifestation of resistance that emerges from working both within and outside of established political and economic systems in the service of Indigenous well-being."[21] While we broadly agree with these sentiments, we wish to add a particular case study that contributes some further specificity and nuance.

First Nations' involvement in the renewable energy sector is often justified in terms of the benefits of energy self-sufficiency, especially for remote communities. It is said to offer alternative, non-extractivist modes of revenue generation, as well as opportunities for capacity building through job creation and technical expertise. Finally, it has been linked to revitalization of traditional practices, marking a transitional shift from "protest" to "proposal" to borrow Canadian social movement scholar Bud Hall's framing.[22] From our perspective, Indigenous involvement in green energy projects holds the most promise where it marks an attempt to extend beyond the typical arrangements negotiated with settler governments to share taxes and resource development royalties with Indigenous communities, and beyond impact benefit agreements as an

[15] In its 2015 report, the National Aboriginal Economic Development Board (NAEDB) raised the estimate to nearly 500 resource projects "announced, proposed, or are underway in Canada, totaling $497.9 billion," two-thirds of which were situated in "treaty lands" (National Aboriginal Economic Development Board, "Enhancing Aboriginal Financial Readiness for Major Resource Development Opportunities," Jan. 2015, p. 3).

[16] J. Winter, "Six Nations of Grand River Lead the Charge on Green Energy," Apr. 26, 2017, www.thestar.com/news/gta/2017/04/26/six-nations-of-grand-river-lead-the-charge-on-green-energy.html.

[17] Lipp and Bale, note 6.

[18] We must also recognize the resistance struggles of Indigenous peoples across the Americas, especially in Latin America, against mining operations of Canadian entities abroad. See J. Webber and T. Gordon, *Blood of Extraction* (Black Point, NS: Fernwood, 2016).

[19] See for example the work of Honor the Earth: "Honor the Earth is interested in the transition from this destructive economy and way of life, back towards land-based economics. In this land based economics, we see that intergenerational and inter-species equity are valued, that cyclical systems are reaffirmed, that not all 'natural resources' are up for extraction, and that we behave responsibly" and "power without pollution, energy without injustice" (Honor the Earth, "About Us," www.honorearth.org/about); C. Henderson, *Aboriginal Power: Clean Energy and the Future of Canada's First Peoples* (Erin, Canada: Rainforest Editions, 2013).

[20] G. Lowan-Trudeau, "Indigenous Environmental Education: The Case of Renewable Energy Projects" (2017) 53 *Educational Studies: A Journal of the American Educational Studies Association* 601–613 at 602.

[21] Ibid.

[22] B. Hall, "A River of Life: Learning and Environmental Social Movements" (2009) 1 *Interface: A Journal for and about Social Movements* 46–78 at 68.

approach through which industry provides annual financial compensation to impacted communities.[23] Instead, we are interested in arrangements that provide varying degrees of ownership and control of renewable energy resources by Indigenous peoples, as expressions of inherent jurisdiction over lands and resources across their traditional territories.[24] That said, it is important to examine, as we do below, the careful and measured critiques of Indigenous investment in large-scale renewable projects that have been leveled from within those communities as well. In the next section, we examine the case of a renewable energy project in which Batchewana First Nation holds a significant equity stake.

25.4 CHINODIN CHIGUMI NODIN KITAGAN/BOW LAKE WIND FARM

Batchewana First Nation is an Anishinaabe community that has ancestral lands around Bawahting, the rapids between Sault Sainte Marie, Ontario and Sault Sainte Marie, Michigan. The elders of the community say that "when the Creator told the Crane to choose a homeland, the Crane flew around and settled at Bawahting where there was an abundance of fish."[25] Bawahting is a gathering area where families met historically to fish for whitefish with gill nets along the rapids. Once fishing season passed, people returned to their family lands that could be found extending all along the north shore of Lake Superior. The once-vast territory has been reduced to four plots of reserve land surrounding Sault Ste. Marie. Nevertheless, the band continues to exercise its inherent jurisdiction over the full extent of its "original, traditional and historic territory."[26]

The Bow Lake wind project, Chinodin Chigumi Nodin Kitagan (Anishinaabemowin for Big-Wind Big-Lake Wind-Garden/Farm) is located in this traditional territory of Batchewana First Nation, northwest of Sault Ste. Marie Ontario. The Batchewana First Nation is a full equity partner with BluEarth Renewables Inc., through establishment of Nodin Kitagan Limited Partnership, said to be "one of the largest economic partnerships between a First Nation and wind energy developer in Canada."[27] It consists of thirty-six turbines perched on a high ridge overlooking the shores of Lake Superior. The project holds a renewable energy approval which

---

[23] For a critical take on impact-benefit agreements (IBAs), see Dayna Nadine Scott, "Extraction Contracting: The Struggle for Control of Indigenous Lands" (2020) 119(2) *South Atlantic Quarterly* 269–299.

[24] We recognize that ownership in the form of "equity stakes" is gaining interest for certain First Nations, even with respect to more conventional extraction projects proposed for their territories (J. Snyder, "A Fair Stake: First Nations Seek Equity Positions in Northern Mining Operations," Mar. 7, 2017, https://business .financialpost.com/commodities/mining/a-fair-stake-first-nations-seek-equity-positions-in-northern-mining-operations). This form of ownership may or may not produce some of the same types of benefits that we describe here. The degree to which it is supportive of Indigenous sovereignty or the exercise of inherent jurisdiction is contingent on the form and quality of "control" a given community can achieve in the arrangement. Certainly, the ability to secure financing is crucial. In the case of the Bow Lake project, the financing hurdle was significantly reduced through statutory enactments made by the province of Ontario through its green energy reforms.

[25] Batchewana First Nation, "Notice of Assertions," http://batchewana.ca/about/sovereignty/.

[26] Ibid. The Batchewana First Nation belongs to the Ojibways of Lake Huron, who are signatories to the 1850 Robinson–Huron treaty with the British Crown.

[27] BluEarth Renewables, "Bow Lake Wind Facility," www.bluearthrenewables.com/portfolio/bow-lake-wind/; Nodin Kitagan Limited Partnership, "Bow Lake Wind Project: Community Liaison Committee," July 23, 2014. BluEarth Renewables is a private equity firm focused on the commercial development and operation of the renewable energy project. The initial relationship between the First Nation and BluEarth Renewables is structured through Nodin Kitagan Limited Partnership and Nodin Kitagan 2 Limited Partnership, by their General Partners Shongwish Nodin Kitagan GP Corp. and Shongwish Nodin Kitagan 2 GP Corp, which are linked back to the Band and BluEarth.

allows for 58 MW of electricity capacity.[28] It secured a twenty-year preferred rate power purchase agreement with Ontario and became operational in September 2015.[29]

In the early planning stages, several local and seasonal residents of Sault Ste. Marie, under the banner of SOAR ("Save the Algoma Region"), brought a challenge to the Bow Lake project to the province's Environmental Review Tribunal.[30] The opposition was largely grounded in concerns about possible detrimental effects on nature, wildlife, tourism industries, and property values.[31] Other groups, such as Wind Concerns Ontario, took the position that renewable power generation should be small-scale and local, and argued that since BluEarth is headquartered in Calgary, and is a larger-scale energy company, the Bow Lake project should not have been approved.

In defense of the project, Batchewana Chief Dean Sayers stated that:

> *Chinodin Chigumi Nodin Kitagan* would help the First Nation meet its basic needs in infrastructure, housing, health care, education . . . [and the] redevelopment of our political systems . . . We are a self-reliant, sovereign nation with inherent jurisdiction over the resources across all of our territory.[32]

The Chief's rationale follows from Batchewana First Nation's 2011 release of a "Notice of Assertions," which stated that the Band would begin issuing permits and demanding consent and full partnership in any resource developments across its traditional territory.[33] It declares that, "[l]ike other Ojibway in the upper Great Lakes, the Batchewana First Nation has exercised its responsibility to use, possess, and protect the waters, lands, and resources from time immemorial."[34] With respect to resources, the Notice identifies fisheries, including commercial fisheries, wildlife, "mines and minerals, waters and watersheds, *wind* and the environment."[35] Chief Sayers has expressly tied the Bow Lake project to the Notice of Assertions, noting:

> The Bow Lake Wind Project is perfectly aligned with our original expectations at Treaty time; those expectations were to benefit from our resources in sustainable ways. The [Batchewana First Nation] will continue to affirm, and benefit from the Letter of Assertions, which outlines our First Nations' expected relationship with resource developers. This assertion was the foundation for our relationship with our partner, BluEarth Renewables.[36]

In some ways, the initial contestation over the Bow Lake project is a reflection of concerns and reactions to the ways in which renewable energy projects, and wind turbines in particular, were rolled out across the province in the preceding years.[37] The source of contention stems from the feed-in-tariff (FIT) program introduced in Ontario's Green Energy and Green

---

[28] Ontario Ministry of the Environment, "Renewable Energy Approval Number 8443–9BMG23, Schedule A: Facility Description (a)," Dec. 16, 2013.

[29] BluEarth Renewables, note 26.

[30] *Fata v. Director, Ministry of the Environment*, [2014] OERTD. No. 42, 90 CELR (3d) 376.

[31] D. Taylor, "Bow Lake Wind Farm Appeal Turned Down," July 11, 2014, www.sootoday.com/local-news/bow-lake-wind-farm-appeal-turned-down-174715.

[32] D. Taylor, "Bow Lake Wind Farm Project Finalized with Batchewana," January 17, 2013, www.sootoday.com/local-news/bow-lake-wind-farm-project-finalized-with-batchewana-updated-164494.

[33] Batchewana First Nation, note 24: The Notice of Assertions is a formal notice from BFN to other governments, to resource users and developers, to its neighbors and to the general public of the rights and interests BFN asserts and will to continue to assert in its original, traditional, and historic territory.

[34] Ibid.

[35] Ibid. (emphasis added).

[36] D. Bailey, "First Nations Turn to Wind for Independence," Feb. 28, 2014, www.windpowermonthly.com/article/1281869/first-nations-turn-wind-independence.

[37] Scott and Smith, note 14.

Economy Act.[38] In the first iteration of the Act, the FIT program permitted more or less any qualifying individual, business, or organization to become power producers. Authorized projects would sell the electricity they generated to the provincial energy grid at a guaranteed price over a twenty-year fixed term. This led to criticisms that the FIT program encouraged projects chiefly led by large energy multinationals, not community-owned power.[39] The program was judged highly effective at driving increased investment into the renewables sector, but not at diversifying ownership.[40]

In the second iteration, in an attempt to encourage participation by First Nation communities, Ontario introduced the "Aboriginal Price Adder."[41] The "Aboriginal Adder," as it became known, increased the price paid by the province per kilowatt hour (kWh) of generation, calculated in increments depending on the level of Aboriginal participation. It reflected the higher development, operation, and maintenance costs that are said to be associated with community-owned projects. The greater the percentage of First Nation ownership of a project, the greater the price received for energy produced. Analysts agreed that relative to the typical prices paid for wind power projects under the FIT program, the adder made a significant difference.[42] The FIT program was placed on hold in December 2016, as the Ontario government was forced to backtrack on its green energy agenda because of political backlash over high electricity prices.[43]

25.5 BOW LAKE WIND FARM: POWER TO THE COMMUNITY?

"Community power" is an umbrella term used to encompass alternative forms of ownership that include the sharing of collective benefits from energy projects leading to enhanced levels of local input and control. Projects with the highest levels of input and control would qualify as "community energy," defined as "collective action to generate or produce, distribute and manage the energy resources of a community."[44] In the Batchewana case, and in FIT scenarios more generally, the energy generated is sold back to the provincial power grid and thus does not, in a strict sense, constitute "the energy resources of the community." It is possible, however, to conceive of potential instances where renewable energy projects developed in more remote Indigenous communities – especially those now reliant on diesel generators – would fall into this category.

---

[38] Green Energy and Green Economy Act, 2009, RSO, c. 12.

[39] L. C. Stokes, "The Politics of Renewable Energy Policies: The Case of Feed-in Tariffs in Ontario, Canada," 56 *Energy Policy* 490 at 493; S. Fast and W. Mabee, 2015, "Place-making and Trust-building: The Influence of Policy on Host Community Responses to Wind Farms" 81 *Energy Policy* 27 at 33.

[40] MacArthur, note 5, p. 107.

[41] Ibid., p. 108; A. Jaffar, "Establishing a Clean Economy or Strengthening Indigenous Sovereignty: Conflicting & Complementary Narratives for Energy Transitions," June 2015 (unpublished MA thesis, University of Guelph).

[42] S. Fonseca and T. Timmins, "Unlocking the Value of Aboriginal Participation in Ontario FIT Program Projects," July 1, 2015, https://gowlingwlg.com/en/canada/insights-resources/unlocking-the-value-of-aboriginal-participation-in-ontario-fit-program-projects.

[43] Glenn Thibeault, Ministry of Energy of Ontario, Dec. 16, 2016 directive to Bruce Campbell, President and CEO of the Independent Electricity System Operator. It is important to point out, however, that most analysts attribute the high cost of electricity to decisions by the utility to refurbish an aging nuclear reactor and the high cost of debt servicing ("Ontario Electricity Rates: Experts Explain How They Would Make Power Cheaper," Nov. 28, 2016, https://globalnews.ca/news/3091320/ontario-electricity-rates-experts-explain-how-they-would-make-power-cheaper/; M. Winfield, "Energy Costs in Ontario," Nov. 2016, http://marksw.blog.yorku.ca/2016/11/28/electricity-costs-in-ontario/).

[44] MacArthur, note 5, p. 15.

Pertinent factors in the classification of projects could include whether the process of planning and implementation is "open and participatory" or "closed and institutional,"[45] and whether the finished project is "local and collective" or distantly and privately run. Ultimately, the extent to which a project can be considered "community power" requires a relatively complex and thorough assessment. Although we cannot undertake such a full assessment here, we wish to draw attention to certain aspects of the Bow Lake Project.

Generally, the Bow Lake Project involved local actors in design, operation, and governance. The extent to which BluEarth's (and its predecessor's) technical know-how shaped the process, however, is not precisely known but assumed to be considerable. Our understanding is that they selected the appropriate site of the turbines and secured all necessary approvals in the regulatory process with the support of external expertise (provided by consulting firms). BluEarth also led the construction and brought the wind farm online. For its part, Batchewana First Nation, through its Natural Resources Department, conducted a site evaluation to assess the impact on wetland – and Band officials later participated in environmental assessment activities. Band Council subsequently issued a permit for activities associated with wind data collection (in August 2008).

In terms of electricity generated, this extends beyond the local community of Batchewana First Nation, but the revenue generated will remain local and collectively held.[46] Batchewana First Nation established a trust to hold the revenues from the Bow Lake Project collectively and initiated the process of establishing criteria and priorities for the allocation of the funds. That allocation, importantly, will be based on the community's own needs and priorities, in accordance with principles derived from their own social, political, and legal order. The process for making decisions, while appearing relatively open and participatory, was constrained due to the reliance on technical knowledge and expertise external to the community and on externally imposed timelines and deadlines, such as those established through the provincial regulatory framework.[47]

The governance structure for the Bow Lake project relied to a certain extent on the particular and specific set of obligations that First Nations leaders owe to their members. Fundamentally, these obligations exist under Anishinaabe law,[48] and in certain respects are set out in Canadian state legislation such as the Indian Act.[49] Taken together, the obligations determine the ways in which project revenues and benefits flow back to the band, and the ways in which decision-making unfolds. As an interviewee explained, "I take a traditional Anishinaabe kwe point of view [so] . . . I see a lot of different law, when it comes to the traditional territory. There is regular law,

---

[45] G. Walker and P. Devine-Wright, "Community Renewable Energy: What Should It Mean?" (2008) 36 *Energy Policy* 497 at 498.

[46] Nodin Kitagan Limited Partnership, "Bow Lake Wind Farm Newsletter No. 1," Fall 2012. This newsletter stated: "one of the most common questions we heard at the Sept. 6 public meeting was, where is the power from the Bow Lake Project going to go? The IESO balances the supply and demand for electricity in Ontario and then directs its flow across the province's transmission lines. According to the IESO, the power produced by the Bow Lake project will be used in and around Sault Ste. Marie, Ontario."

[47] Green Energy and Green Economy Act, note 37.

[48] Anishinaabe legal obligations would be multiple and complex. Anishinaabe legal scholar John Borrows, however, has described some of these obligations in stewardship terms, stating that leaders would strive to ensure the continuity and well-being of all their relations (J. Borrows, "Stewardship and the First Nations Governance Act" (2003) 29 *Queen's Law Journal* 103).

[49] Indian Act, RSC, 1985, c. I-5. The Indian Act structures relations between bands and the federal government, and between Chief and Council and the community (such as in relation to community input and participation). For further detail, see S. Imai, "The Structure of the Indian Act: Accountability in Governance," Research Paper for the National Centre for First Nations Governance, July 2007.

public, private law, but there's also Anishinaabe law. [I think we should] follow the Anishinaabe law first and foremost."[50]

In addressing whether renewable energy projects are consistent with an Anishinaabe legal order and obligations to steward the land for future generations, it is important to recognize that Batchewana First Nation sees itself as managing its inherent obligations according to Natural Law and the Nation's commitments to all of Creation.[51] Many community members felt that the project, as a *renewable* energy project, opened up opportunities for them to honor principles of environmental stewardship, to respect ecological limits, in the sense of taking actions that protect the climate and the environment, rather than engaging in mining or other extractive activities.[52] This calculus is complex and uncertain, however, as one interviewee's comments make clear:

> [W]hat effect does it have on the birds? Some people were saying well we don't see this bird here anymore, we don't see that bird anymore. Ok, well they might leave an area for a little bit but, it's something new to them, just as it is the people who live in the area, they live in the area. It's new. It's a technology and yes it's green. It's not hazardous in any way, so why wouldn't you be patting somebody on the back?[53]

As the community member's reference to her responsibilities as *Anishinaabe kwe* makes clear, obligations under Anishinaabe law vary between individuals. For women (*Anishinaabe kwe*), there is a "special relationship and responsibility to water" as an example.[54] Women may feel obligations to "speak for the water" and to remind others of how water is necessary for all life. Similarly, obligations to future generations figured into the decision-making of community members in Batchewana, as well as obligations to honor ancestors. As Darlene Johnston has shown, this ongoing relationship between ancestors and descendants is central to Anishinaabe law of obligations.[55] One community member, speaking about the Bow Lake Project specifically, noted:

> I was really thinking about my parents and grandparents and [what they would think] . . . would that have been ok to go in there? And destroy the food that's there? The berries, the vegetation, the trees. Would it have been ok to put up these big structures that no one really knows what they are? Would [they] have been ok with us coming in and putting up this big electrical structure that's going to take the wind?[56]

For other community members, the idea of renewable energy was appealing, but the implementation was much more disruptive than they anticipated. One stated: "The natural wildlife wouldn't be the same around there after all of the machinery and the time that it took to build them."[57] Another asked what happens to turbines and infrastructure after the initial twenty-year agreement – what responsibility exists beyond established remediation

---

[50] Interview #7, note 11.

[51] Batchewana First Nation, http: www.batchewana.ca.

[52] Recall that we acknowledge that the manufacture of wind turbines (and solar panels) will require the mining of rare earth minerals, such that it is not possible to draw a bright line between energy generating activities that will and will not require "extraction," note 14.

[53] Interview #4, note 11.

[54] D. McGregor, "Honouring Our Relations", in J. Agyeman, P. Cole, R. Haluza-DeLay, and P. O'Riley (eds.), *Speaking for Ourselves: Environmental Justice in Canada* (Vancouver: UBC Press, 2010), p. 38.

[55] D. Johnston, "Connecting People to Place: Great Lakes Aboriginal History in Cultural Context," Prepared for the Ipperwash Commission of Inquiry, 2006, p.17.

[56] Interview #3, note 11.

[57] Interview #9, note 11.

plans?[58] Will the responsibility and ecological impacts of the project fall on Indigenous communities as the respective territorial authorities? Will it fall on future generations?

Some people attributed their support for the project to the stringency of community standards in relation to provincial standards, intimating that the community was able to assert principles deriving from its own legal order into the approval process:

> We had our natural resources department add certain criteria to the restoration plan that was in addition [to] the Ministry of Environment, so as far as First Nation people, when we were looking at our plan, their standard was down here. Ours was up here [gesturing] because there's so many other things that were happening in our territory that they don't even consider, that they don't even think about that we do.[59]

Many community members also placed a great deal of significance on the community's assertion of its legal authority to exercise inherent jurisdiction across the full extent of their lands.[60] As one person remarked, "This is our territory, this is where we assert ourselves."[61] Several people also urged us to emphasize the source of the authority. In the words of one such interviewee: "the source of authority is the community, the people," in contrast to the authority of Chief and Council as set out in the Indian Act. Many members stated that they have never stopped exercising their jurisdiction, insisting that assertions of inherent jurisdiction "are not a recent phenomenon."[62] Based on the community's experience with commercial fishing and nonrenewable extraction, a member stated:

> [W]e've pretty much always taken that stand . . . whether it be through commercial fishing or whether it be logging or use of our lands. We've kind of taken that. It's who we are, right? So we stand united on that front, we've never swayed. But you know . . . we're trying to take that one step further . . . to have an ownership stake, to have some input into what's actually happening.[63]

The same member went on to address the assertion of inherent jurisdiction in the context of the Band's ownership interest in the wind farm, stating: "We've been saying that, this is our area, this is our land. The way the treaties were, we're supposed to benefit. A lot of times, you kind of lost faith in government to turn around and say, here's your benefit. Unless we [have an] ownership stake, we could [not] have input into what's actually happening."[64] Another person identified a connection between community ownership of the renewable energy generation project and responsibility to future generations: "In terms of looking at ownership and responsibility and looking, as we say, to the next generation, to our youth . . . I think it's a great opportunity for our First Nation to be put on the map as a leader in renewable energy . . . I think in the long run it will be very beneficial."[65]

[58] Stantec Consulting, Bow Lake Wind Farm: Decommissioning Plan Report, Prepared for Kitagan Limited Partnership and Nodin Kitagan 2 Limited Partnership, Jan. 2013. These questions are especially pertinent because, as we have seen in instances of corporate malfeasance, the corporate form can be altered or dissolved with the result of shifting or evading responsibility and liability.
[59] Interview #6, note 11.
[60] Although several members did also describe some of those lands as shared or having been historically shared with neighboring First Nations.
[61] Interview #6, note 11.
[62] Interviewees #1, 6, 7, 8, note 11; quote is from Interview #1, note 11.
[63] Interview #8, note 11.
[64] Ibid.
[65] Interview #3, note 11.

25.6 ENTANGLEMENTS OF OWNERSHIP

A major objective of the Batchewana First Nation in undertaking the Bow Lake project was the generation of what is often called "own-source revenue" (OSR). While the politics around OSR are very complicated, the major benefit that some Indigenous communities see in this revenue is that it can be put to the priorities that they themselves determine, in contrast to federal transfers that are usually ear-marked for certain programs with strict parameters for how funds can be spent.[66] In fact, a central justification that is advanced in favor of Indigenous ownership of renewable energy projects is that the projects can generate revenues that are independent of any external government control, and that can be put toward interests of the band that are outside of what the federal government provides for, such as language revitalization programs, or in addition to the inadequate funds that are provided for certain needs, such as housing.[67] As the Chiefs of Ontario state, Indigenous-led green energy projects "allow First Nations to assert their autonomy by enabling them to generate revenue through the sale of power, thus creating greater economic self-sufficiency so they can address local concerns without external constraints."[68] A community member echoed this sentiment in relation to the Bow Lake project: "To be self-sustaining . . . that's the whole reason behind this. To be self-sustaining, [a] sovereign nation, to take care of its own."[69]

To come back to the central concepts of environmental and energy justice, most accounts would say that these are enhanced when the revenues from the generation and sale of renewable power are "circulated back into the communities bearing the environmental costs of generation."[70] But not all would agree with this framing. Broad criticisms surround Indigenous involvement in capitalist economic development. Taiaiake Alfred (Kanien'kehá:ka), for instance, raises concerns about "business development and job training and other schemes to increase First Nations' participation in the market economy" arguing that they are "irrelevant to the basic problems that are the actual causes of the social and health crises in First Nations' communities and at the root of First Nations' psychological and financial dependency on the state."[71] It is fair to point out, of course, that the larger organizing structure into which the Bow

---

[66] However, this must be approached with caution. The Canadian federal government understands OSR as any revenue that "self-governing groups" are able to generate. The government's OSR policy states that it proposes to "take into account the ability of self-governing groups to contribute to the costs of their own government activities when determining the level of federal transfers. Over time, and based on ability, an Aboriginal government's reliance on federal transfers may be expected to decline." Further, in 2015, Aboriginal Affairs and Northern Development Canada (now called Indigenous and Northern Affairs Canada) released Canada's Fiscal Approach for Self-Government Arrangements which established a policy framework and a revised methodology for calculating OSR offsets. This was said to include details on the protection of program transfers for health, education, and social development. The policy has been highly controversial within Indigenous communities, whose leaders believe that bands should not be under an obligation to disclose all OSR to the federal department. As of April 1, 2017, funding "reductions" under Canada's OSR policy is suspended for up to three years (Government of Canada, "Own-Source-Revenue for Self-Governing Groups," www.rcaanc-cirnac.gc.ca/eng/1354117773784/1539869378991).

[67] Jaffar, note 40, interviewed many of the actors in what she called the "Aboriginal Power" sphere. She found that they overwhelmingly emphasized the "opportunities that sustainable energy development creates for First Nations to assert their independence by strengthening autonomy and sovereignty" (p. 54).

[68] Ibid.

[69] Interview #7, note 11.

[70] MacArthur, note 5, p. 115. Similarly, "[t]ransmission systems come with environmental and monetary costs for the communities in spatial proximity, whereas the benefits accrue to power traders and energy investors." As MacArthur argues, if we are serious about sustainability and the mitigation of climate change, we need to tackle these inequities.

[71] G. T. Alfred, "Colonialism and State Dependency" (2009) 5 *Journal of Aboriginal Health* 42–60 at 44.

Lake project falls and is made possible, is determined according to settler state laws and remains squarely inside capitalist logics.

Other critics may point out that the generation of economic development income through what economists refer to as "resource rents" raises real questions about who truly benefits from the income generated – community members or agents. Termed "principal–agent problems," these problems can arise in an Indigenous ownership scenario between band membership and leadership, and between the band and hired managers and consultants. Issues also surround the accountability of First Nations'-derived entities created to pursue economic development opportunities. Most notably, resource rent capture has fallen to First Nations'-controlled economic development corporations often in partnership with non-Indigenous corporate entities.[72] In this respect, "principal-to-principal problems" emerge as between multiple owners of resource projects, including between the band and non-Indigenous business partners. Ultimately, then, we should temper our conclusions about how partnership arrangements between Indigenous communities and non-Indigenous businesses can contribute to long-term "economic prosperity and self-sufficiency."[73]

Resource revenue generation brings with it additional challenges, including of "fiscal management and prioritization."[74] To meet these challenges, some recommend the creation and use of resource revenue trusts which, according to supporters, help to "strike a balance between sharing the benefits in the present and providing for the needs of future generations."[75] As we see below, however, important questions surround that approach, highlighting the importance of the Indigenous legal order to structure on-the-ground arrangements.

25.7 IN RESOURCE REVENUE WE TRUST?

As a way of ensuring that the Bow Lake project could meet the community's needs and priorities, Batchewana First Nation established an OSR trust in order to manage the revenues generated. Three public meetings were held on reserve in Batchewana First Nation in early October 2016 for the purposes of discussing the establishment of the trust. There were approximately forty Batchewana First Nation Band members in total present at the meetings. A presentation on the potential options for structuring the trust was completed by an outside consultant. A particular trust model was presented as an option for the community. The initial allocation model of the trust included three components: loan repayment, capital preservation (including family, youth, and elders program delivery), and Chief and Council-identified priorities.

Some concerns expressed at the consultations included: the need for more transparency in relation to current investments and other First Nation revenue streams; the need for consultation with elders; the question of whether other options for trust models and modes of allocation had been canvassed, and what the governance structure of the trust would be; whether the trust model would promote inclusivity; the need to clarify who the beneficiaries of the trust would be and what the initial allocation of funds to Chief and Council would support; the options for short-term investment; the need for prioritization of specific community objectives, primarily youth programming; the issue of safeguards built into the trust model and governance structure

[72] The phenomenon is certainly not new. R. B. Anderson, "Corporate/Indigenous Partnerships in Economic Development: The First Nations in Canada" (1997) 25 *World Development* 1483–1503.

[73] NAEDB, note 15.

[74] Ibid., p. 18.

[75] Ibid.

against theft or fraud; and the need to acknowledge that the Bow Lake revenues belong to the whole community collectively.[76] There was a strongly felt need for more community consultation before a final decision on the trust could be made. As one of our interviewees stated, "the collective nature of our rights mean we have to find a way to share the revenues."[77] Another person framed the issue quite starkly: "We can't make a decision on how we're going to disburse the money because half of us want it right now, saying 'we're getting old, you know, you have to take care of your elders . . .' And the other half is saying, 'we have to save that for seven generations down the road.'" Still another interviewee remarked: "It takes a lot of self-control and foresight to work on a trust that you may never see the benefit of. You yourself as a person may never benefit from that. It may be your children or your grandchildren; it takes a strong mind to do that."[78]

Overall, it is clear that the Bow Lake project would be governed with a strong degree of community input, and that the revenues would eventually be held collectively and distributed according to criteria set by the community in accordance with their own priorities, which is not to say that they are not contested. It is also clear that the trust is likely to be governed in a less hierarchical fashion than typical energy utilities, with more opportunities for meaningful deliberation and participation. Less hierarchical governance models are also likely to garner deeper social inclusion. As an example, the governance of typical conventional energy utilities across the world have excluded, and continue to more or less exclude, women. Current estimates on gender diversity in the boardrooms of all major energy utilities have women represented in only 7 percent of board roles, a figure that is increasing at only 1 percent per year.[79] Thus, while it has been recognized that the participation of women in the renewables sector is also lacking,[80] democratization of governance in the energy sector is likely to advance in the direction of deeper social inclusion.

25.8 GENERATING POWER

One of the most exciting dimensions of this shift is that Indigenous communities that undertake renewable energy projects as expressions of their inherent jurisdiction over their lands may do so in a way that honors their meaningful connections to specific places.[81] As John Borrows explains, the details of the Indigenous legal order (structure and organization of laws) vary between

---

[76] As of July 2017, no motion of the government of Batchewana First Nation had been made to support the trust. We are aware that lawyers were at the time putting together draft documents that would be presented to community members. The plan was that different options for the establishment of the trust would be presented to the membership, followed by motions of Chief and Council to formally establish the structure of the trust.

[77] Interview #1, note 11.

[78] Interview #6, note 11.

[79] Ernst & Young Global, "Talent at the Table: Index of Women in Power and Utilities," May 2014; M. B. Orlando, V. L. Janik, P. Vaidya, N. Angelou, I. Zumbyte, and N. Adams, "Getting to Gender Equality in Energy Infrastructure: Lessons from Electricity Generation, Transmission, and Distribution Projects," Energy Sector Management Assistance Program (ESMAP) Technical Report, No. 012/18, World Bank, Jan. 2018.

[80] B. Baruah, "Renewable inequity? Women's Employment in Clean Energy in Industrialized, Emerging and Developing Economies" (2016) *Natural Resource Forum*.

[81] This is not to say that Indigenous communities will (or should) always apply "traditional" norms in their decision-making, nor to deny them the ability to adapt to changing circumstances. It is to say that if they do so, a policy for renewable energy that favors Indigenous ownership of generating resources may – in addition to bringing in a more equitable sharing of economic benefits and a more participatory governance structure – also introduce principles of governance that are oriented toward stewardship obligations with more meaningful connections to a specific set of lands and waters.

communities, depending on the unique "social, political, biological, economic and spiritual circumstances."[82] In this way, the legal order comes from the land; its authority derives from the complex web of relationships between people and their relations, which in the Anishnaabe world view, include the water, rocks, animals, and other elements of the "environment" that non-Indigenous legal orders tend to abstract and instrumentalize.

That said, all community members should not be expected to agree that the details of any particular project – even if owned and governed by the community and undertaken as an expression of inherent jurisdiction – are compatible with the demands of the Indigenous social, political, or legal order, as community members' voices in the Bow Lake example demonstrate. While most community members we spoke to expressed pride and confidence that the project, as a *renewable* energy project, was not only compatible with their obligations to steward the land and to think about future generations, but necessary to fulfill them – others questioned that compatibility. One person said:

> As I just know that when we ask our ancestors in the spirit of the land, my grave concern was the environment. It was the animals, the migration trails . . . the bats, the bears, deer, moose. They've been traveling these trails for thousands, and thousands and thousands of years. And now . . . they have to come along their trail and they've got to move, which is hard for me to accept.[83]

25.9 CONCLUSION

Can Indigenous-led renewable energy initiatives point a path forward toward a more just set of energy relations? Certainly, renewable energy projects can contribute to climate change mitigation insofar as they can reduce reliance on fossil fuels and thus prevent GHG emissions. These projects may also foster a broader sharing of the benefits of energy generation. A greater diversity of ownership of energy assets will help to deepen social inclusion, including the participation of women. Indigenous-owned and controlled renewables might generate momentum for a just transition away from fossil extractivism toward renewable empowerment in ways that begin to confront the undermining of the inherent jurisdiction of Indigenous peoples and their existing social, economic, and legal orders under settler capitalism.

With recognition of the inherent jurisdiction of Indigenous peoples and genuine respect for the complex set of interconnections between people, lands, and livelihoods, we believe it is possible to restructure the ownership and control of energy generation and distribution systems in more equitable ways. In particular, as can be seen through the Bow Lake example – although it is by no means a guaranteed outcome – alternatives exist for structuring projects such that significant control over and governance of projects remains with Indigenous communities themselves, as expressions of their inherent jurisdiction over the lands and waters across their territories. Where Indigenous communities secure ownership and control of energy assets, it results in a wider distribution of economic, social, and political power in society. That those communities hold the resources collectively and deliberate on the principles through which the benefits of the development should be shared between generations (on the basis of their own social, political, and legal orders), provides further inspiration for moving forward in a transformative direction. This kind of governance model greatly enhances the chances of decision-

---

[82] J. Borrows, *Canada's Indigenous Constitution* (Toronto: University of Toronto Press, 2010).
[83] Interview #7, note 11.

making honoring principles of environmental stewardship – emphasizing relations of reciprocity rather than entitlement – and respecting ecological limits.[84]

But we would be mistaken to suggest it represents a panacea. Indeed, while it is not inevitable that the environmental injustices of fossil extractivism be replicated in the green energy economy, there are real concerns about co-optation and the failure to achieve transformative changes. Leadership is needed to articulate a commitment to ongoing deliberation and participation through processes which not only allow for the expression of differences of opinion and dissent but find creative ways to take up the real challenges posed. Most importantly, communities are hampered in their implementation of their existing Indigenous legal and political orders by the imposition of settler state law. Settler capitalism continues to structure the broader set of relations in which renewable energy projects, including those in which Indigenous peoples hold equity stakes, are situated. As mentioned, the Bow Lake project itself was specifically enabled by settler law, as the Green Energy and Economy Act explicitly countered some of the barriers to Indigenous governance by providing access to capital, by guaranteeing returns, and by creating statutory incentives for industry to seek out partnerships with Indigenous communities. Further, settler law continues to govern – as it structures the relationships between the First Nation and its partners through contract law and its remedies, and the wider market economy in which the project is situated.[85]

Indigenous participation in renewable energy projects holds power – for transforming energy generation relations and extractivist, settler capitalist development – when the projects are initiated by Indigenous communities themselves, when those communities are able to exercise their authority within project governance on an ongoing basis, and when they maintain the authority to structure how revenues are shared.

We have argued in the past that a policy emphasis on renewable energy development as climate mitigation should not be expected to overcome the environmental injustices that characterized the fossil era. Instead, we might reasonably expect the benefits and burdens of the green energy economy to flow along the same familiar axes as climate change itself, to the extent that underlying structural relations of power remain unchanged. Here, we attempt to work through an example of how a more fundamental restructuring might take shape. Indigenous participation in renewable energy, figuratively speaking, can disrupt the concentration of power in the energy grid, as a less hierarchical mode of collective governance aimed at promoting community inclusion, adhering to communal notions of environmental stewardship and obligations to protect lands and waters, and fulfilling obligations to future generations. Within and beyond Indigenous communities, a renewed focus on the connections between people, lands, and livelihoods is central to the structural shift necessary for a just transition.

---

[84] This may not always be the case of course. Some Indigenous communities may not maintain strong connections to lands and/or Indigenous legal traditions. Some may choose not to act in accordance with these when making business-oriented decisions. But again, the *structure* of the ownership model, and the fact of collective ownership, means that principles of environmental stewardship are more likely to be honored than in status quo situations. We do not rule out that non-Indigenous community ownership, such as renewable energy coops, may promise many of the same benefits – in fact, we expect that they would, and we support growth in these alternatives as moves toward a more just energy future as well.

[85] See Scott, "Extraction Contracting", supra note 24.

Climate Change

26

Climate Justice and the Social Pillar in California's Climate Policies

Alice Kaswan

26.1 INTRODUCTION

As California legislators first contemplated comprehensive climate action in the early 2000s, environmental justice activists recognized the connection between climate policy and the everyday challenges faced by the state's poorest and most vulnerable residents. They understood the urgency of climate action because their communities were likely to be the least able to cope with impending climate impacts, like sea level rise, heat waves, and wildfires. And they understood that efforts to reduce greenhouse gases (GHGs) could accomplish multiple goals, including reducing the persistent air pollution plaguing many parts of California.

To an unprecedented degree, environmental justice advocacy has resulted in state laws and policies that have steadily reflected climate justice and the social pillar of sustainable development.[1] Though the record is mixed, numerous climate policies acknowledge the state's underlying inequities and simultaneously direct environmental, economic, and other community benefits to the state's most disadvantaged citizens. As the state's 2017 climate plan stated, "California's environmental justice and equity movement is establishing a blueprint for the nation and world."[2]

Climate policies' social development potential has been important in California because, despite its strong economy and progressive reputation, the state continues to suffer longstanding socioeconomic inequities. In urban areas, poor communities of color are often concentrated close to polluting industrial uses, like ports and refineries.[3] Wilmington, California, experiences both, and its poor Latino residents decry continued pollution. Cristina Garcia, a California assemblywoman who represents an LA-area community, has said: "We have left communities like mine behind too long. We get treated like a wasteland."[4] Residents near the port of

---

[1] As one reporter observed after a series of climate justice-related bills were passed in 2016: "All the measures were advanced this year as many lawmakers representing low-income communities of color made themselves a force in the state's climate change debate after complaints that existing policies weren't doing enough to benefit the districts they represent" (L. Dillon, "City and State: Climate Change Funding Climbs," *L.A. Times*, p. 3 (Sept. 15, 2016)).

[2] California Air Resources Board, "California's 2017 Climate Change Scoping Plan: The Strategy for Achieving California's 2030 Greenhouse Gas Target," Nov. 2017, p. ES-6 [CARB (2017A)].

[3] L. Cushing, J. Faust, L. M. August, R. Cendrak, W. Wieland, and G. Alexeff, "Racial/Ethnic Disparities in Cumulative Environmental Health Impacts in California: Evidence from a Statewide Environmental Justice Screening Tool (CalEnviroScreen 1.1)" (2015) 105 *American Journal of Public Health* 2341.

[4] J. Cart, "'Trying to Breathe' – as CA Toasts Environmental Win, Pollution Still Plagues," July 27, 2017, https://calmatters.org/articles/california-environmental-success-poor-communities-remain-polluted/.

Oakland, primarily African-American, have choked on the emissions from port activities and from the diesel trucks radiating from the port to destinations around the country. As one resident observed in connection with a civil rights lawsuit against the port: "Our neighborhood has long endured the unjust burden of toxic pollution and jarring noise from the Port of Oakland."[5] In Richmond, California, the African community experiences ongoing pollution from the Chevron refinery located in the city.[6] The Los Angeles–Long Beach metropolitan region experiences the worst ozone pollution in the country, posing respiratory and coronary risks to almost twenty million people.[7]

Rural agricultural areas like the Central Valley also experience severe air quality challenges. According to the American Lung Association's "State of the Air 2018," four Central Valley cities are among the ten cities experiencing the highest ozone levels in the nation.[8] And five Central Valley cities are among the top-ten cities experiencing the highest levels of average year-round particulate pollution and spikes in particulate pollution.[9] The smog-ridden San Joaquin Valley has some of the highest asthma rates in the country. Exposure to poor air quality is worst for those who work outdoors, including farmworkers – most of whom are immigrants[10] – and construction workers.

California's environmental justice screening methodology bears out these inequities. Racial minorities – particularly Hispanics and African Americans – are more likely to reside in areas suffering high levels of cumulative environmental impacts than White populations.[11] Controlling for other factors, race is strongly correlated with the likelihood of exposure. Poverty is also correlated with cumulative exposures, though less strongly than race.[12]

California has significant economic as well as pollution disparities. Taking into account the cost of living, California has the highest poverty rate in the nation (except for the District of Columbia).[13] At the same time, California has high and steadily increasing levels of income inequality.[14]

Poor and of-color communities are more vulnerable to climate impacts. For example, California agricultural field workers work outside in increasingly blistering heat and risk losing their jobs as projected water shortages impact the agricultural sector.[15] Thirty-six percent of Californians do not have air-conditioning, and low-income residents who do have air-conditioning may not be able to afford to run it.[16] The urban heat island effect, caused by

---

[5] C. Jordan-Bloch, "Community Group Alleges Civil Rights Violations by the City and Port of Oakland in Complaint to Federal Government," Apr. 15, 2017, https://earthjustice.org/news/press/2017/community-group-alleges-civil-rights-violations-by-the-city-and-port-of-oakland-in-complaint-to-federal.

[6] Y. Funes, "The Battle for Environmental Justice Continues 4 Years after Richmond Refinery Explosion," Aug. 5, 2016, www.colorlines.com/articles/battle-environmental-justice-continues-4-years-after-richmond-refinery-explosion.

[7] American Lung Association, "State of the Air 2018," p. 20.

[8] Ibid., p. 20.

[9] Ibid., p. 19 (year-round particulates); p. 18 (short-term particulates).

[10] P. Martin, B. Hooker, M. Akhtar, and M. Stockton, "How Many Workers are Employed in California Agriculture?" (2016) 71 *California Agriculture* 30.

[11] Cushing et al., note 3.

[12] Ibid.

[13] T. Renwick and L. Fox, "The Supplemental Poverty Measure: 2015: Current Population Reports," United States Census Bureau, Sept. 2016, p. 9 (table 4, Number and Percentage of People in Poverty by State Using 3-Year Average over 2013, 2014, and 2015).

[14] S. Bohn and C. Danielson, "Income Inequality and the Safety Net in California," Public Policy Institute of California, May 2016, pp. 4–8. California's income inequality is higher than most other states (ibid., p. 6).

[15] M. Roos et al., *Climate Justice Report, California's Fourth Climate Change Assessment*, 2018, pp. 44–45.

[16] Ibid., p. 45.

multiple factors that combine to increase urban temperatures, affects low-income residents and communities of color who are concentrated in urban areas.[17] The effects of greater exposure to heat in rural and urban areas will adversely impact poor residents, who experience greater underlying health problems and are less likely to have sufficient health insurance.[18] One study shows that African Americans in Los Angeles were two times more likely to die in a heat wave than others.[19] Wildfires are increasingly threatening communities, posing significant risks to poor residents, who confront shortages of affordable housing and, if homeowners, are less likely to have adequate insurance.[20]

Influenced by environmental justice advocacy, the state has recognized that climate change measures will profoundly transform our fossil fuel–based economy, generating environmental, economic, and social risks, and opportunities.[21] Because GHG emissions are closely linked to traditional pollutants, GHG mitigation policies have the potential to reduce the state's persistent air pollution. And new ways of saving and generating energy, like energy efficiency and renewables, create potential employment opportunities for underserved communities and current fossil fuel workers. By reducing the need for electricity from the grid, energy efficiency and distributed renewable resources, like rooftop solar, have the potential to reduce electricity bills and boost the economy with new industries and services. California has recognized that the task at hand is not just reducing a single pollutant but transitioning to a green energy economy.[22]

In this chapter, I first lay out the distributive, participatory, and social justice issues presented by domestic climate policy in California and their connection to the social pillar of sustainable development. Although much of the attention to climate justice focuses on the unequal and unfair *impacts* of climate change and their implications for climate change adaptation,[23] this chapter focuses on the climate justice implications of climate mitigation policies – of policies to reduce emissions. Accordingly, I provide an overview of California's climate mitigation policies, and then explore their distributive and participatory justice implications. Lastly, the chapter considers a few of the broader lessons offered by the California experience.

26.2 THE CLIMATE JUSTICE FRAMEWORK AND THE SOCIAL PILLAR OF SUSTAINABLE DEVELOPMENT

Preventing catastrophic climate change will likely require decarbonization, which in turn will require a transformation in our fossil fuel–driven economy.[24] The policies we use to achieve that transformation will profoundly affect communities and necessarily implicate the social pillar of sustainable development. As elaborated in the Copenhagen Declaration on Social Development, the social pillar is people-centered, and calls for access to basic needs, including

[17] Ibid., p. 40.
[18] Ibid., pp. 42–43.
[19] Ibid., p. 38.
[20] Ibid., pp. 39, 47–48.
[21] CARB (2017A), note 2, p. ES-1 (describing widespread climate and non-climate benefits of state's climate plan)
[22] Ibid.
[23] See, for example, W. N. Adger, J. Paavola, S. Huq, and M. J. Mace, (eds.), *Fairness in Adaptation to Climate Change* (London: MIT Press, 2006).
[24] J. H. Williams, B. Haley, F. Kahrl, et al., "Policy Implications of Deep Decarbonization in the United States," DDRI SciencesPo, Sustainable Development Solutions Network, the US report of the Deep Decarbonization Pathways Project of the Sustainable Development Solutions Network and the Institute for Sustainable Development and International Relations, Nov. 25, 2014.

health, poverty reduction, and the right to a clean environment.[25] The social pillar's focus on absolute well-being as well as on equity in the distribution of resources reflects principles of distributive justice.[26] In addition to its focus on distributive justice, the social pillar recognizes the importance of meaningful engagement in government decision making,[27] reflecting principles of participatory justice. Moreover, improving socioeconomic well-being requires an understanding of the structural reasons for existing inequities,[28] reflecting concern with overarching social justice. This section reviews the distributive, participatory, and social justice implications of a clean energy transition and their relationship to the social pillar of sustainable development.

26.2.1 *Distributive Justice*

The first distributive justice implication of climate policies stems from the close correlation between GHGs and other harmful pollutants. Most GHG emissions come from the production and combustion of fossil fuels, and so climate policies that reduce GHGs have the potential to reduce traditional pollutants, such as particulates (including diesel particulates), sulfur and nitrogen oxides, and a wide range of toxic pollutants.[29] The more that climate policies induce emissions reductions in areas experiencing high levels of traditional air pollution, the greater the distributive justice benefits. Climate policies that improve living conditions and reduce inequalities in exposure align with the Copenhagen Declaration's sixth commitment, to achieve the "highest attainable standard of physical and mental health . . . making particular efforts to rectify inequalities."[30]

In addition, distributive justice questions are raised by the degree to which disadvantaged communities have access to clean energy technologies.[31] Will only rich residents be able to afford solar panels, electric cars, and energy efficient appliances – or will poor communities also have access? The social pillar emphasizes the importance of equitable access to resources that enable social development,[32] and Goal 7 of the Sustainable Development Goals, "Affordable and Clean Energy," explicitly states the objective of "access to affordable, reliable, sustainable, and modern energy for all."[33]

Moreover, new modes of energy conservation and production could lead to employment opportunities for traditionally marginalized communities, including inner-city residents, rural outposts investing in renewable energy, and Native American tribes with renewable resources, consistent with the social pillar's emphasis on increasing employment opportunities in areas

---

[25] UN World Summit for Social Development, Copenhagen Declaration on Social Development, Mar. 14, 1995, UN Doc. A/CONF.166/9.

[26] Ibid., Commitment 2(f).

[27] Ibid., para. 26(o) ("Empowerment requires the full participation of people in the formulation, implementation and evaluation of decisions determining the functioning and well-being of our societies").

[28] Ibid., para. 2.

[29] M. L. Bell, "Ancillary Human Health Benefits of Improved Air Quality Resulting from Climate Change Mitigation" (2008) 7 *Environmental Health* art. no. 41.

[30] UN WSSD, note 25, Commitment 6.

[31] D. Behles, "From Dirty to Green: Increasing Energy Efficiency and Renewable Energy in Environmental Justice Communities" (2013) 58 *Villanova Law Review* 25; B. Bovarnick and D. Banks, "State Policies to Increase Low-Income Communities' Access to Solar Power," Center for American Progress, September 23, 2014; U. Outka, "Fairness in the Low-Carbon Shift: Learning from Environmental Justice" (2017) 82 *Brooklyn Law Review* 791; S. Welton, "Clean Electrification" (2017) 88 *University of Colorado Law Review* 571 at 631–36.

[32] UN WSSD, note 25, Commitment 1(b).

[33] UN Development Program, *Sustainable Development Goals*.

suffering from "structural, long-term unemployment,"[34] and the Sustainable Development Goal of achieving "full and productive employment and decent work for all."[35]

There will also be distributive justice risks. Reductions in coal-fired power could lead to increased operation of natural gas facilities, increasing pollution in neighboring communities as well as generating a range of environmental impacts from fracking.[36] New biomass or biogas facilities, promoted by some as a climate neutral alternative, could create new pollution exposures.[37] Cap-and-trade or carbon tax programs, which allow companies to purchase allowances or pay a tax, could fail to achieve reductions in polluted areas, perpetuating pollution that a more carefully tailored program could have reduced.[38]

There are economic as well as environmental risks. The costs of a new energy infrastructure are likely to be most difficult for the poor, who spend a higher percentage of their income on energy and the basic needs impacted by energy costs.[39] Moreover, although a green energy transition has the potential to increase jobs and provide opportunities for communities that have long suffered from chronic unemployment, the transition will cause disruptions in some areas. For example, in coal country – whether places like West Virginia or Native American lands – lessening reliance on coal will undercut the economic foundation for communities, with social as well as economic implications.[40] Similarly, lessening reliance on oil and gas will have economic and indirect social impacts on communities in the Gulf Coast and other regions that rely heavily on oil, gas, and petrochemicals.

Different policy tools enhance or impede achieving distributive justice. The choice of market-based mechanisms, planning mechanisms, sector-based targets, facility-specific limits, or other tools can affect the ease with which policymakers can simultaneously reduce GHGs, reduce pollution, and provide other benefits, like access to clean energy technology for marginalized communities. They will also shape the extent of the environmental and socioeconomic risks of a transition. The social pillar of development suggests the importance of relying upon policy tools that maximize the benefits of a green transition while simultaneously addressing the needs of those who could be negatively impacted.

26.2.2 *Participatory Justice*

The social pillar of sustainable development includes a strong participatory element. As the Copenhagen Declaration states: "Empowerment requires the full participation of people in the formulation, implementation and evaluation of decisions determining the functioning and well-being of our societies."[41] And Principle 10 of the Environmental Justice Leadership Forum on Climate Change states that "people-of-color, Indigenous peoples, and low-income communities

---

[34] UN WSSD, note 25, Commitment 3(a).

[35] UNDP, note 33, Goal 8.

[36] J. Deyette, S. Clemmer, R. Cleetus, S. Sattler, A. Bailie, and M. Rising, "The Natural Gas Gamble: A Risky Bet on America's Clean Energy Future," Union of Concerned Scientists, Mar. 2015.

[37] R. L. Bain, W. A. Amos, M. Downing, and R. L. Perlack, "Biopower Technical Assessment: State of the Industry and Technology," National Renewable Energy Laboratory, Mar. 2003, pp. 6-1–6-7

[38] A. Kaswan, "Environmental Justice and Domestic Climate Change Policy" (2008) 38 *Environmental Law Reporter* 10287 at 10291–10303.

[39] A. Drehobl and L. Ross, "Lifting the High Energy Burden in America's Largest Cities: How Energy Efficiency Can Improve Low Income and Underserved Communities," American Council for an Energy Efficient Economy, April 2016.

[40] P. McGinley, "Collateral Damage: Turning a Blind Eye to Environmental and Social Injustice in the Coalfields" (2013) 19 *Journal on Environmental and Sustainability Law* 304.

[41] UN WSSD, note 25, para. 26(o).

... have the inalienable right to have our voices shape what is the most significant policy debate of the 21st Century."[42] Participatory justice questions arise at every turn.

Participatory opportunities in developing climate policies are likely to vary depending upon who decides: international bodies, legislative bodies, or administrative agencies, at international, federal, state, or local levels. Some of these forums, like legislative bodies, are democratic but not participatory. Administrative agencies typically provide public hearings. Citizens have opportunities to participate at local levels, while organized environmental justice groups are more likely to represent citizens at the state, federal, and international level.

Of course, an opportunity on paper does not always translate into actual access and influence. Particularly for complex and time-consuming proceedings, like administrative or rule-making actions, low-income communities often lack the information, expertise, and financial resources to participate effectively without outside assistance. And, by definition, marginalized communities may have less influence in the legislative and administrative decisions that affect their fate. Achieving participatory justice for marginalized communities thus requires deliberate attention to enabling access and influence.[43]

Different types of climate policies also provide differing opportunities to participate. Some climate policies begin with a planning phase: for example, an executive or legislative directive requiring an environmental agency to develop a climate action plan. As of 2018, the Center for Climate Strategies' map of completed state climate action plans indicates that 33 states have completed plans,[44] and many local governments have likewise engaged in climate action planning. Climate action planning typically includes opportunities for public participation.[45]

For regulatory approaches, like requirements that certain kinds of facilities reduce emissions by a certain amount, U.S. administrative procedures typically require the implementing agency to provide a public comment period.[46] In addition, regulatory programs imposing facility-specific permitting requirements usually require public hearings on the permits.[47] Although effective participation in administrative proceedings requires resources, expertise, and power, these proceedings can give communities at least the potential to influence decisions.

Market-based mechanisms like cap-and-trade, in contrast, give sources independent discretion to determine their own GHG emissions, so long as they comply with the requirements of the market-based system.[48] By leaving emissions decisions to private entities, market-based mechanisms therefore offer less public participation than other types of climate strategies.[49]

---

[42] "Environmental Justice Leadership Forum on Climate Change," http://ejnet.org/ej/ejlf.pdf.

[43] See S. Kravchenko, "The Myth of Public Participation in a World of Poverty" (2009) 23 *Tulane Environmental Law Journal* 33.

[44] The Center for Climate Strategies, "State and Local Climate," www.climatestrategies.us/policy_tracker/state.

[45] For a local example, see Ascent Environment, Inc., "Public Outreach and Engagement Plan, Climate Action Plan, County of San Diego," Prepared for Planning and Development Services, Mar. 2016. For a non-California state example describing the role of the public in New York state's climate action planning process, see New York State Climate Action Council, "Interim Report," Nov. 2010.

[46] For example, the US Administrative Procedures Act requires that agencies provide public notice and allow for public comment before enacting regulations (5 US Code § 553).

[47] For an example, see the general public participation requirements for Texas environmental permits: Texas Commission on Environmental Quality, "Overview: Public Participation in Environmental Permitting," Sept. 1, 2015.

[48] The public would have the opportunity to comment on administrative decisions setting the emissions cap and establishing the program's parameters, but they would not have the opportunity to influence individual facility decisions.

[49] Kaswan, note 38, pp. 10302–10303.

To meet the social pillar's commitment to including people in the formulation of policies that affect them, a critical factor will thus be the mode and degree of public engagement in the formulation of the green energy policies that could have a profound effect on communities. Moreover, the choice of particular climate strategies – like planning, regulatory, and market-based mechanisms – will offer differing opportunities for ongoing public input.

26.2.3 *Social Justice*

The social pillar is fundamentally grounded in a conception of social justice that recognizes the need for positive action to overcome past inequities. The Sustainable Development Goals similarly emphasize equality.[50] Social justice pervades the distributive and participatory justice contexts described above. Currently disproportionate concentrations of pollution result from a legacy of discrimination and poverty, including land use planning that has disregarded the interests of marginalized communities and a suite of other governmental and civil society factors that have led to existing patterns of segregation and a lower quality of life in poor communities of color.[51] To the degree climate policies can improve existing pollution patterns and economic disparities, they respond to the history and ongoing experience of social injustice.

26.3 CALIFORNIA CLIMATE POLICIES AND THE SOCIAL PILLAR

Before delving into specific climate justice policies, I first provide a broad overview of California's climate initiatives, and then explore the degree to which California has incorporated distributive and participatory justice concerns into its climate policies in ways that reflect the social pillar of sustainable development.

26.3.1 *Overview of California Climate Policies*

California has adopted increasingly stringent GHG reductions targets. In 2006, Assembly Bill 32 (AB 32), California's first comprehensive climate policy, established an emissions reduction goal of achieving 1990 GHG emission levels by 2020.[52] That goal increased in 2016, when California set a GHG reduction target of 40 percent below 1990 emissions by 2030.[53] In 2018, then-Governor Brown established a goal of net carbon neutrality by 2045, a daunting and unprecedented challenge.[54]

A central feature of California's approach has been its statewide planning process. The state's first comprehensive climate bill, AB 32, required the state's Air Resources Board (ARB) to develop a comprehensive "scoping plan" for achieving the law's 2020 emission reduction goal.[55] Working with a wide range of state agencies, including the state's Public Utilities Commission, the Energy Commission, and agencies addressing transportation, solid waste, and other programs, ARB and its sister agencies analyzed all of the state's emission-generating sectors,

---

[50] UNDP, note 33, Goal 10 ("Reduced Inequalities").

[51] L. Cole and S. Foster, *From the Ground up: Environmental Racism and the Rise of the Environmental Justice Movement* (New York: New York University Press, 2001); C. A. Anthony, "Planning Milagros: Environmental Justice and Land Use Regulation" (1998) 76 *Denver Law Review* 1.

[52] California Health & Safety Code, §§ 38500–38599.

[53] Ibid., § 38566.

[54] Executive Department: State of California, "Executive Order B–55–18 to Achieve Carbon Neutrality," Sept. 10, 2018.

[55] California Health & Safety Code, § 38561.

identified potential control strategies in these sectors, and then laid out a proposed plan.[56] The plan has been updated twice, once in 2014[57] and, looking ahead to the 2030 target, in 2017.[58] The executive order establishing the net neutrality goal directs ARB to integrate that objective into future scoping plans.[59]

Climate reduction strategies in the plan have been guided, in many cases, by additional state legislation mandating specific goals or programs, like renewable portfolio standards and mobile source strategies.[60] The scoping plans have integrated these legislative initiatives, as well as administrative initiatives, into a single comprehensive roadmap. In addition to mapping out strategies and implementation steps, each plan has also included an "evaluations" section, which analyzes a wide variety of anticipated impacts, including economic impacts, public health and environmental impacts, as well as a range of other potential consequences.[61]

California's initial 2008 scoping plan established a comprehensive cap-and-trade program intended to cover approximately 85 percent of the state's emissions, and subsequent scoping plans have maintained this program.[62] The cap-and-trade program requires all large emitting sources, including power plants and industrial sources, to hold allowances for their emissions, and requires industrial and transportation fuel suppliers to hold allowances to cover the carbon content of all of the fuels they put into commerce in the state.[63] The program generates revenue that is being returned to consumers and used for a variety of emission-reducing activities.[64]

The cap-and-trade program does not, however, operate in isolation. Many other energy and transportation programs drive the state's emission reductions more directly. In fact, analysts suggest that progress made by 2018 has largely been driven by these more direct measures, not the cap-and-trade program.[65] At least at present, the cap has operated as a backstop that ensures that the target is reached, rather than as a direct driver of emission reductions.

Through both legislative and agency action, the state has adopted a wide range of renewable energy policies over the last two decades, now driven by a 2018 renewable portfolio standard (RPS) mandating 60 percent renewables by 2030[66] and establishing a policy goal of achieving 100 percent renewables by 2045.[67] In addition, notwithstanding a strong history of appliance and building

---

[56] Ibid.

[57] E. G. Brown, M. Rodriguz, M. D. Nichols, and R. W. Corey, "First Update to the Climate Change Scoping Plan: Building on the Framework Pursuant to AB 32: The California Global Warming Solutions Act of 2006," May 2014.

[58] CARB (2017A), note 2.

[59] Brown et al., note 57.

[60] Ibid., p. 1.

[61] The first scoping plan contained a long list of evaluations, including economic, technology, cost-effectiveness, small business, environmental/public health, and other societal benefits. California Air Resources Board, "Climate Change Scoping Plan: A Framework for Change," Dec. 2008, pp. 73–96 [CARB (2008)]. The 2014 update included evaluations of economic impacts, public health, environmental justice and disadvantaged communities, and environmental impacts. Brown et al., note 57, pp. 117–132. The 2017 Scoping Plan again included a long list of evaluations, including a range of both specific and general environmental and economic factors. CARB (2017A), note 2, pp. 35–61.

[62] CARB (2017A), note 2, p. ES-16. The 2017 Scoping Plan anticipated that the cap-and-trade program would cover 80 percent of the state's GHG emissions, ibid., slightly less than the 85 percent initially anticipated. CARB (2008), note 61, p. 31.

[63] C2ES, "California Cap-and-Trade," www.c2es.org/content/california-cap-and-trade/.

[64] CARB (2017A), note 2, p. ES-16–17.

[65] C. Busch, "Comment: California's Cap-and-Trade Program – The Crisis that Wasn't," Aug. 2, 2016, http://carbon-pulse.com/22969/.

[66] California Public Utilities Code, § 399.15(b)(2)(B).

[67] Ibid., § 454.53(a).

efficiency standards, 2016 state legislation requires the state to double energy-efficiency energy savings by 2030.[68]

The state's earliest policies to reduce GHG emissions focused on mobile sources, including cars and freight. The state has addressed multiple dimensions, beginning with required tailpipe standards, standards that ultimately served as the basis for federal auto emission standards.[69] On the fuel side, the state has adopted a low-carbon fuel standard to reduce the presence of carbon in fuels through biofuels and electrification.[70] Diesel fuels, which produce "black carbon" particulates, have received special attention, and are being reduced through the state's Short-lived Climate Pollutant Strategy (SLCP Strategy).[71] Recognizing the strong connection between land use patterns and driving, the legislature adopted a law that requires the state to set transportation-related GHG emissions budgets for each region and then requires regional planning, culminating in "sustainable communities strategies."[72] Although the strategies are not directly enforceable, the law encourages local government cooperation in structuring future housing development to reduce how far people have to drive and, accordingly, reduce GHG emissions.

While the electricity, mobile source, and agricultural[73] sectors of California's economy are or will be subject to sector-specific emission reduction targets, most industrial operations, like refineries, cement production, and food manufacturing, are subject only to the cap-and-trade program.[74] The primary exceptions are methane emission controls on oil-and-gas storage and distribution and controls on discrete pollutants with high global-warming potentials.[75]

26.3.2 *Climate Policies and the Social Pillar*

Recognizing a legacy of discrimination that has resulted in significant pockets of pollution and poverty in communities of color, numerous California policies have incorporated provisions that address both distributive justice and participatory justice and that reflect steps to achieve the social pillar. As discussed below, policies that address the distribution of co-pollutants and clean energy opportunities attempt to improve distributive justice. And the state's planning approach, coupled with specific environmental justice mechanisms, enhance participatory justice. These mechanisms have not fully embodied the environmental justice movement's goals for a more radical reduction in GHG emissions, a speedier and deeper transition to renewable energy, and direct controls on individual facilities to maximize co-pollutant reductions. Nonetheless, they provide a useful example demonstrating one state's effort to incorporate the social pillar of sustainable development into climate policies.

---

[68] California Public Resources Code, § 25301(c)(1).

[69] A. E. Carlson, "The President, Climate Change, and California" (2013) 126 *Harvard Law Review Forum* 156.

[70] California Code Regulations, § 95480.

[71] California Air Resources Board, "Short-Lived Climate Pollutant Reduction Strategy," Mar. 2017, pp. 47–50 [CARB (2017B)].

[72] California Government Code, § 65080(b)(2)(A).

[73] The SLCP Strategy also grapples with methane emissions from the state's massive dairy industry, requiring the development of mechanisms to reduce the sector's contribution by 40 percent from 2013 levels by 2030. CARB (2017B), note 71, p. 63.

[74] The state has adopted direct measures for certain high-global warming potential gases and has set methane limits on oil-and-gas production and transmission activities.

[75] CARB (2017A), note 2, p. 72.

26.3.3 *Distributive Justice and Pollution Impacts*

Facilitated by strategic political pressure from Latinx lawmakers representing communities suffering from significant pollution,[76] California's first comprehensive climate law, AB 32, contained numerous provisions encouraging ARB to take a multi-pollutant approach that would couple GHG and co-pollutant reductions. For example, the law stated that ARB should develop an approach that "maximizes additional environmental and economic co-benefits for California, and complements the state's efforts to improve air quality."[77] The law expressed special concern for low-income communities, stating that the ARB must "[e]nsure that the activities undertaken to comply with [its] regulations do not disproportionately impact low-income communities."[78] And, anticipating that ARB might adopt a cap-and-trade program (as it eventually did), AB 32 stated that ARB must "[c]onsider the potential for direct, indirect, and cumulative emission impacts from these mechanisms, including localized impacts in communities that are already adversely impacted by air pollution."[79]

As implemented through ARB's scoping plan, measures in the electricity and transportation sectors are intended to reduce both GHGs and conventional pollutants.[80] ARB's mobile source strategies, including tailpipe emissions for cars, diesel emission controls, and efforts to reduce pollution from freight transport, were all developed with the goal of achieving combined GHG and co-pollutant reduction benefits,[81] with special attention to concentrated pollution from freight transport near the state's active ports.[82] Although transportation emissions rose slightly between 2013 and 2016, they nonetheless dropped considerably between 2007 and 2016.[83]

Similarly, the state's RPS and multiple initiatives for renewable energy and energy efficiency are anticipated to reduce co-pollutant emissions from the electricity sector. However, in-state emissions have only recently begun to decrease. From 2011 to 2015, in-state emissions increased because utilities decreased carbon-intensive imports and increased in-state generation to make up the difference.[84] By 2016, in-state electricity emissions also began to go down due to increased in-state renewable generation and hydropower, a trend that is likely to continue as state utilities comply with the state's increasingly stringent RPS.[85] That GHG decrease should generate associated co-pollutant reductions.[86]

---

[76] J. Sze, G. Gambrirazzio, A. Karner, D. Rowan, J. London, and D. Niemeier, "Best in Show? Climate and Environmental Justice Policy in California" (2009) 2 *Environmental Justice* 179 at 180–183.

[77] California Health & Safety Code, § 38501(h).

[78] Ibid., § 38562(b)(2).

[79] Ibid., § 38570(b)(1). Moreover, the law required ARB to design any market mechanism "to prevent any increase in the emissions of toxic air contaminants or criteria air pollutants" (ibid., § 38562(b) (2)).

[80] CARB (2017A), note 2, pp. 12–13.

[81] Ibid., p. 47.

[82] California Governor's Office, "Sustainable Freight Action Plan," July 2016.

[83] California Air Resources Board, "2018 Edition: California Greenhouse Gas Emissions from 2000 to 2016: Trends of Emissions and Other Indicators," pp. 5–6 [CARB (2018)].

[84] Ibid., p. 7.

[85] Ibid., pp. 7–8.

[86] Decreases are not, however, certain. ARB acknowledges that utility operational shifts could both decrease and increase emissions in particular locations, and notes that "it is of particular importance to ensure that this transition to a cleaner grid does not result in unintended negative impacts to . . . [disadvantaged] communities" (CARB (2017A), note 2, p. 66). Moreover, as of the summer of 2018, the state legislature is considering a bill that would connect California's grid with that of other western states and transfer authority over the grid to a regional transmission operator. AB-813, *Multi-state Regional Transmission System Organization: Membership*, Feb. 15, 2017; M. Macias, Jr., "California's Controversial Energy-Grid Bill Advances," June 19, 2018, www.courthousenews.com/californias-controversial-energy-grid-bill-advances/. If that occurs, California

As noted above, the state is relying primarily on the cap-and-trade program to reduce industrial emissions. Because the electricity and transportation sectors are subject to regulations that will reduce these sectors' demand for allowances under the cap-and-trade program, more allowances are likely to be available to and inexpensive for industrial sources. If so, industrial sources may disproportionately purchase allowances rather than reducing emissions. Consequently, communities neighboring industrial facilities, like refineries and cement plants, may experience fewer GHG and associated co-pollutant reductions than other communities. Although industry emissions can be affected by multiple factors, not just climate policy, it is worth noting that, since 2007, industry combustion emissions have gradually increased with a growing economy, with the exception of oil-and-gas extraction emissions, which have slightly decreased.[87]

Recent studies assessing the degree to which localized stationary source pollution has gone down in disadvantaged communities suggest a mixed picture. ARB analyzed ten communities to assess emissions trends and found that emissions had stayed the same or gone down in six, while increasing in four communities, including highly populated areas like downtown Los Angeles and Richmond, California.[88] A detailed study evaluating emissions before and after the adoption of the trading program found that neighborhoods experiencing post-trading emissions increases were more likely to be disadvantaged.[89]

Because the state's programs have not placed direct limits on stationary sources, these variations in results are unsurprising. Even though the RPS creates a rigorous statewide goal, it does not control emissions at individual power plants. Utilities could reduce imports, or close or decrease emissions at one plant and increase at others, while still complying with the RPS. As noted above, industrial sources can take advantage of the ample supply of allowances that could result from required reductions in the electricity and transportation sectors. Moreover, the cap-and-trade program allows sources to purchase offsets – credits for emission reductions occurring elsewhere – as well as allowances. California industries have used offsets extensively,[90] and three-quarters of the purchased offsets came from out-of-state projects that promise to reduce GHGs, but which do not provide associated co-benefits within California.[91]

Concerned about cap-and-trade and the lack of facility-specific measures, the California environmental justice community has spearheaded two additional statutes intended to distribute the benefits of climate policies. In 2016, legislators representing low-income communities of color linked their support for a new GHG target bill (SB 32) to passage of AB 197, which instructed ARB to prioritize direct requirements on stationary and mobile sources.[92] The California Alliance for Environmental Justice observed that:

> climate justice can no longer be ignored in state policy. The path to passing SB 32 and AB 197 highlighted the new political reality for climate policy: to win on climate, we've got to include the issues communities of color care about. We need climate solutions that work for

---

utilities might increase generation (and emissions) from underutilized natural gas plants to supply energy to out-of-state consumers.

[87] CARB (2018), note 83, p. 11.

[88] California Air Resources Board, "California's Clean Air Approach and Update on the Cap-and-Trade Adaptive Management Process," Nov. 17, 2016, p. 25.

[89] L. J. Cushing, D. Blaustein-Rejto, M. Wander, et al., "Carbon Trading, Co-pollutants, and Environmental Equity: Evidence from California's Cap-and-Trade Program (2011–2015)" (2018) 15 *PLoS Med* e1002604.

[90] Ibid., pp. 14–15.

[91] Ibid., p. 14.

[92] AB-197, State Air Resources Board: Greenhouse Gases: Regulations, § 5 (2015–2016), California Health & Safety Code, § 38562.5.

communities that have been or will be hit first and worst by climate change and related pollution and addressing equity issues must be a central piece of California policy solutions.[93]

In 2017, as the Governor and state legislature pushed to extend the state's cap-and-trade program, environmental justice interests were again central in forging a legislative compromise.[94] Explaining their effort to condition approval of cap-and-trade on benefits to marginalized communities, assemblywoman Cristina Garcia stated that: "We can be the leaders for the global community, but we're going to be failing if we're not leading with the environmental issues in our backyard."[95] Although assemblywoman Garcia's bill to directly incorporate environmental justice concerns into the operation of the cap-and-trade program failed to garner sufficient votes,[96] legislators representing environmental justice communities secured passage of AB 617, a parallel law directly targeting concentrated pollution.[97] AB 617 initiated a monitoring and planning process for addressing cumulative pollution risks, a measure designed to target pollution reductions where they are most needed.[98] In addition, the law requires facilities to accelerate their adoption of the latest available pollution-control technologies.[99]

Despite these laws, the November 2017 scoping plan, outlining the state's plans for achieving the 2030 target of 40 percent below 1990 emissions, continues to rely largely on the general RPS and energy efficiency in the electricity sector and cap-and-trade in the industrial sector, without the direct limitations expected under AB 197.[100] The agency suggests that AB 197's preference for direct reductions from facilities should be fulfilled through programs focused directly on co-pollutants, including AB 617.[101]

The last mechanism for addressing the distribution of co-pollutants is indirect: Revenue from the sale of allowances in the cap-and-trade program can be used to improve environmental quality in disadvantaged communities. As cap-and-trade became instantiated in the state's climate policy, environmental justice advocates successfully promoted legislation that now requires the state to channel 35 percent of cap-and-trade revenue to (and for the benefit of)

---

[93] California Environmental Justice Alliance, "Environmental Justice Wins in the 2016 Legislative Session," https://caleja.org/2016/09/environmental-justice-in-the-2016-legislative-session/.

[94] M. Mason, "Governor Brown and Democratic Leaders Offer Plan to Extend Cap and Trade, with Aim for Approval this Week," July 11, 2017, www.latimes.com/politics/la-pol-ca-jerry-brown-cap-trade-details-20170710-story.html.

[95] T. Barboza and C. Megerian, "Brown Tours Areas Hit Hard by Pollution," May 24, 2017, www.pressreader .com/, p. 1.

[96] A. Kaswan, "A Broader Vison for Climate Policy: Lessons from California," (2018) 9 *San Diego Journal of Climate and Energy Law* 83 at 114–116.

[97] AB-617, Nonvehicular Air Pollution: Criteria Air Pollutants and Toxic Air Contaminants, 2017–2018, §7; California Health & Safety Code, § 42705.5(b).

[98] Ibid.

[99] AB-617, note 97, § 2; California Health & Safety Code §40920.6(c). The legislative compromise was controversial within the environmental justice community. Some groups believed that the gains achieved through AB 617 did not outweigh the negative features of the cap-and-trade bill, particularly state preemption of local source GHG controls and direct controls on the oil industry. California Environmental Justice Alliance, "Environmental Justice Advances in the 2017 Legislative Session," https://caleja.org/2017/10/environ mental-justice-advances-2017-legislative-session/.

[100] CARB (2018), note 83, pp. 65–73.

[101] Ibid., p. 71. In the January 2017 draft scoping plan, the agency had proposed requiring refineries to reduce GHG emissions by 20 percent (CARB (2017A), note 2, p. 38–39). However, 2017 legislation preempted this facility-specific proposal (Cal. Health & Safety Code § 38592.5(a)(1); M. Mason, C. Megerian, and T. Barboza, "The Environment: Cool Reception: Progressive, Environmentalists Are Ambivalent on Cap-Trade Law," July 12, 2017, www.pressreader.com/).

disadvantaged and low-income communities.[102] "Disadvantage" is determined by location, socioeconomic criteria, and exposure to environmental and public health hazards.[103] Projects for disadvantaged communities must reduce GHGs, as required by California law, and must "[m]aximize economic, environmental, and public health benefits."[104] In addition, state electric car rebates are available only to low-income car buyers,[105] increasing the likelihood that poorer, and potentially more polluted, communities will obtain environmental benefits. To the degree auction revenue projects and other programs provide public health benefits, they improve distributional justice.

Overall, the state's programs for mobile and electricity sources are likely to lead to GHG and associated co-pollutant reductions, and disadvantaged communities are likely (although not certain) to benefit from these reductions. In the industrial sector, however, the lack of direct reduction measures, relative to other sectors, could mean that more allowances and offsets flow to industry rather than the state's other sectors, offering fewer environmental co-benefits near industrial sources. AB 617's requirements could, however, lower emissions in communities experiencing the most pollution, but in a way that is not directly linked to the state's GHG policies. Programs providing revenue for reductions in disadvantaged communities could have positive impacts, but it is unclear whether the funds will be devoted to pollution reduction and how much of a difference they can make in light of a given community's pollution sources. To the degree that California's climate programs improve public health and reduce disparities, they will help achieve the social pillar of development's people-centered equity objectives.

26.3.4 *The Economic and Clean Energy Dimensions of Distributive Justice*

A key climate justice concern is who will bear the costs of a green transition. ARB analysts predict that the average annual cost for achieving the 2030 target is relatively modest, ranging from US$115 to US$280 per household per year, not counting potential benefits, like reduced health costs and increased employment opportunities.[106] While not high, these costs will have the greatest impact on poor households, and California has adopted a variety of measures to mitigate costs.

In addition to general utility support for low-income customers, the cap-and-trade program requires utilities that sell freely obtained allowances to devote the revenue to "rate-payer benefit."[107] Utilities have been sending some of that revenue directly back to customers, who receive funds twice per year.[108]

---

[102] California Health & Safety Code, § 39713. The history behind the first revenue bill is relayed in V. Truong, "Addressing Poverty and Pollution: California's SB 535 Greenhouse Gas Reduction Fund" (2014) 49 *Harvard Civil Rights–Civil Liberties Law Review* 493. In 2016, environmental justice advocates succeeded in increasing the percentage of auction revenue flowing to and on behalf of disadvantaged and low-income communities from 25 percent to 35 percent (E. Wang, "Addressing the Climate Gap: California Legislature Delivers for Frontline Communities," Sept. 14, 2016, http://greenlining.org/blog/2016/addressing-climate-gap-california-legislature-delivers-frontline-communities/; AB-1550, Greenhouse Gases: Investment Plan: Disadvantaged Communities (2015–2016)).

[103] California Health & Safety Code, § 39711.

[104] Ibid., § 39712(b).

[105] SB-1275, Vehicle retirement and replacement: Charge Ahead California Initiative (2013–2014), §3; California Health & Safety Code, § 44258.4(c)(3)(B).

[106] CARB (2018), note 83, p. 50.

[107] California Code Regulations, § 95892(d).

[108] J. Gattaciecca et al., "Protecting the Most Vulnerable: A Financial Analysis of Cap-and-Trade's Impact on Households in Disadvantaged Communities across California," Apr. 2016, p. 4. At the beginning of the program, when costs and revenues have been relatively low, the credits were approximately US$25–30 (ibid.). Investor-owned utilities receive allowances for free but must then sell the allowances and use the revenue they

Another way to lower costs is to reduce the need for electricity from the grid through energy efficiency and distributed renewable energy. In 2016, California environmental justice advocates successfully pushed for a bill that requires the state's utilities to spend one billion dollars (US$100 million per year for ten years) of their allowance revenue on solar power for multi-family affordable housing, which would protect these renters from energy-related price increases.[109] And the funds dedicated to disadvantaged communities from the state's cap-and-trade auctions can be used to finance renewable energy, energy efficiency, and weatherization measures in disadvantaged and low-income neighborhoods, investments that could reduce electricity usage and, accordingly, keep electricity bills low even if the price per kWh rises.[110]

In the transportation sector, providing rebates only for low-income purchasers supports electric car purchases for the residents who most need protection from rising fuel prices. Five percent of the state's auction revenues are dedicated to the "Low Carbon Transit Operations Program,"[111] designed to help transit agencies reduce GHGs and improve mobility, with an emphasis on disadvantaged areas.[112] A key question will be the number of people and communities that benefit from these programs.

Achieving the social pillar of sustainable development is not only about addressing the distribution of costs, but also about ensuring an equitable distribution of benefits. As assemblywoman Garcia has stated, describing Bell Gardens, the low-income community she represents: "You don't see solar panels on rooftops . . . Whether it's electrification or hybrid cars or cleaner air, you don't see it."[113] Programs to develop solar on multifamily affordable housing, use auction revenue for efficiency or renewable energy investments, and support clean car purchases not only reduce pollution; they could help distribute the benefits of a green transition. Though unlikely to be universal, the programs create access to clean energy that would otherwise be virtually nonexistent.

Moreover, investing in disadvantaged communities creates at least the possibility of enhanced employment opportunities, consistent with the Copenhagen Declaration's third commitment, to full employment. These socioeconomic programs could help protect the most vulnerable from the costs of a clean transition and provide economic opportunity and a sense of inclusion to traditionally marginalized communities.

26.3.5 *Participatory Justice*

California's scoping plan process provides a critical forum for participation in shaping the state's climate strategies and its larger transition to a clean economy. Through multiple drafts of sector-by-sector planning, ARB has accepted public comments and held public hearings in the state capitol and has held some meetings in environmental justice communities to facilitate direct

---

receive to benefit ratepayers, thus mitigating potentially increasing costs (D. Burtraw, D. McLaughlin, and S. J. Szambelan, "Resources for the Future Discussion Paper: For the Benefit of California Ratepayers," Resources for the Future, May 2012, p. 6). Publicly owned utilities, like those owned by Los Angeles, are allowed to use the freely obtained allowances for compliance but must use any excess revenue from allowance sales for ratepayer benefit (ibid.).

[109] California Public Utilities Code, § 2870(c).
[110] See note 102.
[111] California Climate Investments, "Annual Report to the Legislature on California Climate Investments Using Cap-and-Trade Auction Proceeds: Greenhouse Gas Reduction Fund Monies," Mar. 2018, p. 6.
[112] A. Cid, "Low Carbon Transit Operations Program," www.dot.ca.gov/drmt/splctop.html.
[113] Barboza and Megerian, note 95.

community participation.[114] State law requires bilingual interpreters for most state functions,[115] and ARB offers to provide interpreters and translate documents for its public hearings.[116]

Recognizing that marginalized communities will nonetheless face challenges in accessing participatory forums due to language barriers, time constraints, and a lack of technical expertise, AB 32, the comprehensive climate law establishing the scoping plan process, required ARB to convene an Environmental Justice Advisory Committee (EJAC).[117] The EJAC draws members from environmental justice groups around the state, including groups with grassroots and technical expertise.[118] In addition to its own public meetings, the EJAC has held local community meetings around the state to engage citizens who have often been marginalized from statewide environmental policy decisions.[119] The EJAC has thus provided a mechanism for organizing grassroots participation and a visible platform for environmental justice views.

These measures increase participation but they do not guarantee influence, and the EJAC and environmental justice groups more broadly have been frustrated by ARB's reluctance to embrace some of their recommendations, like abandoning the cap-and-trade program and establishing a moratorium on oil and gas.[120] In 2016, in the hopes of increasing the voice of environmental justice viewpoints within the key decision-making body, the ARB, the legislature added two slots designated for members likely to represent environmental justice views.[121] While two voices will not dictate decisions on the fourteen-person board, advocates hope that having a presence inside the boardroom will increase their influence.

At the community level, the legislature created a Transformative Climate Communities program that "empowers the communities most impacted by pollution to choose their own goals, strategies, and projects to reduce greenhouse gas emissions and local air pollution[.]"[122] This state grant program, which disperses funds from cap-and-trade auction revenue, provides initial planning grants for disadvantaged communities as well as funding for integrated projects, designed by multi-stakeholder groups, to achieve a "shared transformative vision."

Fresno, with pockets of intense poverty and environmental challenges, received US$70 million to fund the Fresno Transformative Climate Communities Collaborative plan for distributed solar and energy efficiency initiatives, clean transit, car, and bike-sharing programs, greening initiatives, as well as a new satellite college campus.[123] The City of Ontario, a poor community struggling with a wide range of environmental and socioeconomic challenges, received US$35 million to fund the Healthy Ontario Initiative's plan for affordable housing, transit, bike and pedestrian accessibility, and an urban farm using local compost and providing

---

[114] For a list of public meetings on the scoping plan, see California Air Resources Board, "AB 32 Scoping Plan Events," www.arb.ca.gov/cc/scopingplan/meetings/meetings.htm.

[115] California Government Code, §§ 7290–7299.

[116] The California Air Resources Board includes boilerplate language at the end of each official public hearing notice. For an example, see California Air Resources Board, "Workshop to Discuss Opportunities for Additional Greenhouse Gas Reductions from Petroleum Transportation Fuels," Aug. 10, 2018, https://content.govdelivery.com/accounts/CARB/bulletins/205091e.

[117] California Health & Safety Code, § 38591(a).

[118] California Air Resources Board, "Environmental Justice Advisory Committee, Environmental Justice Committee Members," Jan. 17, 2018, www.arb.ca.gov/cc/ejac/ejac.htm#ejlcm.

[119] California Air Resources Board, "Environmental Justice Advisory Committee, Local Community Meetings," www.arb.ca.gov/cc/ejac/ejac.htm#ejlcm.

[120] CARB (2017), note 2; California Air Resources Board, "AB 32 Environmental Justice Advisory Committee (EJAC) Recommendations and CARB Response," May 23, 2017 (within Nov. 2017 document), pp. 4 and 8.

[121] AB-617, note 97, §7; California Health and Safety Code, § 39510(e).

[122] California Strategic Growth Council, "Transformative Climate Communities," http://sgc.ca.gov/programs/tcc/.

[123] California Strategic Growth Council, "Transform Fresno: Transformative Climate Communities."

job training.[124] The Watts neighborhood in Los Angeles likewise received US$35 million for a range of housing, energy, transit, and greening initiatives developed within the community.[125] The program facilitates a more cohesive and participatory process for communities themselves to determine how to apply for and use auction revenue designated for disadvantaged and low-income communities.

For marginalized and disadvantaged groups, meaningful participation with the power to change outcomes has sometimes felt like an oxymoron – marginalization by definition suggests a lack of power. But climate policies that provide opportunities for deep and meaningful engagement, and that meet the social pillar's recognition of people's desire for a voice in the forces that shape their lives, could provide a mechanism for decreasing marginalization

26.4 LESSONS FOR EMERGING CLIMATE POLICY

From the perspective of the social pillar of sustainable development, California's experience offers a largely positive story about how climate policy can be tailored to the much broader socioeconomic context in which it is situated and which it will profoundly alter. Because of its far-reaching impacts, climate policy can be used to address existing disparities and improve socioeconomic equity. At the same time, however, the path is not easy. Even in a progressive state like California, efforts to incorporate the social pillar are likely to encounter persistent challenges and limitations.

26.4.1 *The Value of a Planning Approach*

One of the most important features of California's climate mitigation strategies is that they rest on a foundation of integrated and comprehensive planning provided by the scoping plan process. Although many initiatives have been mandated by specific legislation or developed through independent agency initiatives, the scoping plan process provides a vehicle for assembling the pieces, recognizing connections within and among the different sectors, and identifying duplication, inconsistencies, and gaps. The scoping plan advances social justice by including systematic economic, health, and environmental justice analyses that allow the public to evaluate and debate the distributional implications of the plan.[126]

Moreover, from a participatory standpoint, the planning process involves multiple public hearings, provides opportunities for written comments, and generates extensive interaction between the agency and stakeholders. While that approach could, in theory, perpetuate marginalization by privileging those with the resources to participate, California's EJAC has provided a structural mechanism for gathering and focusing environmental justice community views. Overall, the comprehensive planning process provides a much more robust and holistic comprehensive framework and roadmap than the pure market-based mechanisms that many policy analysts propose.

26.4.2 *The Ability to Improve the Distribution of Co-pollutants through Climate Policies*

The California story demonstrates that, even in a state with unprecedented environmental justice commitments, it is difficult to instantiate climate policies that target GHG reductions where their

---

[124] California Strategic Growth Council, "Ontario Together."
[125] California Strategic Growth Council, "Watts Rising."
[126] CARB (2017A), note 2, pp. 35–61.

associated co-pollutant benefits will do the most good. The state anticipates that its general renewable energy requirements, transportation emission requirements and programs, and over-arching cap-and-trade program will lead to improvements that will benefit the disadvantaged communities most likely to live close to emissions sources. Although the state ultimately adopted AB 617, the bill that requires localized pollution assessment and reduction plans, that bill does not call for integrated climate and co-pollutant controls; it sets up a separate pollution control program.

And in the industrial sector, the ability to adopt targeted climate and co-pollutant limits has become harder, not easier. As local air agencies and the state began to consider direct GHG limits intended to accomplish multi-pollutant objectives, industry, particularly the state's powerful oil-and-gas industry, pushed for limits on direct regulation. The San Francisco Bay Area air agency had been developing programs to control local sources,[127] and ARB had planned to require refineries to reduce emissions by 20 percent in its draft 2017 scoping plan.[128] However, in legislative debates over extending the state's cap-and-trade program to 2030, industry successfully pushed the legislature to preempt local air agencies from imposing any direct controls on stationary sources. The legislation did preserve *state* authority to adopt direct controls, but it prohibited such controls on the oil-and-gas industry, effectively nixing the state's planned refinery controls.[129]

Political pressure is not the only reason the state has been reluctant to establish industry-specific reduction requirements. In the industrial sector, California fears leakage – fears that direct controls will lead industries to shift production elsewhere.[130] While that shift would reduce in-state co-pollutant emissions, GHG and co-pollutant emissions would increase elsewhere, causing in-state economic pain without any net carbon reduction benefits. Consequently, unless other jurisdictions adopt similar restrictions, states are likely to impose least-cost options, like cap-and-trade, on industry. Ultimately, the ability to pursue more direct and substantial measures would improve if the federal government or other jurisdictions also adopted climate policies.

26.4.3 *Market-Based Mechanisms Are Double-edged*

California's inclusion of a cap-and-trade program in its climate strategy has generated frustrations as well as benefits. Cap-and-trade could allow individual facilities to purchase allowances or offsets that allow them to maintain the status quo or increase emissions. And, because facilities themselves decide whether to reduce, maintain, or increase emissions, trading programs do not provide any mechanism for public participation. Cap-and-trade is thus poorly situated to provide distributional and participatory benefits.

On the other hand, requiring polluters to pay a price for their carbon, as occurs to some extent in California's cap-and-trade program, provides critical funds for achieving a wide variety of social justice ends.[131] California's commitment of 35 percent of allowance auction revenue to

---

[127] Kaswan, note 96, p. 145.

[128] Ibid., p. 147

[129] Ibid., pp. 144–148.

[130] CARB (2008), note 61, p. 31; CARB (2017A), note 2, p. 70.

[131] I pointedly do not include one economic justice argument sometimes raised in support of market mechanisms: that their greater cost-effectiveness in achieving reductions reduces the impact on low-income consumers and the economy. A narrow and short-term focus on cost-effectiveness could delay the investments necessary for decarbonization because it could induce companies to buy cheaper allowances or offsets rather than making potentially more expensive transformational investments (D. M. Driesen, "Does Emissions Trading Encourage Innovation?" (2003) 33 *Environmental Law Reporter* 10094). The cost of transformative investments is indeed a concern but is one that should and could be managed through other measures, including investments in energy efficiency, subsidizing distributed renewables and electric transportation,

benefit disadvantaged and low-income communities could generate billions of dollars for these communities. Even if cap-and-trade itself does not target reductions in poor communities, auction revenue can be used to reduce GHG and co-pollutant sources, like diesel buses. And auction revenue can be used to finance energy efficiency and renewables in poor communities, lowering energy costs even if electricity rates go up. Significant rebates for electric vehicles lower costs, provide access, and reduce pollution in poor communities. A nuanced approach to carbon pricing, one that includes pricing as a part of a larger strategy, can thus best meet climate justice goals.

26.4.4 *The Political Value of Incorporating the Social Pillar into Climate Policy*

If we choose to take the risks of climate change seriously, then mitigation policies will have a profound impact. Decarbonizing – eliminating fossil fuels – will transform the way we live, with potential impacts on community structures. That creates socioeconomic risks and opportunities that any wise policy should take into account. Consistent with efforts to achieve the social pillar of sustainable development, using this transition to improve social justice – and avoid increasing social injustice – should be a critical component of climate policy in its own right.

In addition, taking these factors into account – considering mechanisms to address historic environmental and socioeconomic disadvantage – could provide critical political support for often-contested climate policies. For many, climate change still feels remote and abstract, and it is difficult for a given citizen to know what specific consequences flow from climate change. Whether due to uncertainty or the desire not to know, the lack of direct causation and the diffusion of responsibility make it difficult to rally support for fundamental change, particularly when vested fossil fuel interests are fighting to maintain their hold.

Proposals narrowly focused on reducing GHGs, or on imposing a "tax" or "cap," do not provide a compelling vision for how these reductions will play out or offer a socioeconomic agenda. A broader and more inclusive vision for a just transition, and one that touches upon the issues that people experience on a more immediate level, could better garner political support for the climate action the globe so desperately needs.

26.5 CONCLUSION

California's climate policies do not reflect a perfect embodiment of climate justice or the social pillar of sustainable development. Nonetheless, California's programs have gone farther than many jurisdictions in the US in recognizing the ways in which climate policies implicate justice. Other jurisdictions will face different challenges: in some the central issues may be employment opportunities, or distribution of energy costs, or the fate of fossil fuel–dependent communities. In all these instances, however, climate policies would be enhanced by recognizing the underlying socioeconomic contexts and histories in the communities that will be impacted by a green transition. Given the major systemic upheaval necessary to decarbonize, attention to climate justice and the social pillar of sustainable development will lead to better policies – and policies that are more politically viable than narrow, pollutant-specific efforts that ignore the socioeconomic context they face.

and, to the extent necessary, direct financial assistance to pay for higher energy costs (A. Kaswan, "Energy, Governance, and Market Mechanisms" (2018) 72 *University of Miami Law Review* 476 at 561–563).

27

Climate Change–Related Ecohealth Considerations
for Impact Assessments in the Canadian Arctic

Katherine Lofts and Konstantia Koutouki

27.1 INTRODUCTION

Climate change is affecting the Arctic faster and more severely than other parts of the world. Arctic temperatures are rising at over twice the global rate, and it is predicted that the Arctic Ocean could be largely free of summer ice by the late 2030s.[1] Scientists warn that increasing concentrations of greenhouse gases in the atmosphere are now impacting the Arctic's climate, hydrological, and ecological systems to such an extent that the region is actually "shifting to a new state" – "the Arctic as we know it is being replaced by a warmer, wetter, and more variable environment"[2] with "profound implications for people, resources, and ecosystems worldwide."[3]

Climate change is projected to have a disproportionate impact on the health and well-being of Indigenous peoples around the world, due in part to "their greater dependence on local resources, habitation in regions of the world where the environment is changing rapidly, and socio-economic disadvantage."[4] This observation is true for the Inuit, who have been among the first in Canada to feel the effects of climate change on their environment, and to report changes in their social, cultural, spiritual, and economic systems.[5] At the same time, melting sea ice and a warming Arctic are increasing the viability of resource exploration and extraction, and opening

---

[1] Arctic Monitoring and Assessment Programme (AMAP), "Snow, Water, Ice and Permafrost in the Arctic: Summary for Policy-makers," Arctic Council, Apr. 2017, p. 3; C. Woods and R. Cabellero, "The Role of Moist Intrusions in Winter Arctic Warming and Sea Ice Decline" (2016) 29 *American Meteorological Society* 4473 at 4473.

[2] AMAP, note 1. See also D. Gondor, "Inuit Knowledge and Environmental Assessment in Nunavut, Canada" (2016) 11 *Sustainability Science* 153 at 154.

[3] AMAP, note 1, p. 3; Gondor, note 2, p. 154.

[4] A. Durkalec, C. Furgal, M. W. Skinner, and T. Sheldon, "Climate Change Influences on Environment as a Determinant of Indigenous Health: Relationships to Place, Sea Ice, and Health in an Inuit Community" (2015) 136–137 *Social Science and Medicine* 17 at 18.

[5] K. Koutouki, P. Watts, and S. Booth, "The Canadian Arctic Marine Ecological Footprint and Free Prior Informed Consent: Making the Case for Indigenous Public Participation through Inclusive Education" (2015) 24 *Review of European, and International Environmental Law* 160 at 160. See, for example, S. Watt-Cloutier, "Petition to the Inter-American Commission on Human Rights Seeking Relief from Violations Resulting from Global Warming Caused by Acts and Omissions of the United States," Inuit Circumpolar Conference, Dec. 2005.

new transportation routes in the region.[6] This influx of investment and development is putting even greater stress on the region's ecological and social systems.[7]

In this context, the need for environmental impact assessment (EIA) processes capable of protecting and promoting the health and well-being of Inuit communities in the face of climate change is becoming increasingly important. To keep pace with the rapid changes occurring in the Arctic, impact assessment processes must be equipped to evaluate the climate change dimensions of proposed projects, not only in relation to their potential greenhouse gas emissions, but also in terms of how climate change will affect all aspects of a project's life cycle. Moreover, in order to truly contribute to Arctic sustainability, impact assessments must account for the complex and interconnected nature of ecological, social, cultural, and economic systems, and the interactions between these systems at the local, regional, and global levels.

In this chapter, we argue that the emerging field of ecohealth provides valuable insights into the design of impact assessment processes that are more responsive to the changing environmental and human landscapes of the North. The term *ecohealth* encompasses both research and practice focused on the complex social and environmental factors that shape human health,[8] viewing health as a result of dynamic interactions between individuals; social, economic, and cultural conditions; and the natural environment.[9] An ecohealth approach can thus offer guidance on how to better attend to the complex interconnections between the health of ecosystems, humans, and other species in the face of climate change and resource development pressures.[10]

Section 27.2 provides a brief overview of the current legal frameworks for EIA in the Inuit regions of Canada. Following this overview, Section 27.3 considers the impacts of both climate change and increased resource extraction on Inuit communities, examining the interconnected nature of these impacts on the region's ecological, social, cultural, and economic systems, as well as the challenges faced by impact assessment processes in grappling with these complexities. Finally, Section 27.4 introduces the concept of ecohealth as a framework for approaching impact assessment in a more holistic and comprehensive way.

27.2 BRIEF OVERVIEW OF CURRENT LEGAL FRAMEWORKS FOR IMPACT ASSESSMENT IN CANADA

Due to Canada's federal system and the division of powers under the Canadian Constitution, determining the requirements for EIA can be complex.[11] Environmental issues fall under a

---

[6] J. Kapyla and H. Mikkola, "The Promise of the Geoeconomic Arctic: A Critical Analysis" (2016) 14 *Asia Europe Journal* 203–205; K. Koutouki, K. Lofts, and G. Davidian, "A Rights-Based Approach to Indigenous Women and Gender Inequities in Resource Development in Northern Canada" (2018) 27 *Review of European, and International Environmental Law* 63.

[7] C. Emmerson and G. Lahn, "Arctic Opening: Opportunity and Risk in the High North," Lloyd's, ClimateWise, Chatham House, Apr. 2012, p. 18.

[8] M. Berbés-Blázquez, J. S. Oestreicher, F. Mertens, and J. Saint-Charles, "Ecohealth and Resilience Thinking: A Dialog from Experiences in Research and Practice" (2014) 19 *Ecology and Society* 24; S. L. Harper, V. L. Edge, A. Cunsolo Willox, and Rigolet Inuit Community Government, "'Changing Climate, Changing Health, Changing Stories' Profile: Using an EcoHealth Approach to Explore Impacts of Climate Change on Inuit Health" (2012) 9 *EcoHealth* 89 at 90.

[9] See T. Asakura, H. Mallee, S. Tomokawa, K. Moji, and J. Kobayashi "The Ecosystem Approach to Health Is a Promising Strategy in International Development: Lessons from Japan and Laos" (2015) 11 *Global Health* at 2–3.

[10] C. G. Buse, J. S. Oestreicher, N. R. Ellis, et al., "Public Health Guide to Field Developments Linking Ecosystems, Environments and Health in the Anthropocene" (2018) 72 *Journal of Epidemiology and Community Health* 1.

[11] J. MacLean, M. Doelle, and C. Tollefson, "Polyjural and Polycentric Sustainability Assessment: A Once-in-a-Generation Law Reform Opportunity" (2016) 30 *Journal of Environmental Law and Practice* 35 at 39–40.

number of areas of federal, provincial, and territorial jurisdictions,[12] while in many parts of the North, land claims agreements include provisions for impact assessment, vesting jurisdiction in specially constituted review boards or in Inuit regional government authorities. The result is a patchwork of guidelines, procedures, and regulations applicable in different regions and for different project types.[13]

27.2.1 *The Federal Environmental Assessment Process*

Until August 28, 2019, federal EIA processes were governed by the Canadian Environmental Assessment Act 2012 (CEAA 2012). Introduced to replace the Canadian Environmental Assessment Act 1992, the CEAA 2012 was presented as a means of facilitating "more timely assessments focused properly on the most significant projects" and ensuring "robust review."[14] In practice, however, the law largely eliminated federal government involvement in environmental assessments, and "sharply curtail[ed] the scope and potential effectiveness of what remain[ed]."[15] The CEAA 2012 took a "project list" approach, requiring environmental assessment only in cases where a project fell within a list of "designated projects" set out in the Regulations,[16] or in cases where a project was specially designated by the Minister of Environment.[17] Thus, while most projects were automatically covered under the old legislation's "trigger" approach, the approach adopted by the CEAA 2012 can be described as "all out unless specifically included."[18] Moreover, the CEAA 2012 applied only to "specified major individual projects that could affect matters of exclusive federal jurisdiction" – further limiting the scope of application.[19]

In 2016, Canada launched a review of its federal EIA legislation, including within the scope of review the provinces, the Inuvialuit Settlement Region, and certain federally regulated areas,[20] and stating its intention to replace the CEAA 2012 with new federal legislation. To this end, the government introduced the Impact Assessment Act (IAA) through Bill C-69. The Bill, as amended by the Senate, received Royal Assent on June 21, 2019, and came into force on August 28, 2019, bringing numerous changes to the federal impact assessment process.[21]

These changes affect matters of jurisdictional scope, particularly in terms of coordination between the federal government, the provinces, and Indigenous governing bodies.[22] While the CEAA 2012 "focus[ed] on delegation, substitution, equivalency, and narrow scope of federal

---

[12] Ibid., p. 39.

[13] M. Papillon and T. Rodon, "Proponent-Indigenous Agreements and the Implementation of the Right to Free, Prior, and Informed Consent in Canada" (2017) 62 *Environmental Impact Assessment Review* 216 at 219.

[14] R. B. Gibson, "In Full Retreat: The Canadian Government's New Environmental Assessment Law Undoes Decades of Progress" (2012) 30 *Impact Assessment and Project Appraisal* 179 at 180.

[15] Ibid.

[16] Regulations Designating Physical Activities, SOR/2012–147.

[17] Gibson, note 14, p. 181.

[18] Ibid.

[19] Ibid., p. 183.

[20] Northern Affairs Canada, "Environmental Assessments in Canada's North," www.aadnc-aandc.gc.ca/eng/ 1466431262580/1466431344459; Environment and Climate Change Canada, "News Release: Government of Canada Takes Steps to Ensure a Clean Environment and Strong Economy," Feb. 8, 2018, www.canada.ca/en/ environment-climate-change/news/2018/02/government_of_ canadatakesstepstoensureacleanenvironmentandstrong.html.

[21] Bill C-69, An Act to enact the Impact Assessment Act and the Canadian Energy Regulator Act, to amend the Navigation Protection Act and to make consequential amendments to other Acts, 1st Sess., 42nd Parl., 2015.

[22] M. Doelle, "Jurisdictional Cooperation under the Proposed Federal Impact Assessment Act (IAA)," Mar. 10, 2018, https://blogs.dal.ca/melaw/2018/03/10/jurisdictional-cooperation-under-the-proposed-canadian-impact-assess ment-act-ciaa/.

assessments as the preferred approach to harmonization in case of multiple jurisdictions,"[23] the IAA instead seeks "to promote cooperation and coordinated action between federal and provincial governments . . . and the federal government and Indigenous governing bodies," and "to promote communication and cooperation with Indigenous peoples of Canada with respect to impact assessments."[24] The IAA includes provisions for the implementation of these purposes,[25] although their operation in practice and the impact they will have on the assessment process in the North remain to be seen. Moreover, although the preamble to the IAA states that the government of Canada is committed to implementing the United Nations Declaration on the Rights of Indigenous Peoples (UNDRIP), the ways in which the legislation's provisions will interact with the principle of free, prior, and informed consent (FPIC) enshrined in UNDRIP are also unclear.[26]

Finally, the government is in the process of developing a strategic assessment of climate change to provide guidance on how federal impact assessments will consider a project's greenhouse gas emissions, including the quantification of emissions, as well as assessing a project's upstream emissions.[27] Notably, downstream greenhouse gas emissions will not be assessed under the IAA.

27.2.2 *Environmental Assessment Processes in the Canadian North*

Inuit Nunangat refers to the four Inuit regions in Canada (Inuvialuit, Nunavut, Nunavik, and Nunatsiavut), and encompasses all of the land, water, and ice.[28] In Inuit Nunangat, environmental assessment is governed by a variety of processes enshrined in legislation and land claims agreements.[29] In the western Arctic's Inuvialuit Settlement Region, the process for impact assessment is governed by the IAA, as well as by the Inuvialuit Final Agreement (1984), which established two comanagement boards for the review of proposed developments – the Environmental Impact Screening Committee and the Environmental Impact Review Board.[30] The IAA also applies in certain other areas of the Northwest Territories that are federally regulated, including offshore waters.[31]

In Nunavut, the Nunavut Impact Review Board (NIRB) is responsible for the impact assessment of resource projects and new infrastructure in the Nunavut Settlement Area.[32]

---

[23] Ibid.

[24] Bill C-69, note 21, para. 6 (1) e–f.

[25] Doelle, note 22. See Bill C-69, note 21, paras. 21, 31–35, and 39.

[26] See D. V. Wright, "Indigenous Engagement and Consideration in the Newly Proposed Impact Assessment Act: The Fog Persists," Feb. 27, 2018, https://ablawg.ca/2018/02/27/indigenous-engagement-and-consideration-in-the-newly-proposed-impact-assessment-act-the-fog-persists/?utm_source=feedburner&utm_medium=email&utm_campaign=Feed%3A+Ablawg+%28ABlawg%29.

[27] Government of Canada, *Draft Strategic Assessment of Climate Change* (Aug. 2019).

[28] Inuit Tapiriit Kanatami, "Inuit Regions of Canada," www.itk.ca/about-canadian-inuit/#nunangat.

[29] The concept of Inuit Nunangut as encompassing land, ice, and sea has implications for "the enforcement of Inuit rights in the Arctic offshore areas not covered by existing Treaties like the Nunavut or Inuvialuit Land claims" (H. N. Nicol, "From Territory to Rights: New Foundations for Conceptualising Indigenous Sovereignty" (2017) 22 *Geopolitics* 794 at 809). The implication is that Arctic Ocean governance would "include the recognition of [Inuit] offshore rights and their full participation in marine-related development, marine and wildlife management and, the protection of the environment" (P. W. Hutchins, M. Caron, B. Suciu, and R. Campbell, "Setting Out Canada's Obligations to Inuit in Respect of the Extended Continental Shelf in the Arctic Ocean," paper commissioned by Senator Charlie Watt, Oct. 20, 2015).

[30] Northern Affairs Canada, note 20.

[31] Ibid.

[32] Gondor, note 2, pp. 153–154.

Established by the Nunavut Land Claims Agreement (1993) and accompanying legislation,[33] the NIRB has jurisdiction to conduct impact assessments within the land and marine areas of the Nunavut Settlement Area, and the Outer Land Fast Ice Zone off the eastern coast of Baffin Island.[34] Upon request by the government or by a Designated Inuit Organization, the NIRB may also review project proposals located outside this area that may nonetheless have "significant adverse ecosystemic effects on the Nunavut Settlement Area."[35] Inuit organizations play an important part in the composition of the NIRB, which reports to the Canadian Parliament through the responsible minister, and makes recommendations regarding projects to the minister for final decision.[36]

In Nunavik, in northern Quebec, the situation is somewhat more complicated, with four potentially applicable assessment procedures for projects in the region: the Provincial Procedure under the James Bay and Northern Quebec Agreement (1975); the Federal Procedure under the James Bay and Northern Quebec Agreement; the IAA; and the Nunavik Inuit Land Claims Agreement.[37]

In Labrador, the Labrador Inuit Agreement (2005) provides that the Nunatsiavut government has jurisdiction to authorize or refuse projects on Labrador Inuit lands, and delineates how the jurisdiction of the Nunatsiavut government to conduct impact assessments relates to provincial and federal assessment processes. Moreover, the agreement establishes the circumstances under which projects may be assessed under Inuit laws, which are defined to include subordinate legislation under a law of the Nunatsiavut government, as well as Inuit customary law.[38]

As these examples demonstrate, land claims agreements play an important role in determining environmental assessment processes in the North.[39] In broader terms, land claims agreements are also regarded by many Inuit communities as important tools for reestablishing control over their lands and resources, "serv[ing] as a nexus for community action," as well as providing "an opportunity to present historical and contemporary grievances to government bodies."[40]

27.2.3 *Considerations under International Law and Their Application in Canada*

Obligations enshrined in international law must also be brought to bear on the assessment process, particularly with respect to the rights of Indigenous peoples. Chief among these is UNDRIP, which addresses in significant ways "the historical exclusion from, or ineffective

---

[33] This legislation includes the Nunavut Waters and Nunavut Surface Rights Tribunal Act and the Nunavut Planning and Project Assessment Act. See Nunavut Impact Review Board, "Projects Requiring Assessment," www.nirb.ca/content/projects-requiring-assessment.

[34] Nunavut Impact Review Board, "Mandate," www.nirb.ca/mandate-and-mission.

[35] Ibid.

[36] Gondor, note 2, p. 155.

[37] For a guide on the different procedures, see Kativik Environmental Advisory Committee, "Reference Guide on Environmental and Social Impact Assessment Procedures Applicable in Nunavik," Oct. 2017.

[38] See Land Claims Agreement Between the Inuit of Labrador and Her Majesty the Queen in Right of Newfoundland and Labrador and Her Majesty the Queen in Right of Canada at Part 1.1 and Part 11.4.

[39] Other comprehensive land claims agreements currently in effect in the Canadian North include: the Northeastern Quebec Agreement (1978); the Gwich'in Agreement (1992); the Sahtu Dene and Métis Agreement (1994); the Tlicho Agreement (2005); and Labrador Inuit Agreement (2005). Also, in effect are eleven Yukon First Nation Final Agreements based on the Council for Yukon Indians Umbrella Final Agreement (1993) and corresponding Self-Government Agreements.

[40] K. Koutouki and N. Lyons, "Canadian Inuit Speak to Climate Change: Inuit Perceptions on the Adaptability of Land Claims Agreements to Accommodate Environmental Change" (2009) 27 *Wisconsin International Law Journal* 516 at 536.

engagement of, indigenous people in the management of resources in their territories."[41] UNDRIP enshrines the right to FPIC of Indigenous peoples for projects that affect their rights to land and resources.[42] UNDRIP also recognizes the right of Indigenous peoples to maintain, control, protect, and develop their traditional knowledge – an important consideration with respect to the incorporation of such knowledge into environmental assessment processes.[43]

Strictly speaking, as a declaration of the UN General Assembly, UNDRIP is not legally binding. Nevertheless, UNDRIP sets out minimum standards for the rights of Indigenous peoples,[44] and commentators have pointed to the preexisting legal nature of many of the obligations it enshrines.[45] The Inuit Tapiriit Kanatami – the national representational organization for Inuit in Canada – also views the Declaration as authoritative, asserting that UNDRIP "affirms the comprehensive human rights norms that Inuit and other Indigenous peoples have identified as minimum standards for [their] survival, dignity and well-being,"[46] and noting that "Canada has a legal and moral imperative to integrate [UNDRIP] into Canadian domestic law and policy."[47]

The Canadian government's own position on the status of UNDRIP has shifted over time. One of only four countries to vote against the adoption of the Declaration at the UN General Assembly in 2007, Canada eventually signed UNDRIP in 2010, stating that it viewed the document as "aspirational."[48] Canada finally dropped its objector status in May 2016,[49] and despite statements appearing to backpedal on its commitment to fully implement UNDRIP, has since taken steps toward implementation through Bill C-262.[50] It is unclear how this stated commitment to UNDRIP implementation will play out on the Canadian legal landscape, particularly with respect to resource management on Indigenous lands. In the landmark 2014 decision, *Tsilhqot'in Nation v. British Columbia*,[51] the Supreme Court of Canada held that duties of consultation and accommodation were applicable with respect to development on titled and even pre-titled Indigenous lands;[52] at the same time, the decision reproduced the doctrine of *terra nullius*, "presuppos[ing] that Aboriginal land is legally vacant for the

---

[41] Koutouki et al., note 5, p. 161.

[42] UN General Assembly, Declaration on the Rights of Indigenous Peoples, Sept. 13, 2007, UN Doc. A/RES/61/295, Art. 32.

[43] Ibid., Art. 31.

[44] Y. Boyer, "Using the UN Framework to Advance and Protect the Inherent Rights of Indigenous Peoples in Canada," in *The Internationalization of Indigenous Rights: UNDRIP in the Canadian Context: Special Report*, Centre for International Governance Innovation, 2014, p. 13.

[45] Ibid. See also UN General Assembly, *Situation of human rights and fundamental freedoms of indigenous people: Note by the Secretary General, Interim report of the Special Rapporteur on the situation of human rights and fundamental freedoms of Indigenous people*, Aug. 9, 2010, UN Doc. A/65/264, para. 82.

[46] Inuit Tapiriit Kanatami, "Inuit Tapiriit Kanatami Position Paper: Implementing the UN Declaration on the Rights of Indigenous Peoples in Canada," 2017, p. 5.

[47] Ibid., p. 10. The Inuit Circumpolar Council also invoked FPIC in its Circumpolar Inuit Declaration on Resource Development Principles in Inuit Nunaat, stating: "No matter what level or form of self-determination the Inuit of any particular region have achieved, resource development in Inuit Nunaat must proceed only with the free, prior and informed consent of the Inuit of that region" (Principle 2.3).

[48] See T. Rodon, "Offshore Development and Inuit Rights in Inuit Nunangat," in C. Pelaudeix and E. M. Basse (eds.), *Governance of Arctic Offshore Oil and Gas* (Abingdon, UK: Routledge, 2018), p. 172.

[49] T. Fontaine, "Canada Officially Adopts UN Declaration on Rights of Indigenous Peoples," May 10, 2016, www.cbc.ca/news/indigenous/canada-adopting-implementing-un-rights-declaration-1.3575272.

[50] See "Justice Minister Jody Wilson-Raybould Says Adopting UNDRIP into Canadian Law 'Unworkable'" July 12, 2016, http://aptnnews.ca/2016/07/12/justice-minister-jody-wilson-raybould-says-adopting-undrip-into-canadian-law-unworkable/; Bill C-262, An Act to ensure that the laws of Canada are in harmony with the United Nations Declaration on the Rights of Indigenous Peoples, 1st Sess., 42nd Parl., 2016.

[51] *Tsilhqot'in Nation v. British Columbia*, 2014 SCC 44.

[52] Ibid.

purposes of underlying title and overarching governance," and thus continuing to presume Crown title absent proof of Indigenous title.[53] It remains to be seen how this decision will be interpreted, particularly with respect to the government's right to override Indigenous rights on the basis of "national interest."[54] For example, the federal government's recent decision to purchase the Trans Mountain pipeline from Kinder Morgan on the grounds that the project is in the national interest, despite opposition from a number of First Nations[55] (and the subsequent decision of the Federal Court of Appeal in *Tsleil-Waututh Nation*),[56] indicate that the implications of *Tsilhqot'in* are still far from certain.[57]

Finally, the legal norms concerning the participation, consultation, and consent of Indigenous peoples with respect to decisions concerning their lands, resources, and traditional knowledge are reinforced by a range of basic principles of international environmental and health law. These principles provide guidance on how environmental, social, cultural, and economic considerations should be integrated into assessment and approval processes for resource development projects in ways that protect the health of communities and ecosystems and promote more just and sustainable practices. Enshrined in a variety of legal instruments, they include the duty to ensure the sustainable use of natural resources;[58] the principle of equity and the eradication of poverty;[59] the principle of a precautionary approach to human health, natural resources, and ecosystems;[60] the principle of common but differentiated responsibilities;[61] the principle of public participation and access to information and justice;[62] the principle of good governance;[63] the principle of sustainable development;[64] and the principle of

[53] J. Borrows, "Aboriginal Title in *Tsilhqot'in* v. *British Columbia* [2014] SCC 44" (Aug. 2014) *Māori Law Review*.

[54] Ibid., p. 169.

[55] See, for example, E. Paling, "Kinder Morgan Pipeline Won't Be Allowed through First Nations Territories, Leaders Say," Apr. 15, 2018, www.huffingtonpost.ca/2018/04/15/kinder-morgan-pipeline-first-nations-block-trans-mountain-indigenous_a_23411828/.

[56] *Tsleil-Waututh Nation* v. *Canada (Attorney General)* 2018 FCA 153. The Federal Court of Appeal quashed approval of the Trans Mountain pipeline due to Canada's failure to fulfill its consultation and accommodation obligations to First Nations, and on the basis of shortcomings in the National Energy Board's environmental assessment.

[57] The recent decisions of the Supreme Court of Canada in *Clyde River (Hamlet)* v. *Petroleum Geo-Services Inc.*, 2017 SCC 40, and *Chippewas of the Thames First Nation* v. *Enbridge Pipelines Inc.*, 2017 SCC 41, concerning, inter alia, the duty to consult and accommodate, also fall short of enshrining two fundamental principles underpinning FPIC – namely, the "participation of the rights-holding group in the design of the consultation process, and structuring the consultation process around the objective of obtaining reasonable consent" (K. Nerland, M. McPherson, and L. Land, "SCC Decisions: *Chippewas of the Thames & Clyde River Hamlet*," Olthuis Kleer Townshend LLP, p. 11).

[58] See, for example, *UN Framework Convention on Climate Change*, May 9, 1992, UN Doc. FCCC/INFORMAL/84, preamble [UNFCCC]; UN Convention on Biological Diversity, June 5, 1992, UNTS vol. 1760, p. 79, preamble, Art. 3, and Art. 10 [CBD]; UN Convention to Combat Desertification, Oct. 14, 1994, UNTS vol. 1954, p. 3, Art. 3(c), Art. 10.4, Art. 11, Art. 17.1(a), Art 19.1(c) and (e) [CCD].

[59] See, for example, CBD, note 58, Art 15.7; UNFCCC, note 58, preamble and Art. 3; CCD, note 58, Art. 16(g), Art. 17.1, and Art 18.2(b).

[60] See, for example, CBD, note 58, preamble, Art. 14.1(b) and Art 8(g); UNFCCC, note 58, Art. 3.

[61] See, for example, UNFCCC, note 58, preamble, Art. 3, and Art. 4; Kyoto Protocol, Dec. 11, 1997, UNTS vol. 2303, p. 162, Art. 10 and Art. 12; CCD, note 58, Art. 3, Art. 4, Art. 5, Art. 6, and Art. 7.

[62] See, for example, CBD, note 58, Art. 13 and Art. 14.1(a); CCD, note 58, Art. 3(a) and Art. 10.2(f).

[63] See, for example, CCD, note 58, Art. 3(c), Art. 10.2(e), Art. 11, and Art. 12. See also UN Economic and Social Council, *Commission on Human Rights: Report on the Fifty-Seventh Session, Resolution 2001/72, The Role of Good Governance in the Promotion of Human Rights*, Mar. 19–Apr. 27, 2001, UN Doc. E/2001/23.

[64] See, for example, Declaration of the United Nations Conference on the Human Environment, June 5–16, 1972, UN Doc. A/CONF.48/14/REV.1, Principles 13 and 21; Rio Declaration on Environment and Development, Aug. 12, 1992, UN Doc. A//CONF.151/26, Principle 15.

integration and interrelationship, in particular in relation to human rights and social, economic, and environmental objectives.[65]

27.3 THE IMPACTS OF CLIMATE CHANGE AND RESOURCE DEVELOPMENT IN INUIT REGIONS OF CANADA

The Inuit have been among the first to draw attention to the impacts of climate change in the Arctic,[66] in part because of the intimate relationship between the Inuit and their environment.[67] As the 2005 Inuit Petition to the Inter-American Commission on Human Rights – the first case to draw a link between climate change and human rights – states: "Inuit Qaujimajatuqangit [traditional knowledge] tells the Inuit that the weather is not just warmer in the Arctic, but the entire familiar landscape is metamorphosing into an unknown land."[68] The Petition goes on to note that "[f]or the last 15–20 years, Inuit, particularly hunters and elders who have intimate knowledge of their environment, have reported climate-related changes within a context of generations of accumulated traditional knowledge."[69]

The biophysical changes wrought by climate change are also producing a number of secondary effects, impacting social, cultural, and economic facets of Inuit life, including health and well-being.[70] For example, changes to sea ice have made traditional activities such as travel to hunting and harvesting locations, access to culturally significant places, and communication between communities more dangerous and at times impossible.[71] Due to the rapidity of these changes, in addition to increasingly unpredictable weather,[72] traditional knowledge concerning the safety and behavior of sea ice – developed over millennia – is becoming less reliable, posing a greater danger to hunters who are at risk of falling through the ice.[73] Changes to the location, population, and health of plant and animal species are affecting hunting and subsistence activities,[74] which, in turn, threatens the food security and nutritional health of Inuit communities.[75] Subsistence harvesting is also an important spiritual and cultural activity, and is "crucial for passing skills, knowledge and values from one generation to the next, thus ensuring cultural continuity and vibrancy."[76] In addition to changes in ice, higher temperatures and sun intensity are causing increased health risks such as sunburn, skin cancer, and heat-related health problems[77], while melting permafrost and higher water levels threaten homes and infrastructure, and may require communities to relocate in certain cases.[78] The reduced ability of individuals to practice

---

[65] See, for example, CBD, note 58, Art. 6; Cartagena Protocol on Biosafety, Jan. 29, 2000, UNTS, vol. 2226, p. 208, preamble, Arts. 2.4 and 2.5.

[66] Koutouki et al., note 5, p. 160. See also C. Furgal and J. Seguin, "Climate Change, Health, and Vulnerability in Canadian Northern Aboriginal Communities" (2006) 114 *Environmental Health Perspectives* 1964 at 1964 and 1968; Koutouki et al., note 39, pp. 532–534.

[67] Watt-Cloutier, note 5, p. 1.

[68] Ibid., p. 21.

[69] Ibid., p. 35. See also M. Dowsley, S. Gearheard, N. Johnson, and J. Inksetter "Should We Turn the Tent? Inuit Women and Climate Change" (2010) 34 *Études/Inuit/Studies* 151.

[70] Furgal and Seguin, note 66; Dowsley et al., note 69, p. 160. For a discussion of the importance of place to Indigenous health, see Durkalec et al., note 4, p. 19.

[71] Durkalec et al., note 4, p. 18.

[72] Watt-Cloutier, note 5, p. 3.

[73] Ibid., p. 2; Furgal and Seguin, note 66, p. 1966.

[74] Watt-Cloutier, note 5, p. 3.

[75] Furgal and Seguin, note 66, pp. 1966–1967.

[76] Watt-Cloutier, note 5, p. 1.

[77] Ibid., p. 3.

[78] Ibid., pp. 3–4.

aspects of their traditional lifestyles can also take a toll on mental health, as can the threat of relocation.[79] Indeed, Arctic communities have reported increasing anxiety and psychological stress due to the changing environmental conditions.[80]

The changing climate is also facilitating large-scale development in the Arctic, which is experiencing an influx of investment and resource extractive activities.[81] These activities may have a cumulative negative effect on the already stressed Arctic environment, as irreversible changes threaten to overwhelm the adaptive capacity of certain ecosystems.[82] Moreover, the rapidly changing Arctic climate may make these impacts more difficult to accurately assess or predict. And as with climate change itself, the impacts of resource development on Inuit communities are not limited to biophysical effects; resource development can lead to far-reaching social, economic, and cultural changes as well.[83]

The impacts of climate change and resource development on Inuit communities must also be considered in the context of the continuing legacy of colonialism. Durkalec et al. highlight the way in which this legacy intersects with other environmental and social changes occurring in the North:

> In Canada . . . government policies of displacement and assimilation, enacted through Canada's Indian Act and the residential school system . . . affected and continue to impact Indigenous peoples' relationship with the land. These impacts are interacting with rapid social changes taking place in Indigenous communities today related to changing technology use, wage economy participation, changing social and cultural norms, and other changes brought on by the influence and imposition of Western culture, social norms, technologies, economic structures, and governance institutions.[84]

The particularity of this historical context and the importance of place in relation to the well-being of Inuit communities demonstrate the local and geographically specific nature of the impacts of environmental change. At the same time, localized events can also have unexpected, far-reaching effects, as changes in the Arctic affect systems at the global level. For example, scientists are now finding connections between environmental changes in the Arctic and mid-latitude weather, including linkages between Arctic environmental change and the onset and rainfall of monsoons in Southeast Asia.[85] The global scale of climate change impacts also engages issues of climate justice; those least responsible for historical greenhouse gas emissions – including the Inuit – are among the worst affected.[86]

---

[79] Furgal and Seguin, note 66, p. 1968; Harper et al., note 8, pp. 89–90.
[80] Durkalec et al., note 4, p. 18; Dowsley et al., note 69, pp. 158–159.
[81] Durkalec et al., note 4, p. 18.
[82] Furgal and Seguin, note 66, p. 1964; S. J. Hassol, *Impacts of a Warming Arctic: Arctic Climate Impact Assessment* (Cambridge: Cambridge University Press, 2004), p. 5.
[83] See, for example, V. Sweet, "Rising Waters, Rising Threats: The Human Trafficking of Indigenous Women in the Circumpolar Region of the United States and Canada" (2014) 6 *Yearbook of Polar Law Online* 1. See also R. Kohut and T. Prior, "Absence, Not Abundance: Where to Begin with Gender Issues in Arctic Communities?," Nov. 8, 2015, https://medium.com/@PlanArctic/absence-not-abundance-where-to-begin-with-gender-issues-in-arctic-communities-8102d91a219; G. Gibson and J. Klinck, "Canada's Resilient North: The Impact of Mining on Aboriginal Communities" (2005) 3 *Pimatisiwin: A Journal of Aboriginal and Indigenous Community Health* 116, p. 123; R. Deonandan, K. Deonandan, and B. Field, "Mining the Gap: Aboriginal Women and the Mining Industry," University of Ottawa, June 30, 2016, p. 15; "Statement by the UN Special Rapporteur on the Rights of Indigenous Peoples, James Anaya, to the International Expert Group Meeting on the Theme: Sexual Health and Reproductive Rights," Jan. 15–17, 2014; M. J. Taggart, "#AmINext? A Discussion on the Sexual Violence and Trafficking of Aboriginal Women in Canada and the Link to Domestic Extractive Industries," June 2015; Amnesty International, "Out of Sight, Out of Mind: Gender, Indigenous Rights, and Energy Development in Northeast British Columbia, Canada," 2016, p. 49.
[84] Durkalec et al., note 4, p. 18.
[85] AMAP, note 1, p. xiii.
[86] See E. Cameron, T. Shine, and W. Blevins, "Working Paper: Climate Justice: Equity and Justice Informing a New Climate Agreement," World Resources Institute, Mary Robinson Foundation Climate Justice, Sept. 2013.

The foregoing discussion sets out some of the features of the complex terrain within which impact assessments must be situated if they are to take the goal of sustainability seriously. In particular, impact assessment processes must contend with the nested scales, multiple perspectives, interconnectedness, and nonlinearity of ecosocial systems in the Arctic and farther afield.[87] As this discussion also illustrates, concerns regarding the relationship between northern resource development and climate change include not only the social and environmental toll of proposed projects, but also the extent to which the impacts of new resource development will interact with, or exacerbate, social, cultural, and environmental changes currently underway. The next section proposes the adoption of an ecohealth approach to impact assessment as a means of better accounting for these complexities and interactions, providing a framework for the modernization of impact assessment processes in an era of rapid environmental change.

27.4 ADOPTING AN ECOHEALTH APPROACH TO ADDRESS CLIMATE CHANGE–RELATED CONSIDERATIONS IN IMPACT ASSESSMENTS

Ecohealth is an emerging transdisciplinary field that encompasses research and practice focused on the complex social and environmental factors that shape human health.[88] The ecohealth paradigm views the health of ecosystems, humans and other animals as reciprocal and interconnected,[89] recognizing "that human health and well-being are the result of a complex and dynamic set of interactions between people, social and economic conditions, culture, and the natural environment."[90] Rather than simply "the result of the (cumulative) effects of social or environmental determinants,"[91] health and illness are thus linked to interactions between complex, nonlinear ecological, social, cultural, and economic systems.[92]

Recognition of the fundamental relationship between ecology and human health underpinning ecohealth is rooted in the ancient beliefs of a number of cultures, including those of Indigenous peoples around the world.[93] Indeed, the ecohealth perspective appears to be complementary to traditional Inuit approaches to health and well-being, which tend to be more holistic in nature and are intimately tied to the land.[94] As Flint et al. point out, ecohealth for far northern Indigenous communities can be characterized as being "composed of a broad range of values, including harvesting food from the land, environmental stewardship, self-governance, spiritual relations, individual and family well-being, social connectedness, and cultural continuity."[95]

Ecohealth has acquired particular salience in light of the rapid rate of human-induced environmental changes that characterize the Anthropocene.[96] Its systemic orientation and nonlinearity make it particularly well suited to the complexities and uncertainties that

---

[87] D. Waltner-Toews, J. J. Kay, C. Neudoerffer, and T. Gitau, "Perspective Changes Everything: Managing Ecosystems from the Inside Out" (2003) 1 *Frontiers in Ecology and the Environment* 23 at 24.

[88] Berbés-Blázquez et al., note 8, p. 24; Harper et al., note 8, p. 90.

[89] See, for example, Buse et al., note 10, pp. 1–3.

[90] Asakura et al., note 9, pp. 2–3.

[91] D. F. Charron, "Ecosystem Approaches to Health for a Global Sustainability Agenda" (2012) 9 *EcoHealth* 256, p. 257.

[92] Berbés-Blázquez et al., note 8, p. 24.

[93] Charron, note 91, p. 263.

[94] Harper et al., note 8, pp. 94 and 96; Berbés-Blázquez et al., note 8, p. 24; Durkalec et al., note 4, p, 18.

[95] C. G. Flint, E. S. Robinson, J. Kellogg, et al., "Promoting Wellness in Alaskan Villages: Integrating Traditional Knowledge and Science of Wild Berries" (2011) 8 *EcoHealth* 199 at 200.

[96] Buse et al., note 10, p. 1. See also Asakura et al., note 9, p. 2. Although we use the term Anthropocene, we acknowledge the critiques of this terminology, particularly those grounded in the environmental injustices and radical economic inequalities that lie at the heart of our current climate crisis (see, e.g., C. G. Gonzalez,

characterize "wicked problems" such as climate change and its impacts on public health.[97] In addition to serving as a paradigm for research, ecohealth can provide guidance for rethinking approaches to impact assessment in Canada and beyond. Charron highlights six key principles underpinning ecohealth, which "help conceptually frame an effective process of inquiry to generate and apply new knowledge to problems arising from complex interactions of societies and ecosystems."[98] We examine each of these principles in turn to consider their relevance in the context of impact assessments in the Canadian Arctic.

27.4.1 *Systems Thinking*

In the face of the interconnected complexities that characterize processes of environmental and social change, systems thinking can "help connect the already complex social and economic dimensions of health with the ecosystems that underpin human well-being."[99] This approach is crucial for coming to grips with the multi-scalar nature of phenomena like climate change. How do we define the scope of environmental impacts or the concept of an ecosystem when changes to ice and snow cover in the Arctic impact weather patterns as far away as Southeast Asia, and who is permitted to make these determinations? As our understanding of the interconnectedness of global systems increases, so too does our realization that human health is embedded in both local ecosystems and in processes much farther afield.[100] Moreover, the causal pathways that link environmental impacts and determinants of health "are typically long and complex, often involving multiple intervening and potentially interacting factors along the way."[101] These questions of scale and complexity have implications for public engagement and participation in impact assessment processes, as the individuals and communities affected by resource development decisions may not be limited to those in close geographic proximity.

In the context of the new IAA, the shift from the term "environmental impact assessment" to the more inclusive term "impact assessment" shows some promise of moving toward a systems-level understanding of assessment, with a stated aim of broadening the scope of assessments and supporting holistic and integrated decision-making.[102] The IAA also requires consideration of the direct, incidental, and cumulative effects of a project.[103] Nevertheless, while the new legislation may allow for regional and strategic assessments at the discretion of the minister, it lacks robust provisions concerning the triggering and process requirements.[104] Moreover, while consideration of cumulative effects is a requirement under the IAA, there is no obligation to consider historic cumulative impacts, nor is

"Global Justice in the Anthropocene," in Louis Kotzé (ed.), *Environmental Law and Governance for the Anthropocene* (London: Hart, 2017)).

97 W. Parkes, "Diversity, Emergence, Resilience: Guides for A New Generation of Ecohealth Research and Practice" (2012) 8 *EcoHealth* 137 at 138; Harper et al., note 8, pp. 89–90.

98 Charron, note 91, pp. 258–261; see also Berbés-Blázquez et al., note 8, p. 25.

99 Charron, note 91, p. 258.

100 Ibid.

101 P. Mahboubi, M. W. Parkes, and L. Chan, "Challenges and Opportunities of Integrating Human Health into the Environmental Assessment Process: The Canadian Experience Contextualised to International Efforts" (2015) 17 *Journal of Environmental Assessment Policy and Management* 14.

102 Government of Canada, "Better Rules to Protect Canada's Environment and Grow the Economy: Current System and Proposed Impact Assessment System Comparison." https://www.canada.ca/en/services/environment/conservation/assessments/environmental-reviews/environmental-assessment-processes/current-new-system.html

103 West Coast Environmental Law, Centre Quebecois du Droit de L'Environnement, Ecojustice, Environmental Defence, MiningWatch Canada, Nature Canada, and Yellowstone to Yukon Conservation Initiative, "Making the Grade: A Report Card on Canada's New Impact Assessment Act," Aug. 2019, p. 3.

104 Ibid., p. 2.

much guidance given on how climate impacts should be analyzed or factored into decision-making.[105] These omissions may result in incomplete assessments based on a partial analysis of the complex ecosocial factors at play.

27.4.2 *Transdisciplinary Research*

Transdisciplinary research is the second key principle of the ecohealth approach. Ecohealth integrates a number of specialized areas of knowledge across the social, natural, and health sciences, in addition to nonacademic perspectives and expertise.[106] Through participatory processes and methodologies, the ecohealth approach actively seeks out transdisciplinary perspectives, "facilitat[ing] stakeholder participation in the development of new information, strategies, and action."[107]

In the context of impact assessments affecting Inuit communities and lands, the inclusion of traditional knowledge must be a key component of this transdisciplinary approach, "as the Inuit culture is inseparable from the ecosystem itself."[108] While the new IAA does mandate the consideration of Indigenous knowledge,[109] it does not provide guidance concerning the weight such perspective should be given, nor does it address the challenges that may arise in seeking to draw together and integrate different perspectives and world views.[110] Yet in the context of the complex problems that characterize impact assessment, "transcending disciplinary constraints, and learning how to meaningfully respect and engage with other forms knowledge" is vital.[111] Therefore, impact assessment processes must be capable of accounting for and developing indicators concerning the need to "translate these multiple perspectives into an action and learning process."[112]

In addition, the participation of traditional knowledge holders should not be restricted to narrow definitions of what constitutes "tradition" and "knowledge,"[113] nor should such knowledge be "framed in a depoliticized way . . . that excludes claims of environmental injustices and historical dispossession from local resources."[114] Rather, participation must be expansive enough to encompass justice considerations such as the effects of colonization and its continuing impact on ecosocial systems in the North, as well as the fact that the Inuit regions now face a disproportionate share of climate change impacts, despite being among those least responsible for historical emissions.

27.4.3 *Participation*

Linked to the principle of transdisciplinarity, robust and meaningful participation is central to an ecohealth approach and to ensuring "effective, efficient and fair environmental assessment."[115] Such participation is required at all stages of the process, in order to better comprehend the

---

[105] Ibid., p. 4.
[106] D. J. Rapport, "Sustainability Science: An Ecohealth Perspective" (2007) 2 *Sustainability Science* 77 at 259.
[107] Charron, note 91, p. 259.
[108] Koutouki et al., note 5, p. 160.
[109] See, for example, Bill C-69, note 21, preamble, 6(1)(j), 22(1)(g).
[110] See Mahboubi et al., note 101, pp. 10–11.
[111] Parkes, note 97, p. 138.
[112] Waltner-Toews et al., note 87, p. 27.
[113] J. Sandlos and A. Keeling, "Aboriginal Communities, Traditional Knowledge, and the Environmental Legacies of Extractive Development in Canada" (2015) 3 *Extractive Industries and Society* 278 at 285.
[114] Ibid., p. 282.
[115] A. J. Sinclair and A. P. Diduck, "Reconceptualizing Public Participation in Environmental Assessment as EA Civics" (2017) 62 *Environmental Impact Assessment Review* 174.

interrelationships between climate change and health.[116] In the northern context, participation is crucial to understanding Inuit priorities concerning resource use on their territories.[117] Moreover, given the multi-scalar, geographically dispersed impacts of processes such as climate change, it may also be necessary to consider Inuit participation in assessment processes beyond northern territories.[118]

While only narrow windows for public engagement were provided under CEAA 2012,[119] the new IAA includes a mandatory early planning and engagement phase, suggesting some improvement in this respect.[120] But in the context of impact assessments on Indigenous lands, mere *participation* of the Inuit is not equivalent to *partnership*, and is insufficient to meet the requirements for FPIC enshrined under international law.[121] Indeed, although the preamble to the IAA states that the "Government of Canada is committed to implementing the United Nations Declaration on the Rights of Indigenous Peoples," the Act fails to incorporate the FPIC requirements that UNDRIP entrenches.[122] The legislation does require the agency or minister to offer to consult and cooperate on impact assessment with other jurisdictions, including an "Indigenous governing body;"[123] however, final decision-making authority rests with the minister or governor in council.[124] This situation may change if Bill C-262 or similar legislation is adopted, as the government would then be under further pressure to reconcile its position on consultation with more robust obligations under UNDRIP.

27.4.4 *Sustainability*

Ecohealth is underpinned by a commitment to ecological and social sustainability.[125] Yet the very notion of sustainability can be difficult to define, particularly in the context of ecological and social systems that are already changing at a rapid rate.[126] Frequently, sustainability is subsumed under the rubric of "sustainable development," which, in practice, has tended to prioritize economic growth. For example, under CEAA 2012, the economic objective of the EIA process often "overshadow[ed] other objectives, especially under external influences such as Canadian economic development policies and federal budget obligations."[127]

While the IAA establishes sustainability (as opposed to "sustainable development") as a core objective of the assessment process, it nevertheless leaves significant discretion to the minister and cabinet concerning the role of sustainability considerations in the decision-making

---

[116] Harper et al., note 8, p. 90.

[117] Koutouki et al., note 5, p. 168.

[118] For example, the 2016 report of the UN Special Rapporteur on human rights and the environment, John Knox, points to an enlarged concept of the assessment of climate impacts, particularly when vulnerable communities are concerned (A/HRC/31/52 at para. 54).

[119] Gibson, note 14, p.184.

[120] Government of Canada, "A Proposed New Impact Assessment System," www.canada.ca/en/services/environ ment/conservation/assessments/environmental-reviews/environmental-assessment-processes.html.

[121] UNDRIP, note 42, Arts. 10, 11(2), 19, 28, and 29(2).

[122] Canadian Environmental Law Association, "The Federal Government's Proposed Impact Assessment Act: Some Forward Progress, But Changes Needed to Ensure Sustainability," Feb. 8, 2018, www.cela.ca/newse vents/media-release/impact-assessment-act-some-forward-progress.

[123] Bill C-69, note 21, as defined in S.2.

[124] D. V. Wright, "Indigenous Engagement and Consideration in the Newly Proposed Impact Assessment Act: The Fog Persists," Feb. 27, 2018, https://ablawg.ca/2018/02/27/indigenous-engagement-and-consideration-in-the-newly-proposed-impact-assessment-act-the-fog-persists/.

[125] Charron, note 91, p. 259.

[126] MacLean et al., note 11, p. 37.

[127] Mahboubi et al., note 101, p. 15.

process.[128] Moreover, its limited scope makes it ill-suited to addressing sustainability as encompassing "the complex interactions among and effects of economic activity, cultural, political, and legal arrangements, and the Earth's biophysical environment, including the planetary boundaries we are currently exceeding."[129] While the federal government is required to consider a proposed project's contribution to sustainability, as well as whether it hinders Canada's ability to meet its climate change commitments, the IAA does not set out a substantive standard or bottom line in this respect.[130]

27.4.5 *Gender and Social Equity*

With respect to considerations of gender and social equity, Charron states that "[e]cohealth research explicitly addresses unequal and unfair conditions impinging on the health and well-being of women and other disadvantaged groups," emphasizing that health research must be attentive to differences between members of different social, economic, class, age, or gender groups, which are "reflected in their relationships with ecosystems, their exposure to different health risks, their health status, and their well-being."[131]

To this end, it is important to note that Inuit women are disproportionately affected by the impacts of both climate change and resource development in direct and indirect ways,[132] and that "[I]ndigenous women in remote northern communities may experience intersectional forms of discrimination and harm due to overlapping social categorizations of gender, race and indigeneity, and socio-economic status."[133] In addition to differential impacts on women, there has also been a tendency to pay greater attention to Inuit men's experience and knowledge of environmental change.[134] This may be due in part to the traditional division of labor between women and men, which "has led to different pathways through which women and men make observations and assess environmental change."[135] As Kafarowski notes, while women's and men's traditional knowledge is often distinct, such differences are frequently "conflated into one traditional knowledge system – a knowledge system that too often privileges the male perspective."[136] As a result, "critical natural resource decisions and policies . . . are made without the substantive input of women,"[137] meaning that women's disparate experience of social and environmental impacts may not be taken into account. Attention to the harms experienced by individuals by virtue of their intersecting identities and experiences must therefore be a core component of the assessment process at every stage, rather than an afterthought or an additional box to tick, and the participation of women in decision-making processes must be facilitated.

---

[128] WCEL et al., note 103, p. 2.

[129] MacLean et al., note 11, p. 54.

[130] Martin Olszynski, "In Search of #BetterRules: An Overview of Federal Environmental C-68 and C-69," Feb. 15, 2018, https://ablawg.ca/2018/02/15/in-search-of-betterrules-an-overview-of-federal-environmental-bills-c-68-and-c-69/. See also Bill C-69, note 21, ss. 22(1)(i), 63(a) and (e).

[131] Charron, note 91, p. 259.

[132] See Koutouki, et al., note 6.

[133] Ibid., pp. 64–65.

[134] Dowsley et al., note 69, pp. 153 and 155.

[135] Ibid.

[136] J. Kafarowski, "'Everyone Should Have a Voice, Everyone's Equal': Gender, Decision-Making and Environmental Policy in the Canadian Arctic" (2005) 24 *Canadian Woman Studies/Les cahiers de la femme* 12. See also K. Staples and D. C. Natcher, "Gender, Decision Making, and Natural Resource Co-management in Yukon" (2015) 68 *Arctic* 356 at 362–365.

[137] Kafarowski, note 136.

The IAA does make some progress in this respect, with references to differential impacts on women and gender-diverse people, and to the knowledge of Indigenous women.[138]

27.4.6 *Knowledge-to-Action*

Finally, the ecohealth approach focuses on linking research and knowledge to action in an iterative manner, as "[e]cosystem approaches to health inform an action-oriented research endeavor where knowledge gains are applied in some way to improve health and well-being, and to promote equity and sustainability," in turn generating "additional knowledge about the problem, leading to further changes and actions."[139] In the context of impact assessment, this principle means that knowledge gained through the assessment process itself must be fed back into that process, with the aim of ensuring more sustainable and better-informed decision-making. This notion of iterative adaptation is congruent with a key principle of Inuit Qaujimajatuqangiit – namely, "the need to constantly adapt in new and emerging ways to present circumstances, rather than being constrained by established patterns."[140]

To this end, assessment processes should include provisions for follow-up, monitoring, and enforcement, all of which are essential to the ongoing generation of knowledge and its application to improve health and well-being.[141] Adaptive management strategies may be used as a means to anticipate, plan for, and respond to uncertainties, such as climate-sensitive health outcomes,[142] although these processes should not take the place of the precautionary principle in impact assessment.

27.5 CONCLUSION

The regulatory landscape of impact assessment in Canada is evolving, but its ability to keep pace with rapid and unprecedented environmental and social change in the Canadian North is questionable. While a comprehensive analysis of impact assessment regulations in the Canadian North is beyond the scope of this chapter, we have suggested that assessing the efficacy of impact assessment through the lens of an ecohealth approach can help guide processes and implementation in ways that better integrate Indigenous world views and knowledge; account for the complexity and interconnectedness of environmental, social, cultural, and economic systems across temporal and spatial scales; and provide the flexibility and adaptability needed to adjust to a rapidly changing environment.

We also emphasize that the modernization of impact assessment processes presents a key opportunity for the implementation of UNDRIP in Canada, as a concrete means by which Indigenous peoples may exercise self-determination in the management of their lands and resources, and by extension, over their own health and well-being. To this end, the ecohealth approach aligns well with UNDRIP's provisions concerning the participation and FPIC of Indigenous peoples, its protections for intellectual property, including traditional knowledge and traditional cultural expressions, and its recognition of Indigenous legal orders and self-governance.

---

[138] Bill C-69, note 21, preamble, ss. 9(2) and 96(2).
[139] Kafarowski, note 136, p. 260.
[140] Koutouki et al., note 39, p. 540.
[141] See WCEL et al., note 103, p. 5.
[142] K. Ebi, "Climate Change and Health Risks: Assessing and Responding to Them through 'Adaptive Management'" (2011) 30 *Health Affairs* 924.

28

Climate Justice, Sustainable Development, and Small Island States

A Case Study of the Maldives

Sumudu A. Atapattu and Andrea C. Simonelli

28.1 INTRODUCTION

The prospect of total submergence of small island states due to sea level rise associated with climate change raises several legal issues such as those relating to statehood and nationality, the right to self-determination of the people, and the whole array of rights that would be at jeopardy as a result of states disappearing. Climate change raises profound justice issues – those who contributed most to the problem are not those who will suffer the most, with the poor and the marginalized being disproportionately affected. At the same time, the inhabitants of these countries badly need to "develop." What does development mean in the context of climate change? What does the social pillar of sustainable development mean for the people of small island states? What is the role of government? What is the responsibility of the international community, especially the major emitters and rich, oil-producing countries to provide climate finance, if not compensation for the damage caused? This chapter seeks to examine some of these questions through a case study of the Maldives. The chapter also sheds light on the role of governance and politics in relation to climate change and sustainable development as its leaders have vacillated between being climate crusaders and promoters of economic development.

There has been growing acceptance from the academic community that the causes and consequences of both slow-onset events (such as sea level rise) and sudden events (such as cyclones) are not "natural" because they involve human actions, decisions, governance, and values.[1] In the context of climate justice, the Maldives is a case study in divided blame, ineffective response, and human-induced vulnerabilities. A small island state made up of atoll islands, the Maldives is low-lying in relation to sea level and lacks capital and resources needed to adapt to the impacts of climate change on its own. Government measures to combat climate impacts have been inadequate and have created additional vulnerabilities for its poorer sections of society. For the Maldives, the conundrum of climate justice lies at the intersection of its national government's development initiatives, the international community's less than ambitious emissions targets, and the reluctance of the major emitters to acknowledge responsibility, fund adaptation programs, and provide for loss and damage under the Paris Agreement. The last three governments have reacted to climate change in different ways but none has been sufficiently thorough, adequate, or proactive to

---

[1] I. Kelman, "No Change from Climate Change: Vulnerability and Small Island Developing States" (2014) 180 *Geographical Journal* 120–129; Global Network of Civil Society Organizations for Disaster Reduction, "If We Do Not Join Hands: Views from the Front Line," May 2011; T. Steinberg, *Acts of God: The Unnatural History of Natural Disaster in America* (New York: Oxford University Press, 2000).

actually help the Maldivian people as a whole. There is a progression from "hard" development projects to "soft" adaptation measures and from urban development to ecosystem destruction for more tourism, leaving most islands in continual disrepair. At the same time, global emissions are not decreasing, and the successive governments have done little to address climate impacts despite their vocal participation in international meetings.

Climate change disproportionately affects the poor and the vulnerable and the Maldives is no exception. As this chapter shows, the mega-development projects that the government envisages (including luxury resorts, technology centers, and foreign universities) cater to the global elite and could adversely impact the livelihoods of ordinary Maldivians. While these projects could create more employment, it is not clear whether Maldivians will have the necessary skills or education to engage in them. Moreover, government plans to relocate people to the larger islands could affect the rights of those who do not want to move. It seems clear from the chapter that most efforts have focused on developing the capital Male' and not on improving the day-to-day lives of ordinary people.

This chapter proceeds in five sections. Section 28.2 examines the unique vulnerability of small island states to climate change through the framework of justice and sustainable development. It provides an overview of relevant international instruments. Section 28.3 is a case study of the Maldives, its vulnerability and its response to climate change. Section 28.4 discusses intersections of politics, governance, and development, while Section 28.5 offers some concluding thoughts.

28.2 CLIMATE CHANGE, SMALL ISLAND STATES, AND JUSTICE: FRAMING THE ISSUES WITHIN THE SOCIAL PILLAR OF SUSTAINABLE DEVELOPMENT

Small island states are especially vulnerable to the impacts of climate change[2] as they stand to lose everything they have, including their territory and with it perhaps, statehood.[3] The UN Framework Convention on Climate Change (UNFCCC) recognized that: low-lying and other small island countries, countries with low-lying coastal, arid and semi-arid areas or areas susceptible to floods, drought, and desertification, and developing countries with fragile mountainous ecosystems are particularly vulnerable to the adverse effects of climate change.[4]

---

[2] This section draws from coauthor's previous work (S. Atapattu, *Human Rights Approaches to Climate Change: Challenges and Opportunities* (Abingdon, UK: Routledge, 2016); S. Atapattu, "Justice for Small Island States: Intersections of Equity, Human Rights and Environmental Justice," in R. Abate (ed.), *Climate Justice: Case Studies in Global and Regional Governance Challenges* (Washington, DC: Environmental Law Institute, 2016), p. 299).

[3] Whether entities will cease to be states if they lose any attributes of statehood is a hotly debated issue. See J. McAdam, "'Disappearing States', Statelessness and the Boundaries of International Law," in J. McAdam (ed.), *Climate Change and Displacement: Multidisciplinary Perspectives* (London: Hart, 2010), p. 105; M. Burkett, "The Nation Ex-Situ: On Climate Change, Deterritorialized Nationhood, and the Post-Climate Era" (2011) 2 *Climate Law* 345; M. B. Gerrard and G. E. Wannier (eds.), *Threatened Island Nations: Legal Implications of Rising Seas and a Changing Climate* (Cambridge: Cambridge University Press, 2013); D. Wong, "Statehood & Sovereignty: Sovereignty Sunk? The Position of 'Sinking States' at International law" (2014) 14 *Melbourne Journal of International Law* 346; W. Burns, "Global Warming – The United Nations Framework Convention on Climate Change and the Future of Small Island States" (1997) 6 *Dickinson Journal of Environmental Law and Policy* 147.

[4] See UN General Assembly, UN Framework Convention on Climate Change, Jan. 20, 1994, UN Doc. A/RES/48/189, preamble [UNFCCC].

28.2.1 *Alliances and Coalitions*

Small island states have been at the forefront of action relating to climate change but because their bargaining power is weak individually, they have formed alliances to negotiate at the international level, often collaborating with NGOs based in the Global North. Three major alliances are visible at international negotiations – Small Island Developing States (SIDS),[5] the Alliance of Small Island States (AOSIS),[6] and the Pacific Islands Forum.[7] These coalitions have adopted several declarations at regular intervals to highlight the impact of climate change on these states.[8] They have used international forums like the UN General Assembly and the Conference of the Parties (COP) to the UNFCCC to draw attention to their plight. However, not all small islands are equally exposed to climate risks. Some larger islands have, in fact, offered to host inhabitants of smaller islands, and Kiribati and Tuvalu have bought land from Fiji to settle its people and to cultivate food crops due to increasing salinity of their own land.[9]

The Male' Declaration on Global Warming and Sea Level Rise adopted in 1989 recognized that with the increase of global mean temperatures, sea levels are rising which will cause extensive damage to the land and infrastructure of island states and even threaten their very survival.[10] Noting that the primary reason for this is rapid industrialization which resulted in overloading the atmosphere with greenhouse gases (GHGs), the Declaration emphasized that industrialized nations have a moral obligation to take urgent action[11] to reduce their emissions and to provide developing countries with necessary resources and technology.[12] It urged industrialized countries to facilitate funding, technology transfer, and training, giving priority to those states facing immediate threat. It called upon developing countries to transition to a more environmentally sound program of sustainable development.[13]

The 2007 Male' Declaration on Human Dimension of Global Climate Change[14] highlighted, yet again, the vulnerability of small island, low-lying coastal and atoll states to climate change, sea level

---

[5] There is no official definition of small island states. Wikipedia quoting the UN Department of Economic and Social Affairs lists fifty-seven states as SIDS. The official UN grouping is Least Developed Countries, Landlocked Developing Countries, and Small Island Developing States (https://en.wikipedia.org/wiki/Small_Island_Developing_States).

[6] AOSIS is a coalition of forty-four small island and low-lying coastal developing states, including five observers. See www.aosis.org/about/.

[7] It is an intergovernmental organization with observer status at UN General Assembly. See www.forumsec.org/. In addition, a few small island states are members of the Climate Vulnerable Forum, https://thecvf.org/category/member-states/.

[8] While declarations are not binding under international law, they have played an important role contributing to the development of law, clarifying the law, or simply drawing attention to a particular issue. The role of declarations and their legal status vary. See S. Atapattu, "International Environmental law and Soft Law: A New Direction or a Contradiction?," in C. M. Bailliet (ed.), *Non-State Actors, Soft law and Protective Regimes: From the Margins* (Cambridge: Cambridge University Press, 2012), p. 200.
    The year 2014 was declared the Year of the Small Island States. See www.un.org/en/events/islands2014/#&panel1-1.

[9] L. Caramel, "Besieged by the Rising Tides of Climate Change, Kiribati Buys Land in Fiji," July 1, 2014, www.theguardian.com/environment/2014/jul/01/kiribati-climate-change-fiji-vanua-levu; FHTA Secretariat, "Tuvalu Buys 5000 Acres of Land in Fiji," Feb. 20, 2018, https://fhta.com.fj/tuvalu-buys-5000-acres-land-fiji/.

[10] Small States Conference on Sea Level Rise, *Male' Declaration on Global Warming and Sea Level* Rise, Nov. 14–18, 1989, MLV/SLR/15, preamble.

[11] However, categorizing this as a mere moral obligation is problematic. We argue that as parties to the UNFCCC process, there is a legal obligation on these states to reduce their emissions.

[12] Small States Conference on Sea Level Rise, note 10.

[13] Ibid.

[14] Maldives Ministry of Foreign Affairs, Male' Declaration on the Human Dimension of Global Climate Change, Nov. 14, 2007.

rise, and severe weather events. The Declaration expressed concern that climate change has clear and immediate implications for the full enjoyment of human rights.[15] It called upon (a) the international community to commit at the Conference of Parties meeting in Bali to take urgent action to stabilize the temperature increase to well below 2° C above pre-industrial levels; (b) the Office of the UN High Commissioner for Human Rights (OHCHR) to conduct a detailed study on the effects of climate change on the full enjoyment of human rights; and (c) the UN Human Rights Council to convene a debate on human rights and climate change.[16]

The Male' Declaration was among the catalysts for the adoption of Resolution 7/23 on climate change and human rights by the UN Human Rights Council[17] which requested OHCHR to prepare a study on the relationship between climate change and human rights. The OHCHR's report[18] discussed, inter alia, the unique situation of small island states and the impact on protected rights. It recognized that the disappearance of states for climate-related reasons would give rise to a range of legal questions but there are no precedents to follow.[19] A possible scenario of forcible displacement across borders would be the total submergence of small island states. However, human rights law does not provide clear answers and the report noted that we need to adopt political solutions, rather than new legal instruments.[20] It is problematic that the report did not stress the need for legal solutions, especially in light of its own assertation that disappearance of states gives rise to "a range of legal questions."[21] The report concluded that further study was needed of protection mechanisms for those who will be permanently displaced by inundation of low-lying areas and island states.[22]

In its 2009 Declaration on Climate Change issued at a meeting of heads of state in New York, the AOSIS expressed grave concern that despite mitigation commitments made by parties to the UNFCCC and the Kyoto Protocol, GHG emissions continued to increase.[23] It also expressed disappointment at the lack of ambition within UNFCCC negotiations to protect SIDS and other vulnerable countries, their people, culture, land, and ecosystems from the impacts of climate change. The Declaration called upon the international community, with developed countries taking the lead, to undertake urgent action to significantly reduce GHG emissions and to establish a mechanism to address loss and damage from climate change comprising a disaster risk component, insurance, and compensation funds.

The AOSIS Leaders Declaration in 2012 called upon the UN General Assembly to declare 2014 as the International Year of Small Island Developing States[24] to raise awareness of their special situation.[25] The Declaration expressed grave concern that: climate change threatened the very existence of the small island states; international action to address climate change is grossly inadequate; people have been forcibly displaced from their homes; and entire islands

---

[15] Small States Conference on Sea Level Rise, note 10.
[16] Ibid.
[17] UN Human Rights Council, Resolution 7/23, Human Rights and Climate Change, Mar. 28, 2008, UN Doc. A/HRC/RES/27/3.
[18] UN Human Rights Council, *Report of the United Nations High Commissioner for Human Rights on the relationship between Climate Change and Human Rights*, Jan. 15, 2009, UN Doc. A/HRC/10/61.
[19] Ibid., para. 41.
[20] Ibid., para. 60.
[21] Ibid.
[22] Ibid., para. 98.
[23] Alliance of Small Island States, Declaration on Climate Change, Sept. 21, 2009.
[24] States of the Alliance of Small Island States, Alliance of Small Island States Leaders' Declaration, Sept. 27, 2012.
[25] 2014 was declared the Year of the Small Island States (www.un.org/en/events/islands2014/#&panel1-1).

may become uninhabitable or entirely submerged.[26] It referred to the urgent need to consider forced displacement, the human dimension of climate change, and initiatives to prepare communities for eventual relocation.[27] The Declaration referred to the extreme vulnerability of SIDS to climate change[28] which is undermining their efforts to achieve sustainable development. It called upon the international community to ensure that the temperature increase does not exceed 1.5 °C above pre-industrial levels and for the urgent operationalization of the fund on loss and damage.[29]

Despite the recognition by the IPCC of the unique susceptibility of small island states to climate change and the disproportionate impacts they experience relative to their minimal contribution to the problem,[30] these countries and their people continue to suffer the adverse consequences of climate change. Some villages such as that of Vunidogoloa in Fiji have been abandoned because of king tides and extreme weather events associated with climate change.[31] Similarly, five islands that were part of the Solomon Islands have been claimed by the ocean, and six other islands had large areas of land washed to the sea destroying villages, and forcing people to relocate.[32]

The small island states have had successes too. They succeeded in getting states to pledge to limit the temperature increase to 1.5 °C at COP21 in Paris,[33] generated support from the international community to commission a special IPCC report on 1.5 °C, and persuaded states to pledge billions of dollars in financial commitments.[34] However, unless major emitters reduce their GHG emissions significantly and fulfill their pledges to provide climate finance,[35] the plight of the inhabitants of small island states will be exacerbated. What will happen to these people? What will happen to the states as sovereign entities? We will explore these issues through the justice framework, discussed next.

28.2.2 *Climate Justice and Sustainable Development*

Distinguishing between environmental justice and climate justice, some scholars argue that the former is considered a local or national issue, while the latter is a global justice issue.[36] Others,

---

[26] AOSIS, note 24, s. 3.

[27] Ibid.

[28] Ibid.

[29] Ibid.

[30] According to the IPCC, SIDS account for less than 1 percent of global GHG emissions but "are among the most vulnerable of all locations to the potential adverse effects of climate change and sea-level rise" (J. J. McCarthy, O. F. Canziani, N. A. Leary, D. J. Dokken, and K. S. White (eds.), *Third Assessment Report Climate Change 2001: Impacts, Adaptation, and Vulnerability* (Cambridge: Cambridge University Press, 2001), ch. 17, executive summary).

[31] A. Piggot-McKellar, K. E. McNamara, and P. D. Nunn, "September 17, 2019, Fiji's Climate Change Refugees," Apr. 30, 2019, www.newsweek.com/fiji-climate-change-refugees-relocate-1409518.

[32] "Five Pacific Islands Lost to Rising Seas as Climate Change Hits," May 10, 2016, www.theguardian.com/environment/2016/may/10/five-pacific-islands-lost-rising-seas-climate-change.

[33] See T. Ourbak and A. K. Magnan, "The Paris Agreement and Climate Change Negotiations: Small Islands, Big Players," (2018) 18 *Regional Environmental Change* 2201.

[34] States pledged US$100 billion per year for climate finance by 2020. See J. Waslander and N. M. Amerasinghe, "How Much Should Countries Contribute to the Green Climate Funds Replenishment?" Apr. 3, 2019, www.wri.org/blog/2019/04/how-much-should-countries-contribute-green-climate-funds-replenishment.

[35] Ibid. Only a fraction of that has been actually paid.

[36] See H. Shue, *Climate Justice: Vulnerability and Protection* (Oxford: Oxford University Press, 2014); D. Jamieson, "Two Cheers for Climate Justice" (2015) 82 *Social Research* 791, who at times refers to global justice; D. Scholsberg and L. B. Collins, "From Environmental to Climate Justice: Climate Change and the Discourse of Environmental Justice" (2014) 5 *WIREs Climate Change* 359.

however, believe that the environmental justice framework is wide enough to encompass climate justice.[37] For all forms of justice, notions of fairness and equity are central[38] and human rights form their essential core. According to the Mary Robinson Foundation: "Climate justice links human rights and development to achieve a human-centred approach, safeguarding the rights of the most vulnerable and sharing the burdens and benefits of climate change and its resolution equitably and fairly."[39] This definition is closely aligned with distributive justice. The International Bar Association adopts a human rights–centered definition framed around the right to a healthy environment.[40]

Judiciaries have also begun discussing climate justice. In *Asghar Leghari v. Federation of Pakistan and Others*,[41] Chief Justice Ali Shah of Lahore High Court distinguished between environmental justice and climate justice, and noted that with climate change, the construct of environmental justice needs reconsideration:

> Climate Justice links human rights and development to achieve a human-centered approach, safeguarding the rights of the most vulnerable people and sharing the burdens and benefits of climate change and its impacts equitably and fairly. Climate justice is informed by science, responds to science and acknowledges the need for equitable stewardship of the world's resources . . . Climate Change has moved the debate from a linear local environmental issue to a more complex global problem. In this context of climate change, the identity of the polluter is not clearly ascertainable and by and largely falls outside the national jurisdiction.[42]

The Chief Justice noted that adaptation seeks to reduce the vulnerability of people to the adverse effects of climate change,[43] engages many stakeholders who were not traditionally part of the national environmental dialogue, and embraces a wide variety of issues such as health, food security, water security, energy security, human displacement, human trafficking, and disaster management. He believes that while mitigation can be addressed through environmental justice, adaptation can only be addressed through climate justice with the engagement of multiple stakeholders.

The distinction that the court made here suggests that while the state is primarily responsible for mitigation and ensuring environmental justice, a wider array of stakeholders including corporations, NGOs, and even the international community have a role to play in adaptation.[44]

---

[37] See C. Gonzalez, "Environmental Justice and International Environmental Law," in S. Alam, J. H. Bhuiyan, T. M. R. Chowdhury, and E. Techera (eds.), *Routledge Handbook of International Environmental Law* (Abingdon, UK: Routledge, 2013), pp. 79–80; R. Anand, *International Environmental Justice: A North–South Dimension* (London: Routledge, 2004); J. Brunnee, "Climate Change, Global Environmental Justice and International Environmental Law," in J. Ebbeson and P. Okowa (eds.), *Environmental Law and Justice in Context* (Cambridge: Cambridge University Press, 2009), p. 318, who believes that there is no compelling reason not to apply the overarching principles of justice internationally; C. Gonzalez, "Global Justice in the Anthropocene," in L. Kotzé (ed.) *Environmental Law and Governance for the Anthropocene* (London: Hart, 2017).

[38] See F. Soltau, *Fairness in international Climate Change Law and Policy* (Cambridge: Cambridge University Press, 2009).

[39] See Mary Robinson Foundation Climate Justice, "Principles of Climate Justice," www.mrfcj.org/pdf/Principles-of-Climate-Justice.pdf.

[40] See International Bar Association, "Achieving Justice and Human Rights in an Era of Climate Disruption," Climate Change Justice and Human Rights Task Force Report, July 2014, www.ibanet.org/Article/Detail.aspx?ArticleUid=96b93592-3761-4418-8a52-54a81b02c5f1.

[41] Case No. WP No. 25501/2015, in the Lahore High Court, Lahore Judicial Department (references omitted).

[42] Ibid., para. 21.

[43] Ibid.

[44] The Chief Justice did not elaborate on who these stakeholders are.

However, this distinction is hard to maintain as many stakeholders[45] must be involved in mitigation action too. While states are largely responsible for mitigation measures, the Paris Agreement recognizes the need to incentivize and facilitate participation by public and private entities.[46] Thus, we argue that environmental justice can be taken as the overarching framework with other forms of justice as its subcategories. The fact that the perpetrator and victim do not fall within the same polity[47] is not a crucial factor for the justice framework.[48] The justice framework relies on allocating responsibility for climate change and several principles can be used to do so: the historic responsibility principle, the equal entitlement principle, the polluter-pays principle, the common but differentiated responsibility principle,[49] strict liability, and collective theories of liability.[50]

Small island states recognized as early as 1994 that there is a close link between climate change, sustainable development, and poverty alleviation. The Barbados Declaration[51] affirmed that the survival of SIDS is firmly rooted in their human resources and cultural heritage which are under severe stress and that sustainable development programs must enhance the quality of life of peoples, their health, safety, and well-being. It recognized the need to give full attention to gender equity, and the needs of women, children, youth, and Indigenous people.[52] The Program of Action devoted a separate section to climate change and recognized that any rise in sea level will have a significant impact on the living conditions of people and the economy.[53]

Thus, achieving social justice is an objective of both sustainable development and environmental justice.[54] Human rights with its emphasis on nondiscrimination and protection of marginalized and subordinated groups is a tool to achieve both.[55] The social pillar of sustainable development has brought human rights law within the sustainable development paradigm.[56] Examining the link between environmental justice and sustainability, Agyeman et al. propose

---

[45] Whether "stakeholder" is the correct term here is arguable. "Actors" or "participants" might be a better word.

[46] UNFCCC, Paris Agreement, Dec. 12, 2015, UN Doc. FCCC/CP/2015/L.9, Art. 6(4) on the sustainable development mechanism.

[47] J. Knox, "Climate Change and Human Rights Law" (2009) 50 *Virginia Journal of International Law* 163, 200.

[48] The landmark Advisory Opinion of the Inter-American Court of Human Rights recognized that if pollution can travel across international borders, so can legal responsibility. It was, however, careful to say that the exercise of extraterritorial jurisdiction was exceptional (www.corteidh.or.cr/docs/opiniones/seriea_23_esp.pdf and for discussion: www.asil.org/insights/volume/22/issue/6/inter-american-court-human-rights-advisory-opin ion-environment-and-human). On the other hand, international environmental law clearly prohibits significant transboundary damage. See also, S. Seck, "Transnational Business and Environmental Harm: TWAIL and the Universality of International Law" (2011) 3 *Trade and Development* 164.

[49] The CBDR was originally adopted as a way of allocating obligations, rather than responsibility. However, legally, there is no reason why the CBDR cannot be applied in relation to responsibility as well.

[50] See R. Lord, S. Goldberg, L. Rajamani, and J. Brunnee (eds.), *Climate Change Liability: Transnational Law and Practice* (Cambridge: Cambridge University Press, 2012).

[51] UN General Assembly, *Report of the Global Conference on the Sustainable Development of Small Island Developing States*, 26 Apr.–6 May, 1994, UN Doc. A/CONF.167/9.

[52] Opening Statement by H. E. Sandiford, LE, Prime Minister of Barbados and President of the Global Conference, Annex II, p. 78.

[53] Ibid., s. II.

[54] See J. Agyeman, R. D. Bullard, and B. Evans (eds.), *Just Sustainabilities: Development in an Unequal World* (Boston: MIT Press, 2003), p. 7, who believe that "one explanation for the success of the environmental justice movement can be seen in the mutual benefits of a coalition between environmental and social concerns."

[55] In the *Leghari* case, the court recognized the need to protect marginalized groups.

[56] See S. Atapattu, "From 'Our Common Future' to Sustainable Development Goals: Evolution of Sustainable Development under International Law" (2019) 36 *Wisconsin International Law Journal* 215.

"just sustainability" as a framework which they define as "the need to ensure a better quality of life for all, now, and into the future, in a just and equitable manner, while living within the limits of supporting ecosystems."[57] This framing encompasses fairness, equity, inter and intra-generational equity, precaution, environmental sustainability, and social justice. Environmental justice encompasses distributive, procedural, and corrective justice[58] while social justice is common to both frameworks. Applying these two frameworks together would require SIDS, including the Maldives, to ensure that they fulfill their mitigation commitments and increase their ambition incrementally; they need to ensure a better standard of living for all its people, paying particular attention to marginalized and vulnerable groups, and protecting the environment. This framing also needs to encompass principles of good governance,[59] which plays an important role in relation to environmental justice and sustainable development.

In addition, *distributive justice* would require taking responsibility for historic emissions by major emitters including corporations[60] and acknowledging the impact of these unabated GHG emissions on the present plight of SIDS. It would also require ensuring that benefits and burdens of industrialization that gave rise to climate change are distributed equally. The common but differentiated responsibility principle (CBDR) that forms part of the legal framework governing climate change,[61] sought to redress past imbalances. *Participatory justice* requires the provision of relevant and timely information and ensuring the equal participation by these countries in the COP negotiations, paying particular attention to gender balance and recognizing the free, prior, and informed consent of Indigenous groups. *Corrective justice* requires, inter alia, punishing wrongdoers,[62] correcting past wrongs, offering compensation for the damage caused,[63] providing assistance with adaptation, and reducing emissions in earnest by all states, especially the major emitters. We also need to seriously explore the need to relocate the inhabitants of SIDS and adopt new legal principles to accommodate "disappearing states" and their people.[64] The major emitters including corporations should at least contribute to a global fund for these inhabitants if they are unwilling to provide compensation for the damage they are suffering. It is unfortunate (though not surprising) that the loss-and-damage mechanism which seeks to address this aspect and which SIDS fought hard for, excludes liability and compensation.[65] We now turn to a case study of the Maldives, that highlights many of these intersections.

---

[57] Ibid., p. 2.

[58] See R. Kuehn, "A Taxonomy of Environmental Justice" (2000) 30 *Environmental Law Reporter* 10681, who recognizes the all-encompassing and multilevel nature of environmental justice disputes.

[59] According to the former UN Commission on Human Rights, key attributes of good governance are: transparency, responsibility, accountability, participation, and responsiveness (to the needs of the people) (UN Commission on Human Rights, Commission on Human Rights Resolution 2000/64, The Role of Good Governance in the Promotion of Human Rights, Apr. 27, 2000, UN Doc. E/CN.4/RES/2000/64). See also, OHCHR, "Good Governance Practices for the Protection of Human Rights," 2007.

[60] See R. Heede, "Carbon Majors: Update of Top Twenty Companies 1965–2017," Climate Accountability Institute, Oct. 9, 2019. The top twenty companies include state-owned companies from the Global South.

[61] See UNFCCC, note 4, Art. 3. For a detailed analysis of the CBDR, see L. Rajamani, *Differential Treatment in International Environmental Law* (Oxford: Oxford University Press, 2006).

[62] See *People of the State of New York* v. *Exxon Mobil Corporation* (2018) (http://climatecasechart.com/case/people-v-exxon-mobil-corporation/).

[63] The loss-and-damage mechanism seems to address this situation even though liability and compensation are excluded. See UNFCCC, note 46, Art. 8; M. Burkett, "Loss and Damage" (2014) 4 *Climate Law* 119–130.

[64] See Gerrard and Wannier, note 3, chs. 3 and 4.

[65] UNFCCC, *Decisions adopted by the Conference of the Parties 21, Decision 1/CP.21*, Jan. 29, 2016, UN Doc. FCCC/CP/2015/10/Add.1.

28.3 CASE STUDY OF THE MALDIVES: VULNERABILITY AND THE RESPONSE TO CLIMATE CHANGE

28.3.1 *Vulnerability*

The Maldives is an archipelago consisting of 1,192 islands, most of which are less than 2 meters above sea level with the highest ridge on survey at 3.2 meters.[66] Much of the land is lower than the expected sea level rise projected by 2100.[67] This statement is not meant to assume that the archipelago is simply static; islands change and morph over time. Atolls are low-lying and dynamic accumulations of sands and gravels which rely on locally generated sediments, making them particularly vulnerable to sea level rise.[68] If increasing storm surge takes away the new accumulation of local sand, atoll islands may not be able to grow back successfully. Thus, the "loss" of atoll land is complicated by geological factors compounding climate impacts. With only 3,000 hectares of arable land, most agriculture is subsistence farming mainly native crops such as coconuts, yams, and other tree fruits. Additionally, there has been a diversification in the fishing industry away from traditional dry fish productions toward processing for developed country markets; over half of the total catch is exported.[69] However, tourism is the driving force of the Maldivian economy. It is the biggest foreign currency earner[70] with the service industry accounting for 81 percent of the Maldives' GDP.[71]

The Maldives provides a provocative case study of vulnerabilities that are both inherent and created. Small islands are often characterized by narrow resource bases and dependency on links to the outside world[72] but these alone do not make them inherently vulnerable. Both human actions and social structure are integral to nature; hence, the distinction between social and natural systems is arbitrary.[73] However, natural systems occur without any forethought or ethics, allowing the human component to ameliorate or exacerbate environmental threats to societal structures. Social actors can mismanage ecological systems which otherwise function without any human involvement. If vulnerability is the state of susceptibility to harm from exposure to stresses associated with environmental and social change and the absence of capacity to adapt,[74] then exposure can be mitigated by human actions such as planning, social structures, and adaptation measures. However, structural inequalities purposefully place those on a lower socioeconomic status in harm's way. Poor planning, unsuccessful planning, or the refusal to plan for disaster can often determine how societies are impacted by environmental hazards. Varying levels of social capital also serve unevenly to benefit those with stronger social ties.

---

[66] C. D. Woodroffe, "Reef-Island Topography and the Vulnerability of Atolls to Sea-Level Rise" (2008) *Global and Planetary Change* 62 at 77–96.

[67] See IPCC, "Fifth Assessment Report," Intergovernmental Panel on Climate Change, Geneva, 2014.

[68] P. S. Kench, R. F. McLean, and S. L. Nichol, "New Model of Reef-Island Revolution: Maldives, Indian Ocean" (2005) 33 *Geology* 145–148.

[69] P. C. Athukorala, "Trade Policy Making in a Small Island Economy: The WTO Review of the Maldives" (2004) 27 *World Economy* 1401–1419.

[70] A. C. Simonelli, "A Good Economy in Rising Seas: Kandholhudhoo, Dhuvaafaru, and the need for a Development-based Island Migration Policy," in A. Milan, B. Schraven, K. Warner, and N. Cascone (eds.), *Migration, Risk Management and Climate Change: Evidence and Policy Responses* (Switzerland: Springer, 2016).

[71] Moody's Analytics, "Maldives – Economic Indicators," 2018, www.economy.com/maldives/indicators.

[72] G. Baldacchino and D. Niles (eds.), *Island Futures: Conservation and Development across the Asia-Pacific Region* (Tokyo: Springer, 2011).

[73] W. N. Adger, "Vulnerability" (2006) 16 *Global Environmental Change* 268–281.

[74] Ibid.

Even if the overall susceptibility of a country to climate change is low, particular groups of the population may still be disproportionately affected.[75] Vulnerability is often assessed for the express purpose of resource allocation and to provide recommendations for mitigation and adaptation measures.[76] Vulnerability assessments are usually directed toward entire nations or regions even though it is *people* who are vulnerable.[77] Islands produce pollution and are sites for deforestation, overexploitation of resources, and even nuclear testing. In addition, all hazards can lead to acquired vulnerability over time with successive years of damage without full recovery between events.[78] This is made starkly obvious in the Maldives where roughly 50 percent of all human structures in the entire country are less than 100 meters from the shore, including 70 percent of critical infrastructure such as hospitals, government buildings, sewage systems, and ports.[79]

While climate change tends to dominate the conversation, day-to-day environmental issues such as pollution and sewage are of immediate concern in the Maldives. The jetties in Male' are littered with Styrofoam and other forms of packaging (plastic wrappers and take-out containers are very prevalent). This is the same on neighboring islands where there is no garbage collection service. The remnants of imported food stuffs, and household trash such as water bottles and diapers litter the small islands and collect in their lagoons.[80] Male' and many of the resort islands are able to send trash to what is dubbed the "trash island," literally a separate island that specifically serves as a trash dump site. Most inhabited islands do not have this luxury and either have a dump site on their small acreage or simply burn what they can.[81] The trash is no better in the outer atolls where water bottles by the hundreds float in their harbors, discarded televisions litter the shorelines, and tuna cans wash up from neighboring islands.[82] "Development" may provide new commerce, but it comes with an environmental price. When large waves hit and the atolls are inundated by sea water, the trash has nowhere to go but across the island surface, contaminating the homes of its inhabitants.[83]

Poverty and political instability have also exacerbated social vulnerabilities. The capital Male' continues to grow. Only families who are originally from Male' can own land there, and rentals are very expensive.[84] Most people stay with family or friends during the week in Male' and go back to their native islands on weekends.[85] Young Maldivians yearn for the high standard of

[75] H. M. Fussel and R. J. T. Klein, "Climate Change Vulnerability Assessments: An Evolution of Conceptual Thinking" (2006) 75 *Climatic Change* 301–329.

[76] Ibid.

[77] N. Brooks, W. N. Adger, and P. M. Kelly, "The Determinants of Vulnerability and Adaptive Capacity at the National Level and the Implications for Adaptation" (2005) 15 *Global Environmental Change* 151–163.

[78] U. Kaly, C. Pratt, and R. Howorth "A Framework for Managing Environmental Vulnerability in Small Islands Developing States" (2002) 58 *Development Bulletin* 33–39.

[79] B. K. Sovacool, "Expert Views on Climate Change Adaptation in the Maldives" (2012) 114 *Climatic Change* 295–300.

[80] A. C. Simonelli, *Perceptions and Understandings of Climate Change and Migration: Conceptualising and Contextualising for Lakshadweep and the Maldives (Field Report 1)* (Norway: Norwegian Research Institute, 2013).

[81] Ibid.

[82] A. C. Simonelli, *Perceptions and Understandings of Climate Change and Migration: Conceptualising and Contextualising for Lakshadweep and the Maldives (Field Report 2)* (Norway: Norwegian Research Institute, 2013).

[83] S. Malatesta and M. Schmidt di Friedberg, "Environmental Policy and Climate Change Vulnerability in the Maldives: From the 'Lexicon of Risk' to Social Response to Change" (2017) 12 *Island Studies Journal* 53–70.

[84] J. Orlowaka, "Risk Ranking according to Maldivians," in "Living on the Sinking Islands: Social Aspects of Climate Change on Example of Maldives" (doctoral dissertation, Institute of Philosophy and Sociology Polish Academy of Sciences, Graduate School for Social Research, 2015).

[85] Simonelli, note 80.

living seen on the nearby resorts, but most regular jobs do not provide the earnings to fulfill this desire.[86] Healthcare is extremely expensive for the average Maldivian. Most islands have a small basic clinic, but if an islander needs to be hospitalized, the whole family needs to collect money for transportation and treatment in Male'.[87] During fieldwork carried out in the Maldives, individuals expressed the view that there was less community tension before the country divided into political parties (prior to the democratic transition of 2008). Researchers note that the ways in which locals use the colors of the national political parties to paint their shops and houses can make those who support the opposition uncomfortable. Visible displays such as these make and keep political divides fresh.[88]

While domestically climate change did not receive much attention, the Maldives played a key role at the international level. It was instrumental in getting climate change and human rights topic on the UN agenda and lobbied tirelessly to get the OHCHR to prepare a report on the link. In its submission to the OHCHR, the Maldives stated that it is especially vulnerable to the impacts of climate change, including: sea level rise causing permanent inundation and flooding; increases in sea and surface temperatures causing changes to island and marine ecosystems including coral reefs and other aquatic life; increases in intensity of extreme weather events; changes in precipitation; increased salinity; displacement of people; and transmission of diseases.[89] Stressing that many of their protected rights could be violated as a result of climate change, the Maldives contended that states should ensure that the multilateral climate change negotiations discuss human rights considerations while the international human rights discourse incorporates climate change considerations. After much political wrangling, the Paris Agreement finally included a provision in the preamble on human rights.[90]

28.3.2 *Response to Climate Change*

The Maldives proclaimed in its National Adaptation Program of Action (NAPA) of 2006 that over 80 percent of its total land area is less than 1 meter above sea level, and 44 percent of the population lives within 100 meters of the coastline.[91] Consequently, "the small size, extremely low elevation[,] and unconsolidated nature of the coral islands place the people and their livelihoods at very high risk from climate change, particularly sea level rise."[92] The NAPA referred to the scarcity of land in the Maldives, and its extreme low elevation and pointed out that "unless expensive coastal protection measures are undertaken the human settlements face the threat of inundation."[93]

---

[86] Orlowaka, note 84.

[87] Ibid.

[88] Simonelli, note 82; Orlowaka, note 84.

[89] Submission of the Maldives to the Office of the UN High Commissioner for Human Rights, Human Rights Council Resolution 7/23 "Human Rights and Climate Change," Sept. 25, 2008.

[90] UNFCCC, note 46.

[91] Ministry of Environment, Energy and Water, Republic of Maldives, "National Adaptation Program of Action," Dec. 27, 2006. Adopted during President Gayoom's time, the report was prepared by the Integrated Climate Change Strategy (ICCS) Projects of Ministry of Environment, Energy and Water with the support of the Global Environment Facility and the United Nations Development Programme. It was adopted through a consultative process with different stakeholders consisting of government officials, the private sector, and representatives from atolls. A national workshop was also held to discuss the report. The report does not, however, mention either the general public or civil society groups as being part of this process.

[92] Ibid.

[93] Ibid.

The NAPA also acknowledged that human pressures such as population increase and human intervention including land reclamation are aggravating the problem. While the NAPA deals with diverse issues (e.g. tourism, fisheries, water resources, food security, human health, and flood protection), it failed to address the issue of relocation en masse. The NAPA prioritized population consolidation and the development of "Safer Islands" for communities.[94] The program was supported by three out of the five political parties and would produce lower costs for service delivery as well as be a strategy for adaptation to climate change. But, as noted by the World Bank, the islands would need to be selected by detailed scientific assessments based on climate risk, but current decisions do not appear to be guided by them.[95]

The Maldivian government, with the help of the Least Developed Countries Fund (LDCF) and the United Nations Development Programme (UNDP) implemented a four-year US$9.3 million adaptation project starting in 2012. "Integrating Climate Change risks into Resilient Planning in the Maldives" or ICCR, an island level investment in climate adaptation, provided four different types of demonstration projects that involved the replenishment of natural ridges, coral restoration, coral sea wall repair, and mangrove planting respectively.[96] As "soft" projects, they seek to improve the resilience of the natural environment in contrast to "hard" projects such as infrastructure and sea walls.[97]

The Maldives Strategic National Action Plan for Disaster Risk Reduction and Climate Change Adaptation (SNAP), developed by the Maldives and the UN Disaster arm, aims to strengthen four strategic areas from 2010 to 2020: an enabling environment toward good governance, empowered and capable communities, communities with access to technology, knowledge and other resources, and risk-sensitive regional and local development. The Maldives Climate Change Policy Framework (2015) developed with UNDP and financed by the LDC Fund, seeks to ensure (1) sustainable financing, (2) a low-emission development for the future and creating energy security, (3) developing adaptation actions and opportunities and building appropriate infrastructure and communities, (4) playing a leading role in various international negotiations, and (5) fostering sustainable development.

Despite the prospect of eventual submergence of islands, none of the formal policies and communications relating to climate change in the Maldives discuss plans for out-migration. Former President Nasheed voiced his intention to purchase land in Australia or Sri Lanka to resettle the people.[98] New research shows that the perception of Maldivians is nuanced; they do not see out-migration as a direct response to climate impacts.[99] Maldivians have a deep sense of home and community. Even those who were completely inundated during the 2004 tsunami and know that this is what climate change will eventually bring are in no hurry to leave.[100] Working together with aid agencies their new, reclaimed island is larger and higher than their

[94] U. Kothari, "Political Discourses of Climate Change and Migration: Resettlement Policies in the Maldives" (2014) 180 *Geographical Journal* 130– 140.

[95] World Bank, "Maldives – Country Assistance Strategy," Washington, DC, World Bank, 2007.

[96] B. K. Sovacool, "Perceptions of Climate Change Risks and Resilient Island Planning in the Maldives" (2012) 17 *Mitigation and Adaptation Strategies for Global Change* 731–752.

[97] UNDP, "Integrating Climate Change Risks into Resilient Island Planning in the Maldives," 2015, www .adaptation-undp.org/projects/ldcf-resilient-island-planning-maldives.

[98] E. Hirsch, "'It Won't Be Any Good to Have Democracy If We Don't Have a Country': Climate Change and the Politics of the Synecdoche in the Maldives" (2015) 35 *Global Environmental Change* 190–198; Kothari, note 94; I. Kelman, H. Upadhyay, A. C. Simonelli, et al., "Here and Now: Perceptions of Indian Ocean Islanders on the Climate Change and Migration Nexus" (2017) 99 *Geografiska Annaler: Series B, Human Geography* 284–303.

[99] I. Kelman, J. Orlowska, H. Upadhyay, et al., "Does Climate Change Influence People's Migration Decisions in Maldives?," (2019) 153 *Climatic Change* 285–299.

[100] Simonelli, note 82.

old one, leading most to feel safer there. However, they share a calm acceptance that one day they may have to leave, but that if it is as a community, they are ready to accept that fate.[101]

28.4 INTERSECTIONS OF POLITICS, GOVERNANCE, AND DEVELOPMENT

The Maldives case study highlights the crucial intersection of governance, politics, human rights, sustainable development, and environmental protection. The democratic experiment in the Maldives has not been easy. The nation has become a victim to severe political infighting, breakdown of the administrative machinery, emergence of fundamentalism, increasing intolerance toward other religions and cultures, economic growing pains, environmental issues, indolence on the part of the administrators, and undue external influences.[102] For thirty years, Maumoon Abdul Gayoom held full power in the Maldives with only promises of democratic reforms in 2004[103] becoming mandated reforms as a condition of the European aid post-Indian Ocean tsunami.[104] Mohammad Nasheed won the first free and competitive presidential election in Maldives in 2008. However, he inherited a government that was economically bankrupt, politically nascent, and prone to infighting.[105] Nasheed is internationally noted for his flamboyant use of the media to bring attention to the Maldives' climate vulnerabilities, but global popularity did not translate into approval at home. In February 2012, tensions came to a head. Nasheed resigned in the wake of a mass protest and mounting political violence.[106] The Maldivian economy and political system plunged into instability as Vice President Waheed took over the highest office and parceled out ministries among the political parties; in the two years that followed, just who held power was hard to say.[107] In 2013, the alliances flipped nearly completely from 2008: parties that had sided with Nasheed against Gayoom in that year now opted for Yameen and the Progressive Party of the Maldives (PPM), a Gayoom creation. From September to November of that year, people voted for the president three times in just nine weeks.[108]

The position on climate change has also changed drastically from president to president. Former President of the Maldives, Mohammed Nasheed, dubbed "the Island President,"[109] strove to bring global attention to the consequences of climate change on his people. He announced that he would like to buy or lease land to resettle the people when the islands are no longer habitable even though this issue was never put to the people. He said he would look for a place that is culturally appropriate.[110] In 2009 he even held a cabinet meeting under water in an effort to draw attention to the plight of his country and its people.[111]

However, President Abdulla Yameen, who succeeded him, believed that economic development was more important. He acknowledged that climate change is happening; weather patterns are changing; there are higher waves and salt water intrusion; and farming and fishing

---

[101] Ibid.
[102] J. A. Bonofer, "The Challenges of Democracy in Maldives" (2010) 3 *International Journal of South Asian Studies* 433–449.
[103] Ibid.
[104] Hirsch, note 98.
[105] Bonofer, note 102.
[106] Hirsch, note 98.
[107] F. Musthaq, "Tumult in the Maldives" (2014) 25 *Journal of Democracy* 164– 170.
[108] Ibid.
[109] The Island President documentary was released in 2011. Trailer available here: www.imdb.com/title/tt1990352/.
[110] R. Rameesh, "Paradise Almost Lost: Maldives Seeks to Buy a New Homeland," Nov. 10, 2008, www.theguardian.com/environment/2008/nov/10/maldives-climate-change.
[111] Ibid.

are affected.[112] But he emphasized that climate change is just one problem; more pressing are water and sanitation, waste, and coastal protection.[113] He stressed: "We need development."[114]

According to President Yameen, mass tourism and mega-developments, rather than solar power and carbon neutrality, will enable the country to adapt to climate change. How tourism would be used to do so was never specified. He negotiated with the King of Saudi Arabia to sell an entire atoll consisting of nineteen coral islands for US$10 billion. This is not compensation for Saudi Arabia's historical use of and sale of fossil fuels, but a playground for the superrich to enjoy before it "disappears." Using tourism this way allows the worst emitters to participate in morbid voyeurism of their inaction on climate change. In addition, he had plans to geoengineer artificial islands, relocate populations, and attract millions of additional tourists by creating fifty more resorts with six-star hotels. He also proposed to construct high-tech centers and to establish foreign universities to attract the global elite. He offered free housing on larger islands to relocated families, stating that "development must go on, we need jobs, we have the same aspirations as US and Europe."[115] It is not clear what kind of employment will be generated by these mega-development projects, but since tourism is the main focus, most employment opportunities will likely be in this sector. However, the Maldivians who currently work on resorts are most often relegated to the lower-level jobs;[116] internationally owned hotels bring in their best workers from all over the world with many years' experience and the ability to speak multiple languages. It is also not clear whether the government has any plans to provide training to enhance the skills of its workforce.

This is in stark contrast to the position taken by the previous president, who gave primacy to climate change. President Yameen clearly put economic development first at the expense of people (especially, rural communities) and the environment. While he offered free housing to relocated populations, relocation plans were not developed with their participation.[117] It is not clear whether sufficient information was provided to these communities and whether he consulted with anybody before selling islands to a foreign sovereign.[118] The political situation changed again in the Maldives in 2018.[119] There was hope for improvement in the human rights situation in the Maldives after joint opposition candidate Ibrahim Mohamed Solih defeated then President Yameen in September 2018. Solih took office in November 2018 and vowed to implement judicial reform, restore fundamental rights, and investigate the murder of a political activist and the forced disappearance of a prominent journalist.[120]

Even during the years of political turmoil, the main focus of the Maldives has continued: economic development and tourism. Development is considered necessary to prepare for climate impacts under the concept of building back better which could be used as an opportunity to deal with ongoing development challenges such as overcoming ingrained power structures and promoting fairness and equality in SIDS communities.[121] In the case of the Maldives, government decision makers are still choosing the way forward for the fledgling

[112] J. Vidal, "Maldives Switches Focus from Climate Threat to Mass Tourism," Mar. 3, 2017, www.theguardian .com/environment/2017/mar/03/maldives-plan-to-embrace-mass-tourism-sparks-criticism-and-outrage.

[113] Ibid.

[114] Ibid.

[115] Ibid. It is interesting that the USA and Europe are identified as the development model to aspire to.

[116] Simonelli, note 80.

[117] Ibid.

[118] Ibid.

[119] Human Rights Watch, "Maldives: Events of 2018," www.hrw.org/world-report/2019/country-chapters/maldives.

[120] Ibid.

[121] Kelman, note 1.

democracy. President Yameen focused on mass tourism and mega-developments, which he claimed would enable the Maldives to adapt itself to climate change and give its young population hope for the future.[122] It appears the country will sell its beauty to outsiders until it can no longer do so.

Under President Yameen, plans were underway to relocate people to bigger islands so that the smaller ones can be "developed." Many are fishermen who lead a very simple way of life and do not want to move to the bigger islands.[123] While Maldives is not the only country facing these challenges, it does have a rather unique situation of being especially vulnerable to climate change to the point of extinction in the future. The country built an artificial island called Hulhumalé Island at a cost of US$63 million[124] to meet housing, industrial, and commercial development demands of the Male' region. It was inaugurated by President Gayoom in 2004.[125] While some scholars contend that this could be a solution to "disappearing states,"[126] the cost would be rather prohibitive for many small island states.

28.5 CONCLUSION

The Maldives case study highlighted the tensions among climate change, economic development, sustainable development, environmental justice, and the role played by politics and politicians. How do we reconcile these tensions? Should economic development trump environmental protection and social development, including social justice? Who decides this? Have people been consulted on the government's proposals? Are they in favor of selling their islands to a foreign sovereign? What about the self-determination of the people of the Maldives?

The political roller-coaster in the Maldives has ranged from being climate champions to climate disregarders, giving primacy to short-term economic gain at the expense of people and the environment. Cynics might argue that they should sell those islands before they get completely submerged. What if the people of Maldives decide, at a future date, to sell some of the islands and use that money to buy land elsewhere so that they can migrate with dignity? If this is what the people want as a manifestation of their right to self-determination,[127] then how should the government facilitate this? What is the role of the international community, especially of the major emitters? The ultimate responsibility to ensure that the rights of people are protected, their views heard and respected, and their eventual out-migration facilitated rests

---

[122] Vidal, note 112.

[123] Ibid.

[124] See M. Gagain, "Climate Change, Sea Level Rise, and Artificial Islands: Saving the Maldives' Statehood and Maritime Claims through the 'Constitution of the Oceans'" (2012) 23 *Colorado Journal of International Law and Policy* 77.

[125] "Hulhumalé: The Artificial Island Now a Tropical Paradise," May 11, 2019, www.island.lk/index.php?page_cat=article-details&page=article-details&code_title=204030.

[126] See Gagain, note 124.

[127] Self-determination is embodied in Article 1 of the two UN Human Rights Covenants – International Covenant on Economic, Social and Cultural Rights and International Covenant on Civil and Political Rights both adopted in 1966. According to Article 1(1), "All peoples have the right of self-determination. By virtue of that right they freely determine their political status and freely pursue their economic, social and cultural development." While self-determination outside the colonial context is subject to debate, it is generally accepted that "peoples" have the right to determine for themselves their political status and economic and cultural development, including freedom and independence. See UN General Assembly, Declaration on Principles of International Law concerning Friendly Relations and Cooperation among States in accordance with the Charter of the United Nations, Oct. 24, 1970, UN Doc. A/RES/2625(XXV), p. 121.

with the government. Regrettably, the current political wrangling does not offer much hope for the poor and marginalized people of the Maldives.

These competing interests are not easy to reconcile in any country. The Maldives case study brings these issues to the forefront. Ordinary people are suffering the negative consequences not only of climate change but also of the wrangling and flip-flopping by political parties. The case study also highlights the disproportionate impact of political vacillation on the poor and marginalized while those who are in the capital city are less affected by these policies and by environmental degradation. This is a far cry from the "human-centered" development that sustainable development envisages.

PART III

Conclusion

29

Toward a Law and Political Economy Approach to Environmental Justice

Angela P. Harris

29.1 INTRODUCTION

Time is running out for the earth's ecosystem as our species has known it and still, in the words of critical race theorist Derrick Bell, "we are not saved."[1] In this afterword, I reflect on the lessons of this volume from a perspective newly emergent in legal scholarship: "law and political economy" (LPE).

Environmental justice begins with the recognition of the disproportionate environmental burdens shouldered by minorities and the poor at all levels of governance.[2] Beyond resistance and protest, the quest for environmental justice unites ecology, economics, and equity in the search for "just sustainabilities."[3] The contributors to this book, in keeping with these principles, promote legal and policy initiatives that unite environmental, economic, and social regulation with an understanding of scientific realities. Some of the challenges to realizing environmental justice are technical, requiring empirical study.[4] The most difficult challenges, however, are political, economic, and social.

From an LPE perspective, some of the most intractable obstacles to promoting just sustainabilities are the result of structural limitations of modern governance. This afterword attempts to describe some of these limitations. Because these limitations are endogenous to the current global political economy, an open question is whether legal and political reforms within the existing system can surmount them.

Section 29.2 briefly describes the LPE approach to political and legal theory and provides an LPE-inspired genealogy of the present global political economy. Section 29.3 argues that from an LPE perspective, some of the recurring problems faced by environmental justice advocates and scholars around the world are the product of legal institutions and a legal–political imaginary indebted to colonial empire. Section 29.4 argues that the best hope for achieving

---

[1] D. Bell, *And We Are Not Saved* (New York: Basic Books, 2008).

[2] See Chapter 3 in this volume, pp. oo–oo (environmental justice "stems from centuries of environmental degradation as a result of colonization and the oppression of communities of color worldwide – communities that carried the burden of Western industrialization through loss of land, livelihood, and life so that elites could profit").

[3] J. Agyeman, *Introducing Just Sustainabilities: Policy, Planning, and Practice* (New York: Zed Books, 2013), p. 7 (defining "just sustainabilities" as combining four dimensions of human justice – distributive, procedural, corrective, and social – with commitments to living within the limits of the planet's ecosystem, improving the quality of life for all, and meeting the needs of both present and future generations).

[4] See, for example, Chapter 7 in this volume.

environmental justice thus lies in initiatives directed at disrupting some of the fundamental principles and structures of modern governance.

29.2 EMPIRES OF EXTRACTION: AN LPE PERSPECTIVE

LPE builds on, and is indebted to, the critical legal scholarship tradition, including the literatures of legal realism, critical legal studies, Third World Approaches to International Law (TWAIL), and "outsider jurisprudence" (especially feminist legal theory, critical race theory, and LatCrit theory).[5] This section provides a brief introduction to the LPE approach and an LPE-influenced genealogy of modern patterns of governance.

29.2.1 *LPE: an Overview*

Like its critical legal theory predecessors, the central commitment of LPE is to what used to be called "emancipatory critique." The goal of emancipatory critique, as Max Horkheimer famously put it, is to help "create a world which satisfies the needs and powers" of human beings, by developing theories that "explain what is wrong with current social reality, identify the actors to change it, and provide both clear norms for criticism and achievable practical goals for social transformation."[6]

As its name suggests, LPE is devoted to investigating the material and ideological functions of contemporary law, with a special focus on how liberal political–legal thought portrays the production of unequal subjects and the extractive foundations of contemporary economic and political governance as natural, normal, and either impossible or imprudent to alter – effectively beyond the reach of policy. LPE attempts to make these dynamics visible and subject to change through collective struggle.[7] In keeping with the critical theory tradition, LPE scholars have adopted the methods of "critique:" reading texts with a strong moral commitment to liberal ideals of freedom and equality, and taking an attitude toward textual interpretation that Paul Ricoeur once called "the hermeneutics of suspicion."[8] This commitment gives LPE a tragic vision of the world – a strikingly different affective stance than the eternal optimism of liberalism.[9] It also tends to direct our attention to the past, in search of moments when history went astray and the ways in which it could have been otherwise.

Such a moment in the formation of our present global political economy is the period of European colonialism. In her chapter in this volume, Carmen Gonzalez argues that this period saw the invention of both "race" and "capitalism" as we know them, that the two are indissoluble, and that the global political economy of racial capitalism continues to shape international relations today.[10] LPE embraces this perspective, arguing that the production of unequal subjects in states, markets, and civil societies is inextricably intertwined with the mechanisms

---

[5] For a recent careful intellectual analysis of this tradition, see C. Blalock, "Neoliberalism and the Crisis of Legal Theory" (2014) 77 *Law & Contemporary Problems* 71.

[6] *Stanford Encyclopedia of Philosophy*, "Critical Theory," https://plato.stanford.edu/entries/critical-theory/.

[7] See Blalock, note 5, p. 102 ("[C]ritique is simply a means of asserting that things can be different than they are in a world that constantly insists that there is no alternative").

[8] See R. Felski, "Critique and the Hermeneutics of Suspicion" (2011) 15 *M/C Journal*, http://journal.media-culture.org.au/index.php/mcjournal/article/view/431.

[9] See A. Gross, "When Is the Time of Slavery? The History of Slavery in Legal and Political Argument" (2008) 96 *California Law Review* 283 (providing an example of the affective contrast between critical and liberal interpretation).

[10] Chapter 5 in this volume.

of economic–political governance we are accustomed to associate with capitalism, especially in liberal democracies. LPE scholars focus on the role of law in this project.

Many of the chapters in this volume describe the distribution of benefits and burdens of economic activity and environmental extraction as lopsided, with the burdens falling disproportionately on the world's Indigenous peoples and people racialized as non-White.[11] Meanwhile, the human world seems to be busily committing suicide – and ecocide.[12] Why? The next two sections sketch an account drawn from LPE principles.

29.2.2 *The Political Economy of Colonial Empire*

In 1976, the ecologist Barry Commoner published a book titled *The Poverty of Power*, in which he argued that three apparently separate crises then besetting the United States – a crisis of environmental pollution, the "energy crisis," and an economic crisis of simultaneous recession and inflation ("stagflation") – could be traced to a "single basic defect – a fault that lies deep in the design of modern society."[13] He argued that three basic material systems provide the skeleton for all contemporary human societies: the ecosystem, the production system, and the financial system.[14] The financial system (earnings, profit, credit and debt, savings, investment, and taxes) depends on the production of goods and services in the "real economy," which in turn depends on "the great natural, interwoven, ecological cycles that comprise the planet's skin, and the minerals that lie beneath it."[15] Logically, human societies should make ecosystem protection their first priority and the financial system their last.[16] Instead, Commoner argues, the international economic system has done the reverse. In contemporary capitalism, for example, the pursuit of financial profit directs the terms of economic production, which in turn directs the terms of human–nonhuman relations.[17] The discovery of oil and gas extraction as a cheap source of energy, moreover, has allowed this upside-down design to become entrenched, making possible continuous increases in economic productivity and steep decreases in poverty.[18] But ceaseless growth in the means and pace of extraction without attention to the ecological consequences, driven by the remorseless search for financial profit, has resulted in linked crises that now threaten life on the planet.[19]

---

[11] See Ibid., Chapter 3 (arguing that the environmental justice paradigm is relevant to the Global South generally); Chapter 28 (the Maldives); Chapter 24 (sub-Saharan Africa); Chapter 18 (the Marshall Islands); Chapters, 4, 11, 12, 14, 21, 23, 27 (Indigenous peoples in several countries).

[12] See Intergovernmental Panel on Climate Change, "Climate Change and Land: An IPCC Special Report on Climate Change, Desertification, Land Degradation, Sustainable Land Management, Food Security, and Greenhouse Gas Fluxes in Terrestrial Ecosystems" (2019), www.ipcc.ch/report/srccl/.

[13] B. Commoner, *The Poverty of Power: Energy and the Economic Crisis* (New York: Knopf, 1976), p. 3.

[14] Commoner refers to the financial system as the "economic system" (ibid., p. 2).

[15] Ibid.

[16] Ibid.

[17] Although not all societies consider themselves capitalist, the major nation-states that once embraced a planned economy – including China, Russia, and the former communist states of east-central Europe – have now pivoted toward capitalist-style economic practices, particularly in their international relations, to the extent that some scholars call their economies "post-socialist." See, for example, C. Candland and R. Sil, "The Politics of Labor in Late-Industrializing and Post-Socialist Economies: New Challenges in a Global Age," in *The Politics of Labor in a Global Age: Continuity and Change in Late-Industrializing and Post-Socialist Economies* (New York: Oxford University Press, 2001), p. 4.

[18] See S. Igbatayo and O. A. Bosedi, "Exploring Inclusive Growth and Poverty Reduction Strategies in the BRICS Economies: A Multi-Country Study of Brazil, China and South Africa" (2014) 5 *IOSR Journal of Economics and Finance (IOSR-JEF)* 54 (attributing significant poverty reduction in all three countries to policies of "inclusive growth").

[19] Observers today concur (K. P. Gallagher and J. Ghosh, "Introducing the Triple Crisis Blog," Feb. 1, 2010, http://triplecrisis.com/introducing-the-triplecrisis-blog/).

In the book widely considered his most important legacy, *The Closing Circle*,[20] Commoner identified the period immediately following World War II as the starting point of this "blind, mindless chain of events."[21] As he pointed out, the decades before the war had seen revolutionary advances in basic science, especially physics and chemistry. Much of this new science was first adopted for military purposes, but rapidly migrated into industrial and agricultural production in the postwar period. "The period of World War II is, therefore, a great divide between the scientific revolution that preceded it and the technological revolution that followed it."[22] The spectacular postwar expansion of the petroleum and petrochemical industries produced products and wastes that nature could not recycle and simultaneously stimulated a huge expansion in the amount of energy used in production and transportation. Low-energy manufacturing gave way to high-energy processes and natural products were replaced by synthetic ones that required petroleum, both as raw material and for energy. The result was a steep increase in productive power, but at the cost of far more (and different kinds of) waste than the planet's ecological systems could handle.[23]

In addition to being one of the first outspoken voices to recognize that this moment marked a new era for the planet – the so-called Anthropocene – Commoner recognized that environmental crises are the result of what Marx called a "metabolic rift," a broken link between human systems of production and the ecological systems that make production possible.[24] What Commoner did not adequately address in his work, however, was the role of social and political relations in the "Great Acceleration" of economic production and environmental destruction.[25]

Recent scholarship on "racial capitalism" has begun to develop a story of the Great Acceleration that identifies European colonial empire as a crucial precursor.[26] By definition, empires function to extract wealth from their subject territories. The European imperial project of the fifteenth century and beyond did so, however, not simply by requiring tributes, but by reshaping the political economies and cultural patterns of their subject peoples and territories to their own advantage. European colonial empire unleashed a type and degree of economic extraction and political subjection new in global history.[27]

---

[20] B. Commoner, *The Closing Circle: Nature, Man, and Technology* (New York: Knopf, 1971).

[21] Ibid., p. 129.

[22] Ibid.

[23] Ibid., p. 144 (summarizing the displacement of older, less-polluting technologies by more productive and more highly polluting technologies in a string of industries).

[24] Commoner put it this way: "The environment makes up a huge, enormously complex living machine that forms a thin dynamic layer on the earth's surface, and every human activity depends on the integrity and the proper functioning of this machine . . . If we destroy it, our most advanced technology will become useless and any economic and political system that depends on it will founder" (ibid., p. 16). Compare J. B. Foster, "Marx's Theory of Metabolic Rift: Classical Foundations for Environmental Sociology" (1999) 105 *American Journal of Sociology* 366.

[25] W. Steffen, J. Grinevald, P. Crutzen, and J. McNeill, "The Anthropocene: Conceptual and Historical Perspectives" (2011) 369 *Philosophical Transactions, Royal Society Association* 842 at 851–852 (charting various measures of human activity from 1750 to 2000 and describing a "Great Acceleration" following World War II). See also J. G. Speth, *The Bridge at the Edge of the World* (New Haven, CT: Yale University Press, 2008), pp. xx–xxi (presenting similar "hockey stick" shaped charts).

[26] On racial capitalism, see Chapter 5 in this volume; see also A. P. Harris, "The Treadmill and the Contract: A Classcrits Guide to the Anthropocene" (2016) 5 *Tennessee Journal of Race, Gender, & Social Justice* 1. I borrow the term "colonial empire" from Onur Ince (O. Ince, "Primitive Accumulation, New Enclosures, and Global Land Grabs: A Theoretical Intervention" (2014) 79 *Rural Sociology* 104). Some climate scientists have also suggested that European colonialism, not the post-industrial "Great Acceleration," should mark the beginning of the Anthropocene (S. L. Lewis and M. A. Maslin, "Defining the Anthropocene" (2015) 519 *Nature* 171).

[27] L. Lowe, *The Intimacies of Four Continents* (Durham, NC: Duke University Press, 2015).

European imperialism and settler colonialism, particularly in the New World, became the source of technological innovations in agriculture, such as the cotton gin and the mechanical loom,[28] as well as myriad economic innovations, from new financial practices[29] to novel forms of economic enterprise[30] and the development of sophisticated global finance systems.[31] Meanwhile, the violent destruction of cultural and social bonds and norms that accompanied New World slavery made it possible to subjugate human life to profit to an extent never before seen, intensifying means of labor and resource extraction.[32]

As well as a laboratory for turning land and bodies into economic profits, colonial empire was a laboratory for new forms of political and social governance founded on assumptions about human capacities rather than divine authority. In a process that crystallized in the nineteenth century, for example, a system of governance based on the nation-state emerged. This "law of nations" was ostensibly founded on principles of human equality. But the "family of nations" to which this law applied, like the new political theory of domestic government "by the people and for the people," was only for peoples deemed "civilized," not for "savages" who needed to be ruled by others.[33]

Historians typically emphasize the centrality of fixations on skin color, nose shape, and skull size in the new language of "race." Just as crucial, however, were the historical and cultural "just-so stories" that established certain European peoples at the top of a global hierarchy of cultural development.[34] The civilized-savage gradient, for instance, originated in the religious distinction between "Christian" and "heathen" (or "infidel").[35] The two sides of the coin of race – the language of "culture," and the language of color and blood – reflected a philosophical upheaval within European culture that begat the key terms within which the majority of the world now thinks, works, and desires: nature, science, and man. Decolonial scholars call this discursive structure "European modernity/rationality," the "modern/colonial" world, or simply modernity.[36]

Aníbal Quijano observes that modernity rests on a "radical dualism" between reason and nature, subject and object.[37] Haunted by its Christian origins, this dualism is reflected in an

---

[28] See S. Beckert, *Empire of Cotton: A Global History* (New York: Knopf, 2014).

[29] See K. S. Park, "Money, Mortgages, and the Conquest of America" (2016) 41 *Law & Social Inquiry* 1006. See also C. Rosenthal, *Accounting for Slavery: Masters and Management* (Cambridge, MA: Harvard University Press, 2018).

[30] The joint-stock company, for example, a forerunner of the multinational corporation, was instrumental to the wealth accumulated in European colonialism (H. V. Bowen, *The Business of Empire: The East India Company and Imperial Britain, 1756–1833* (Cambridge: Cambridge University Press, 2006); N. B. Dirks, *The Scandal of Empire: India and the Creation of Imperial Britain* (Cambridge, MA: Harvard University Press, 2006).

[31] See P. J. Hudson, *Bankers and Empire: How Wall Street Colonized the Caribbean* (Chicago: University of Chicago Press, 2017).

[32] See W. Johnson, *River of Dark Dreams: Slavery and Empire in the Cotton Kingdom* (Cambridge, MA: Harvard University Press, 2013) (exploring the material and cultural consequences of commodifying human flesh in the context of American chattel slavery).

[33] See W. Mignolo, "Who Speaks for the 'Human' in Human Rights?" (2009) 5 *Hispanic Issue Series: University of Minnesota Digital Conservancy*; J. Barker, *Native Acts: Law, Recognition, and Cultural Authenticity* (Durham, NC: Duke University Press, 2011).

[34] Mignolo, note 33; I. Hannaford, *Race: The History of an Idea in the West* (Washington, DC: Woodrow Wilson Center, 1996).

[35] Mignolo, note 33, p. 14; R. A. Williams, *The American Indian in Western Legal Thought* (Oxford: Oxford University Press, 1990).

[36] See Mignolo, note 33, p. 11 (using the term "modern-colonial"); A. Quijano, "Coloniality and Modernity/ Rationality" (2007) 21 *Cultural Studies* 168 at 171 (using the term "European modernity/rationality").

[37] Quijano, note 36, pp. 172–173.

imagined binary opposition between "humans" and "the environment."[38] The effort to master the nonhuman world through human reason, justified by the Christian language of "dominion," gave rise to modern science and technology as the preeminent way of knowing the world – and a view of the nonhuman as lifeless, inert, and passive.[39]

Modernity's philosophical dualism between reason and nature, subject and object, human and nonhuman, is intertwined with an imagined order of human existence, which Sylvia Wynter calls "the coloniality of being."[40] Within this order, a new historical figure – man – appeared, defined not by his relationship to God but by his ability to reason, and understood through the new "sciences of man," the forerunners of biology and anthropology. European man, of course, stood at the pinnacle of human development and all the world's peoples would henceforth be measured for their fitness against a European yardstick represented as universal.

Decolonial scholars argue that colonial empire was both cause and effect of modernity. Race, science, and capitalism emerged in the struggle to extract wealth and power from the colonial encounter. These new discourses in turn became assemblages of power deployed to govern a colonized world.[41] Under this account, modern freedom and equality were invented along with and through modern slavery, just as modern notions of legal property took shape through colonial dispossession.[42]

European sex/gender hierarchies are also key features of both colonial empire and modernity. In both modern and premodern times, European patriarchal norms structured family relations and organized social roles along a male–female binary.[43] Sex and gender were also crucial to the ways and means of colonial empire.[44] For example, English colonists legitimated capitalist expansion in North America through gendered metaphors, such as the "extraction of resources from 'nature's bosom'" and the "penetration of 'her womb' by science and technology."[45] English conceptions of patriarchal family governance structured the Anglo-American common law of slavery, as well. Legally, for example, the master–slave relationship was classified as a

---

[38] W. Cronon, "The Trouble with Wilderness: Or, Getting Back to the Wrong Nature," in W. Cronon (ed.), *Uncommon Ground: Rethinking the Human Place in Nature* (New York: Norton, 1995), p. 80 (criticizing the opposition between "humans" and "the environment" as it has shaped Western conceptions of "wilderness").

[39] For an example of this process in the English colonization of the "new world," see C. Merchant, "Reinventing Eden: Western Culture as a Recovery Narrative," ibid., p. 132. See also I. Porras, "Appropriating Nature: Commerce, Property, and the Commodification of Nature in the Law of Nations" (2014) 27 *Leiden Journal of International Law* 641.

[40] S. Wynter, "Unsettling the Coloniality of Being/Power/Truth/Freedom: Towards the Human, after Man, Its Overrepresentation – An Argument" (2003) 3 *CR: The New Centennial Review* 257 at 287.

[41] As Ivan Hannaford puts it, the invention of "laws of nature, based on principles of self-preservation and self-interest, 'opened up new worlds for occupation and conquest – geographical, physiological, biological, psychological, and economic – without regard for the political elements that had dominated the thought of Church and State in Western Europe since Aristotle and Augustine'" (note 34, p. 192).

[42] On modern property and its formation in the context of colonial empire (which the author argues is an ongoing rather than historical event), see B. Bhandar, *Colonial Lives of Property: Law, Land, and Racial Regimes of Ownership* (Durham, NC: Duke University Press, 2018). On the dialectical emergence of Atlantic slavery and liberal discourses of equality, see G. M. Fredrickson, *Racism: A Short History* (Princeton, NJ: Princeton University Press, 2002).

[43] See F. Valdes, "Queers, Sissies, Dykes, and Tomboys: Deconstructing the Conflation of 'Sex,' 'Gender,' and 'Sexual Orientation' in Euro-American Law and Society" (1995) 83 *California Law Review* 3 (describing this conflation as central to heteropatriarchy).

[44] A. McClintock, *Imperial Leather: Race, Gender, and Sexuality in the Colonial Contest* (New York: Routledge, 1995), p. 7 (arguing that sex/gender dynamics were central to the way Europeans understood and pursued colonial empire). My use of "sex/gender" reflects the social constructionist view that culture shapes both what we see as "natural" and what we see as "cultural" with respect to sexual difference, gender performance, and sexuality. See J. Butler, *Gender Trouble* (2nd ed.) (London: Routledge, 1999), pp. 10–11.

[45] Merchant, note 39, p. 145.

"domestic relation," and understood, like other domestic relations (husband–wife, parent–child, employer–servant), to be inherently unequal, granting one party the authority to govern the other.[46] That party, in each case, was the master of a household: the common law granted a master private authority to direct the lives of his wife, his children, his servants, and his slaves.[47] European gender norms also shaped the land rights of Indigenous peoples. As late as the early twentieth century in Canada, for example, the Crown allotted land to private individuals through a "homesteading" system. A man who was 18 years of age could apply for a homestead; a woman, however, could do so only on provision that she was a single mother, abandoned, or widowed; and the homestead program did not apply to "aborigines" at all, unless they had obtained "special permission."[48]

Colonial empire also disrupted and transformed European sex/gender norms in sometimes unexpected ways. Atlantic slavery, for instance, "un-gendered" captive African men and women, withholding from them the right to marry and directing both men and women to perform heavy manual labor.[49] The imperial mission enabled White privileged women to serve as authorities on "proper" family life and to wield power over native men and women.[50] The emergence of racial difference also produced new directions of sexual desire, as some Europeans came to crave the "forbidden fruit" of the Other.[51] Notwithstanding these changes, the political economy that came to be identified with modernity preserved the central features of the European sex/gender system, such as the alliance of economic power and control with male authority and men's interests. For instance, where the law of slavery diverged from European gender norms, it did so in such a way as to empower free White men to enjoy the sexual and economic benefits of power over enslaved women, without disturbing their authority over their White wives and daughters – thus preserving patriarchal norms.[52] Industrial capitalism, as it emerged, defined the economy itself in terms of gender, in ways that are with us today. For example, while wage work performed in the production of commodities is considered economic production, care work in the home is deemed a product of "love" rather than labor,[53] care work in the marketplace is generally undercompensated,[54] and sex work is regulated in most countries through the carceral system, treated as criminal rather than economic behavior.[55] Forms of labor assigned to women by mainstream sex/gender norms, thus, are often treated as peripheral or supplementary to

---

[46] See N. F. Cott, *Public Vows: A History of Marriage and the Nation* (Cambridge, MA: Harvard University Press, 2000), pp. 6–7.

[47] L. VanderVelde, "Servitude and Captivity in the Common Law of Master-Servant: Judicial Interpretations of the Thirteenth Amendment's Labor Vision Immediately after Its Enactment" (2019) 27 *William & Mary Bill of Rights Journal* 1079 at 1081.

[48] Bhandar, note 42, pp. 59–60.

[49] H. J. Spillers, "Mama's Baby, Papa's Maybe: An American Grammar Book" (1987) 17 *Diacritics* 64.

[50] See McClintock, note 44.

[51] See R. J. C. Young, *Colonial Desire: Hybridity in Theory, Culture and Race* (New York: Routledge, 1994).

[52] See A. D. Davis, "The Private Law of Race and Sex: An Antebellum Perspective" (1999) 51 *Stanford Law Review* 221 (explaining how antebellum judicial decisions in property, contract, and estate law directed economic wealth and decision-making power toward White masters and away from White wives, children, and the enslaved).

[53] J. Acker, "Gender, Capitalism, and Globalization" (2004) 30 *Critical Sociology* 17 at 23; K. Silbaugh, "Turning Labor into Love: Housework and the Law" (1996) 91 *Northwestern University Law Review* 1; K. Silbaugh, "Commodification and Women's Household Labor" (1997) 9 *Yale Journal of Law and Feminism* 81.

[54] N. Folbre, *The Invisible Heart: Economics and Family Values* (New York: New Press, 2001).

[55] See J. Halley, P. Kotiswaran, H. Shamir, and C. Thomas, "From the International to the Local in Feminist Legal Responses to Rape, Prostitution/Sex Work, and Sex Trafficking: Four Studies in Contemporary Governance Feminism" (2006) 29 *Harvard Journal of Law & Gender* 335.

economic production or are left outside the boundaries of economic analysis altogether.[56] Meanwhile, although women now work for wages around the globe, they continue to face gendered exclusion, harassment, and exploitation. In this way, the nineteenth-century Anglo-American ideology of "domesticity," under which men belong in the workplace and women at home, still shapes economic relations.

Ideologies of gender, race, and nationalism have been mutually reinforcing in the realm of political governance. In the heyday of European imperialism, for instance, family metaphors were used to justify the control of imperial nations over subject nations: colonized nations were likened to immature children needing the steady hand of the colonizer.[57] Well into the present day, efforts to encourage nationalism are often linked to efforts to get female citizens of the preferred type to bear more children; conversely, campaigns to sterilize women of the non-preferred type have been justified by appeals to the need for a pure, strong nation.[58] Similarly, White fears of being "replaced" by people of color often feature, along with calls for greater national immigration restrictions, calls for White women to leave the workplace and "return" to the home and patriarchal control.[59] Finally, as feminist legal theorists have recognized, the idea of the "autonomous individual" at the center of liberal theory incorporated European sex/gender norms into modern concepts of political citizenship.[60]

29.2.3 *From Colonial Empire to the Upside-Down World*

Today's global political economy continues to reflect the "upside-down" priorities Barry Commoner decried. Worldwide, the needs of finance capital drive economic production and the needs of economic production in turn drive human–nonhuman relationships. Economic production remains primarily reliant on carbon extraction, resulting in escalating rates of pollution, resource depletion, greenhouse gas production, and waste.

In addition to being unsustainable, this carbon-driven political economy remains unjust and racialized, following paths of exploitation and marginalization developed in colonial empire and reflected in modern conceptions of science, nature, and man. This section surveys key characteristics of the contemporary global political economy and sketches an LPE account of the role of legal institutions and concepts in maintaining the injustice and unsustainability of the upside-down world.

In terms of political governance, the world in which a handful of European nation-states maintained vast empires is gone. Indeed, at first impression, it might appear that the postcolonial world has been radically restructured. Collective action by workers and peasants in the colonized world – including strikes and uprisings made possible by the emergence of industrial capitalism – forced economic and political elites to retreat from the imperial project. Moreover, today's global order no longer mirrors the hierarchies of colonial empire. Several formerly poor and colonized nation-states – notably India, China, Brazil, and South Africa – have achieved explosive economic growth and increased political voice, and China in particular

---

[56] See Folbre, note 54.

[57] See McClintock, note 44; see also N. Yuval-Davis, "Gender and Nation" (1993) 16 *Ethnic and Racial Studies* 621.

[58] See P. Hill Collins, "It's All in the Family: Intersections of Gender, Race, and Nation" (1998) 13 *Hypatia* 62 at 75.

[59] See P. Huang, "Anchor Babies, Over-Breeders, and the Population Bomb: The Re-emergence of Nativism and Population Control in Anti-Immigrant Policies" (2008) 2 *Harvard Law & Policy Review* 385.

[60] C. Pateman, *The Sexual Contract* (Stanford, CA: Stanford University Press, 1988); S. M. Okin, *Justice, Gender and the Family* (Oxford: Oxford University Press, 1989).

has become a major world power.[61] Meanwhile, Indigenous peoples (traditionally not considered "states" under international law) have recently achieved, through long struggle, the international recognition of collective rights, such as the right to maintain and develop their own political, economic, and social systems.[62]

The world economy has changed dramatically since the period of colonial empire, as well. By the mid-twentieth century, "[m]ost of the world's people were . . . inextricably tied to both commodity production and consumption."[63] Today's capitalists work to "organize production globally, and to create branded goods and the sales channels to offer them for purchase all over the world."[64] The preeminent actors in this endeavor are multinational corporations, able to organize across national borders and pit nation-states against one another in a competition for lax environmental and labor protections.[65]

Despite these changes, transnational and national patterns of economic extraction and structures of political and economic governance continue to bear the traces of colonial empire in at least four intertwined ways, thwarting the quest for a just and sustainable world. First, international institutions of political and economic governance tend to be most responsive to the interests of the richest nation-states, perpetuating economic inequalities secured by colonial empire and distributing environmental consequences along the same unequal lines. Second, nation-states prioritize economic growth over environmental protection – which often means supporting destructive forms of resource extraction and ignoring the complaints of the people most harmed by it. Third, economic relations and their regulation continue to reflect the interests of patriarchal power in both the center and the peripheries of the world system. Fourth and finally, the international legal regulation of political economy (and in many countries, domestic regulation as well) continues to reflect the ontologies of man, nature, and science first developed in colonial empire. Each of these features of contemporary political economy tends to promote short-term economic growth over long-term ecological sustainability; place disproportionate burdens of environmental extraction on traditionally vulnerable groups, including women, the poorest countries and peoples, national minorities, and Indigenous peoples; and/or make it difficult to redress environmental injustices.

29.2.3.1 International Institutions and the Legacy of Colonial Empire

Some international law scholars agree that "while international law guarantees sovereign equality and self-determination, it carries forward the legacy of imperialism and colonial

---

[61] See R. Gordon, "The Dawn of a New, New International Economic Order?" (2009) 72 *Law and Contemporary Problems* 131 at 132 (identifying a new "Southern Tier" of formerly colonized, now middle-income nations who are demanding a voice in shaping international economic relations); H. Campbell, "China in Africa: Challenging US Global Hegemony" (2008) 28 *Third World Quarterly* 89 (noting China's explosive economic growth and arguing that China's investment in Africa signals its rise to hegemonic power); C. G. Gonzalez, "China in Latin America: Law, Economics, and Sustainable Development" (2010) 40 *Environmental Law Reporter* 10171 at 10175–10176 (discussing the social and economic costs of China's explosive economic growth).

[62] See UN General Assembly, *United Nations Declaration on the Rights of Indigenous Peoples*, Oct. 2, 2007, UN Doc. A/RES/61/195. For a critical examination of the Declaration and the unfinished business that remains, see A. Moreton-Robinson, *The White Possessive: Property, Power, and Indigenous Sovereignty* (Minneapolis: University of Minnesota Press, 2015).

[63] Beckert, note 28, p. 437.

[64] Ibid.

[65] A. D. Chandler and B. Mazlish, *Leviathans: Multinational Corporations and the New Global History* (Cambridge: Cambridge University Press, 2005).

conquest."[66] B. S. Chimni, for example, argues that today's global political economy should be deemed a form of "global imperialism,"[67] sustained by key international legal institutions. For example, the World Trade Organization's Agreement on Agriculture benefits consumers in rich countries and a small number of multinational agricultural concerns, while hurting small farmers, especially those in poor countries.[68] Meanwhile, poor and formerly colonized nations, such as those in sub-Saharan Africa, are systematically disadvantaged within international trade, finance, and development institutions by a lack of resources.[69] Indeed, scholars argue that these institutions, led by the former colonizing nations, have deliberately resisted collective efforts by the poorer countries to correct the economic legacy of colonial empire.[70]

Chimni argues that global imperialism today involves the emergence of a transnational capitalist class, comprising an alliance between national elites and professional and corporate elites.[71] Maintaining the power of this class are the international financial institutions, such as the World Bank and the International Monetary Fund.[72] Economic pressures exerted by these institutions, he argues, reduce the discretion of poorer countries in the realm of "monetary, industrial, technology, trade, and environmental policies."[73] The result of this tilted system is disproportionate economic and environmental benefits for the rich within and across countries, and, conversely, disproportionate economic privation and environmental harms to the poor.[74]

29.2.3.2 The "Law beyond Law": the Priority of Economic Growth

A second feature of the contemporary political–economic landscape traceable to colonial empire is the prioritization of economic development over environmental protection – which, given the path dependencies of global political economy, disproportionately harms the poor. For instance, Sabaa Khan argues that despite the objectives of a "Pollution-Free Planet" and a "Future Detoxified" identified by the third United Nations Environment Assembly and the 2017 Conference of the Parties to the Basel, Rotterdam, and Stockholm Conventions, the existing global regulatory regime places the economic interests of industry stakeholders over human rights and ecosystem health concerns – an international version of the "upside down" world.[75] The same priorities are visible in domestic law and policy. For example, China's

---

[66] J. T. Gathii, "TWAIL: A Brief History of Its Origins, Its Decentralized Network, and a Tentative Bibliography" (2011) 3 *Trade, Law & Development* 26 at 30–31 (arguing that this idea is characteristic of scholars who identify with the literature of TWAIL).

[67] B. S. Chimni, "Capitalism, Imperialism, and International Law in the Twenty-First Century" (2012) 14 *Oregon Review of International Law* 17.

[68] C. G. Gonzalez, "The Global Food Crisis: Law, Policy, and the Elusive Quest for Justice" (2010) 13 *Yale Human Rights & Development Law Journal* 462 at 470 (arguing that the Agreement "enabled developed countries to maintain high levels of agricultural protectionism," while "prohibiting developing countries from raising tariffs to regulate the flow of agricultural imports into their markets so as to protect small farmers from economically ruinous surges of cheap imported food products").

[69] R. Gordon, "Contemplating the WTO from the Margins" (2006) 14 *Berkeley La Raza Law Journal* 95 at 102.

[70] See R. Gordon, "Racing U.S. Foreign Policy" (2002) 17 *National Black Law Journal* 1 at 7–8 (identifying the New International Economic Order, the Charter of Economic Rights and the Duties of States, and the Right to Development as examples of initiatives meant to redress colonial economic injustice that were blocked by the rich countries).

[71] Chimni, note 67, p. 19.

[72] Ibid., p. 31.

[73] Ibid.

[74] See, for example, Chapters 3, 5, 16, 18, 20, 28 in this volume.

[75] Ibid., Chapter 16.

emphasis on economic growth over environmental protection has led to the emergence of "cancer villages."[76] In North America, environmental protection is similarly treated as secondary to economic production, a policy some call the "law beyond law."[77] Even where environmental justice struggles have been successful in achieving law reform, it is often at the cost of accepting environmental protection as secondary to economic growth.[78]

To some extent, the priority of economic growth over environmental protection is the result of the failure, discussed below, of economic analysis to concern itself with ecological knowledge – a failure traceable to the internal construction of modern economics.[79] Timothy Mitchell suggests that widespread inattention to environmental protection is due to a sense of abundance permitted by fossil fuel reliance.[80] Fossil fuel reliance has also encouraged undemocratic alliances among multinational oil corporations, rich countries, and the elites of countries possessed of oil and gas reserves.[81] The biggest losers in these alliances are often Indigenous peoples. In Africa and Latin America, Indigenous attempts to protest the rapacious environmental destruction caused by oil and gas extraction have been met with violence and murder.[82] In many countries and internationally, Indigenous rights frameworks have been subordinated to conventional economic "development" concerns.[83]

29.2.3.3 Gendered Governance

A third legacy of colonial empire is the patriarchal design of governance. For example, international political governance was built on state sovereignty, "the acknowledgement of political control by a government over a people and territory."[84] Except for the limited protections available under international human rights law, this "statist" approach treats family and civil society as beyond the purview of international law, preserving key modes of gendered domination.[85] Statism in international law thus tends to under-protect the rights of women and children to a clean and safe environment – and the rights of subnational minorities.[86]

Meanwhile, economic law reinforces the marginalization and disempowerment of women. For example, Damilola Olawuyi notes that the colonial regime in Nigeria replaced the authority of customary leaders with state control over land tenure, imposing a uniform, nationwide land tenure system; today this regulatory regime contributes to a "cycle of [women's] perpetual dependence on men for accessing land as well as financial and technical resources needed to participate in cash crop schemes."[87] With respect to energy production, Guruswamy notes that in some regions of sub-Saharan Africa and developing Asia, women suffer disproportionately

---

[76] Ibid., Chapter 17.

[77] See M. M'Gonigle and L. Takeda. "The Liberal Limits of Environmental Law: A Green Legal Critique" (2012) 30 *Pace Environmental Law Review* i.

[78] See Chapters 9 and 26 in this volume.

[79] See Section 29.4.

[80] T. Mitchell, *Carbon Democracy: Political Power in the Age of Oil* (New York: Verso, 2011).

[81] Ibid., p. 10.

[82] R. Nixon, *Slow Violence and the Environmentalism of the Poor* (Cambridge, MA: Harvard University Press, 2011).

[83] See, for example, Chapters 4, 11, 21, 23 in this volume.

[84] K. Knop, "Re/Statements: Feminism and State Sovereignty in International Law" (1993) 3 *Transnational Law and Contemporary Problems* 293 at 296.

[85] Ibid., p. 295.

[86] See Chapters 10, 13, 14 in this volume.

[87] Ibid., Chapter 14, p. 000.

from indoor pollution caused by biomass-generated fires, due to cultural norms that assign cooking responsibilities to women.[88]

Economic activity is designed around patriarchal cultural norms in rich countries as well. Sara Seck and Penelope Simons, for example, note that "in rich settler states of the Global North, like Canada, there are few, if any, sustainable mining practices that are truly respectful of the environmental and other human rights of women and girls."[89] Economic activity organized around gender leads to gendered environmental harm in so-called clean industries as well as traditionally "dirty" ones.[90] These gendered systems of production, as we have seen, can be traced back to colonial empire and sometimes beyond. The maldistribution of harms they create persist in an international legal regime that treats human rights, environmental, and labor protections as secondary to trade and investment protections.

29.2.3.4 Colonial Grammars of Governance

Fourth and finally, the internal organization of legal governance regimes internationally and in the rich nations continues to reflect many of the basic assumptions embraced by the architects of colonial modernity. An example is the designation of society into two complementary spheres, "public" and "private." This split is often linked with two other assumed oppositions: between "the family" and "the market," and between "the state" and "civil society."[91] The public–private distinction distributes authority between institutions and styles of governance and sets the terms for conventional political debate. At the national level, for instance, the distinction shapes debates between liberals and conservatives about whether and to what extent the state should "interfere" in the "private" workings of the market or the family.[92] Within international law, as we have seen, the distinction has contributed to a systemic failure to adequately protect women's rights.[93] More generally, it fragments state obligations in economic, political, and social relations, contributing to "siloed" regulatory regimes that fail to adequately address environmental injustice.[94] In the era of neoliberal regulation, the supposed superiority of "market-based" over

---

[88] Ibid., Chapter 24, p. 000. See also ibid., Chapter 21, p. 000 (noting that "Toxic pollution of water and the environment may have a greater impact on women in the Global South due to their traditional roles as collectors of water and preparers of food, and as small-scale farmers with responsibilities for subsistence agriculture"); p. 000 (noting that land and water pollution may disproportionately burden women in Indigenous communities where women are responsible for harvesting or for food provision generally).

[89] See ibid., Chapter 21, p. 000.

[90] For example, Lisa Sun Hee Park and David Pellow found that 70 to 80 percent of electronics workers in California's "Silicon Valley" were Asian and Latino immigrants, and 60 percent of them were women. Their hiring was justified with reference to "their alleged greater manual dexterity and mental tolerance for tedious work" (Ibid), but they also were burdened with levels of environmental illness higher than that found in other industries (L. S. H. Park and D. N. Pellow, "Racial Formation, Environmental Racism, and the Emergence of Silicon Valley" (2004) 4 *Ethnicities* 403 at 418).

[91] F. E. Olsen, "The Family and the Market: A Study of Ideology and Legal Reform" (1983) 96 *Harvard Law Review* 1497; B. Harcourt, *The Illusion of Free Markets* (Chicago: University of Chicago Press, 2011). As Olsen notes, the designations are not fixed: in the family–market distinction, the family is deemed private and the market public, but in the state–civil society distinction, the market is deemed private and the state, public.

[92] Ibid.

[93] H. Charlesworth, "The Public/Private Distinction and the Right to Development in International Law" (1988–1989) 12 *Australian Year Book of International Law* 190; C. Romany, "Women as Aliens: A Feminist Critique of the Public/Private Distinction in International Human Rights Law" (1993) 6 *Harvard Human Rights Journal* 87.

[94] See S. L. Seck, "Transnational Labour Law and the Environment: Beyond the Bounded Autonomous Worker" (2018) 33 *Canadian Journal of Law and Society* 137 at 138.

"state-based" governance regimes has entrenched old colonial patterns of extraction.[95] It also legitimates the notion of a minimal, rather than a responsive, state.[96]

These pathologies of colonial imperial governance are not only present in the structures of international and domestic legal governance. They are also buried in perhaps the most important link between colonial empire and the present moment: the ideology of political–economic "development." This ideology was famously born at the end of World War II, when the decolonized nations constituting the "Third World" were exhorted by President Harry S. Truman to remake themselves in the image of the "First World."[97] In Truman's vision, "capital, science, and technology were the main ingredients that would make this massive revolution possible."[98] Development would "bring about the conditions necessary to replicating the world over the features that characterized the 'advanced' societies of the time – high levels of industrialization and urbanization, technicalization of agriculture, rapid growth of material production and living standards, and the widespread adoption of modern education and cultural values."[99]

Although the narrative of development abandoned the old language of a fixed racial order in favor of an account that promoted the goal of abundance and self-determination for all, it preserved the familiar ranking of peoples and nation-states along a single axis, with "White" peoples from settler colonial and imperial states at the top and Indigenous peoples, immigrant laborers, and the descendants of slaves at the bottom.[100] Indeed, some scholars argue that "development" simply took up where colonial empire left off.[101]

Perhaps the central intellectual tool of development was twentieth-century economics. The modern discipline of economics absorbed the colonial–modern distinction between humans and nature, representing the nonhuman world as an infinite resource for exploitation.[102] In the postcolonial period, development economics became key to statecraft. Countries that had served largely as sources of resource extraction under colonialism were now exhorted to follow the ostensibly universal rules of neoclassical economics and pursue "comparative advantage" in world markets, rather than nurturing their domestic production capacities.[103] Measures of macroeconomic performance also absorbed gendered norms. For example, neither gross national product (GNP) nor its successor gross domestic product (GDP) – key indices of

---

[95] See, for example, C. G. Gonzalez, "Beyond Eco-Imperialism: An Environmental Justice Critique of Free Trade" (2001) 78 *Denver University Law Review* 979; C. G. Gonzalez, "An Environmental Justice Critique of Comparative Advantage: Indigenous Peoples, Trade Policy, and the Mexican Neoliberal Economic Reforms" (2011) 32 *University of Pennsylvania Journal of International Law* 723.

[96] See M. A. Fineman, "The Vulnerable Subject and the Responsive State" (2010) 60 *Emory Law Journal* 251; Chapter 6 in this volume.

[97] A. Escobar, *Encountering Development: The Making and Unmaking of the Third World* (Princeton, NJ: Princeton University Press, 1995). Escobar notes that whereas Europe, the "Second World," received massive amounts of capital from the United States under the Marshall Plan to rebuild itself, the Third World was directed to private capital – and this capital came with preconditions, including "a commitment to capitalist development; the curbing of nationalism; and the control of the Left, the working class, and the peasantry" (ibid., p. 33).

[98] Ibid., p. 4.

[99] Ibid.

[100] See J. Sylvester and R. Gordon, "Deconstructing Development" (2004) 22 *Wisconsin International Law Journal* 1 at p. 16 (noting Eugene Rostow's division of world cultures into "stages" of development from traditional to modern society).

[101] Ibid., p. 5.

[102] U. Natarajan and K. Khoday, "Locating Nature: Making and Unmaking International Law" (2014) 27 *Leiden Journal of International Law* 573; U. Natarajan, "TWAIL and the Environment: The State of Nature, the Nature of the State and the Arab Spring" (2012) 14 *Oregon Review of International Law* 177.

[103] Gonzalez, "Beyond Eco-Imperialism," note 95; Gonzalez, "Environmental Justice Critique," note 95.

national economic accounting – counts unwaged labor, whether in the home or for subsistence – the kind of work predominantly performed by the world's women.[104]

Armed with these discourses of expertise, the international institutions tasked with promoting development, such as the World Bank and the International Monetary Fund (IMF), enthusiastically lent money to the poorer nations for activities that would bind them more securely into international production and finance markets designed to favor the richer nations, including expensive infrastructure projects such as dams and roads; "Green Revolution" technology transfers that substituted capital-intensive and monoculture-based, export-focused agriculture for peasant-driven, diversified subsistence agriculture;[105] and social programs intended to foster national prosperity by reducing the number of births in poor countries.[106] Law was also a subject of technology transfer: experts held that adopting Western legal systems was central to enjoying the material and cultural benefits of development.[107]

Despite the official death of "law and development" in the early 1970s, these ideas were reincarnated in the 1990s as "marketization" and "democratization," and reinvented again in the early 2000s as "good governance."[108] They are circulated not only as "conventional wisdom," but also through the international financial institutions that "virtually control the policy-making processes of some debtor countries."[109] Even the nations that have risen to middle-income status in the international economic order find themselves unable to stray very far from conventional economic wisdom, lest they find themselves punished by "the market." As a result, countries whose economies were ravaged by colonial empire are repeatedly dissuaded from, or punished for, embarking on transformative social projects.[110] Conversely, countries whose elites are willing to collude with the interests of finance capital and multinational corporations have bought market favor at the price of highly unequal societies maintained by authoritarian governments.[111] These structural pressures on poor countries are only intensified by the ravages of climate change.[112]

Finally, exacerbating the upside-down world and its concomitant unequal distribution of environmental health are the persistent racial connotations of political belonging itself. In settler colonial states, such as the United States, Brazil, Canada, and Australia, as well as former seats of empire, such as England and the states of western Europe, immigrants, and refugees are increasingly viewed as toxic substances, dangerous to national culture and social and political norms. As climate change accelerates, creating unprecedented numbers of refugees, the resurfacing of tropes of race and nation first invented in colonial empire portends a frightening era of

---

[104] M. Murphy, *The Economization of Life* (Durham, NC: Duke University Press, 2017), pp. 26–27.

[105] See Escobar, note 97, pp. 113–153; C. G. Gonzalez, "The Global Food System, Environmental Protection, and Human Rights" (2012) 26 *Natural Resources & Environment* 7; C. G. Gonzalez, "Climate Change, Food Security, and Agrobiodiversity: Toward a Just, Resilient, and Sustainable Food System" (2011) 22 *Fordham Environmental Law Review* 493.

[106] See Murphy, note 104, pp. 74–75 (describing the activities of US-funded family planning initiatives in India).

[107] Sylvester and Gordon, note 100, p. 19.

[108] Ibid., p. 21.

[109] Ibid., pp. 22–23.

[110] Anne Orford argues that Western liberal economists moved to block postcolonial states from enacting land reform, labor rights, education, and redistribution initiatives, using the language of "development through trade liberalization" (A. Orford, "Food Security, Free Trade, and the Battle for the State" (2015) 11 *Journal of International Law & International Relations* 1). See also C. G. Gonzalez, "Environmental Justice and International Environmental Law," in S. Alam, J. H. Bhuiyan, T. M. R. Chowdury, and E. J. Techerais (eds.), *Routledge Handbook of International Environmental Law* (Abingdon, UK: Routledge, 2012), pp. 77–98.

[111] A. Mbembe, *On the Postcolony* (Berkeley, CA: University of California Press, 2001).

[112] Chapter 28 in this volume (describing a "political roller coaster" of state policy in the Maldives between confrontational and accommodationist approaches to global elites, as rising waters threaten the nation's territory).

global and local conflicts in which the poorest and most powerless people will be the first to be displaced, only to be met with indifference at best, violence at worst.[113]

29.3 WHAT, THEN, IS TO BE DONE?

One of the invaluable contributions of the environmental justice movement has been to recognize the indissolubility of environmental and economic sustainability and social justice. This recognition is now embodied in the 2002 Johannesburg Declaration on Sustainable Development, which identifies three "pillars" of development: economic, social, and environmental.[114] Promoting forms of governance that integrate these three pillars is an important step forward in crafting effective responses to the crises engulfing our planet.[115]

International human rights law provides an example. In recent years, human rights has emerged as a means of incorporating environmental and economic sustainability into campaigns for social justice.[116] Several regional human rights treaties recognize the right to a healthy environment, meaning that it can be treated as an emerging principle of customary international law; rights to life or to property can be argued to contain the right to a safe and healthy environment as a prerequisite; and the right to a healthy environment, scholars argue, is an apt subject for international treaty-making.[117] Latin American countries have taken the lead in incorporating the "three pillars" framework into domestic constitutional law[118] and several of the chapters in this volume describe strategies for moving this project forward.[119] Yet, it remains unclear whether advocacy under the banner of human rights or human dignity has the capacity to overcome the legacy of colonial empire buried within contemporary frameworks of political–economic governance.[120] One concern is whether the idea of "the human" central to human rights language is inextricable from the ontology of colonial modernity. Decolonial scholar, Walter Mignolo, for instance, argues that despite its liberatory potential, "human rights" discourse is an imperial tool, to the extent that elites continue to define the "human" along the familiar continuum of developed versus developing, civilized versus savage.[121] A second concern is that human rights discourse does not directly address the need to reconstitute corporate personality. Building on the work of Anna Grear,[122] Seck argues for more legal and policy tools to hold corporations responsible for human rights and environmental abuses, such as lifting the corporate veil to hold individual actors responsible for harm, and endorses the search for alternative forms of business enterprise to replace the for-profit corporation.[123]

---

[113] Ibid.

[114] See Chapter 9 in this volume.

[115] Ibid. (discussing public interest litigation in South Asia that draws upon the Sustainable Development Goals to develop a "right to development" that incorporates all three pillars).

[116] See C. G. Gonzalez and S. Atapattu, "International Environmental Law, Environmental Justice, and the Global South" (2017) 26 *Transnational Law & Contemporary Problems* 229 at 235 ("Human rights has become one of the dominant discourses for the articulation and adjudication of environmental disputes").

[117] Ibid., p. 236. Daly and May add that the language of "dignity" inherent in human rights discourse represents a similar opportunity for environmental justice advocacy (Chapter 2 in this volume).

[118] See Chapter 11 in this volume.

[119] Ibid., Chapters 9, 19, 22.

[120] Ibid., Chapter 20.

[121] Mignolo, note 33, p. 17.

[122] A. Grear, "Vulnerability, Advanced Global Capitalism and Co-symptomatic Injustice: Locating the Vulnerable Subject," in M. A. Fineman and A. Grear, *Vulnerability: Reflections on a New Ethical Foundation for Law and Politics* (Farnham, UK: Ashgate, 2013).

[123] S. L. Seck, "Relational Law and the Reimagining of Tools for Environmental and Climate Justice" (2019) 31 *Canadian Journal of Women and the Law* 151 at 161.

Relational theory provides another way forward. In the sciences, ecology has led the way in recognizing the interdependence of human and nonhuman beings and processes.[124] Legal and political theory has only begun to catch up. Some scholars have drawn on Martha Fineman's "vulnerability" theory to reject the increasingly problematic distinction between human and nonhuman subjects in a world made precarious by the specter of ecological collapse.[125] For example, noting that international human rights seems to privilege labor rights over environmental rights, Seck suggests that the tension might be resolved if workers, whose interests are to be represented by labor law, were seen as "corporeal citizens embedded in material environments."[126]

Relational theory holds the potential to restructure the upside-down design of contemporary world political economy that Barry Commoner condemned decades ago. The value of relational discourse is its refusal to accept the basic terms of colonial modernity – in particular, its potential to undermine the privileging of finance and production over the sustenance of human and nonhuman life. The emergence of Indigenous communities and philosophies into leadership in environmental justice struggles is emblematic in this regard.[127] As McGregor's chapter in this volume notes, Indigenous advocates have trenchantly critiqued international agreements that accept the conventional terms of debate, such as "the portrayal of the earth as 'natural capital' which would drive the 'green economy.'"[128] More importantly, Indigenous philosophies offer perspectives and approaches outside the box of colonial empire, rewriting the nature–society distinction so dear to Western epistemology.

McGregor notes that "Indigenous intellectual and legal systems draw on a set of Indigenous metaphysical, ontological, and epistemological assumptions about the place of humanity in the world which describe how people should relate to all of creation."[129] These assumptions are linked to ways of knowing that acknowledge nonhuman beings as relatives and teachers, transforming ecological knowledge and action.[130] Embracing these ways of knowing is not an attempt to return to a romanticized, ahistorical, and unattainable past in which "humans lived in harmony with nature." Rather, Indigenous political philosophers are alive to the task of healing the planet in the wake of colonial empire's depredations and the looming catastrophe of global climate change. Kyle Powys Whyte, for instance, argues for the Indigenous value of "collective continuance," which he defines as "a community's aptitude for being adaptive in ways sufficient for the livelihoods of its members to flourish into the future."[131] Whyte argues that "emerging systems of responsibilities include the new relationships that are needed for communities to relocate because of environmental change, as well as accommodate new species in their territories, cope with losses and begin to use science and other technical support as part of their collective knowledge systems, among other possibilities."[132] Indigenous philosophies also make

[124] See Chapter 27 in this volume (describing "ecohealth" as recognizing "that human health and well-being are the result of a complex and dynamic set of interactions between people, social and economic conditions, culture, and the natural environment"); Ibid., Chapter 7 (drawing on ecology to propose "resilience" as a master framework for confronting climate change).
[125] See, for example, Chapter 6 in this volume; Fineman and Grear, note 122; Harris, note 26; Seck, note 123.
[126] Seck, note 123, p. 156.
[127] See in this volume, for example, Chapters 11, 12, 25.
[128] Ibid., Chapter 4.
[129] Ibid., pp. 00–00.
[130] Ibid., pp. 00–00.
[131] K. P. Whyte, "Indigenous Women, Climate Change Impacts, and Collective Action" (2014) 29 *Hypatia* 599 at 602.
[132] K. P. Whyte, "Justice Forward: Tribes, Climate Adaptation, and Responsibility" (2013) 120 *Climatic Change Journal* 117.

room for reconceptualizing ways of knowing outside modernist scientific rationality, which represents humans as active knowers and the nonhuman world as inert. McGregor argues that "the knowledge we need to survive as humanity may not derive strictly from the 'human realm'; we need to revitalize and relearn the traditions that will ensure all knowledge is respected, including that from our various nonhuman relatives."[133]

Indigenous answers to "Who are we?" provide an alternative to the conventional answer (that is, "human individuals and groups with the capacity for self-governance"). This, in turn, makes possible very different approaches to the question "Can we live together?"[134]

With the example and leadership of Indigenous communities, nonhuman subjects in several countries have begun to be granted legal rights.[135] Indigenous communities themselves, meanwhile, have begun to win greater control over the governance of environmental and energy systems in their territories.[136] The open question is whether such projects will be able to surmount the structures and path dependencies of colonial empire before the planet is overwhelmed.[137]

29.4 CONCLUSION

As Gonzalez argues, "[T]he colonization of the Americas and the transatlantic slave trade established the material and ideological foundations of capitalism – a system based on extraction, accumulation through dispossession, and white supremacy."[138] The upside-down logic of planetary environmental–economic relations treats nonhuman resources and dynamics as infinite and eternal, while the colonial subject Sylvia Wynter describes as "bio-economic Man"[139] sutures politics and economics into an unequal but ostensibly nonpolitical hierarchy of being. These entwined dynamics have produced great wealth for some humans at the expense of others. They have also created the climate emergency in which all of us on the planet currently live. The good news is that environmental justice advocates and their allies are beginning to face the problem squarely. The bad news, of course, is that time is already too short "and we are not saved." We are in a race between catastrophe and transformation.

---

[133] Chapter 4 in this volume; see R. W. Kimmerer, *Braiding Sweetgrass: Indigenous Wisdom, Scientific Knowledge and the Teachings of Plants* (Minneapolis: Milkweed Editions, 2013) (demonstrating how to combine Indigenous and Western ways of knowing).

[134] Compare B. Latour, *Politics of Nature* (Cambridge, MA: Harvard University Press, 1999), p. 8 (arguing that the central questions for governance in a decolonized world are "how many are we?" and "can we live together?"); Whyte, *Justice Forward*, note 132, pp. 519–520; Chapter 23 in this volume (arguing that "both environmental justice and the social pillar of sustainable development (including the SDGs) must be interpreted through an Indigenous rights lens").

[135] See Chapter 12 in this volume.

[136] See, for example, ibid., Chapters 11, 25.

[137] Ibid.

[138] Ibid., Chapter 5, pp. 00–00.

[139] Wynter, note 40, p. 263.

30

Beyond Fragmentation

Reflections, Strategies, and Challenges

Sumudu A. Atapattu, Carmen G. Gonzalez, and Sara L. Seck

In this volume, we examined examples of environmental injustice and unsustainable development from around the world, emphasizing multiple, overlapping forms of subordination and the legal tools used by communities in their struggles to seek remedy and redress. In this concluding chapter, we offer some reflections on moving beyond fragmentation and toward holistic and just solutions. We also provide some clarifications and discuss some of the challenges we encountered as we compiled and edited this volume.

While many of the case studies in this book paint a dismal picture, the volume also contains success stories. These chapters enable us to reflect on the strategies that worked and the challenges that lie ahead as we strive for sustainable development and environmental justice among a series of rapidly intensifying ecological and economic crises.

Despite its shortcomings, sustainable development (or sustainability as some prefer to call it)[1] has moved from being a "slippery concept"[2] to one of the most influential concepts of our time that has been accepted by all segments of the global community.[3] Many scholars believe that sustainable development is an umbrella concept embodying both substantive and procedural components.[4]

---

[1] H. Washington, "Is 'Sustainability' the Same as 'Sustainable Development,'" in H. Kopnina and E. Shoreman-Ouimet (eds.), *Sustainability: Key Issues* (London: Routledge, 2015), pp. 359–376. According to Washington: "'Sustainability' to my mind has to be a much broader concept than 'sustainable development.' It should focus on sustainability in the long-term for all aspects of the human and natural environment. It should certainly not be about growth in numbers, resource use or GDP. As Shiva (1992) predicted, 'sustainable development' has been co-opted by neoliberal ideology to continue 'business as usual' growth. However, growth is the cause of escalating degradation of the biosphere. If we are to demystify 'sustainability' then our focus must (first and foremost) center on being sustainable, not on endless growth on a finite planet – an impossibility" (p. 365).

[2] See C. Stone, "Deciphering Sustainable Development" (1994) 69 *Chicago-Kent Law Review* 997.

[3] See D. Hunter, J. Salzman, and D. Zaelke, *International Environmental Law and Policy* (5th ed.) (Sunderland, UK: Foundation Press, 2015), p. 169 who believe that this acceptance is partly due to its "brilliant ambiguity."

[4] See generally, A. Dobson, "Fairness and Futurity: Essays on Environmental Sustainability and Social Justice" (1999), excerpts in Hunter et al, note 3, p. 170; N. Schrijver, *The Evolution of Sustainable Development in International Law: Inception, Meaning and Status* (Leiden: Brill, 2008); C. Voigt, *Sustainable Development as a Principle of International Law: Resolving Conflicts between Climate Measures and WTO Law* (Leiden: Martinus Nijhoff, 2008); L. Kotzé (ed.), *Environmental Law and Governance for the Anthropocene* (Oxford: Hart, 2017); S. Atapattu, *Emerging Principles of International Environmental Law* (Leiden: Brill, 2006), ch. 2; S. Atapattu, "From 'Our Common Future' to Sustainable Development Goals: Evolution of Sustainable Development under International Law" (2019) 36 *Wisconsin International Law Journal* 215; M. Redclift and D. Springett (eds.), *Routledge International Handbook of Sustainable Development* (Abingdon, UK: Routledge, 2015).

The substantive components include inter and intragenerational equity, sustainable use of natural resources, and the principle of integration.[5] The procedural components consist of access to information, public participation and access to remedies,[6] and overlap with principles of good governance and existing obligations under international human rights law.[7] European and Latin American states, among others, have adopted treaties to give effect to these procedural rights in environmental matters.[8] Many countries have adopted laws requiring impact assessments integrating environment protection and economic development,[9] and some are adopting broader impact assessment laws designed to capture an even more fulsome integrated approach to sustainability assessment.[10] A handful of countries have also adopted sustainable development laws,[11] while a few others have established institutions to look after future generations.[12] Thus, the view that sustainable development is vague and lacks meaning is no longer tenable. The real issue is how sustainable development has been applied in practice.

Many lessons can be learned from traditional societies and diverse cultures in harmonizing the various dimensions of sustainable development. As Justice Weeramantry observed in 1997, drawing extensively from the wisdom of ancient civilizations and practices of Indigenous peoples:

> When Native American wisdom, with its deep love of nature, ordained that no activity affecting the land should be undertaken without giving thought to its impact on the land for seven generations to come; when African tradition viewed the human community as three-fold – past, present and future – and refused to adopt a one-eyed vision of concentration on the present; when Pacific tradition despised the view of land as merchandise that could be bought and sold like a common article of commerce . . . when Chinese and Japanese culture stressed the need for harmony with nature; and when Aboriginal custom, while maximizing the use of all species of plant and animal life, yet decreed that no land should be used by man to the point where it could not replenish itself, these varied cultures were reflecting the ancient wisdom of the human family which the legal systems of the time and the tribe absorbed, reflected and turned into principles whose legal validity cannot be denied. Ancient Indian teaching so respected the environment that it was illegal to cause wanton damage, even to an enemy's territory in the course of military conflict.[13]

---

5   See UN General Assembly, *Rio Declaration on Environment and Development*, Aug. 12, 1992, UN Doc. A/CONF.151/26 (Vol. I), Principles 3–5.

6   See ibid., Principle 10. See further elaboration of the components of procedural environmental rights in UN Human Rights Council, *Report of the Special Rapporteur on the issue of human rights obligations relating to the enjoyment of a safe, clean, healthy and sustainable environment: framework principles, John Knox*, Jan. 24, 2018, UN Doc. A/HRC/37/59 [Framework Principles].

7   See UN Human Rights Council, *Report of the Independent Expert on the issue of human rights obligations relating to the enjoyment of a safe, clean, healthy and sustainable environment, John H. Knox (Mapping Report)*, Dec. 30, 2013, UN Doc. A/HRC/25/53; Framework Principles, note 6.

8   See UN, Convention on Access to Information, Public Participation in Decision-Making and Access to Justice in Environmental Matters (Aarhus Convention), June 25, 1998, 2161 UNTS 447; UN, "Regional Agreement on Access to Information, Public Participation and Justice in Environmental Matters in Latin America and the Caribbean," ECLAC, 2018. Importantly, the Aarhus Convention is open to ratification by any state.

9   See N. Craik, *The International Law of Environmental Impact Assessment: Process, Substance and Integration* (Cambridge: Cambridge University Press, 2008).

10 See Canada's new impact assessment legislation, as discussed in Chapter 21 in this volume.

11 Canada and Sri Lanka are examples (see Chapter 15 in this volume).

12 Hungary has an Ombudsman for Future Generations, see "Hungarian Parliament's Deputy Commissioner for Fundamental Rights, the Ombudsman for Future Generations," www.fdsd.org/ideas/the-hungarian-parliaments-ombudsman-for-future-generations/.

13 ICJ, *Gabčíkovo–Nagymaros Project*, Separate Opinion of Justice Weeramantry, Reports, 1997, pp. 108–109 (fn. omitted).

Environmental stewardship and prudent management of resources goes back centuries. As Arahat Mahinda, son of the Emperor Asoka of India, preached to King Devanampiya Tissa (247–207 BC) who was on a hunting trip (around 223 BC): "O great King, the birds of the air and the beasts have as equal a right to live and move about in any part of the land as thou. *The land belongs to the people and all living beings; thou art only the guardian of it.*"[14] This was the origin of the modern public trust doctrine,[15] a doctrine that is increasingly being called into play by child and youth plaintiffs seeking to ensure that their governments live up to their obligations to protect public trust assets, including a safe climate, by meeting their greenhouse gas emissions reduction obligations.[16]

Regrettably, the track record of contemporary societies on sustainability is not promising. As many of the case studies highlight, despite three decades of action and scholarship on sustainable development, many states and other actors still promote economic growth (which is captured by elites) over environmental protection and social development. The SDGs reinforce this trend to the extent that they promote the acceleration of economic growth in poor countries without a corresponding reduction in economic growth and consumption in affluent countries, instead of addressing the structural causes of poverty and environmental degradation.[17] Nevertheless, there are also signs of good practices, such as New Zealand's legislative integration of Māori Indigenous laws[18] and increasing global recognition of children's rights,[19] among others.

We do not argue that combating poverty and deprivation is not important. On the contrary, improving the living standards of people in the Global South and in impoverished communities in the Global North is essential. However, this cannot be accomplished by destroying the environment or violating the rights of people. What is needed is a holistic, sustainable approach that promotes the flourishing of both humans and nature and welcomes world views that understand reciprocal relations and responsibilities among people and the natural world, including ancestors and future generations.[20]

This volume raises numerous questions for future inquiry and research. One of the unexpected revelations we experienced while compiling the book was the seeming reluctance of scholars to address gender justice as an integral part of environmental justice, unless it intersected with race, poverty, or indigeneity.[21] The same may be true of child rights. While the contributors to this book rightfully strive to steer clear of gender essentialism, it is important to recognize that there are biological reasons that explain differences between the responses of men and women to toxic exposures, including women's higher percentage of body fat (and greater

---

[14] Ibid., p. 102 (emphasis added).

[15] Ibid. See S. Atapattu, "The Role of Human Rights Law in Protecting Environmental Rights in South Asia," in L. Haglund and R. Stryker (eds.), *Closing the Rights Gap: From Human Rights to Social Transformation* (California: University of California Press, 2015), p. 105.

[16] *La Rose v. Her Majesty the Queen* 2019 FCC, Court File No. T-1750–19 (Statement of Claim of the Plaintiff); *Juliana et al. v. United States of America*, 217 F Supp 3d 1224 (D Or 2016). See generally Our Children's Trust, www.ourchildrenstrust.org.

[17] See, for example, SDG Goal 8.1 ("Sustain per capita economic growth in accordance with national circumstances and, in particular, at least 7 percent gross domestic product growth per annum in the least developed countries"). See further S. Alam, S. Atapattu, C. G. Gonzalez, and J. Razzaque (eds.), *International Environmental Law and the Global South* (Cambridge: Cambridge University Press, 2015).

[18] Chapter 12 in this volume.

[19] Ibid., Chapter 10.

[20] Ibid., Chapter 4.

[21] See also L. A. Malone, "Environmental Justice Reimagined Through Human Security and Post-Modern Ecological Feminism: A Neglected Perspective on Climate Change" (2015) 38 *Fordham International Law Journal* 1445 (arguing that ecofeminist perspectives are underrepresented in international environmental law scholarship).

storage of lipophilic chemicals) and women's vulnerability to reproductive toxins.[22] Similarly, children of all ethnic, racial, and socioeconomic backgrounds are more susceptible to environmental hazards because their immune systems are still developing.[23] When risk assessments of toxic chemicals rely on epidemiological studies based on studies of healthy White male workers, these risk assessments systematically fail to protect women and children – as well as persons with disabilities and older adults.[24] Gender justice is an integral part of environmental justice. Are there strategic reasons for the reluctance to address gender? Have scholars and activists concluded that certain identity categories are more likely than others to be favorably received by the judiciary? This is a topic worthy of further research.

Another issue that needs additional attention is the role of non-state actors whose actions are being increasingly scrutinized under international law due to their role in relation to both environmental and human rights abuses around the world. Is corrective justice limited to state enforcement of environmental laws? Or does it encompass other dispute resolution mechanisms? As several case studies in this volume illustrate, environmental justice has been achieved, at least in part, through participation in the legislative process and through civil litigation, including citizen suits, public interest litigation, private prosecutions, and tort actions. In addition, Pillar 3 of the UN Guiding Principles on Business and Human Rights on access to remedy, includes judicial and nonjudicial, state-based, and non-state-based mechanisms, and even those at the company level.[25] How do these non-state-based mechanisms challenge our understanding of environmental justice? What potential do they hold?

Similarly, there is increasing recognition of community institutions of justice such as Indigenous institutions that apply Indigenous laws. This underscores the potential limitations of a state-centric approach to environmental justice. While states are generally understood to be the ultimate enforcers of human rights law, we cannot ignore the increasingly important role played by other actors, both as protectors and violators of human rights. We invite scholars to conduct both empirical and theoretical research on ways to move beyond the state-centric quest for environmental justice.

Another issue we grappled with is how to reconcile the right to development with self-governance aspirations and self-determination. The UN Declaration on the Rights of Indigenous Peoples endorses the right of self-determination of Indigenous peoples.[26] As the chapters in this volume illustrate, under the Anishnabee concept of Indigenous environmental justice, development is less important than self-governance.[27] Similarly, the Te Urewera Act of New Zealand gives legal personhood to a former national park and requires that it be managed in a manner that preserves "Indigenous ecological systems and biodiversity."[28]

However, this raises the question about rural (local) communities who are not Indigenous. Do they similarly have self-governance aspirations? In an important development, the UN

---

[22] See, generally, K. Bell, "Bread and Roses: A Gender Perspective on Environmental Justice and Public Health" (2016) 13 *International Journal of Environmental Research and Public Health* 1005.

[23] See, generally, P. Grandjean et al., (2007) "The Faroes Statement: Human Health Effects of Developmental Exposure to Chemicals in Our Environment" 102 *Basic and Clinical Pharmacology and Toxicology* 73.

[24] See R. R. Kuehn, "The Environmental Justice Implications of Quantitative Risk Assessment" (1996) *University of Illinois Law Review* 103.

[25] See UNOHCHR, "Guiding Principles on Business and Human Rights," (2011). See further UNOHCHR, "Accountability and Remedy Project III: Enhancing effectiveness of non-state-based grievance mechanisms in case of business-related human rights abuse," www.ohchr.org/EN/Issues/Business/Pages/ARP_III.aspx.

[26] See UN, *Declaration on the Rights of Indigenous Peoples*, Sept. 13, 2007, UN Doc. A/RES/61/295, Art. 3.

[27] See Chapter 4 in this volume.

[28] Ibid., Chapter 12.

adopted the Declaration on Rights of Peasants and other People Working in Rural Areas in 2018, which protects the rights of rural communities, including the rights to land, seeds, and an adequate standard of living, the right to participate in any project or program affecting their land and territories, and the right to define their own food and agriculture systems.[29] The Declaration adopts an intersectional approach:

> Particular attention shall be paid in the implementation of the present Declaration to the rights and special needs of peasants and other people working in rural areas, including older persons, women, youth, children and persons with disabilities, taking into account the need to address multiple forms of discrimination.[30]

It is noteworthy that the Declaration's definition of peasants, includes Indigenous peoples and local communities working on the land,[31] as well as migrant workers regardless of their migrant status, landless and hired workers, and nomadic people.[32]

The evolving right to self-determination is an important question for further research. Are nominally independent states controlled by a small number of powerful elites capable of achieving a just transition to sustainability? While appeals to state institutions are an essential part of environmental justice struggles, might it be more fruitful for legal scholars to examine alternative conceptions of sustainable development (and alternatives to the idea of "development") grounded in the internationally recognized right of *peoples* to self-determination?[33]

30.1 SUCCESSES AND STRATEGIES

The case studies highlight several strategies that have been used by civil society groups and vulnerable states to combat environmental injustice and unsustainable development. Public interest litigation is one such tool which has been extensively used in South Asia. The chapters by Puvimanasinghe and Jolly[34] highlight creative uses of existing constitutional provisions (such as the right to life, the right to dignity, and the right to equality) to articulate a right to a healthy environment in South Asia.

Coalitional strategies have also been successful. As the chapter by Atapattu and Simonelli illustrates, the small island states have used this strategy to enhance their bargaining power in the climate negotiations.[35] The chapters by Bratspies and Kaswan demonstrate that environmental justice advocacy can be successful in some instances when environmental justice NGOs work in

---

[29] UN, *Declaration on the Rights of Peasants and Other People Working in Rural Areas*, Oct. 8, 2018, UN Doc. A/HRC/RES/39/12; "UN rights chief welcomes new text to protect rights of peasants and other rural workers," Dec. 18, 2018, https://news.un.org/en/story/2018/12/1028881. Article 1(1) of the Declaration defines peasants as "any person who engages or who seeks to engage alone, or in association with others or as a community, in small-scale agricultural production for subsistence and/or for the market, and who relies significantly, though not necessarily exclusively, on family or household labour and other non-monetized ways of organizing labour, and who has a special dependency on and attachment to the land."

[30] Ibid., Art. 2(2).

[31] Ibid., Art. 1(3).

[32] Ibid., Art. 1(4).

[33] See, generally, R. Ehrenreich Brooks, "Failed States, or the State as Failure?" (2005) 72 *University of Chicago Law Review* 1159; E. A. Daes, "An Overview of the History of Indigenous Peoples: Self-Determination and the United Nations" (2008) 21 *Cambridge Review of International Affairs* 7; H. J. Vogel, "Reframing Rights from the Ground Up: The Contribution of the New UN Law of Self-Determination to Recovering the Principle of Sociability on the Way to a Relational Theory of International Human Rights" (2006) 20 *Temple International and Comparative Law Journal* 443.

[34] Chapters 9 and 19, respectively.

[35] Chapter 28.

partnership with other organizations to influence public policy and legislation.[36] The chapter by Smith and Scott reveals that community-led energy generation based on Indigenous values and participation can be successful.[37] Similarly, as Lofts and Koutouki demonstrate in their chapter, integrating eco-health concerns into environmental impact assessments that incorporate Inuit world views and knowledge can lead to better adaptation outcomes.[38]

30.2 FINAL REFLECTIONS, CHALLENGES, AND CONTRADICTIONS

The compartmentalization of justice issues or the "silo mentality" is a major obstacle to achieving sustainable development and addressing environmental injustice. As Boaventura de Sousa Santos observes, transnational coalitions organized by feminist, ecological, and Indigenous groups have been more successful at "overcoming territorial separation than separation derived from the different forms of discrimination and oppression"[39] even though many of these injustices have common roots and deeply intertwined histories. For example, the chapters on the Tudor Shaft case in South Africa and nuclear testing in the Marshall Islands reveal the multiple and interconnected past and present injustices that produce inequitable social and environmental outcomes.[40] Many environmental justice struggles are often intertwined with issues of good governance as the chapters on the Port City Project in Sri Lanka and climate change in the Maldives illustrate.

These case studies also highlight the contradictory approaches to "economic growth" and sustainable development. While there is a clear articulation of the need to limit economic growth, and even decrease it (for example, the "degrowth" movement), states and international institutions continue to emphasize economic growth as the panacea for environmental and social ills. As mentioned in Chapter 1 of this volume, even the UN, in the context of SDGs laments that economic growth has slowed down in recent years. While appreciating the need for poor and middle-income countries to provide a decent standard of living for their people as many live below the poverty line without access to basic necessities, there is an urgent need to reduce consumption in affluent countries. Regrettably, the sustainable development agenda does not emphasize the need to do so with the required urgency.

We had many constituencies in mind when we embarked on this project. First, for scholars and teachers, this volume provides rich examples of environmental justice struggles from all over the world and insights on the theory and practice of environmental justice movements. Second, for civil society groups and activists, the case studies in this volume illustrate that these struggles are not isolated, and they often reflect patterns of abuse and injustice dating back to the colonial era. We hope that readers of this volume will learn from the successes and failures of these struggles. Finally, for students, this volume offers hope and perhaps direction for future careers.

This volume is only the first step toward identifying the many systems of power that intersect to create environmental injustice and unsustainable development. Despite the breadth and depth of this volume, we were not able to include chapters related to persons with disabilities, migrant workers, climate refugees, and aging populations. Another growing area of concern that is not reflected in this volume is the plight of environmental defenders, who are being harassed,

---

[36] Chapters 22 and 26, respectively
[37] Chapter 25.
[38] Chapter 27.
[39] B. de Sousa Santos, *Epistemologies of the South: Justice Against Epistemicide* (Boulder, CO: Paradigm, 2014), p. 90.
[40] See Chapters 14, 18, and 20.

intimidated, beaten, tortured, and in some cases killed for trying to protect vulnerable populations and the environment.[41] We encourage scholars and activists to supplement this work through additional case studies and interpretive frameworks, including assessment of responsible business conduct guidance tools designed to help businesses to support environmental human rights defenders against rights-violating governments.[42]

The road to achieving justice and sustainability is long and arduous. We hope that this volume will inspire scholars and activists to supplement this volume with their own examples, documenting additional struggles and sharing legal and extralegal strategies. One of the great tragedies of the modern era is that environmental justice is often regarded as an issue of concern only to environmental law specialists. One of the goals of this volume is to highlight the interconnectedness of seemingly unrelated struggles so as to foster the coalitions necessary to achieve lasting systemic change.

---

[41] See Global Witness, "Defenders of the Earth: Global killings of land and environmental defenders in 2016," 2017.

[42] See for example Business and Human Rights Resource Centre and International Service for Human Rights, "Shared Space under Pressure: Business Support for Civic Freedoms and Human Rights Defenders, Guidance for Companies," Sept. 2018.

Index

Printed in the USA
CPSIA information can be obtained
at www.ICGtesting.com
LVHW010638071123
763254LV00007B/470